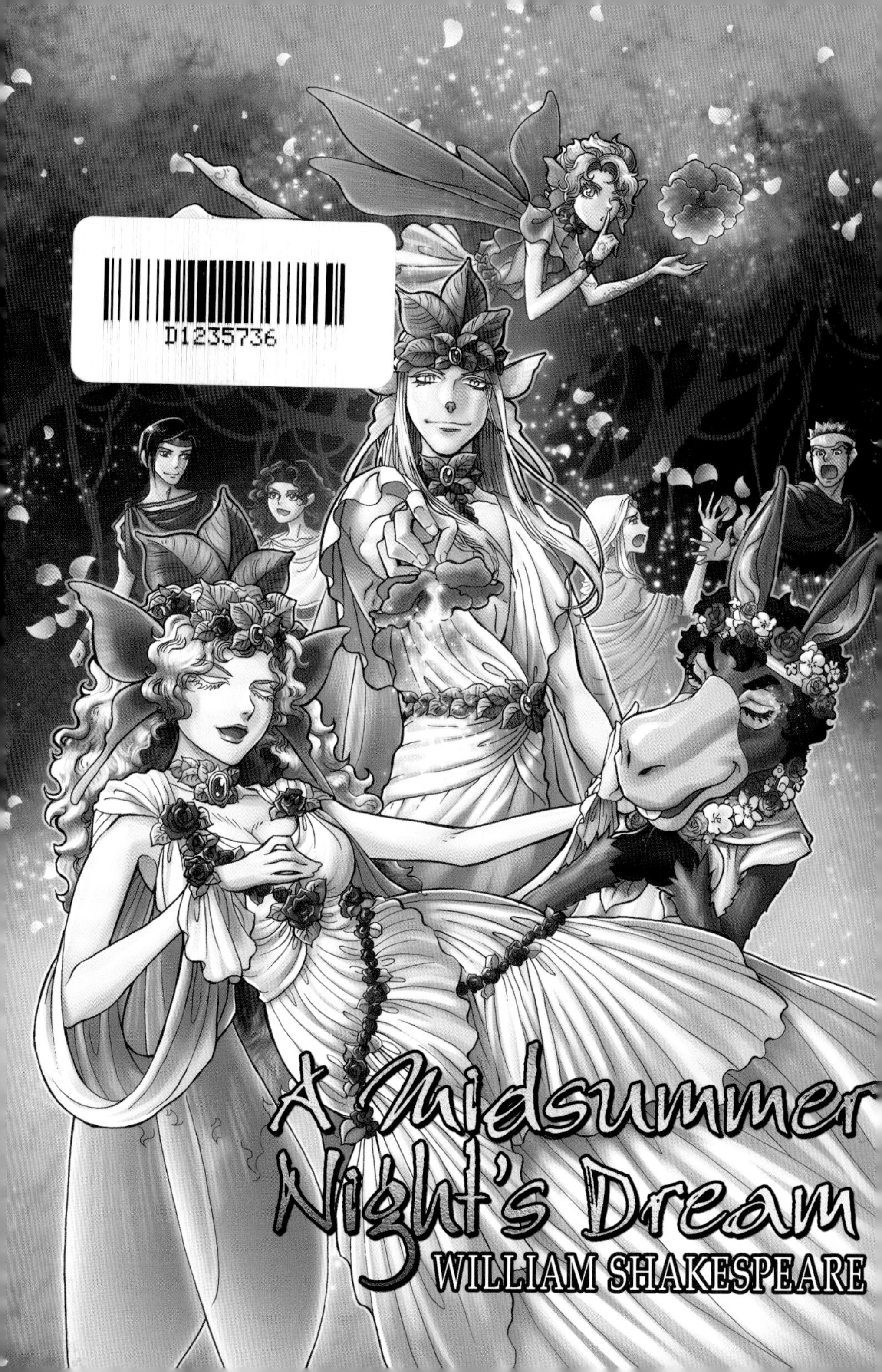
A Midsummer
Night's Dream
WILLIAM SHAKESPEARE

THE CAST

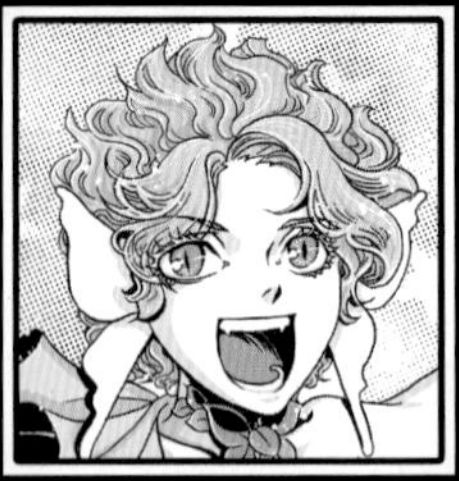
PUCK

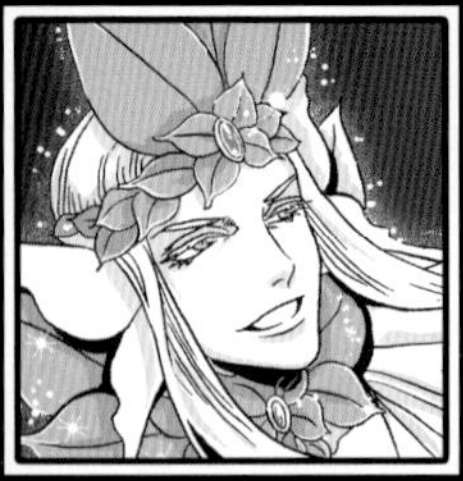
OBERON

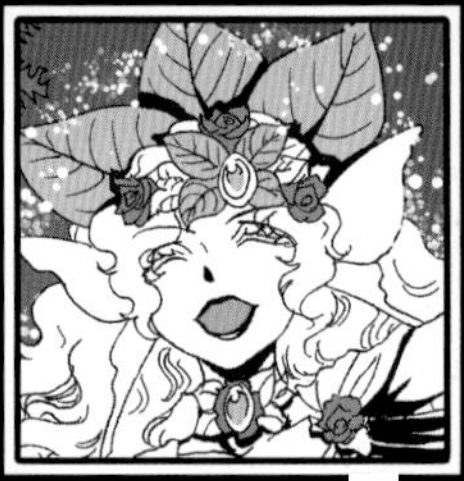
TITANIA

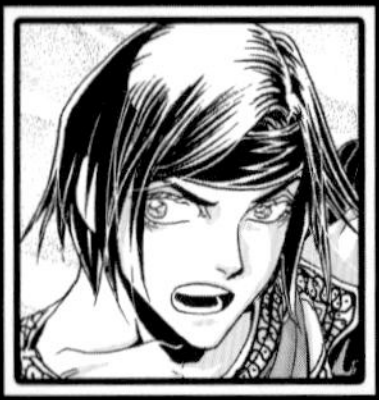
LYSANDER

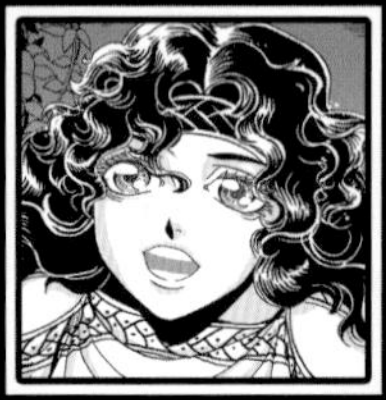
HERMIA

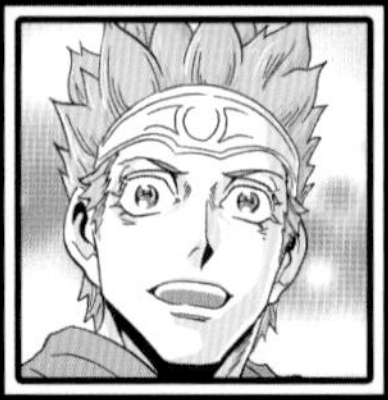
DEMETRIUS

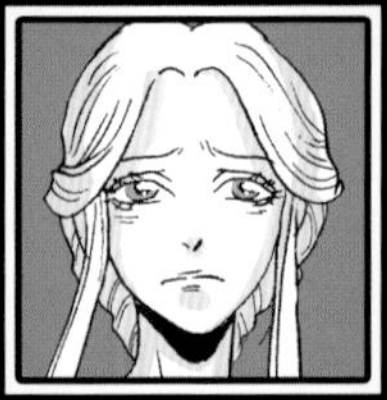
HELENA

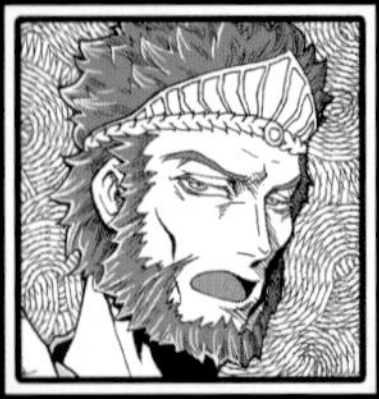
THESEUS

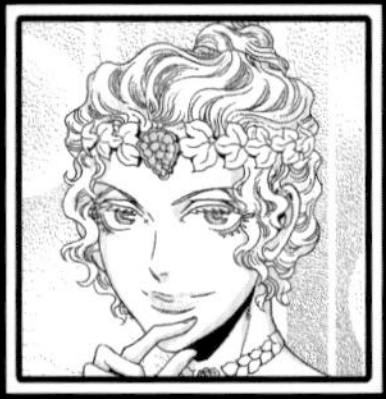
HIPPOLYTA

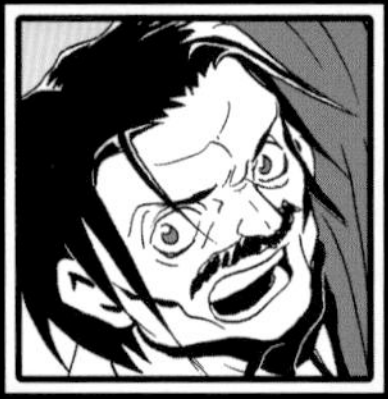
EGEUS

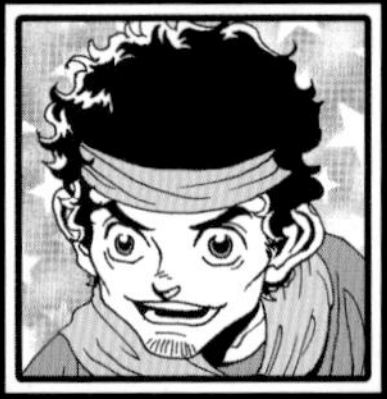
NICK BOTTOM

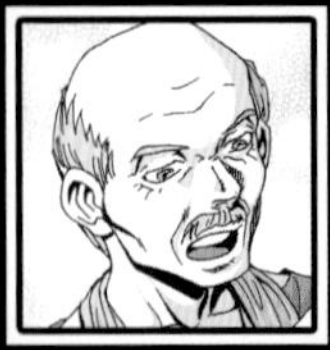
PETER QUINCE

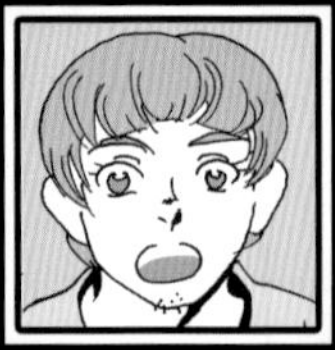
FRANCIS FLUTE

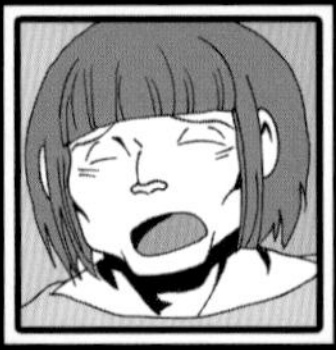
TOM SNOUT

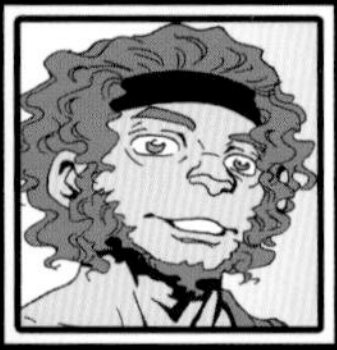
SNUG

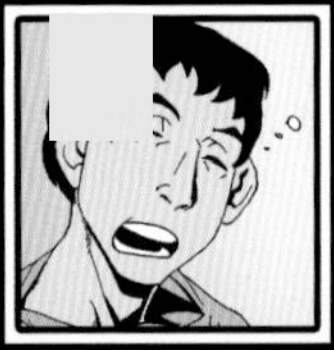
ROBIN STARVELING

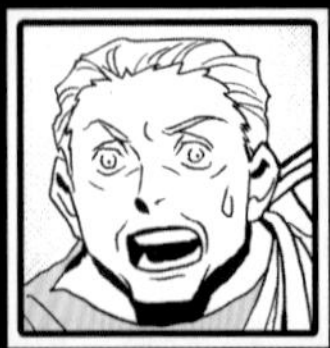
PHILOSTRATE

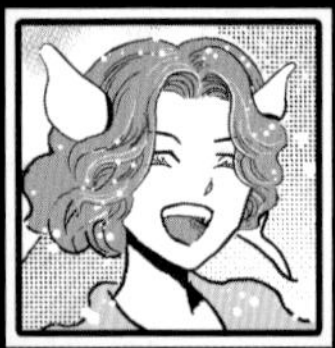
PEASE-BLOSSOM

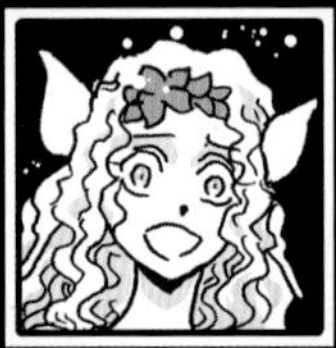
COBWEB

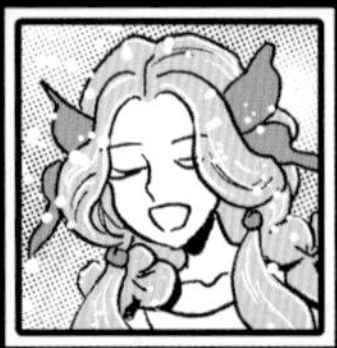
MUSTARDSEED

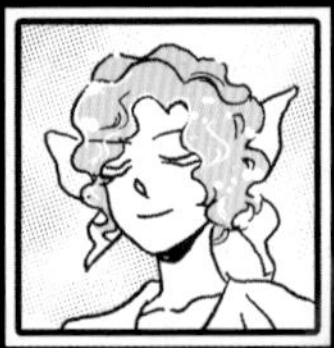
MOTH

CONTENTS

ACT I

ACT II

A Midsummer Night's Dream

WILLIAM SHAKESPEARE

ACT III

ACT IV

ACT V

HOW TO READ MANGA!

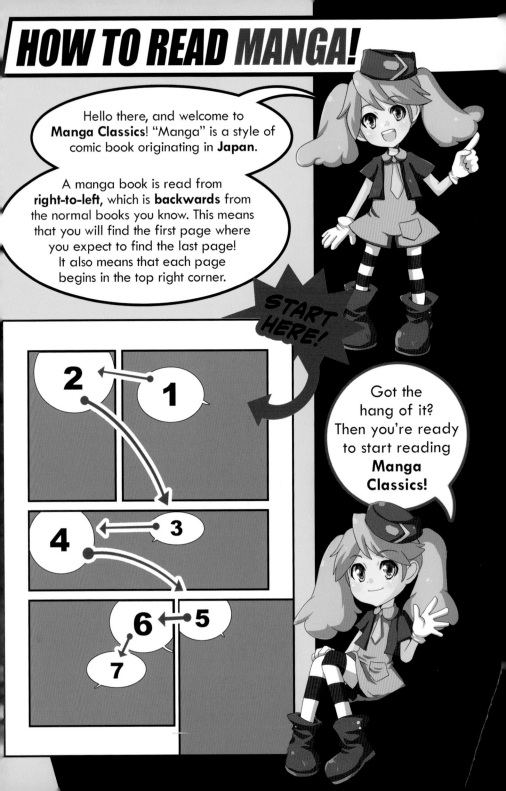

Hello there, and welcome to **Manga Classics!** "Manga" is a style of comic book originating in **Japan**.

A manga book is read from **right-to-left**, which is **backwards** from the normal books you know. This means that you will find the first page where you expect to find the last page! It also means that each page begins in the top right corner.

START HERE!

Got the hang of it? Then you're ready to start reading **Manga Classics!**

2 1
4 3
6 5
7

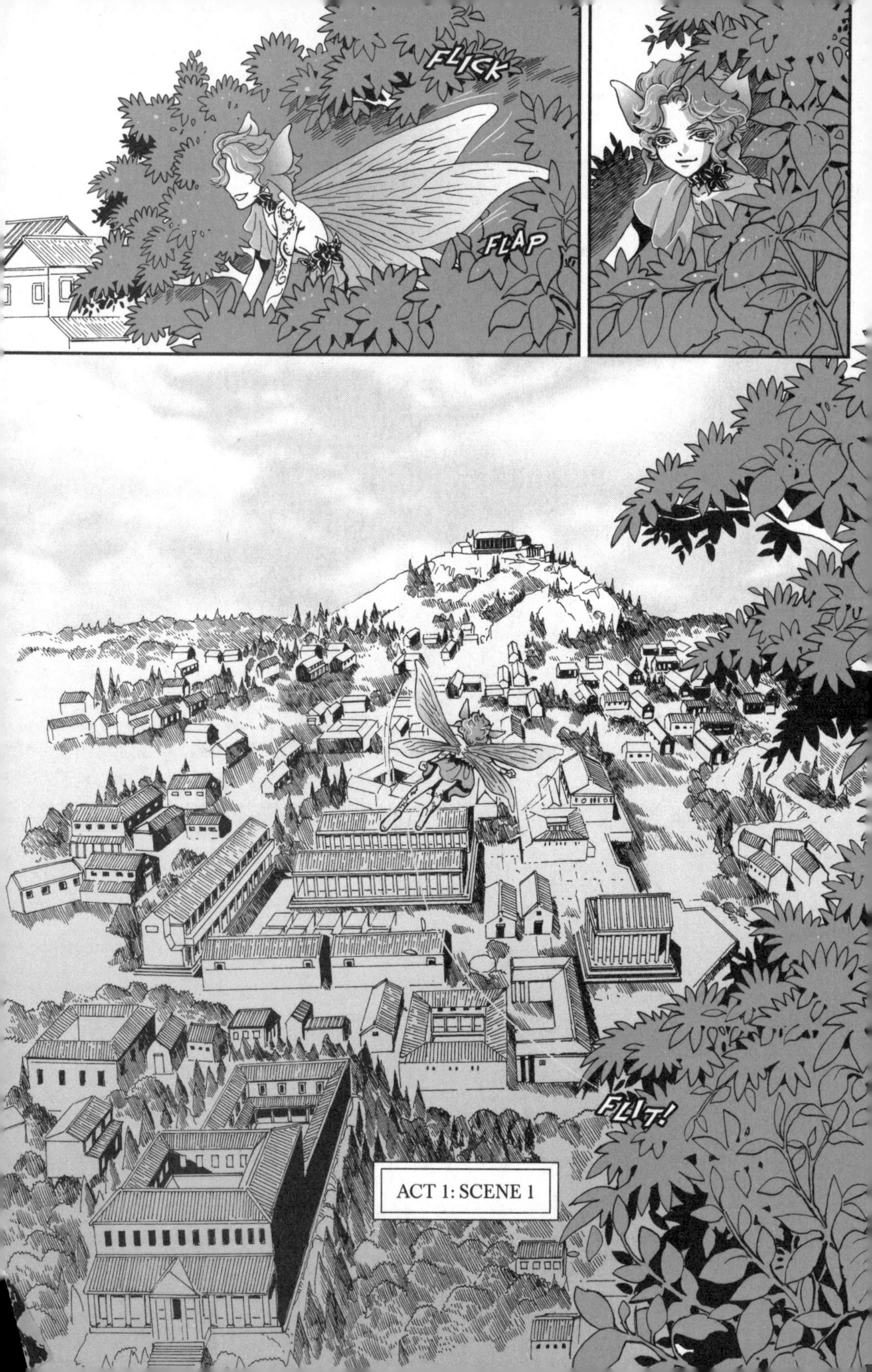
FLICK
FLAP
FLIT!
ACT 1: SCENE 1

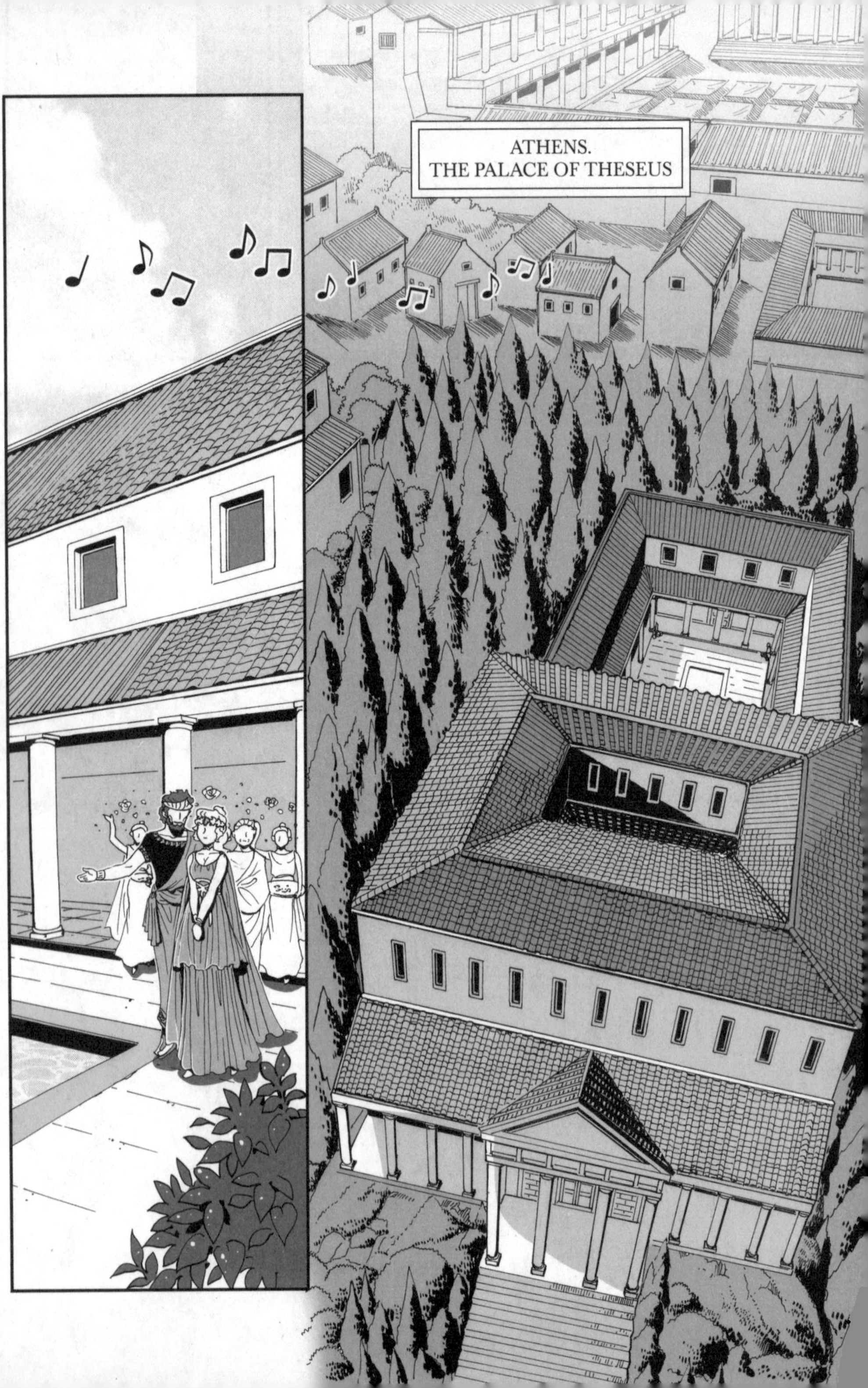
ATHENS.
THE PALACE OF THESEUS

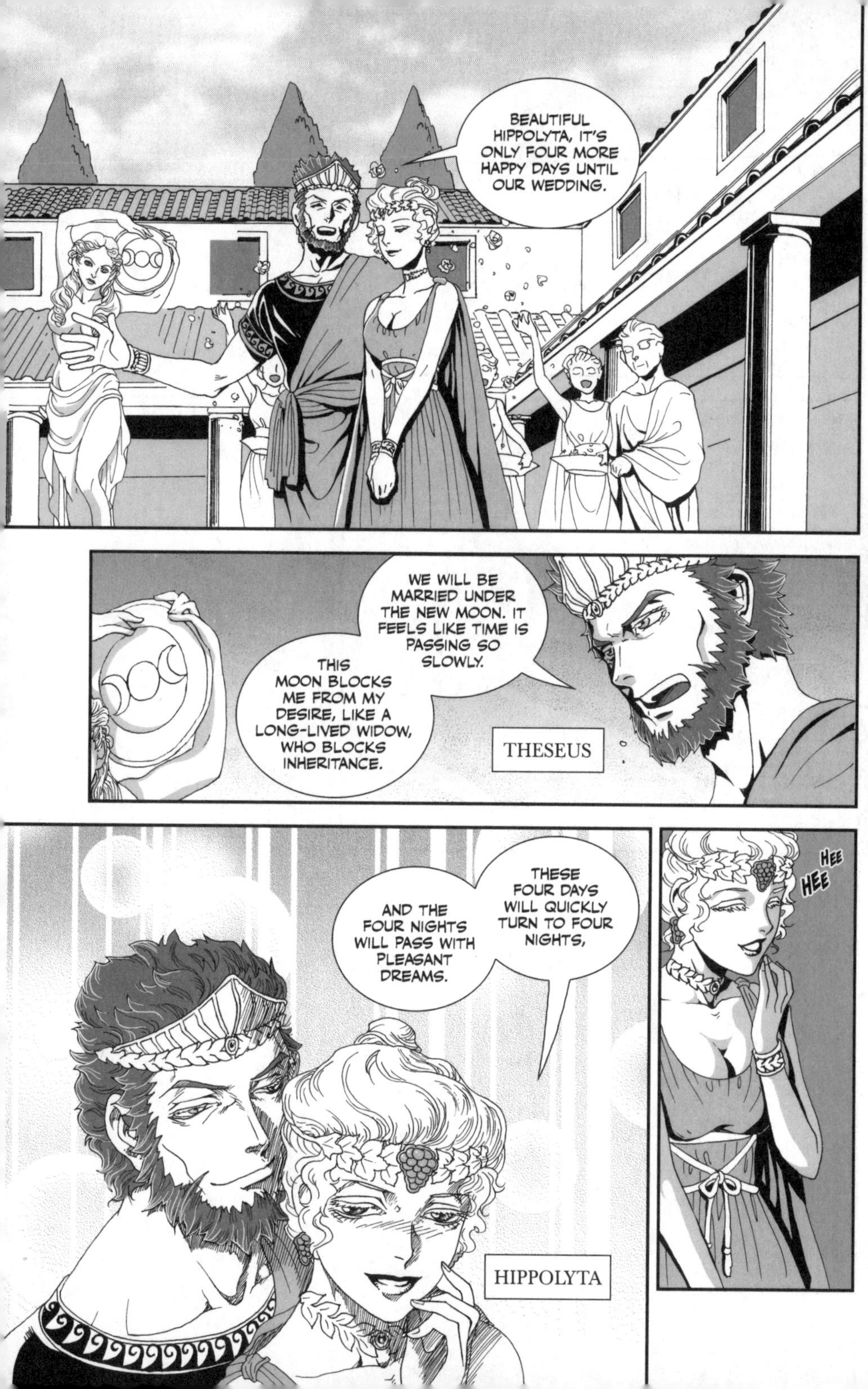
BEAUTIFUL HIPPOLYTA, IT'S ONLY FOUR MORE HAPPY DAYS UNTIL OUR WEDDING.
WE WILL BE MARRIED UNDER THE NEW MOON. IT FEELS LIKE TIME IS PASSING SO SLOWLY.
THIS MOON BLOCKS ME FROM MY DESIRE, LIKE A LONG-LIVED WIDOW, WHO BLOCKS INHERITANCE.
THESEUS
HEE HEE
THESE FOUR DAYS WILL QUICKLY TURN TO FOUR NIGHTS,
AND THE FOUR NIGHTS WILL PASS WITH PLEASANT DREAMS.
HIPPOLYTA

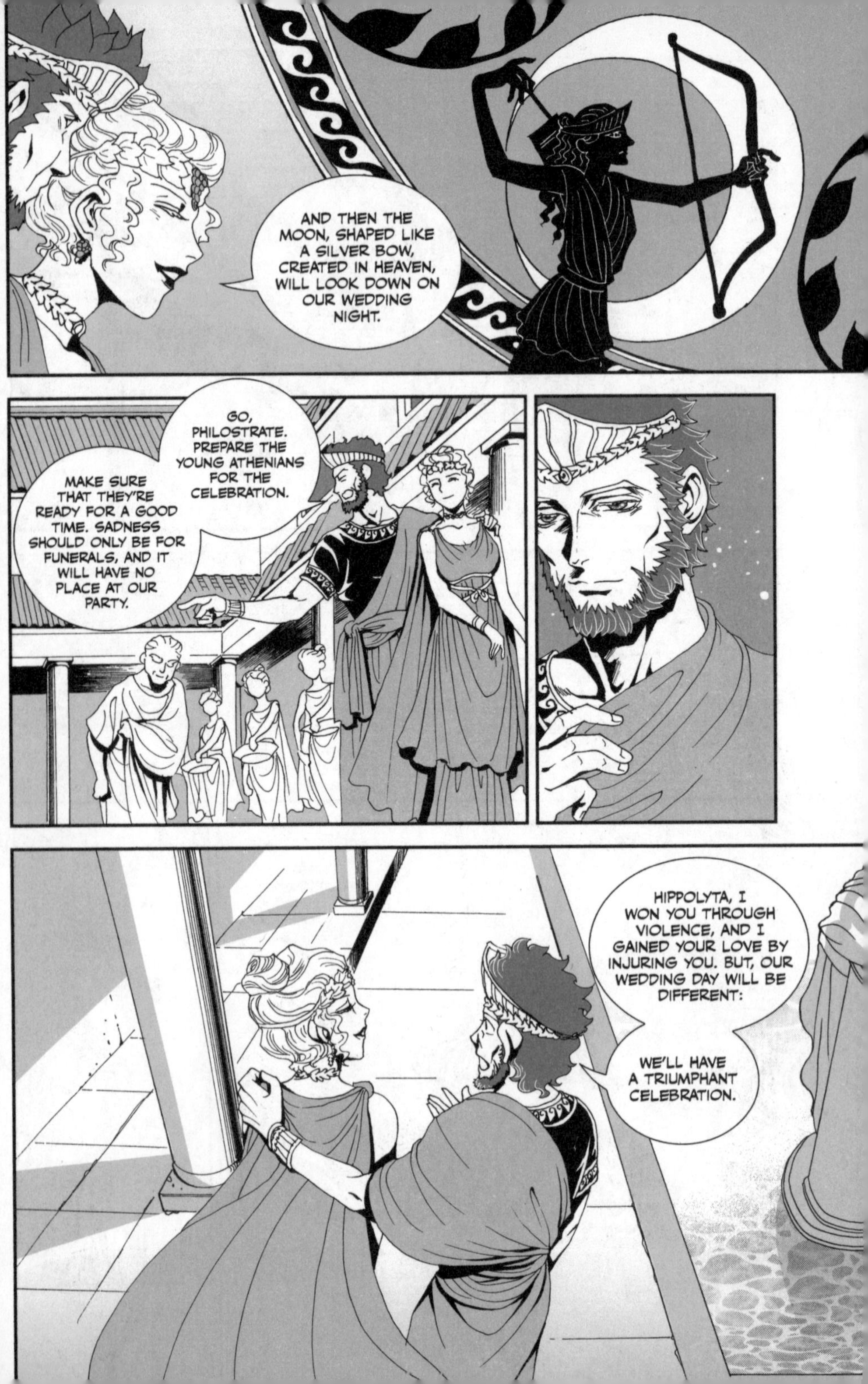
AND THEN THE MOON, SHAPED LIKE A SILVER BOW, CREATED IN HEAVEN, WILL LOOK DOWN ON OUR WEDDING NIGHT.
GO, PHILOSTRATE. PREPARE THE YOUNG ATHENIANS FOR THE CELEBRATION.
MAKE SURE THAT THEY'RE READY FOR A GOOD TIME. SADNESS SHOULD ONLY BE FOR FUNERALS, AND IT WILL HAVE NO PLACE AT OUR PARTY.
HIPPOLYTA, I WON YOU THROUGH VIOLENCE, AND I GAINED YOUR LOVE BY INJURING YOU. BUT, OUR WEDDING DAY WILL BE DIFFERENT:
WE'LL HAVE A TRIUMPHANT CELEBRATION.

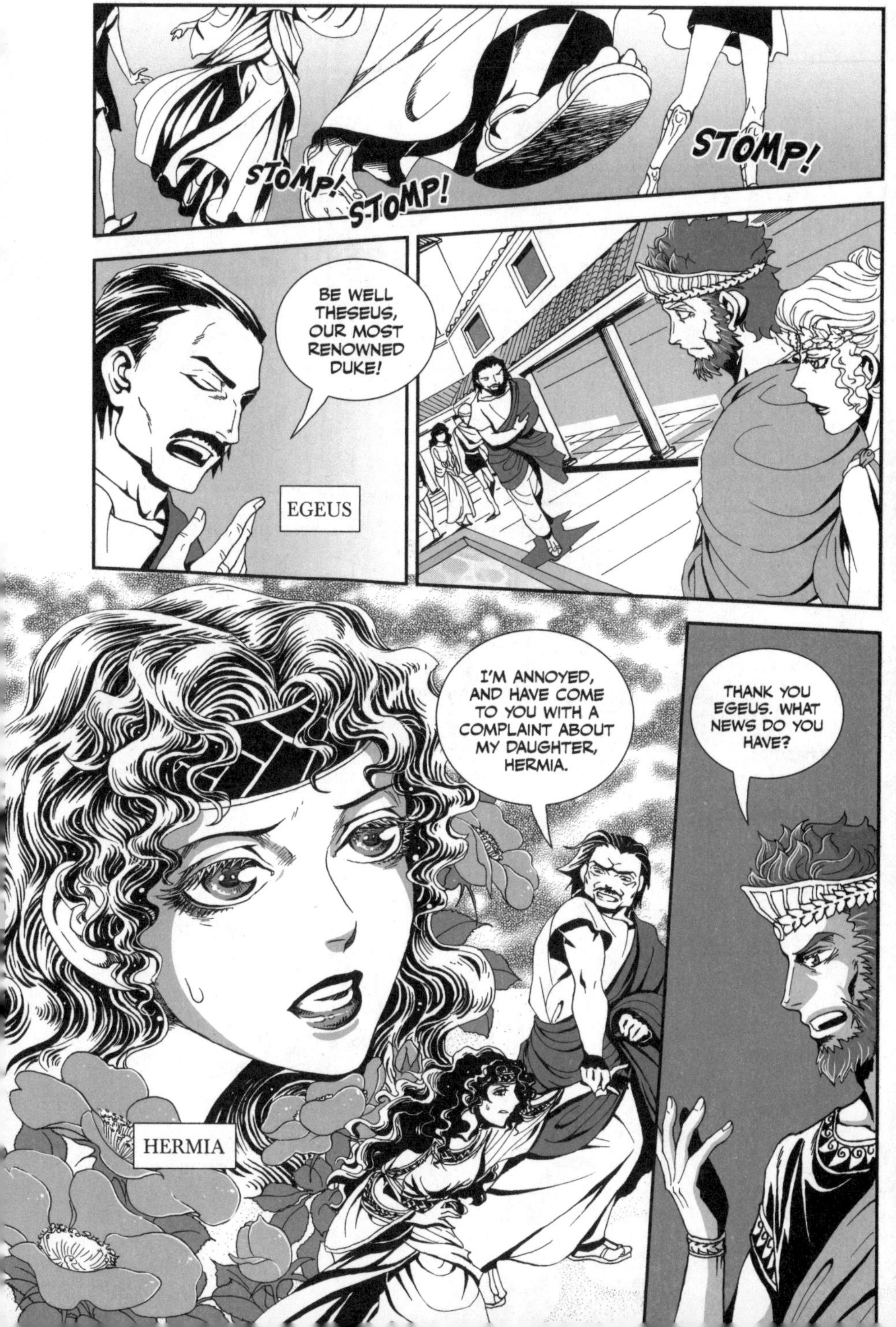
STOMP!
S-TOMP!
STOMP!
BE WELL THESEUS, OUR MOST RENOWNED DUKE!
EGEUS
THANK YOU EGEUS. WHAT NEWS DO YOU HAVE?
I'M ANNOYED, AND HAVE COME TO YOU WITH A COMPLAINT ABOUT MY DAUGHTER, HERMIA.
HERMIA

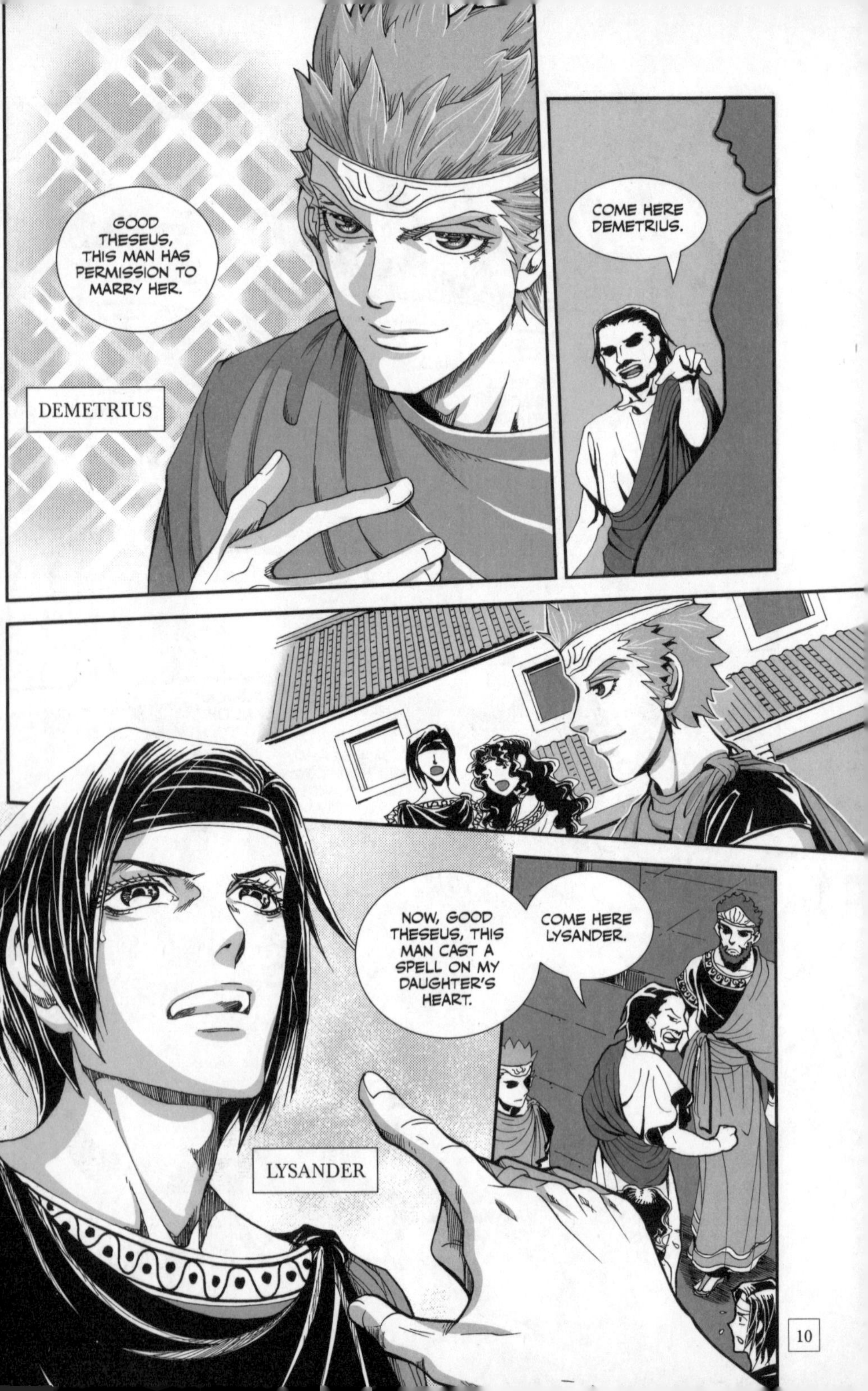
COME HERE DEMETRIUS.
GOOD THESEUS, THIS MAN HAS PERMISSION TO MARRY HER.
DEMETRIUS
COME HERE LYSANDER.
NOW, GOOD THESEUS, THIS MAN CAST A SPELL ON MY DAUGHTER'S HEART.
LYSANDER

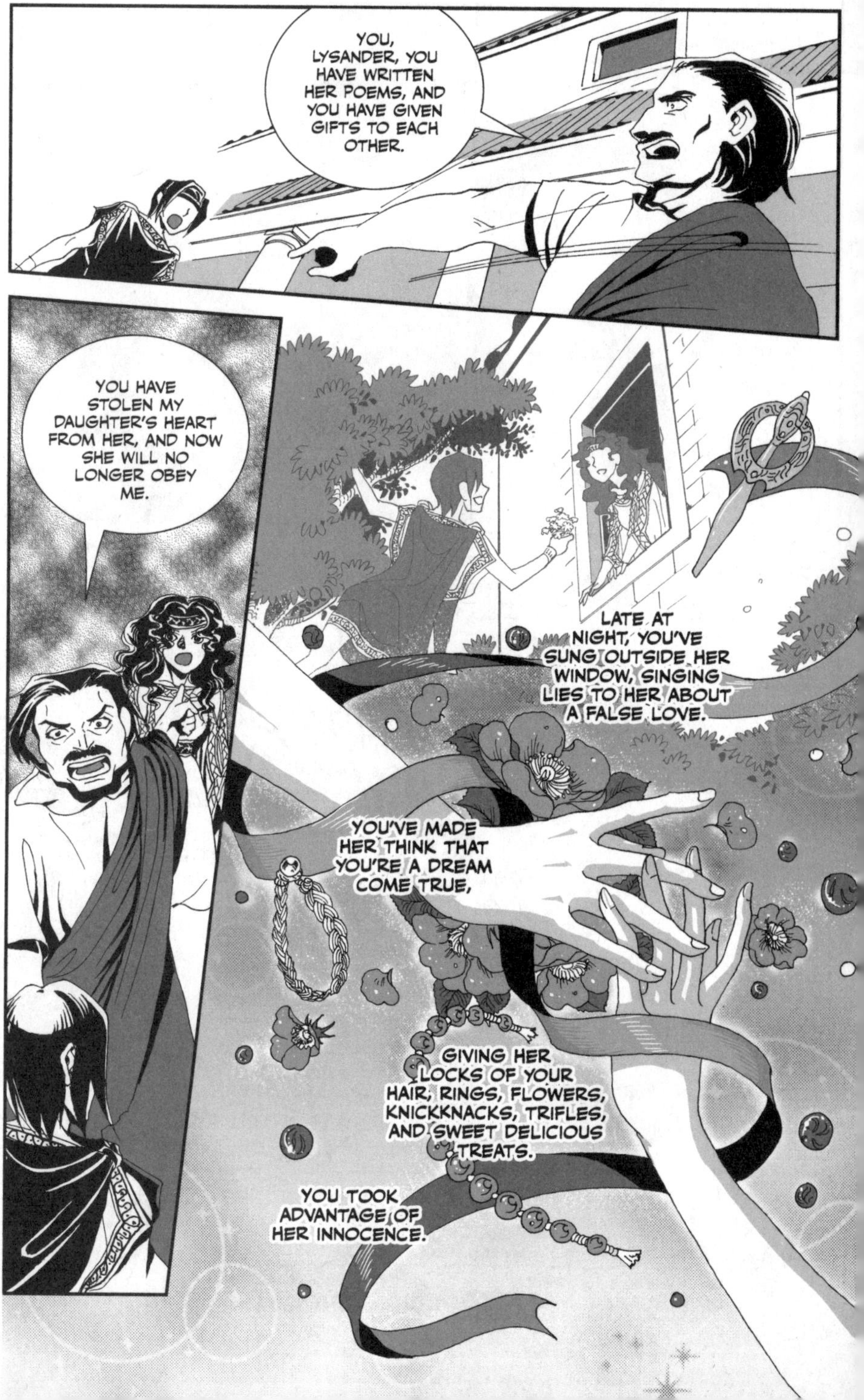
YOU, LYSANDER, YOU HAVE WRITTEN HER POEMS, AND YOU HAVE GIVEN GIFTS TO EACH OTHER.
LATE AT NIGHT, YOU'VE SUNG OUTSIDE HER WINDOW, SINGING LIES TO HER ABOUT A FALSE LOVE.
YOU'VE MADE HER THINK THAT YOU'RE A DREAM COME TRUE,
GIVING HER LOCKS OF YOUR HAIR, RINGS, FLOWERS, KNICKKNACKS, TRIFLES, AND SWEET DELICIOUS TREATS.
YOU TOOK ADVANTAGE OF HER INNOCENCE.
YOU HAVE STOLEN MY DAUGHTER'S HEART FROM HER, AND NOW SHE WILL NO LONGER OBEY ME.

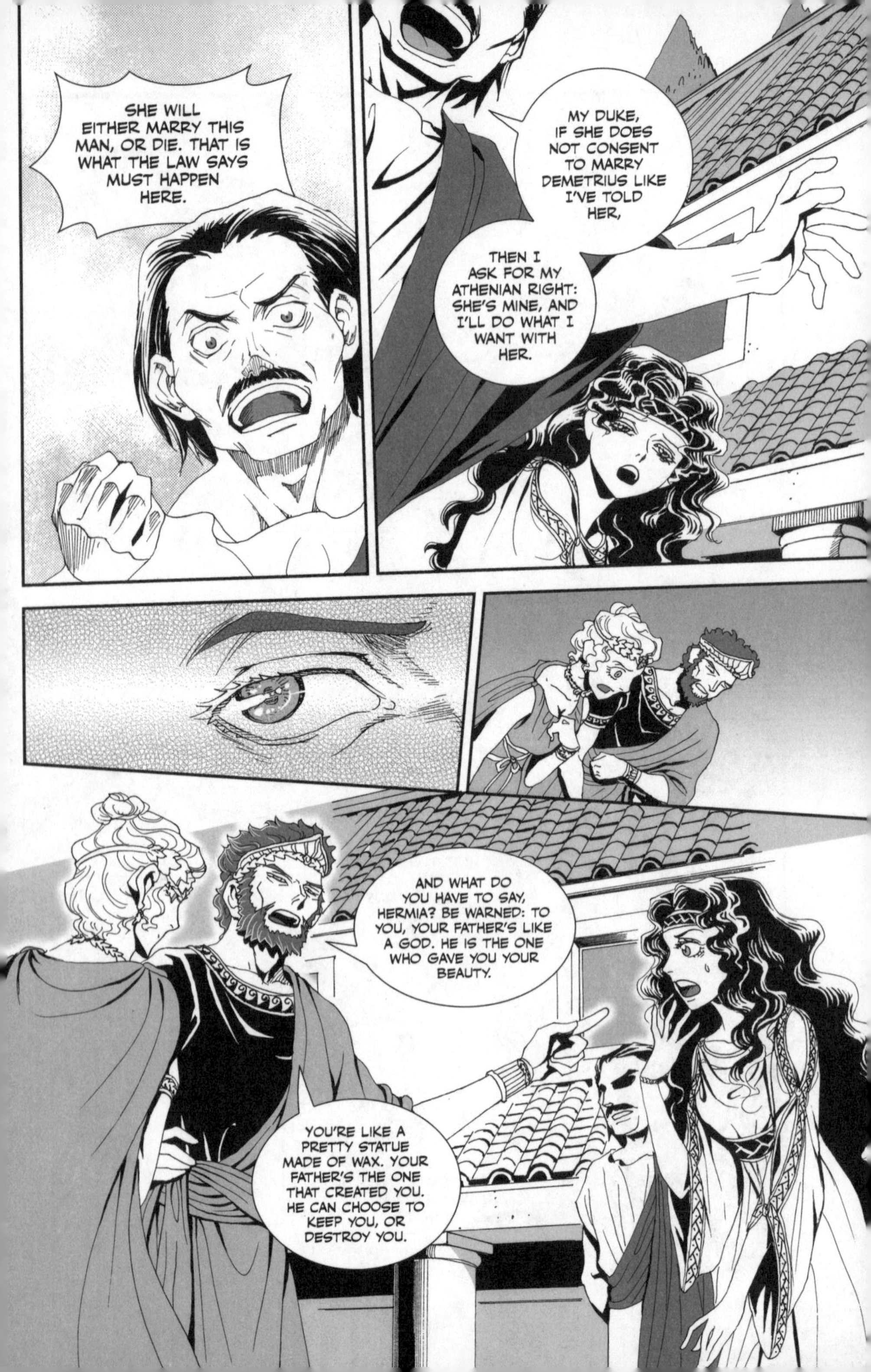
MY DUKE, IF SHE DOES NOT CONSENT TO MARRY DEMETRIUS LIKE I'VE TOLD HER,
THEN I ASK FOR MY ATHENIAN RIGHT: SHE'S MINE, AND I'LL DO WHAT I WANT WITH HER.
SHE WILL EITHER MARRY THIS MAN, OR DIE. THAT IS WHAT THE LAW SAYS MUST HAPPEN HERE.
AND WHAT DO YOU HAVE TO SAY, HERMIA? BE WARNED: TO YOU, YOUR FATHER'S LIKE A GOD. HE IS THE ONE WHO GAVE YOU YOUR BEAUTY.
YOU'RE LIKE A PRETTY STATUE MADE OF WAX. YOUR FATHER'S THE ONE THAT CREATED YOU. HE CAN CHOOSE TO KEEP YOU, OR DESTROY YOU.

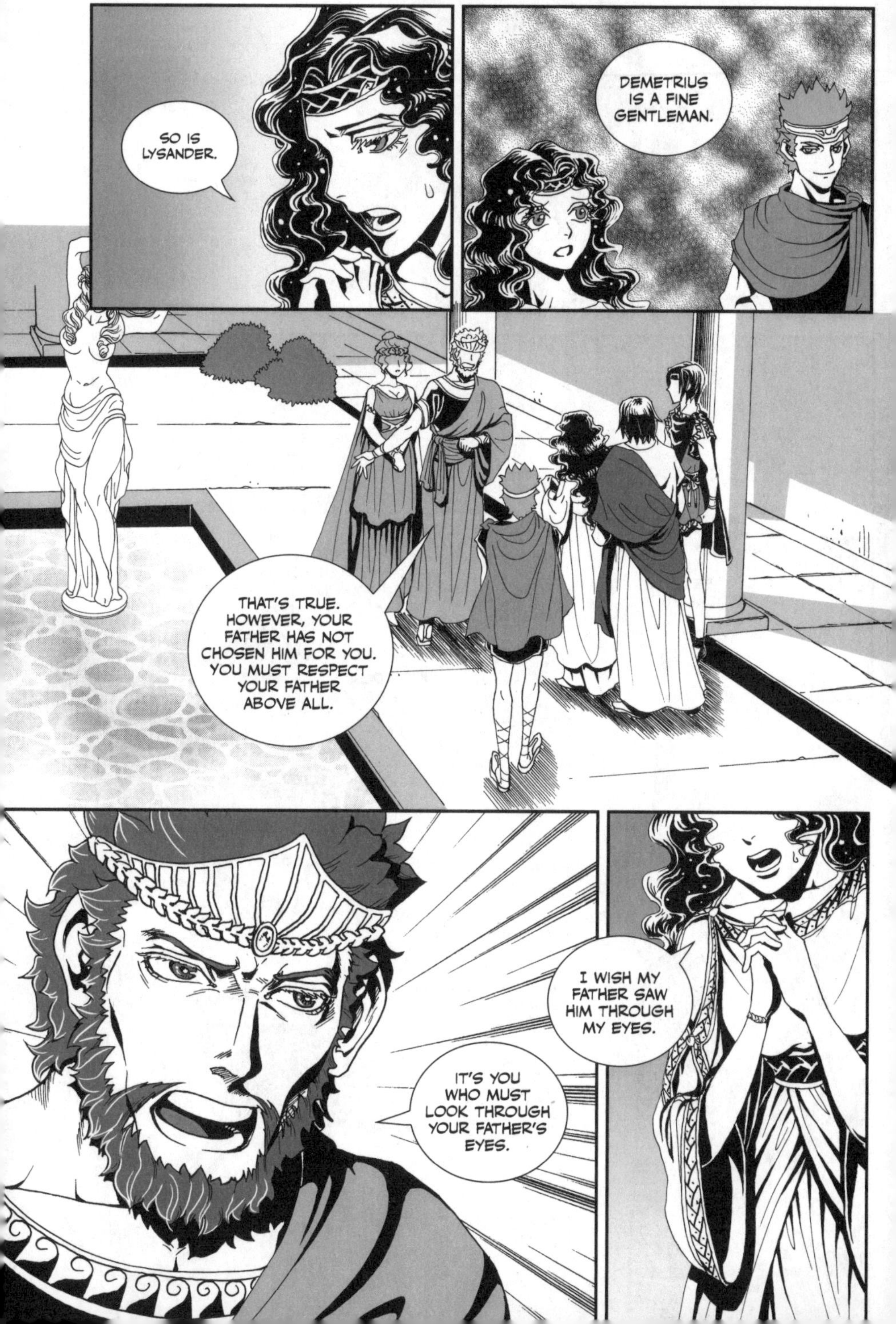
DEMETRIUS IS A FINE GENTLEMAN.
SO IS LYSANDER.
THAT'S TRUE. HOWEVER, YOUR FATHER HAS NOT CHOSEN HIM FOR YOU. YOU MUST RESPECT YOUR FATHER ABOVE ALL.
I WISH MY FATHER SAW HIM THROUGH MY EYES.
IT'S YOU WHO MUST LOOK THROUGH YOUR FATHER'S EYES.

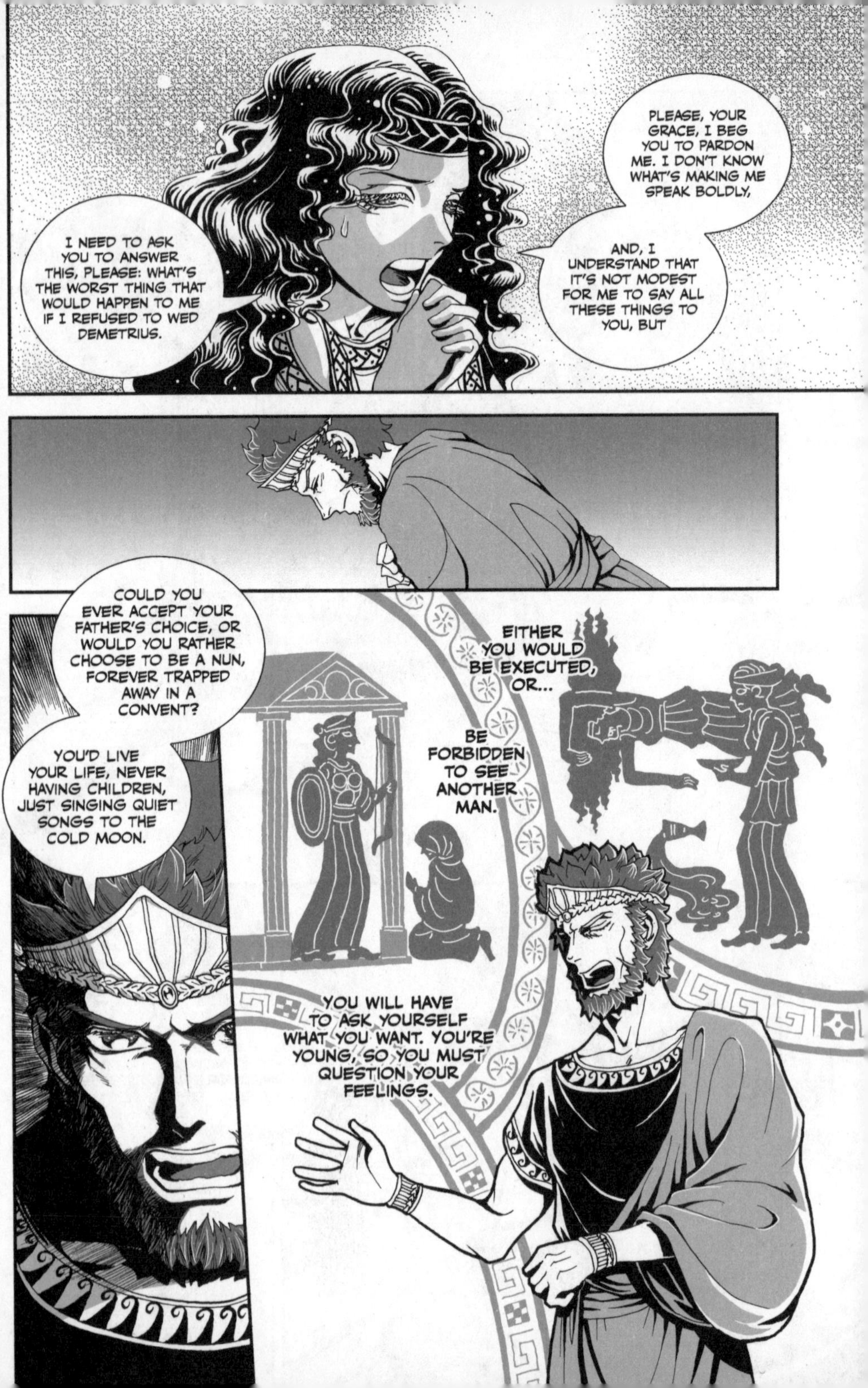
PLEASE, YOUR GRACE, I BEG YOU TO PARDON ME. I DON'T KNOW WHAT'S MAKING ME SPEAK BOLDLY,
AND, I UNDERSTAND THAT IT'S NOT MODEST FOR ME TO SAY ALL THESE THINGS TO YOU, BUT
I NEED TO ASK YOU TO ANSWER THIS, PLEASE: WHAT'S THE WORST THING THAT WOULD HAPPEN TO ME IF I REFUSED TO WED DEMETRIUS.
EITHER YOU WOULD BE EXECUTED, OR...
BE FORBIDDEN TO SEE ANOTHER MAN.
YOU WILL HAVE TO ASK YOURSELF WHAT YOU WANT. YOU'RE YOUNG, SO YOU MUST QUESTION YOUR FEELINGS.
COULD YOU EVER ACCEPT YOUR FATHER'S CHOICE, OR WOULD YOU RATHER CHOOSE TO BE A NUN, FOREVER TRAPPED AWAY IN A CONVENT?
YOU'D LIVE YOUR LIFE, NEVER HAVING CHILDREN, JUST SINGING QUIET SONGS TO THE COLD MOON.

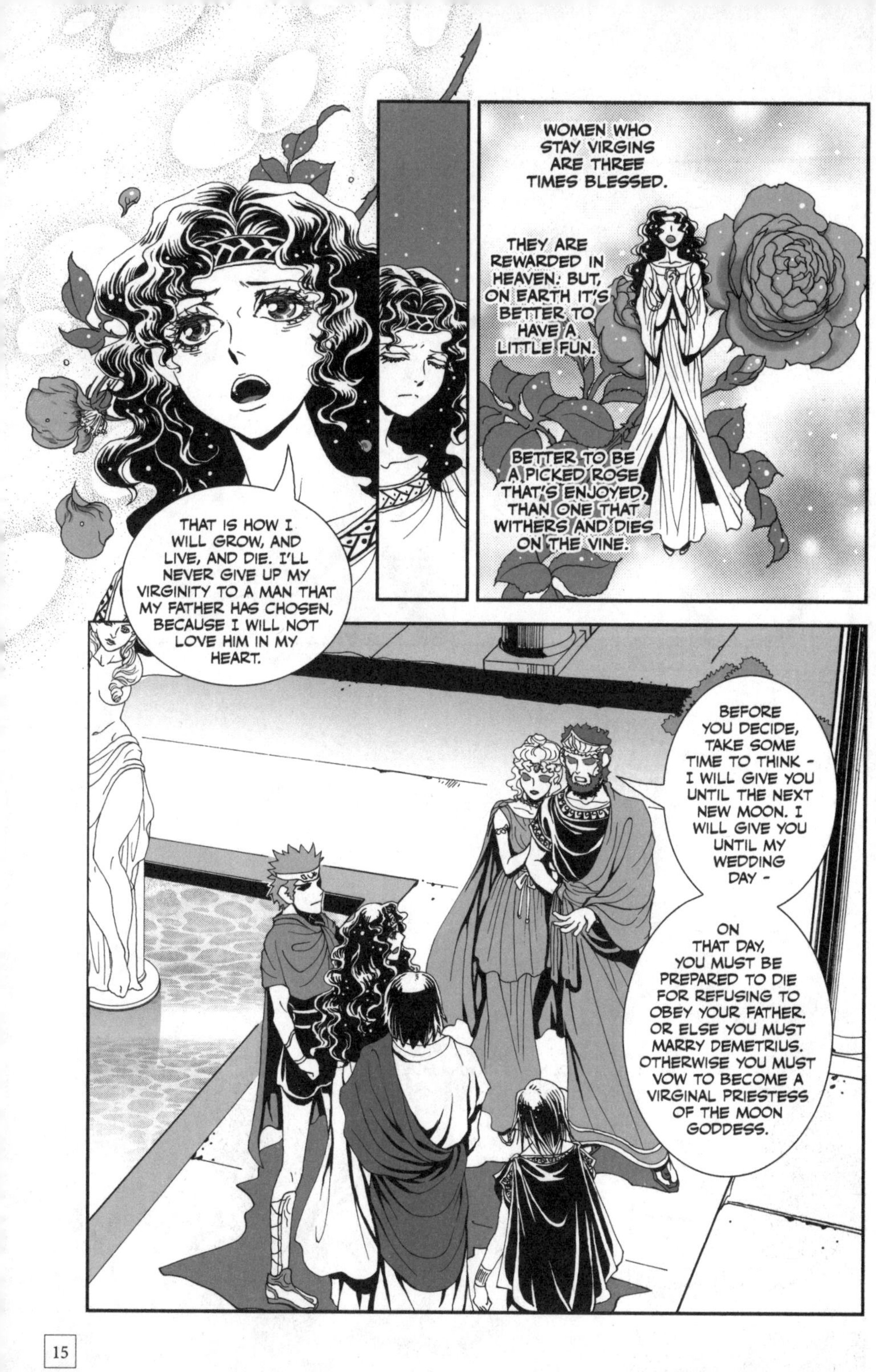
WOMEN WHO STAY VIRGINS ARE THREE TIMES BLESSED.
THEY ARE REWARDED IN HEAVEN. BUT, ON EARTH IT'S BETTER TO HAVE A LITTLE FUN.
BETTER TO BE A PICKED ROSE THAT'S ENJOYED, THAN ONE THAT WITHERS AND DIES ON THE VINE.
THAT IS HOW I WILL GROW, AND LIVE, AND DIE. I'LL NEVER GIVE UP MY VIRGINITY TO A MAN THAT MY FATHER HAS CHOSEN, BECAUSE I WILL NOT LOVE HIM IN MY HEART.
BEFORE YOU DECIDE, TAKE SOME TIME TO THINK - I WILL GIVE YOU UNTIL THE NEXT NEW MOON. I WILL GIVE YOU UNTIL MY WEDDING DAY -
ON THAT DAY, YOU MUST BE PREPARED TO DIE FOR REFUSING TO OBEY YOUR FATHER. OR ELSE YOU MUST MARRY DEMETRIUS. OTHERWISE YOU MUST VOW TO BECOME A VIRGINAL PRIESTESS OF THE MOON GODDESS.

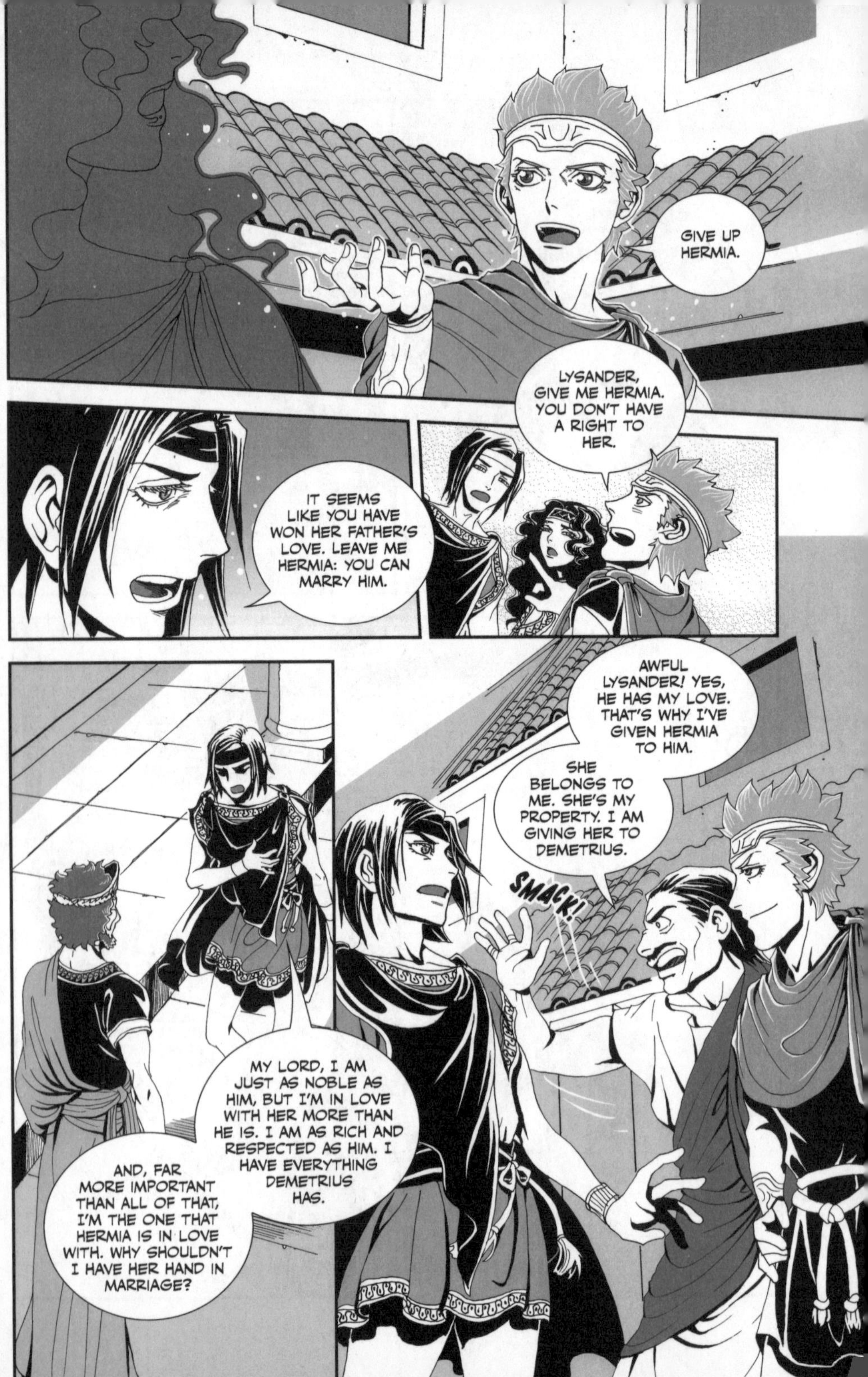
GIVE UP HERMIA.
LYSANDER, GIVE ME HERMIA. YOU DON'T HAVE A RIGHT TO HER.
IT SEEMS LIKE YOU HAVE WON HER FATHER'S LOVE. LEAVE ME HERMIA: YOU CAN MARRY HIM.
AWFUL LYSANDER! YES, HE HAS MY LOVE. THAT'S WHY I'VE GIVEN HERMIA TO HIM.
SHE BELONGS TO ME. SHE'S MY PROPERTY. I AM GIVING HER TO DEMETRIUS.
SMACK!
MY LORD, I AM JUST AS NOBLE AS HIM, BUT I'M IN LOVE WITH HER MORE THAN HE IS. I AM AS RICH AND RESPECTED AS HIM. I HAVE EVERYTHING DEMETRIUS HAS.
AND, FAR MORE IMPORTANT THAN ALL OF THAT, I'M THE ONE THAT HERMIA IS IN LOVE WITH. WHY SHOULDN'T I HAVE HER HAND IN MARRIAGE?

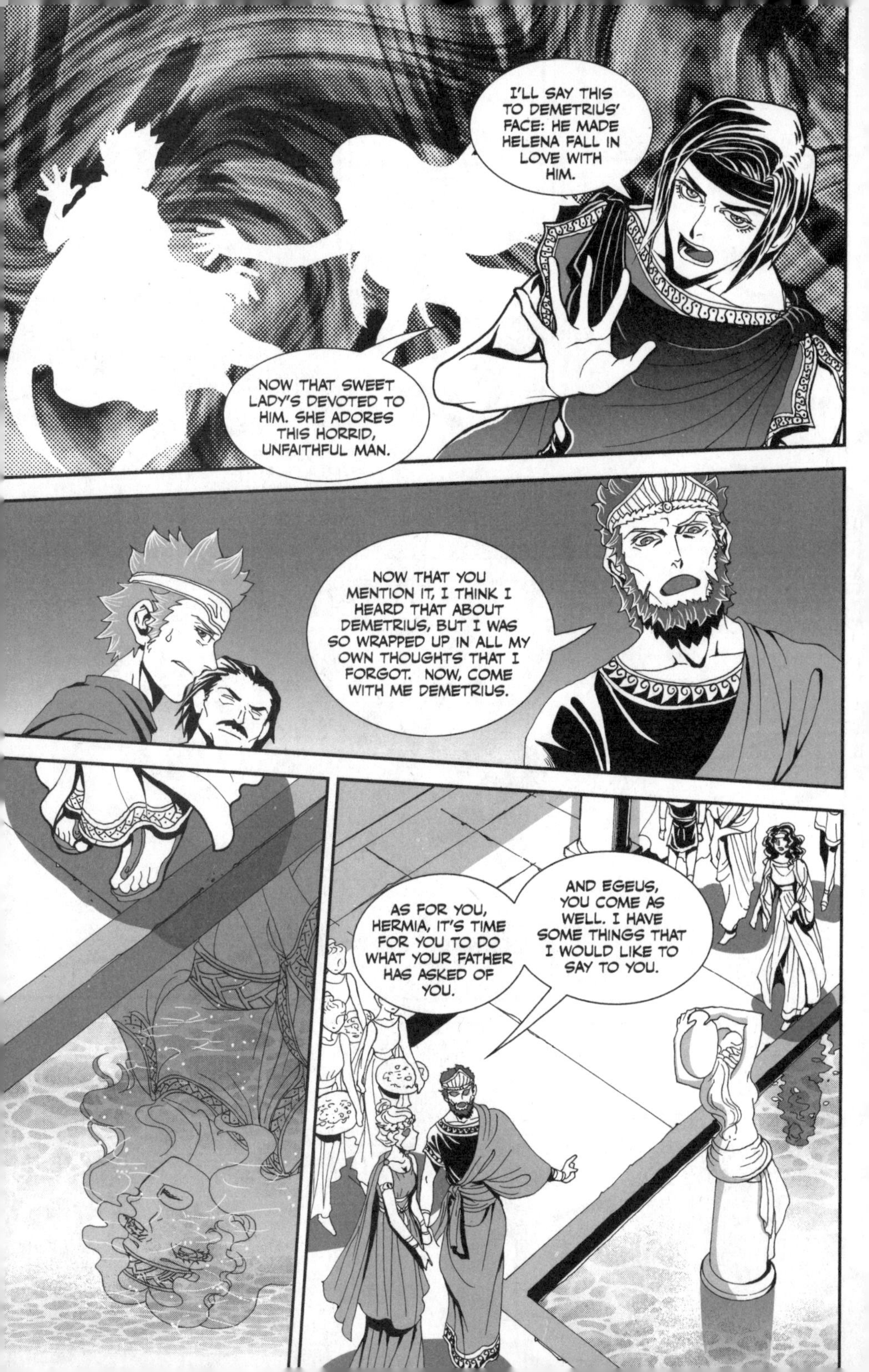
I'LL SAY THIS TO DEMETRIUS' FACE: HE MADE HELENA FALL IN LOVE WITH HIM.
NOW THAT SWEET LADY'S DEVOTED TO HIM. SHE ADORES THIS HORRID, UNFAITHFUL MAN.
NOW THAT YOU MENTION IT, I THINK I HEARD THAT ABOUT DEMETRIUS, BUT I WAS SO WRAPPED UP IN ALL MY OWN THOUGHTS THAT I FORGOT. NOW, COME WITH ME DEMETRIUS.
AND EGEUS, YOU COME AS WELL. I HAVE SOME THINGS THAT I WOULD LIKE TO SAY TO YOU.
AS FOR YOU, HERMIA, IT'S TIME FOR YOU TO DO WHAT YOUR FATHER HAS ASKED OF YOU.

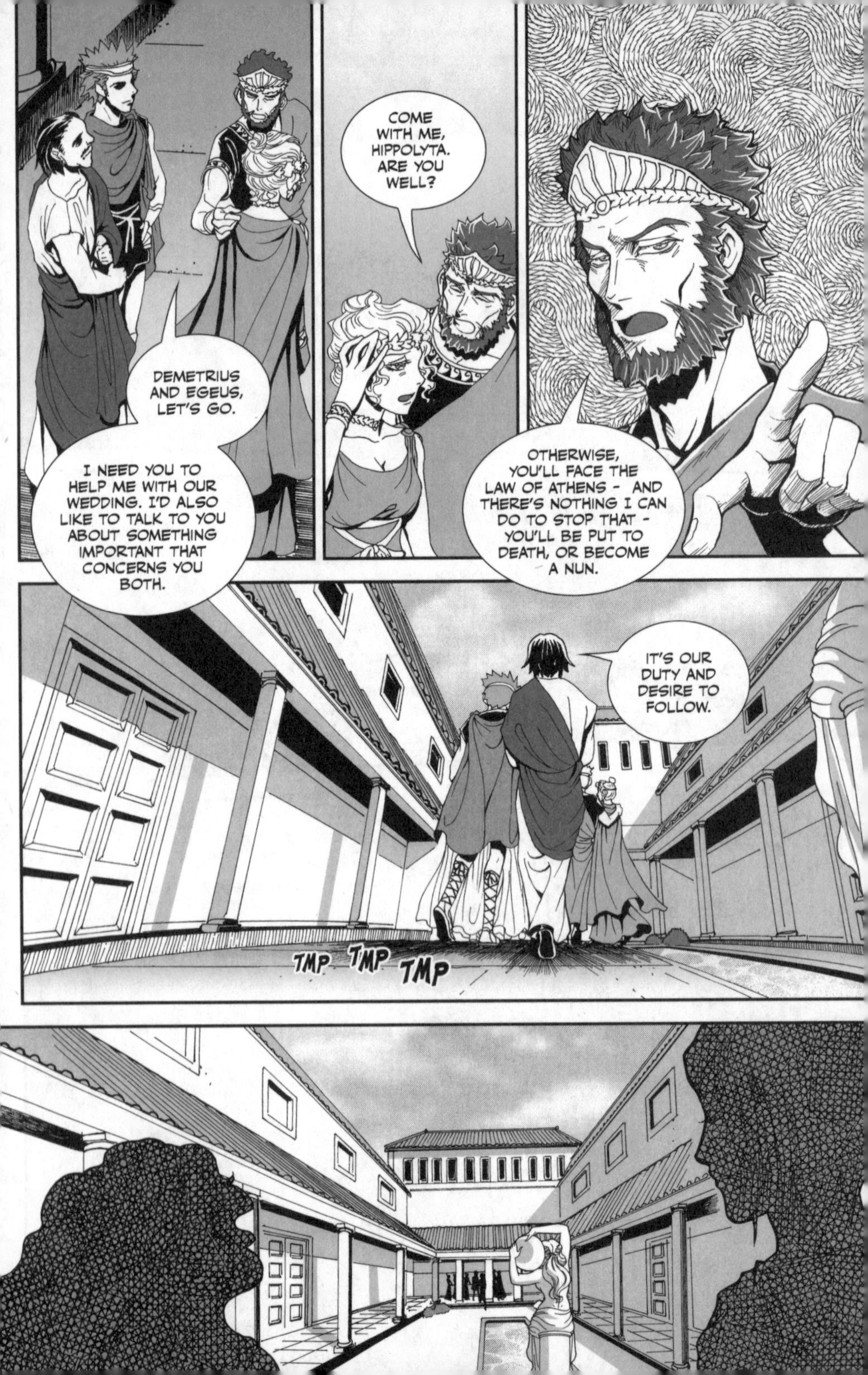
OTHERWISE, YOU'LL FACE THE LAW OF ATHENS - AND THERE'S NOTHING I CAN DO TO STOP THAT - YOU'LL BE PUT TO DEATH, OR BECOME A NUN.
COME WITH ME, HIPPOLYTA. ARE YOU WELL?
DEMETRIUS AND EGEUS, LET'S GO.
I NEED YOU TO HELP ME WITH OUR WEDDING. I'D ALSO LIKE TO TALK TO YOU ABOUT SOMETHING IMPORTANT THAT CONCERNS YOU BOTH.
IT'S OUR DUTY AND DESIRE TO FOLLOW.
TMP TMP TMP

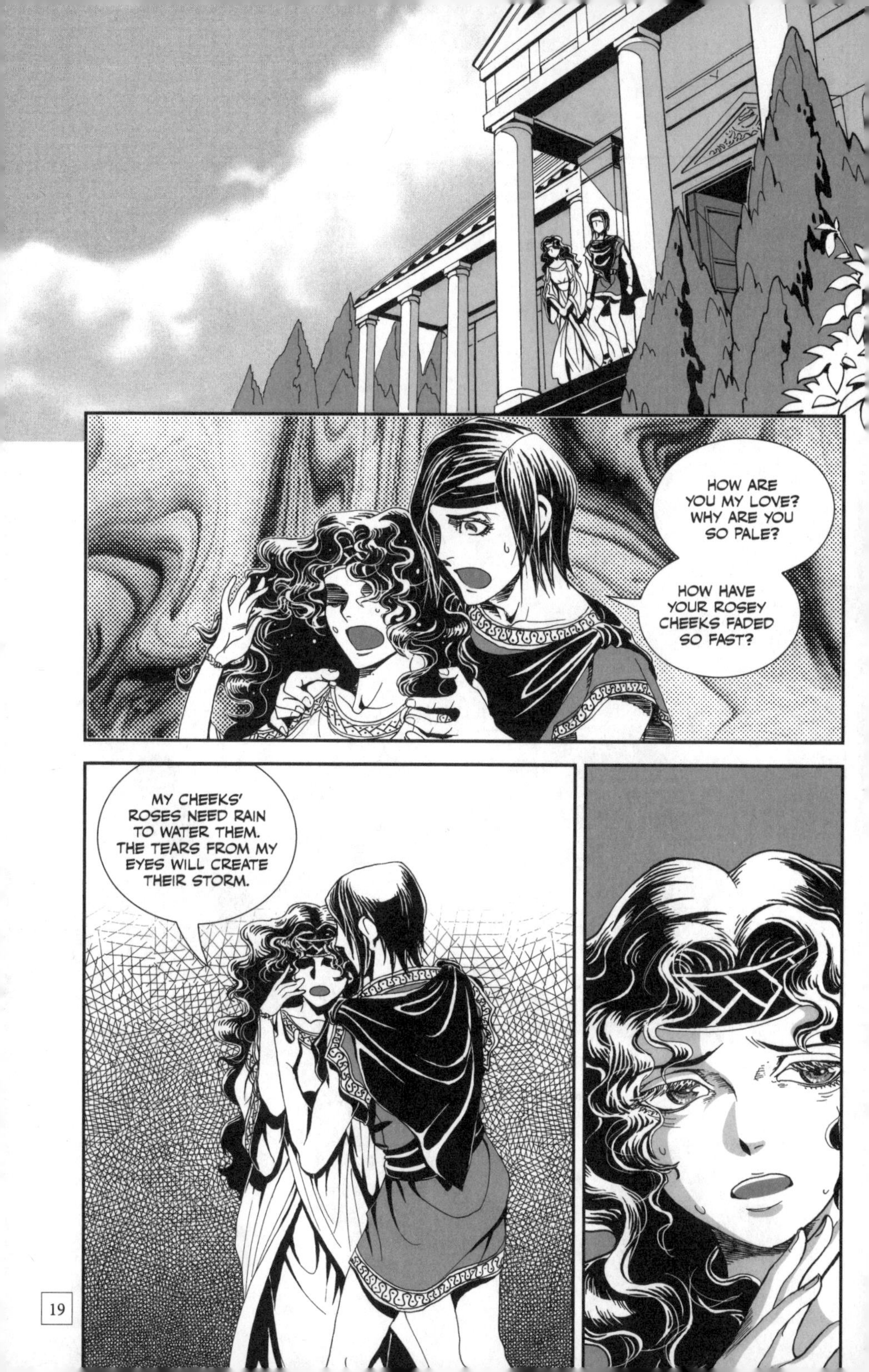
HOW ARE YOU MY LOVE? WHY ARE YOU SO PALE?
HOW HAVE YOUR ROSEY CHEEKS FADED SO FAST?
MY CHEEKS' ROSES NEED RAIN TO WATER THEM. THE TEARS FROM MY EYES WILL CREATE THEIR STORM.

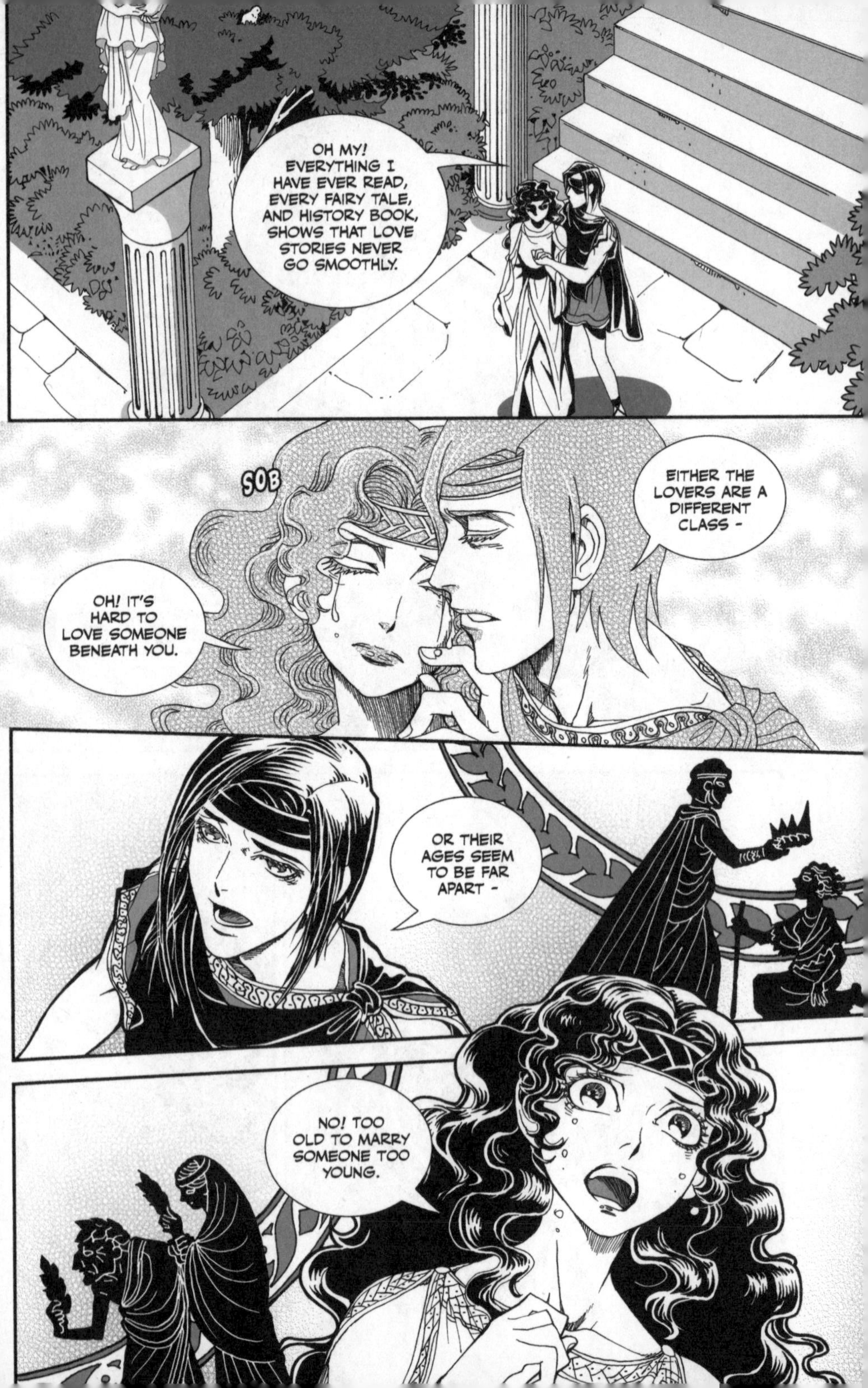
OH MY! EVERYTHING I HAVE EVER READ, EVERY FAIRY TALE, AND HISTORY BOOK, SHOWS THAT LOVE STORIES NEVER GO SMOOTHLY.
EITHER THE LOVERS ARE A DIFFERENT CLASS -
SOB
OH! IT'S HARD TO LOVE SOMEONE BENEATH YOU.
OR THEIR AGES SEEM TO BE FAR APART -
NO! TOO OLD TO MARRY SOMEONE TOO YOUNG.

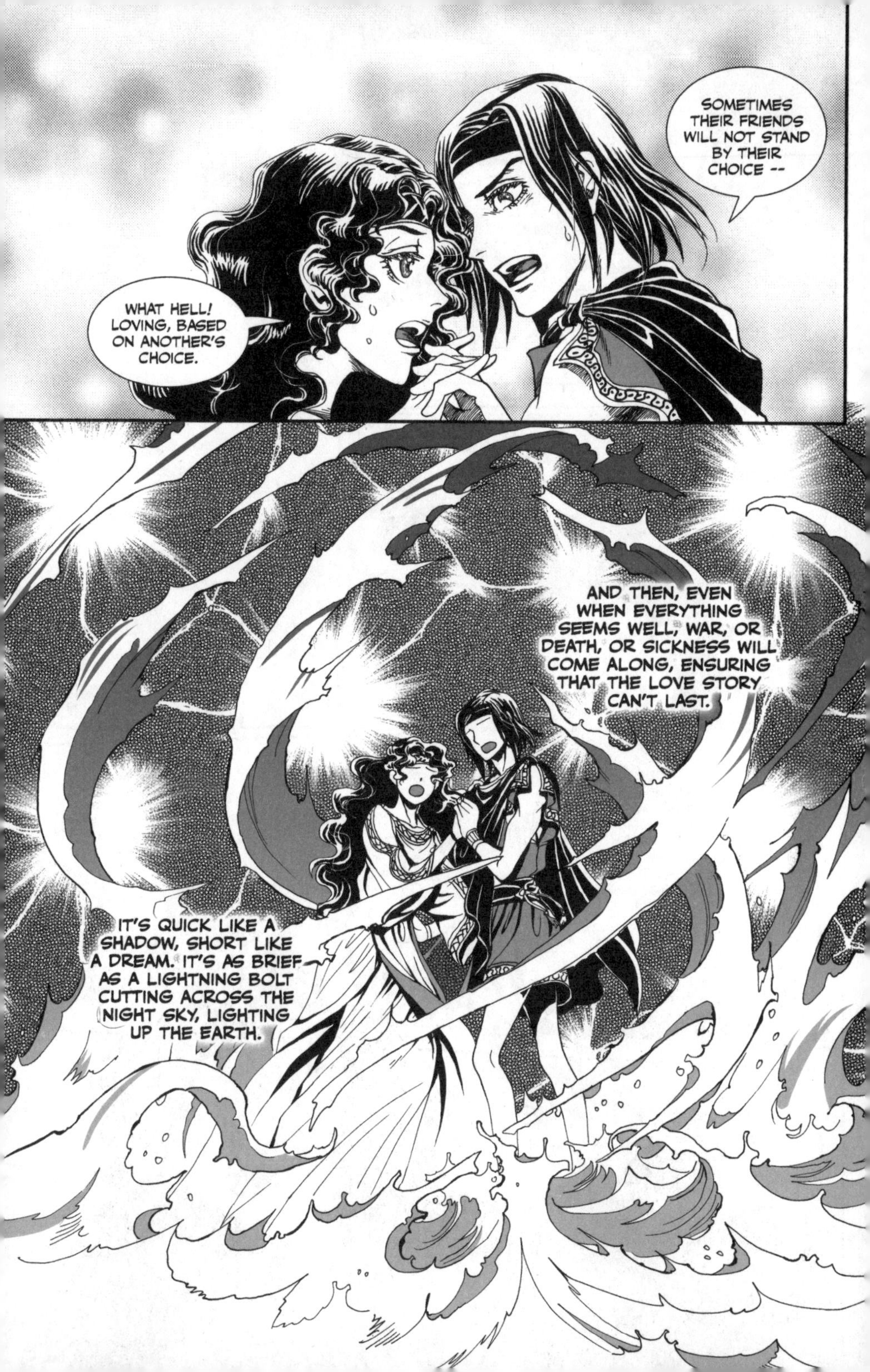
SOMETIMES THEIR FRIENDS WILL NOT STAND BY THEIR CHOICE --
WHAT HELL! LOVING, BASED ON ANOTHER'S CHOICE.
AND THEN, EVEN WHEN EVERYTHING SEEMS WELL, WAR, OR DEATH, OR SICKNESS WILL COME ALONG, ENSURING THAT THE LOVE STORY CAN'T LAST.
IT'S QUICK LIKE A SHADOW, SHORT LIKE A DREAM. IT'S AS BRIEF AS A LIGHTNING BOLT CUTTING ACROSS THE NIGHT SKY, LIGHTING UP THE EARTH.

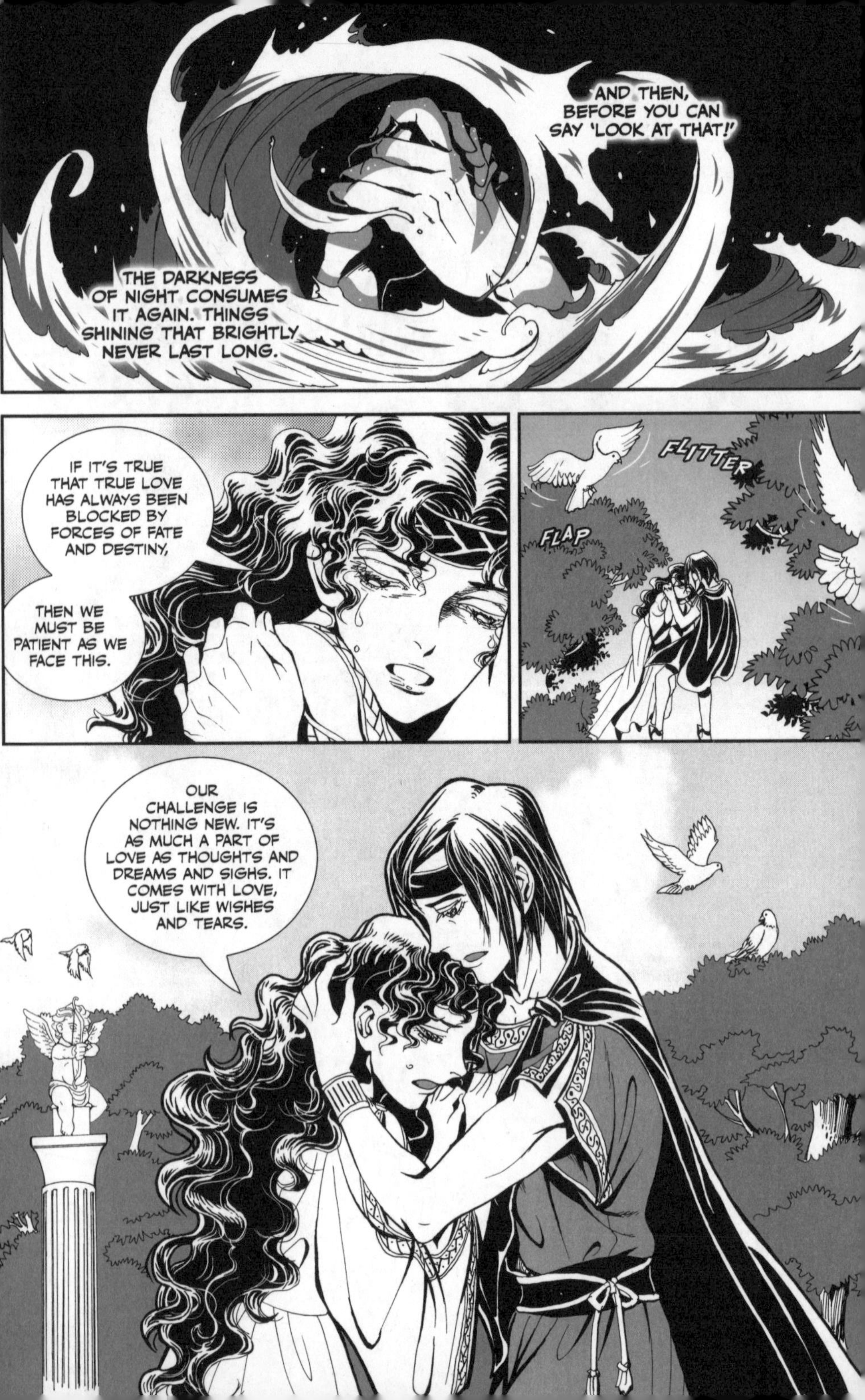
AND THEN, BEFORE YOU CAN SAY 'LOOK AT THAT!'
THE DARKNESS OF NIGHT CONSUMES IT AGAIN. THINGS SHINING THAT BRIGHTLY NEVER LAST LONG.
FLITTER
FLAP
IF IT'S TRUE THAT TRUE LOVE HAS ALWAYS BEEN BLOCKED BY FORCES OF FATE AND DESTINY,
THEN WE MUST BE PATIENT AS WE FACE THIS.
OUR CHALLENGE IS NOTHING NEW. IT'S AS MUCH A PART OF LOVE AS THOUGHTS AND DREAMS AND SIGHS. IT COMES WITH LOVE, JUST LIKE WISHES AND TEARS.

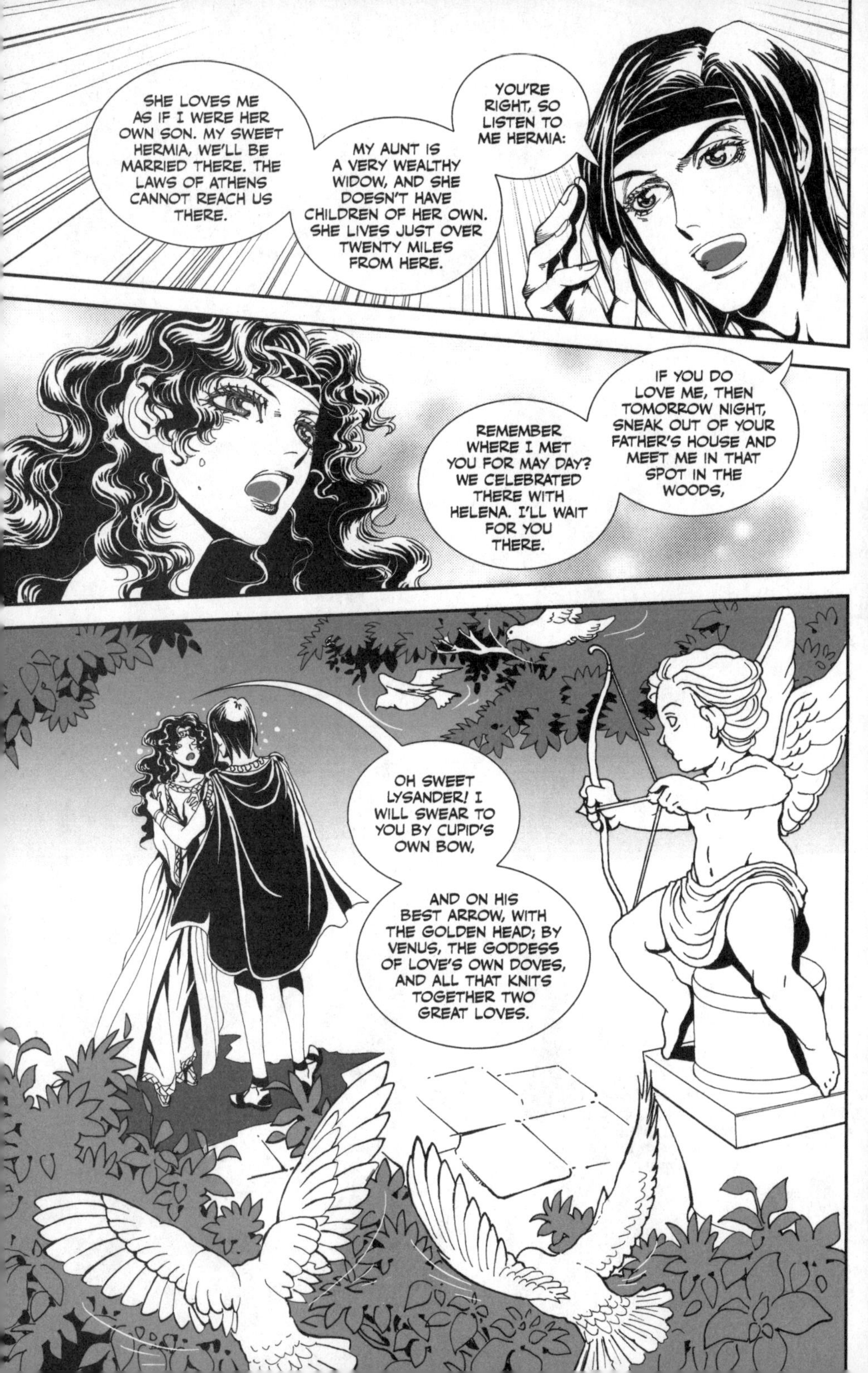
YOU'RE RIGHT, SO LISTEN TO ME HERMIA:
MY AUNT IS A VERY WEALTHY WIDOW, AND SHE DOESN'T HAVE CHILDREN OF HER OWN. SHE LIVES JUST OVER TWENTY MILES FROM HERE.
SHE LOVES ME AS IF I WERE HER OWN SON. MY SWEET HERMIA, WE'LL BE MARRIED THERE. THE LAWS OF ATHENS CANNOT REACH US THERE.
IF YOU DO LOVE ME, THEN TOMORROW NIGHT, SNEAK OUT OF YOUR FATHER'S HOUSE AND MEET ME IN THAT SPOT IN THE WOODS,
REMEMBER WHERE I MET YOU FOR MAY DAY? WE CELEBRATED THERE WITH HELENA. I'LL WAIT FOR YOU THERE.
OH SWEET LYSANDER! I WILL SWEAR TO YOU BY CUPID'S OWN BOW,
AND ON HIS BEST ARROW, WITH THE GOLDEN HEAD; BY VENUS, THE GODDESS OF LOVE'S OWN DOVES, AND ALL THAT KNITS TOGETHER TWO GREAT LOVES.

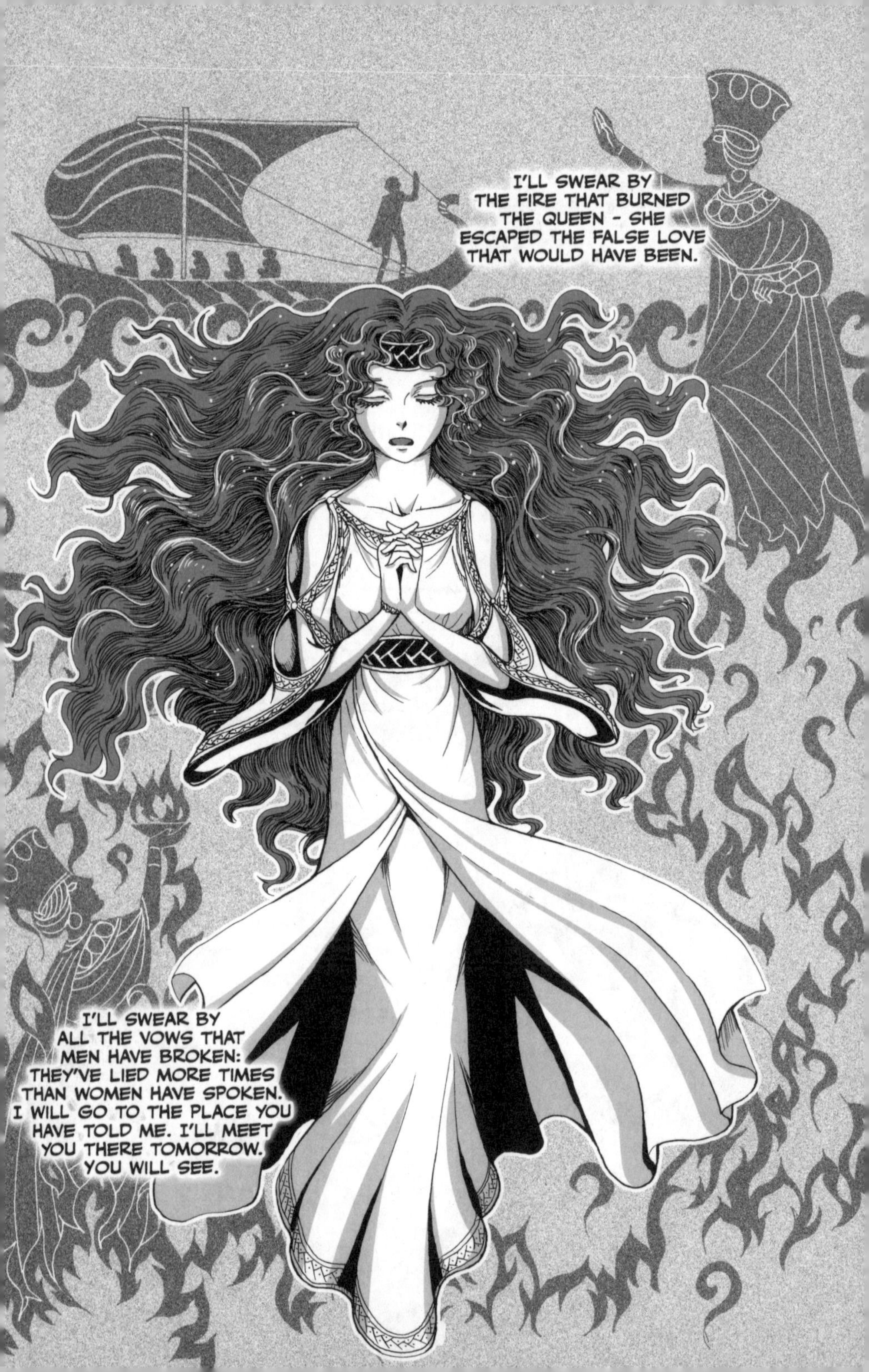
I'LL SWEAR BY THE FIRE THAT BURNED THE QUEEN - SHE ESCAPED THE FALSE LOVE THAT WOULD HAVE BEEN.
I'LL SWEAR BY ALL THE VOWS THAT MEN HAVE BROKEN: THEY'VE LIED MORE TIMES THAN WOMEN HAVE SPOKEN. I WILL GO TO THE PLACE YOU HAVE TOLD ME. I'LL MEET YOU THERE TOMORROW. YOU WILL SEE.

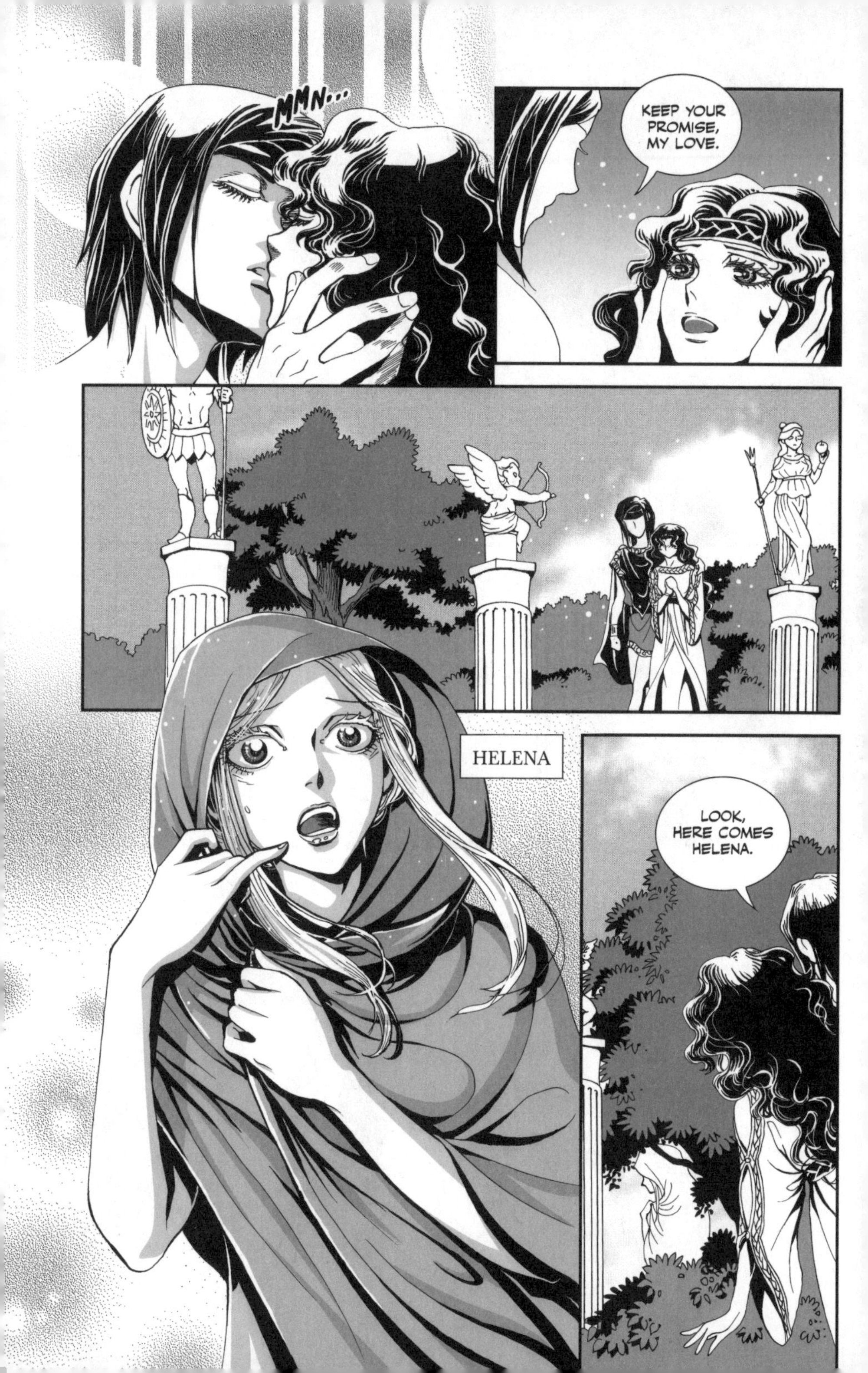
KEEP YOUR PROMISE, MY LOVE.
MMN...
LOOK, HERE COMES HELENA.
HELENA

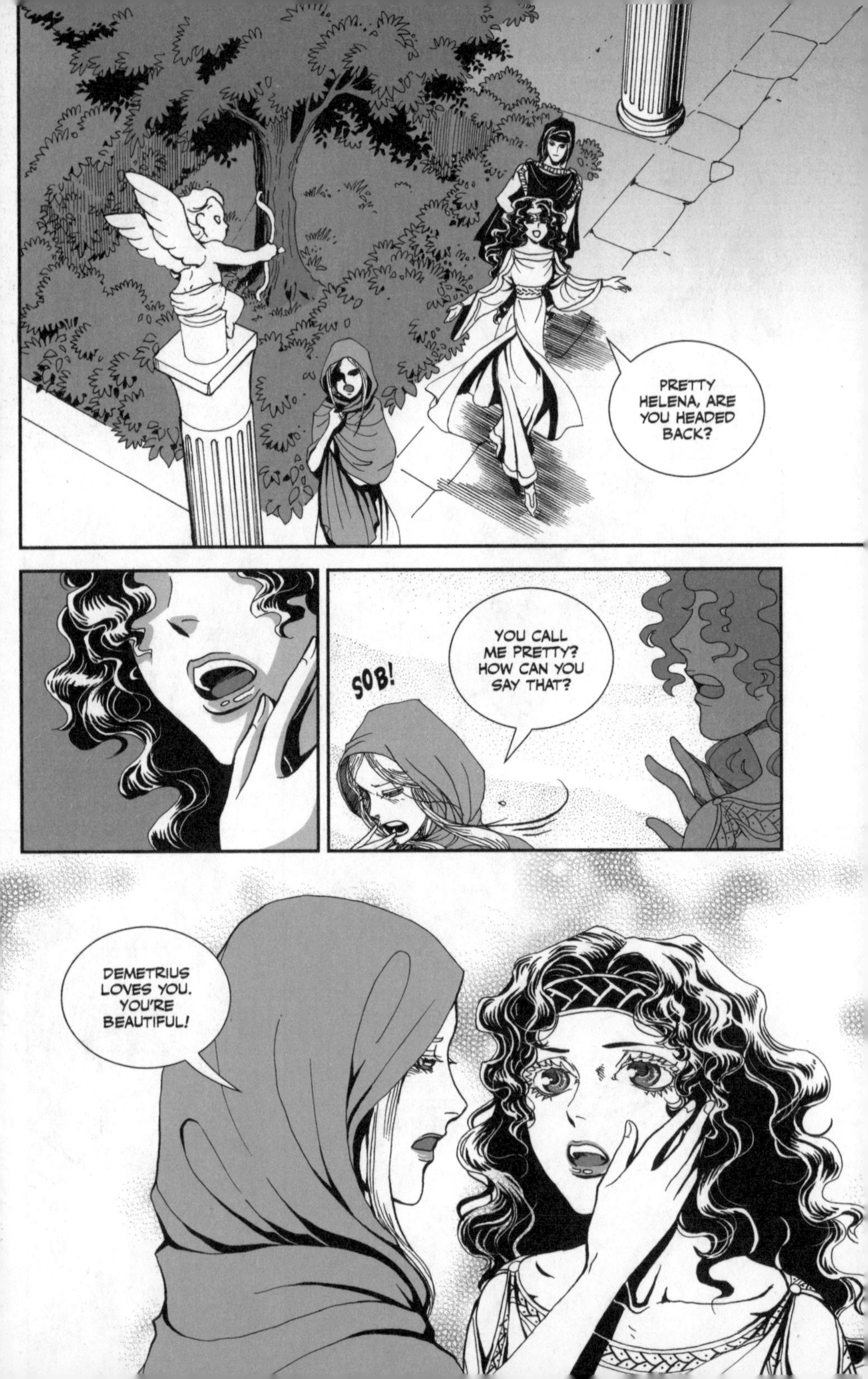
PRETTY HELENA, ARE YOU HEADED BACK?
YOU CALL ME PRETTY? HOW CAN YOU SAY THAT?
SOB!
DEMETRIUS LOVES YOU. YOU'RE BEAUTIFUL!

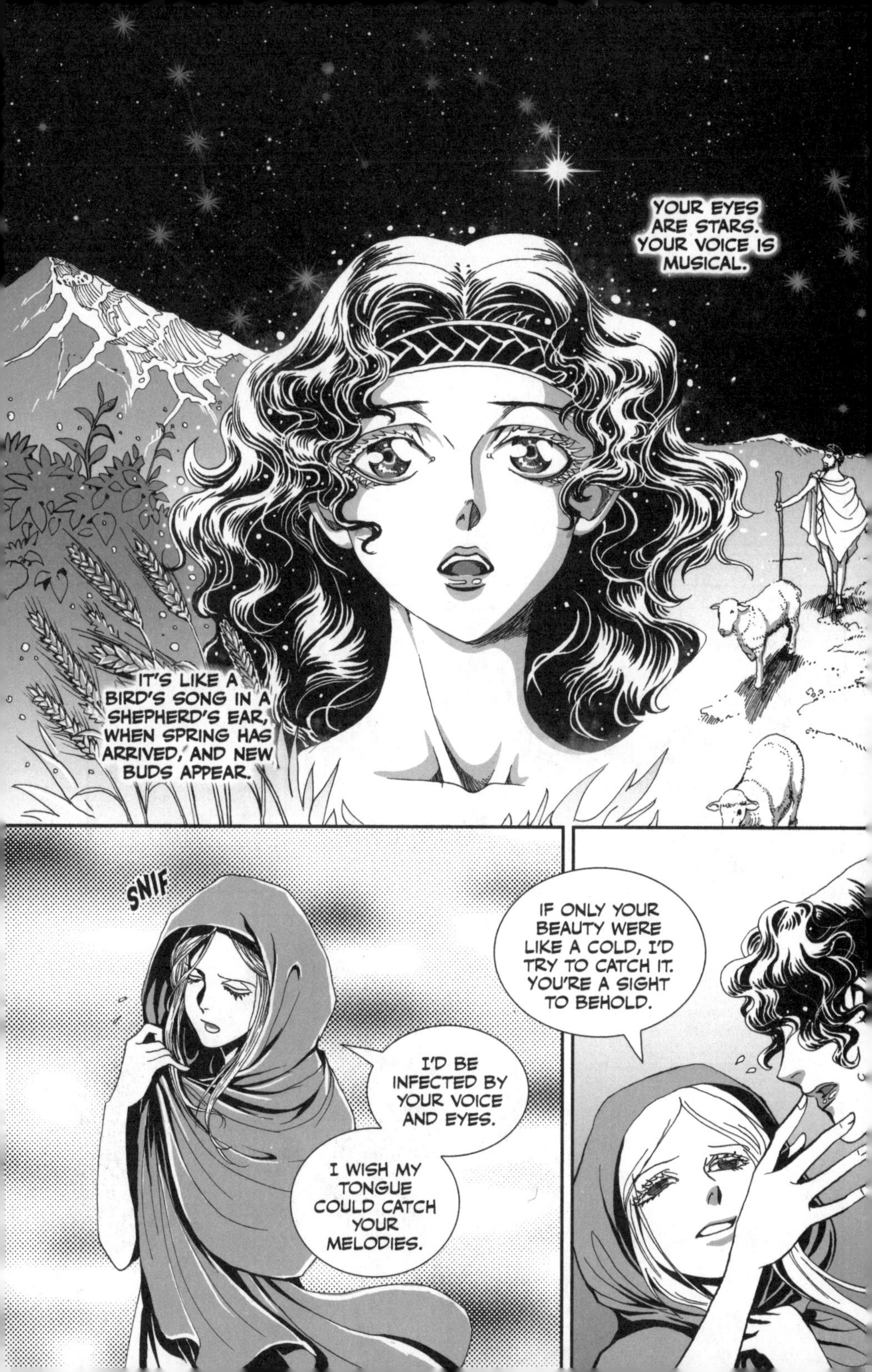
YOUR EYES ARE STARS. YOUR VOICE IS MUSICAL.
IT'S LIKE A BIRD'S SONG IN A SHEPHERD'S EAR, WHEN SPRING HAS ARRIVED, AND NEW BUDS APPEAR.
IF ONLY YOUR BEAUTY WERE LIKE A COLD, I'D TRY TO CATCH IT. YOU'RE A SIGHT TO BEHOLD.
SNIF
I'D BE INFECTED BY YOUR VOICE AND EYES.
I WISH MY TONGUE COULD CATCH YOUR MELODIES.

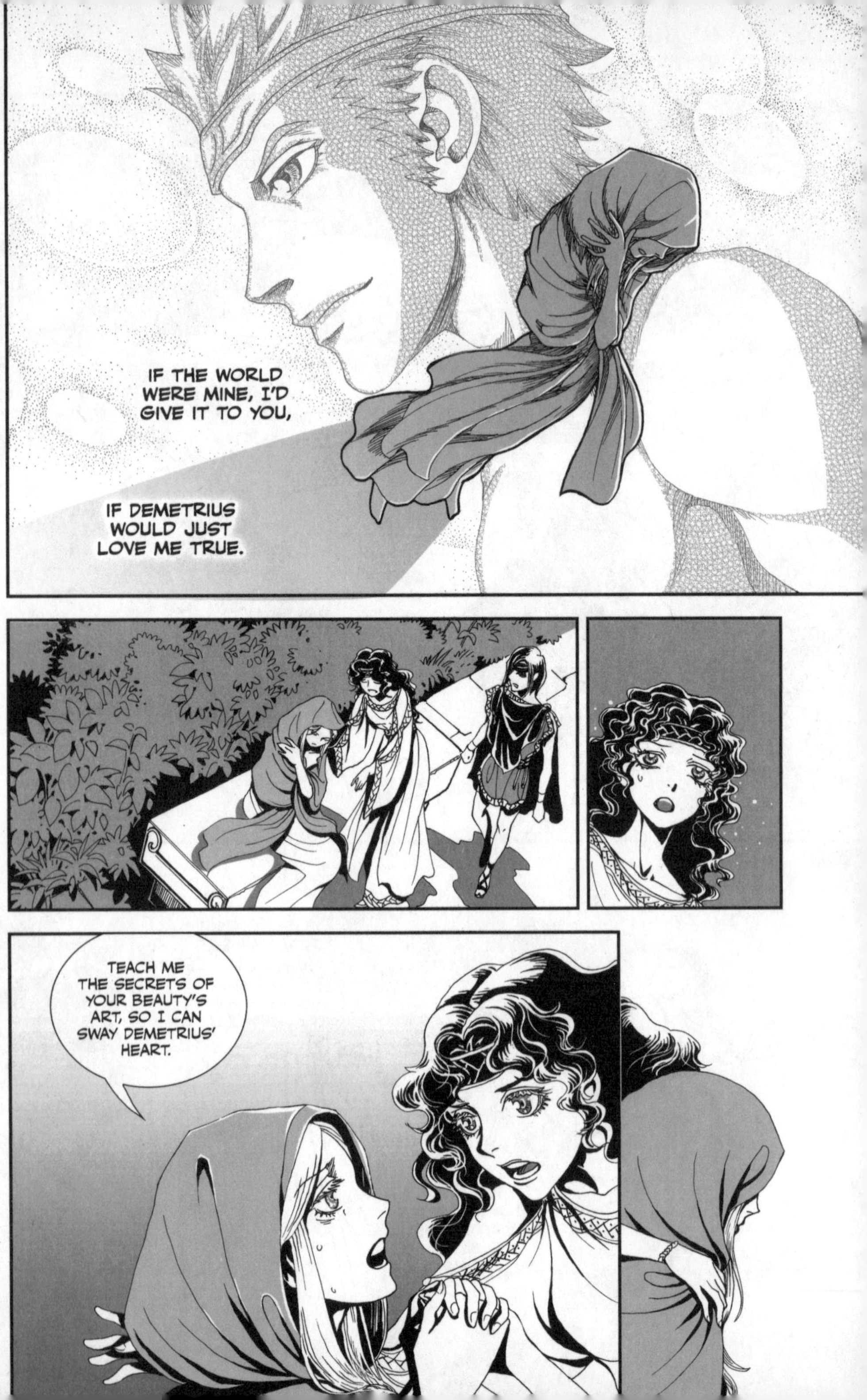
IF THE WORLD WERE MINE, I'D GIVE IT TO YOU,
IF DEMETRIUS WOULD JUST LOVE ME TRUE.
TEACH ME THE SECRETS OF YOUR BEAUTY'S ART, SO I CAN SWAY DEMETRIUS' HEART.

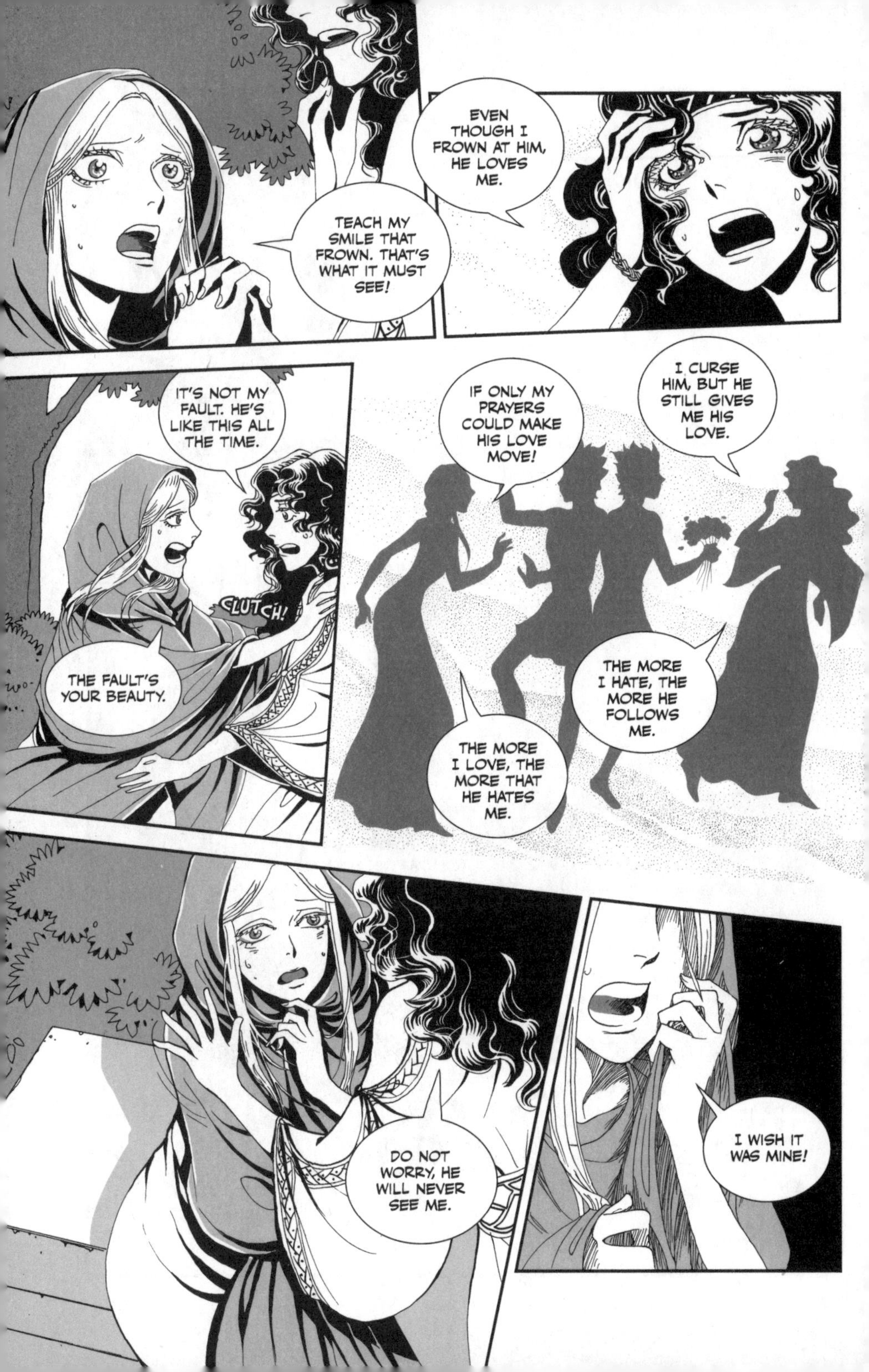
EVEN THOUGH I FROWN AT HIM, HE LOVES ME.
TEACH MY SMILE THAT FROWN. THAT'S WHAT IT MUST SEE!
I CURSE HIM, BUT HE STILL GIVES ME HIS LOVE.
IF ONLY MY PRAYERS COULD MAKE HIS LOVE MOVE!
THE MORE I HATE, THE MORE HE FOLLOWS ME.
THE MORE I LOVE, THE MORE THAT HE HATES ME.
IT'S NOT MY FAULT. HE'S LIKE THIS ALL THE TIME.
CLUTCH!
THE FAULT'S YOUR BEAUTY.
I WISH IT WAS MINE!
DO NOT WORRY, HE WILL NEVER SEE ME.

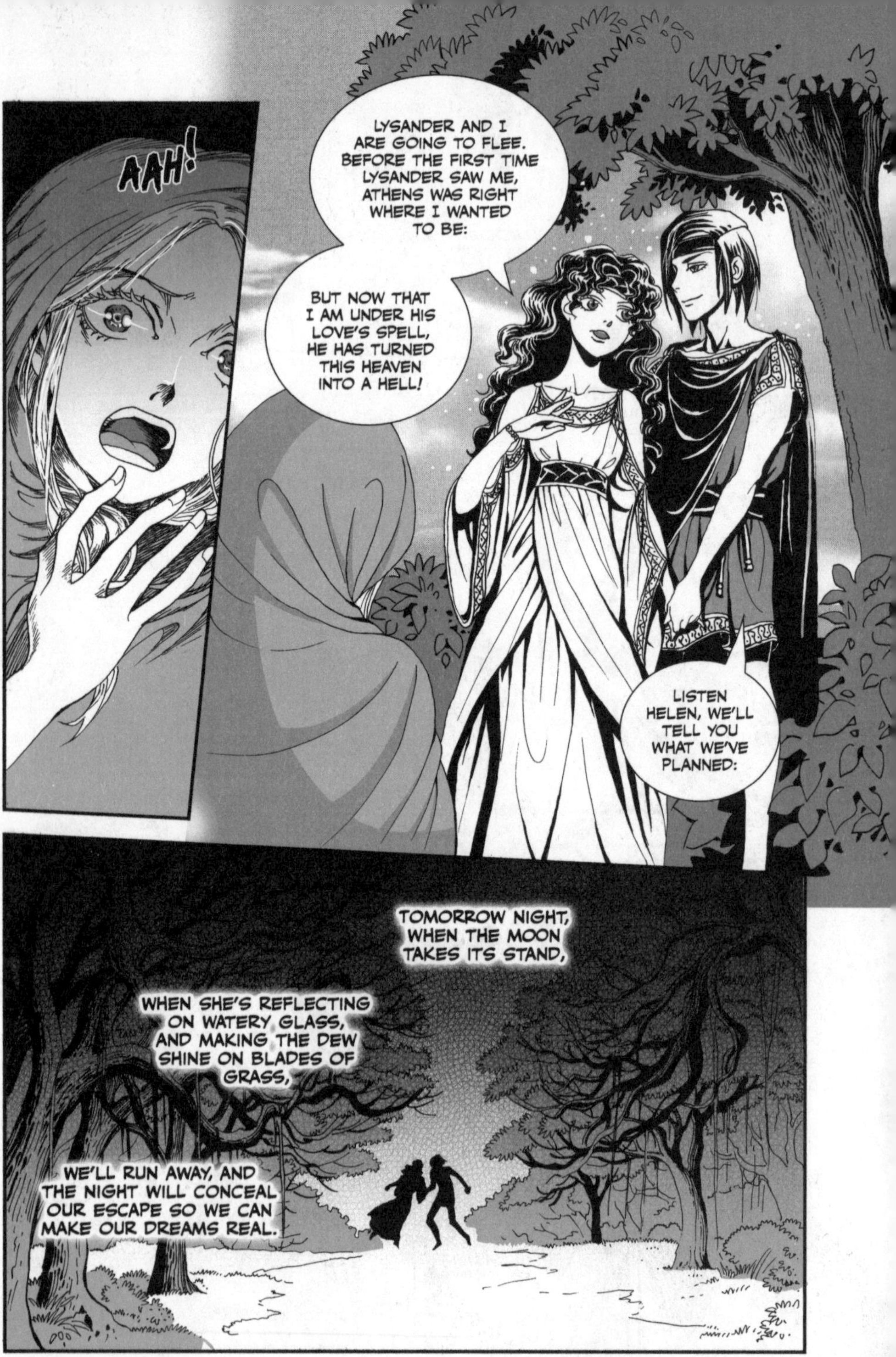
LYSANDER AND I ARE GOING TO FLEE. BEFORE THE FIRST TIME LYSANDER SAW ME, ATHENS WAS RIGHT WHERE I WANTED TO BE:
BUT NOW THAT I AM UNDER HIS LOVE'S SPELL, HE HAS TURNED THIS HEAVEN INTO A HELL!
LISTEN HELEN, WE'LL TELL YOU WHAT WE'VE PLANNED:
AAH!
TOMORROW NIGHT, WHEN THE MOON TAKES ITS STAND,
WHEN SHE'S REFLECTING ON WATERY GLASS, AND MAKING THE DEW SHINE ON BLADES OF GRASS,
WE'LL RUN AWAY, AND THE NIGHT WILL CONCEAL OUR ESCAPE SO WE CAN MAKE OUR DREAMS REAL.

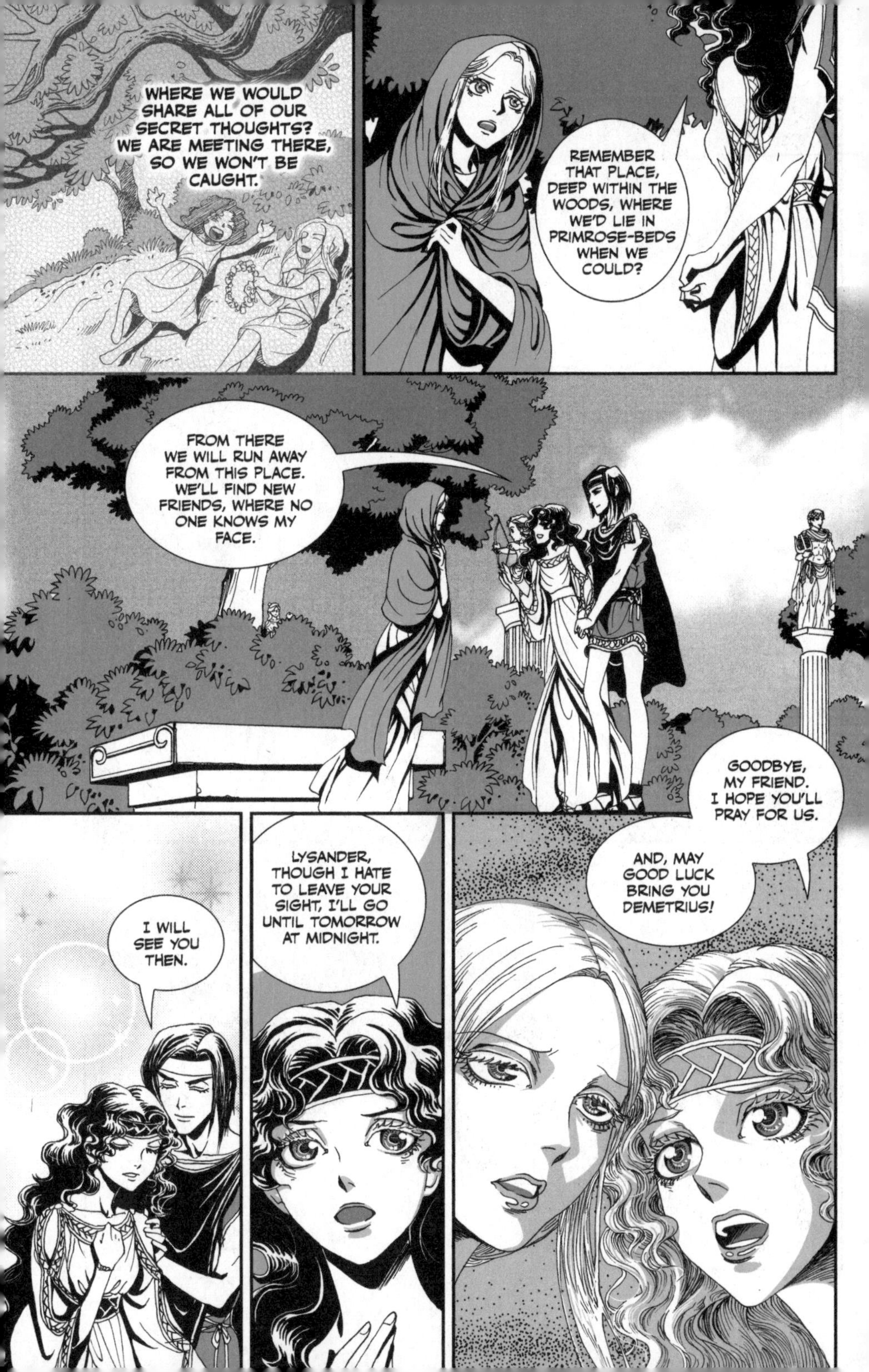
REMEMBER THAT PLACE, DEEP WITHIN THE WOODS, WHERE WE'D LIE IN PRIMROSE-BEDS WHEN WE COULD?
WHERE WE WOULD SHARE ALL OF OUR SECRET THOUGHTS? WE ARE MEETING THERE, SO WE WON'T BE CAUGHT.
FROM THERE WE WILL RUN AWAY FROM THIS PLACE. WE'LL FIND NEW FRIENDS, WHERE NO ONE KNOWS MY FACE.
GOODBYE, MY FRIEND. I HOPE YOU'LL PRAY FOR US.
AND, MAY GOOD LUCK BRING YOU DEMETRIUS!
LYSANDER, THOUGH I HATE TO LEAVE YOUR SIGHT, I'LL GO UNTIL TOMORROW AT MIDNIGHT.
I WILL SEE YOU THEN.

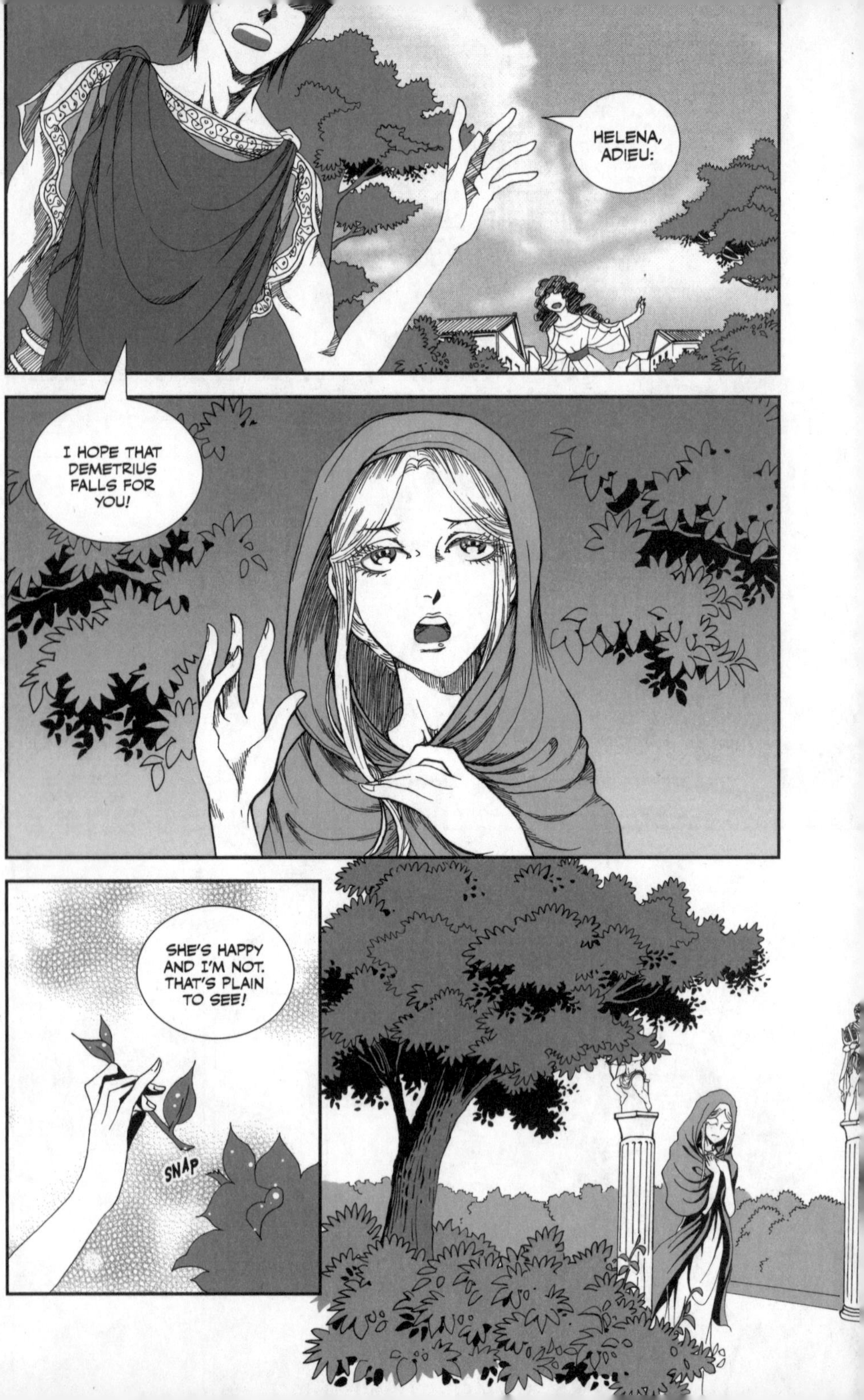
HELENA, ADIEU:
I HOPE THAT DEMETRIUS FALLS FOR YOU!
SHE'S HAPPY AND I'M NOT. THAT'S PLAIN TO SEE!
SNAP

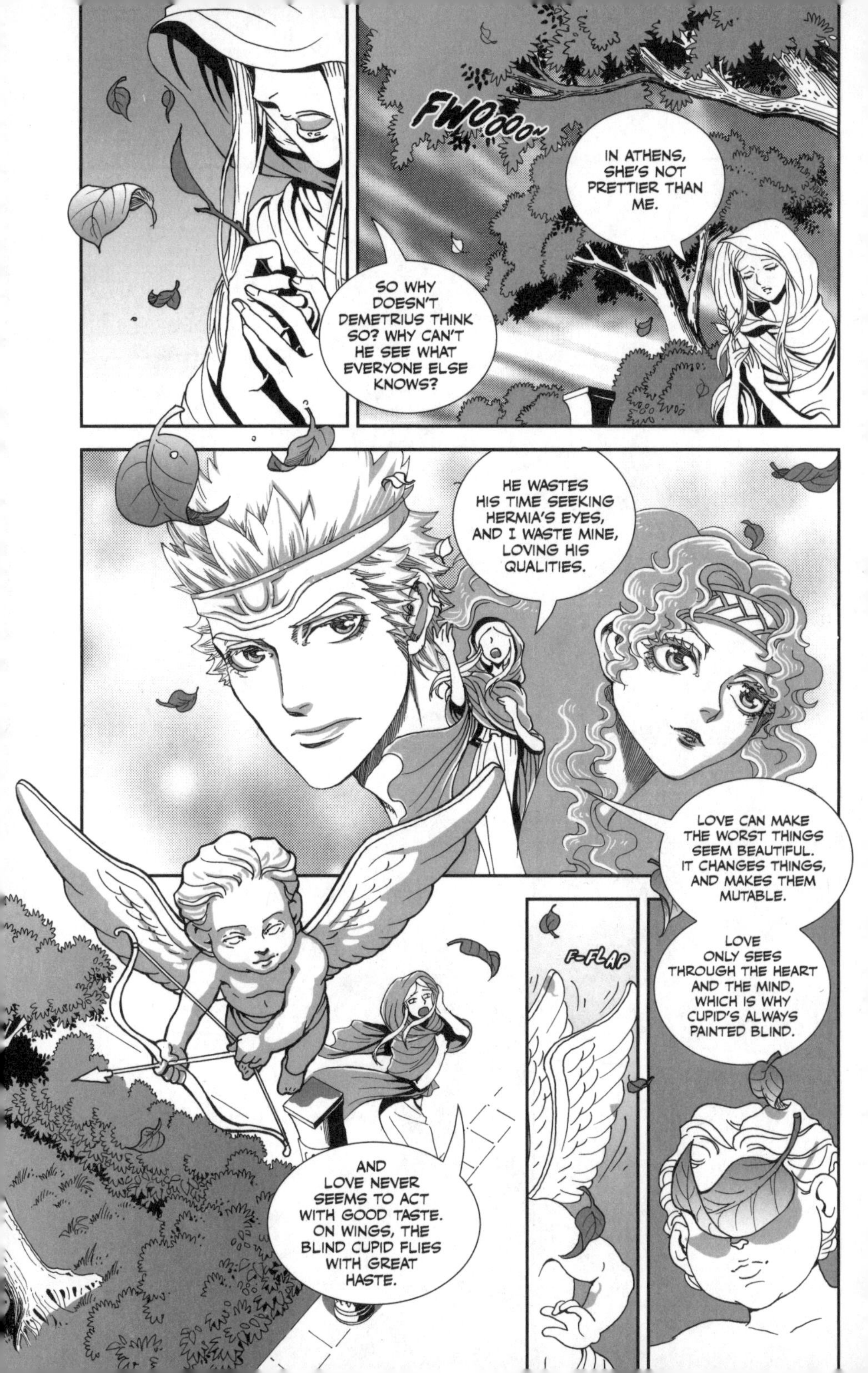
FWOOOOO~
IN ATHENS, SHE'S NOT PRETTIER THAN ME.
SO WHY DOESN'T DEMETRIUS THINK SO? WHY CAN'T HE SEE WHAT EVERYONE ELSE KNOWS?
HE WASTES HIS TIME SEEKING HERMIA'S EYES, AND I WASTE MINE, LOVING HIS QUALITIES.
LOVE CAN MAKE THE WORST THINGS SEEM BEAUTIFUL. IT CHANGES THINGS, AND MAKES THEM MUTABLE.
LOVE ONLY SEES THROUGH THE HEART AND THE MIND, WHICH IS WHY CUPID'S ALWAYS PAINTED BLIND.
F-FLAP
AND LOVE NEVER SEEMS TO ACT WITH GOOD TASTE. ON WINGS, THE BLIND CUPID FLIES WITH GREAT HASTE.

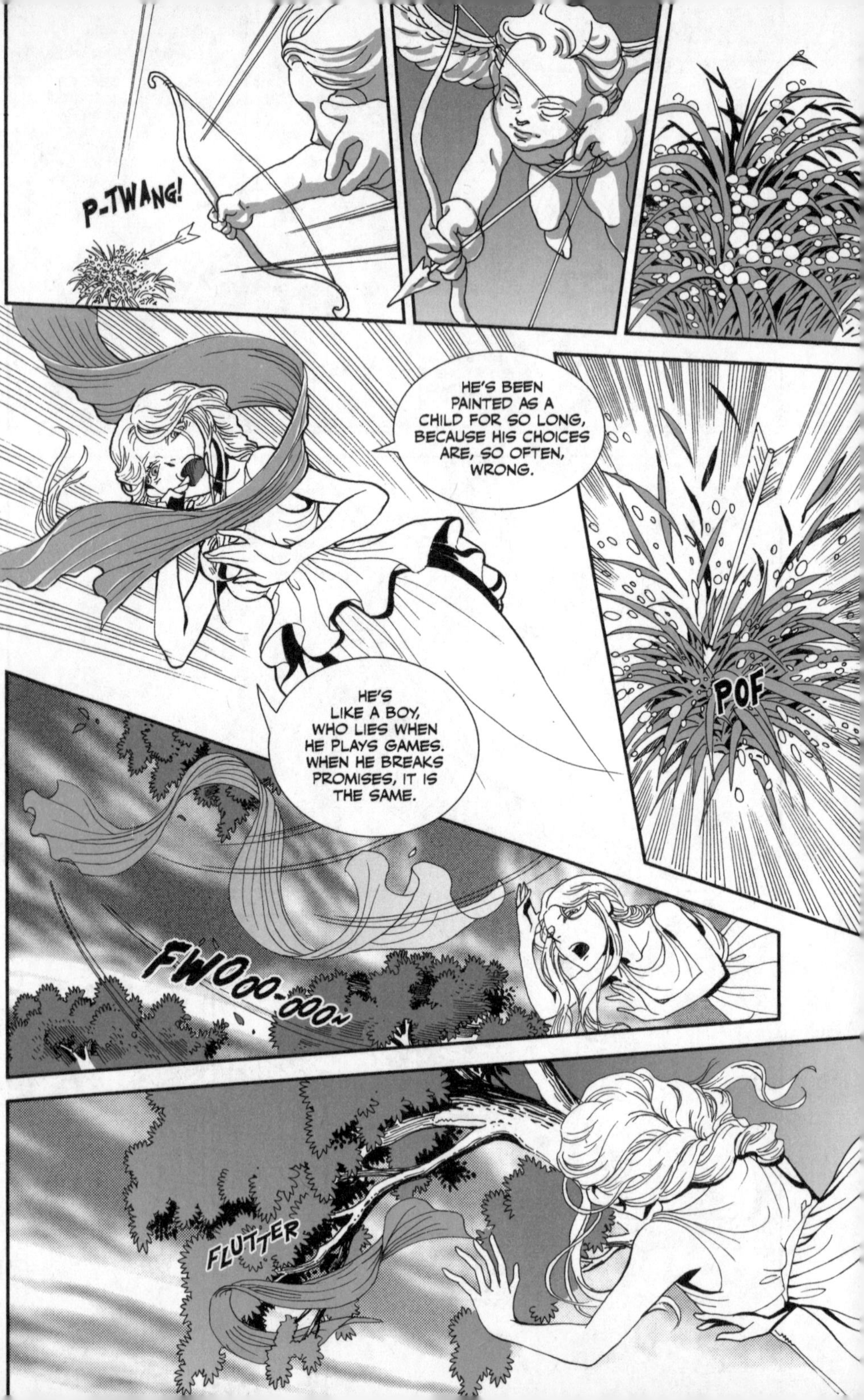
P-TWANG!
POF
HE'S BEEN PAINTED AS A CHILD FOR SO LONG, BECAUSE HIS CHOICES ARE, SO OFTEN, WRONG.
HE'S LIKE A BOY, WHO LIES WHEN HE PLAYS GAMES. WHEN HE BREAKS PROMISES, IT IS THE SAME.
FWOOO-OOO~
FLUTTER

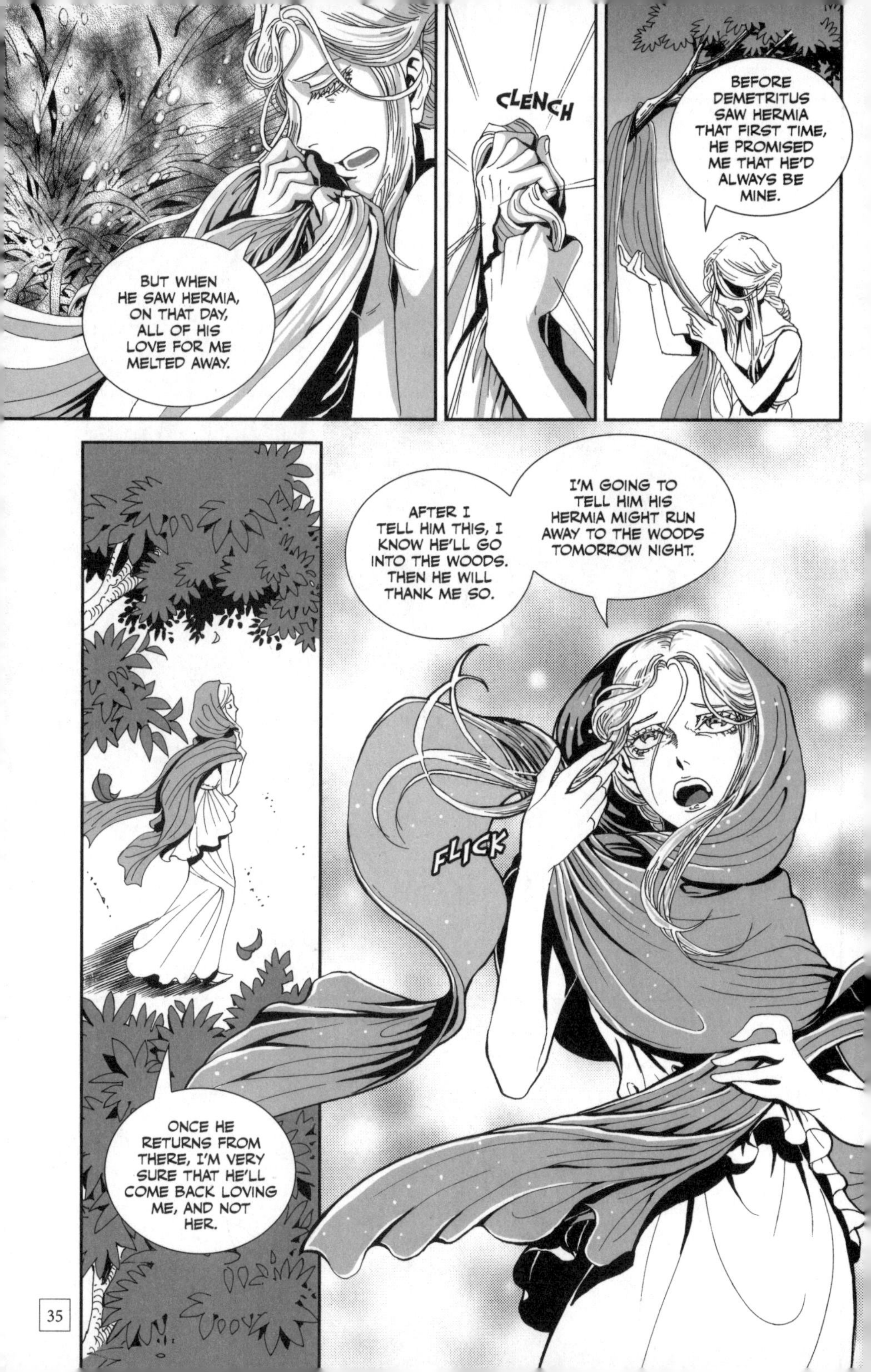
BEFORE DEMETRITUS SAW HERMIA THAT FIRST TIME, HE PROMISED ME THAT HE'D ALWAYS BE MINE.
CLENCH
BUT WHEN HE SAW HERMIA, ON THAT DAY, ALL OF HIS LOVE FOR ME MELTED AWAY.
I'M GOING TO TELL HIM HIS HERMIA MIGHT RUN AWAY TO THE WOODS TOMORROW NIGHT.
AFTER I TELL HIM THIS, I KNOW HE'LL GO INTO THE WOODS. THEN HE WILL THANK ME SO.
FLICK
ONCE HE RETURNS FROM THERE, I'M VERY SURE THAT HE'LL COME BACK LOVING ME, AND NOT HER.

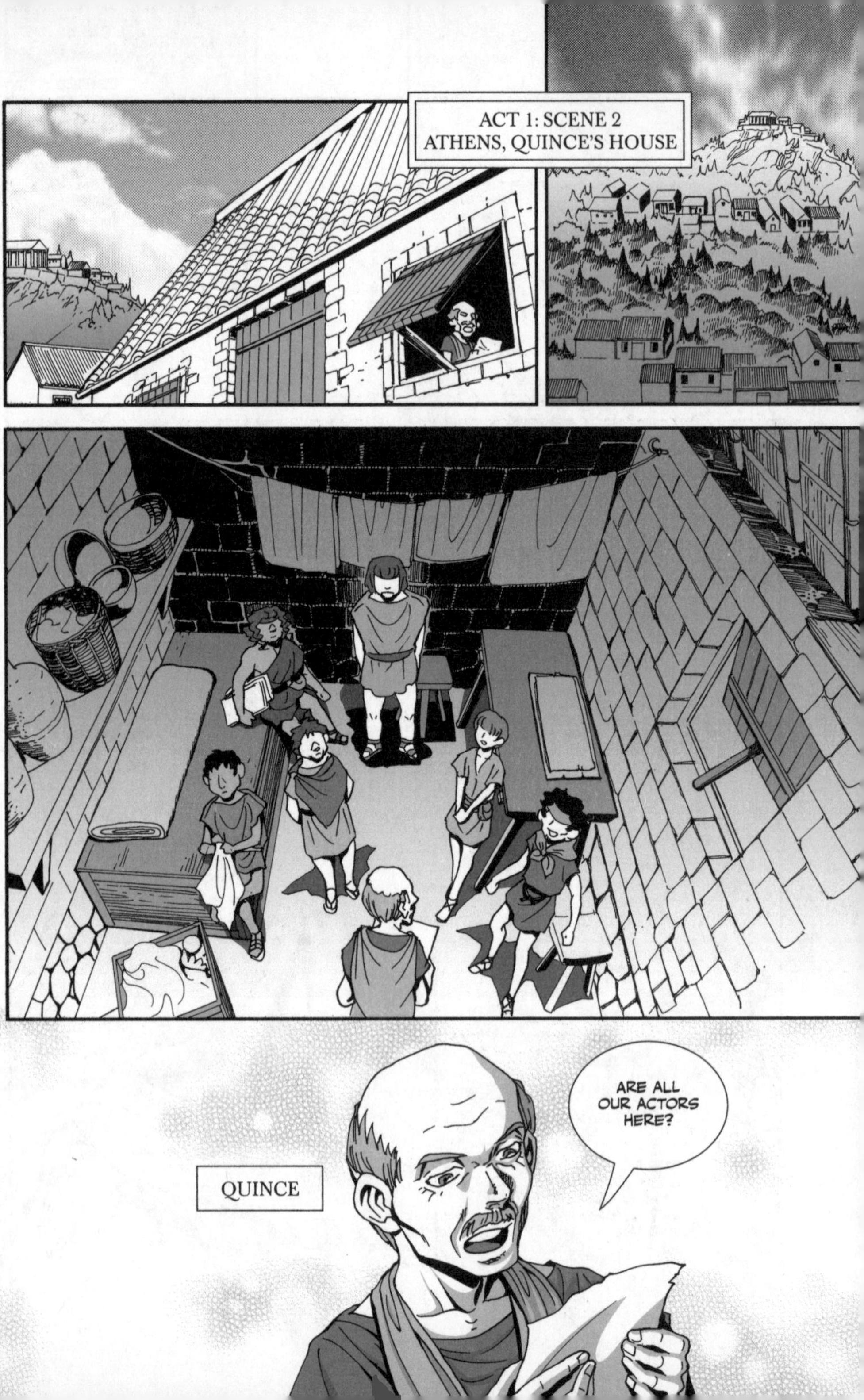
ACT 1: SCENE 2
ATHENS, QUINCE'S HOUSE
QUINCE
ARE ALL OUR ACTORS HERE?

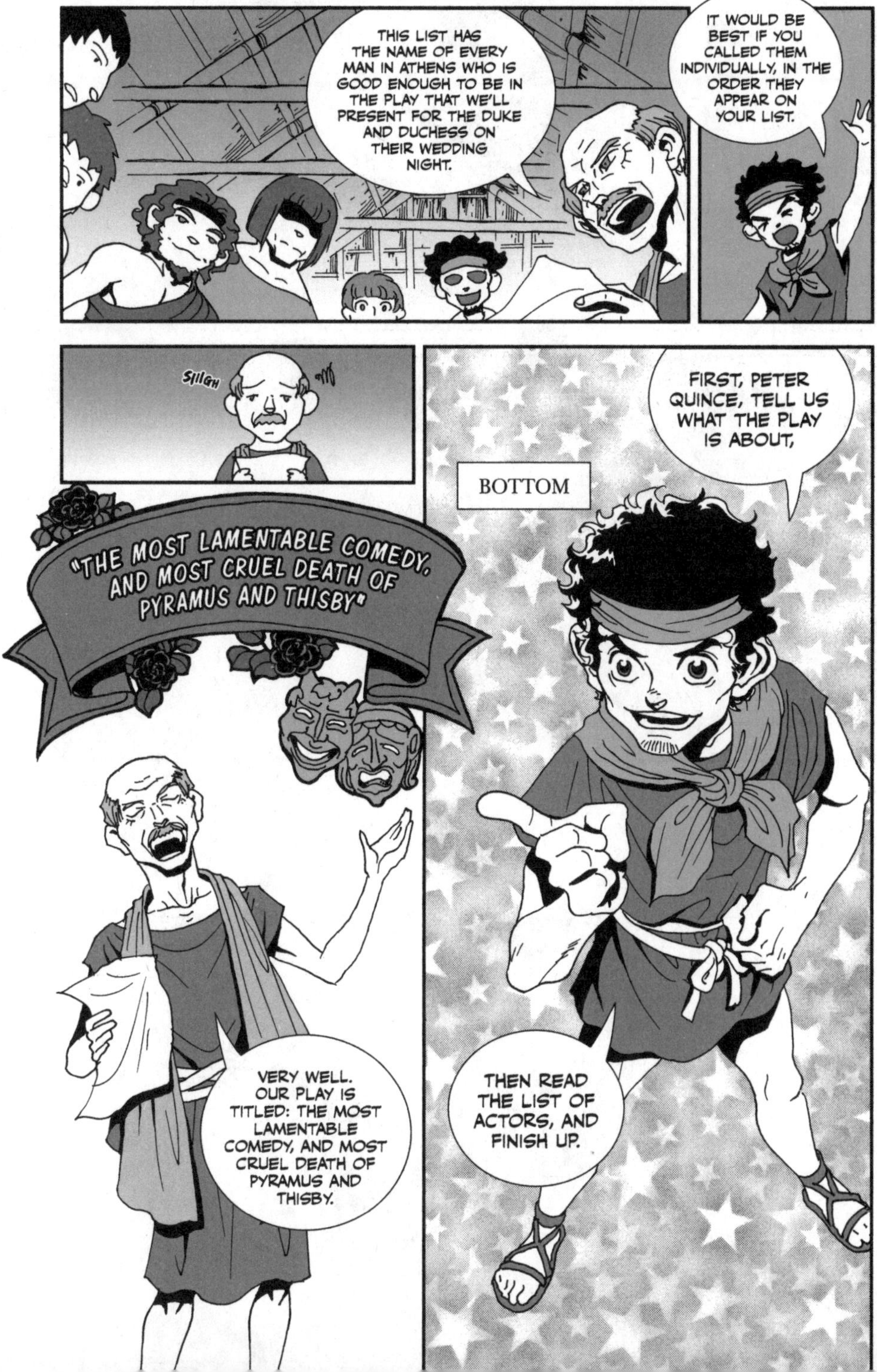
IT WOULD BE BEST IF YOU CALLED THEM INDIVIDUALLY, IN THE ORDER THEY APPEAR ON YOUR LIST.
THIS LIST HAS THE NAME OF EVERY MAN IN ATHENS WHO IS GOOD ENOUGH TO BE IN THE PLAY THAT WE'LL PRESENT FOR THE DUKE AND DUCHESS ON THEIR WEDDING NIGHT.
BOTTOM
FIRST, PETER QUINCE, TELL US WHAT THE PLAY IS ABOUT,
THEN READ THE LIST OF ACTORS, AND FINISH UP.
SIIGH
"THE MOST LAMENTABLE COMEDY, AND MOST CRUEL DEATH OF PYRAMUS AND THISBY"
VERY WELL. OUR PLAY IS TITLED: THE MOST LAMENTABLE COMEDY, AND MOST CRUEL DEATH OF PYRAMUS AND THISBY.

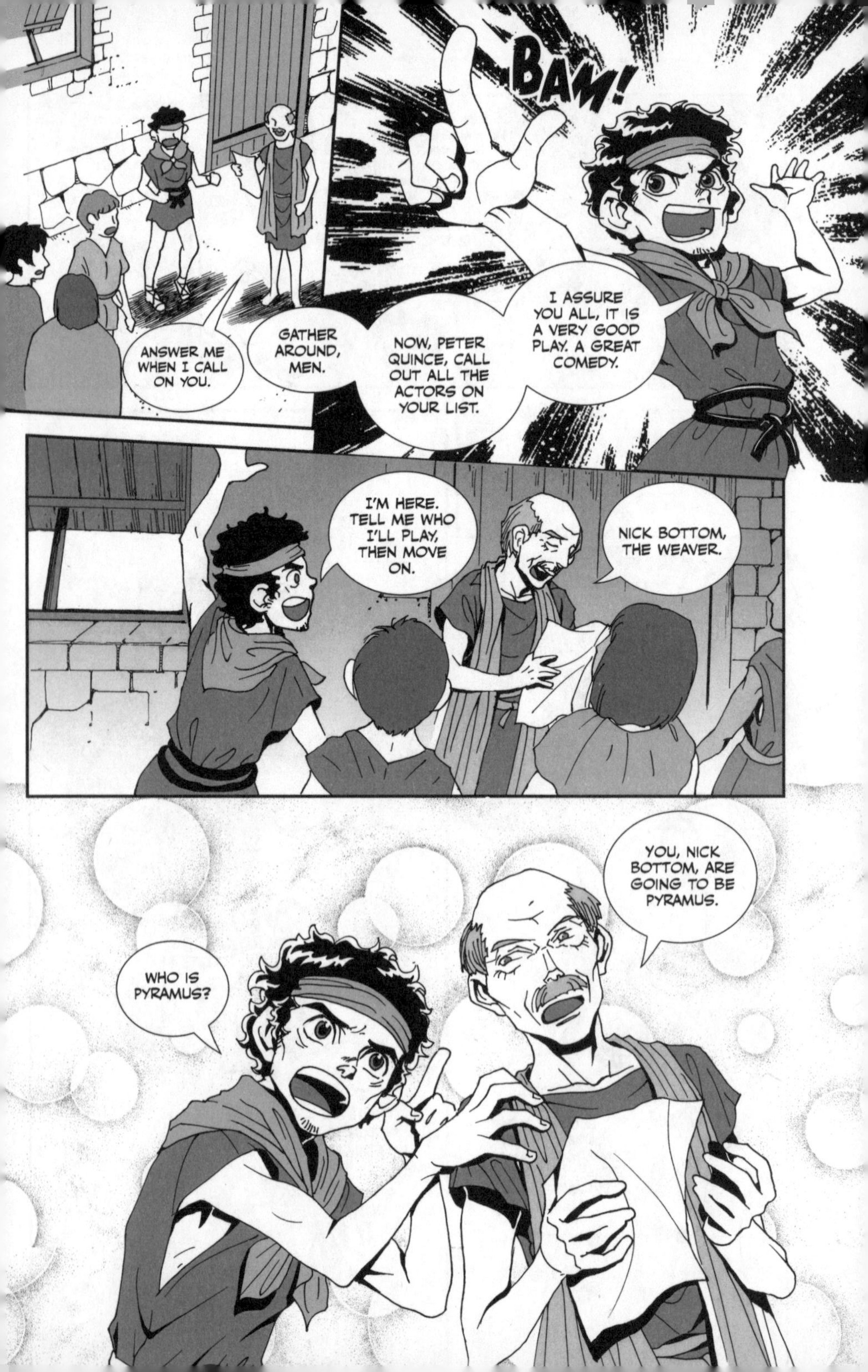
BAM!
I ASSURE YOU ALL, IT IS A VERY GOOD PLAY. A GREAT COMEDY.
NOW, PETER QUINCE, CALL OUT ALL THE ACTORS ON YOUR LIST.
GATHER AROUND, MEN.
ANSWER ME WHEN I CALL ON YOU.
NICK BOTTOM, THE WEAVER.
I'M HERE. TELL ME WHO I'LL PLAY, THEN MOVE ON.
YOU, NICK BOTTOM, ARE GOING TO BE PYRAMUS.
WHO IS PYRAMUS?

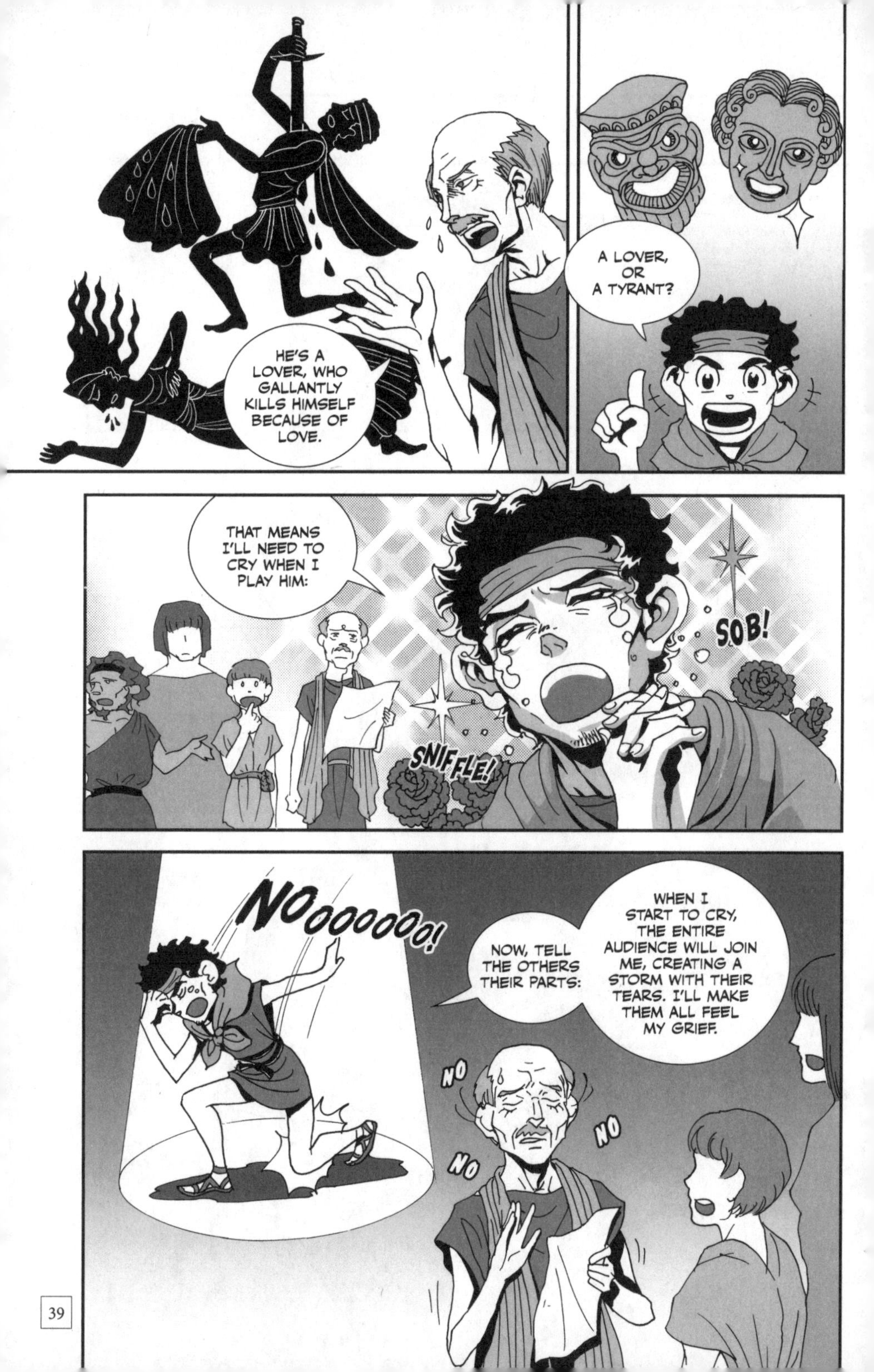
A LOVER, OR A TYRANT?
HE'S A LOVER, WHO GALLANTLY KILLS HIMSELF BECAUSE OF LOVE.
THAT MEANS I'LL NEED TO CRY WHEN I PLAY HIM:
SOB!
SNIFFLE!
WHEN I START TO CRY, THE ENTIRE AUDIENCE WILL JOIN ME, CREATING A STORM WITH THEIR TEARS. I'LL MAKE THEM ALL FEEL MY GRIEF.
NOW, TELL THE OTHERS THEIR PARTS:
NOoooooo!
NO
NO
NO

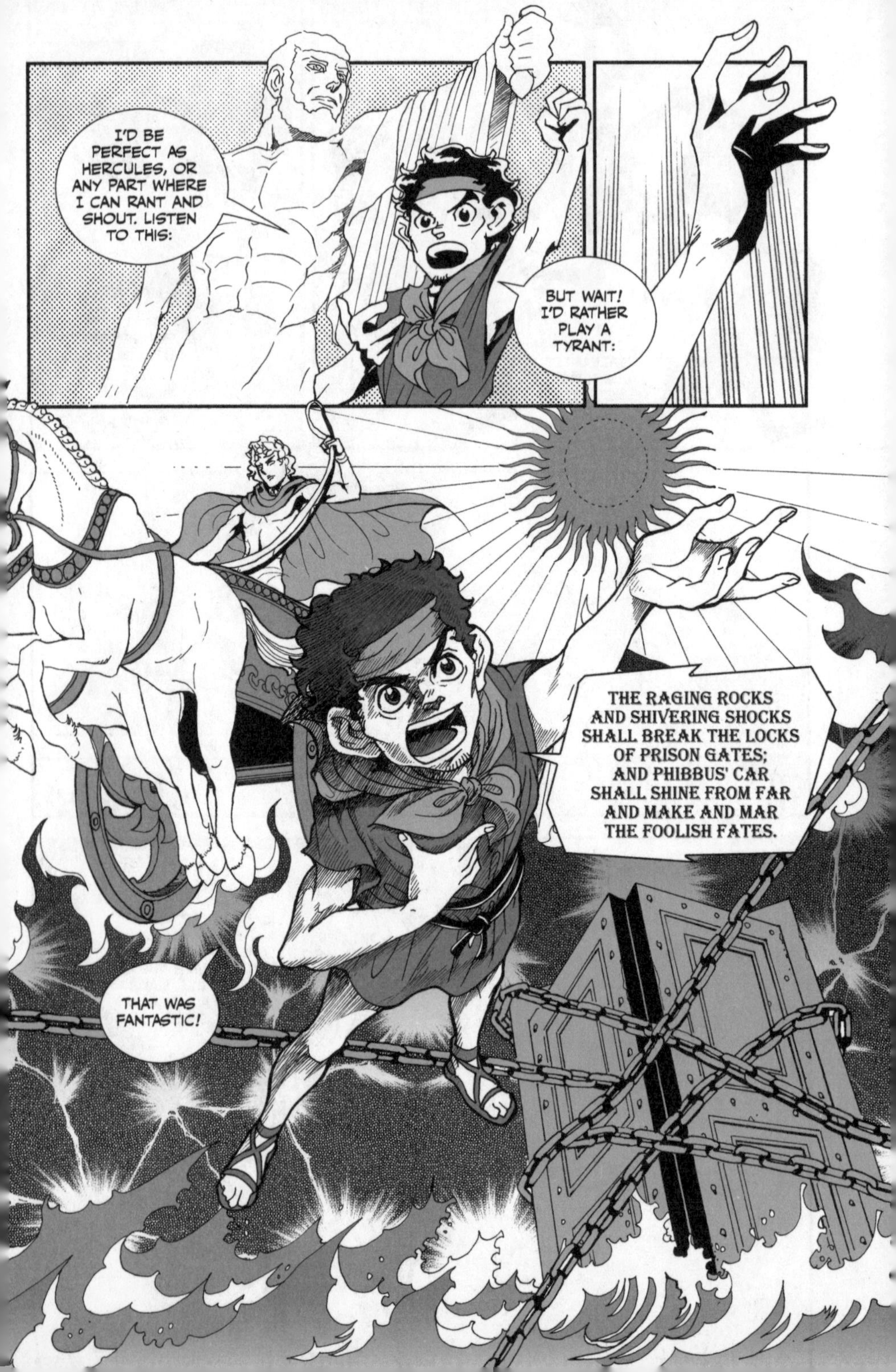
I'D BE PERFECT AS HERCULES, OR ANY PART WHERE I CAN RANT AND SHOUT. LISTEN TO THIS:
BUT WAIT! I'D RATHER PLAY A TYRANT:
THE RAGING ROCKS AND SHIVERING SHOCKS SHALL BREAK THE LOCKS OF PRISON GATES; AND PHIBBUS' CAR SHALL SHINE FROM FAR AND MAKE AND MAR THE FOOLISH FATES.
THAT WAS FANTASTIC!

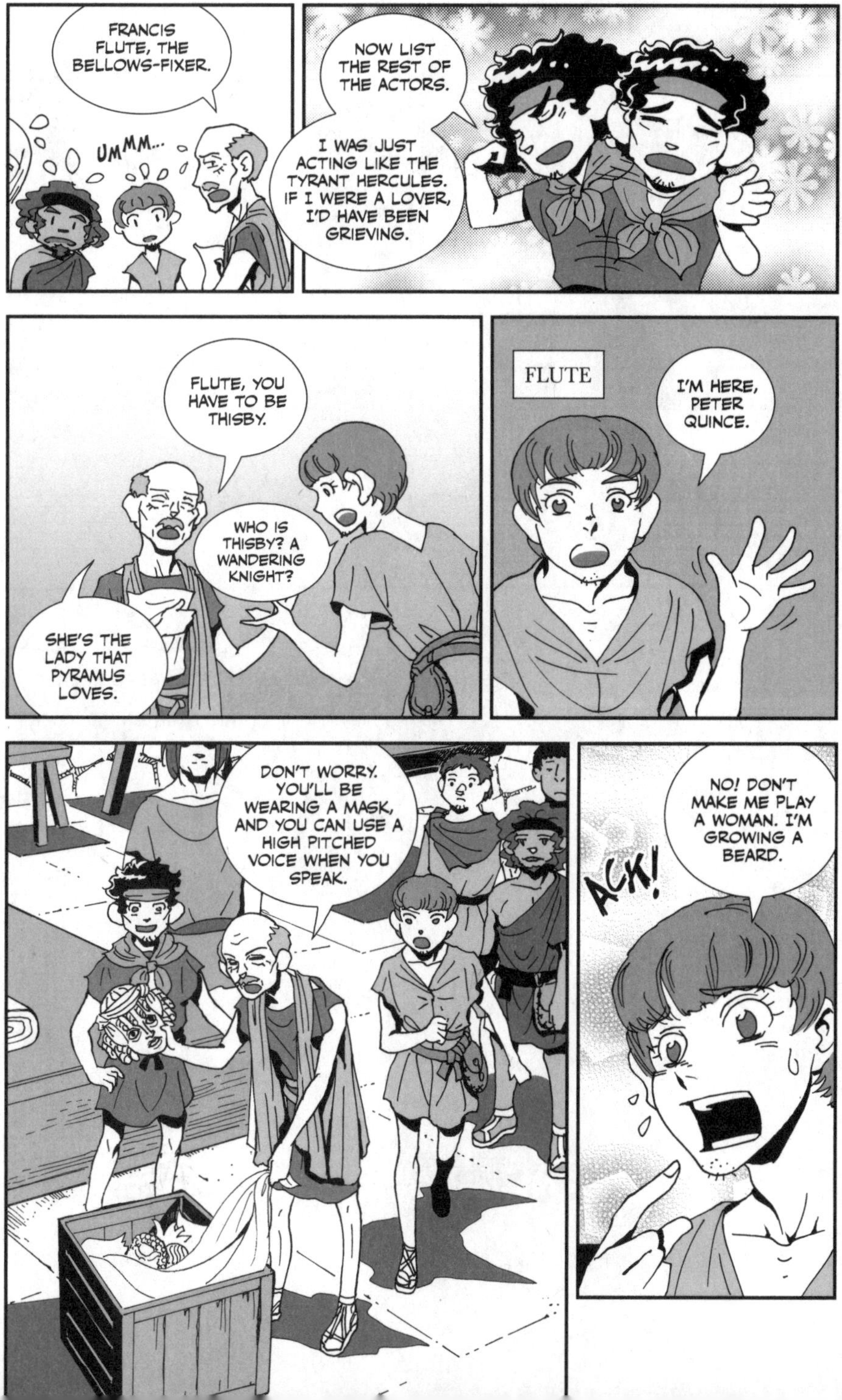
NOW LIST THE REST OF THE ACTORS.
I WAS JUST ACTING LIKE THE TYRANT HERCULES. IF I WERE A LOVER, I'D HAVE BEEN GRIEVING.
FRANCIS FLUTE, THE BELLOWS-FIXER.
UMMM...
FLUTE
I'M HERE, PETER QUINCE.
FLUTE, YOU HAVE TO BE THISBY.
WHO IS THISBY? A WANDERING KNIGHT?
SHE'S THE LADY THAT PYRAMUS LOVES.
NO! DON'T MAKE ME PLAY A WOMAN. I'M GROWING A BEARD.
ACK!
DON'T WORRY. YOU'LL BE WEARING A MASK, AND YOU CAN USE A HIGH PITCHED VOICE WHEN YOU SPEAK.

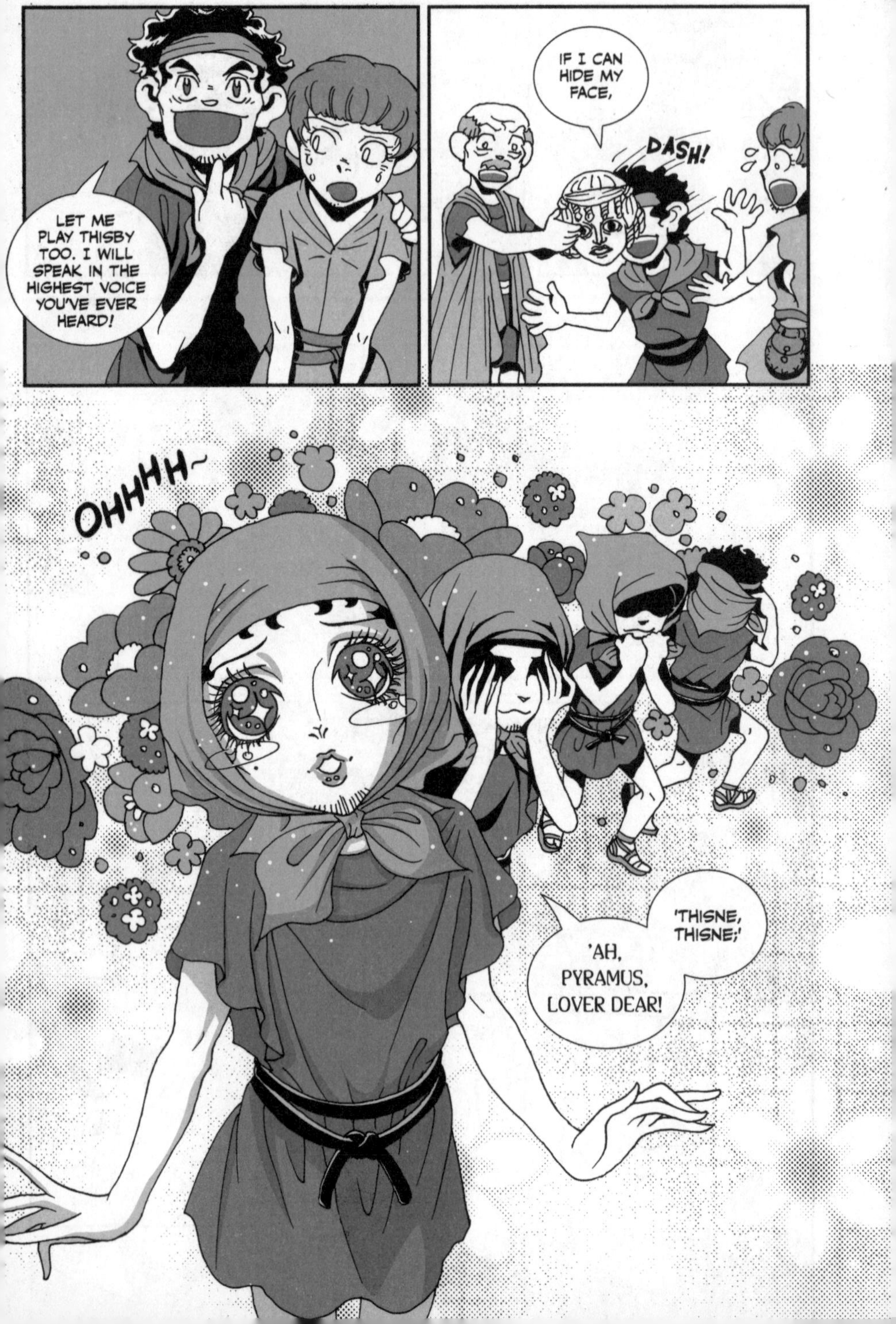
IF I CAN HIDE MY FACE,
DASH!
LET ME PLAY THISBY TOO. I WILL SPEAK IN THE HIGHEST VOICE YOU'VE EVER HEARD!
OHHHH~
'THISNE, THISNE;'
'AH, PYRAMUS, LOVER DEAR!

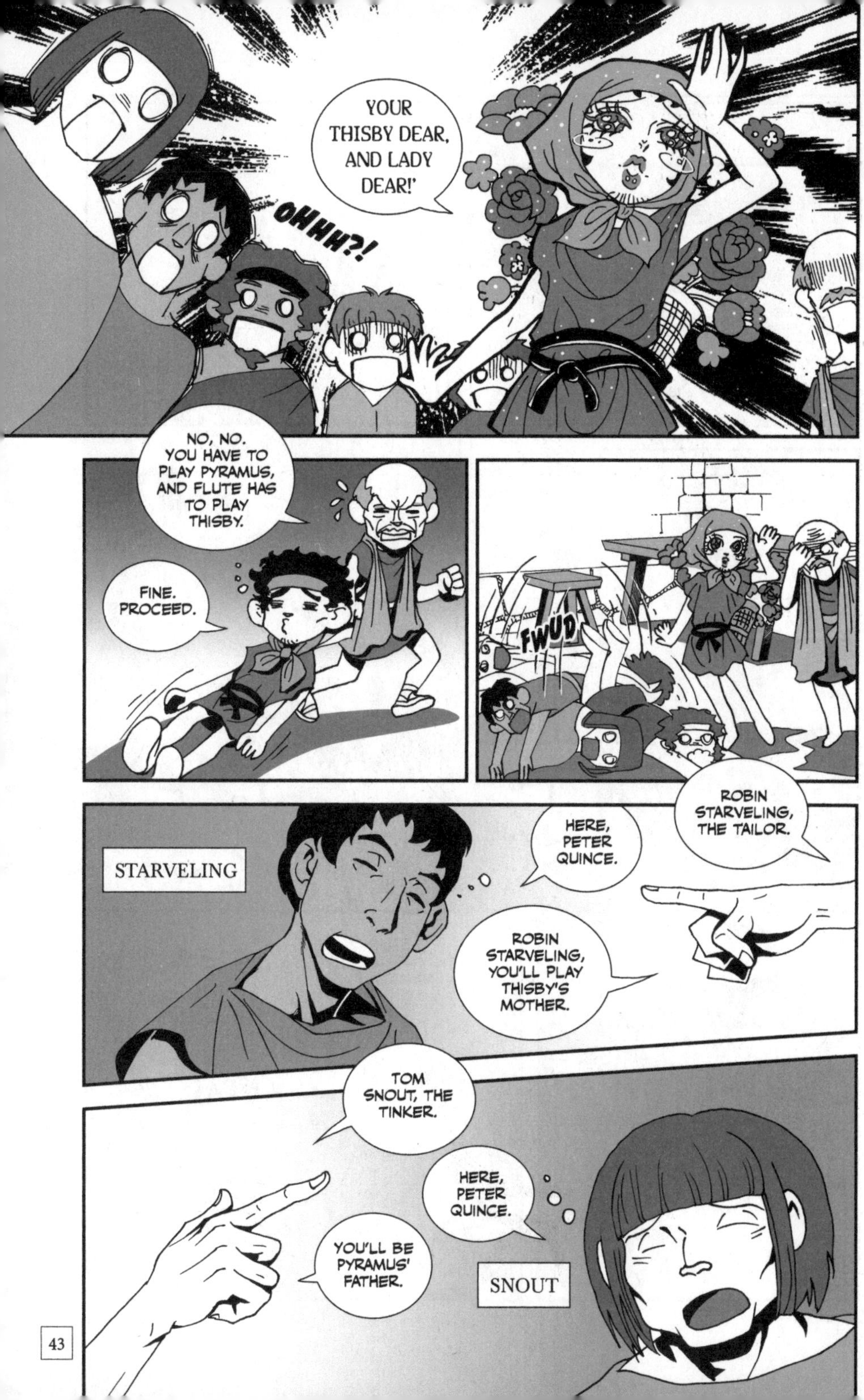
YOUR THISBY DEAR, AND LADY DEAR!'
OHHH?!
FWUD
NO, NO. YOU HAVE TO PLAY PYRAMUS, AND FLUTE HAS TO PLAY THISBY.
FINE. PROCEED.
ROBIN STARVELING, THE TAILOR.
HERE, PETER QUINCE.
STARVELING
ROBIN STARVELING, YOU'LL PLAY THISBY'S MOTHER.
TOM SNOUT, THE TINKER.
HERE, PETER QUINCE.
SNOUT
YOU'LL BE PYRAMUS' FATHER.

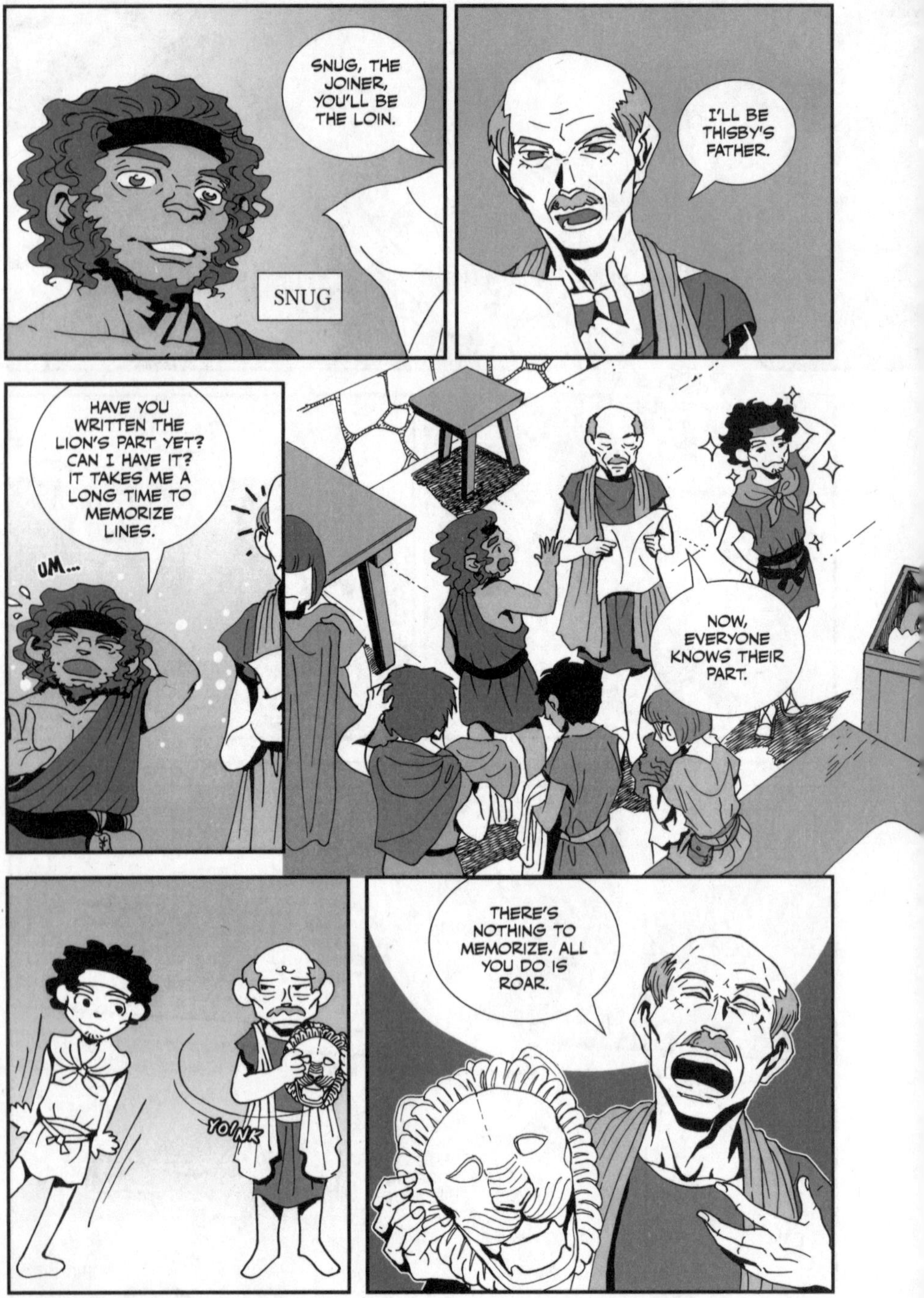
I'LL BE THISBY'S FATHER.
SNUG, THE JOINER, YOU'LL BE THE LOIN.
SNUG
NOW, EVERYONE KNOWS THEIR PART.
HAVE YOU WRITTEN THE LION'S PART YET? CAN I HAVE IT? IT TAKES ME A LONG TIME TO MEMORIZE LINES.
UM...
THERE'S NOTHING TO MEMORIZE, ALL YOU DO IS ROAR.
YOINK

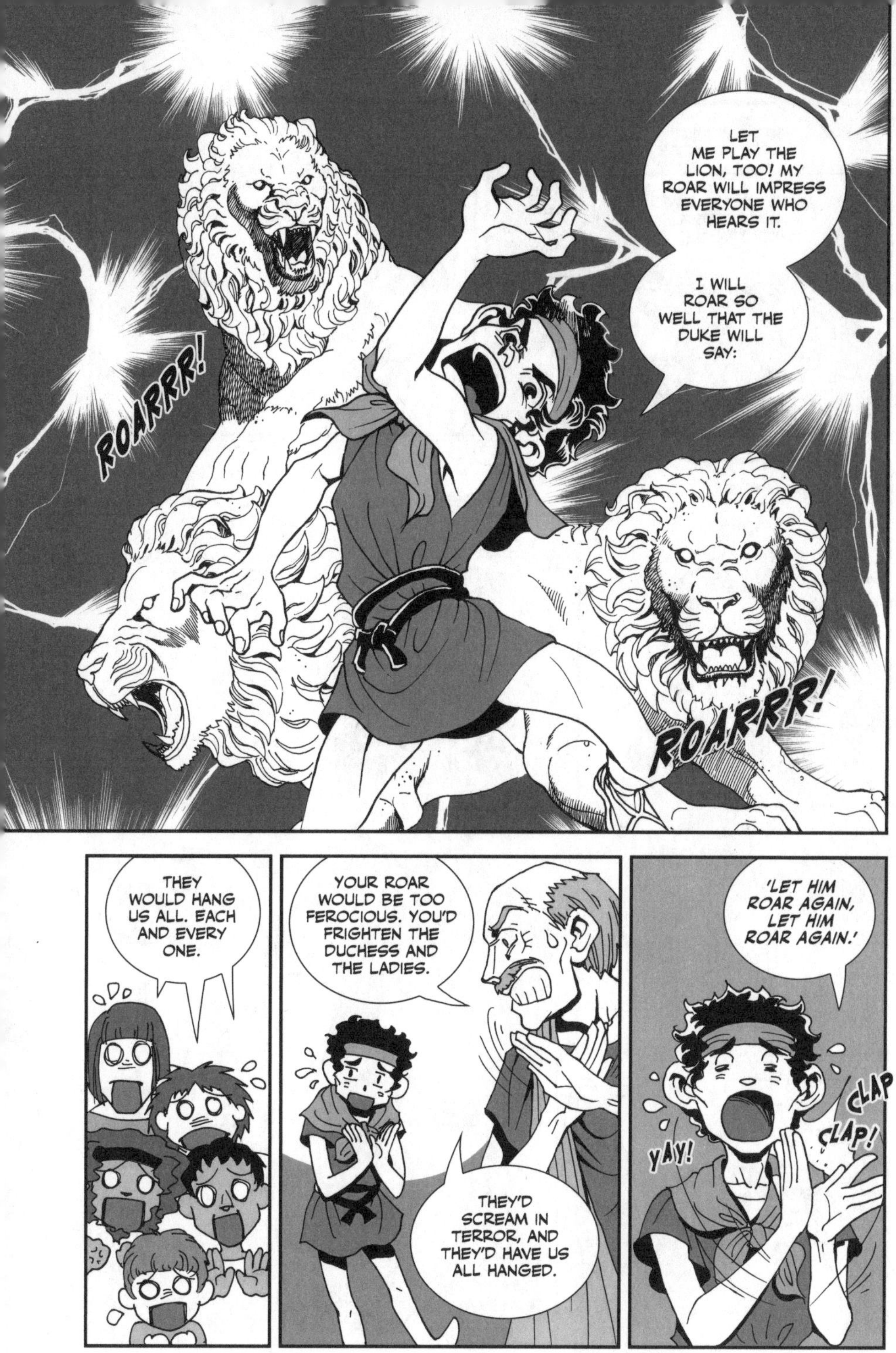
LET ME PLAY THE LION, TOO! MY ROAR WILL IMPRESS EVERYONE WHO HEARS IT.
I WILL ROAR SO WELL THAT THE DUKE WILL SAY:
ROARRR!
ROARRR!
'LET HIM ROAR AGAIN, LET HIM ROAR AGAIN.'
CLAP
CLAP!
YAY!
YOUR ROAR WOULD BE TOO FEROCIOUS. YOU'D FRIGHTEN THE DUCHESS AND THE LADIES.
THEY'D SCREAM IN TERROR, AND THEY'D HAVE US ALL HANGED.
THEY WOULD HANG US ALL. EACH AND EVERY ONE.

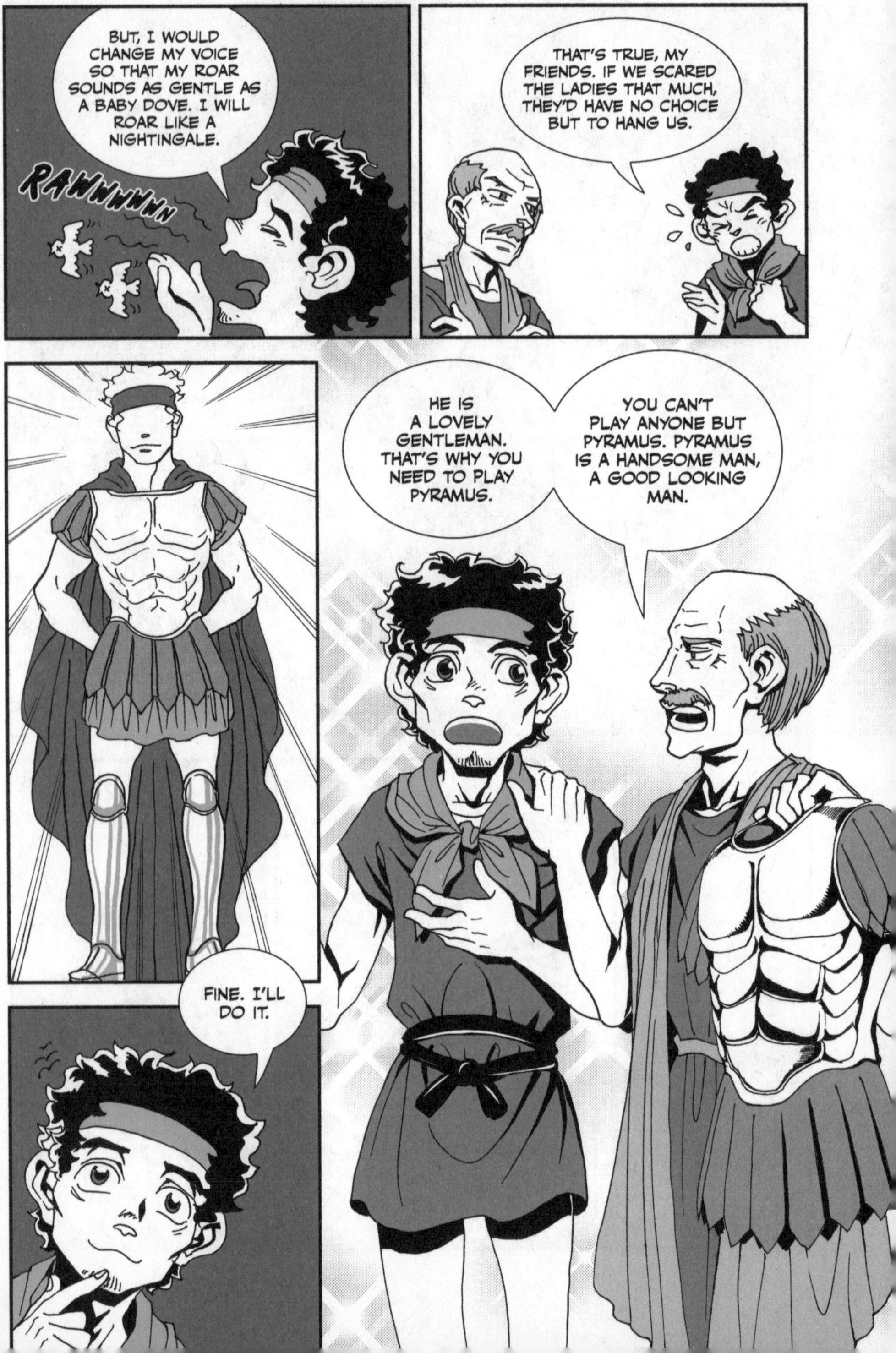
THAT'S TRUE, MY FRIENDS. IF WE SCARED THE LADIES THAT MUCH, THEY'D HAVE NO CHOICE BUT TO HANG US.
BUT, I WOULD CHANGE MY VOICE SO THAT MY ROAR SOUNDS AS GENTLE AS A BABY DOVE. I WILL ROAR LIKE A NIGHTINGALE.
RAWWWWWN
YOU CAN'T PLAY ANYONE BUT PYRAMUS. PYRAMUS IS A HANDSOME MAN, A GOOD LOOKING MAN.
HE IS A LOVELY GENTLEMAN. THAT'S WHY YOU NEED TO PLAY PYRAMUS.
FINE. I'LL DO IT.

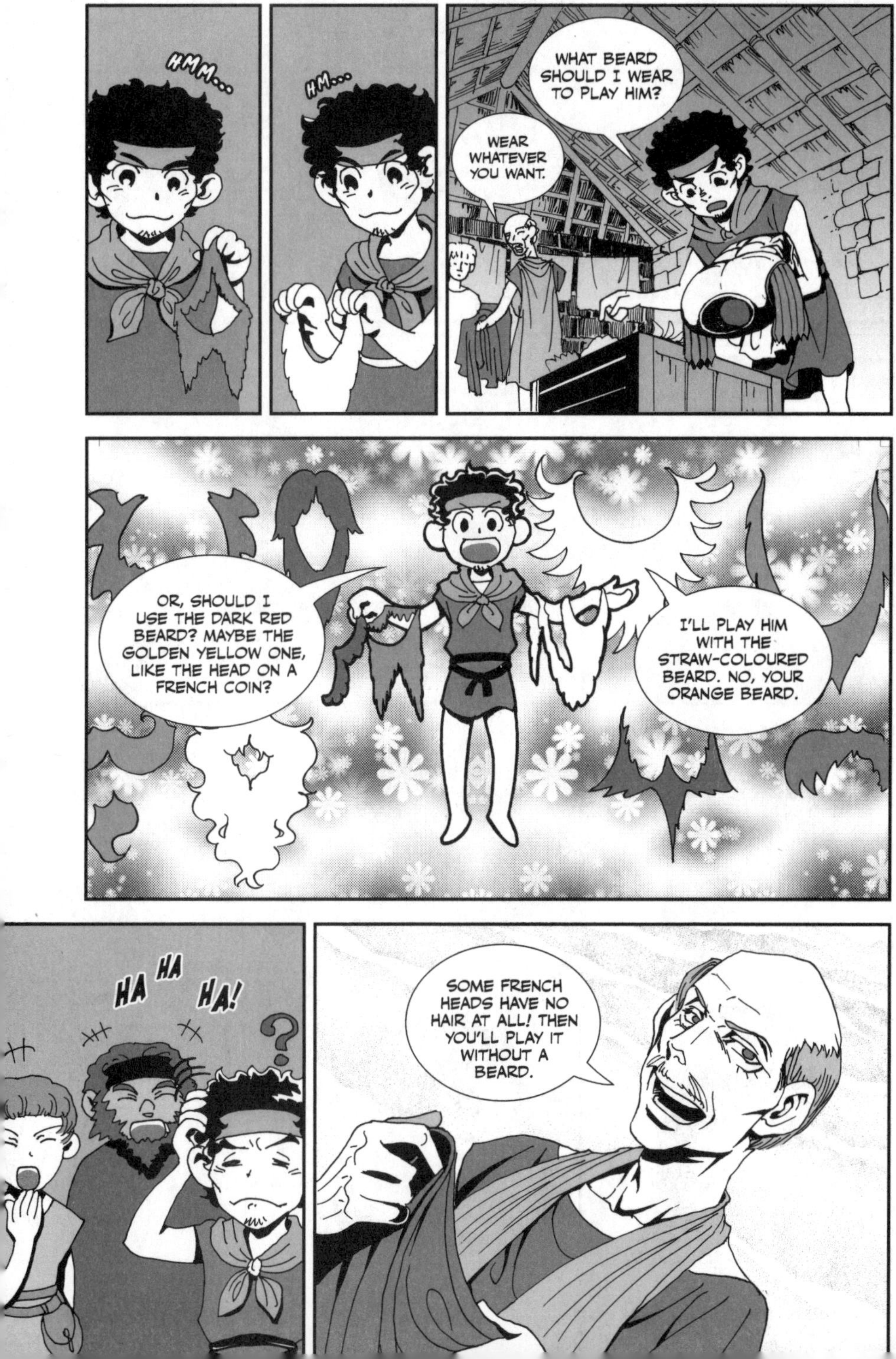
WHAT BEARD SHOULD I WEAR TO PLAY HIM?
WEAR WHATEVER YOU WANT.
HM...
HMM...
I'LL PLAY HIM WITH THE STRAW-COLOURED BEARD. NO, YOUR ORANGE BEARD.
OR, SHOULD I USE THE DARK RED BEARD? MAYBE THE GOLDEN YELLOW ONE, LIKE THE HEAD ON A FRENCH COIN?
SOME FRENCH HEADS HAVE NO HAIR AT ALL! THEN YOU'LL PLAY IT WITHOUT A BEARD.
HA HA HA!

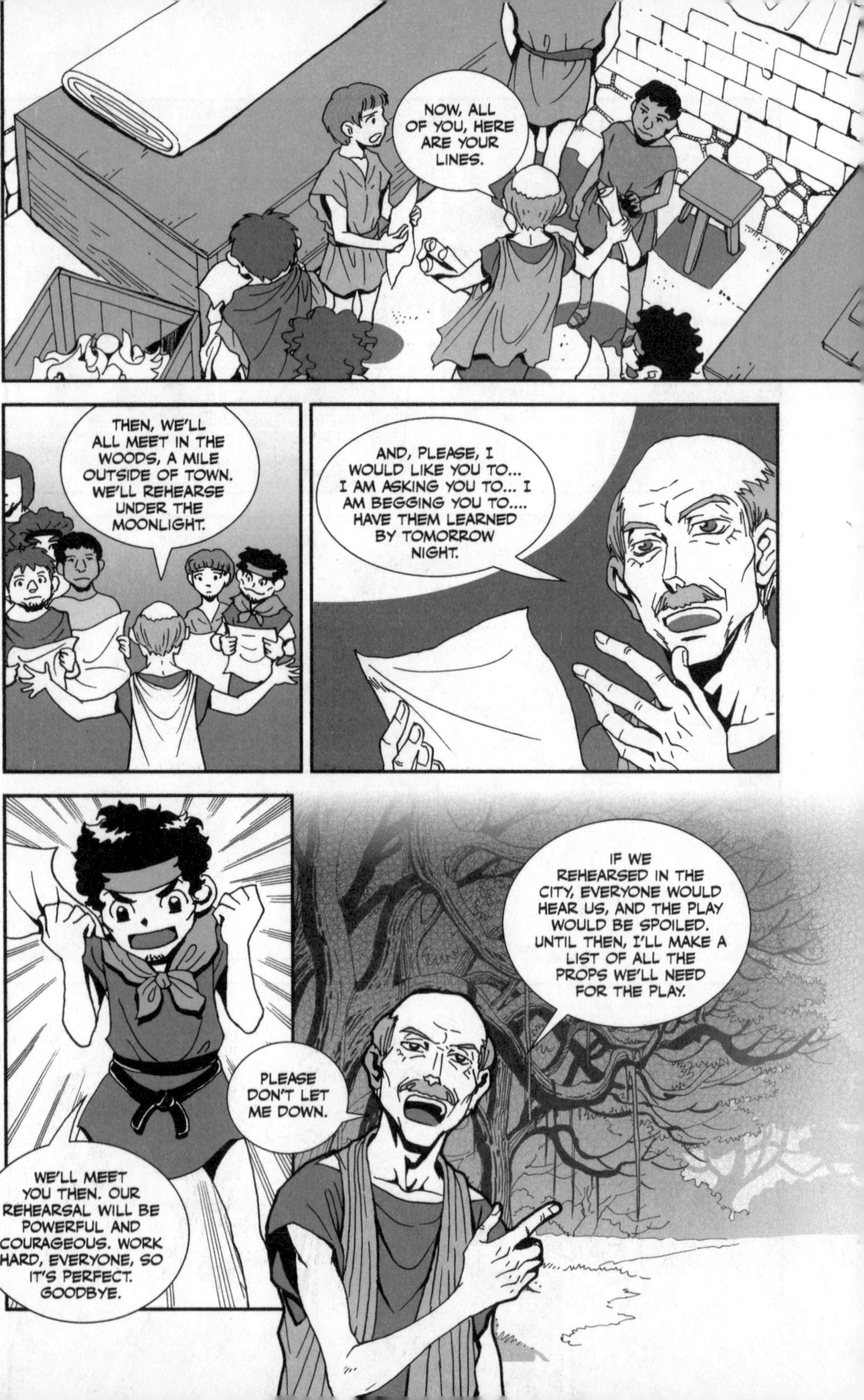
NOW, ALL OF YOU, HERE ARE YOUR LINES.
AND, PLEASE, I WOULD LIKE YOU TO... I AM ASKING YOU TO... I AM BEGGING YOU TO.... HAVE THEM LEARNED BY TOMORROW NIGHT.
THEN, WE'LL ALL MEET IN THE WOODS, A MILE OUTSIDE OF TOWN. WE'LL REHEARSE UNDER THE MOONLIGHT.
IF WE REHEARSED IN THE CITY, EVERYONE WOULD HEAR US, AND THE PLAY WOULD BE SPOILED. UNTIL THEN, I'LL MAKE A LIST OF ALL THE PROPS WE'LL NEED FOR THE PLAY.
PLEASE DON'T LET ME DOWN.
WE'LL MEET YOU THEN. OUR REHEARSAL WILL BE POWERFUL AND COURAGEOUS. WORK HARD, EVERYONE, SO IT'S PERFECT. GOODBYE.

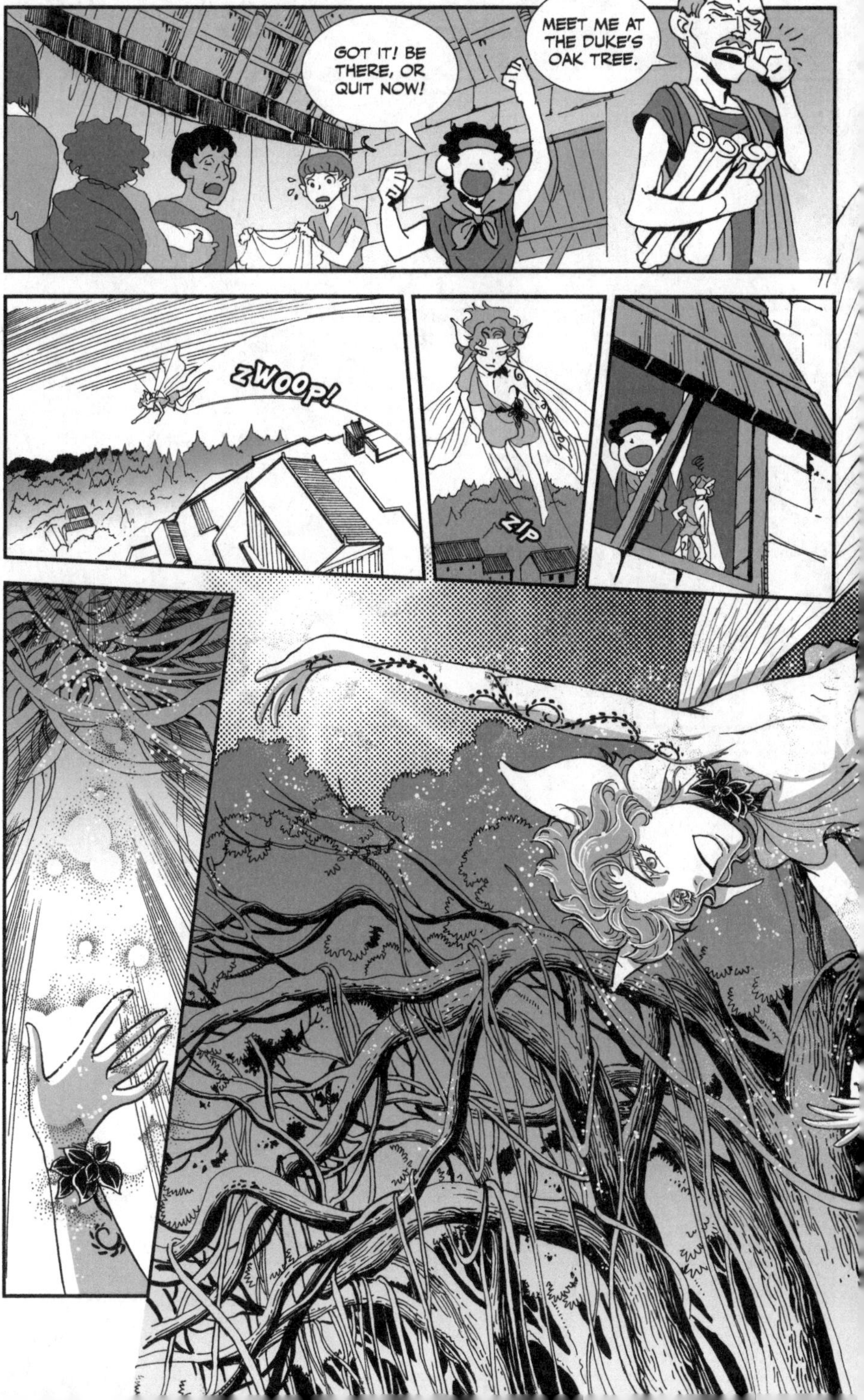
MEET ME AT THE DUKE'S OAK TREE.
GOT IT! BE THERE, OR QUIT NOW!
ZIP
ZWOOP!

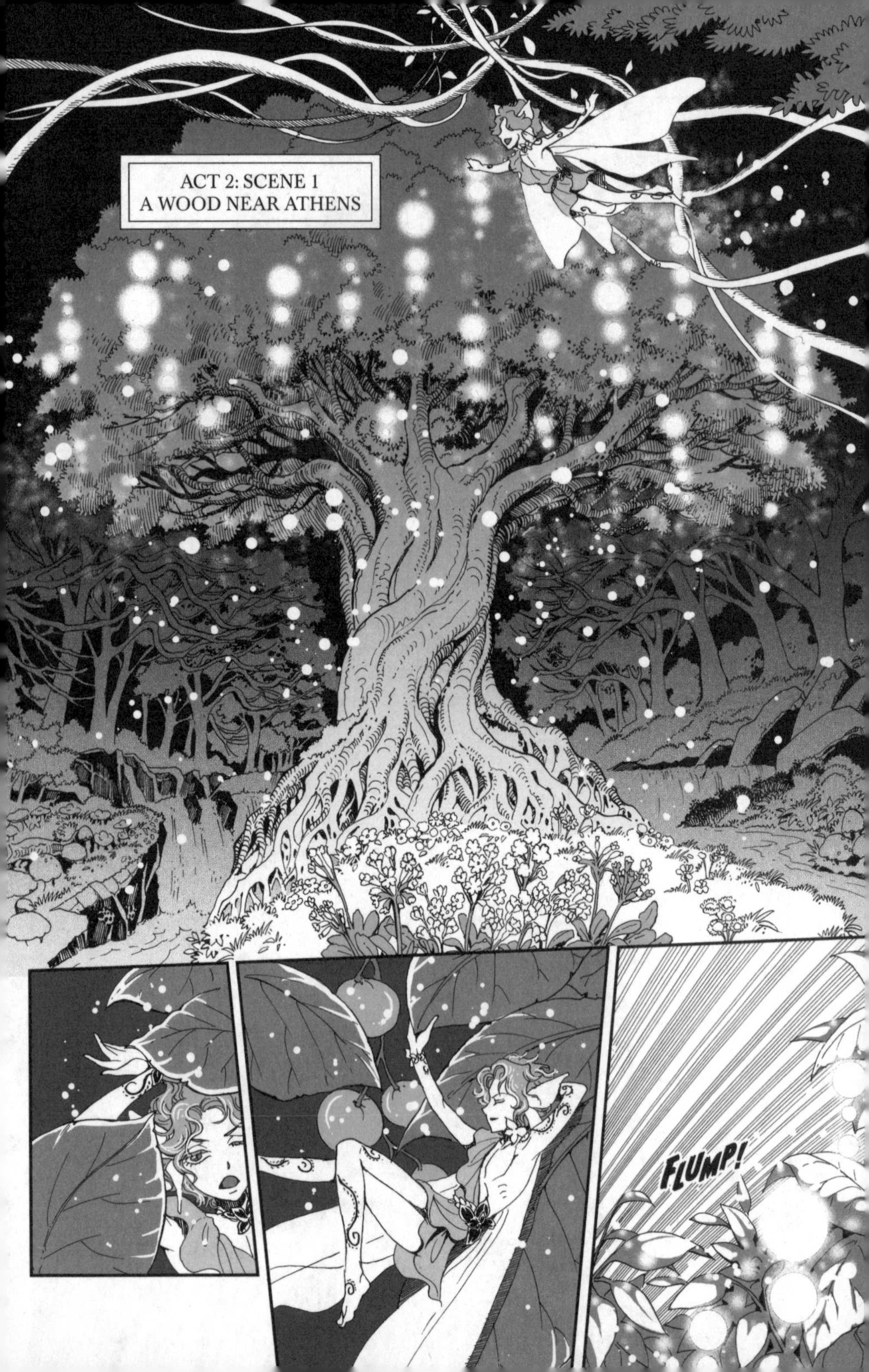
ACT 2: SCENE 1
A WOOD NEAR ATHENS
FLUMP!

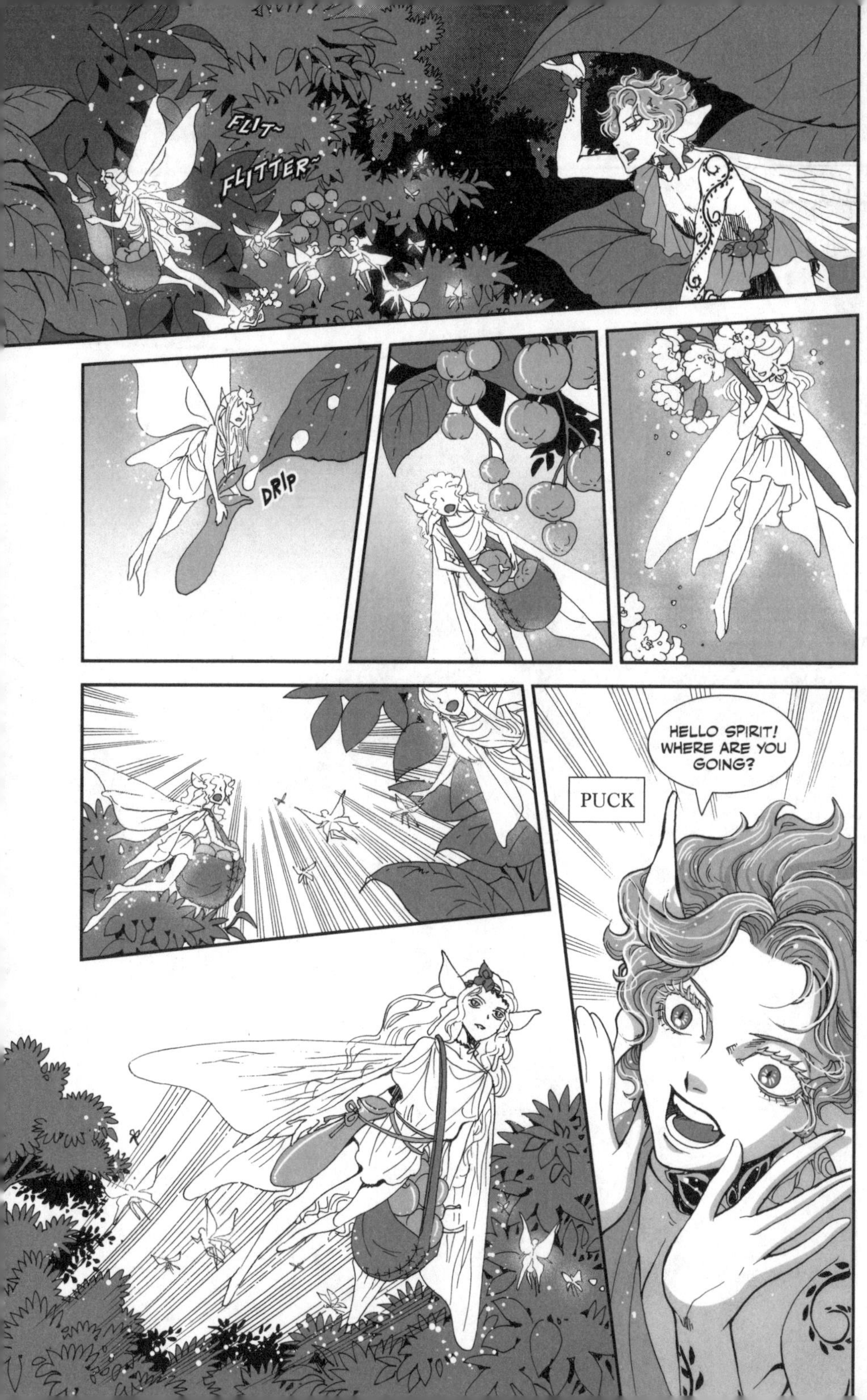
FLIT~
FLITTER~
DRIP
PUCK
HELLO SPIRIT! WHERE ARE YOU GOING?

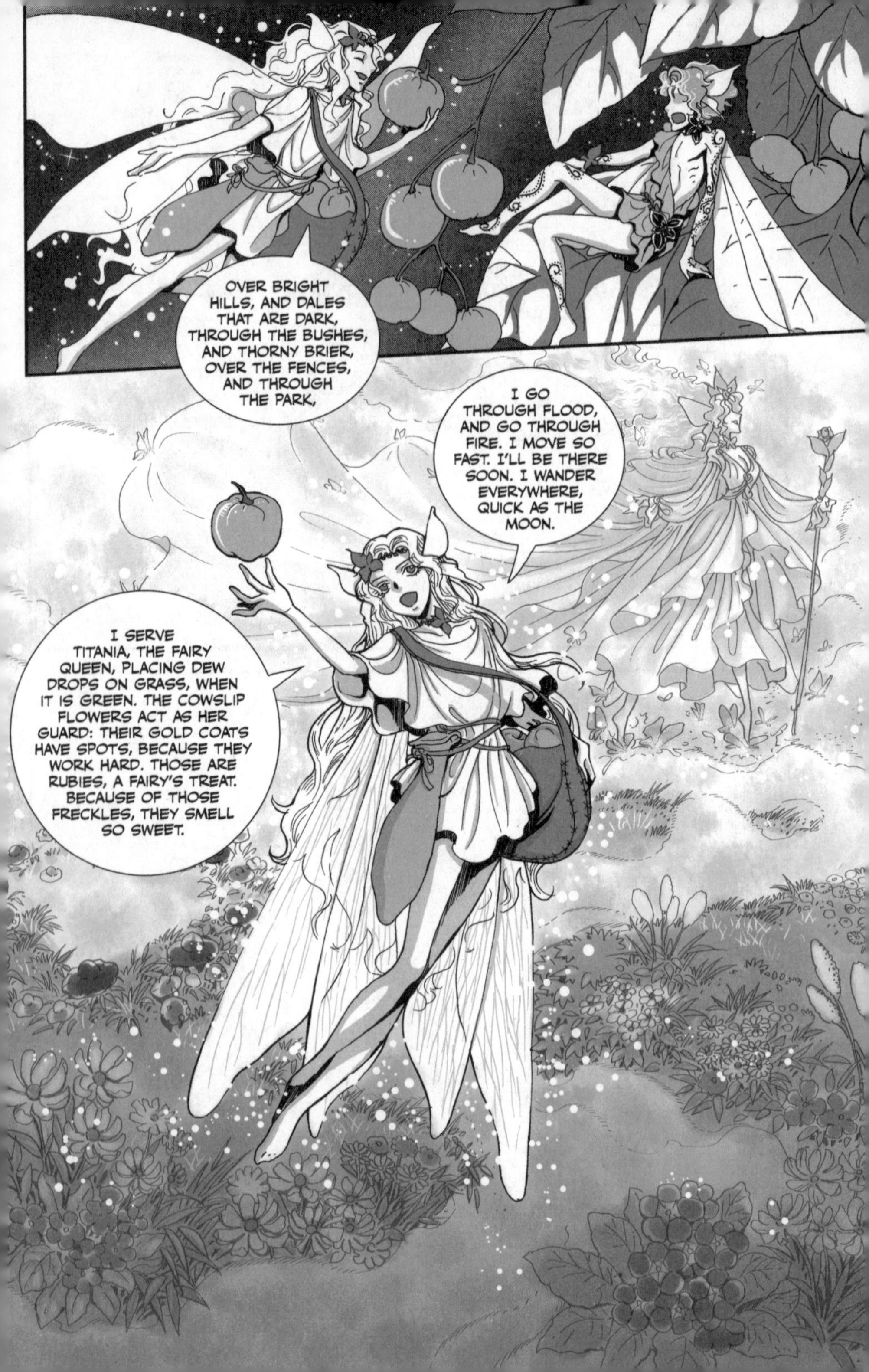
OVER BRIGHT HILLS, AND DALES THAT ARE DARK, THROUGH THE BUSHES, AND THORNY BRIER, OVER THE FENCES, AND THROUGH THE PARK,
I GO THROUGH FLOOD, AND GO THROUGH FIRE. I MOVE SO FAST. I'LL BE THERE SOON. I WANDER EVERYWHERE, QUICK AS THE MOON.
I SERVE TITANIA, THE FAIRY QUEEN, PLACING DEW DROPS ON GRASS, WHEN IT IS GREEN. THE COWSLIP FLOWERS ACT AS HER GUARD: THEIR GOLD COATS HAVE SPOTS, BECAUSE THEY WORK HARD. THOSE ARE RUBIES, A FAIRY'S TREAT. BECAUSE OF THOSE FRECKLES, THEY SMELL SO SWEET.

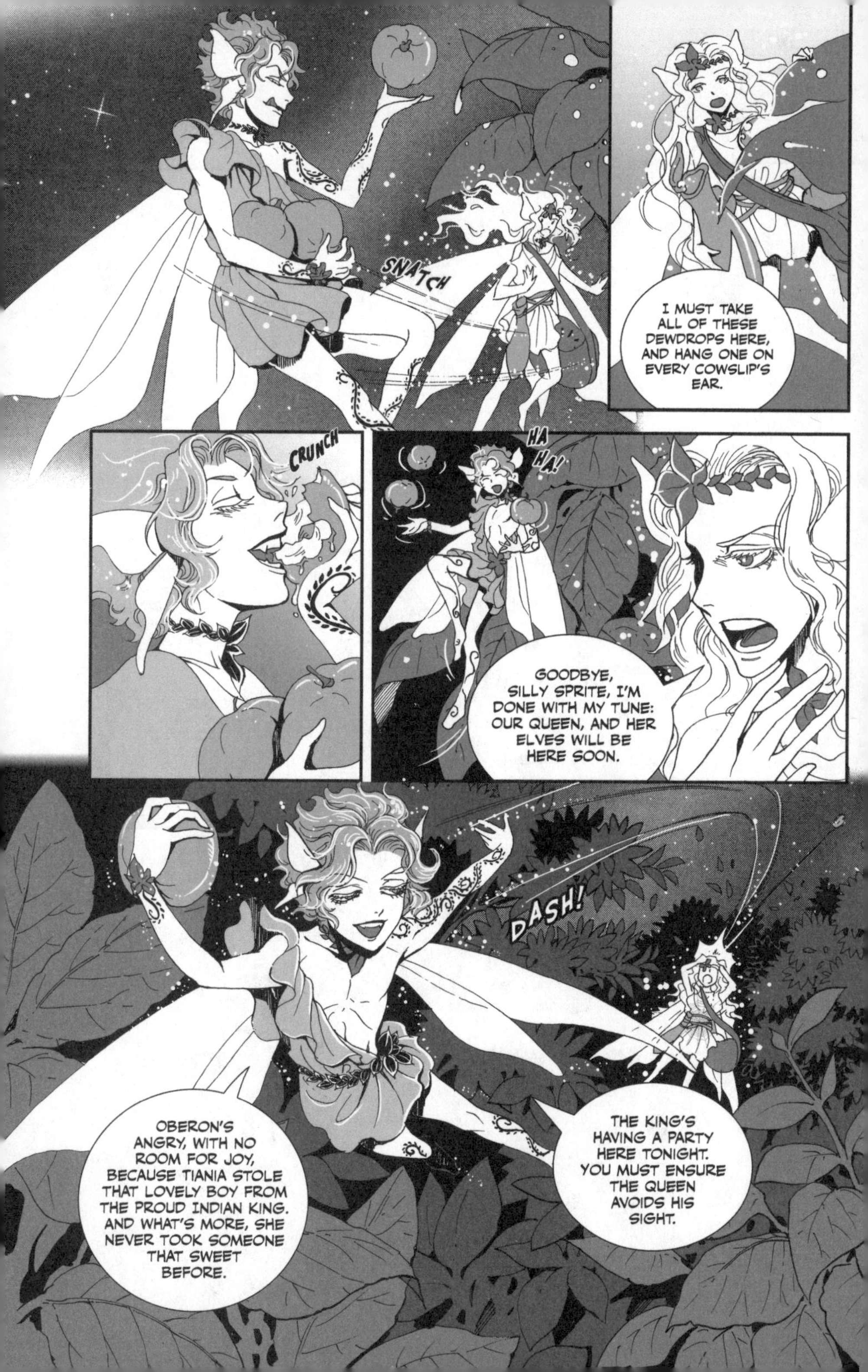
I MUST TAKE ALL OF THESE DEWDROPS HERE, AND HANG ONE ON EVERY COWSLIP'S EAR.
SNATCH
HA HA!
GOODBYE, SILLY SPRITE, I'M DONE WITH MY TUNE: OUR QUEEN, AND HER ELVES WILL BE HERE SOON.
CRUNCH
DASH!
THE KING'S HAVING A PARTY HERE TONIGHT. YOU MUST ENSURE THE QUEEN AVOIDS HIS SIGHT.
OBERON'S ANGRY, WITH NO ROOM FOR JOY, BECAUSE TIANIA STOLE THAT LOVELY BOY FROM THE PROUD INDIAN KING. AND WHAT'S MORE, SHE NEVER TOOK SOMEONE THAT SWEET BEFORE.

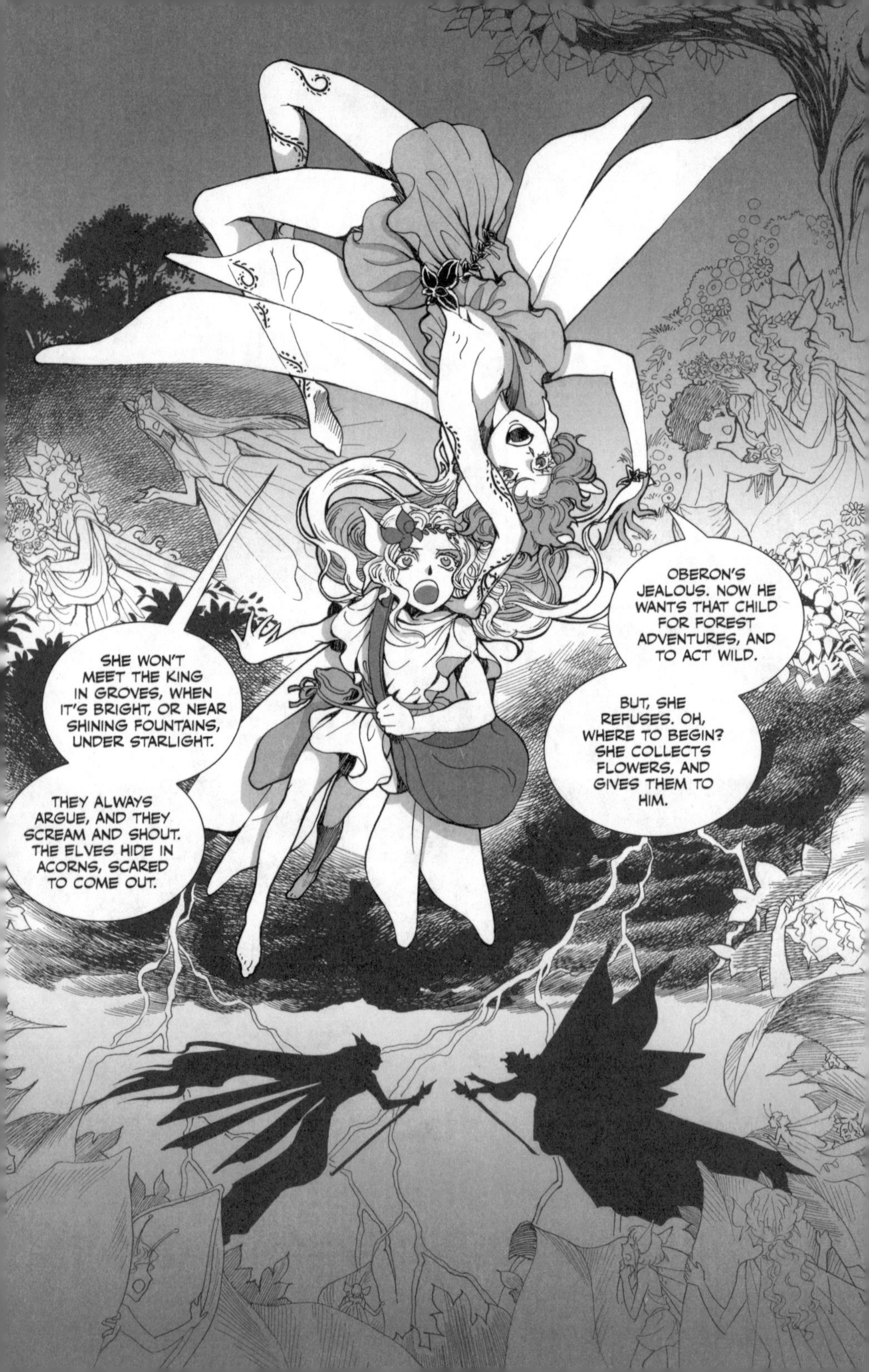
OBERON'S JEALOUS. NOW HE WANTS THAT CHILD FOR FOREST ADVENTURES, AND TO ACT WILD.
BUT, SHE REFUSES. OH, WHERE TO BEGIN? SHE COLLECTS FLOWERS, AND GIVES THEM TO HIM.
SHE WON'T MEET THE KING IN GROVES, WHEN IT'S BRIGHT, OR NEAR SHINING FOUNTAINS, UNDER STARLIGHT.
THEY ALWAYS ARGUE, AND THEY SCREAM AND SHOUT. THE ELVES HIDE IN ACORNS, SCARED TO COME OUT.

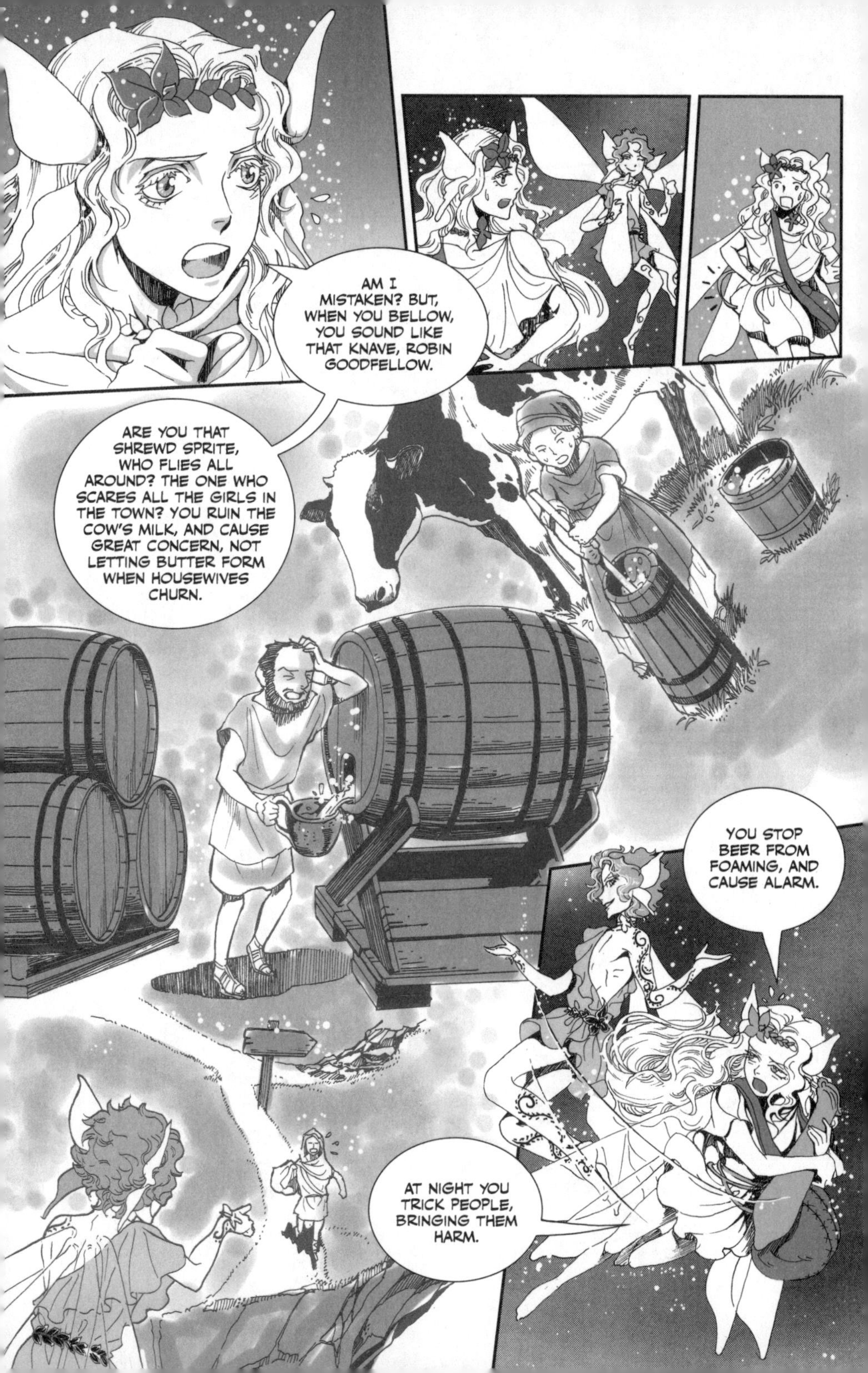

AM I MISTAKEN? BUT, WHEN YOU BELLOW, YOU SOUND LIKE THAT KNAVE, ROBIN GOODFELLOW.
ARE YOU THAT SHREWD SPRITE, WHO FLIES ALL AROUND? THE ONE WHO SCARES ALL THE GIRLS IN THE TOWN? YOU RUIN THE COW'S MILK, AND CAUSE GREAT CONCERN, NOT LETTING BUTTER FORM WHEN HOUSEWIVES CHURN.
YOU STOP BEER FROM FOAMING, AND CAUSE ALARM.
AT NIGHT YOU TRICK PEOPLE, BRINGING THEM HARM.

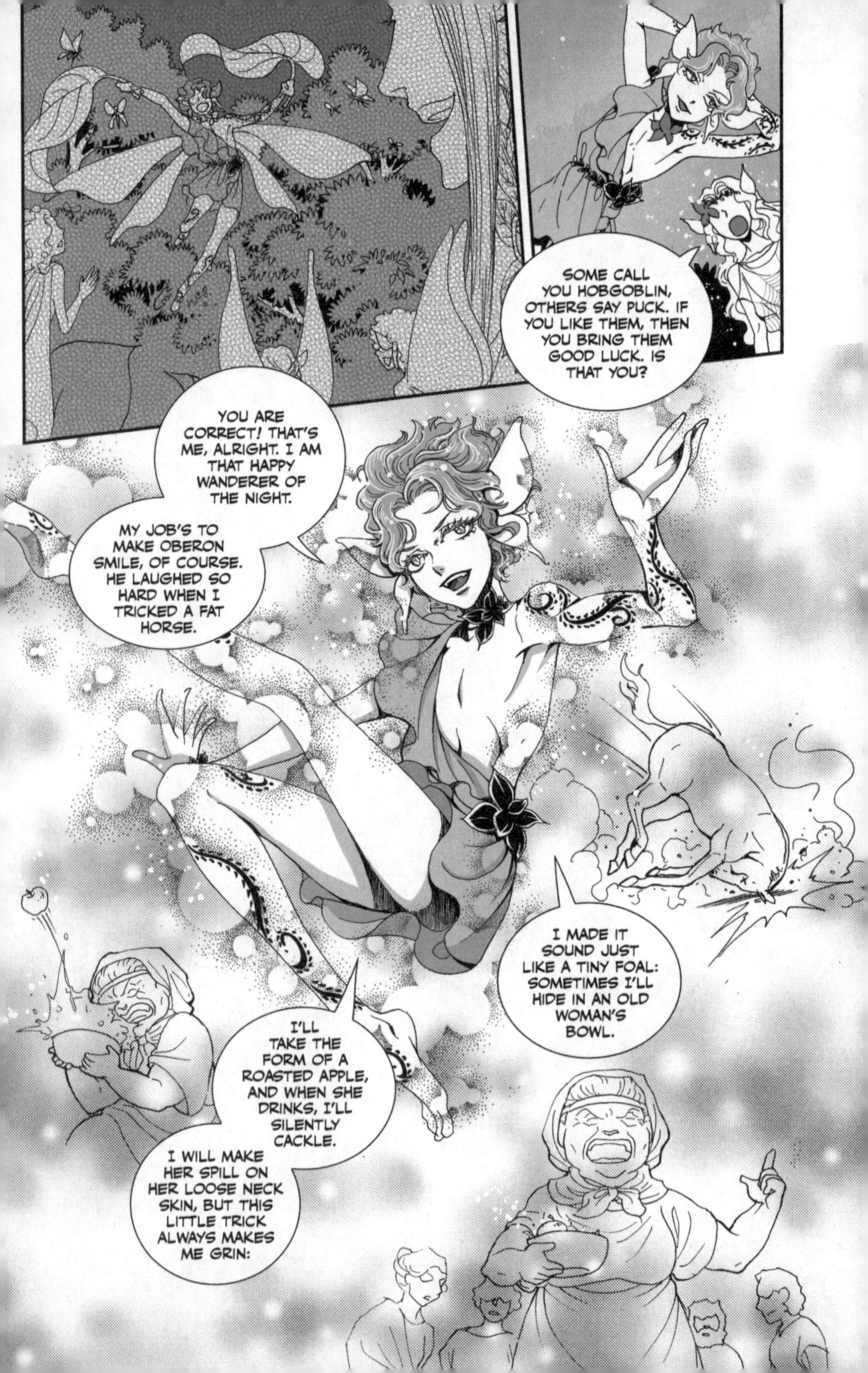
SOME CALL YOU HOBGOBLIN, OTHERS SAY PUCK. IF YOU LIKE THEM, THEN YOU BRING THEM GOOD LUCK. IS THAT YOU?
YOU ARE CORRECT! THAT'S ME, ALRIGHT. I AM THAT HAPPY WANDERER OF THE NIGHT.
MY JOB'S TO MAKE OBERON SMILE, OF COURSE. HE LAUGHED SO HARD WHEN I TRICKED A FAT HORSE.
I MADE IT SOUND JUST LIKE A TINY FOAL: SOMETIMES I'LL HIDE IN AN OLD WOMAN'S BOWL.
I'LL TAKE THE FORM OF A ROASTED APPLE, AND WHEN SHE DRINKS, I'LL SILENTLY CACKLE.
I WILL MAKE HER SPILL ON HER LOOSE NECK SKIN, BUT THIS LITTLE TRICK ALWAYS MAKES ME GRIN:

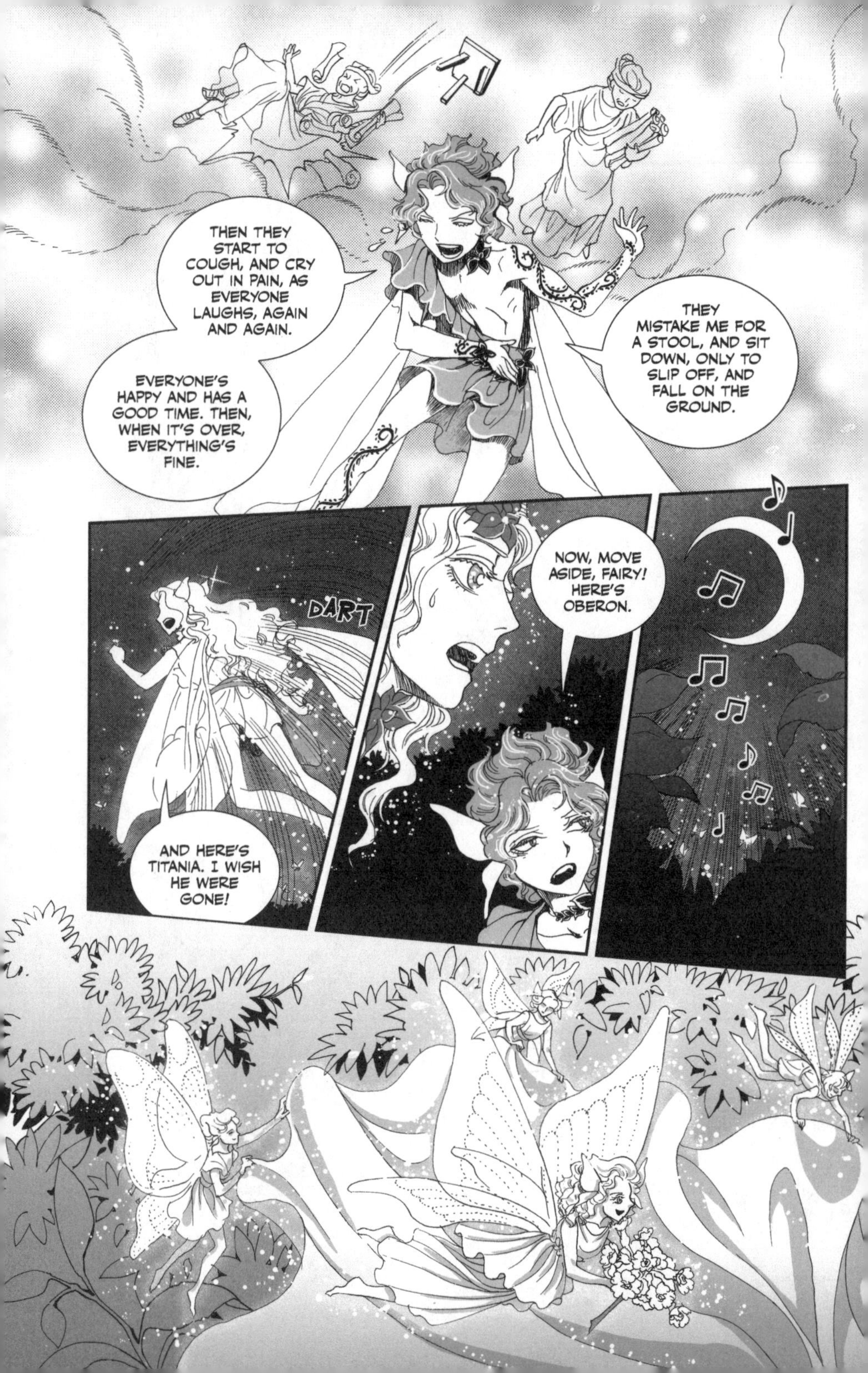
THEY MISTAKE ME FOR A STOOL, AND SIT DOWN, ONLY TO SLIP OFF, AND FALL ON THE GROUND.
THEN THEY START TO COUGH, AND CRY OUT IN PAIN, AS EVERYONE LAUGHS, AGAIN AND AGAIN.
EVERYONE'S HAPPY AND HAS A GOOD TIME. THEN, WHEN IT'S OVER, EVERYTHING'S FINE.
NOW, MOVE ASIDE, FAIRY! HERE'S OBERON.
DART
AND HERE'S TITANIA. I WISH HE WERE GONE!

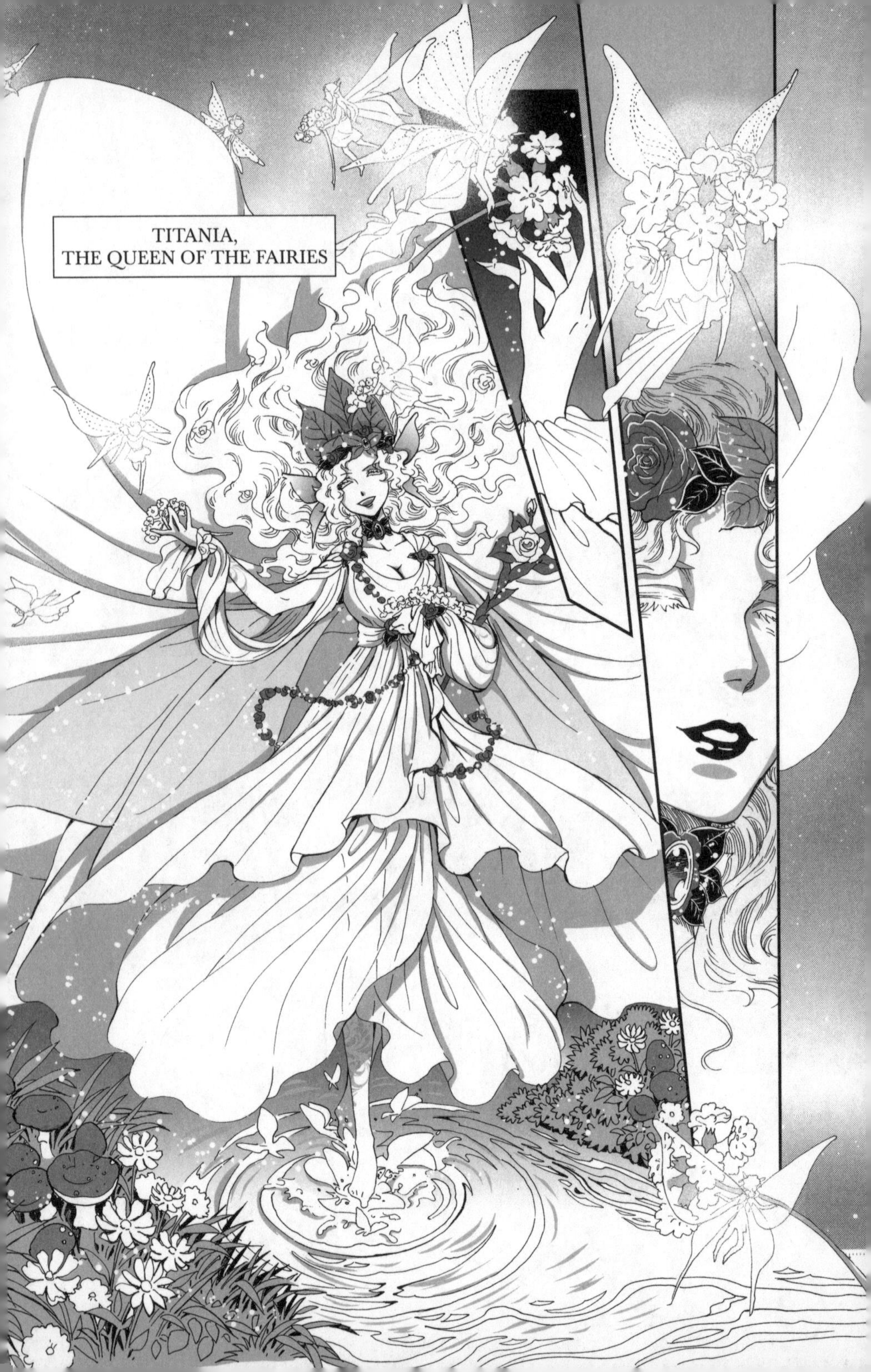
TITANIA,
THE QUEEN OF THE FAIRIES

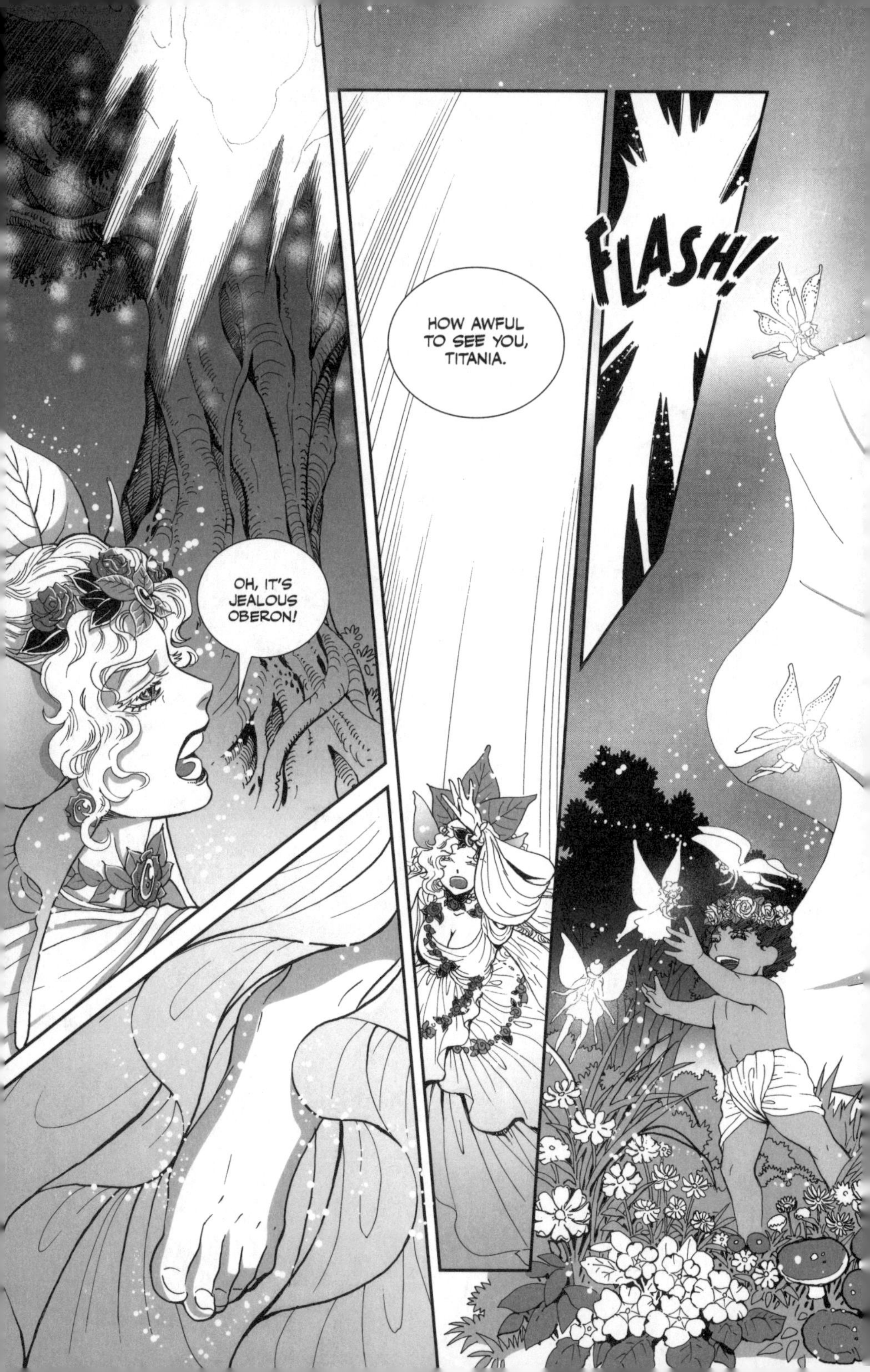
FLASH!
HOW AWFUL TO SEE YOU, TITANIA.
OH, IT'S JEALOUS OBERON!

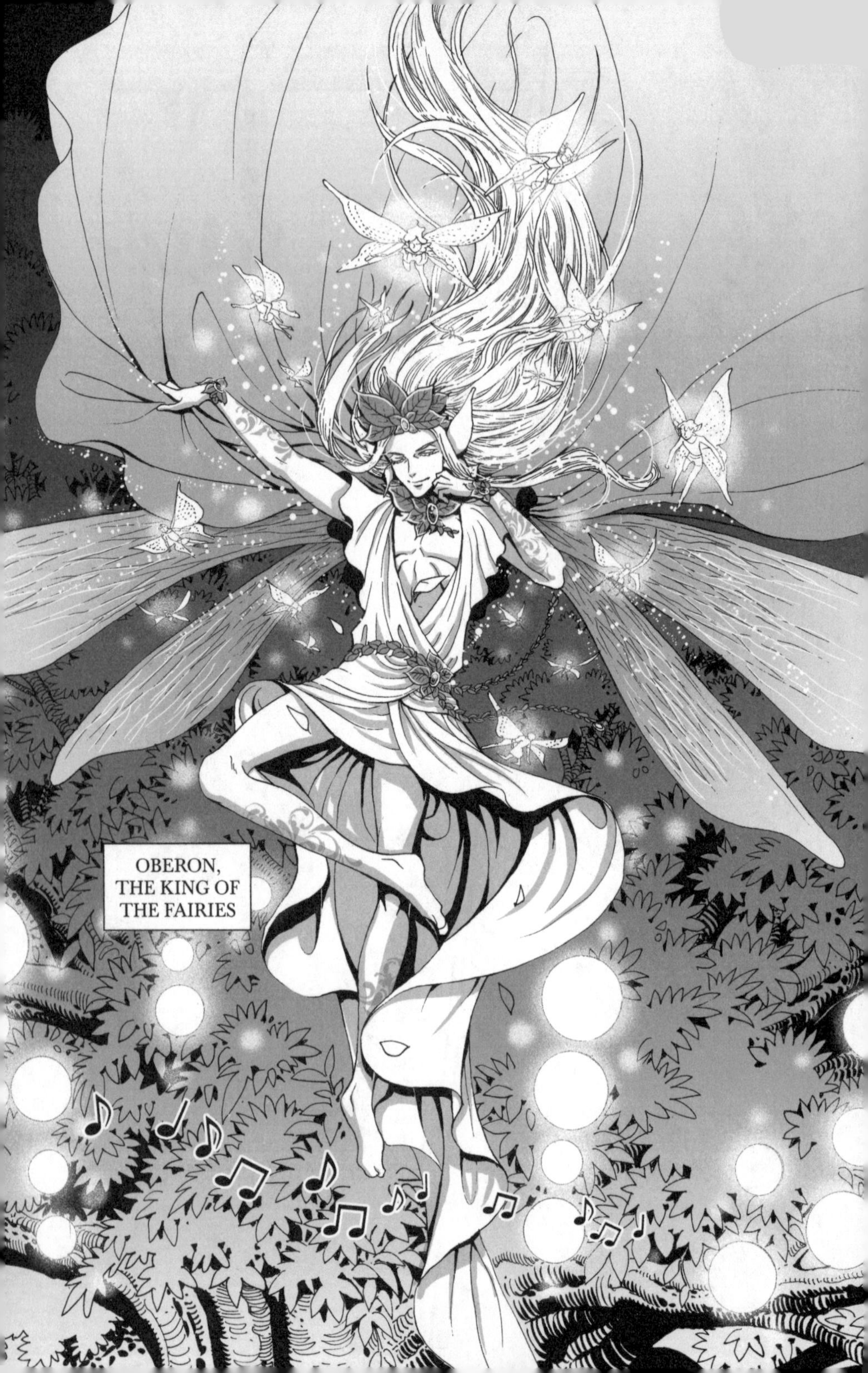
OBERON,
THE KING OF
THE FAIRIES

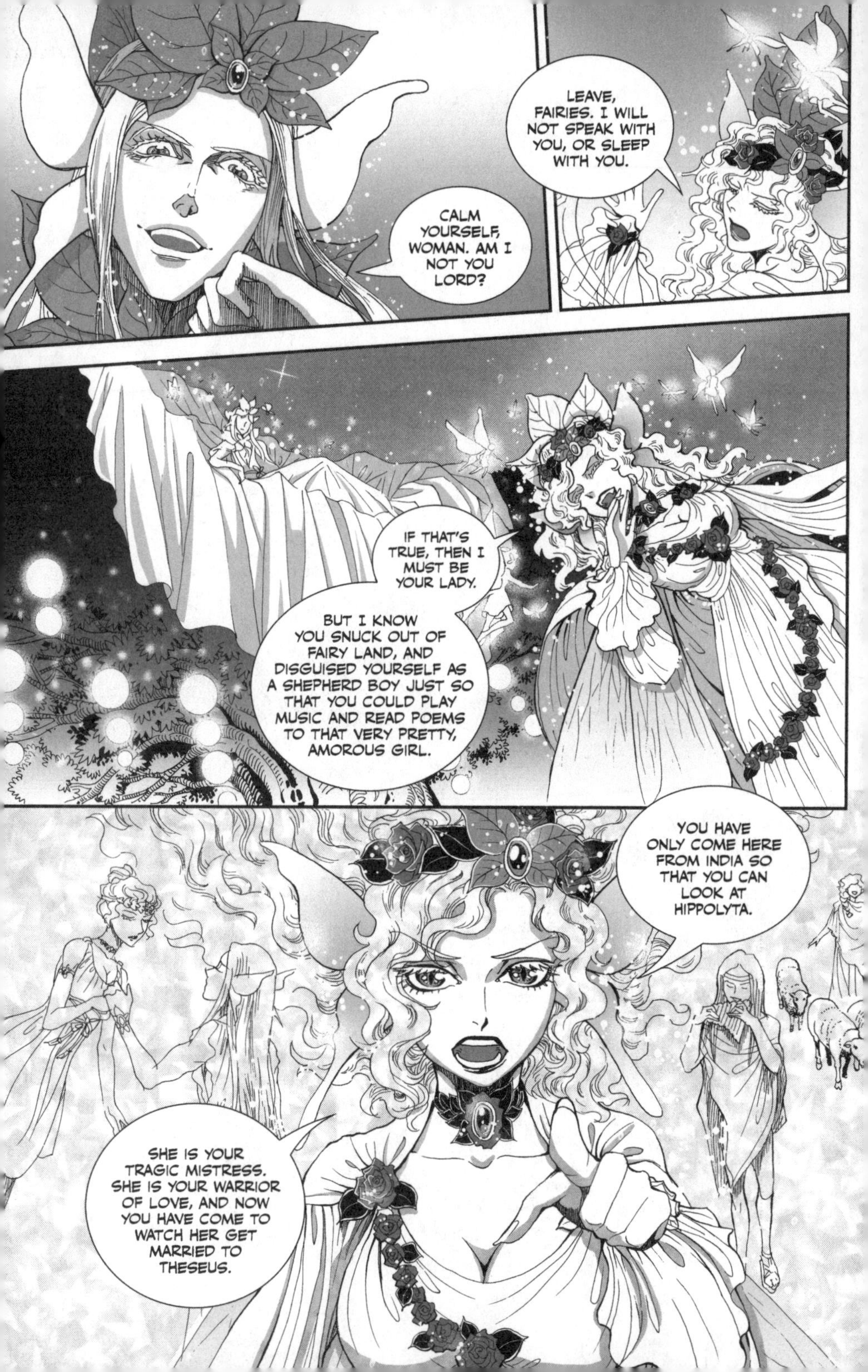

LEAVE, FAIRIES. I WILL NOT SPEAK WITH YOU, OR SLEEP WITH YOU.
CALM YOURSELF, WOMAN. AM I NOT YOU LORD?
IF THAT'S TRUE, THEN I MUST BE YOUR LADY.
BUT I KNOW YOU SNUCK OUT OF FAIRY LAND, AND DISGUISED YOURSELF AS A SHEPHERD BOY JUST SO THAT YOU COULD PLAY MUSIC AND READ POEMS TO THAT VERY PRETTY, AMOROUS GIRL.
YOU HAVE ONLY COME HERE FROM INDIA SO THAT YOU CAN LOOK AT HIPPOLYTA.
SHE IS YOUR TRAGIC MISTRESS. SHE IS YOUR WARRIOR OF LOVE, AND NOW YOU HAVE COME TO WATCH HER GET MARRIED TO THESEUS.

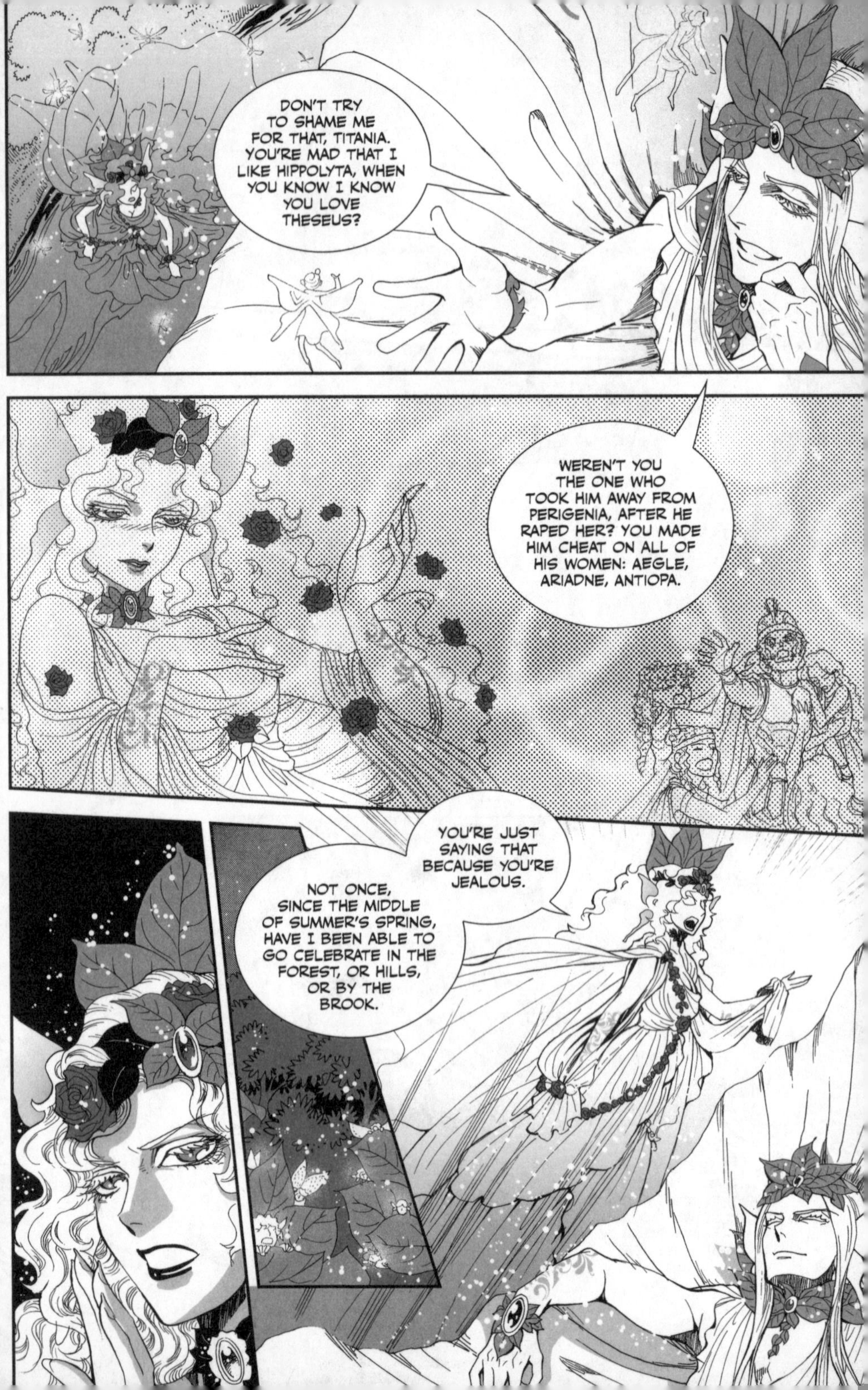
DON'T TRY TO SHAME ME FOR THAT, TITANIA. YOU'RE MAD THAT I LIKE HIPPOLYTA, WHEN YOU KNOW I KNOW YOU LOVE THESEUS?
WEREN'T YOU THE ONE WHO TOOK HIM AWAY FROM PERIGENIA, AFTER HE RAPED HER? YOU MADE HIM CHEAT ON ALL OF HIS WOMEN: AEGLE, ARIADNE, ANTIOPA.
YOU'RE JUST SAYING THAT BECAUSE YOU'RE JEALOUS.
NOT ONCE, SINCE THE MIDDLE OF SUMMER'S SPRING, HAVE I BEEN ABLE TO GO CELEBRATE IN THE FOREST, OR HILLS, OR BY THE BROOK.

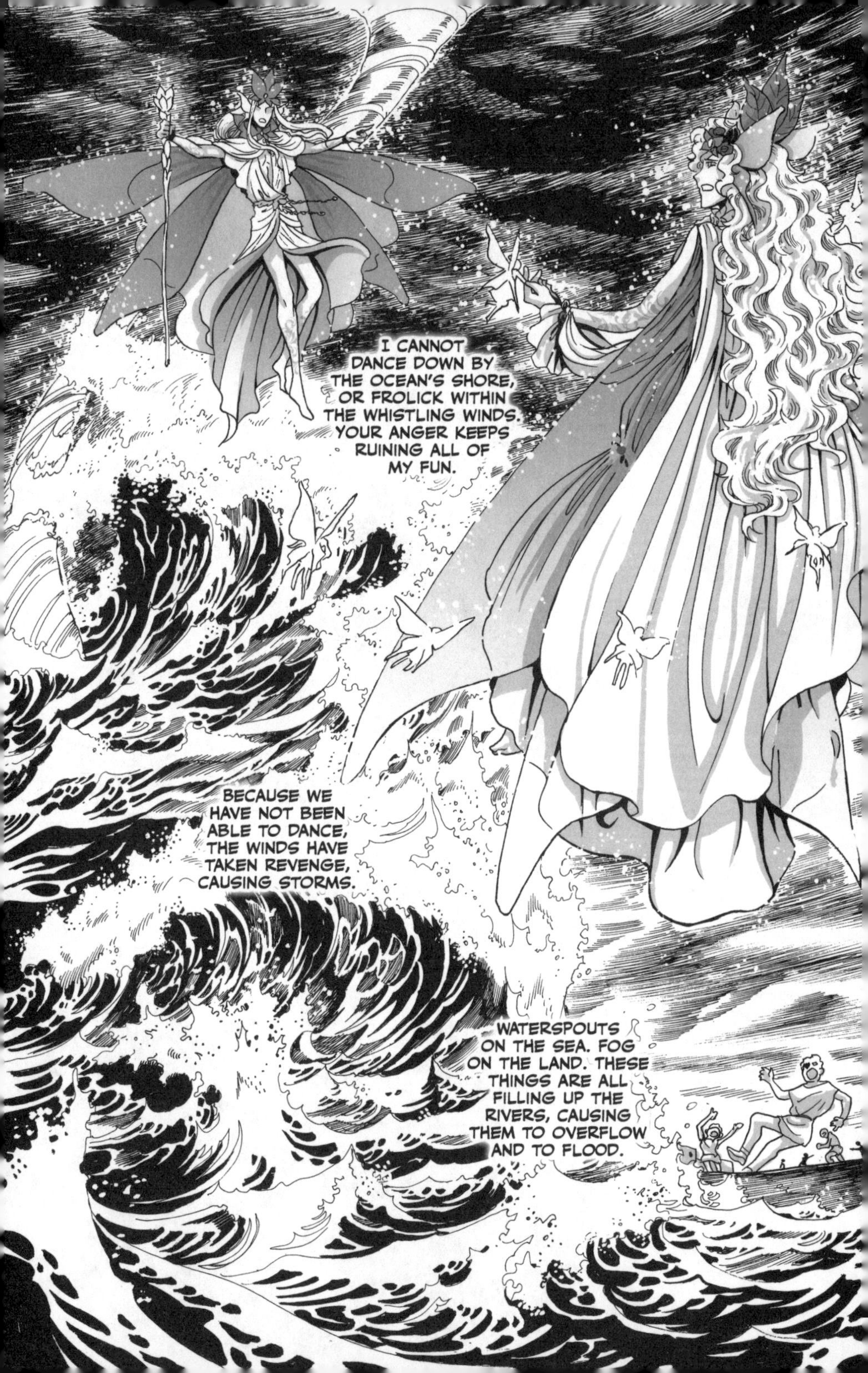
I CANNOT DANCE DOWN BY THE OCEAN'S SHORE, OR FROLICK WITHIN THE WHISTLING WINDS. YOUR ANGER KEEPS RUINING ALL OF MY FUN.
BECAUSE WE HAVE NOT BEEN ABLE TO DANCE, THE WINDS HAVE TAKEN REVENGE, CAUSING STORMS.
WATERSPOUTS ON THE SEA. FOG ON THE LAND. THESE THINGS ARE ALL FILLING UP THE RIVERS, CAUSING THEM TO OVERFLOW AND TO FLOOD.

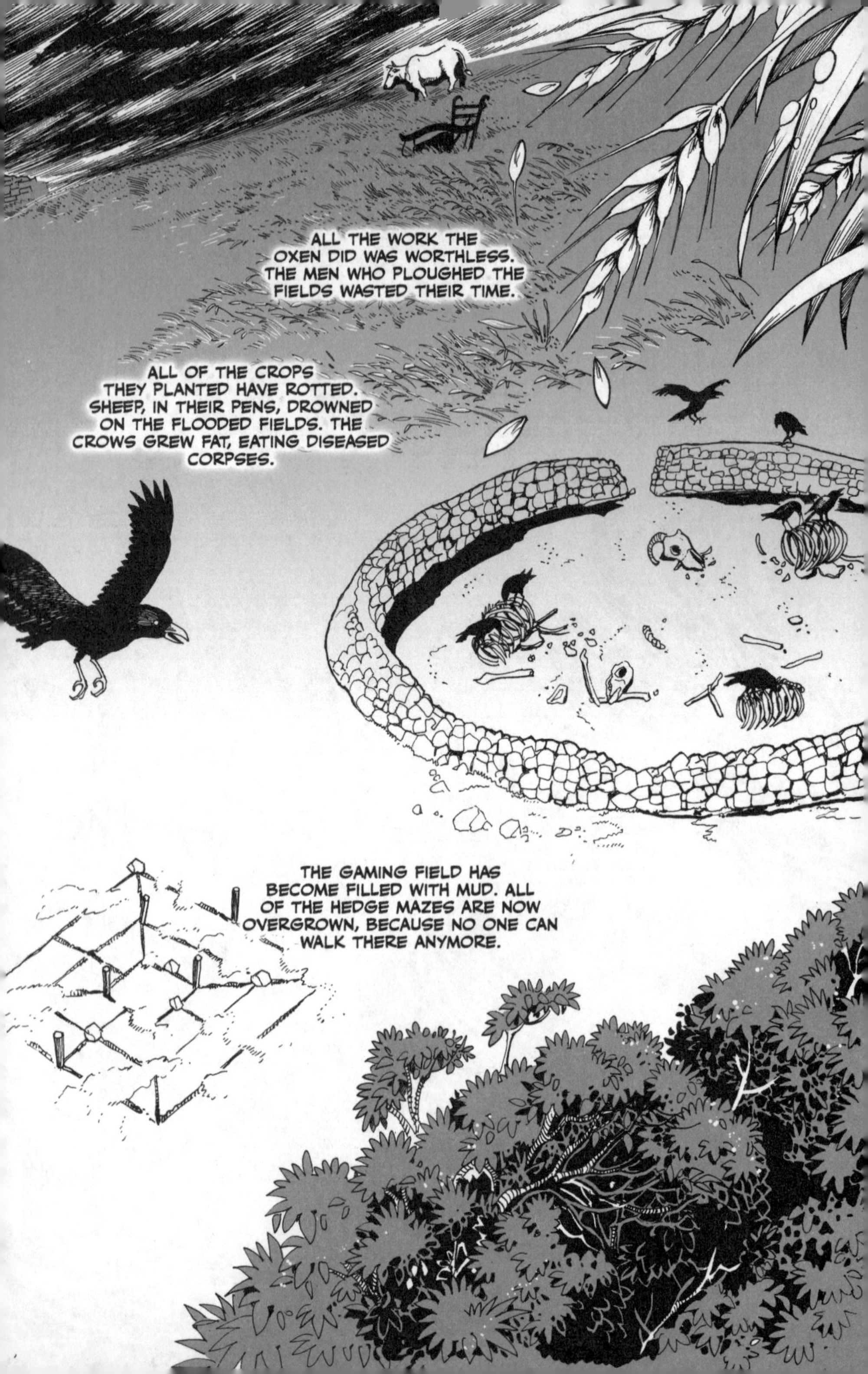
ALL THE WORK THE OXEN DID WAS WORTHLESS. THE MEN WHO PLOUGHED THE FIELDS WASTED THEIR TIME.
ALL OF THE CROPS THEY PLANTED HAVE ROTTED. SHEEP, IN THEIR PENS, DROWNED ON THE FLOODED FIELDS. THE CROWS GREW FAT, EATING DISEASED CORPSES.
THE GAMING FIELD HAS BECOME FILLED WITH MUD. ALL OF THE HEDGE MAZES ARE NOW OVERGROWN, BECAUSE NO ONE CAN WALK THERE ANYMORE.

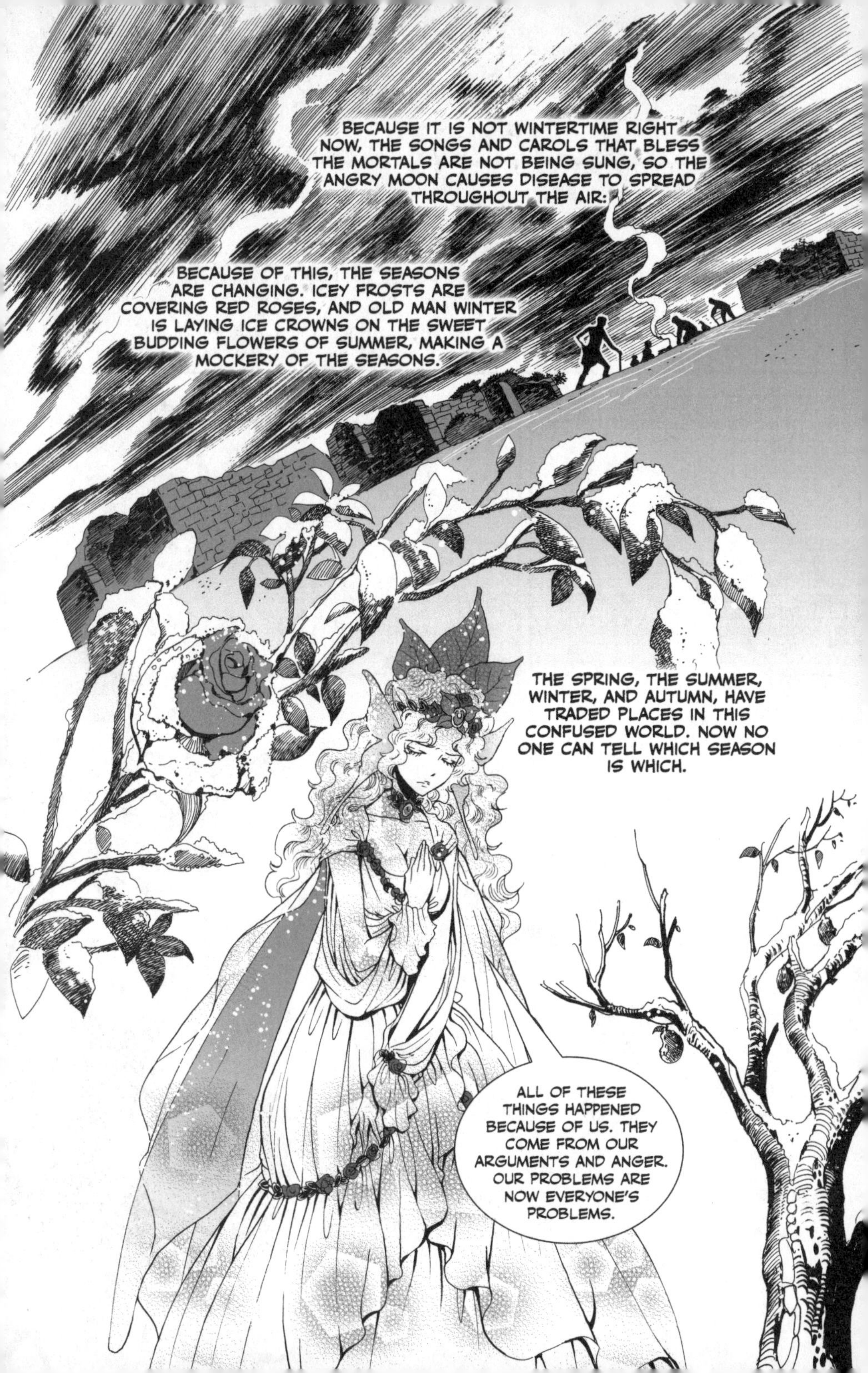
BECAUSE IT IS NOT WINTERTIME RIGHT NOW, THE SONGS AND CAROLS THAT BLESS THE MORTALS ARE NOT BEING SUNG, SO THE ANGRY MOON CAUSES DISEASE TO SPREAD THROUGHOUT THE AIR.
BECAUSE OF THIS, THE SEASONS ARE CHANGING. ICEY FROSTS ARE COVERING RED ROSES, AND OLD MAN WINTER IS LAYING ICE CROWNS ON THE SWEET BUDDING FLOWERS OF SUMMER, MAKING A MOCKERY OF THE SEASONS.
THE SPRING, THE SUMMER, WINTER, AND AUTUMN, HAVE TRADED PLACES IN THIS CONFUSED WORLD. NOW NO ONE CAN TELL WHICH SEASON IS WHICH.
ALL OF THESE THINGS HAPPENED BECAUSE OF US. THEY COME FROM OUR ARGUMENTS AND ANGER. OUR PROBLEMS ARE NOW EVERYONE'S PROBLEMS.

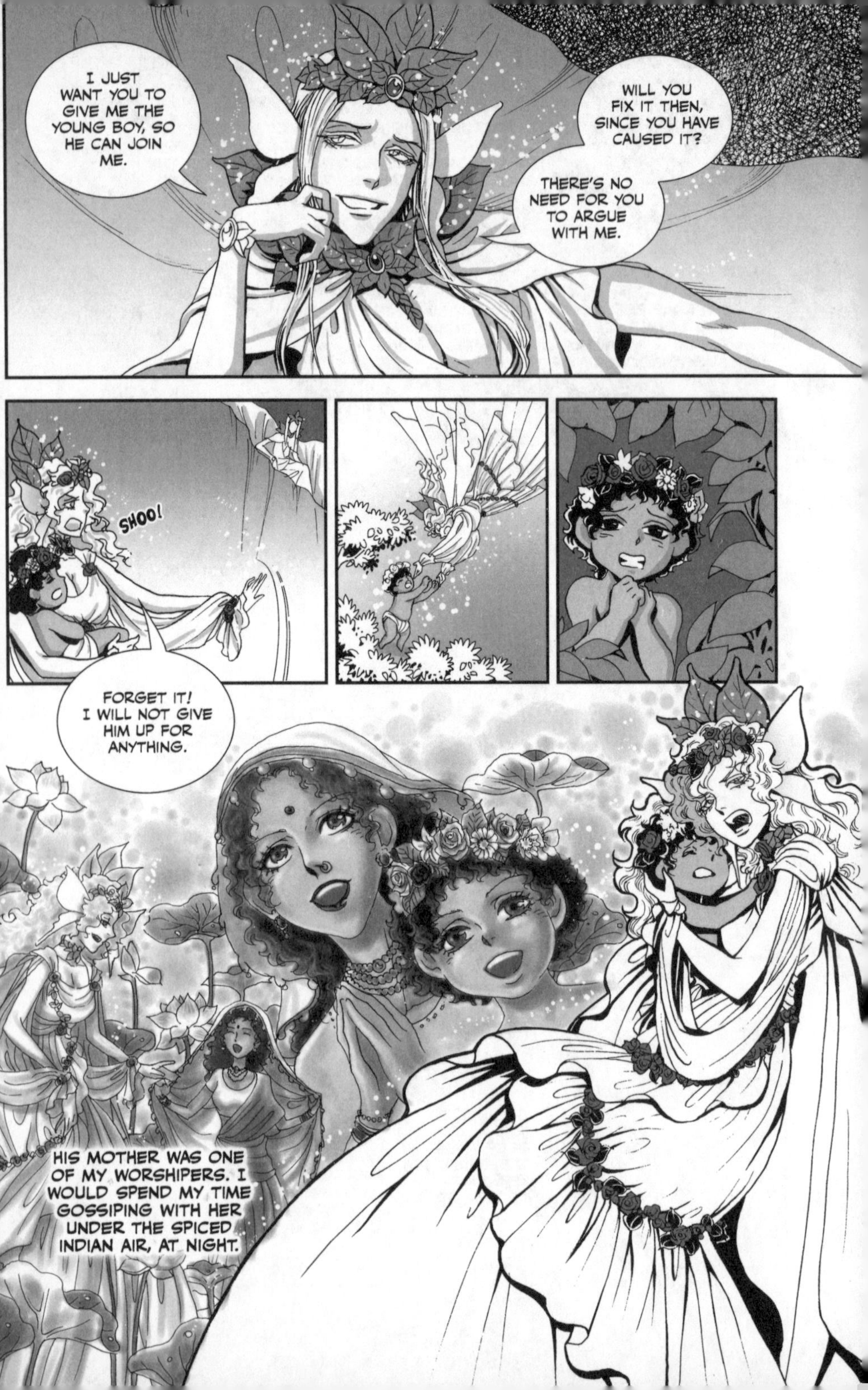
WILL YOU FIX IT THEN, SINCE YOU HAVE CAUSED IT?
THERE'S NO NEED FOR YOU TO ARGUE WITH ME.
I JUST WANT YOU TO GIVE ME THE YOUNG BOY, SO HE CAN JOIN ME.
SHOO!
FORGET IT! I WILL NOT GIVE HIM UP FOR ANYTHING.
HIS MOTHER WAS ONE OF MY WORSHIPERS. I WOULD SPEND MY TIME GOSSIPING WITH HER UNDER THE SPICED INDIAN AIR, AT NIGHT.

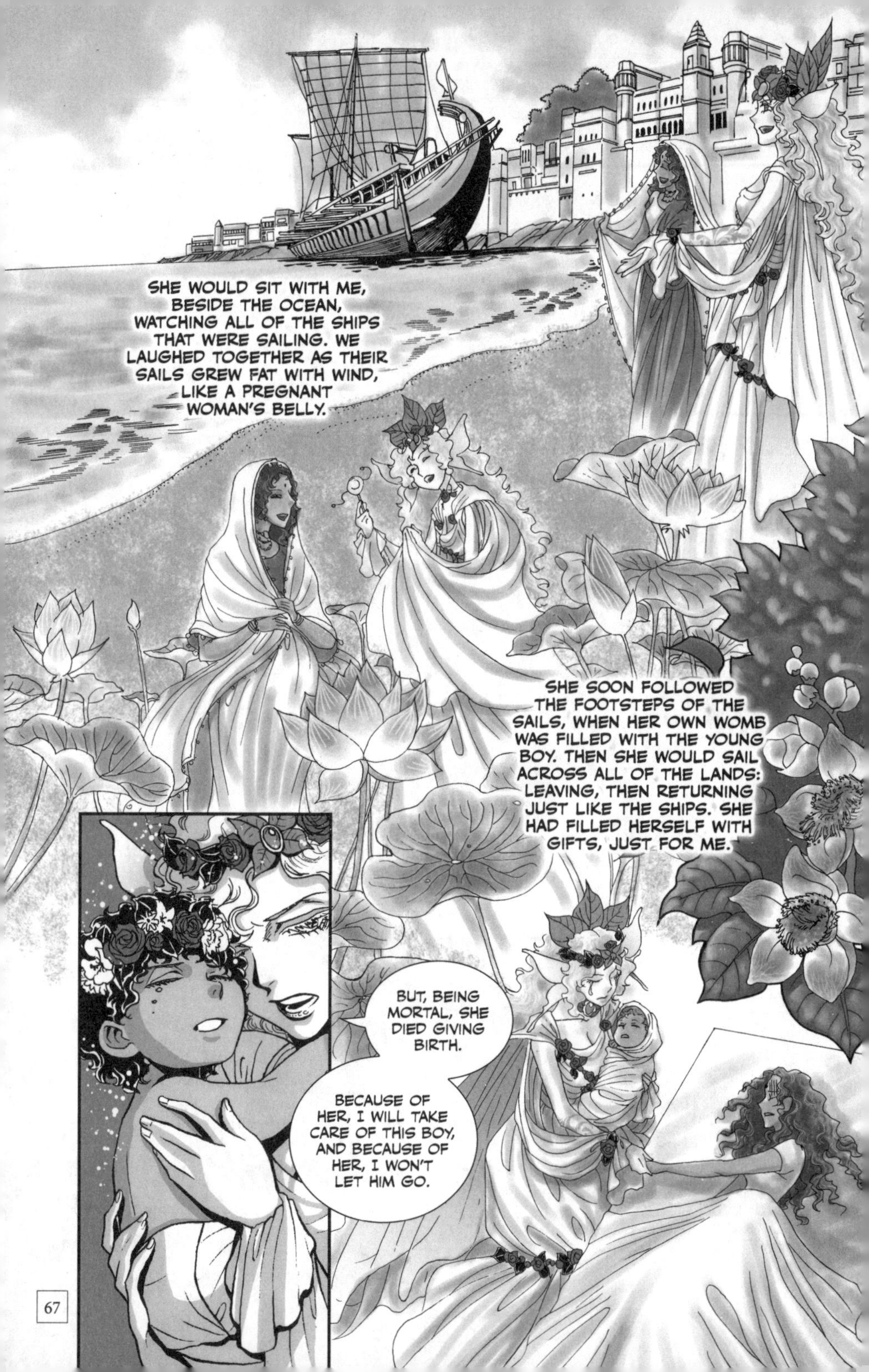
SHE WOULD SIT WITH ME, BESIDE THE OCEAN, WATCHING ALL OF THE SHIPS THAT WERE SAILING. WE LAUGHED TOGETHER AS THEIR SAILS GREW FAT WITH WIND, LIKE A PREGNANT WOMAN'S BELLY.
SHE SOON FOLLOWED THE FOOTSTEPS OF THE SAILS, WHEN HER OWN WOMB WAS FILLED WITH THE YOUNG BOY. THEN SHE WOULD SAIL ACROSS ALL OF THE LANDS: LEAVING, THEN RETURNING JUST LIKE THE SHIPS. SHE HAD FILLED HERSELF WITH GIFTS, JUST FOR ME.
BUT, BEING MORTAL, SHE DIED GIVING BIRTH.
BECAUSE OF HER, I WILL TAKE CARE OF THIS BOY, AND BECAUSE OF HER, I WON'T LET HIM GO.

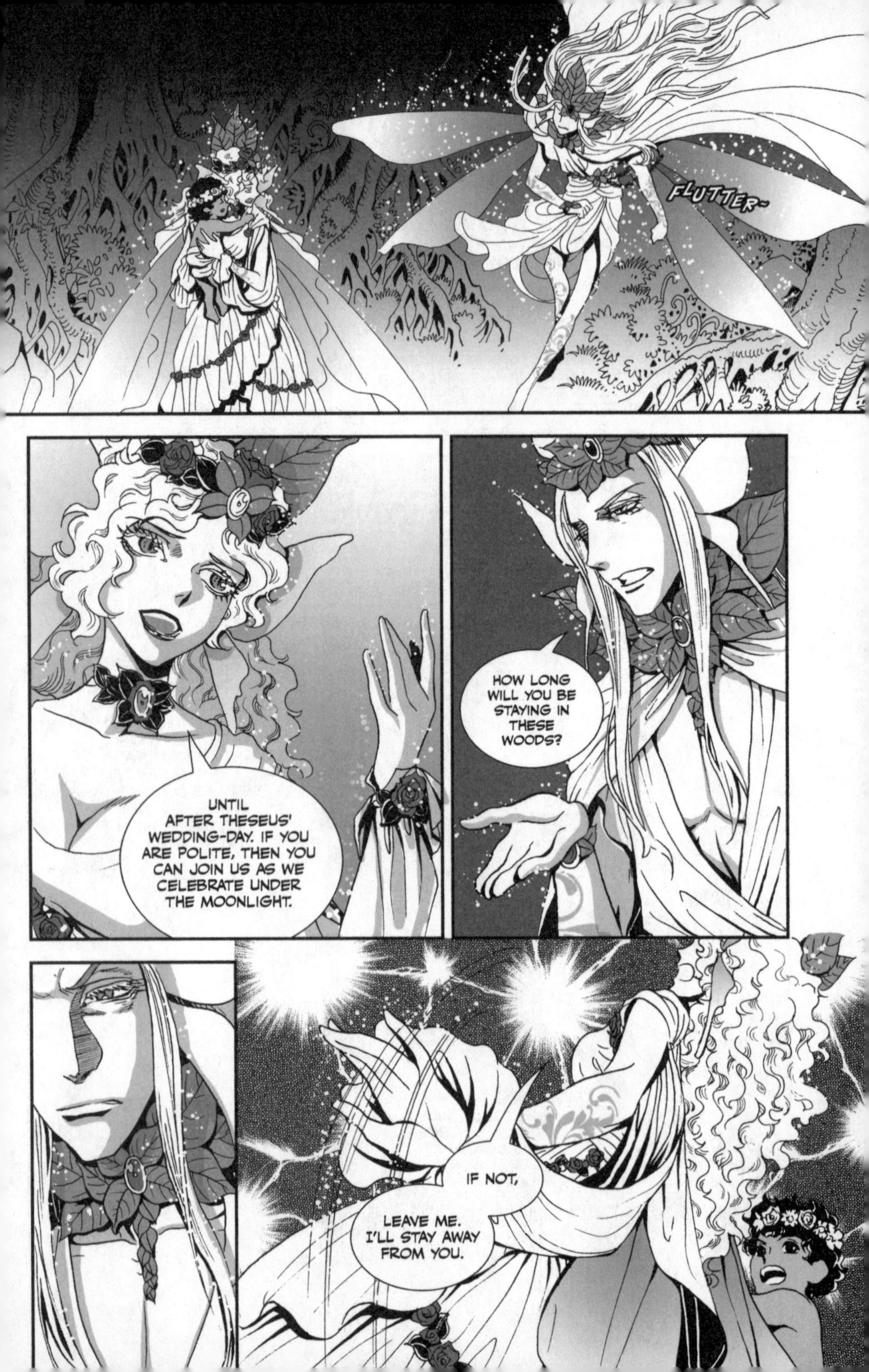
FLUTTER-
HOW LONG WILL YOU BE STAYING IN THESE WOODS?
UNTIL AFTER THESEUS' WEDDING-DAY. IF YOU ARE POLITE, THEN YOU CAN JOIN US AS WE CELEBRATE UNDER THE MOONLIGHT.
IF NOT,
LEAVE ME. I'LL STAY AWAY FROM YOU.

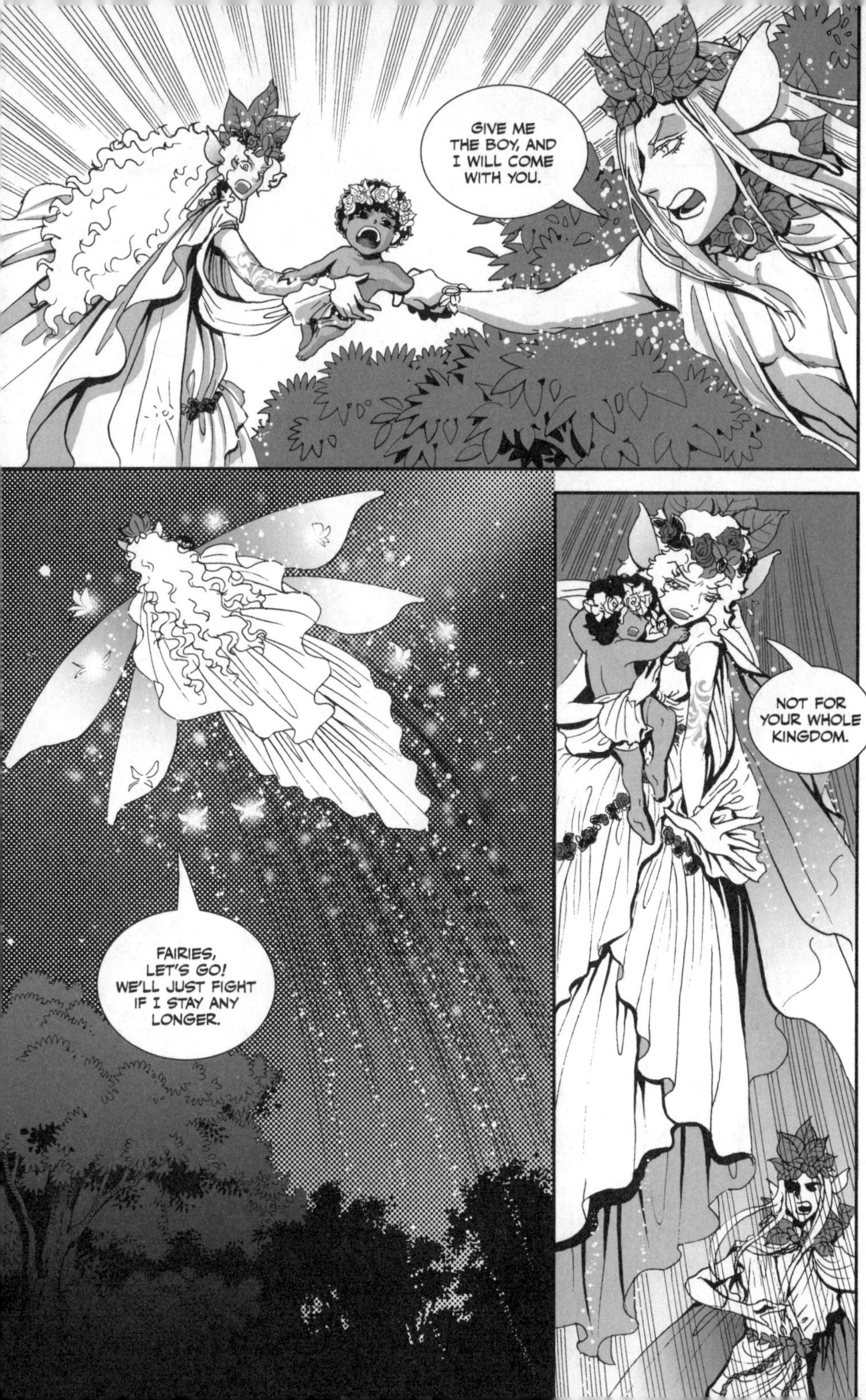
GIVE ME THE BOY, AND I WILL COME WITH YOU.
NOT FOR YOUR WHOLE KINGDOM.
FAIRIES, LET'S GO! WE'LL JUST FIGHT IF I STAY ANY LONGER.

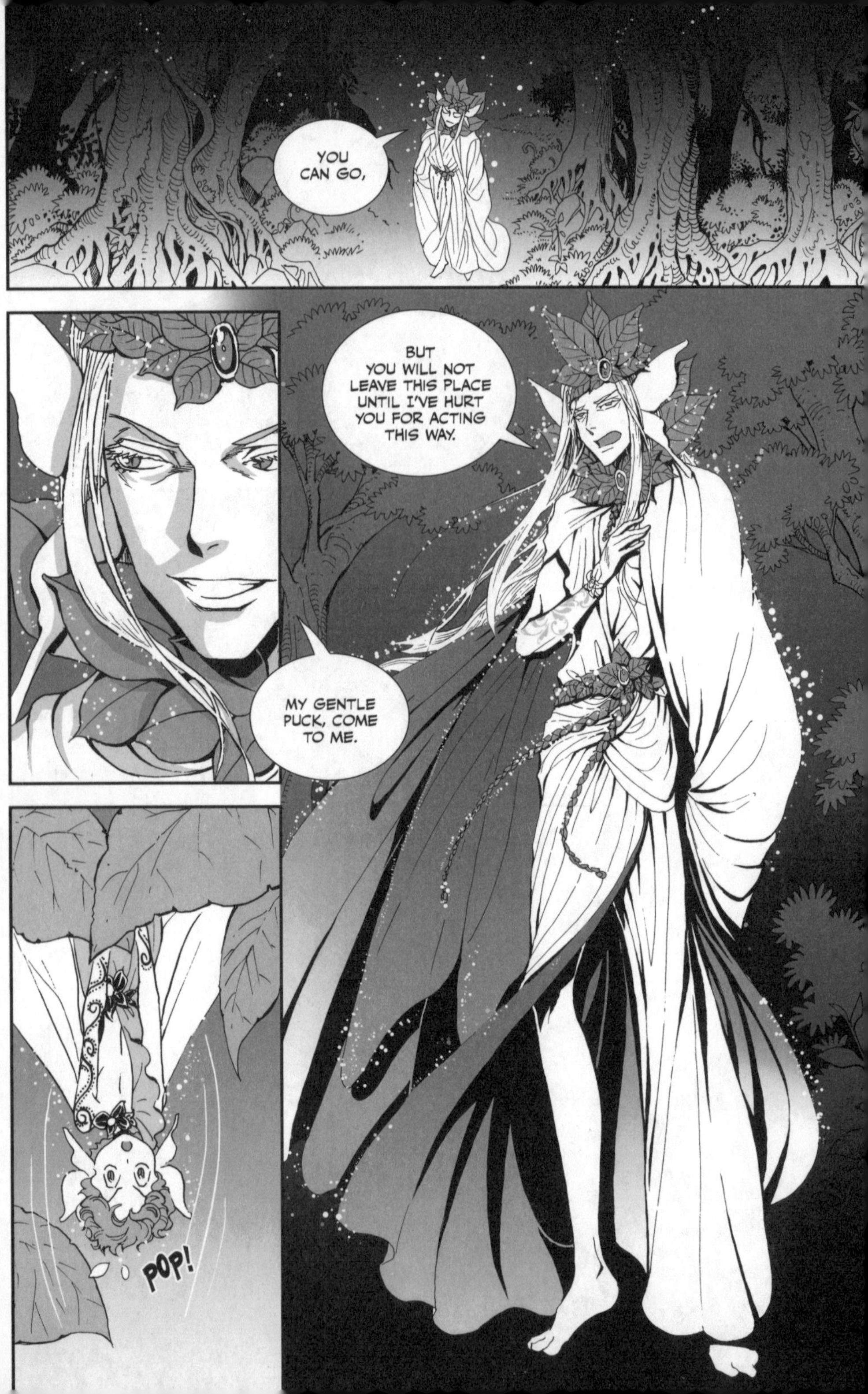
YOU CAN GO,
BUT YOU WILL NOT LEAVE THIS PLACE UNTIL I'VE HURT YOU FOR ACTING THIS WAY.
MY GENTLE PUCK, COME TO ME.
POP!

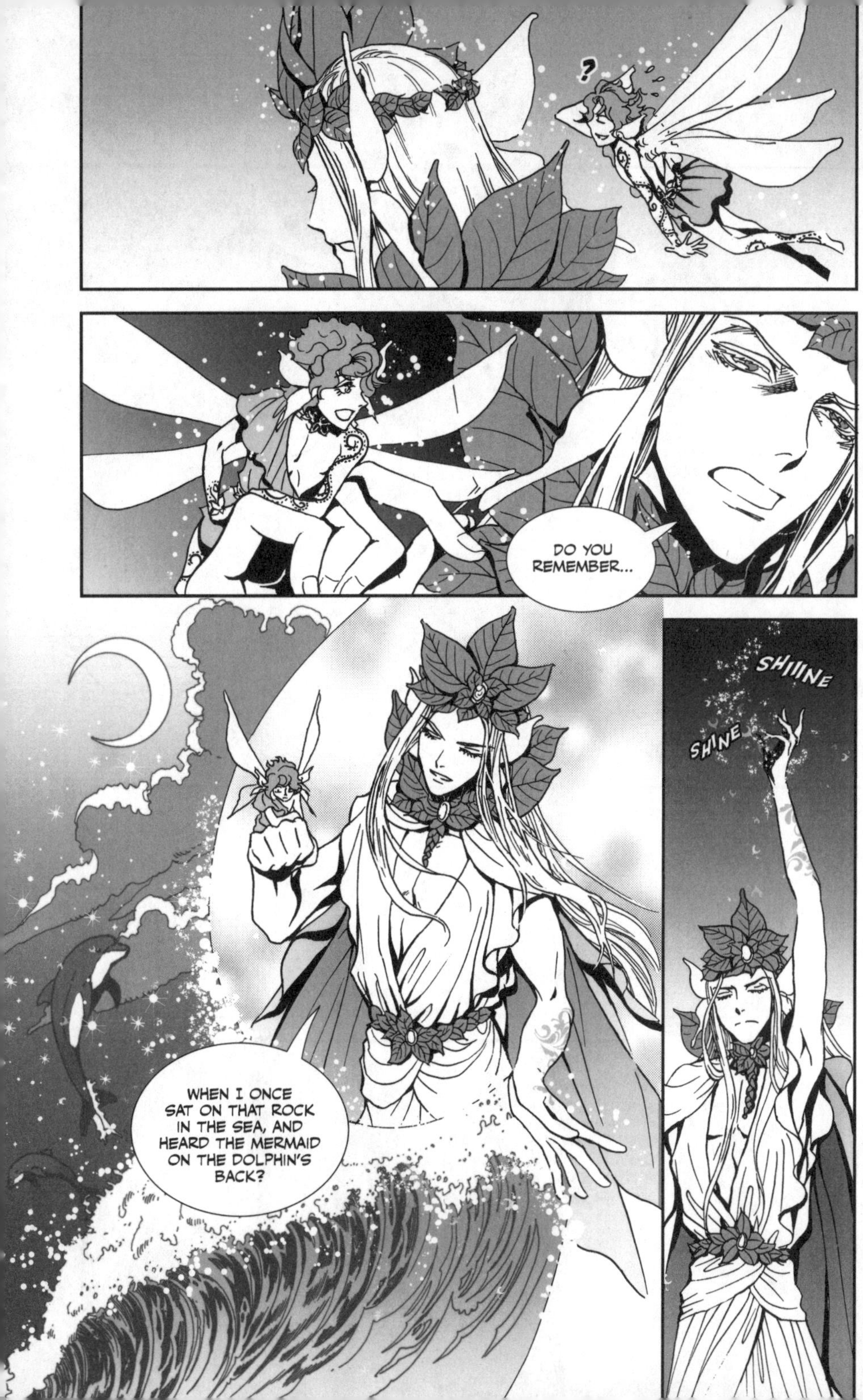
?
DO YOU REMEMBER...
SHIIINE
SHINE
WHEN I ONCE SAT ON THAT ROCK IN THE SEA, AND HEARD THE MERMAID ON THE DOLPHIN'S BACK?

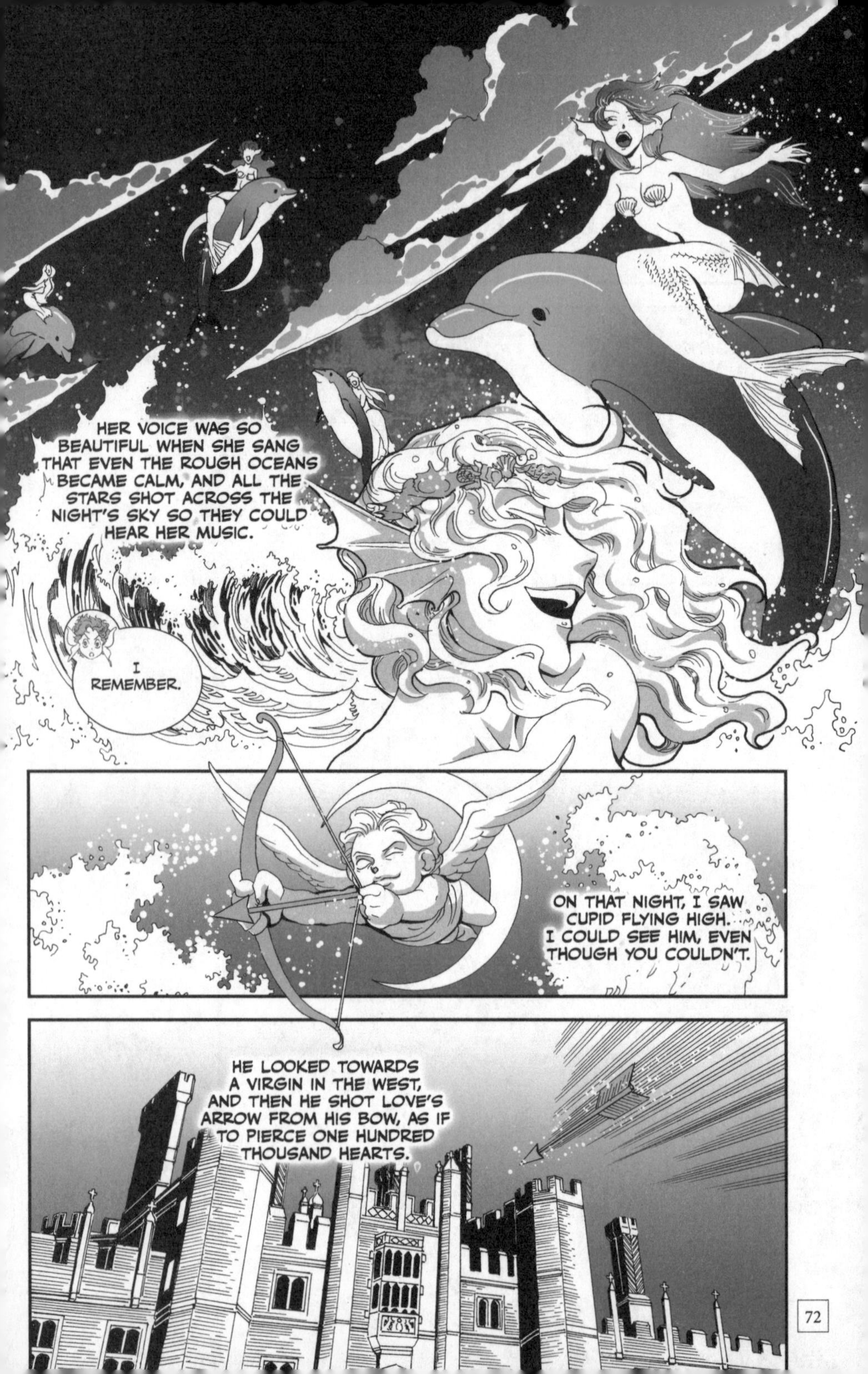
HER VOICE WAS SO BEAUTIFUL WHEN SHE SANG THAT EVEN THE ROUGH OCEANS BECAME CALM, AND ALL THE STARS SHOT ACROSS THE NIGHT'S SKY SO THEY COULD HEAR HER MUSIC.
I REMEMBER.
ON THAT NIGHT, I SAW CUPID FLYING HIGH. I COULD SEE HIM, EVEN THOUGH YOU COULDN'T.
HE LOOKED TOWARDS A VIRGIN IN THE WEST, AND THEN HE SHOT LOVE'S ARROW FROM HIS BOW, AS IF TO PIERCE ONE HUNDRED THOUSAND HEARTS.

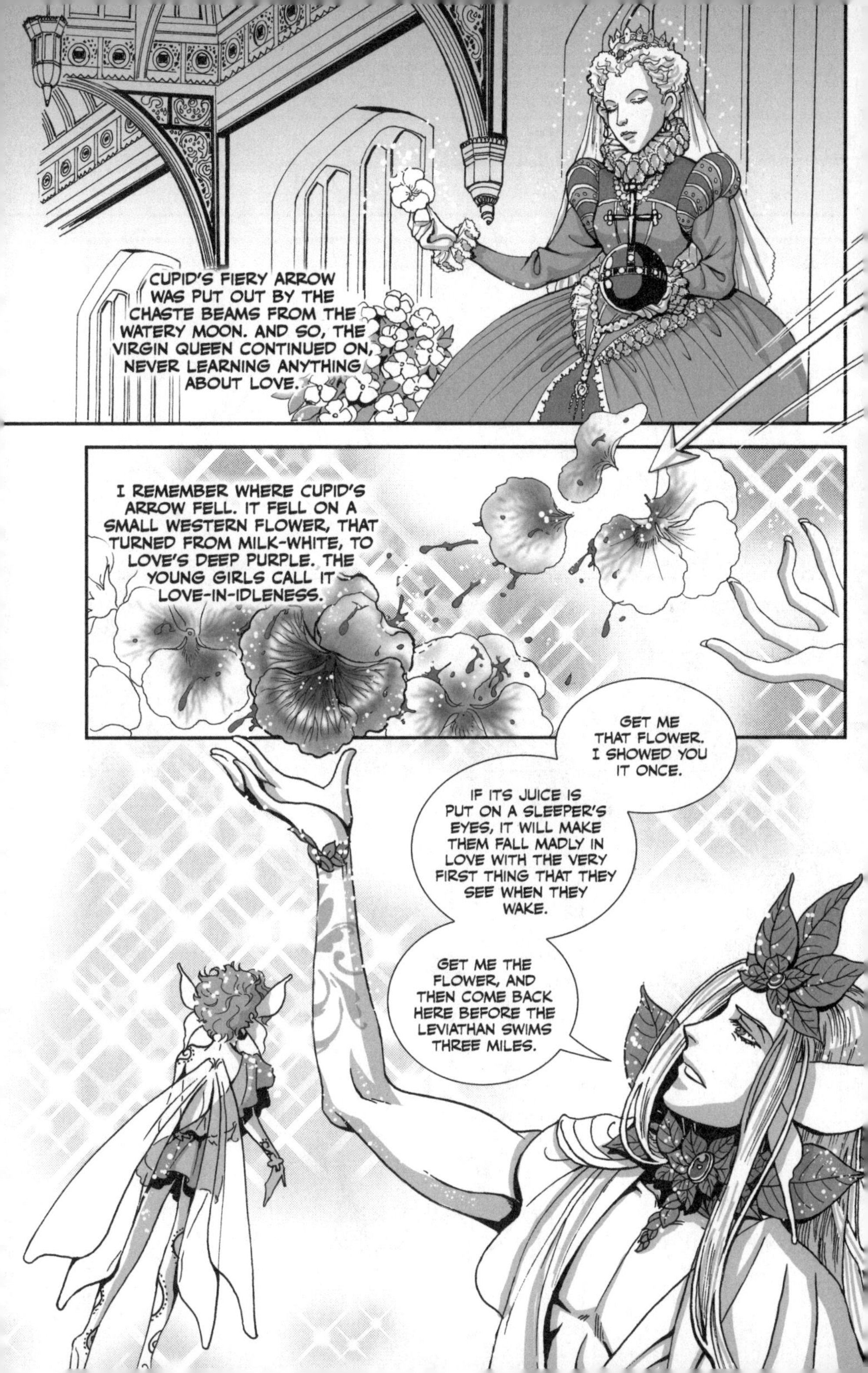
CUPID'S FIERY ARROW WAS PUT OUT BY THE CHASTE BEAMS FROM THE WATERY MOON. AND SO, THE VIRGIN QUEEN CONTINUED ON, NEVER LEARNING ANYTHING ABOUT LOVE.
I REMEMBER WHERE CUPID'S ARROW FELL. IT FELL ON A SMALL WESTERN FLOWER, THAT TURNED FROM MILK-WHITE, TO LOVE'S DEEP PURPLE. THE YOUNG GIRLS CALL IT LOVE-IN-IDLENESS.
GET ME THAT FLOWER. I SHOWED YOU IT ONCE.
IF ITS JUICE IS PUT ON A SLEEPER'S EYES, IT WILL MAKE THEM FALL MADLY IN LOVE WITH THE VERY FIRST THING THAT THEY SEE WHEN THEY WAKE.
GET ME THE FLOWER, AND THEN COME BACK HERE BEFORE THE LEVIATHAN SWIMS THREE MILES.

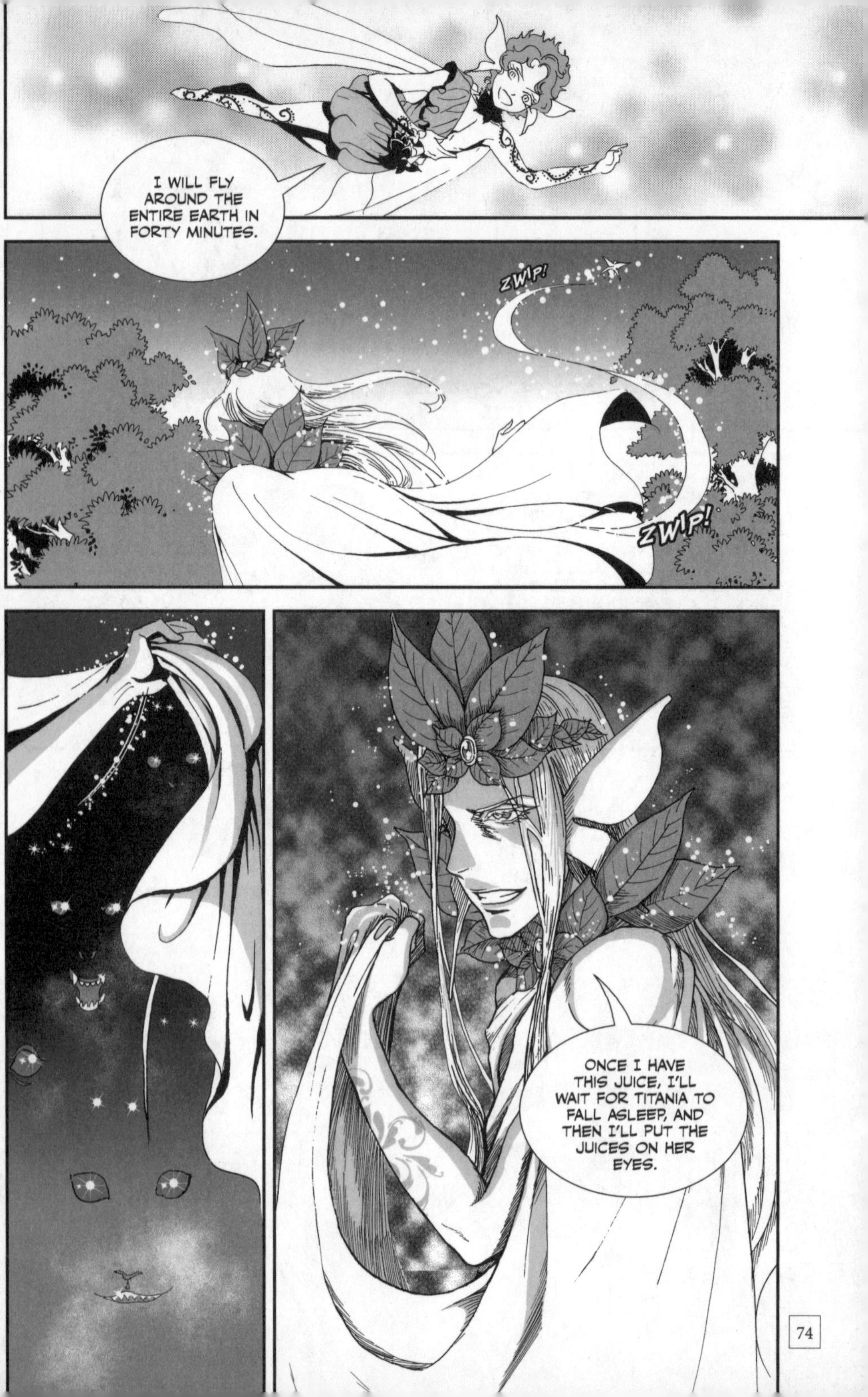
I WILL FLY AROUND THE ENTIRE EARTH IN FORTY MINUTES.
ZWIP!
ZWIP!
ONCE I HAVE THIS JUICE, I'LL WAIT FOR TITANIA TO FALL ASLEEP, AND THEN I'LL PUT THE JUICES ON HER EYES.

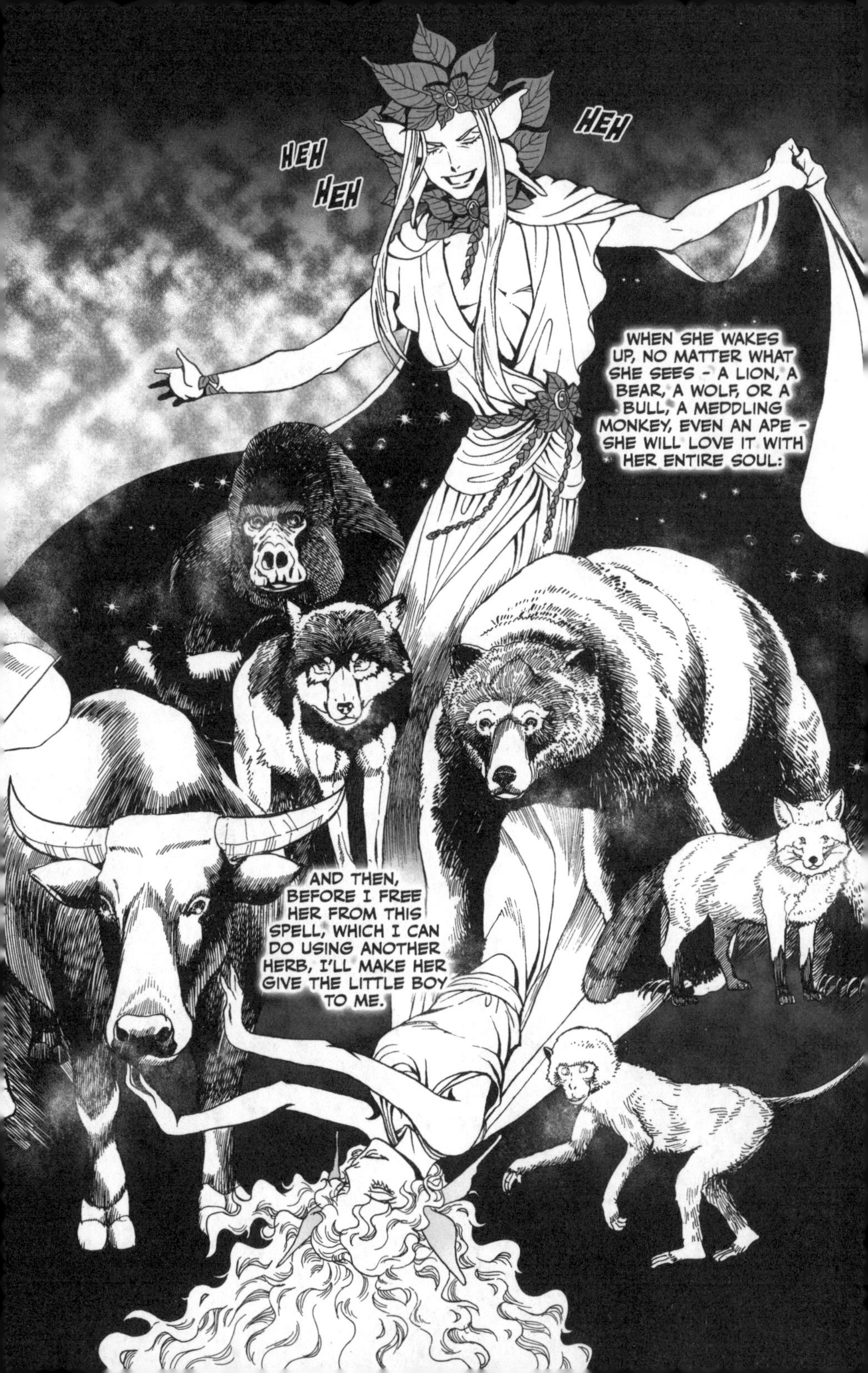
HEH
HEH HEH
WHEN SHE WAKES UP, NO MATTER WHAT SHE SEES - A LION, A BEAR, A WOLF, OR A BULL, A MEDDLING MONKEY, EVEN AN APE - SHE WILL LOVE IT WITH HER ENTIRE SOUL:
AND THEN, BEFORE I FREE HER FROM THIS SPELL, WHICH I CAN DO USING ANOTHER HERB, I'LL MAKE HER GIVE THE LITTLE BOY TO ME.

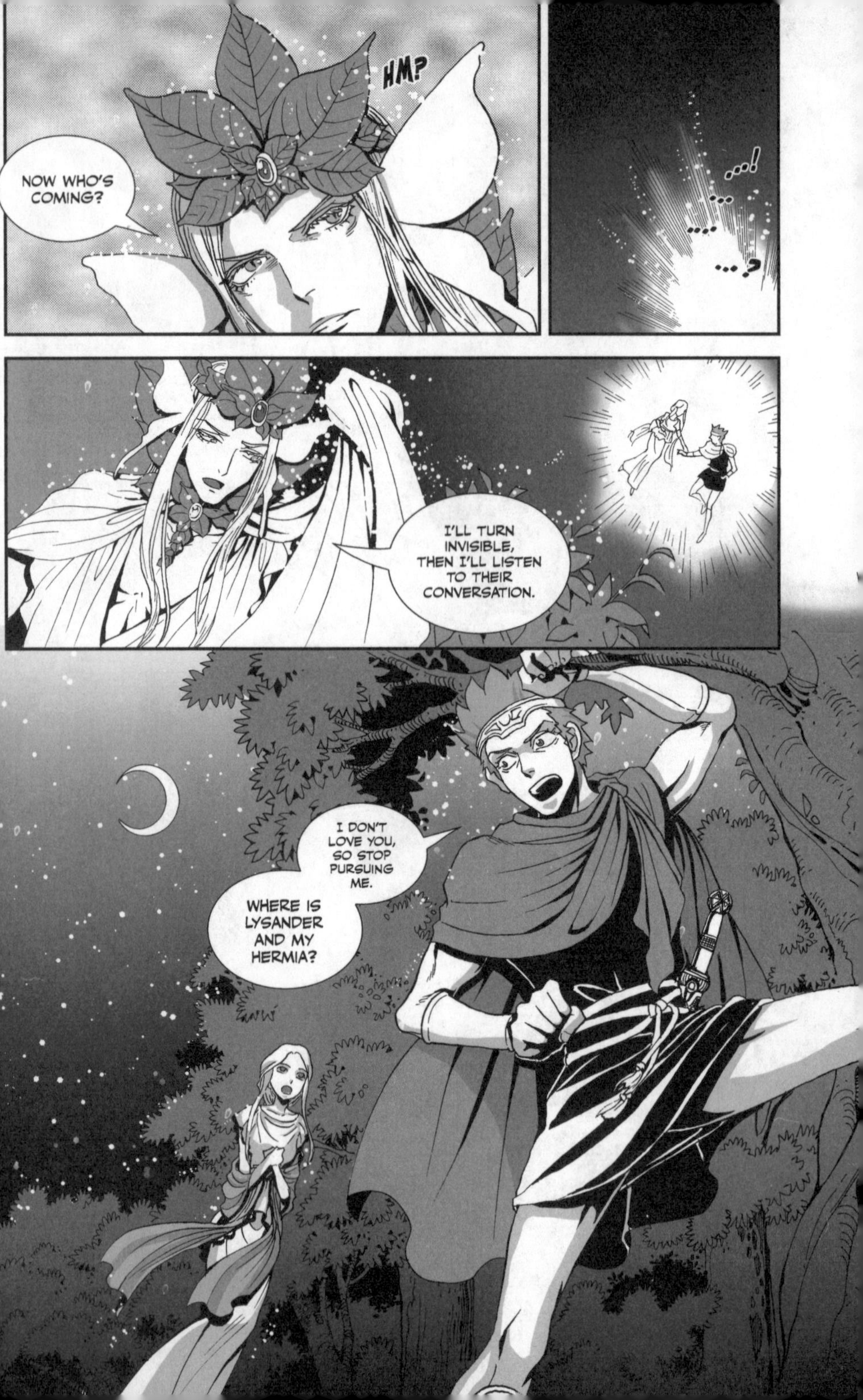
...!
...
...
...?
HM?
NOW WHO'S COMING?
I'LL TURN INVISIBLE, THEN I'LL LISTEN TO THEIR CONVERSATION.
I DON'T LOVE YOU, SO STOP PURSUING ME.
WHERE IS LYSANDER AND MY HERMIA?

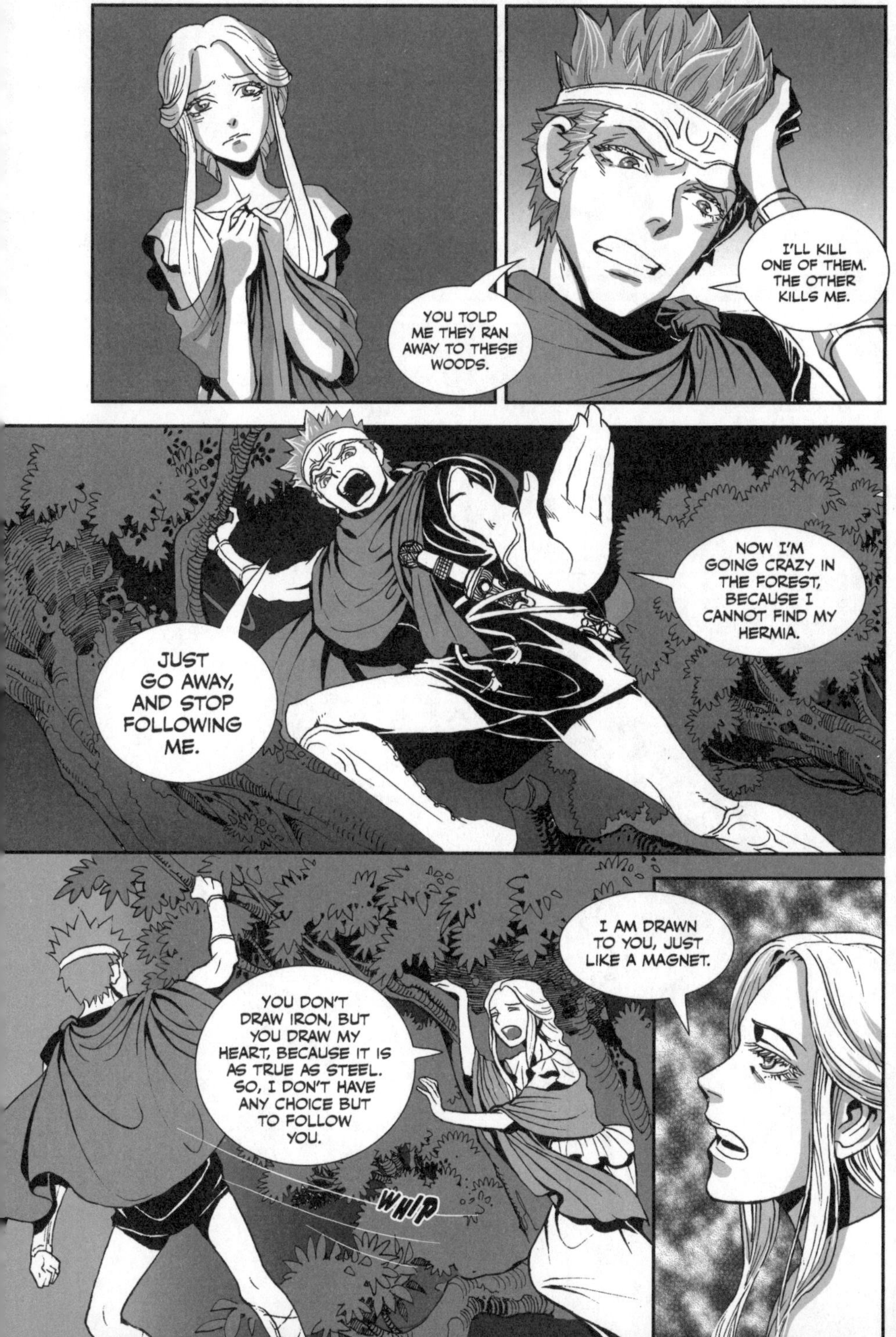
I'LL KILL ONE OF THEM. THE OTHER KILLS ME.
YOU TOLD ME THEY RAN AWAY TO THESE WOODS.
NOW I'M GOING CRAZY IN THE FOREST, BECAUSE I CANNOT FIND MY HERMIA.
JUST GO AWAY, AND STOP FOLLOWING ME.
I AM DRAWN TO YOU, JUST LIKE A MAGNET.
YOU DON'T DRAW IRON, BUT YOU DRAW MY HEART, BECAUSE IT IS AS TRUE AS STEEL. SO, I DON'T HAVE ANY CHOICE BUT TO FOLLOW YOU.
WHIP

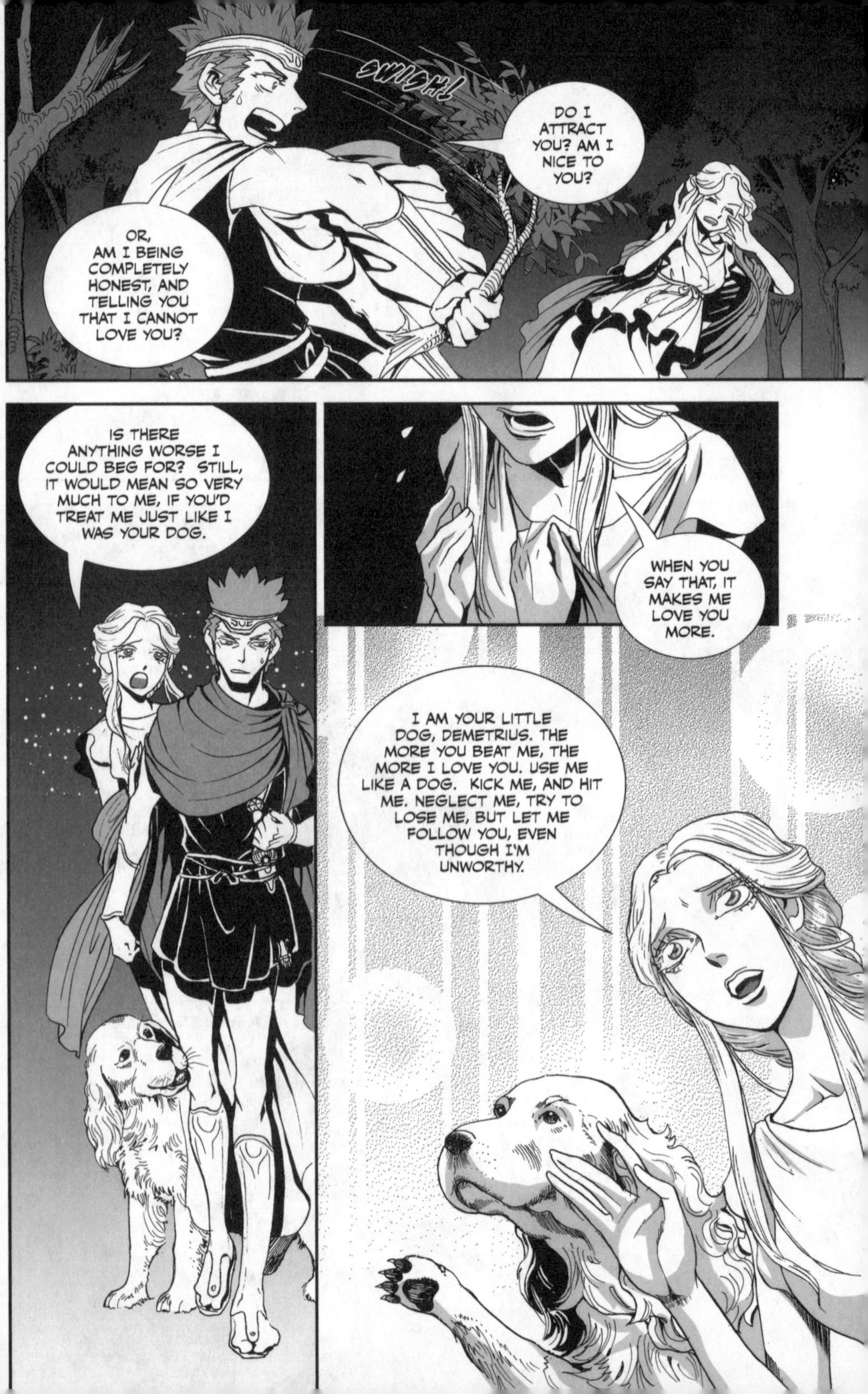
THWING
DO I ATTRACT YOU? AM I NICE TO YOU?
OR, AM I BEING COMPLETELY HONEST, AND TELLING YOU THAT I CANNOT LOVE YOU?
WHEN YOU SAY THAT, IT MAKES ME LOVE YOU MORE.
I AM YOUR LITTLE DOG, DEMETRIUS. THE MORE YOU BEAT ME, THE MORE I LOVE YOU. USE ME LIKE A DOG. KICK ME, AND HIT ME. NEGLECT ME, TRY TO LOSE ME, BUT LET ME FOLLOW YOU, EVEN THOUGH I'M UNWORTHY.
IS THERE ANYTHING WORSE I COULD BEG FOR? STILL, IT WOULD MEAN SO VERY MUCH TO ME, IF YOU'D TREAT ME JUST LIKE I WAS YOUR DOG.

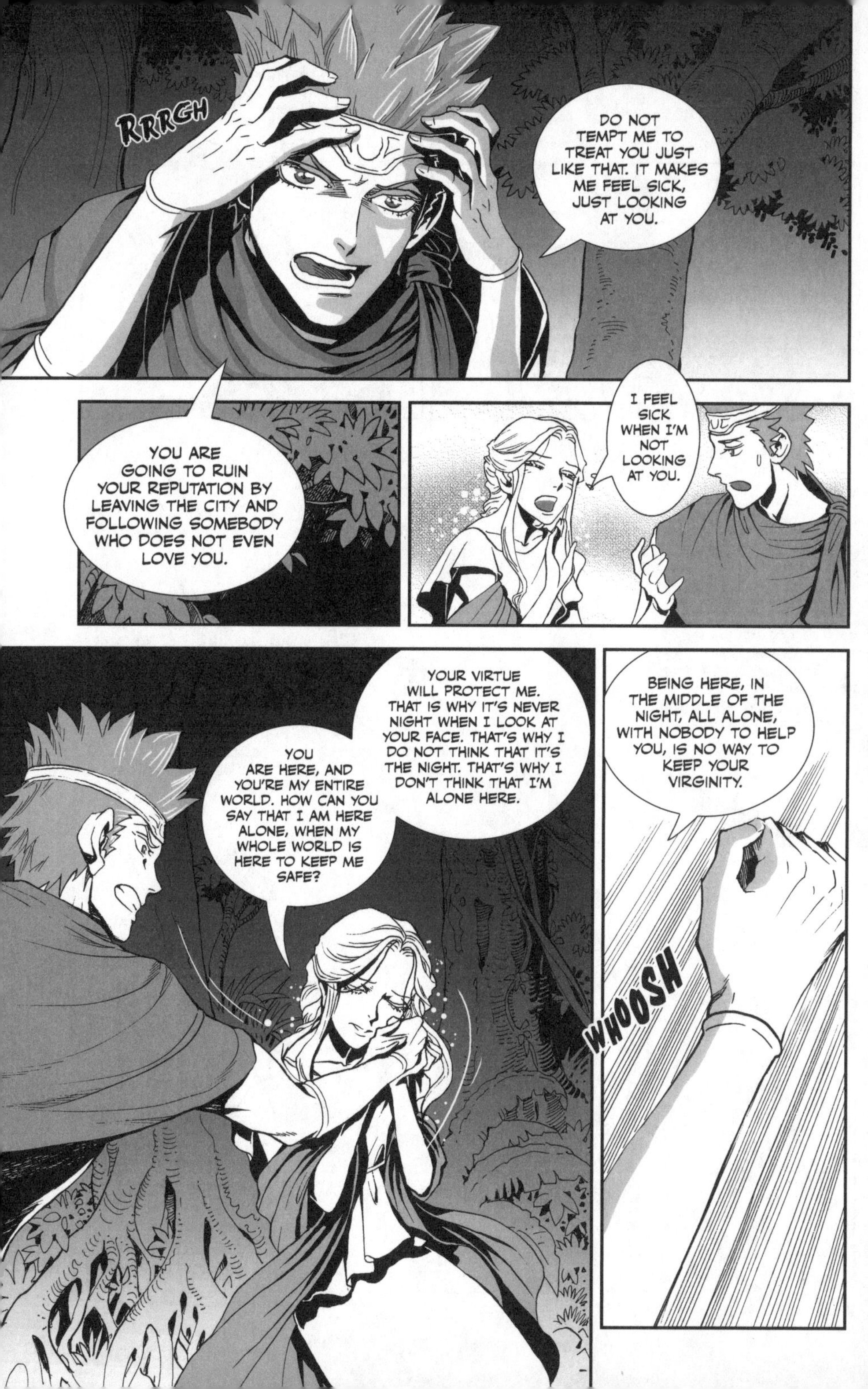
RRRGH
DO NOT TEMPT ME TO TREAT YOU JUST LIKE THAT. IT MAKES ME FEEL SICK, JUST LOOKING AT YOU.
I FEEL SICK WHEN I'M NOT LOOKING AT YOU.
YOU ARE GOING TO RUIN YOUR REPUTATION BY LEAVING THE CITY AND FOLLOWING SOMEBODY WHO DOES NOT EVEN LOVE YOU.
BEING HERE, IN THE MIDDLE OF THE NIGHT, ALL ALONE, WITH NOBODY TO HELP YOU, IS NO WAY TO KEEP YOUR VIRGINITY.
WHOOSH
YOUR VIRTUE WILL PROTECT ME. THAT IS WHY IT'S NEVER NIGHT WHEN I LOOK AT YOUR FACE. THAT'S WHY I DO NOT THINK THAT IT'S THE NIGHT. THAT'S WHY I DON'T THINK THAT I'M ALONE HERE.
YOU ARE HERE, AND YOU'RE MY ENTIRE WORLD. HOW CAN YOU SAY THAT I AM HERE ALONE, WHEN MY WHOLE WORLD IS HERE TO KEEP ME SAFE?

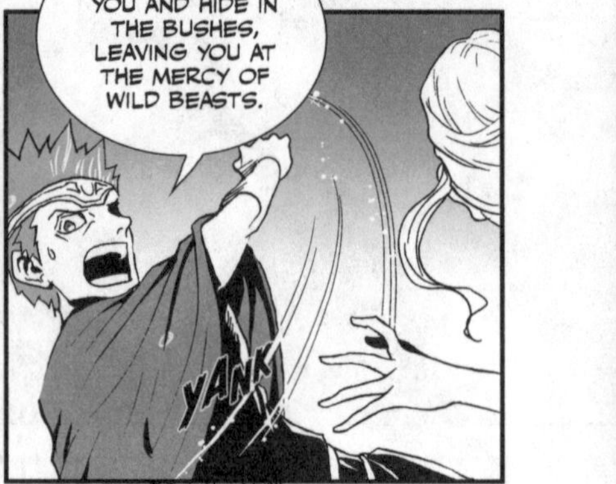
I'D RUN FROM YOU AND HIDE IN THE BUSHES, LEAVING YOU AT THE MERCY OF WILD BEASTS.
YANK

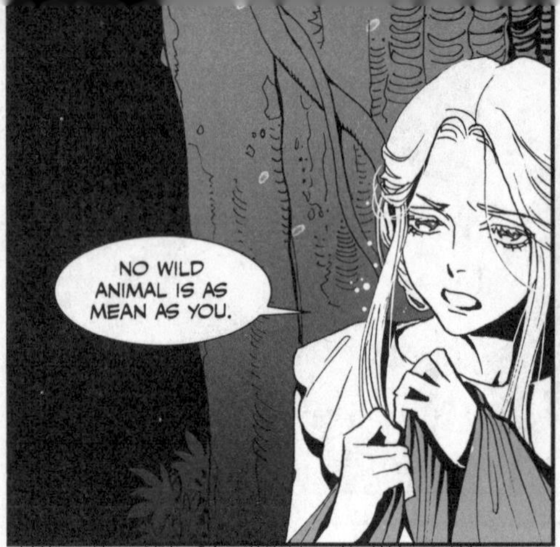
NO WILD ANIMAL IS AS MEAN AS YOU.

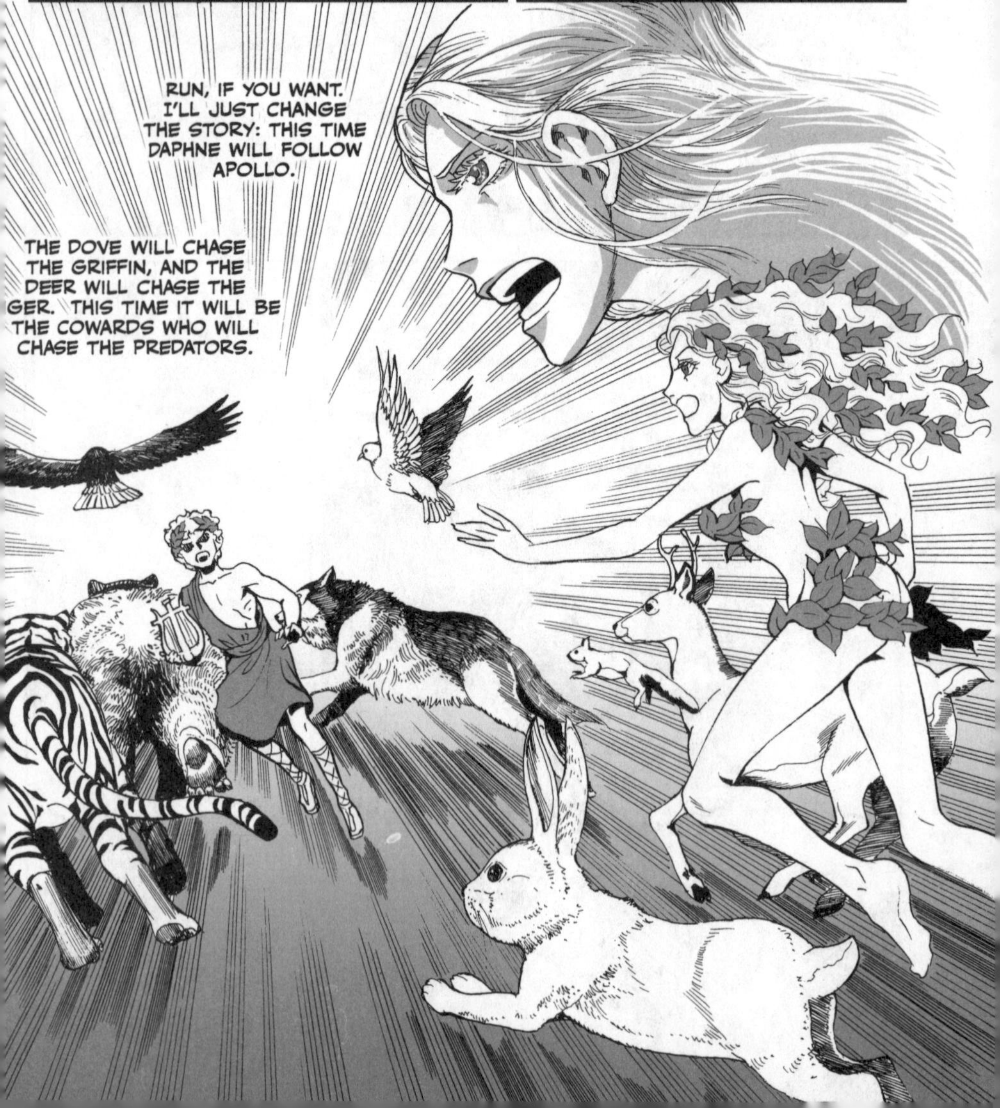
RUN, IF YOU WANT. I'LL JUST CHANGE THE STORY: THIS TIME DAPHNE WILL FOLLOW APOLLO.
THE DOVE WILL CHASE THE GRIFFIN, AND THE DEER WILL CHASE THE GER. THIS TIME IT WILL BE THE COWARDS WHO WILL CHASE THE PREDATORS.

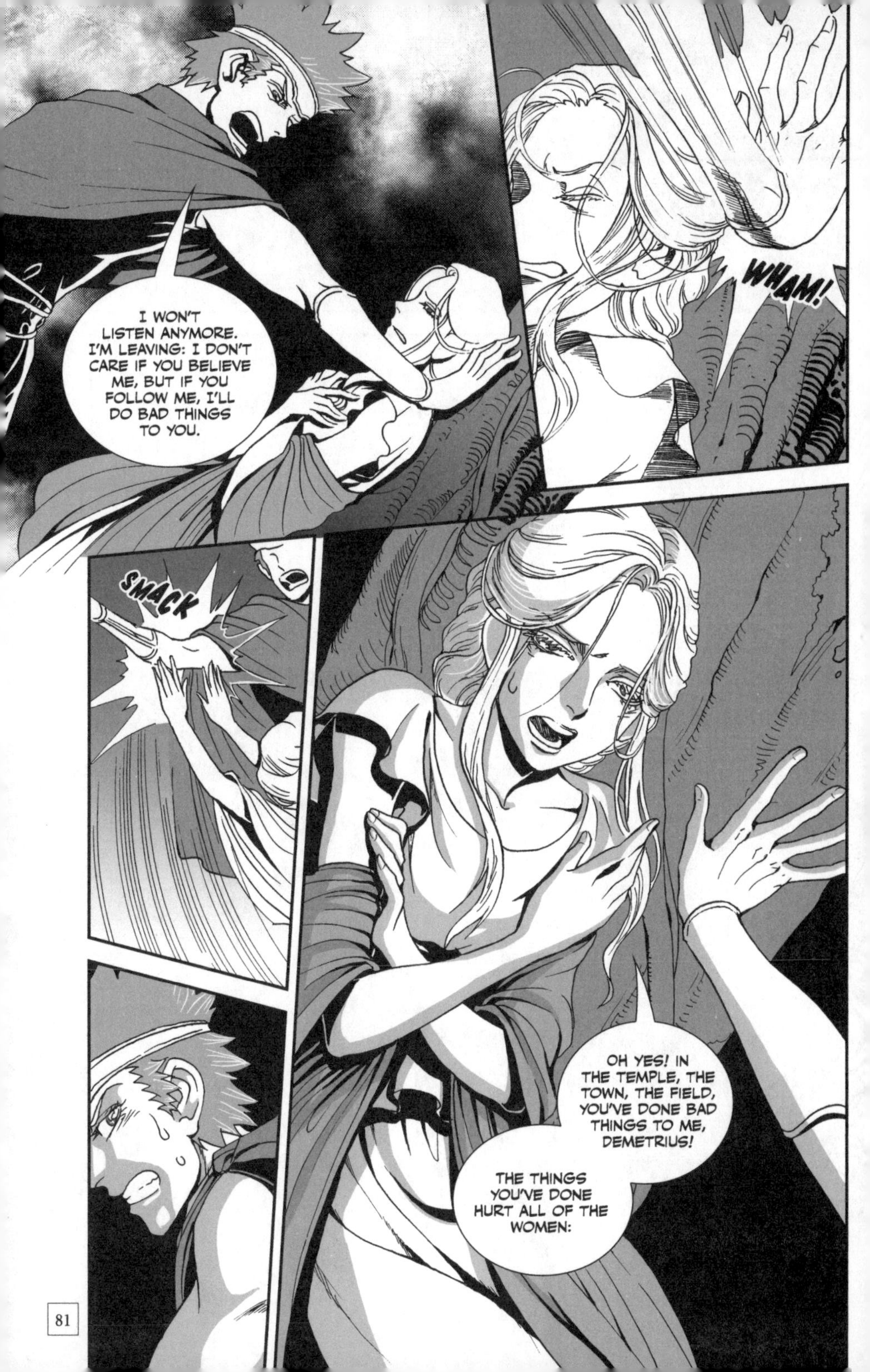
WHAM!
I WON'T LISTEN ANYMORE. I'M LEAVING: I DON'T CARE IF YOU BELIEVE ME, BUT IF YOU FOLLOW ME, I'LL DO BAD THINGS TO YOU.
OH YES! IN THE TEMPLE, THE TOWN, THE FIELD, YOU'VE DONE BAD THINGS TO ME, DEMETRIUS!
THE THINGS YOU'VE DONE HURT ALL OF THE WOMEN:
SMACK

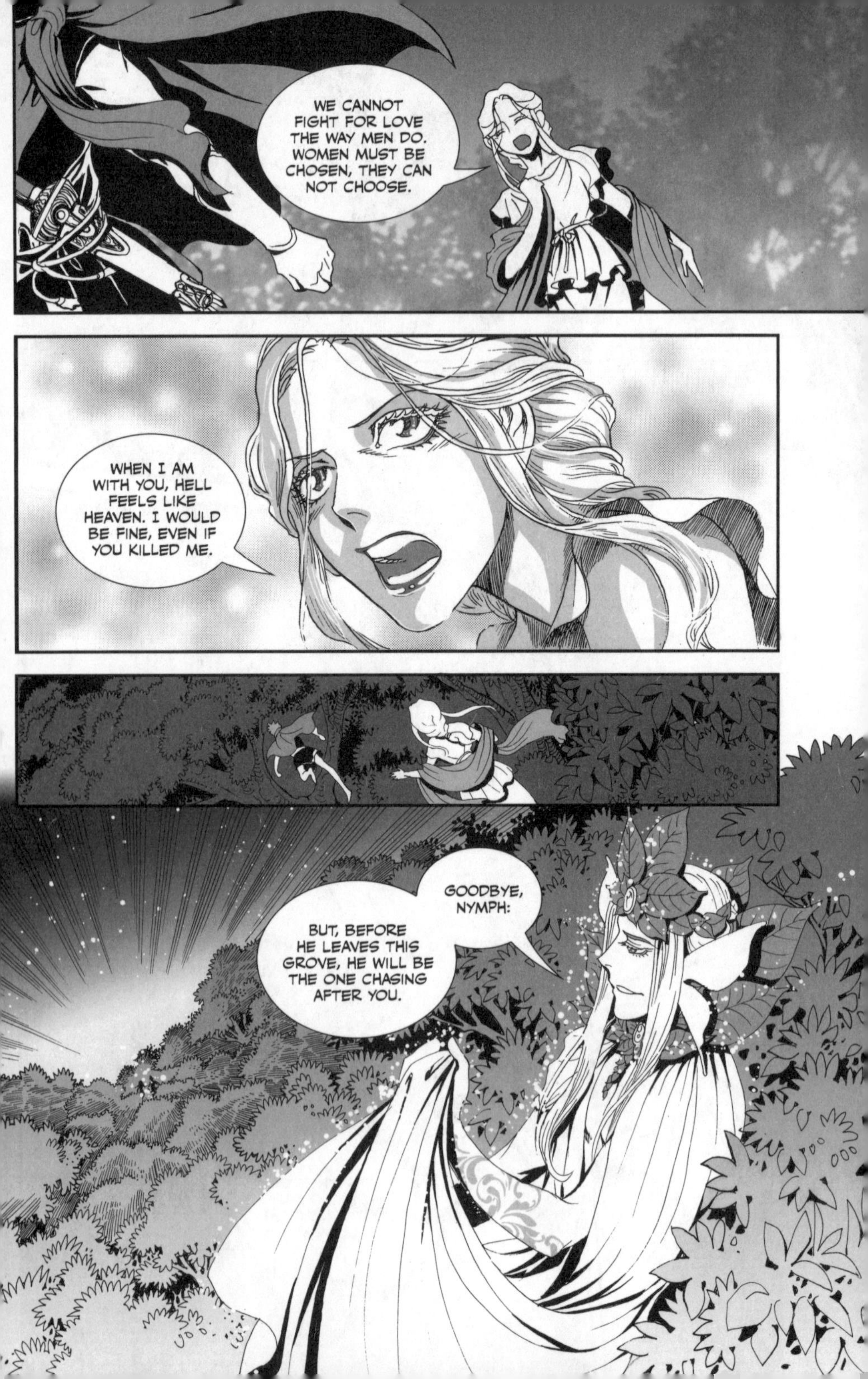
WE CANNOT FIGHT FOR LOVE THE WAY MEN DO. WOMEN MUST BE CHOSEN, THEY CAN NOT CHOOSE.
WHEN I AM WITH YOU, HELL FEELS LIKE HEAVEN. I WOULD BE FINE, EVEN IF YOU KILLED ME.
GOODBYE, NYMPH:
BUT, BEFORE HE LEAVES THIS GROVE, HE WILL BE THE ONE CHASING AFTER YOU.

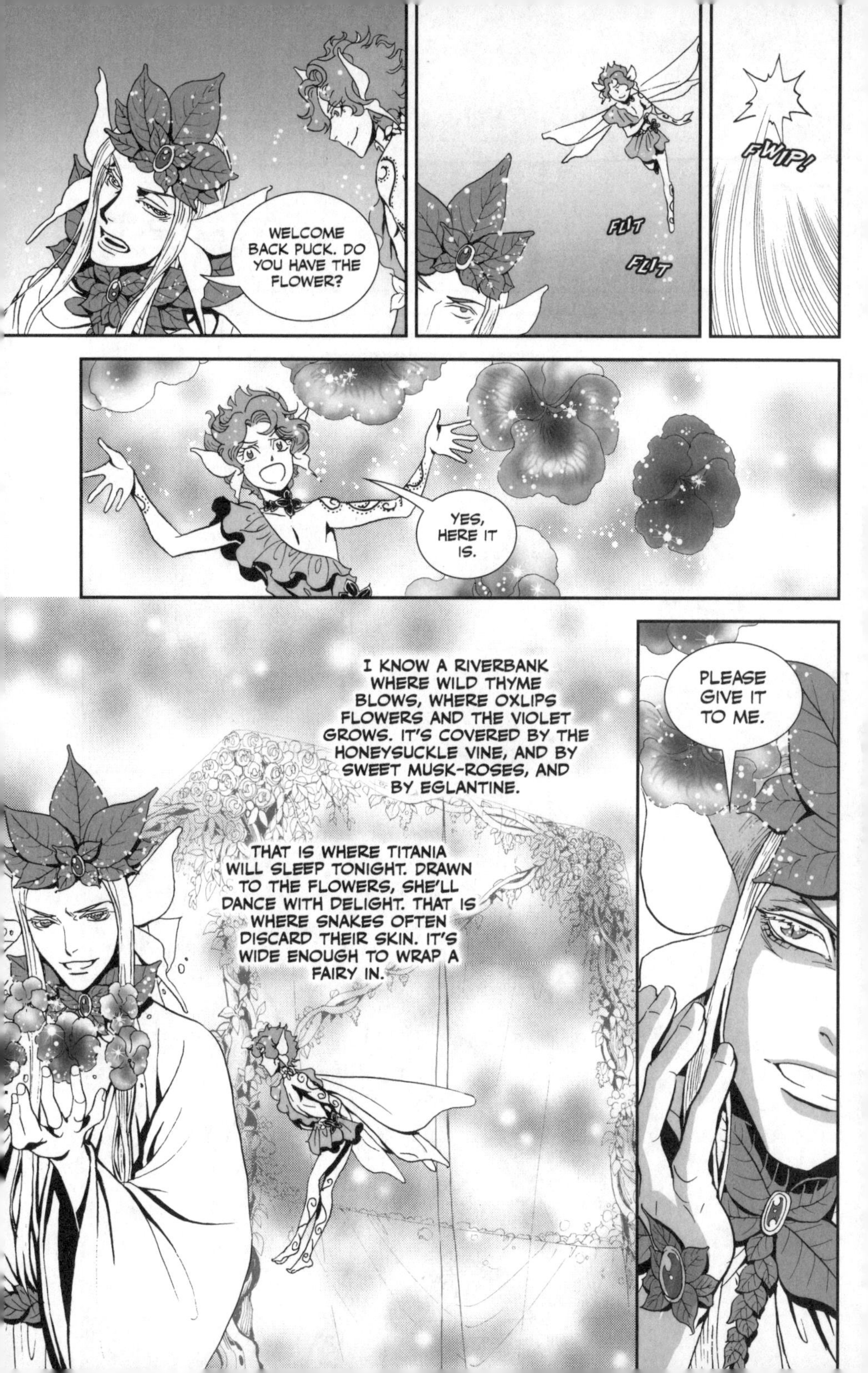
FWIP!
FLIT
FLIT
WELCOME BACK PUCK. DO YOU HAVE THE FLOWER?
YES, HERE IT IS.
PLEASE GIVE IT TO ME.
I KNOW A RIVERBANK WHERE WILD THYME BLOWS, WHERE OXLIPS FLOWERS AND THE VIOLET GROWS. IT'S COVERED BY THE HONEYSUCKLE VINE, AND BY SWEET MUSK-ROSES, AND BY EGLANTINE.
THAT IS WHERE TITANIA WILL SLEEP TONIGHT. DRAWN TO THE FLOWERS, SHE'LL DANCE WITH DELIGHT. THAT IS WHERE SNAKES OFTEN DISCARD THEIR SKIN. IT'S WIDE ENOUGH TO WRAP A FAIRY IN.

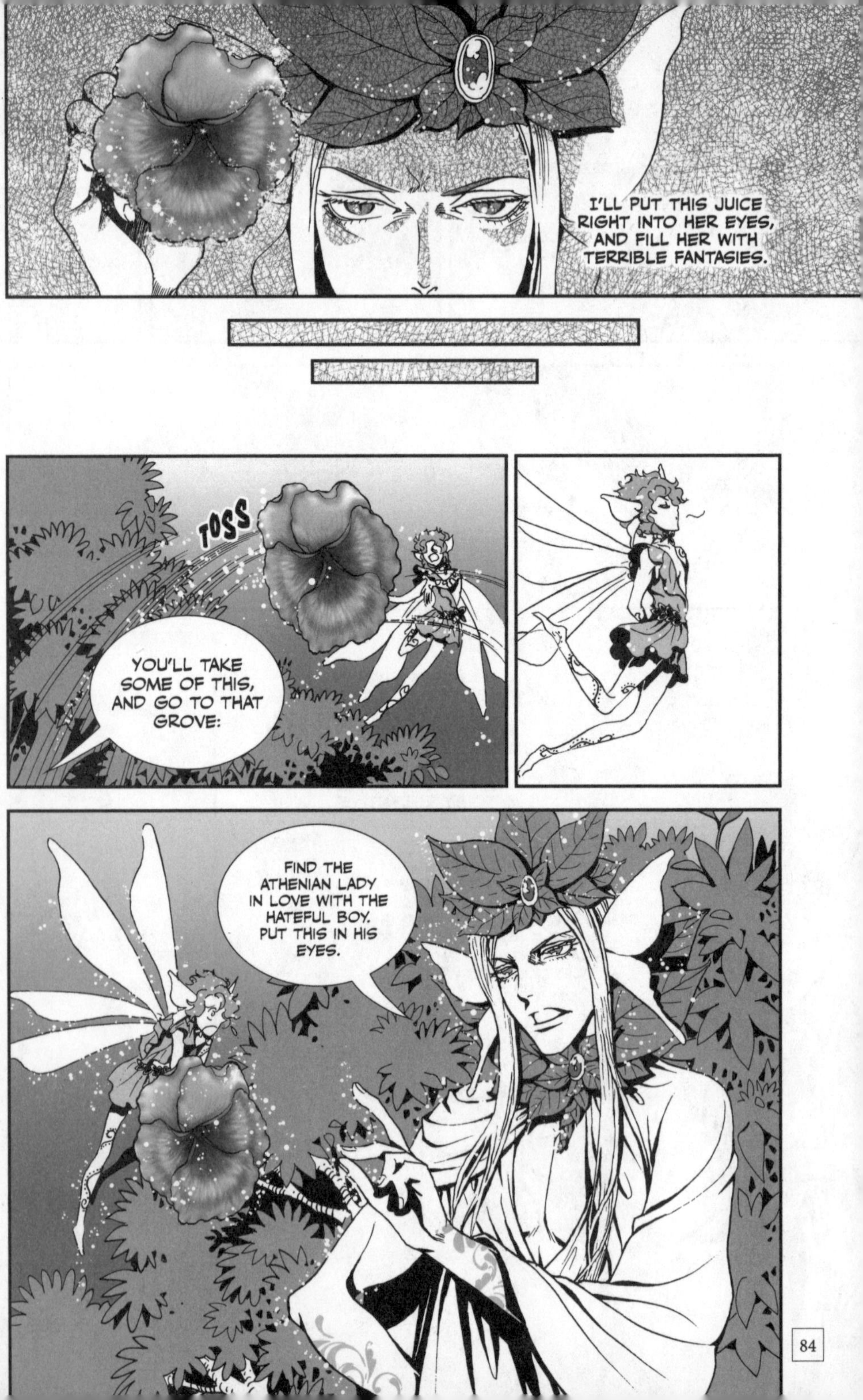
I'LL PUT THIS JUICE RIGHT INTO HER EYES, AND FILL HER WITH TERRIBLE FANTASIES.
TOSS
YOU'LL TAKE SOME OF THIS, AND GO TO THAT GROVE:
FIND THE ATHENIAN LADY IN LOVE WITH THE HATEFUL BOY. PUT THIS IN HIS EYES.

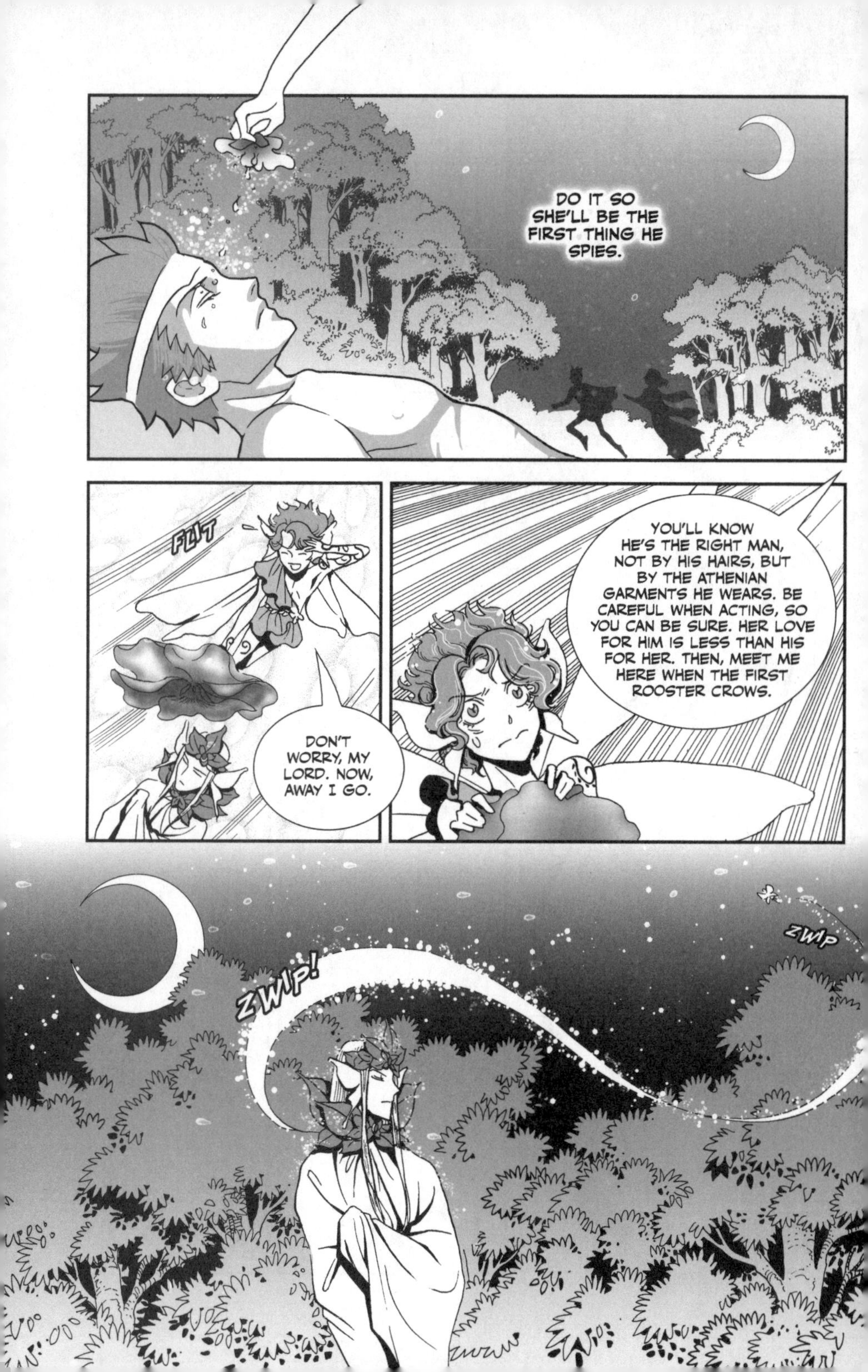
DO IT SO SHE'LL BE THE FIRST THING HE SPIES.
YOU'LL KNOW HE'S THE RIGHT MAN, NOT BY HIS HAIRS, BUT BY THE ATHENIAN GARMENTS HE WEARS. BE CAREFUL WHEN ACTING, SO YOU CAN BE SURE. HER LOVE FOR HIM IS LESS THAN HIS FOR HER. THEN, MEET ME HERE WHEN THE FIRST ROOSTER CROWS.
FLIT
DON'T WORRY, MY LORD. NOW, AWAY I GO.
ZWIP
ZWIP!

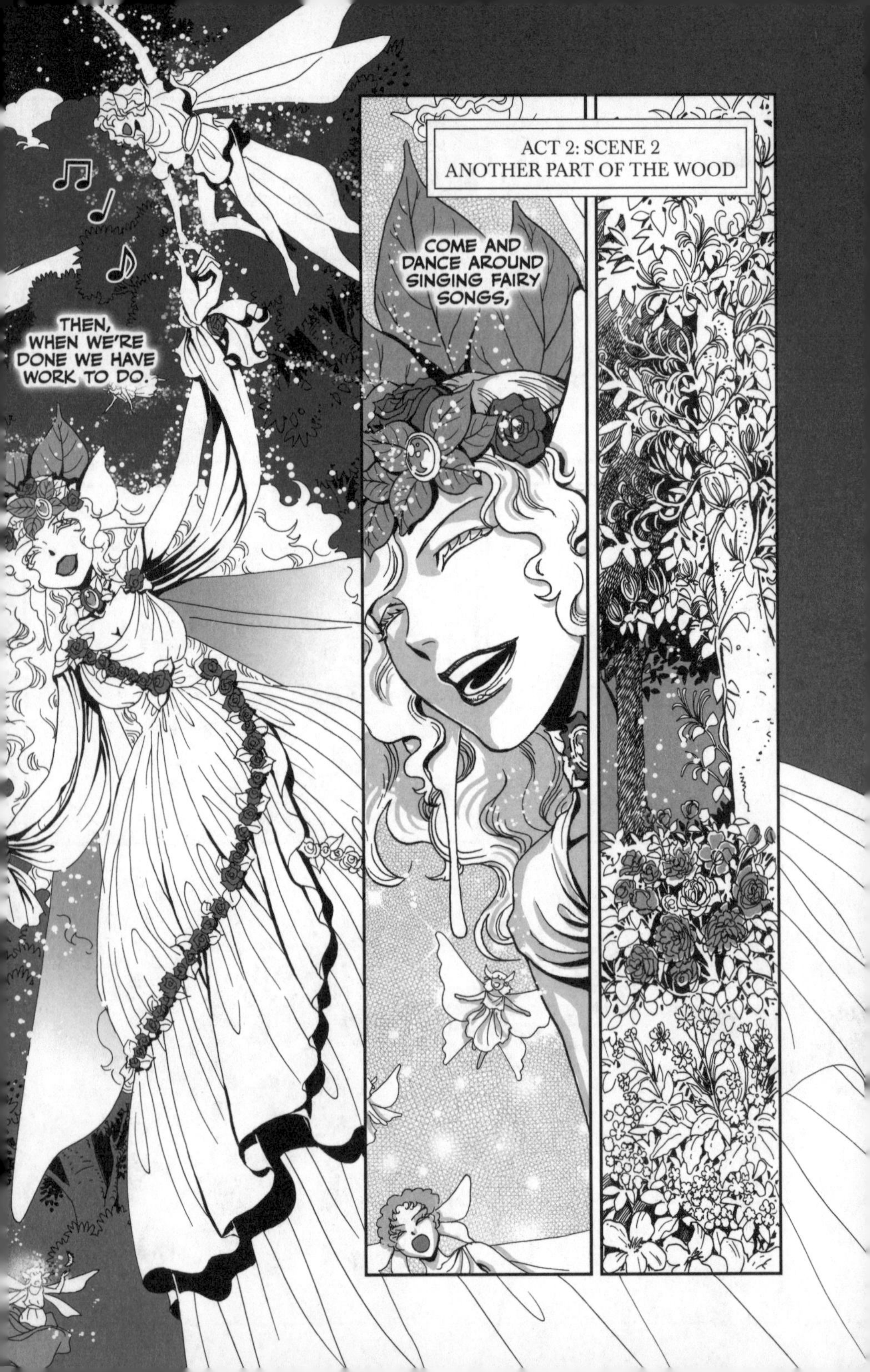
ACT 2: SCENE 2
ANOTHER PART OF THE WOOD
COME AND DANCE AROUND SINGING FAIRY SONGS,
THEN, WHEN WE'RE DONE WE HAVE WORK TO DO.

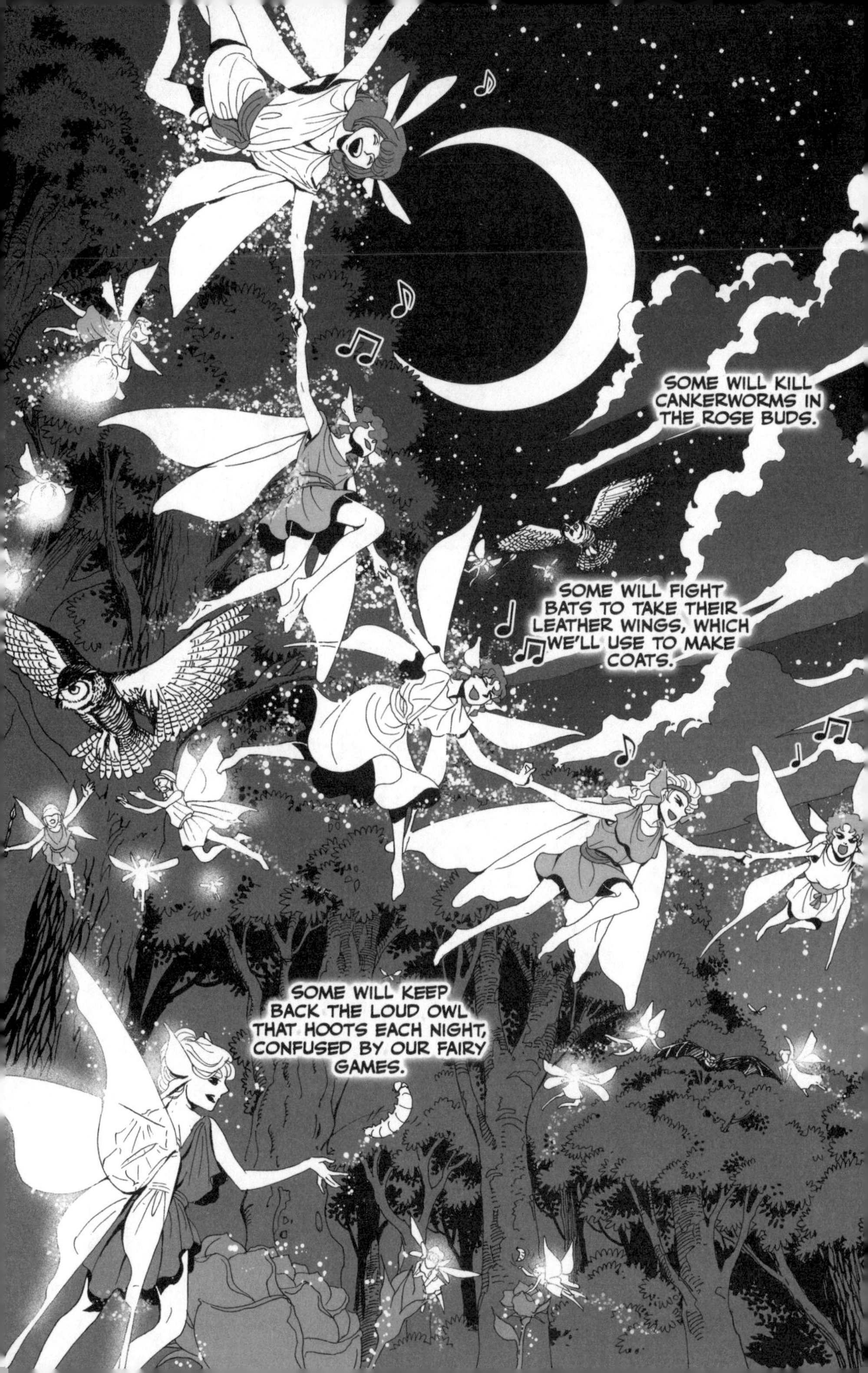
SOME WILL KILL CANKERWORMS IN THE ROSE BUDS.
SOME WILL FIGHT BATS TO TAKE THEIR LEATHER WINGS, WHICH WE'LL USE TO MAKE COATS.
SOME WILL KEEP BACK THE LOUD OWL THAT HOOTS EACH NIGHT, CONFUSED BY OUR FAIRY GAMES.

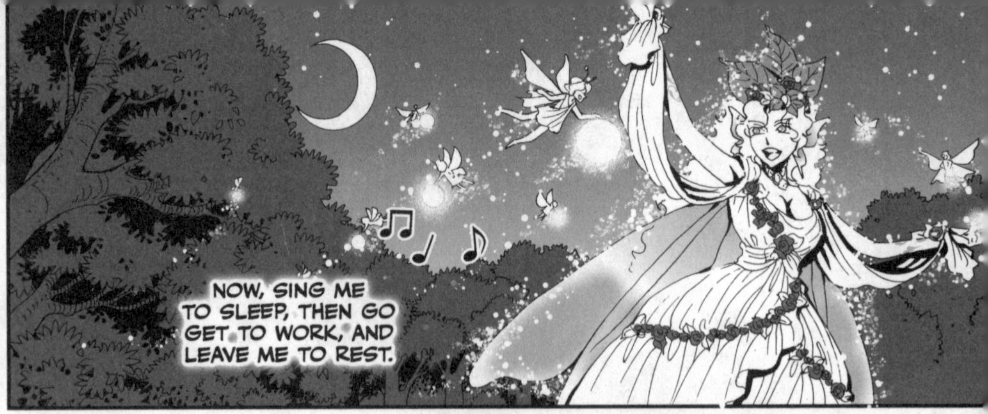
NOW, SING ME TO SLEEP, THEN GO GET TO WORK, AND LEAVE ME TO REST.

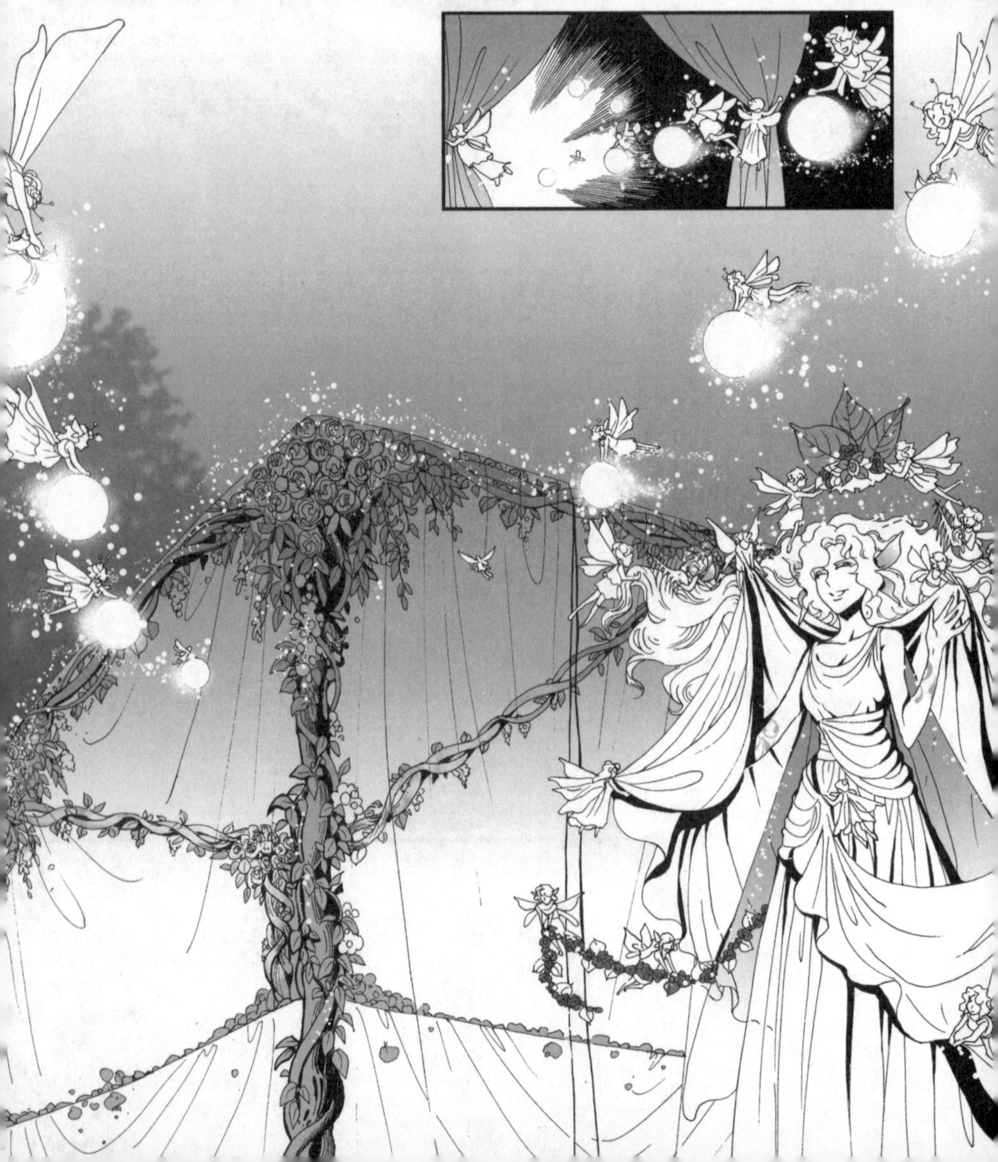

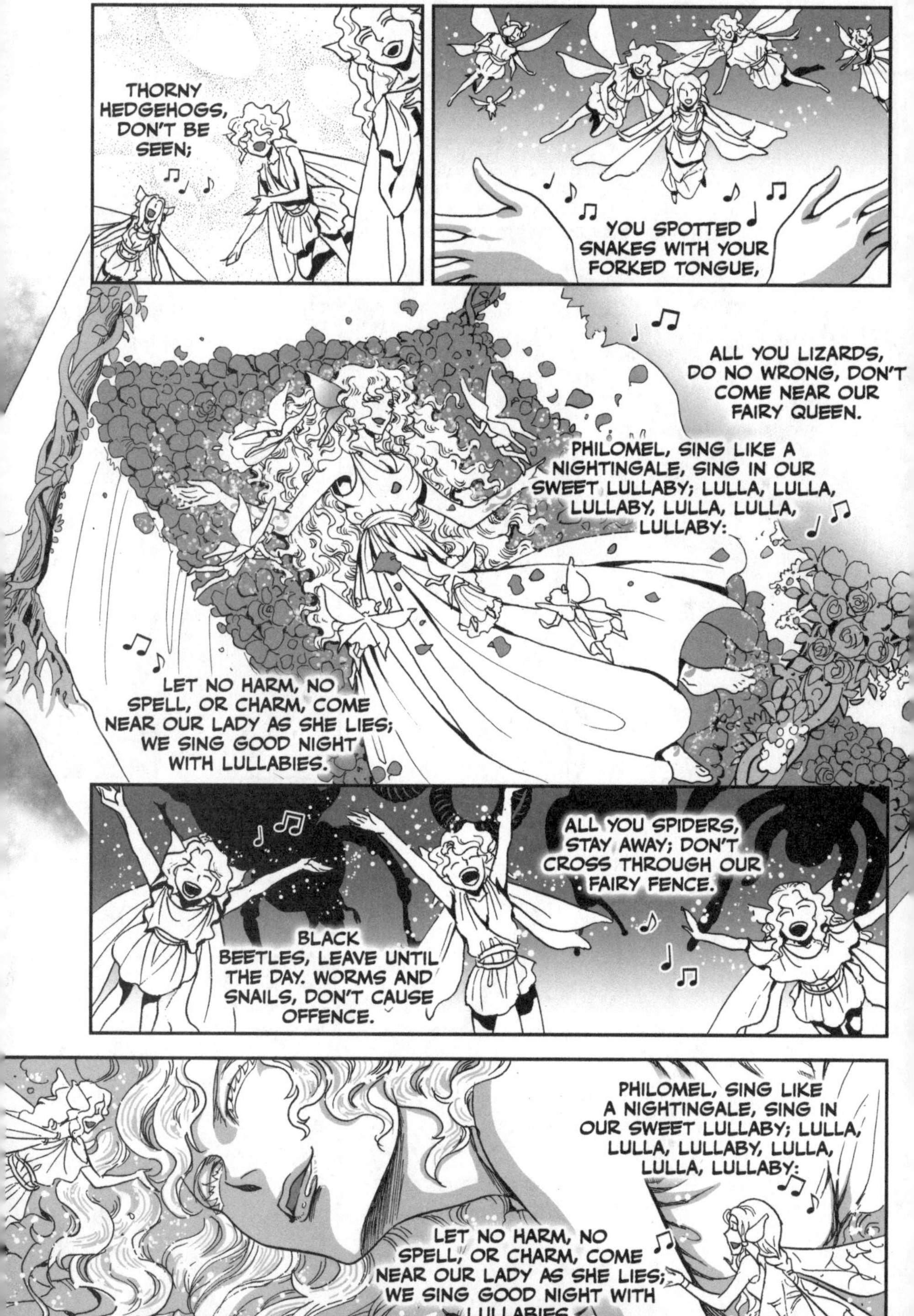
YOU SPOTTED SNAKES WITH YOUR FORKED TONGUE,
THORNY HEDGEHOGS, DON'T BE SEEN;
ALL YOU LIZARDS, DO NO WRONG, DON'T COME NEAR OUR FAIRY QUEEN.
PHILOMEL, SING LIKE A NIGHTINGALE, SING IN OUR SWEET LULLABY; LULLA, LULLA, LULLABY, LULLA, LULLA, LULLABY:
LET NO HARM, NO SPELL, OR CHARM, COME NEAR OUR LADY AS SHE LIES; WE SING GOOD NIGHT WITH LULLABIES.
ALL YOU SPIDERS, STAY AWAY; DON'T CROSS THROUGH OUR FAIRY FENCE.
BLACK BEETLES, LEAVE UNTIL THE DAY. WORMS AND SNAILS, DON'T CAUSE OFFENCE.
PHILOMEL, SING LIKE A NIGHTINGALE, SING IN OUR SWEET LULLABY; LULLA, LULLA, LULLABY, LULLA, LULLA, LULLABY:
LET NO HARM, NO SPELL, OR CHARM, COME NEAR OUR LADY AS SHE LIES; WE SING GOOD NIGHT WITH LULLABIES.

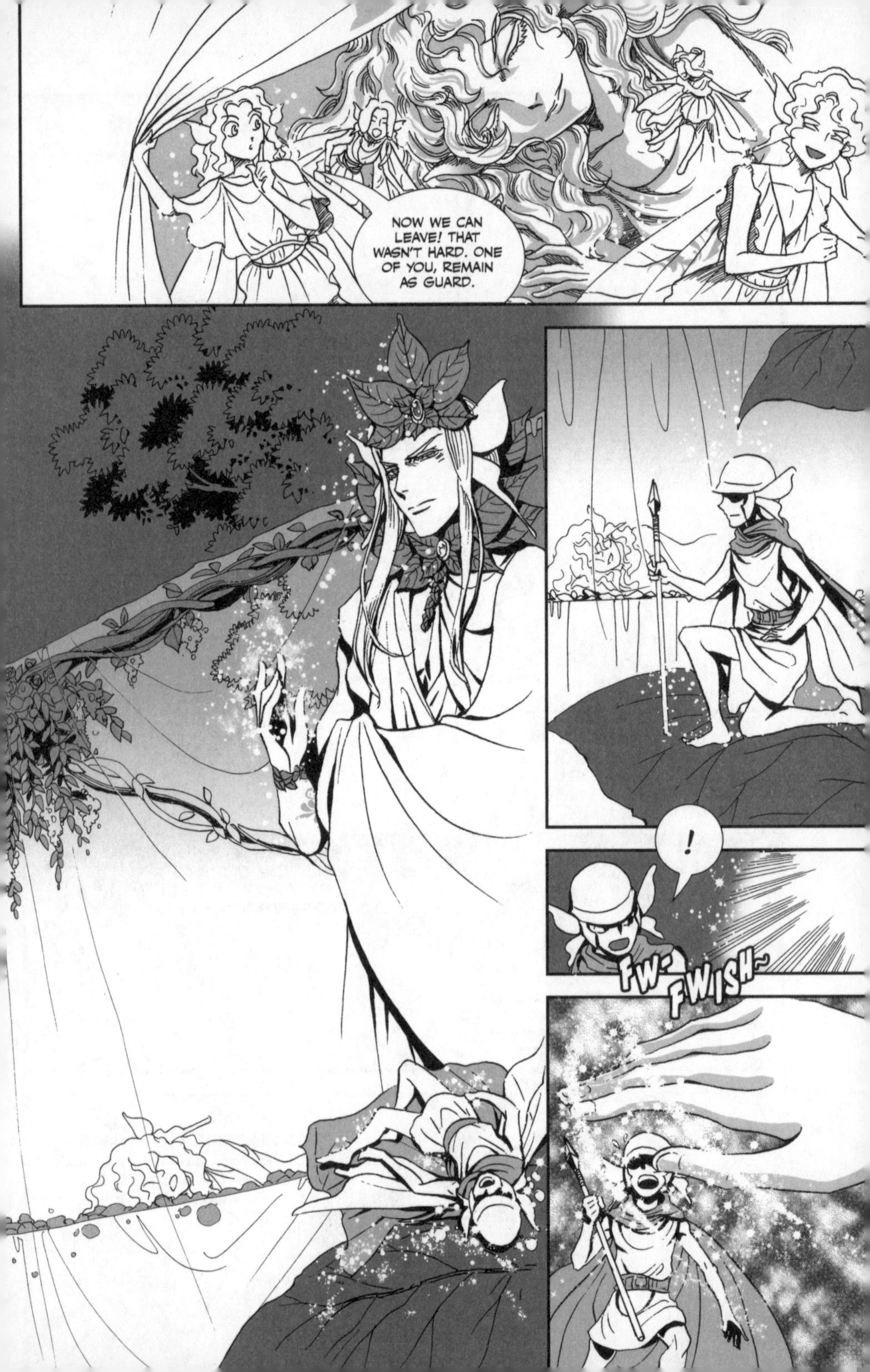
NOW WE CAN LEAVE! THAT WASN'T HARD. ONE OF YOU, REMAIN AS GUARD.
!
FW-FWISH~

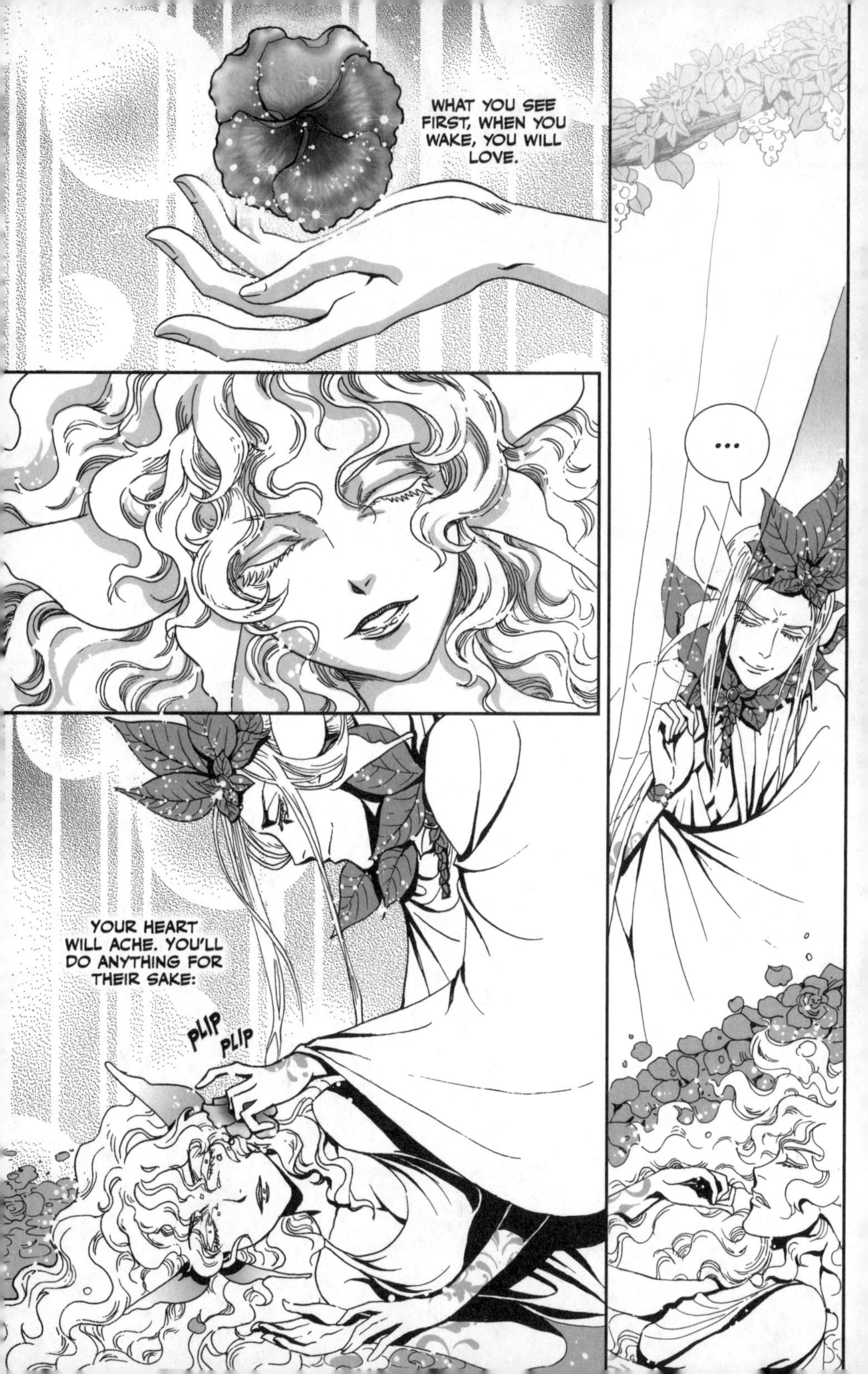
...
WHAT YOU SEE FIRST, WHEN YOU WAKE, YOU WILL LOVE.
YOUR HEART WILL ACHE. YOU'LL DO ANYTHING FOR THEIR SAKE:
PLIP
PLIP

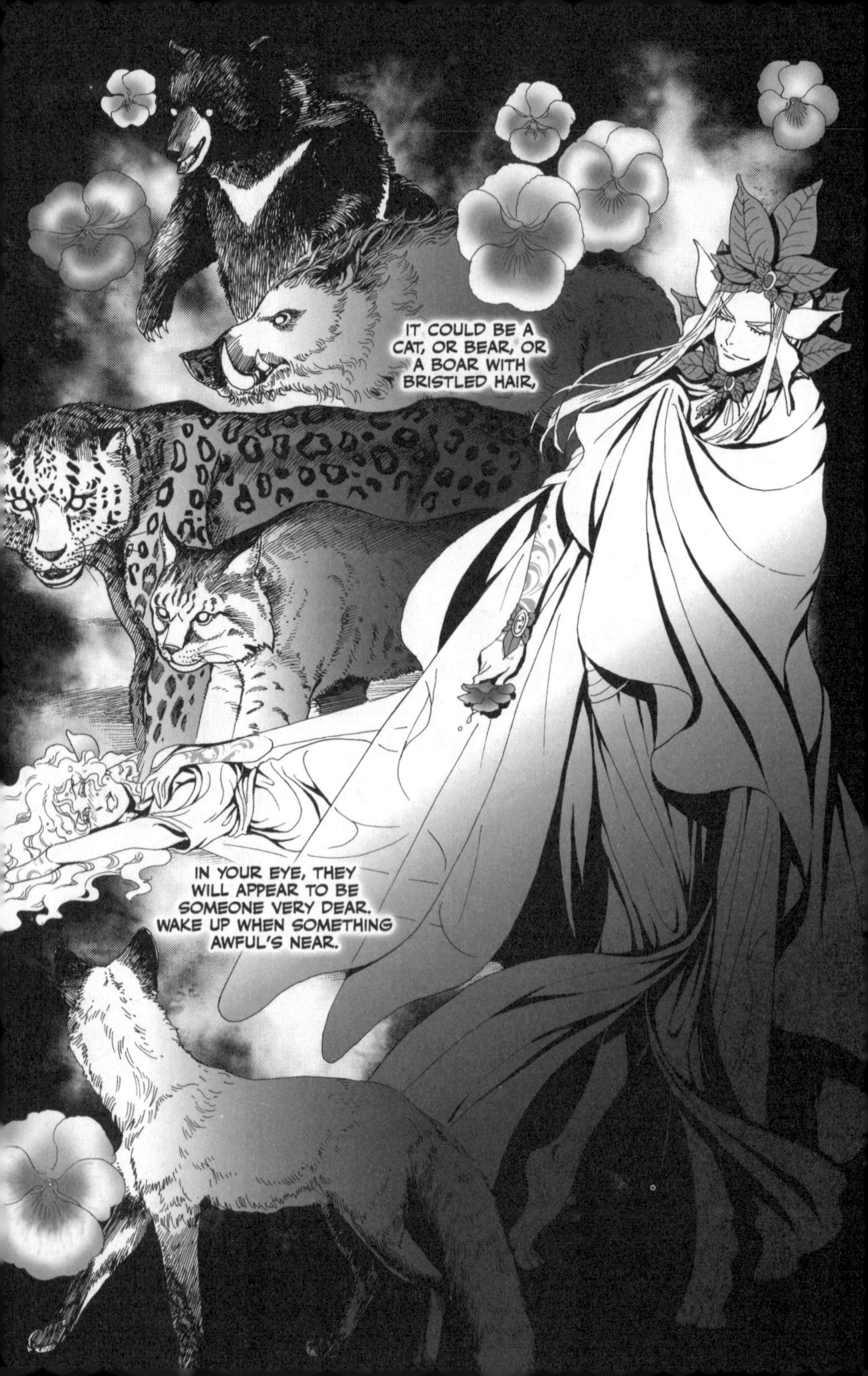
IT COULD BE A CAT, OR BEAR, OR A BOAR WITH BRISTLED HAIR,
IN YOUR EYE, THEY WILL APPEAR TO BE SOMEONE VERY DEAR. WAKE UP WHEN SOMETHING AWFUL'S NEAR.

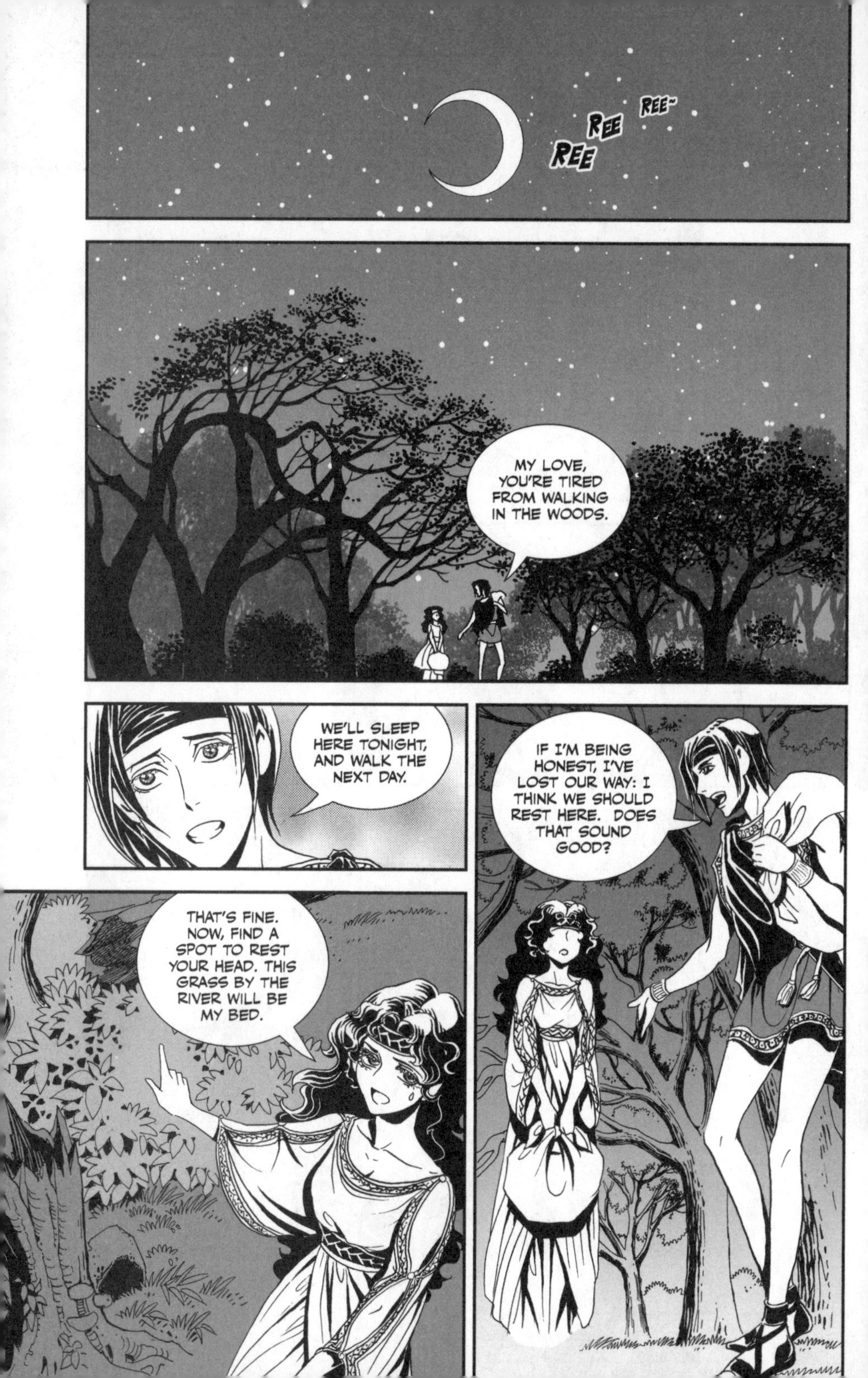
REE~
REE
REE
MY LOVE, YOU'RE TIRED FROM WALKING IN THE WOODS.
IF I'M BEING HONEST, I'VE LOST OUR WAY: I THINK WE SHOULD REST HERE. DOES THAT SOUND GOOD?
WE'LL SLEEP HERE TONIGHT, AND WALK THE NEXT DAY.
THAT'S FINE. NOW, FIND A SPOT TO REST YOUR HEAD. THIS GRASS BY THE RIVER WILL BE MY BED.

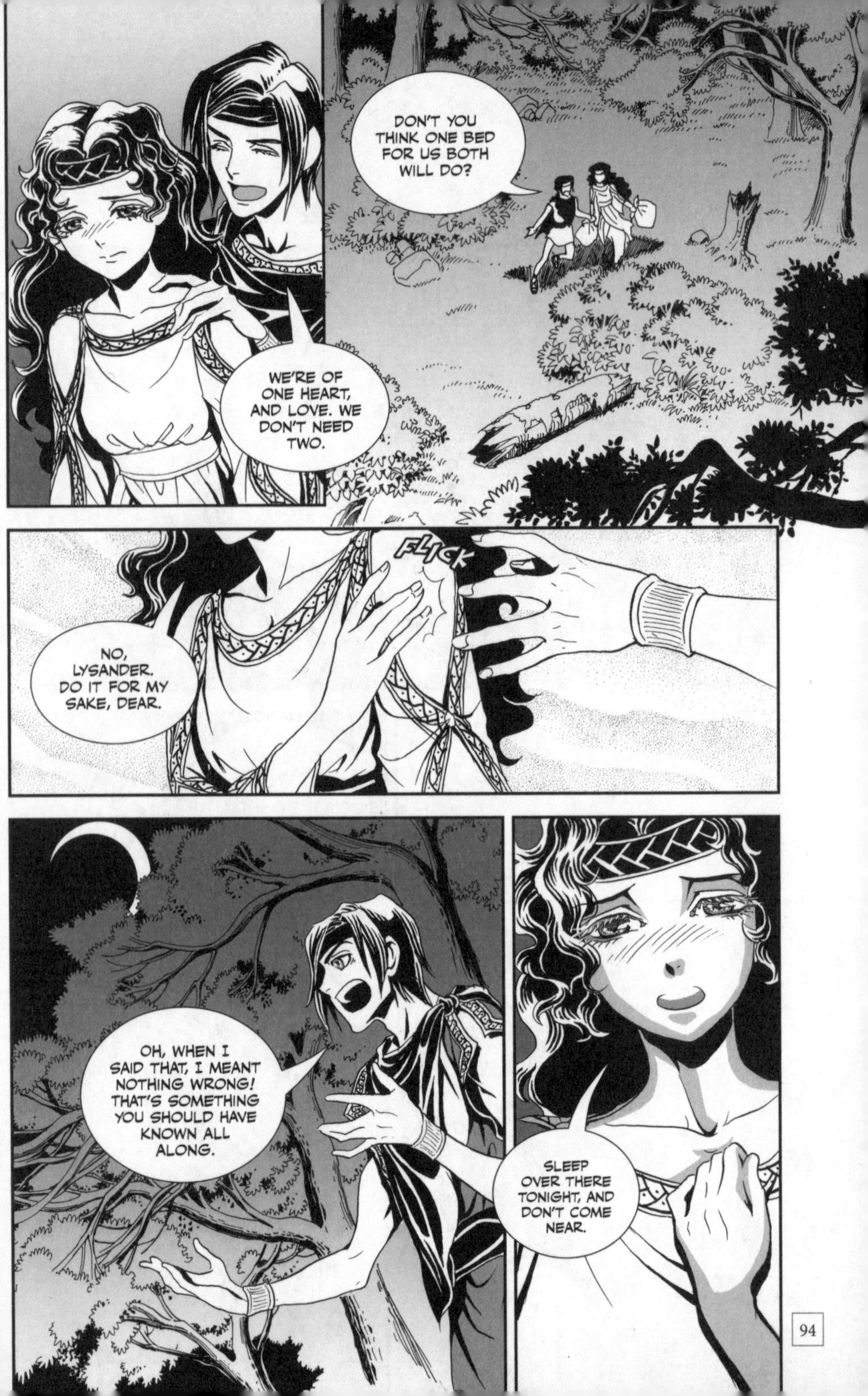
DON'T YOU THINK ONE BED FOR US BOTH WILL DO?
WE'RE OF ONE HEART, AND LOVE. WE DON'T NEED TWO.
FLICK
NO, LYSANDER. DO IT FOR MY SAKE, DEAR.
SLEEP OVER THERE TONIGHT, AND DON'T COME NEAR.
OH, WHEN I SAID THAT, I MEANT NOTHING WRONG! THAT'S SOMETHING YOU SHOULD HAVE KNOWN ALL ALONG.

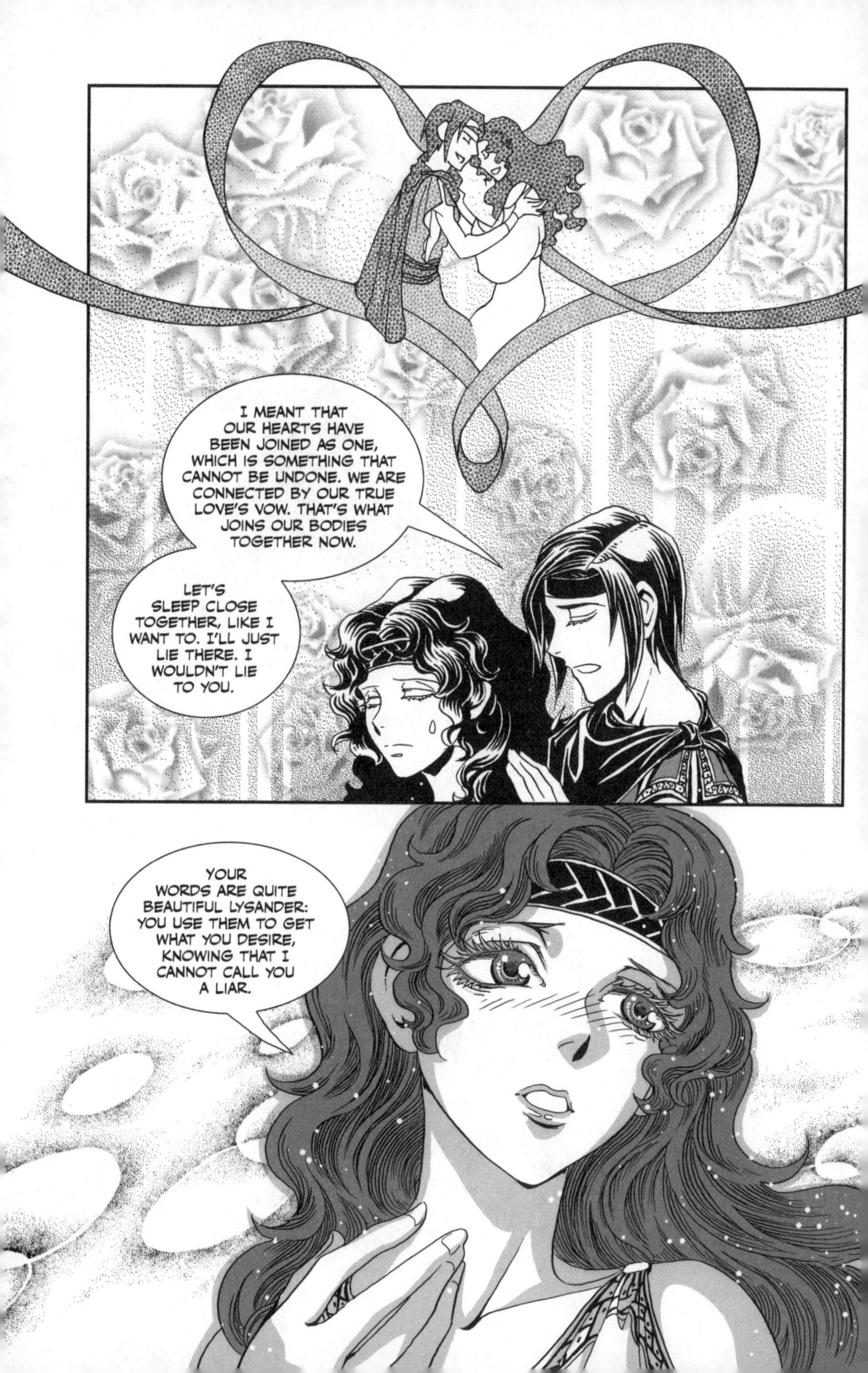
I MEANT THAT OUR HEARTS HAVE BEEN JOINED AS ONE, WHICH IS SOMETHING THAT CANNOT BE UNDONE. WE ARE CONNECTED BY OUR TRUE LOVE'S VOW. THAT'S WHAT JOINS OUR BODIES TOGETHER NOW.
LET'S SLEEP CLOSE TOGETHER, LIKE I WANT TO. I'LL JUST LIE THERE. I WOULDN'T LIE TO YOU.
YOUR WORDS ARE QUITE BEAUTIFUL LYSANDER: YOU USE THEM TO GET WHAT YOU DESIRE, KNOWING THAT I CANNOT CALL YOU A LIAR.

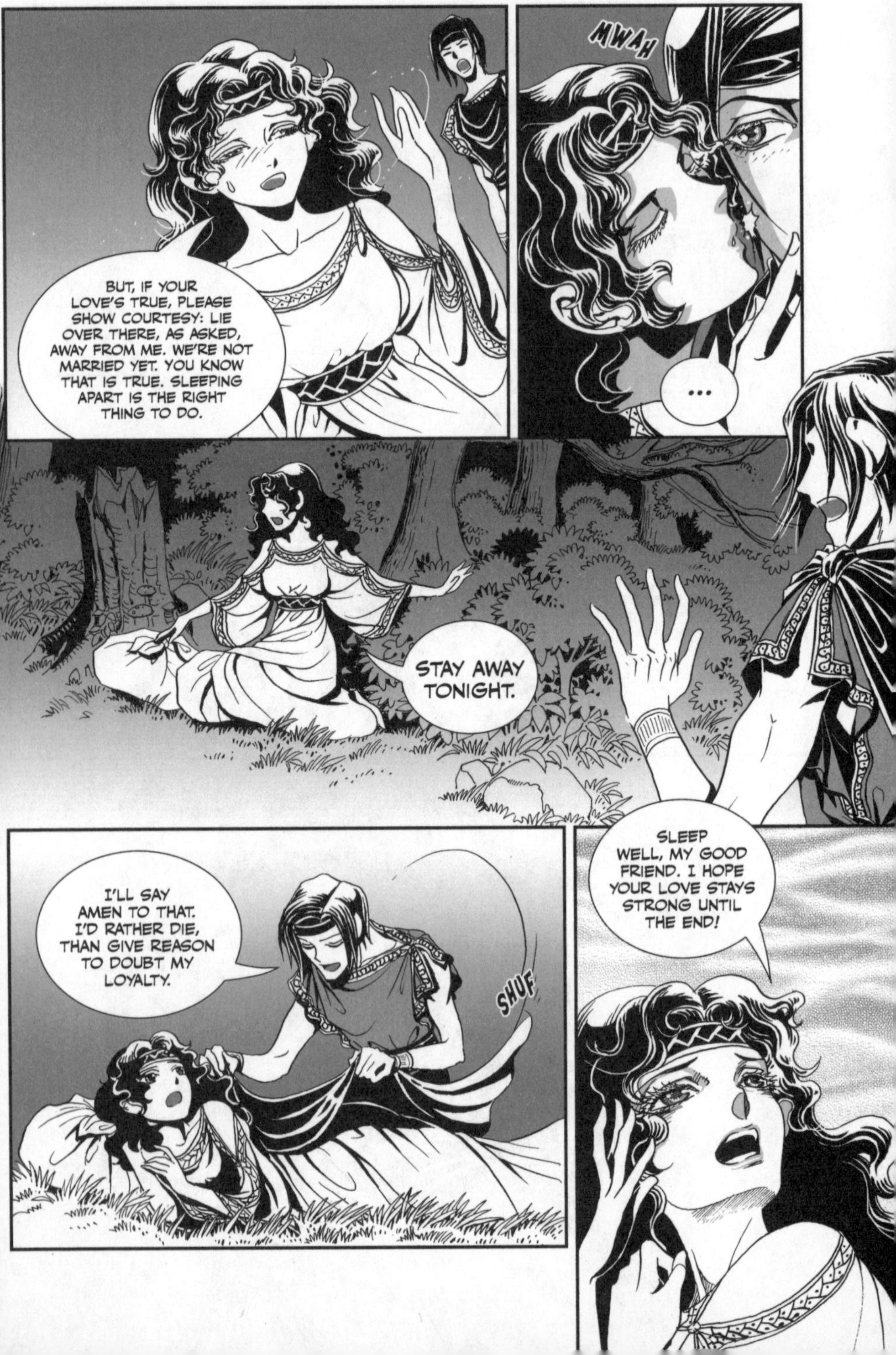
MWAH
...
BUT, IF YOUR LOVE'S TRUE, PLEASE SHOW COURTESY: LIE OVER THERE, AS ASKED, AWAY FROM ME. WE'RE NOT MARRIED YET. YOU KNOW THAT IS TRUE. SLEEPING APART IS THE RIGHT THING TO DO.
STAY AWAY TONIGHT.
SLEEP WELL, MY GOOD FRIEND. I HOPE YOUR LOVE STAYS STRONG UNTIL THE END!
I'LL SAY AMEN TO THAT. I'D RATHER DIE, THAN GIVE REASON TO DOUBT MY LOYALTY.
SHUF

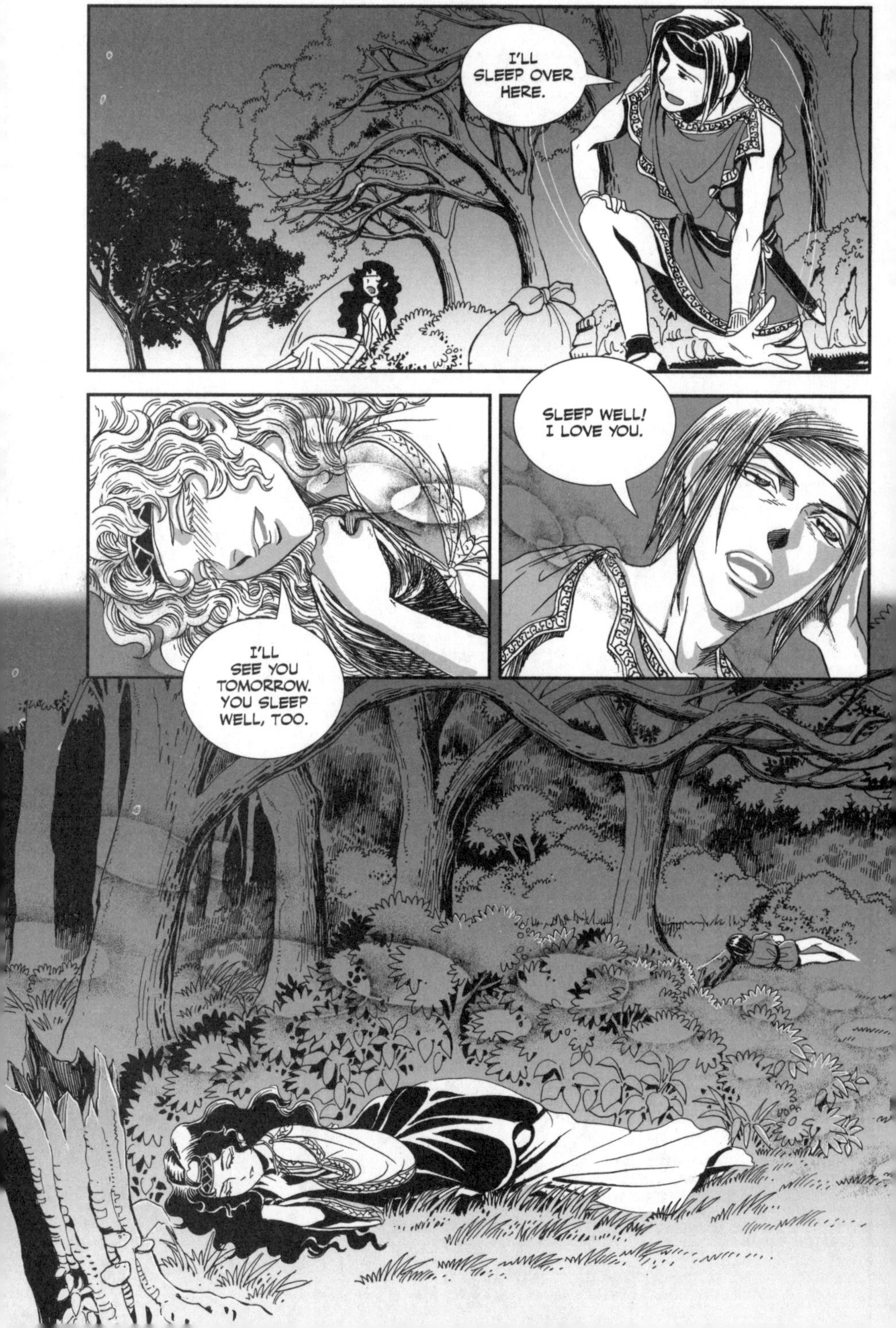
I'LL SLEEP OVER HERE.
SLEEP WELL! I LOVE YOU.
I'LL SEE YOU TOMORROW. YOU SLEEP WELL, TOO.

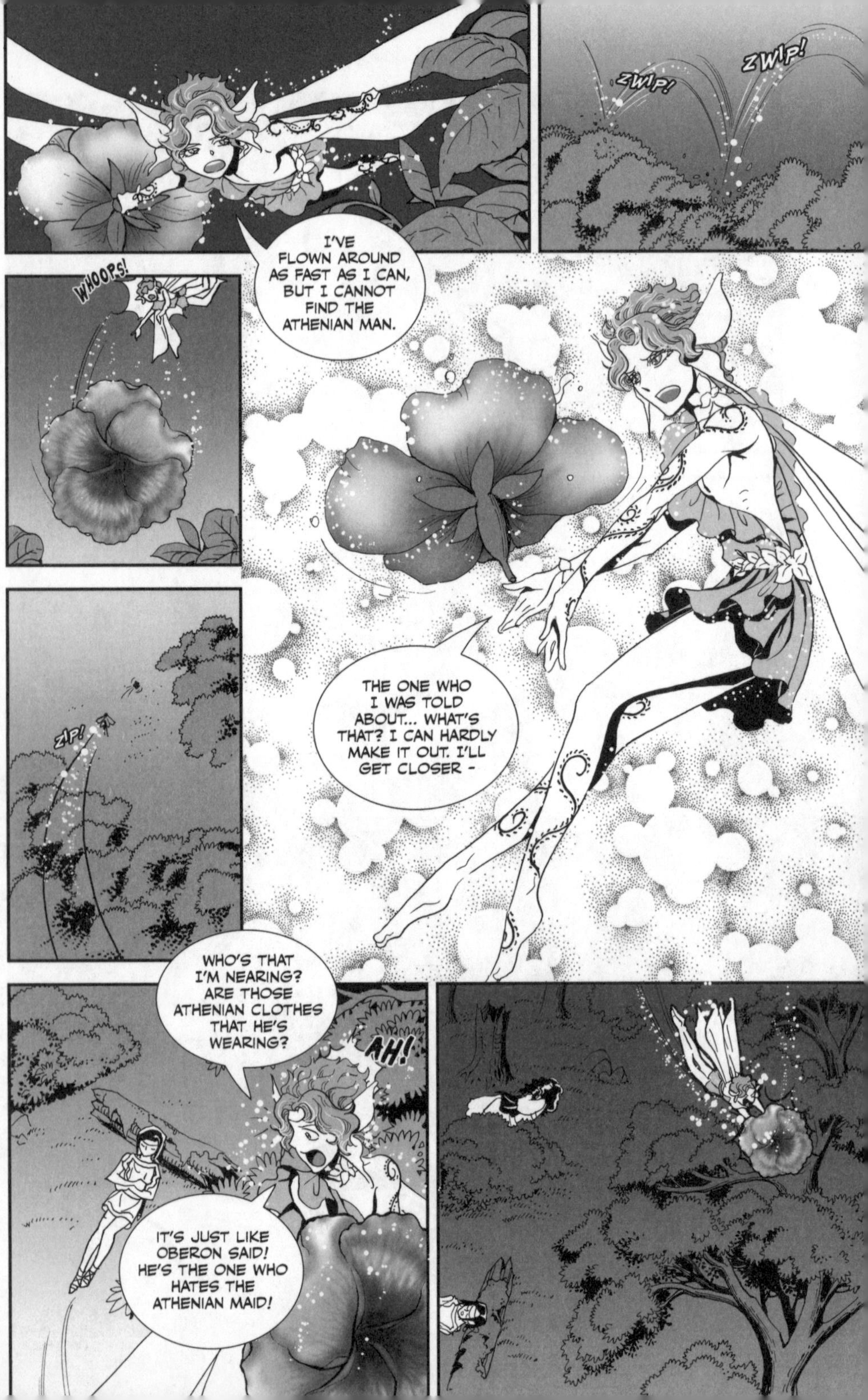
ZWIP!
ZWIP!
I'VE FLOWN AROUND AS FAST AS I CAN, BUT I CANNOT FIND THE ATHENIAN MAN.
THE ONE WHO I WAS TOLD ABOUT... WHAT'S THAT? I CAN HARDLY MAKE IT OUT. I'LL GET CLOSER -
WHOOPS!
ZIP!
WHO'S THAT I'M NEARING? ARE THOSE ATHENIAN CLOTHES THAT HE'S WEARING?
AH!
IT'S JUST LIKE OBERON SAID! HE'S THE ONE WHO HATES THE ATHENIAN MAID!

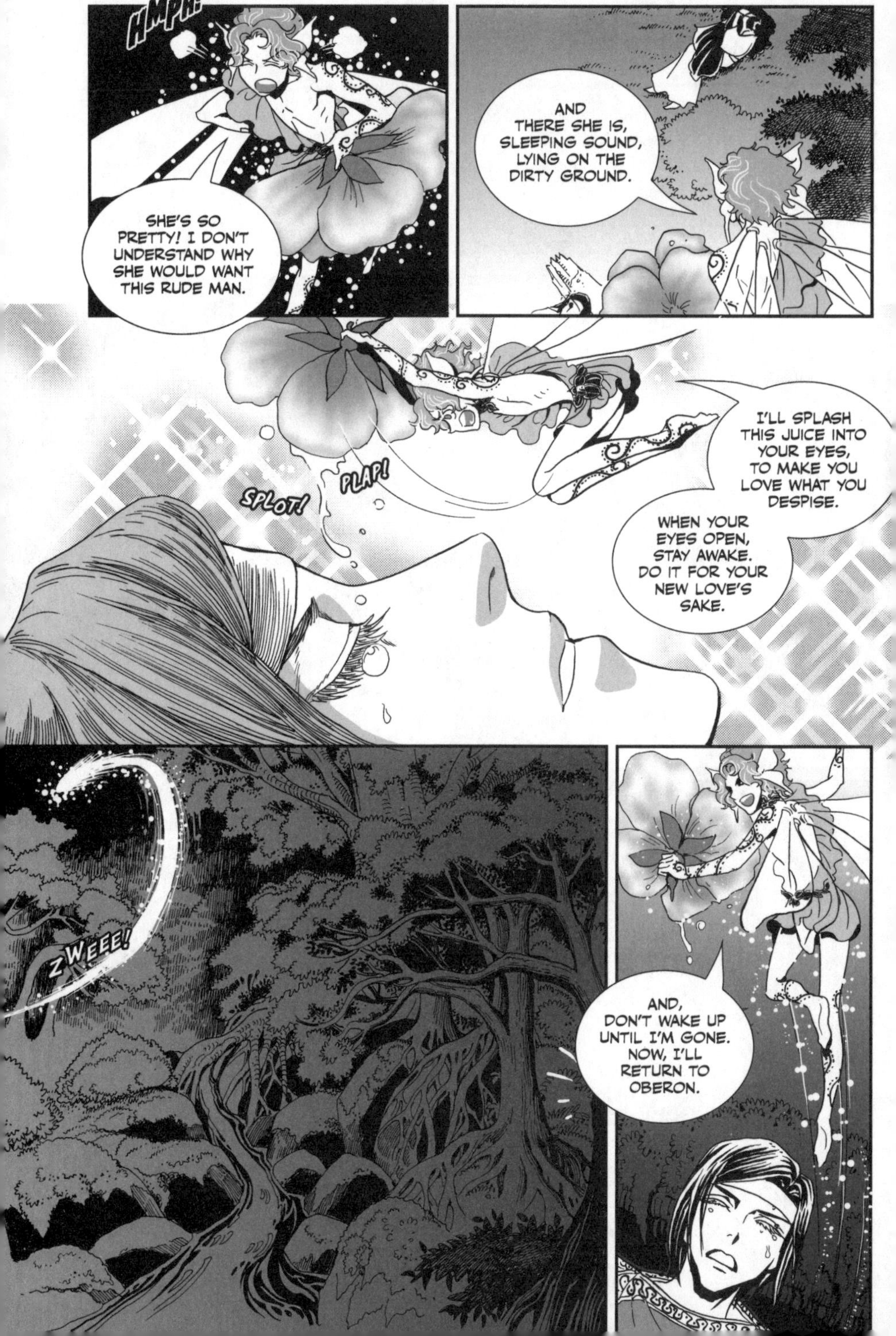
AND THERE SHE IS, SLEEPING SOUND, LYING ON THE DIRTY GROUND.
HMPH!
SHE'S SO PRETTY! I DON'T UNDERSTAND WHY SHE WOULD WANT THIS RUDE MAN.
I'LL SPLASH THIS JUICE INTO YOUR EYES, TO MAKE YOU LOVE WHAT YOU DESPISE.
WHEN YOUR EYES OPEN, STAY AWAKE. DO IT FOR YOUR NEW LOVE'S SAKE.
PLAP!
SPLOT!
AND, DON'T WAKE UP UNTIL I'M GONE. NOW, I'LL RETURN TO OBERON.
ZWEEE!

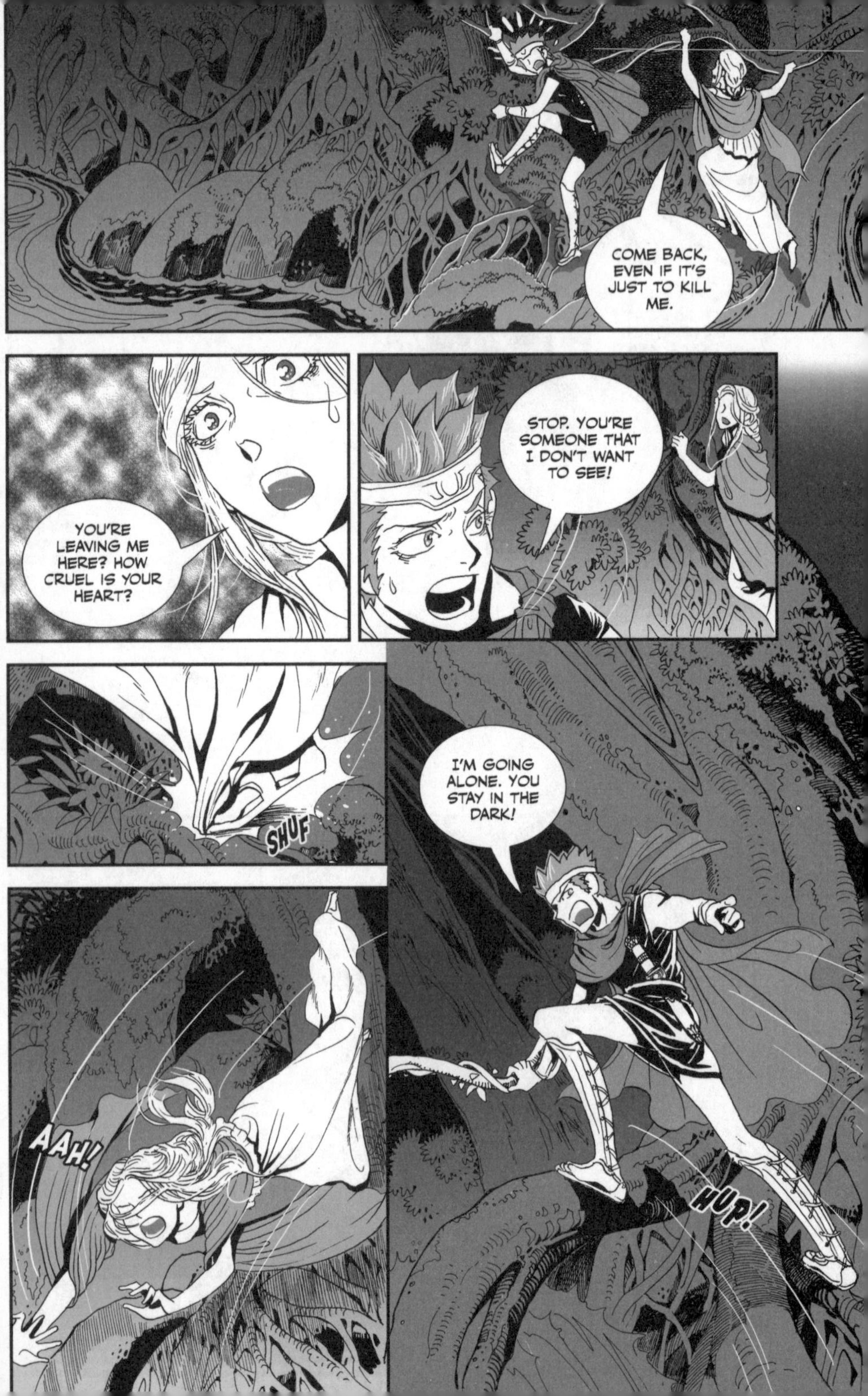
COME BACK, EVEN IF IT'S JUST TO KILL ME.
STOP. YOU'RE SOMEONE THAT I DON'T WANT TO SEE!
YOU'RE LEAVING ME HERE? HOW CRUEL IS YOUR HEART?
I'M GOING ALONE. YOU STAY IN THE DARK!
HUP!
SHUF
AAH!

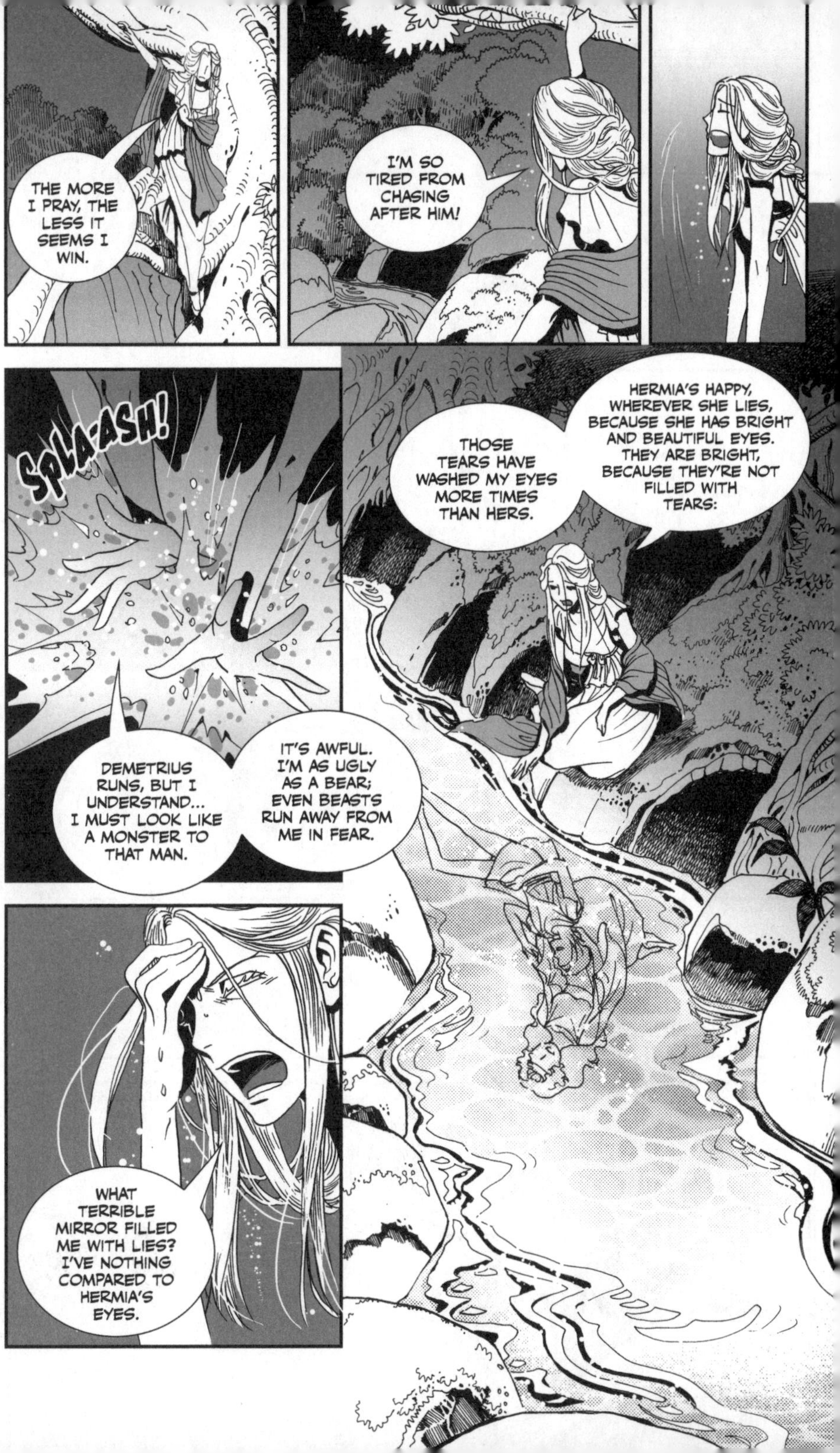

I'M SO TIRED FROM CHASING AFTER HIM!
THE MORE I PRAY, THE LESS IT SEEMS I WIN.
HERMIA'S HAPPY, WHEREVER SHE LIES, BECAUSE SHE HAS BRIGHT AND BEAUTIFUL EYES. THEY ARE BRIGHT, BECAUSE THEY'RE NOT FILLED WITH TEARS:
THOSE TEARS HAVE WASHED MY EYES MORE TIMES THAN HERS.
SPLA-ASH!
IT'S AWFUL. I'M AS UGLY AS A BEAR; EVEN BEASTS RUN AWAY FROM ME IN FEAR.
DEMETRIUS RUNS, BUT I UNDERSTAND... I MUST LOOK LIKE A MONSTER TO THAT MAN.
WHAT TERRIBLE MIRROR FILLED ME WITH LIES? I'VE NOTHING COMPARED TO HERMIA'S EYES.

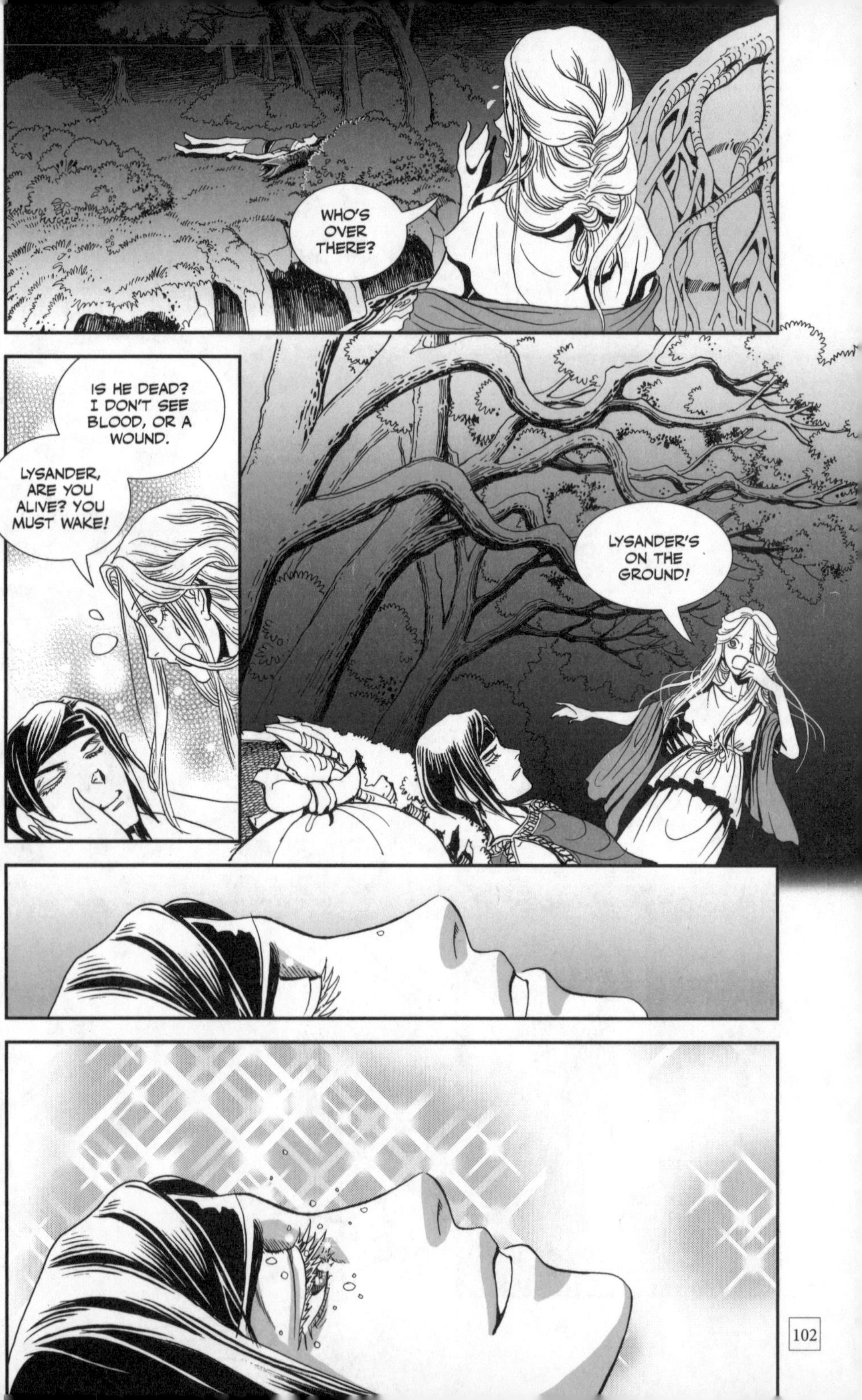
WHO'S OVER THERE?
LYSANDER'S ON THE GROUND!
IS HE DEAD? I DON'T SEE BLOOD, OR A WOUND.
LYSANDER, ARE YOU ALIVE? YOU MUST WAKE!

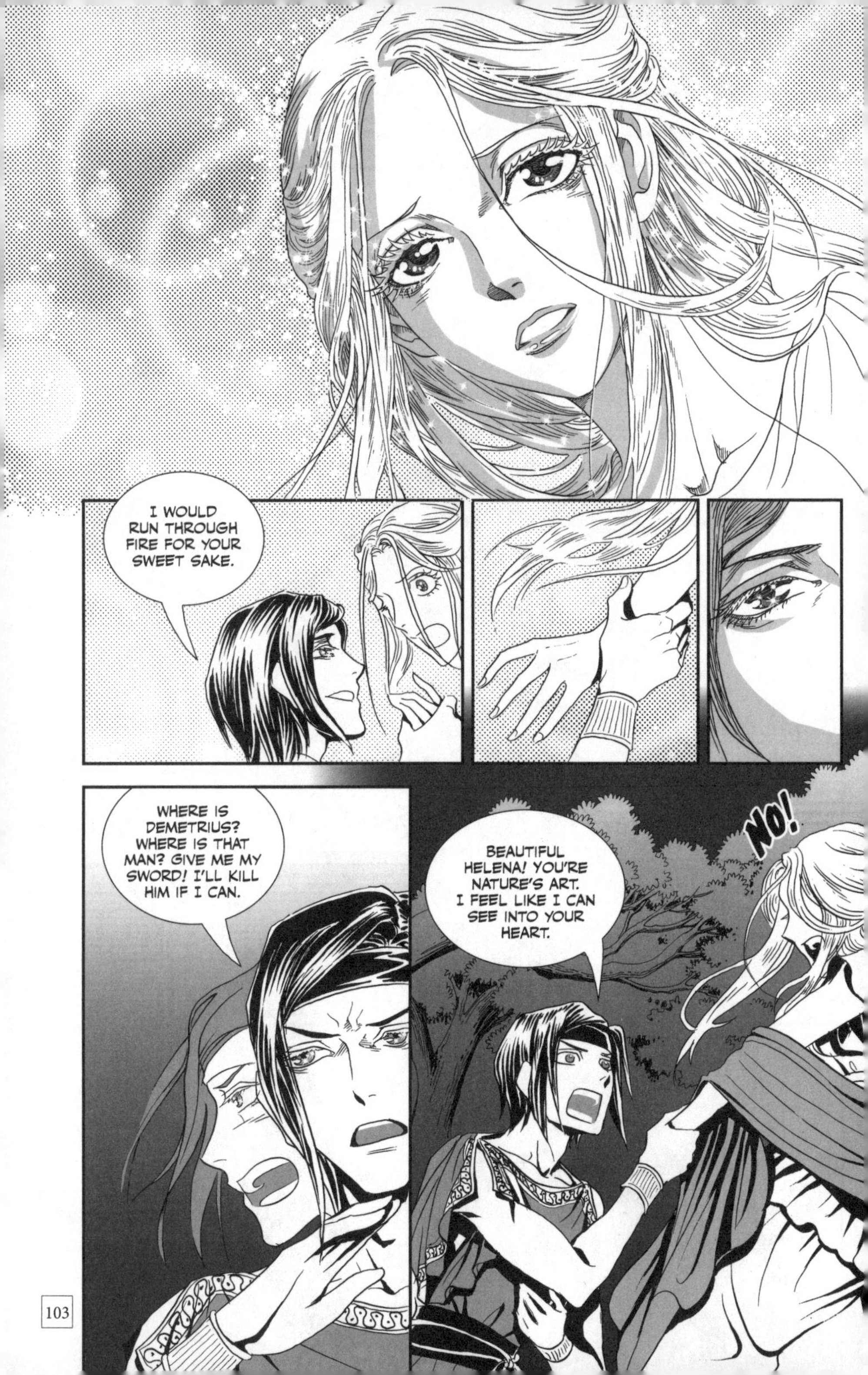
I WOULD RUN THROUGH FIRE FOR YOUR SWEET SAKE.
NO!
BEAUTIFUL HELENA! YOU'RE NATURE'S ART. I FEEL LIKE I CAN SEE INTO YOUR HEART.
WHERE IS DEMETRIUS? WHERE IS THAT MAN? GIVE ME MY SWORD! I'LL KILL HIM IF I CAN.

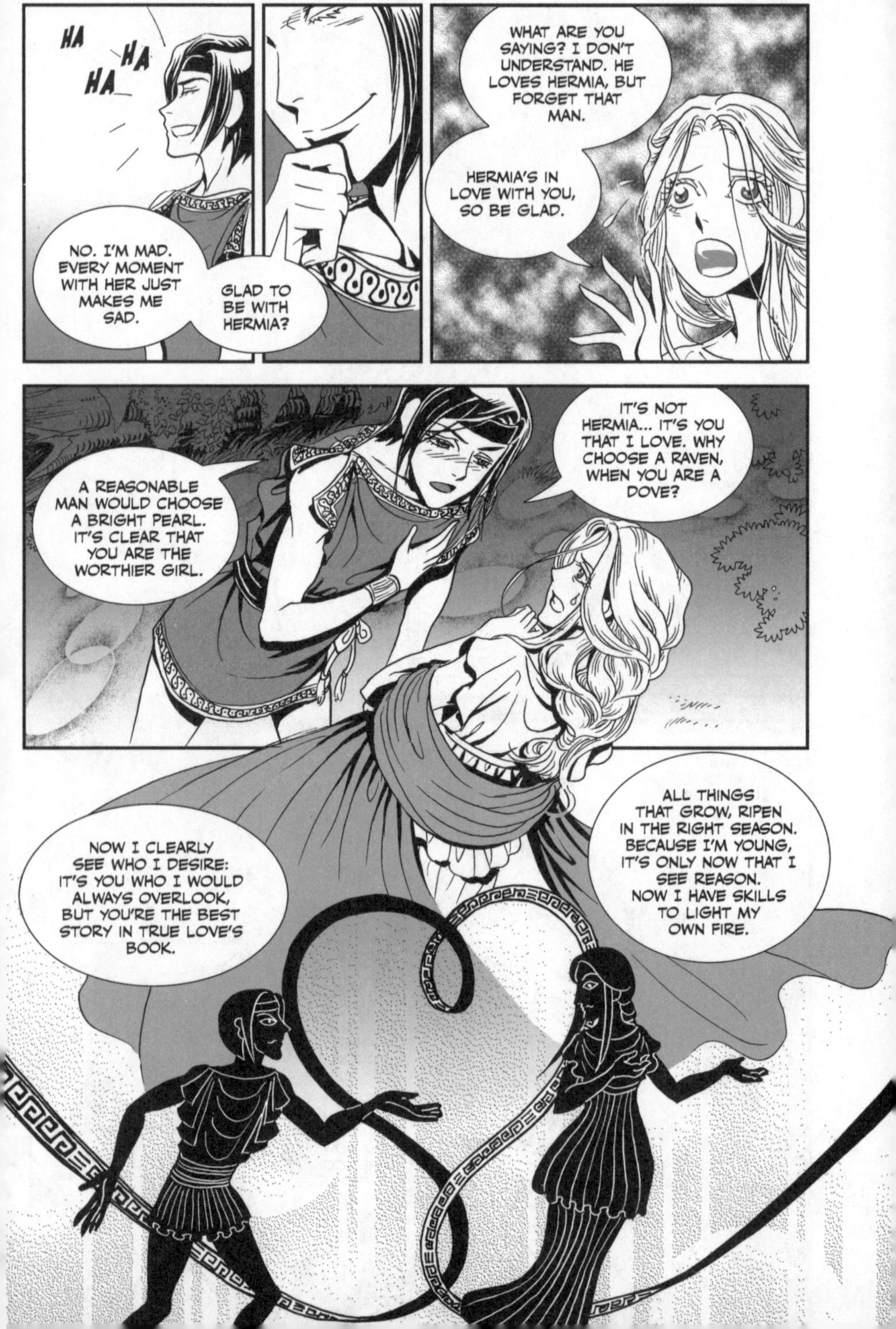
WHAT ARE YOU SAYING? I DON'T UNDERSTAND. HE LOVES HERMIA, BUT FORGET THAT MAN.
HERMIA'S IN LOVE WITH YOU, SO BE GLAD.
GLAD TO BE WITH HERMIA?
HA HA HA
NO. I'M MAD. EVERY MOMENT WITH HER JUST MAKES ME SAD.
IT'S NOT HERMIA... IT'S YOU THAT I LOVE. WHY CHOOSE A RAVEN, WHEN YOU ARE A DOVE?
A REASONABLE MAN WOULD CHOOSE A BRIGHT PEARL. IT'S CLEAR THAT YOU ARE THE WORTHIER GIRL.
ALL THINGS THAT GROW, RIPEN IN THE RIGHT SEASON. BECAUSE I'M YOUNG, IT'S ONLY NOW THAT I SEE REASON. NOW I HAVE SKILLS TO LIGHT MY OWN FIRE.
NOW I CLEARLY SEE WHO I DESIRE: IT'S YOU WHO I WOULD ALWAYS OVERLOOK, BUT YOU'RE THE BEST STORY IN TRUE LOVE'S BOOK.

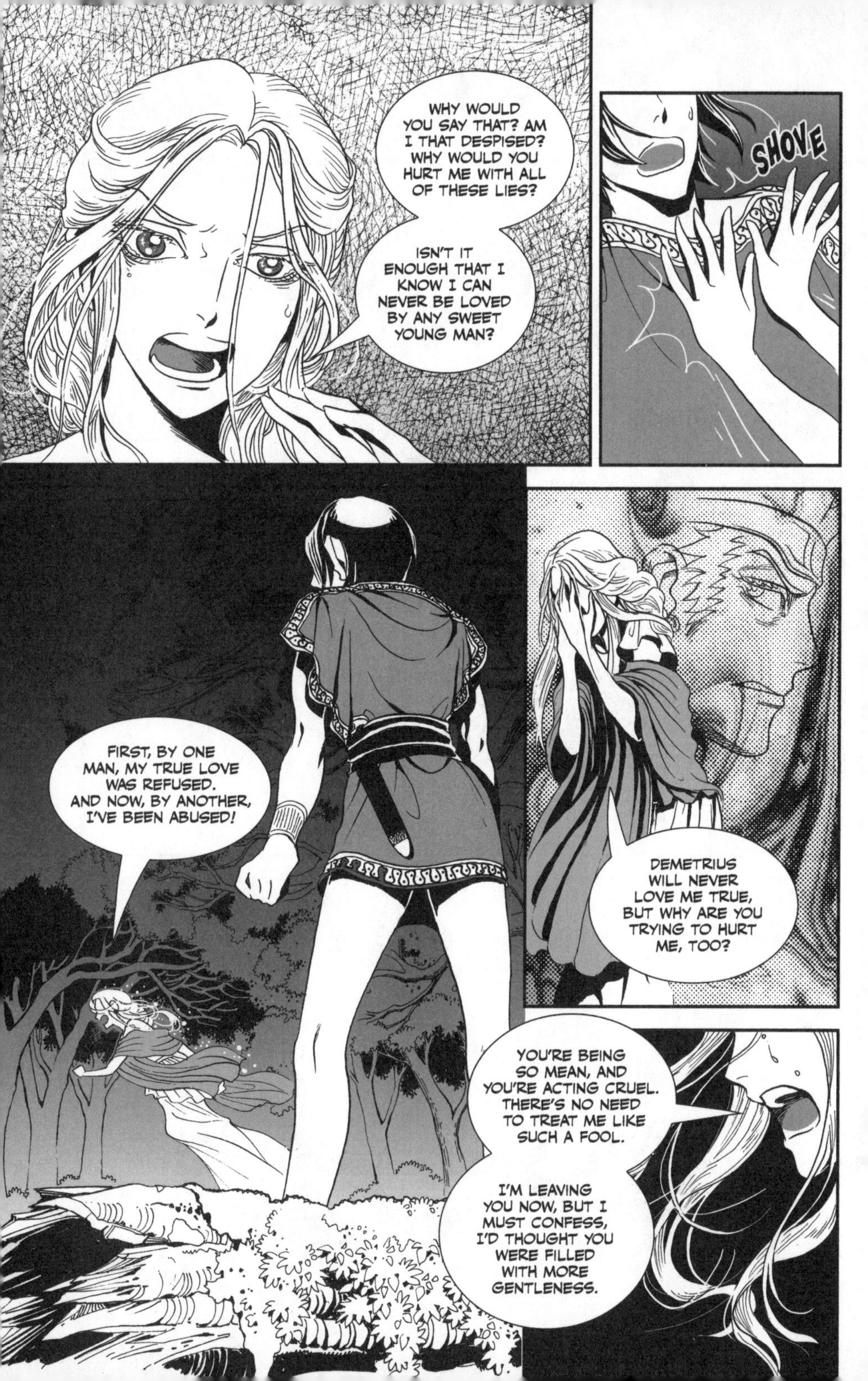
SHOVE
WHY WOULD YOU SAY THAT? AM I THAT DESPISED? WHY WOULD YOU HURT ME WITH ALL OF THESE LIES?
ISN'T IT ENOUGH THAT I KNOW I CAN NEVER BE LOVED BY ANY SWEET YOUNG MAN?
DEMETRIUS WILL NEVER LOVE ME TRUE, BUT WHY ARE YOU TRYING TO HURT ME, TOO?
YOU'RE BEING SO MEAN, AND YOU'RE ACTING CRUEL. THERE'S NO NEED TO TREAT ME LIKE SUCH A FOOL.
I'M LEAVING YOU NOW, BUT I MUST CONFESS, I'D THOUGHT YOU WERE FILLED WITH MORE GENTLENESS.
FIRST, BY ONE MAN, MY TRUE LOVE WAS REFUSED. AND NOW, BY ANOTHER, I'VE BEEN ABUSED!

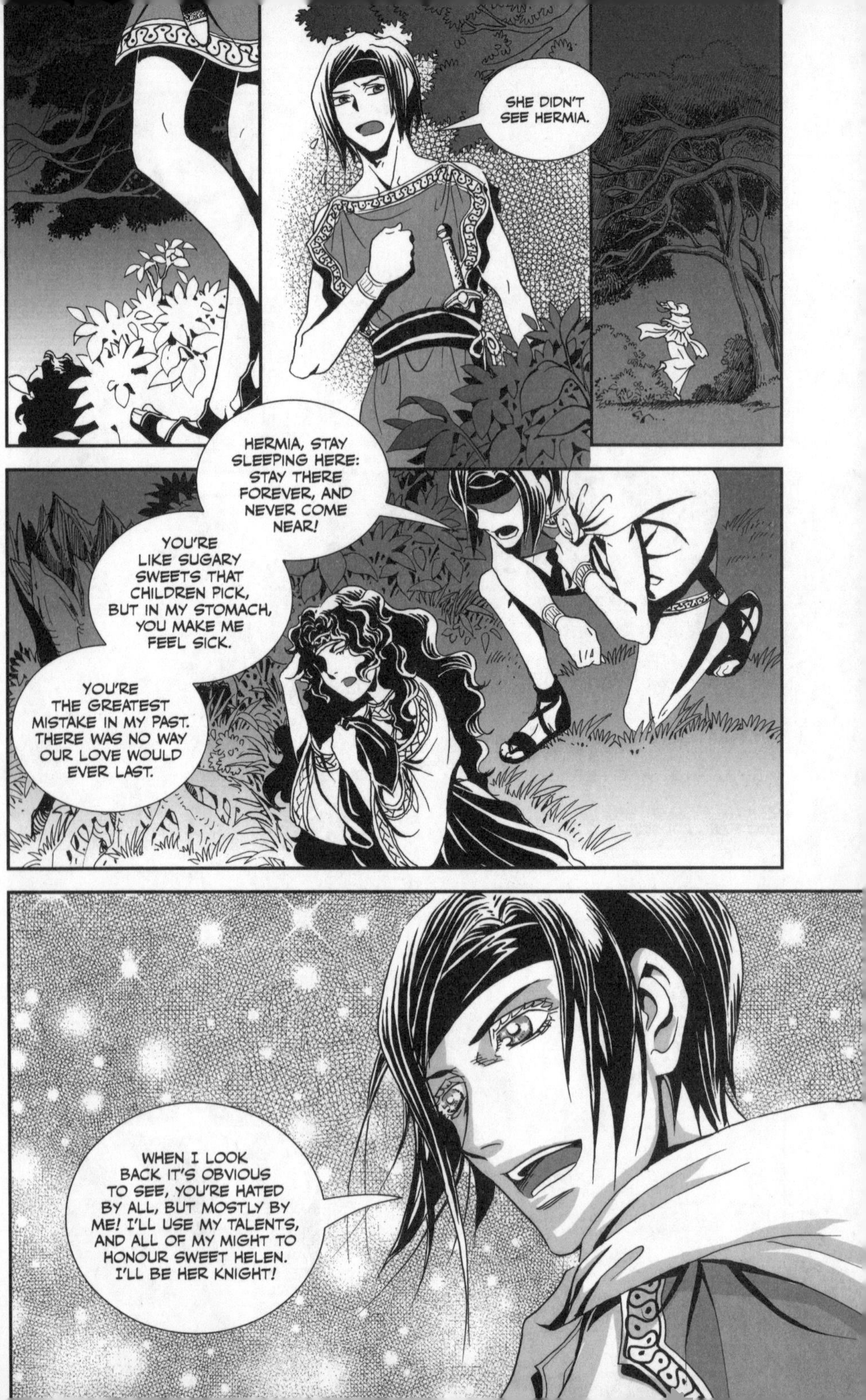
SHE DIDN'T SEE HERMIA.
HERMIA, STAY SLEEPING HERE: STAY THERE FOREVER, AND NEVER COME NEAR!
YOU'RE LIKE SUGARY SWEETS THAT CHILDREN PICK, BUT IN MY STOMACH, YOU MAKE ME FEEL SICK.
YOU'RE THE GREATEST MISTAKE IN MY PAST. THERE WAS NO WAY OUR LOVE WOULD EVER LAST.
WHEN I LOOK BACK IT'S OBVIOUS TO SEE, YOU'RE HATED BY ALL, BUT MOSTLY BY ME! I'LL USE MY TALENTS, AND ALL OF MY MIGHT TO HONOUR SWEET HELEN. I'LL BE HER KNIGHT!

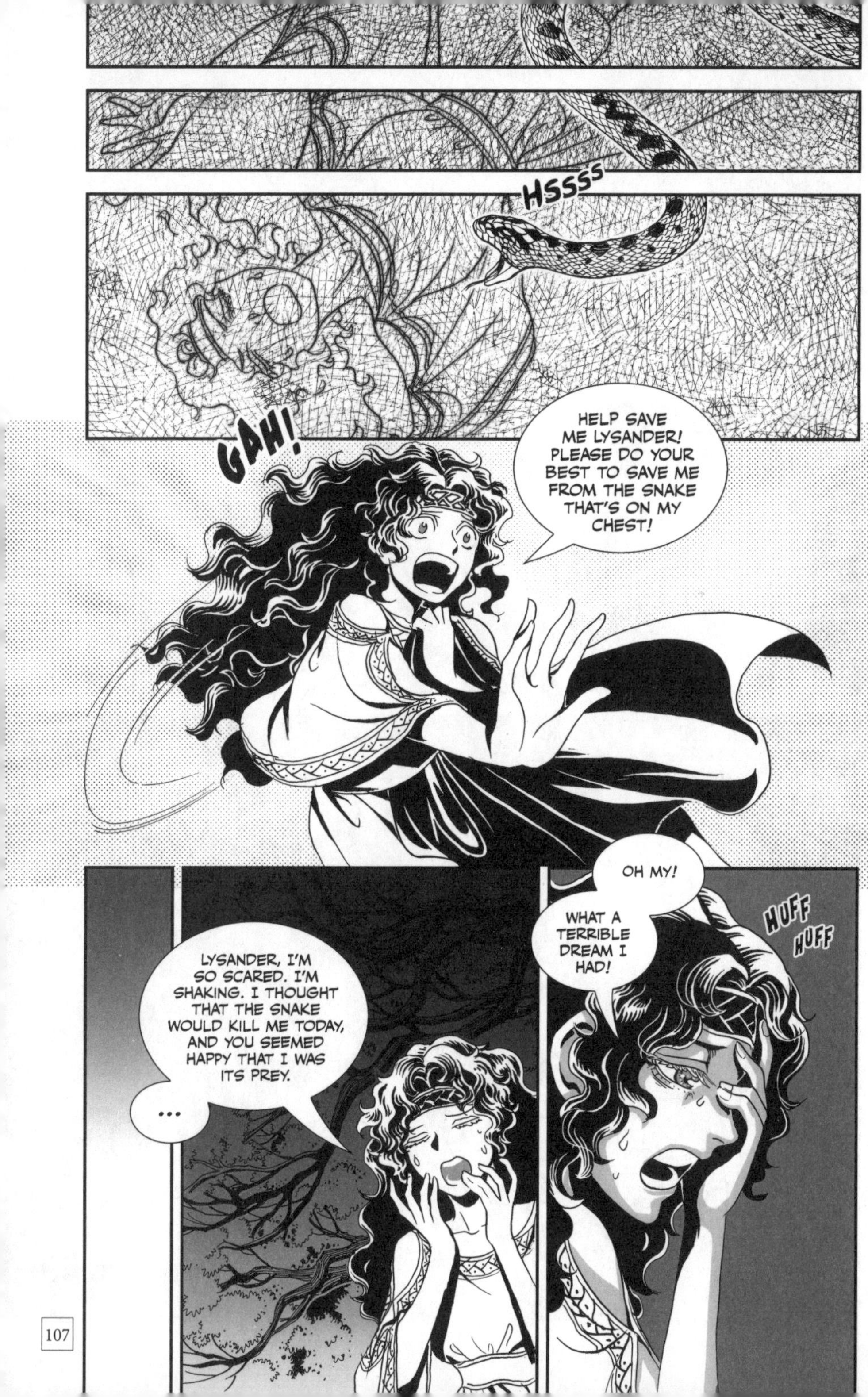
HSSSS
GAH!
HELP SAVE ME LYSANDER! PLEASE DO YOUR BEST TO SAVE ME FROM THE SNAKE THAT'S ON MY CHEST!
OH MY!
WHAT A TERRIBLE DREAM I HAD!
HUFF HUFF
LYSANDER, I'M SO SCARED. I'M SHAKING. I THOUGHT THAT THE SNAKE WOULD KILL ME TODAY, AND YOU SEEMED HAPPY THAT I WAS ITS PREY.
...

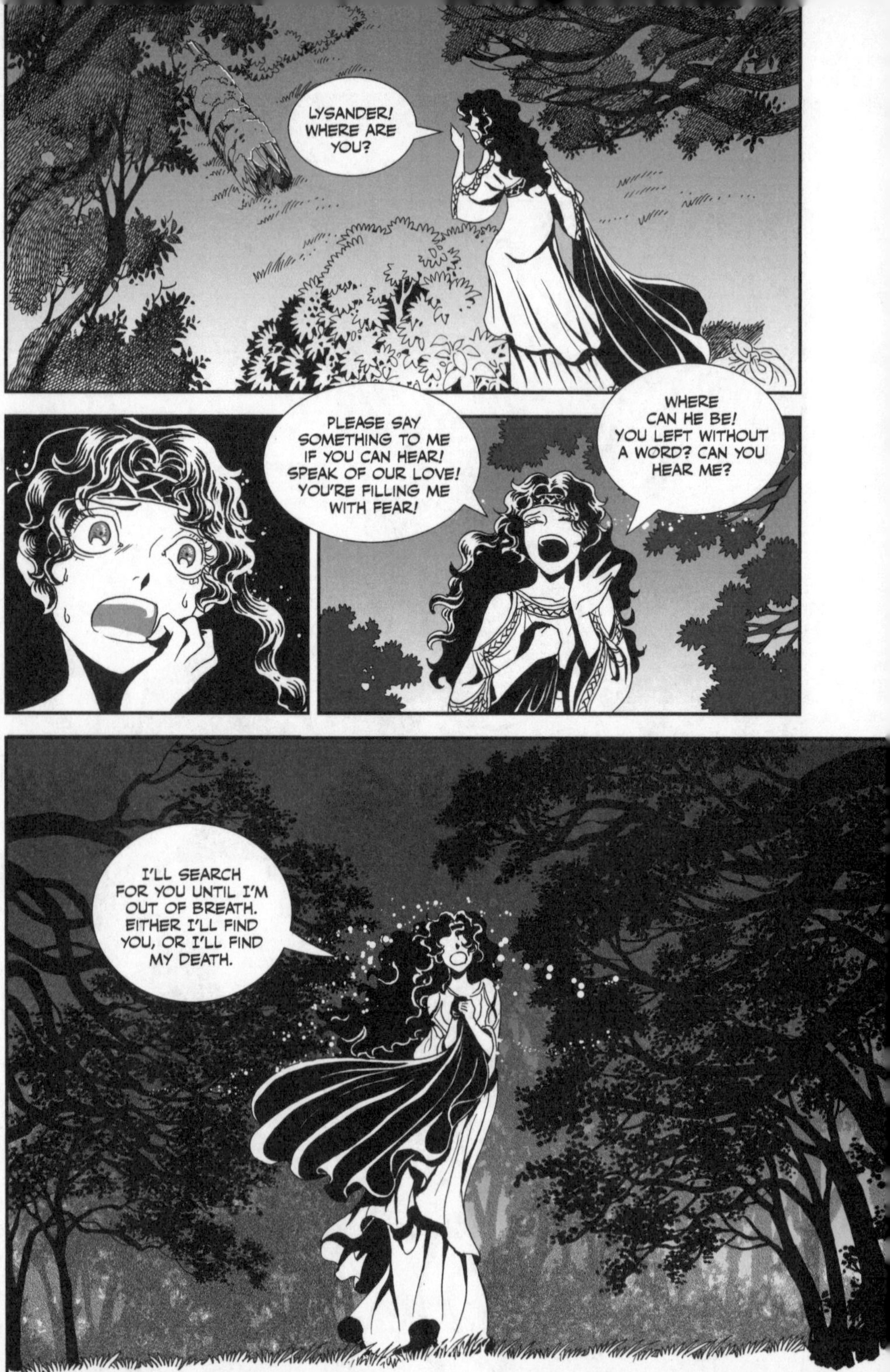
LYSANDER! WHERE ARE YOU?
WHERE CAN HE BE! YOU LEFT WITHOUT A WORD? CAN YOU HEAR ME?
PLEASE SAY SOMETHING TO ME IF YOU CAN HEAR! SPEAK OF OUR LOVE! YOU'RE FILLING ME WITH FEAR!
I'LL SEARCH FOR YOU UNTIL I'M OUT OF BREATH. EITHER I'LL FIND YOU, OR I'LL FIND MY DEATH.

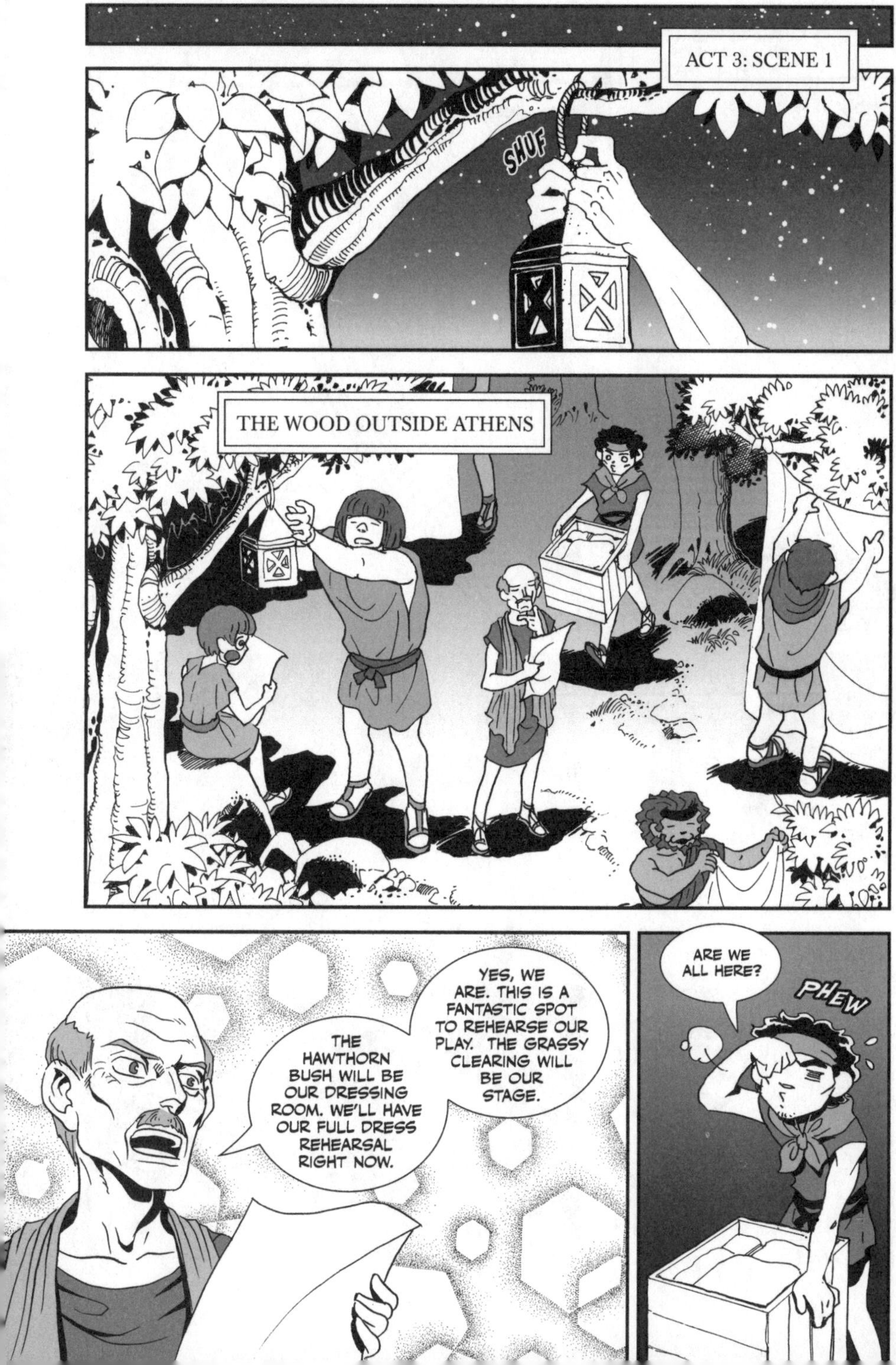
ACT 3: SCENE 1
SHUF
THE WOOD OUTSIDE ATHENS
ARE WE ALL HERE?
PHEW
YES, WE ARE. THIS IS A FANTASTIC SPOT TO REHEARSE OUR PLAY. THE GRASSY CLEARING WILL BE OUR STAGE.
THE HAWTHORN BUSH WILL BE OUR DRESSING ROOM. WE'LL HAVE OUR FULL DRESS REHEARSAL RIGHT NOW.

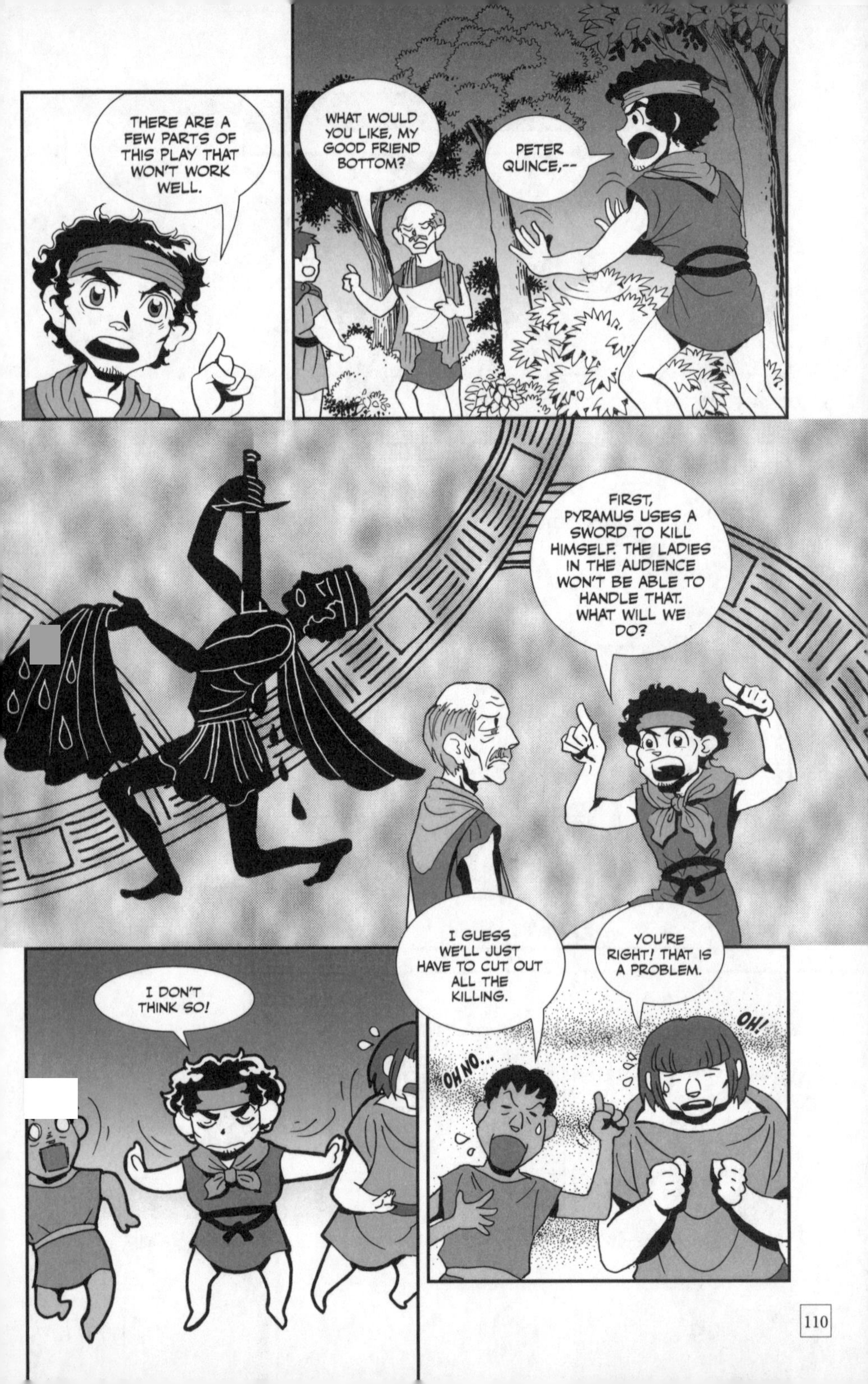
PETER QUINCE,--
WHAT WOULD YOU LIKE, MY GOOD FRIEND BOTTOM?
THERE ARE A FEW PARTS OF THIS PLAY THAT WON'T WORK WELL.
FIRST, PYRAMUS USES A SWORD TO KILL HIMSELF. THE LADIES IN THE AUDIENCE WON'T BE ABLE TO HANDLE THAT. WHAT WILL WE DO?
YOU'RE RIGHT! THAT IS A PROBLEM.
OH!
I GUESS WE'LL JUST HAVE TO CUT OUT ALL THE KILLING.
OH NO...
I DON'T THINK SO!

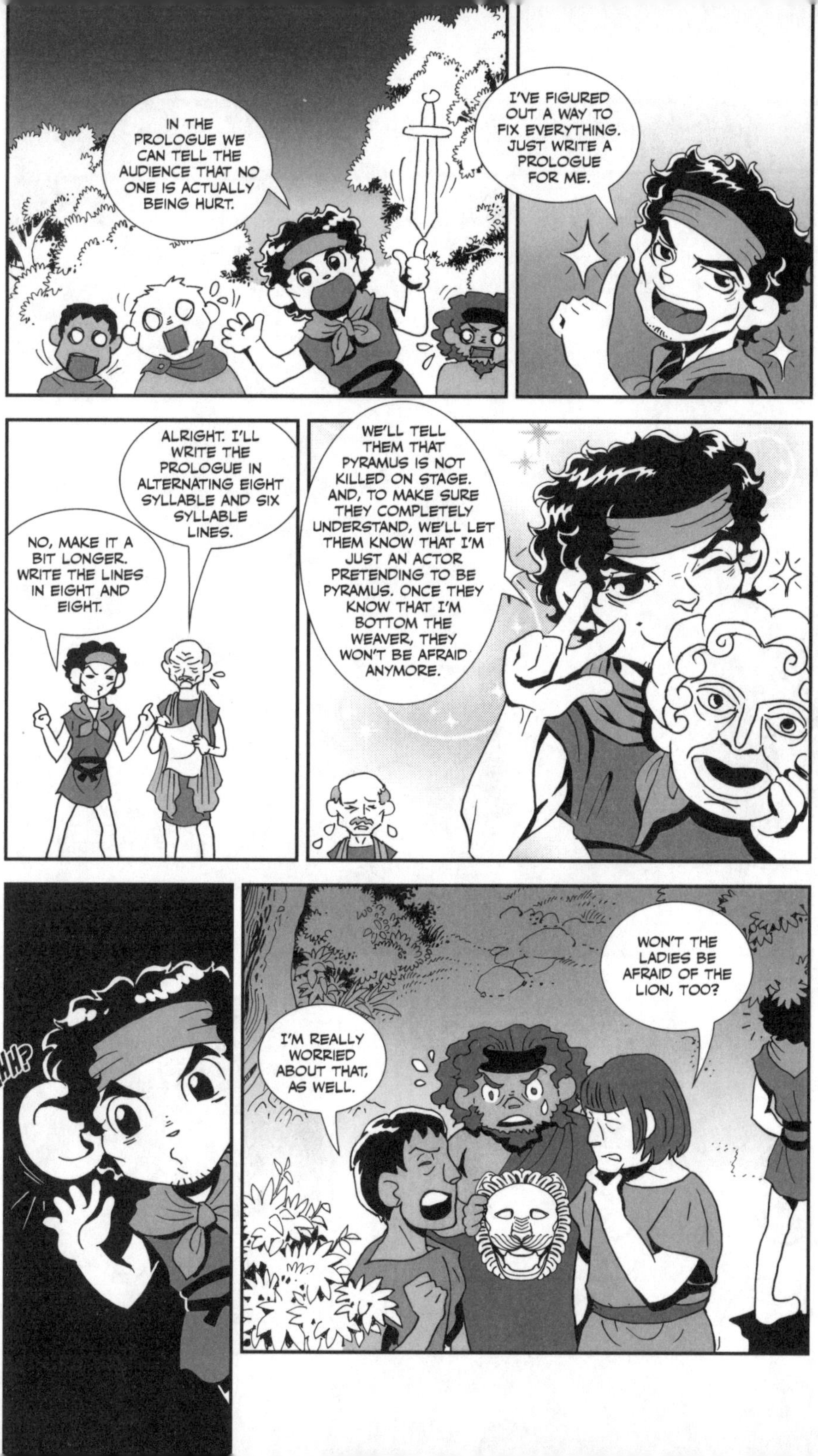
I'VE FIGURED OUT A WAY TO FIX EVERYTHING. JUST WRITE A PROLOGUE FOR ME.
IN THE PROLOGUE WE CAN TELL THE AUDIENCE THAT NO ONE IS ACTUALLY BEING HURT.
WE'LL TELL THEM THAT PYRAMUS IS NOT KILLED ON STAGE. AND, TO MAKE SURE THEY COMPLETELY UNDERSTAND, WE'LL LET THEM KNOW THAT I'M JUST AN ACTOR PRETENDING TO BE PYRAMUS. ONCE THEY KNOW THAT I'M BOTTOM THE WEAVER, THEY WON'T BE AFRAID ANYMORE.
ALRIGHT. I'LL WRITE THE PROLOGUE IN ALTERNATING EIGHT SYLLABLE AND SIX SYLLABLE LINES.
NO, MAKE IT A BIT LONGER. WRITE THE LINES IN EIGHT AND EIGHT.
WON'T THE LADIES BE AFRAID OF THE LION, TOO?
I'M REALLY WORRIED ABOUT THAT, AS WELL.
EHH?

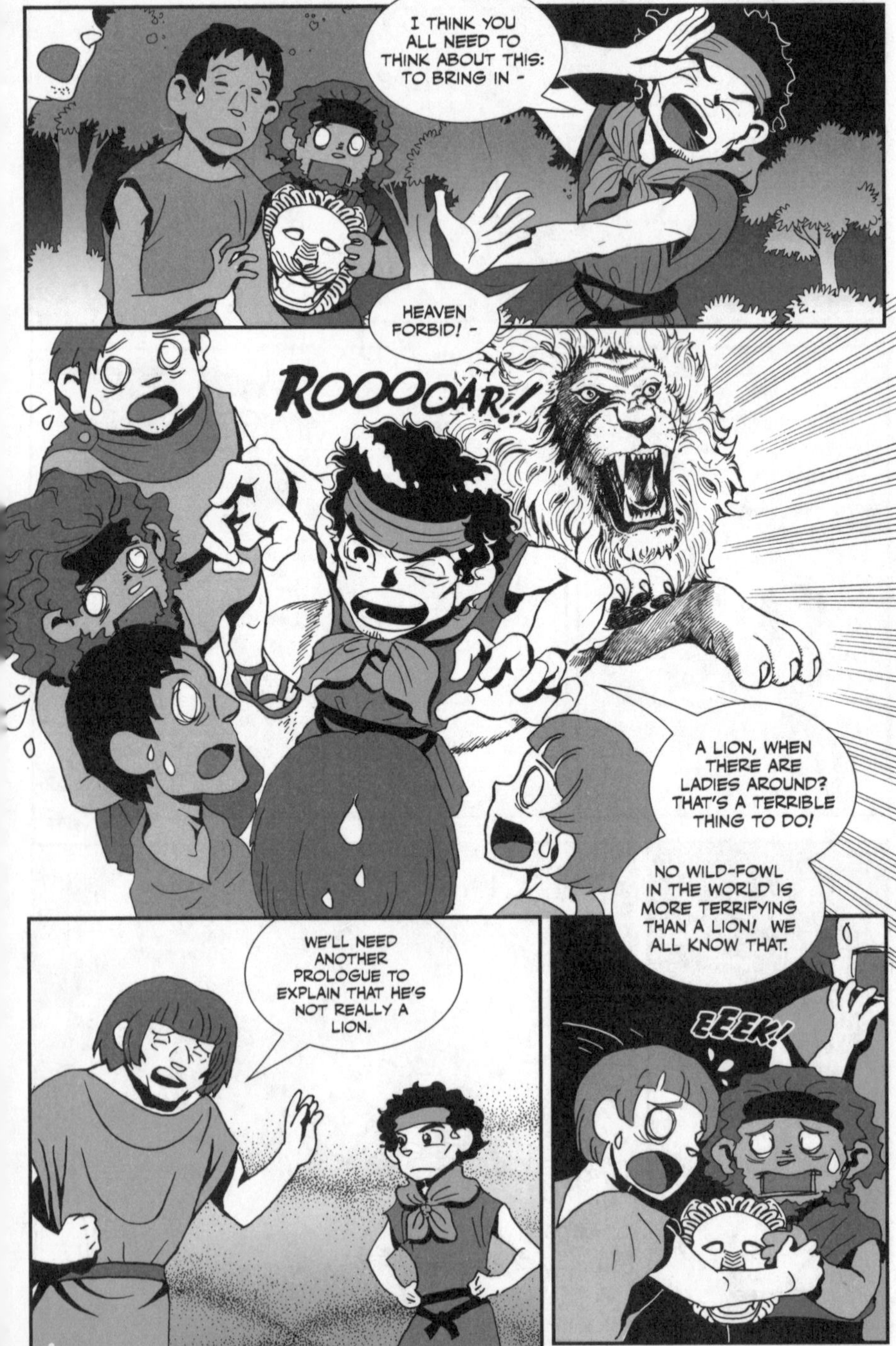
I THINK YOU ALL NEED TO THINK ABOUT THIS: TO BRING IN -
HEAVEN FORBID! -
ROOOOAR!!
A LION, WHEN THERE ARE LADIES AROUND? THAT'S A TERRIBLE THING TO DO!
NO WILD-FOWL IN THE WORLD IS MORE TERRIFYING THAN A LION! WE ALL KNOW THAT.
EEEK!
WE'LL NEED ANOTHER PROLOGUE TO EXPLAIN THAT HE'S NOT REALLY A LION.

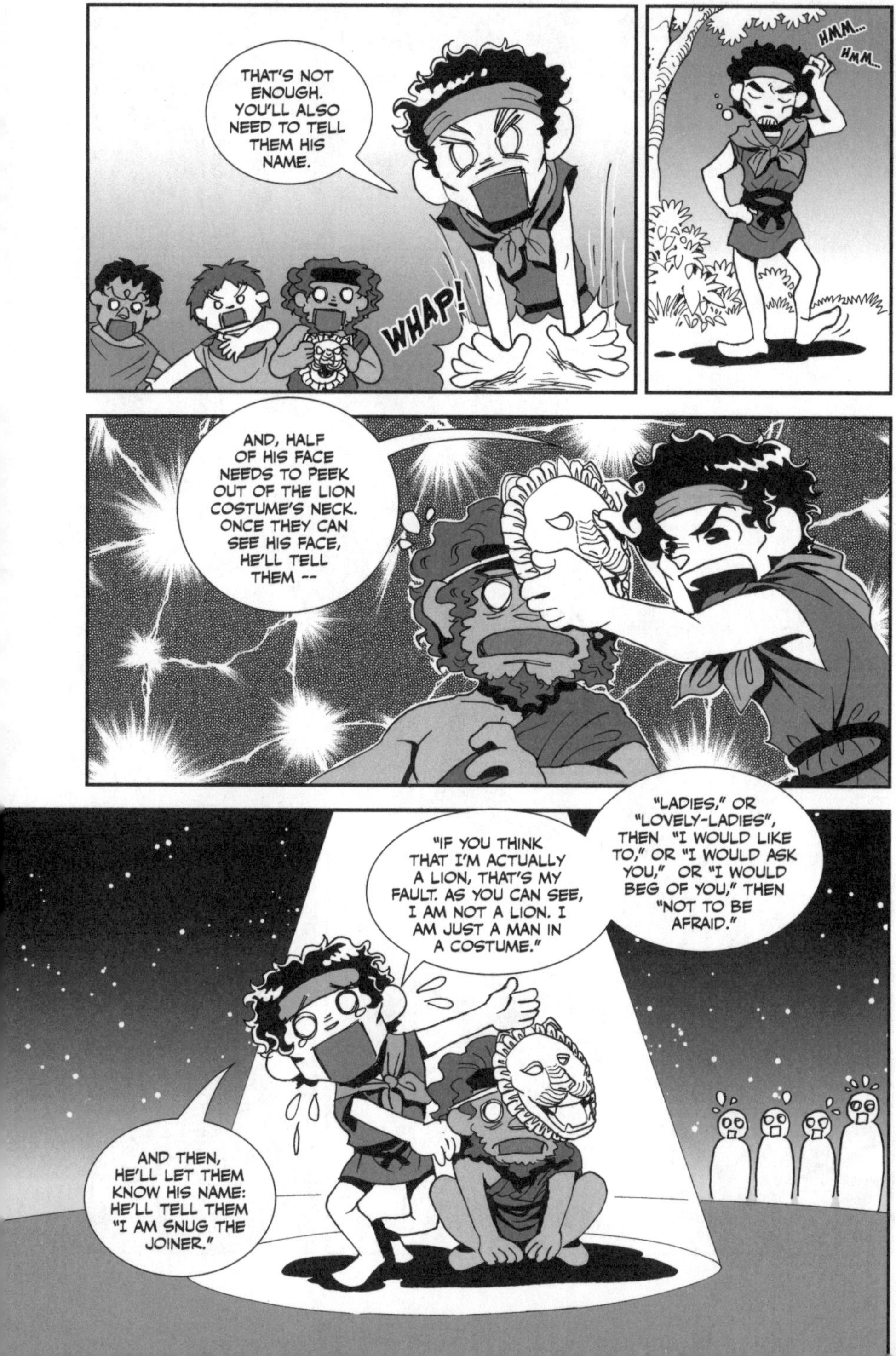
HMM... HMM...
THAT'S NOT ENOUGH. YOU'LL ALSO NEED TO TELL THEM HIS NAME.
WHAP!
AND, HALF OF HIS FACE NEEDS TO PEEK OUT OF THE LION COSTUME'S NECK. ONCE THEY CAN SEE HIS FACE, HE'LL TELL THEM --
"LADIES," OR "LOVELY-LADIES", THEN "I WOULD LIKE TO," OR "I WOULD ASK YOU," OR "I WOULD BEG OF YOU," THEN "NOT TO BE AFRAID."
"IF YOU THINK THAT I'M ACTUALLY A LION, THAT'S MY FAULT. AS YOU CAN SEE, I AM NOT A LION. I AM JUST A MAN IN A COSTUME."
AND THEN, HE'LL LET THEM KNOW HIS NAME: HE'LL TELL THEM "I AM SNUG THE JOINER."

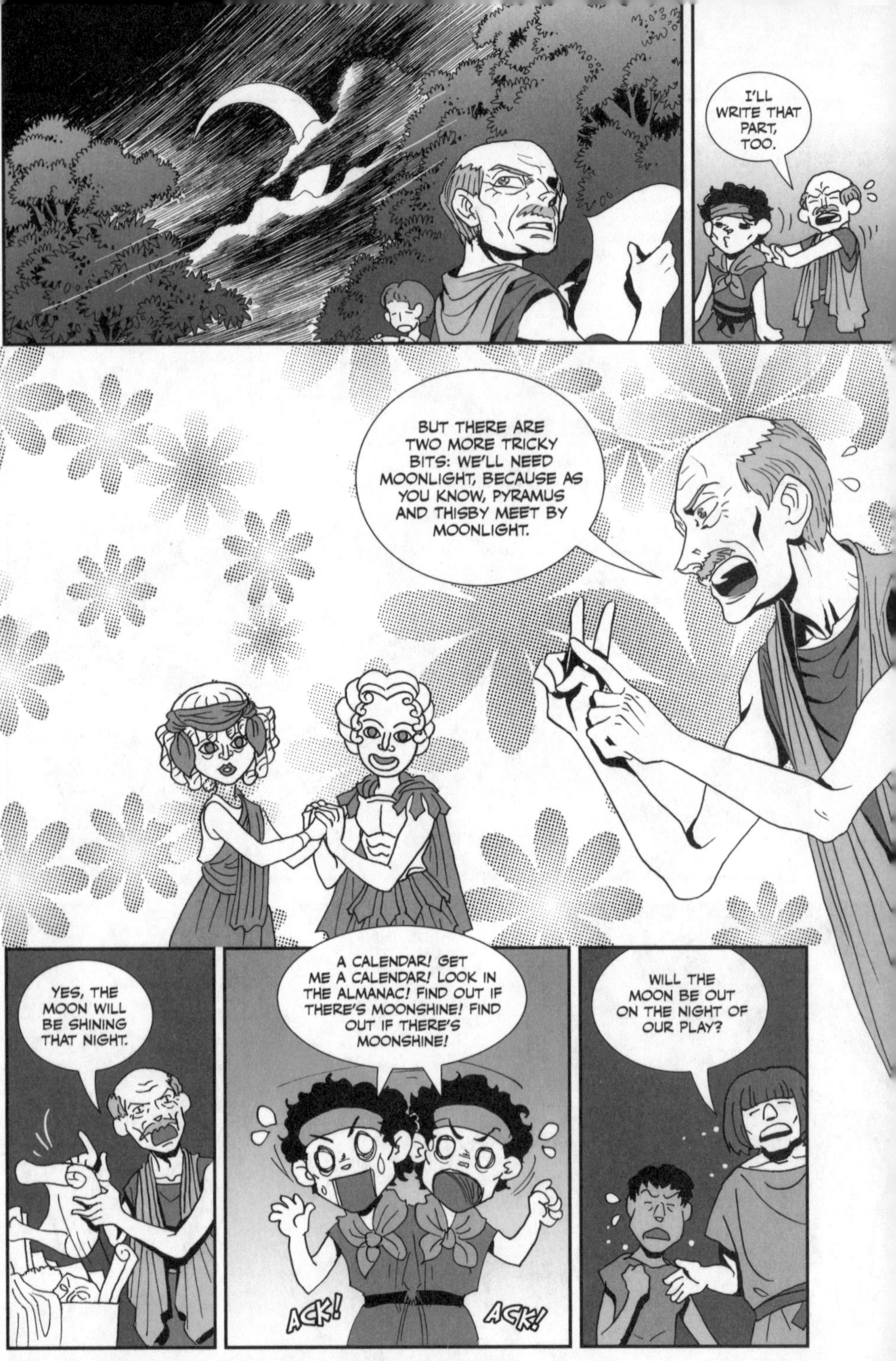
I'LL WRITE THAT PART, TOO.
BUT THERE ARE TWO MORE TRICKY BITS: WE'LL NEED MOONLIGHT, BECAUSE AS YOU KNOW, PYRAMUS AND THISBY MEET BY MOONLIGHT.
WILL THE MOON BE OUT ON THE NIGHT OF OUR PLAY?
A CALENDAR! GET ME A CALENDAR! LOOK IN THE ALMANAC! FIND OUT IF THERE'S MOONSHINE! FIND OUT IF THERE'S MOONSHINE!
ACK!
ACK!
YES, THE MOON WILL BE SHINING THAT NIGHT.

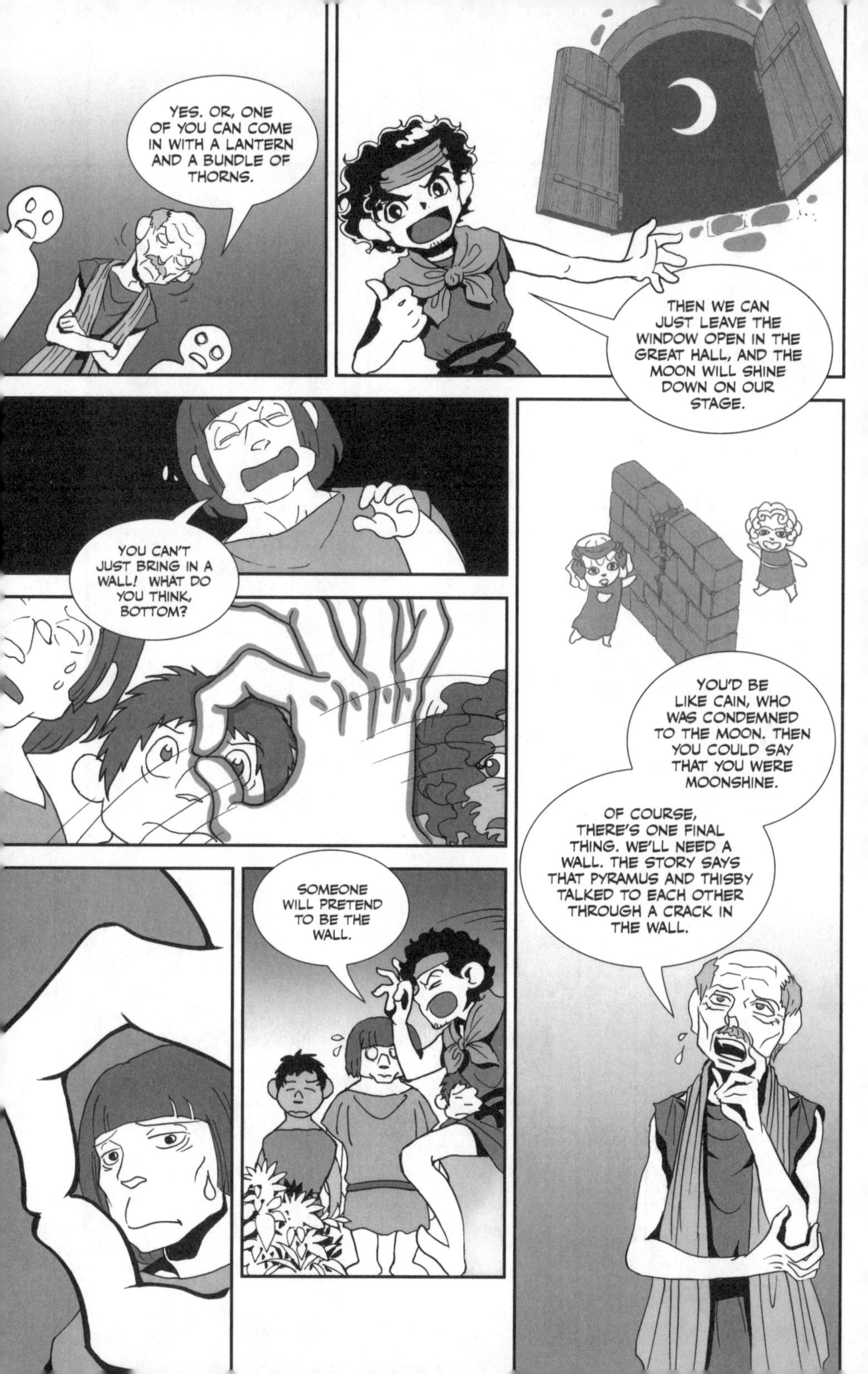
THEN WE CAN JUST LEAVE THE WINDOW OPEN IN THE GREAT HALL, AND THE MOON WILL SHINE DOWN ON OUR STAGE.
YES. OR, ONE OF YOU CAN COME IN WITH A LANTERN AND A BUNDLE OF THORNS.
YOU'D BE LIKE CAIN, WHO WAS CONDEMNED TO THE MOON. THEN YOU COULD SAY THAT YOU WERE MOONSHINE.
OF COURSE, THERE'S ONE FINAL THING. WE'LL NEED A WALL. THE STORY SAYS THAT PYRAMUS AND THISBY TALKED TO EACH OTHER THROUGH A CRACK IN THE WALL.
YOU CAN'T JUST BRING IN A WALL! WHAT DO YOU THINK, BOTTOM?
SOMEONE WILL PRETEND TO BE THE WALL.

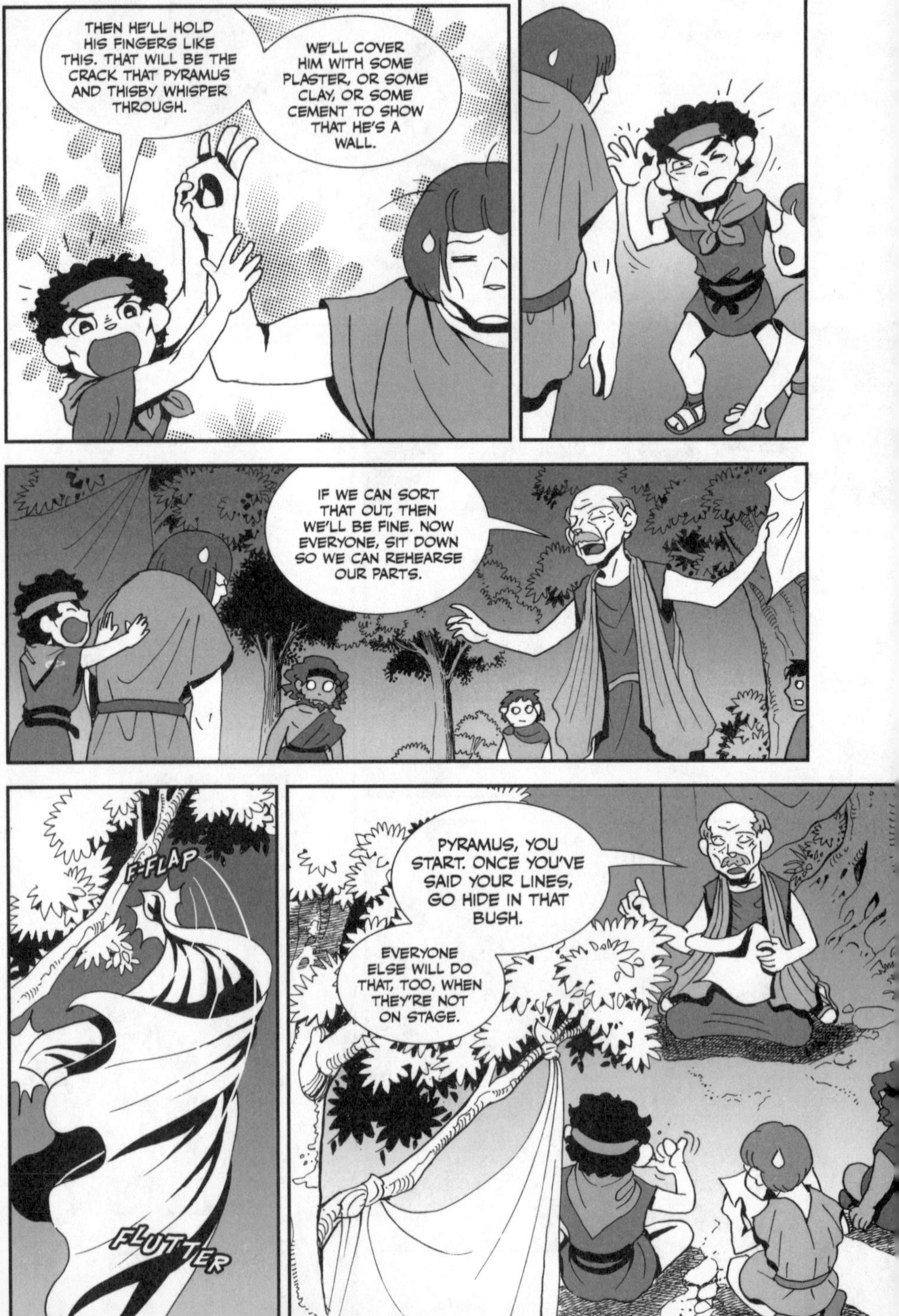
WE'LL COVER HIM WITH SOME PLASTER, OR SOME CLAY, OR SOME CEMENT TO SHOW THAT HE'S A WALL.
THEN HE'LL HOLD HIS FINGERS LIKE THIS. THAT WILL BE THE CRACK THAT PYRAMUS AND THISBY WHISPER THROUGH.
IF WE CAN SORT THAT OUT, THEN WE'LL BE FINE. NOW EVERYONE, SIT DOWN SO WE CAN REHEARSE OUR PARTS.
PYRAMUS, YOU START. ONCE YOU'VE SAID YOUR LINES, GO HIDE IN THAT BUSH.
EVERYONE ELSE WILL DO THAT, TOO, WHEN THEY'RE NOT ON STAGE.
F-FLAP
FLUTTER

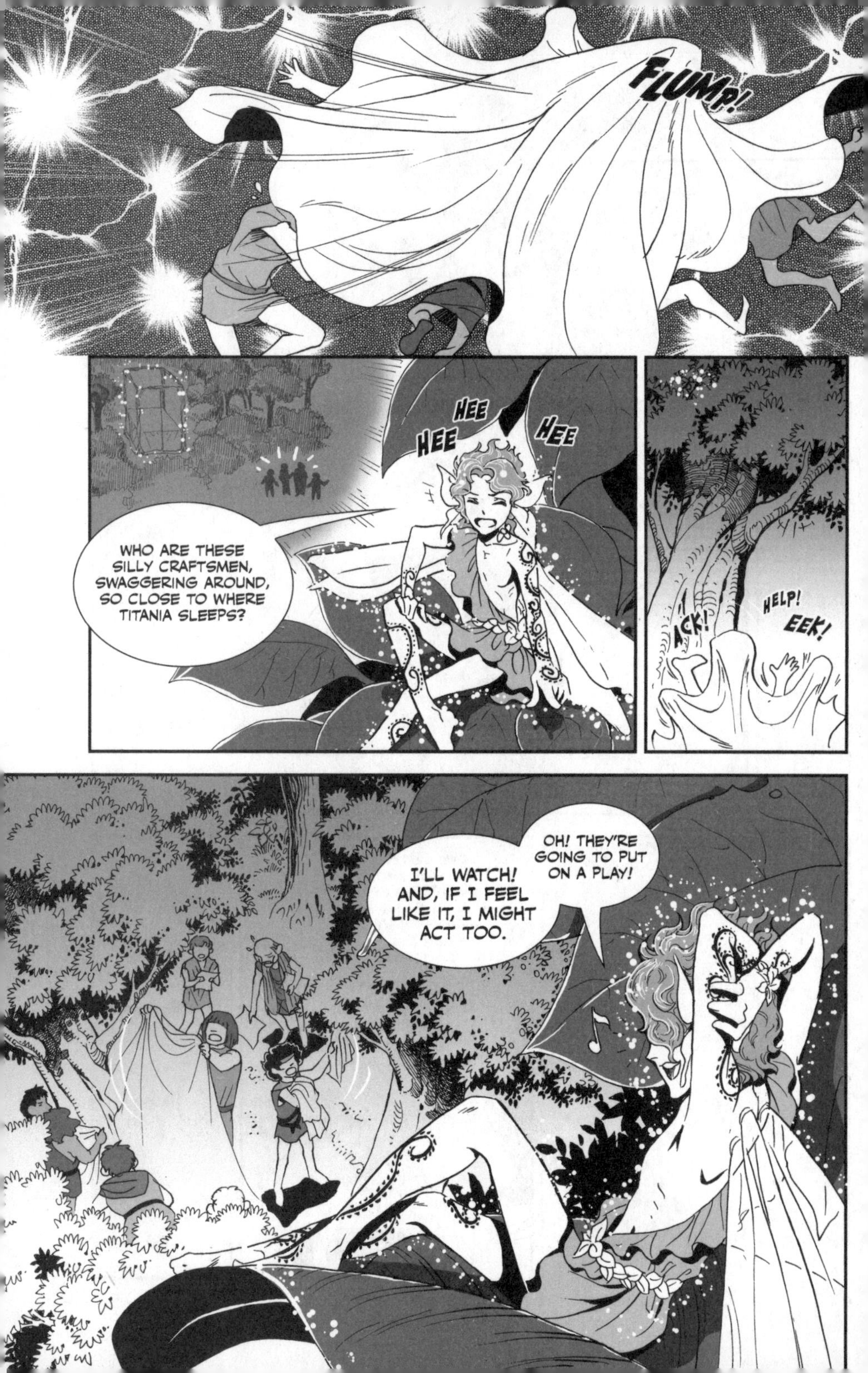
FLUMP!
HELP!
EEK!
ACK!
HEE HEE HEE
WHO ARE THESE SILLY CRAFTSMEN, SWAGGERING AROUND, SO CLOSE TO WHERE TITANIA SLEEPS?
OH! THEY'RE GOING TO PUT ON A PLAY!
I'LL WATCH! AND, IF I FEEL LIKE IT, I MIGHT ACT TOO.

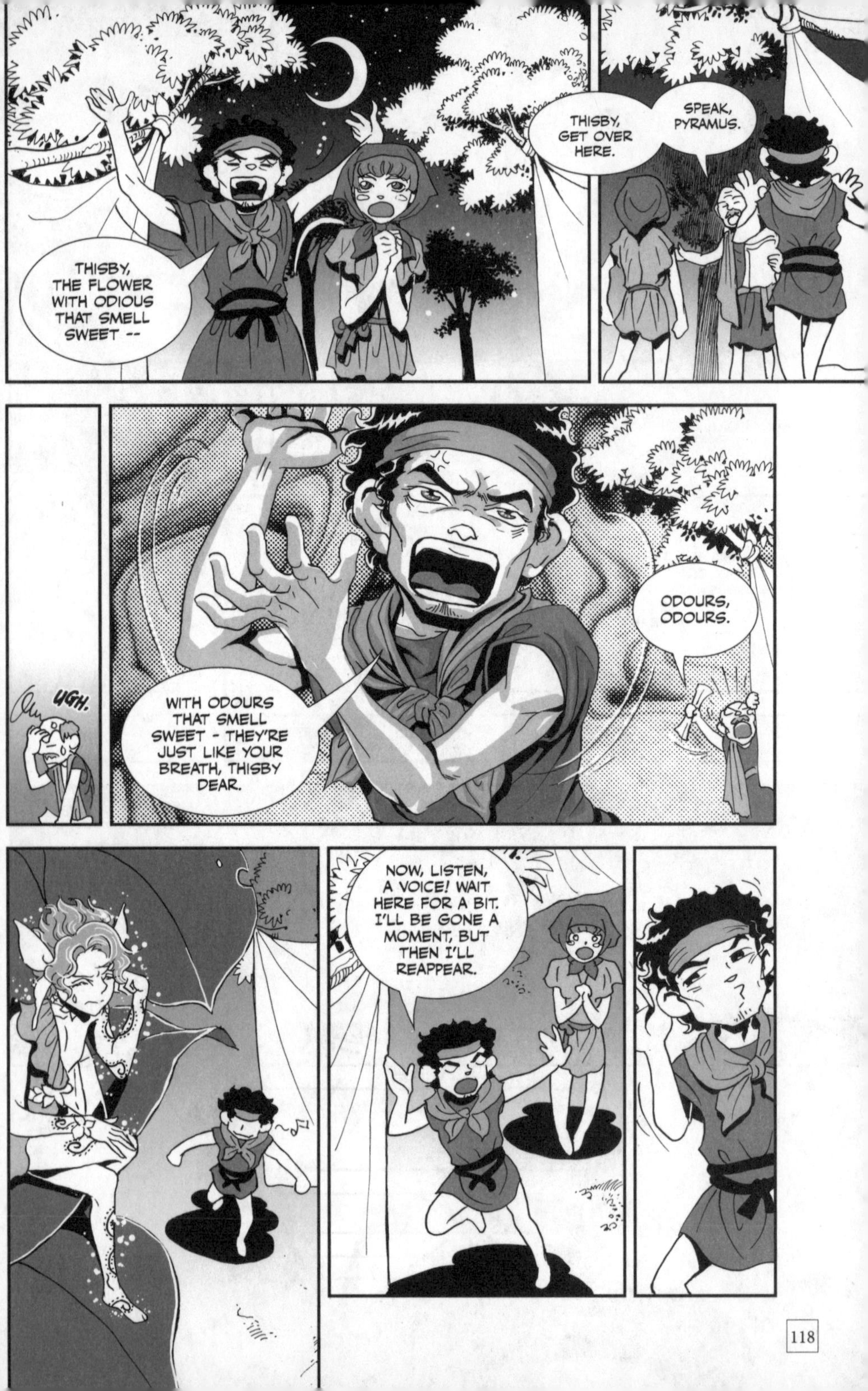
SPEAK, PYRAMUS.
THISBY, GET OVER HERE.
THISBY, THE FLOWER WITH ODIOUS THAT SMELL SWEET --
ODOURS, ODOURS.
WITH ODOURS THAT SMELL SWEET - THEY'RE JUST LIKE YOUR BREATH, THISBY DEAR.
UGH.
NOW, LISTEN, A VOICE! WAIT HERE FOR A BIT. I'LL BE GONE A MOMENT, BUT THEN I'LL REAPPEAR.

HMM...

EE HEE HEE!

YAWWWW

THIS IS THE STRANGEST PYRAMUS I'VE EVER SEEN.

GLINT~

GLIMMER

GLEEEEAM

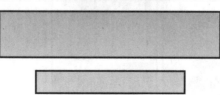

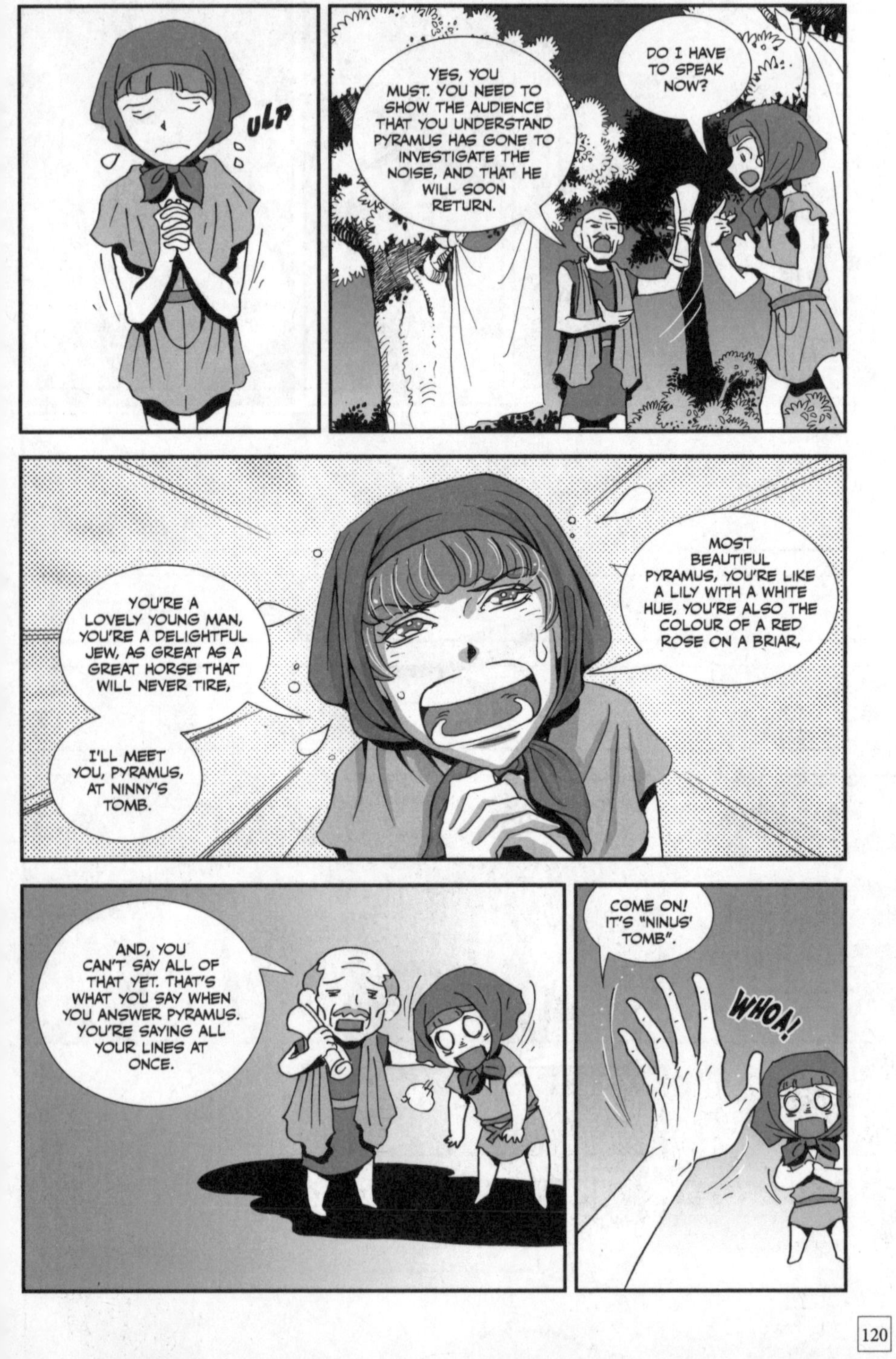
DO I HAVE TO SPEAK NOW?
YES, YOU MUST. YOU NEED TO SHOW THE AUDIENCE THAT YOU UNDERSTAND PYRAMUS HAS GONE TO INVESTIGATE THE NOISE, AND THAT HE WILL SOON RETURN.
ULP
MOST BEAUTIFUL PYRAMUS, YOU'RE LIKE A LILY WITH A WHITE HUE, YOU'RE ALSO THE COLOUR OF A RED ROSE ON A BRIAR,
YOU'RE A LOVELY YOUNG MAN, YOU'RE A DELIGHTFUL JEW, AS GREAT AS A GREAT HORSE THAT WILL NEVER TIRE,
I'LL MEET YOU, PYRAMUS, AT NINNY'S TOMB.
COME ON! IT'S "NINUS' TOMB".
WHOA!
AND, YOU CAN'T SAY ALL OF THAT YET. THAT'S WHAT YOU SAY WHEN YOU ANSWER PYRAMUS. YOU'RE SAYING ALL YOUR LINES AT ONCE.

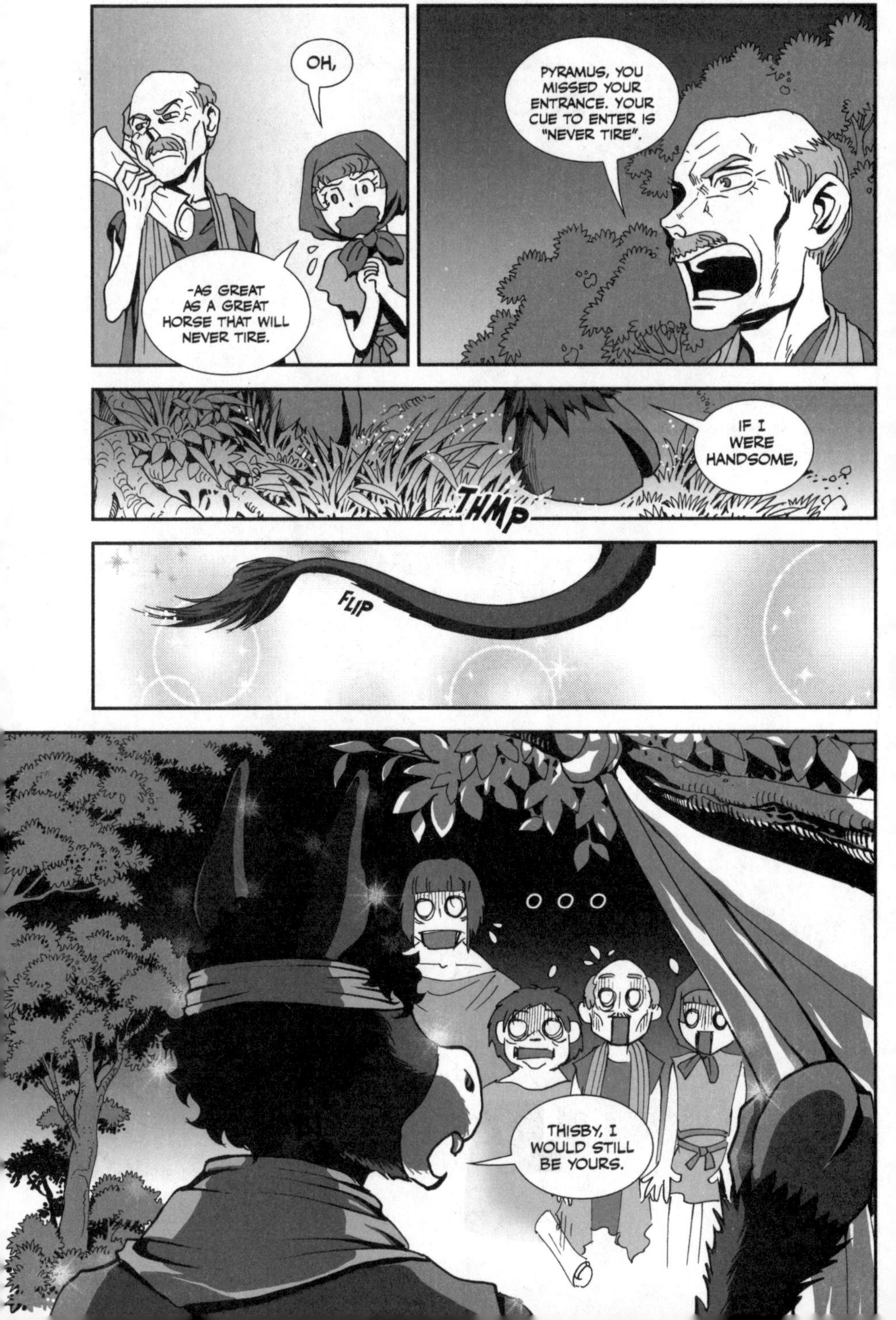
OH,
-AS GREAT AS A GREAT HORSE THAT WILL NEVER TIRE.
PYRAMUS, YOU MISSED YOUR ENTRANCE. YOUR CUE TO ENTER IS "NEVER TIRE".
IF I WERE HANDSOME,
THMP
FLIP
o o o
THISBY, I WOULD STILL BE YOURS.

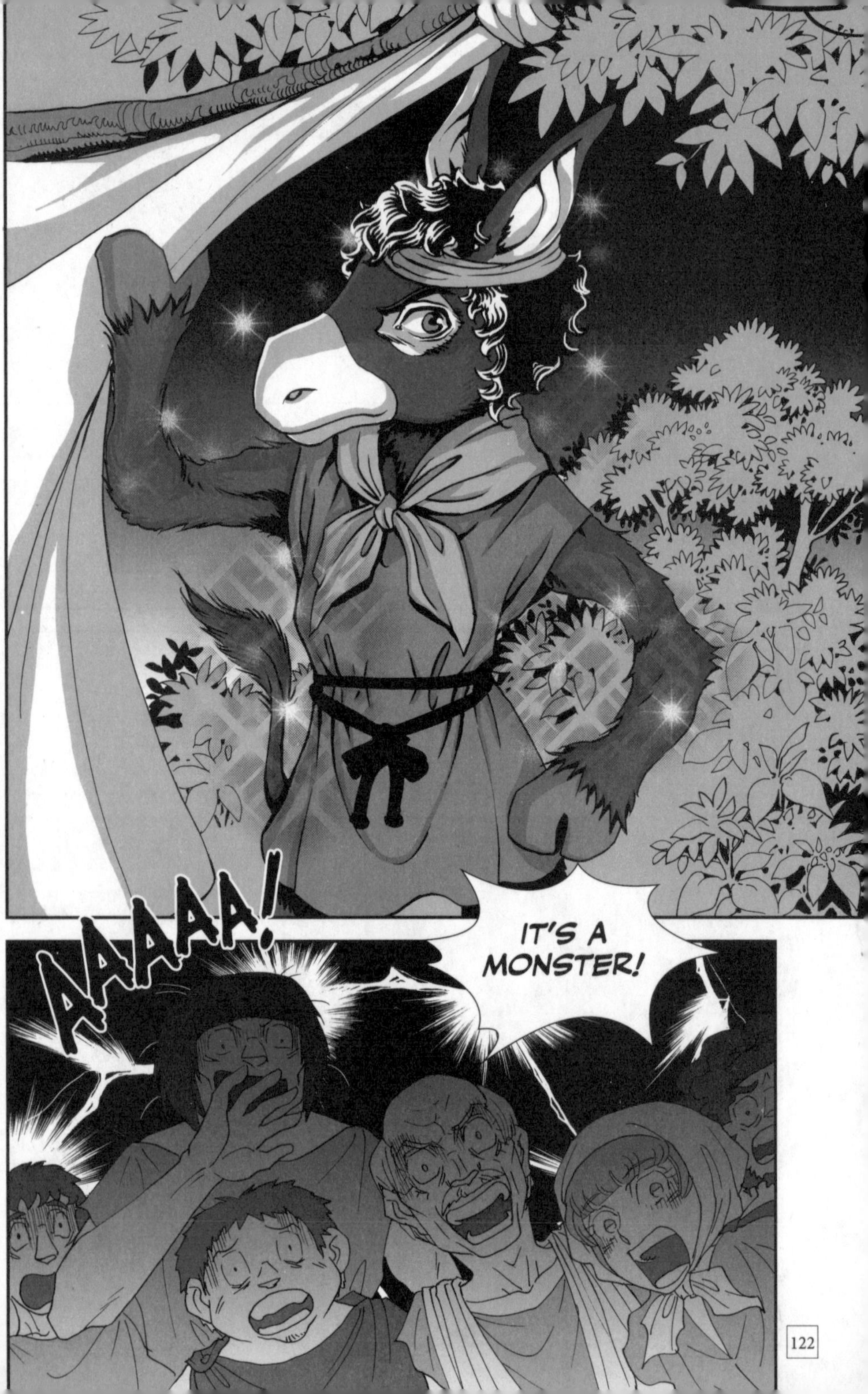
IT'S A MONSTER!
AAAAA!

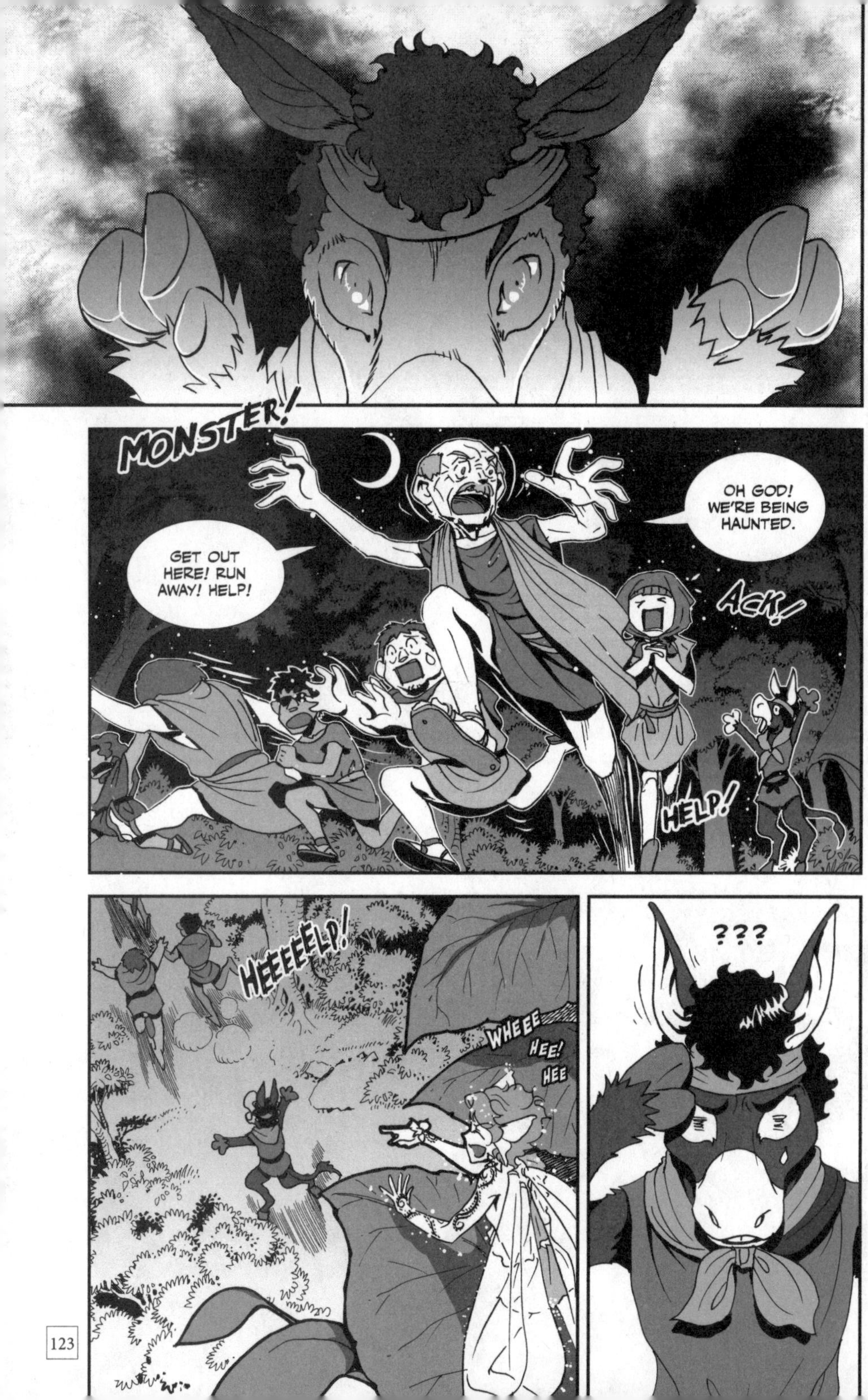
OH GOD! WE'RE BEING HAUNTED.
MONSTER!
ACK!
GET OUT HERE! RUN AWAY! HELP!
HELP!
???
HEEEEELP!
WHEEE
HEE!
HEE

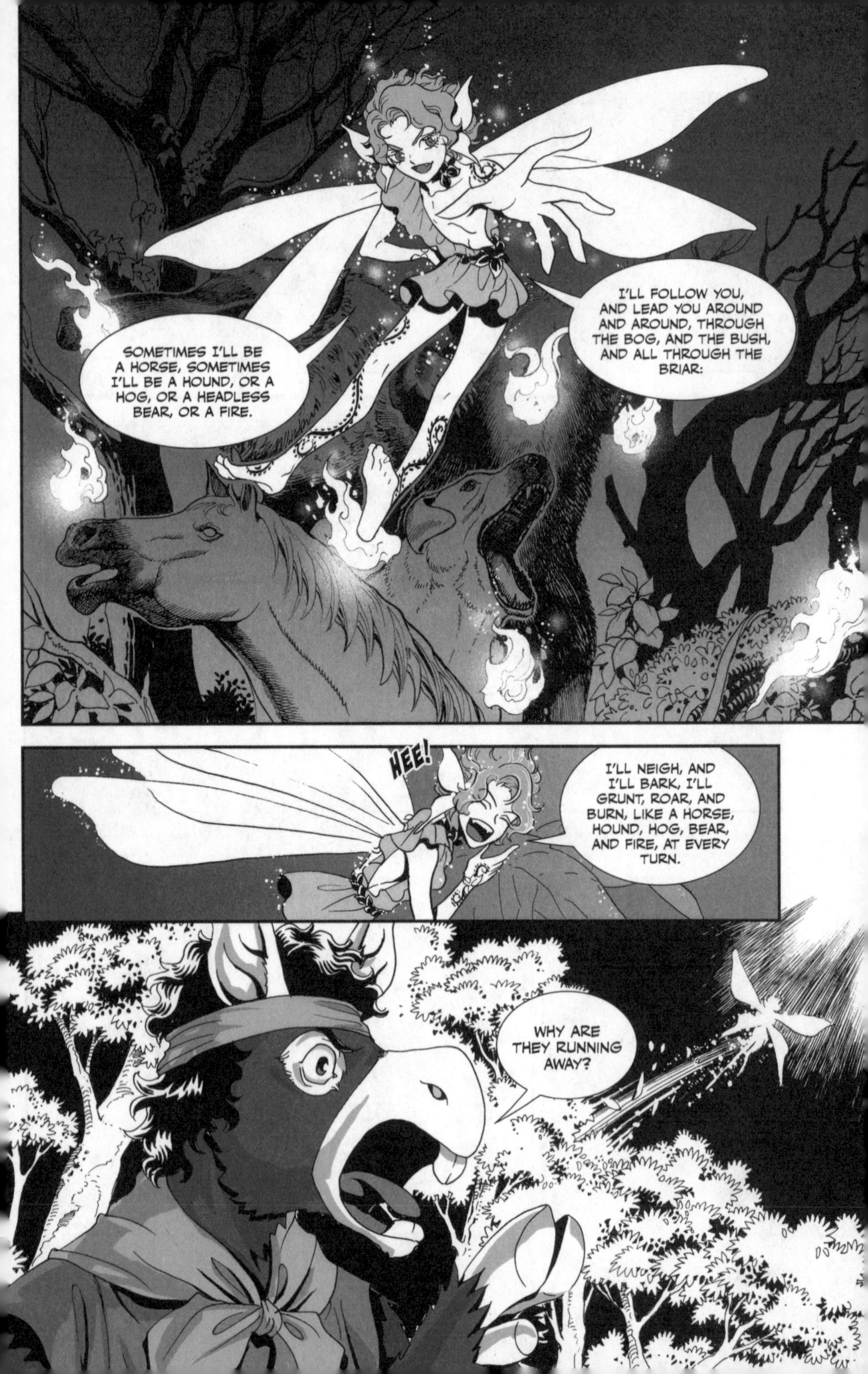
I'LL FOLLOW YOU, AND LEAD YOU AROUND AND AROUND, THROUGH THE BOG, AND THE BUSH, AND ALL THROUGH THE BRIAR:
SOMETIMES I'LL BE A HORSE, SOMETIMES I'LL BE A HOUND, OR A HOG, OR A HEADLESS BEAR, OR A FIRE.
I'LL NEIGH, AND I'LL BARK, I'LL GRUNT, ROAR, AND BURN, LIKE A HORSE, HOUND, HOG, BEAR, AND FIRE, AT EVERY TURN.
HEE!
WHY ARE THEY RUNNING AWAY?

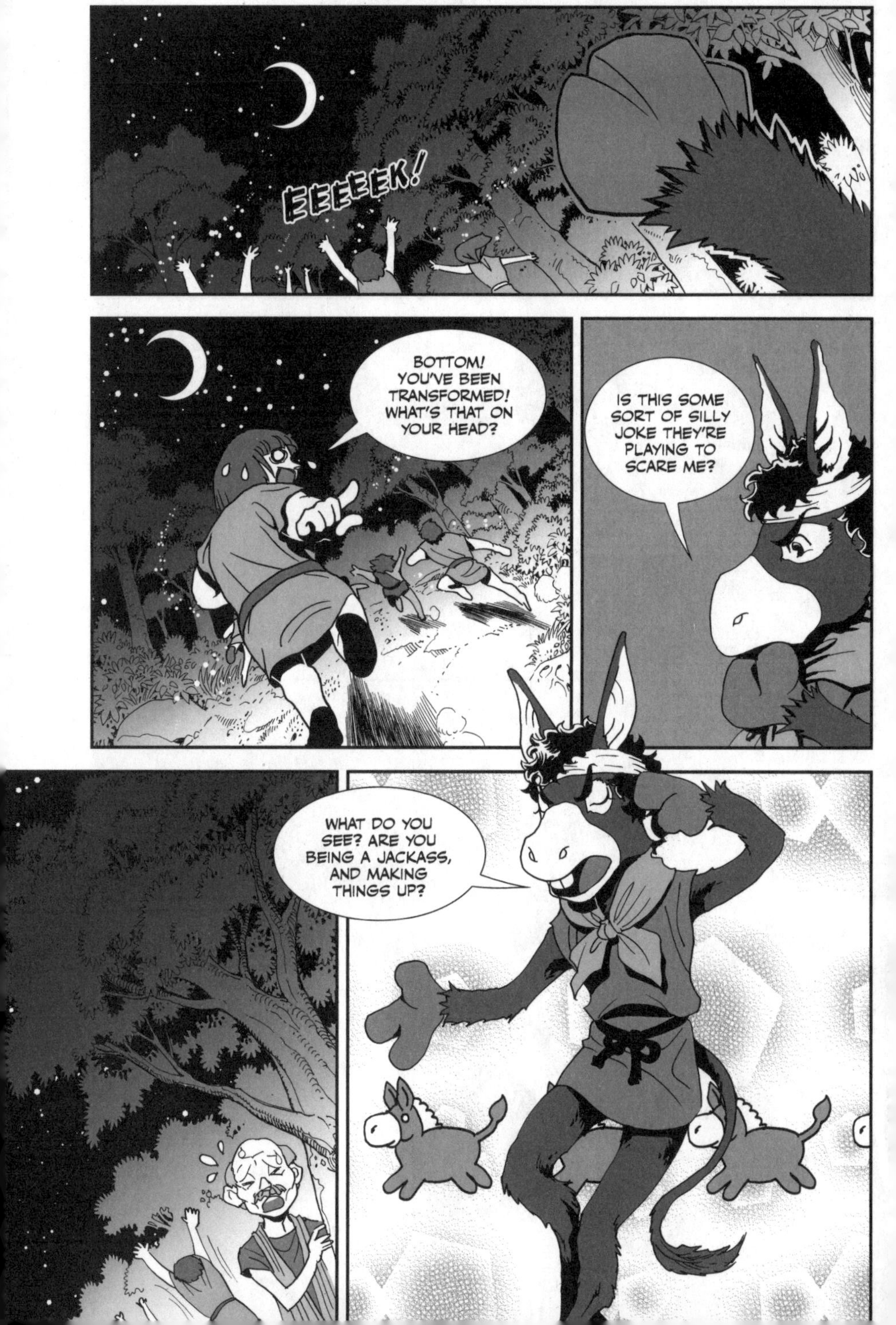
EEEEEK!
IS THIS SOME SORT OF SILLY JOKE THEY'RE PLAYING TO SCARE ME?
BOTTOM! YOU'VE BEEN TRANSFORMED! WHAT'S THAT ON YOUR HEAD?
WHAT DO YOU SEE? ARE YOU BEING A JACKASS, AND MAKING THINGS UP?

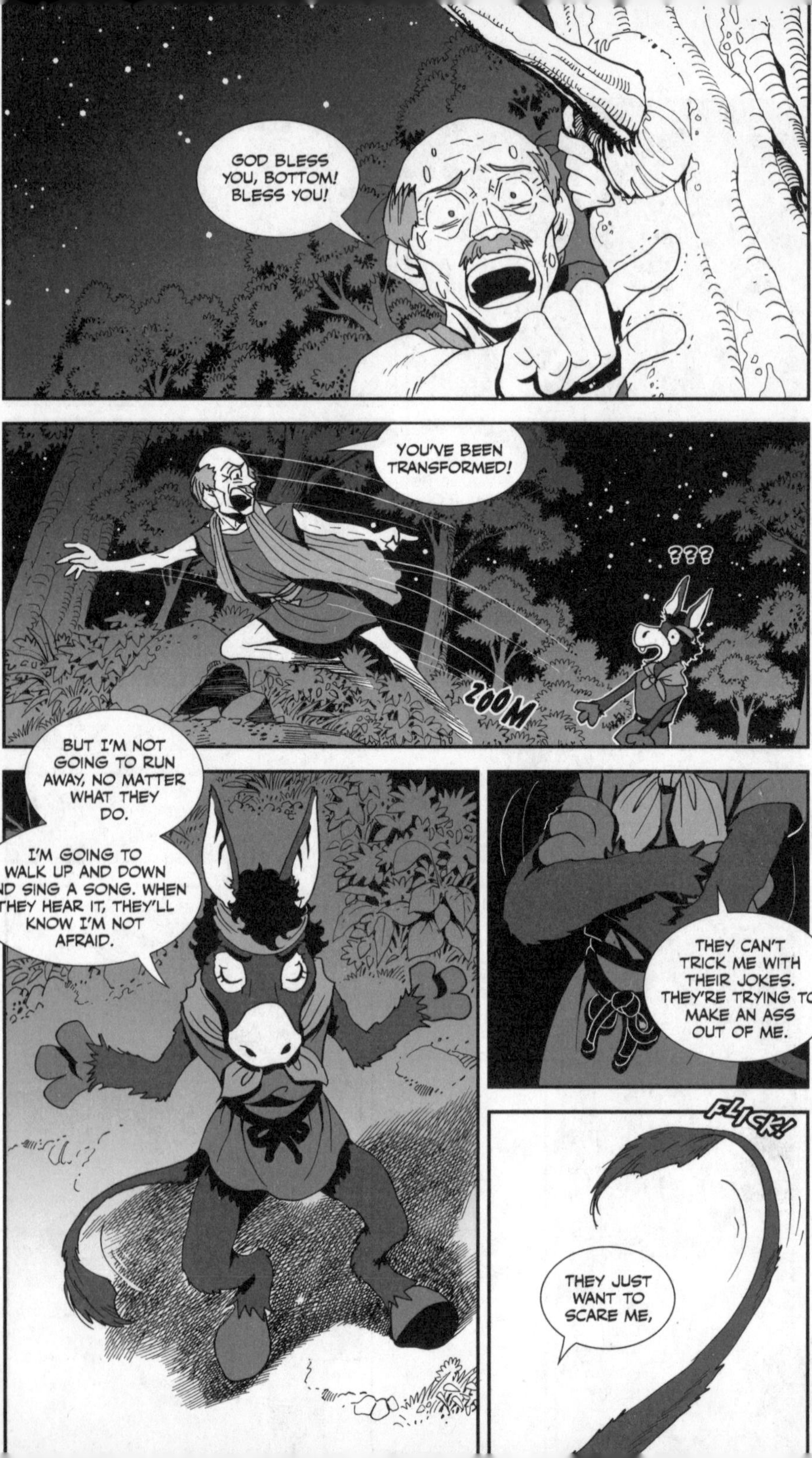
GOD BLESS YOU, BOTTOM! BLESS YOU!
YOU'VE BEEN TRANSFORMED!
???
ZOOM
THEY CAN'T TRICK ME WITH THEIR JOKES. THEY'RE TRYING TO MAKE AN ASS OUT OF ME.
FLICK!
THEY JUST WANT TO SCARE ME,
BUT I'M NOT GOING TO RUN AWAY, NO MATTER WHAT THEY DO.
I'M GOING TO WALK UP AND DOWN AND SING A SONG. WHEN THEY HEAR IT, THEY'LL KNOW I'M NOT AFRAID.

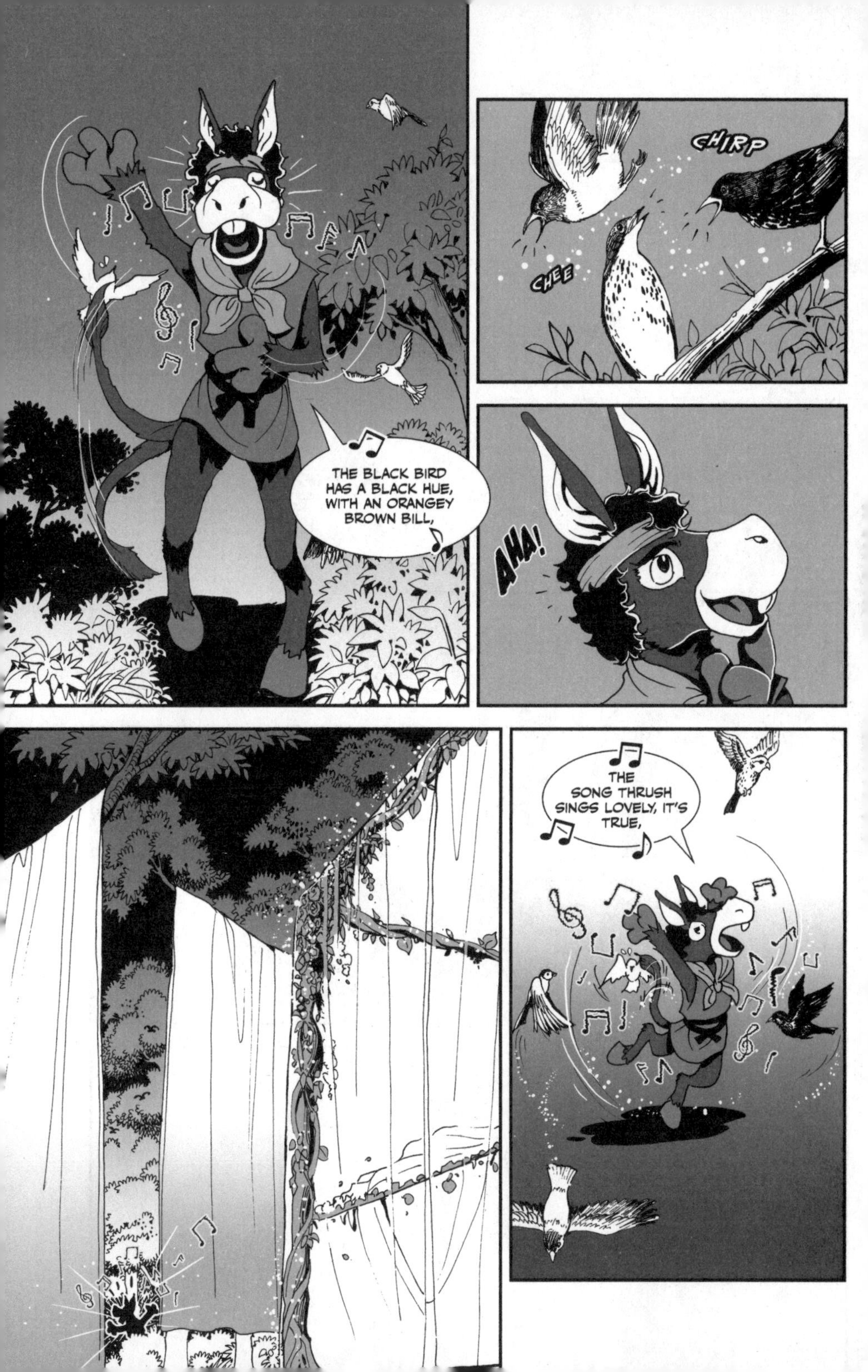
CHIRP
CHEE
AHA!
THE BLACK BIRD HAS A BLACK HUE, WITH AN ORANGEY BROWN BILL,
THE SONG THRUSH SINGS LOVELY, IT'S TRUE,

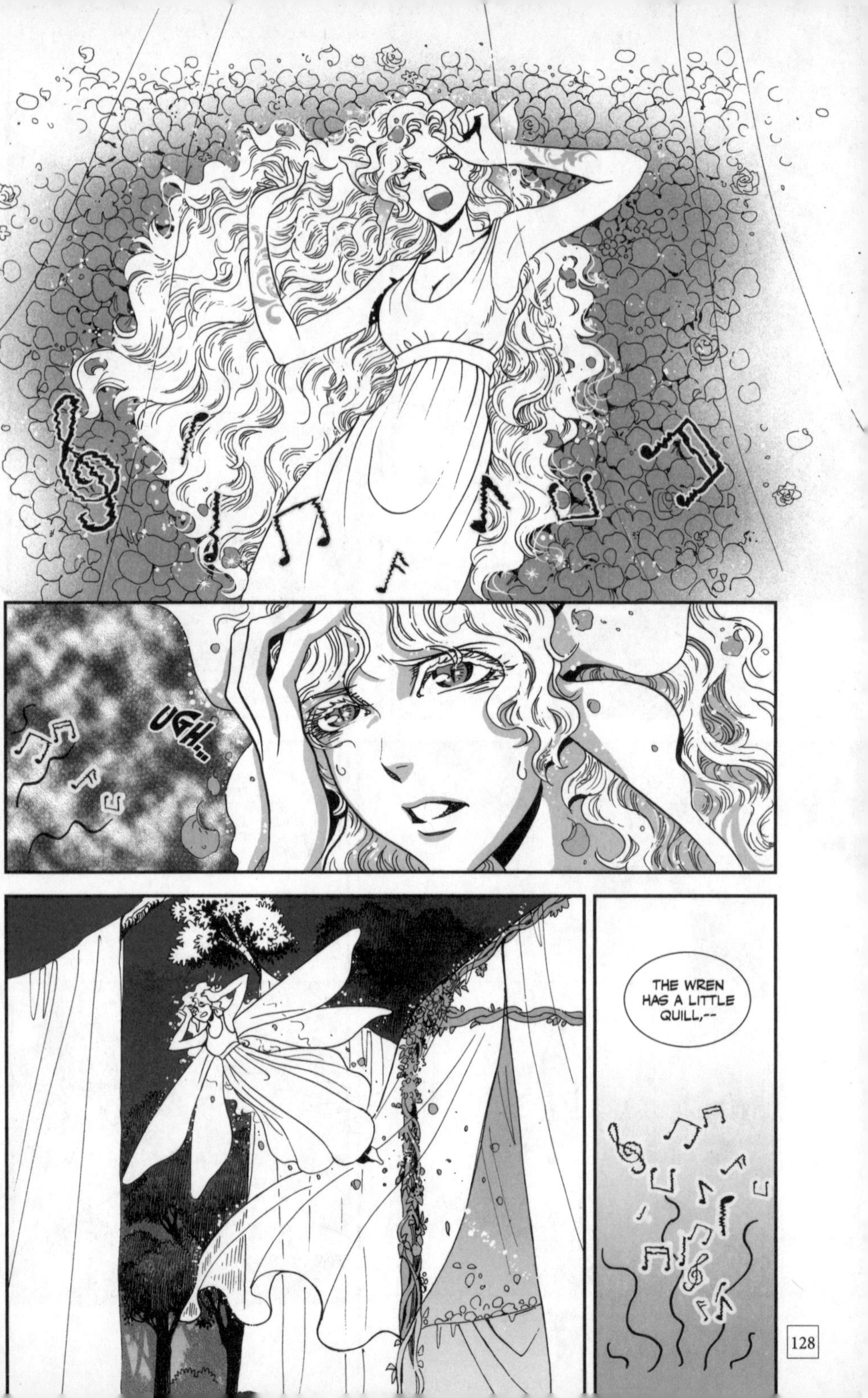
UGH..
THE WREN HAS A LITTLE QUILL,--

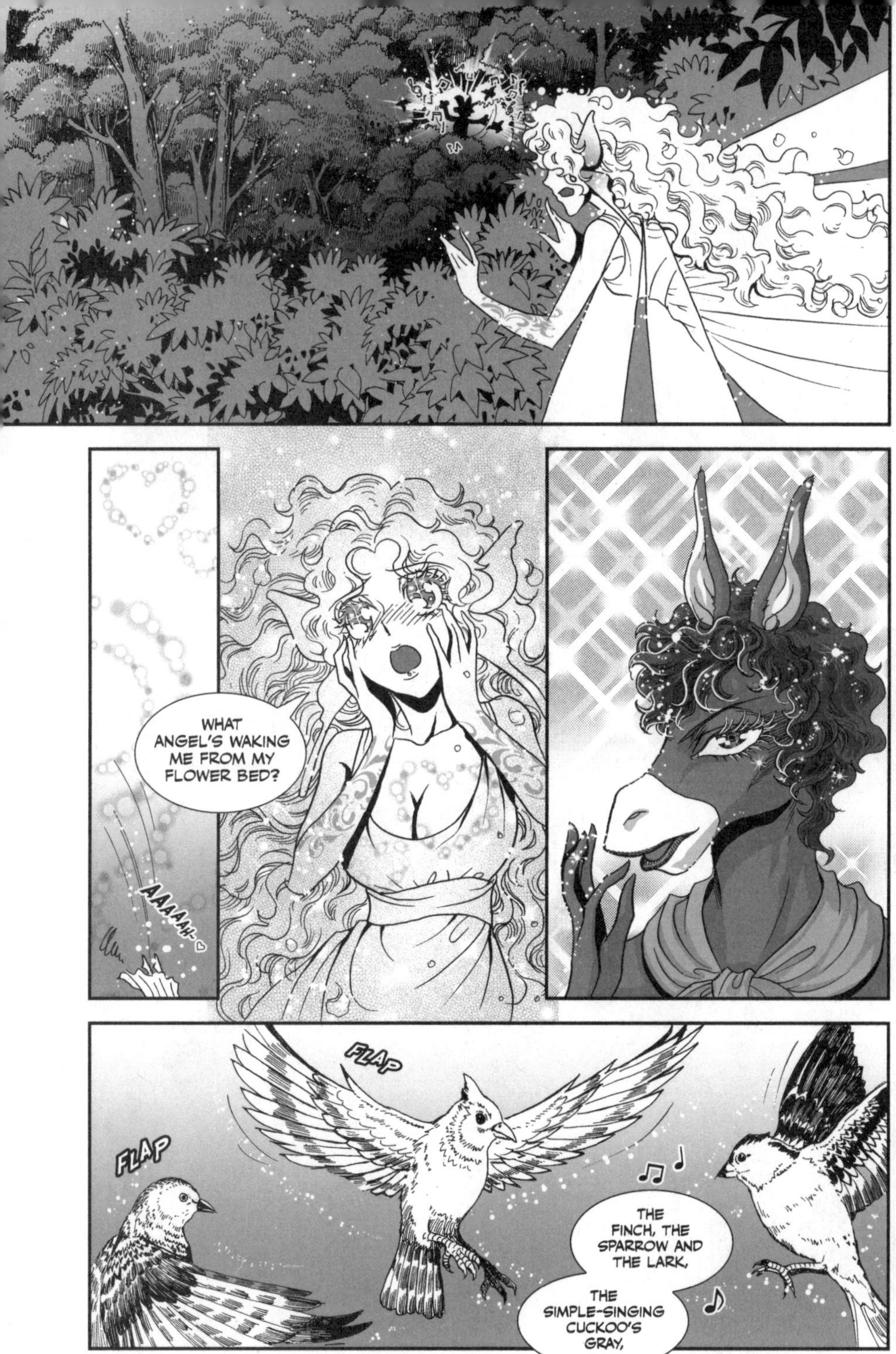
WHAT ANGEL'S WAKING ME FROM MY FLOWER BED?
AAAAAH-♡
THE FINCH, THE SPARROW AND THE LARK,
THE SIMPLE-SINGING CUCKOO'S GRAY,
FLAP
FLAP

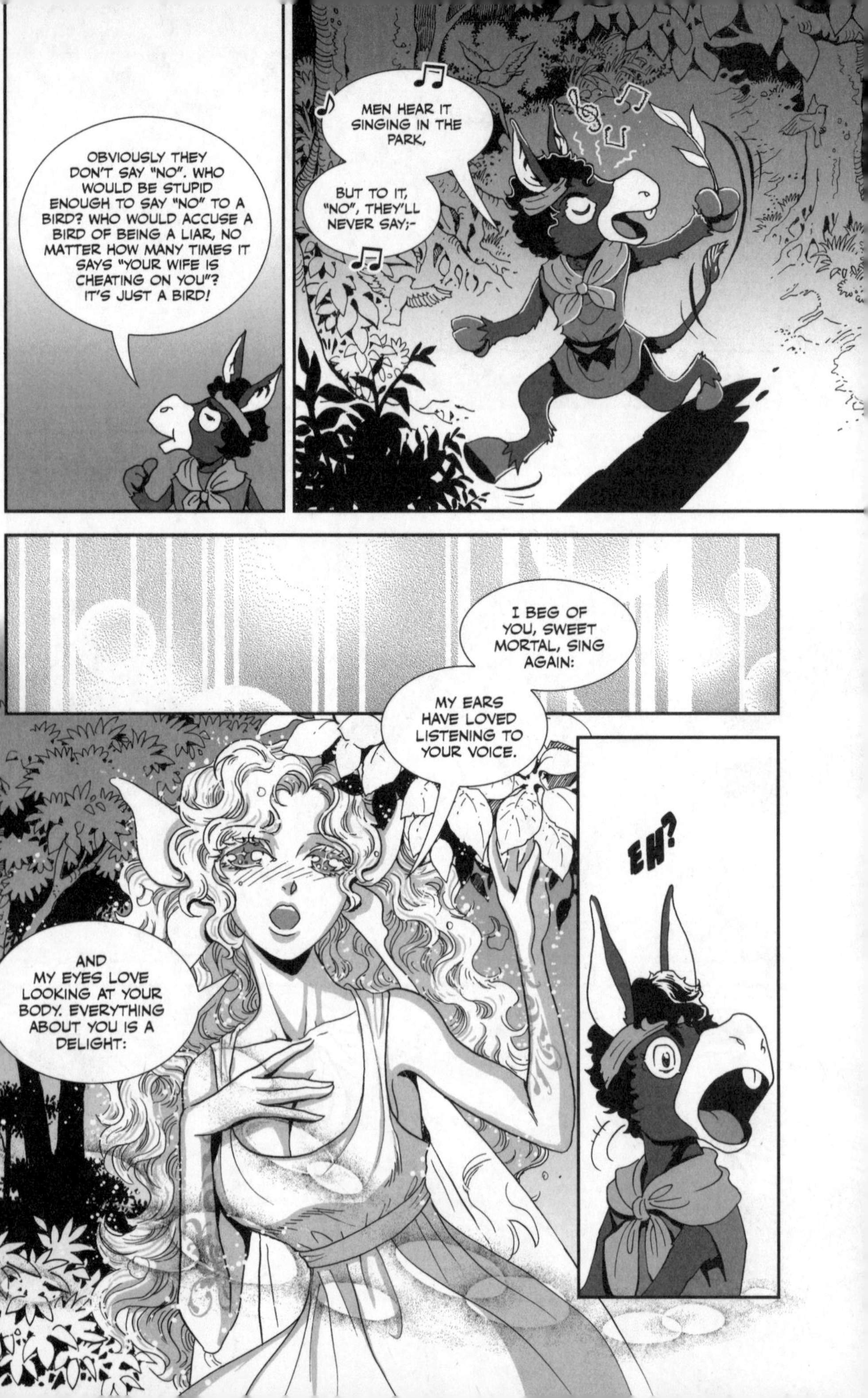
MEN HEAR IT SINGING IN THE PARK,
BUT TO IT, "NO", THEY'LL NEVER SAY;-
OBVIOUSLY THEY DON'T SAY "NO". WHO WOULD BE STUPID ENOUGH TO SAY "NO" TO A BIRD? WHO WOULD ACCUSE A BIRD OF BEING A LIAR, NO MATTER HOW MANY TIMES IT SAYS "YOUR WIFE IS CHEATING ON YOU"? IT'S JUST A BIRD!
I BEG OF YOU, SWEET MORTAL, SING AGAIN:
MY EARS HAVE LOVED LISTENING TO YOUR VOICE.
AND MY EYES LOVE LOOKING AT YOUR BODY. EVERYTHING ABOUT YOU IS A DELIGHT:
EH?

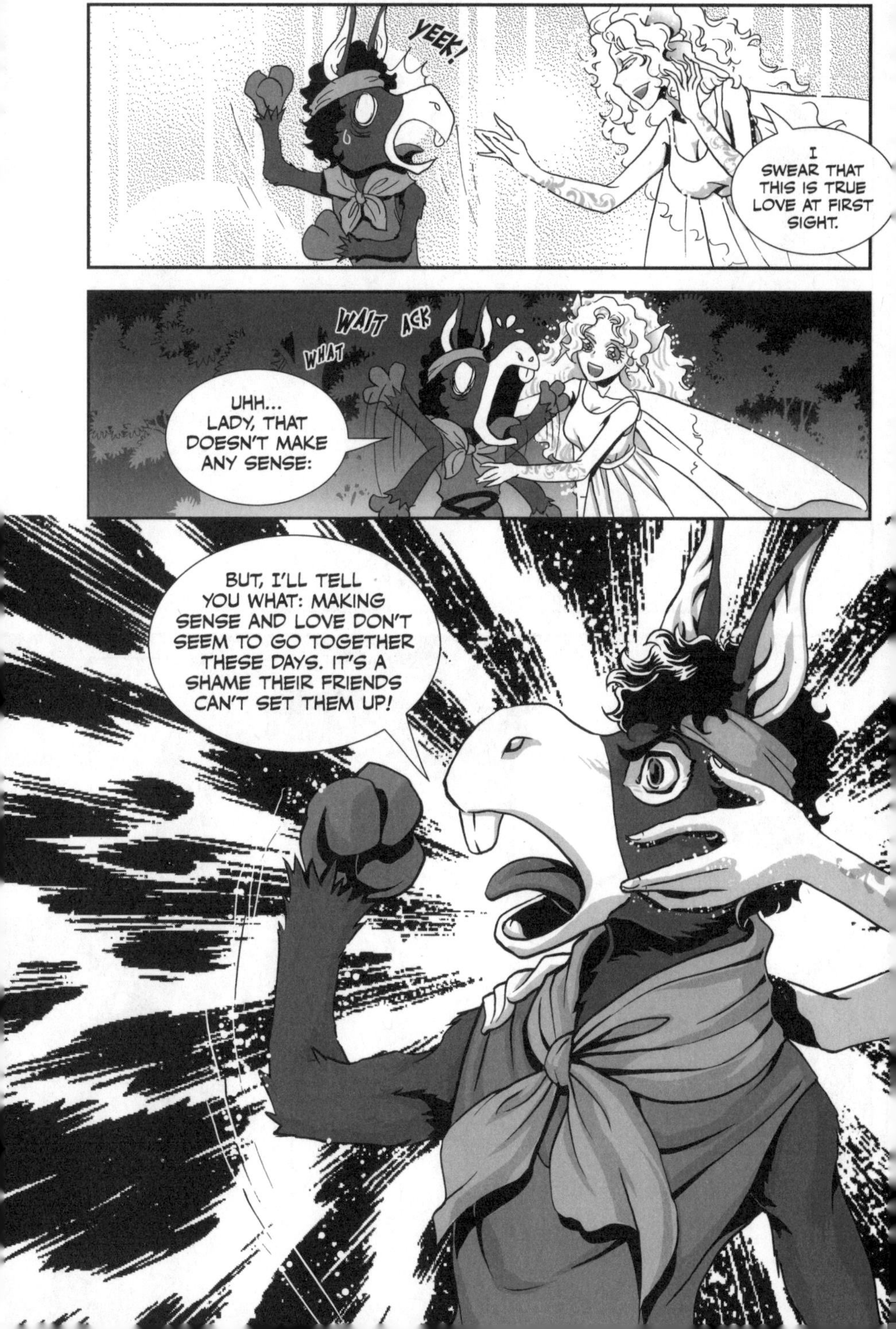
I SWEAR THAT THIS IS TRUE LOVE AT FIRST SIGHT.
YEEK!
ACK
WAIT
WHAT
UHH... LADY, THAT DOESN'T MAKE ANY SENSE:
BUT, I'LL TELL YOU WHAT: MAKING SENSE AND LOVE DON'T SEEM TO GO TOGETHER THESE DAYS. IT'S A SHAME THEIR FRIENDS CAN'T SET THEM UP!

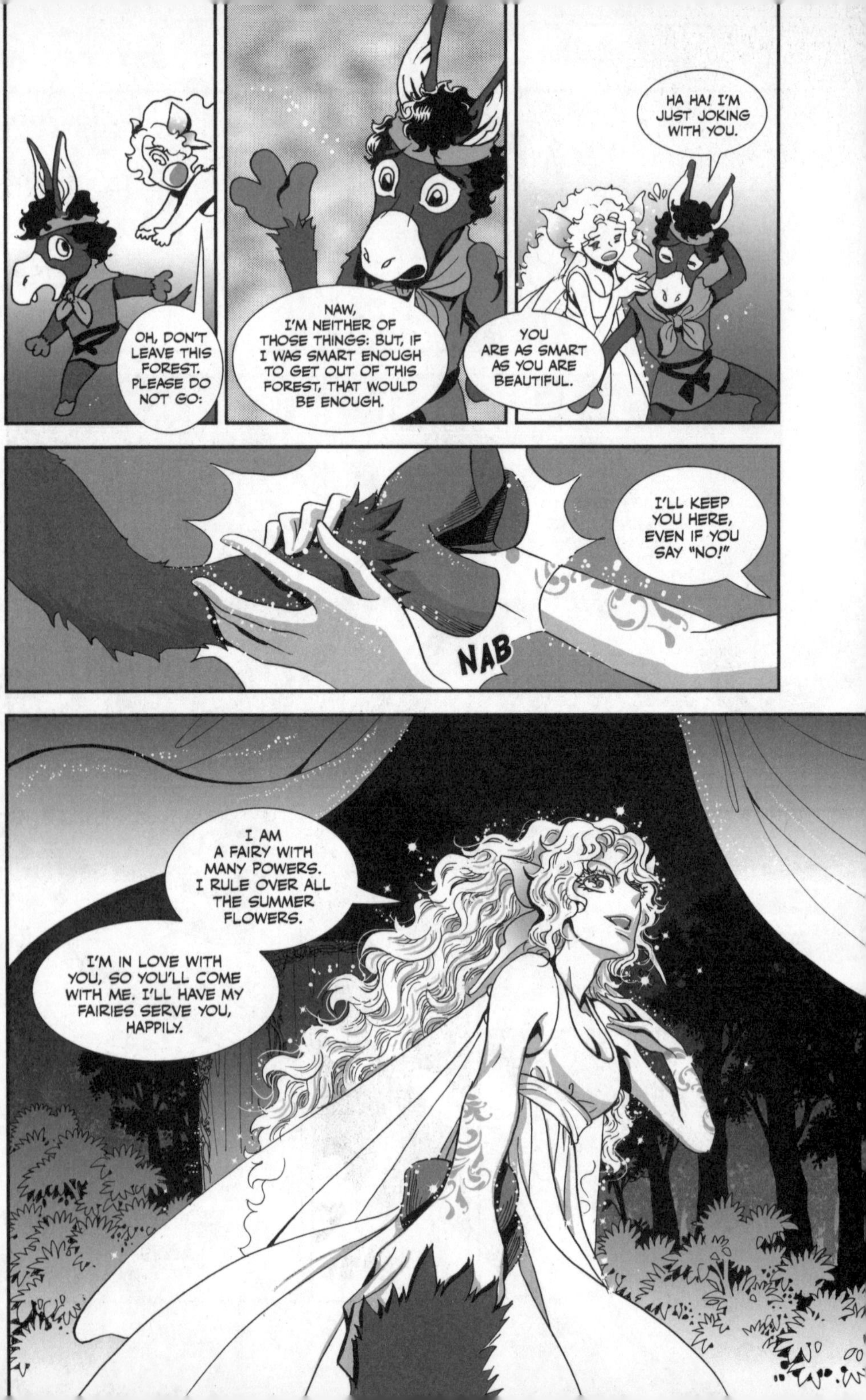
HA HA! I'M JUST JOKING WITH YOU.
YOU ARE AS SMART AS YOU ARE BEAUTIFUL.
NAW, I'M NEITHER OF THOSE THINGS: BUT, IF I WAS SMART ENOUGH TO GET OUT OF THIS FOREST, THAT WOULD BE ENOUGH.
OH, DON'T LEAVE THIS FOREST. PLEASE DO NOT GO:
I'LL KEEP YOU HERE, EVEN IF YOU SAY "NO!"
NAB
I AM A FAIRY WITH MANY POWERS. I RULE OVER ALL THE SUMMER FLOWERS.
I'M IN LOVE WITH YOU, SO YOU'LL COME WITH ME. I'LL HAVE MY FAIRIES SERVE YOU, HAPPILY.

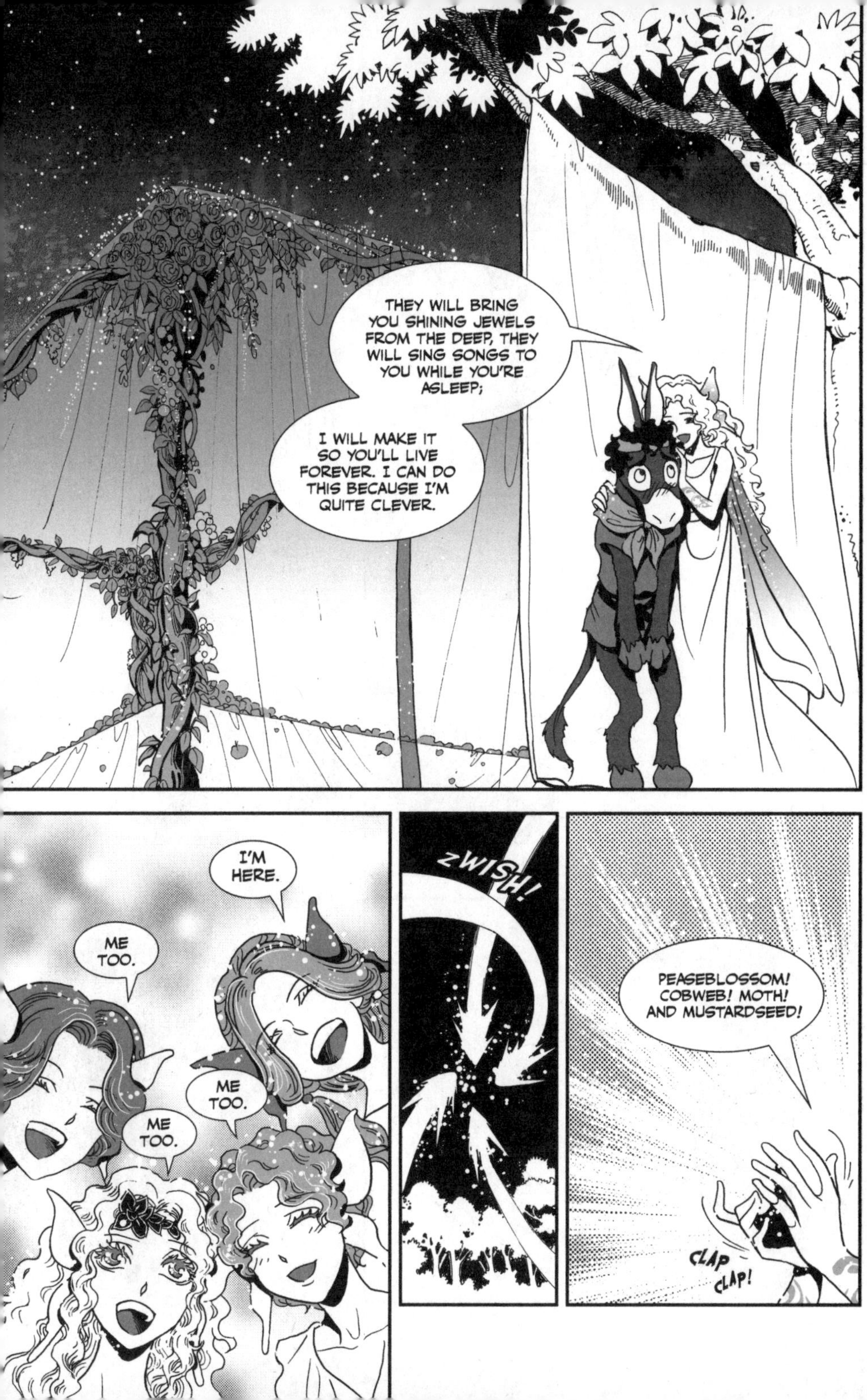
THEY WILL BRING YOU SHINING JEWELS FROM THE DEEP, THEY WILL SING SONGS TO YOU WHILE YOU'RE ASLEEP;
I WILL MAKE IT SO YOU'LL LIVE FOREVER. I CAN DO THIS BECAUSE I'M QUITE CLEVER.
PEASEBLOSSOM! COBWEB! MOTH! AND MUSTARDSEED!
CLAP
CLAP!
ZWISH!
I'M HERE.
ME TOO.
ME TOO.
ME TOO.

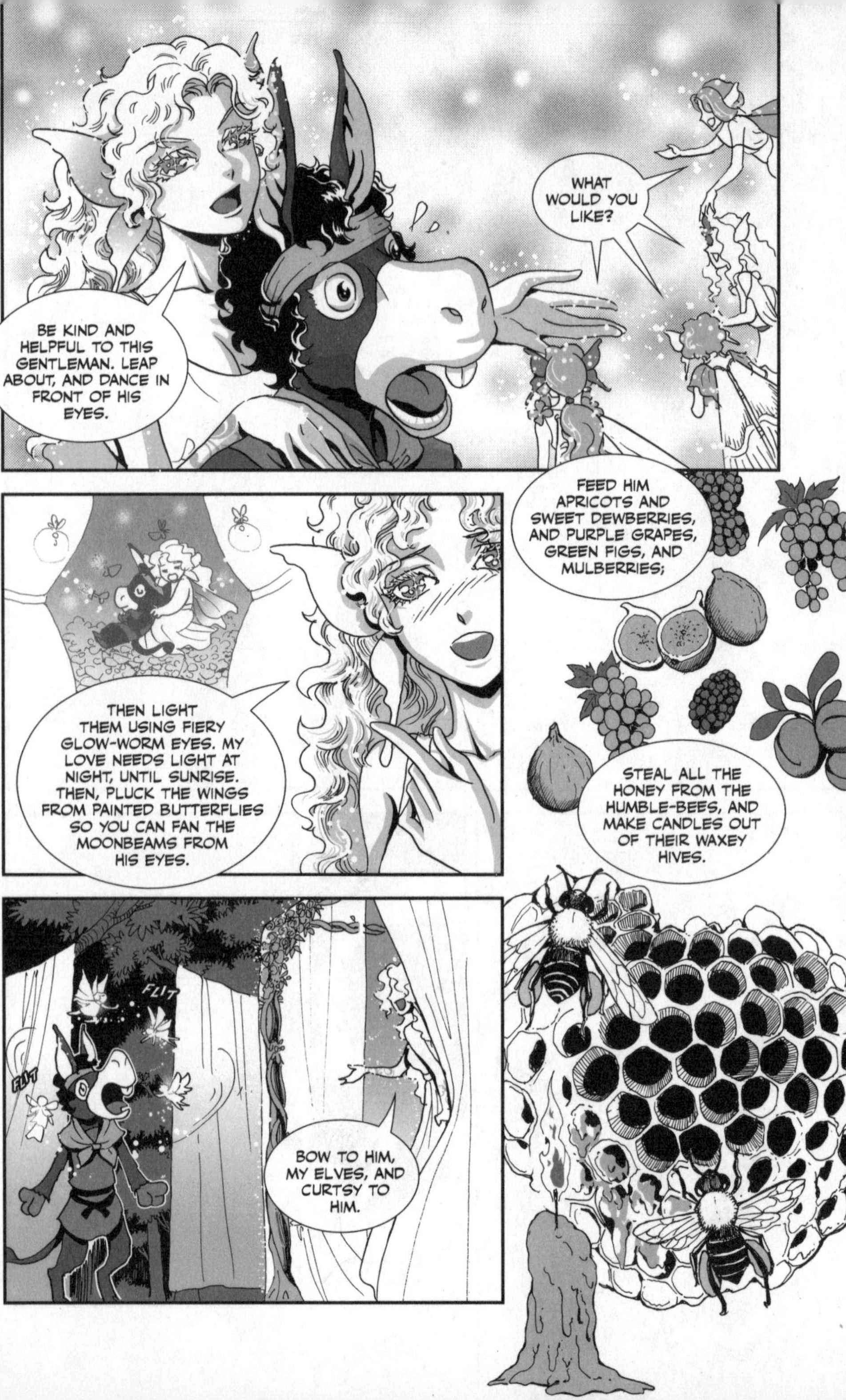
WHAT WOULD YOU LIKE?
BE KIND AND HELPFUL TO THIS GENTLEMAN. LEAP ABOUT, AND DANCE IN FRONT OF HIS EYES.
FEED HIM APRICOTS AND SWEET DEWBERRIES, AND PURPLE GRAPES, GREEN FIGS, AND MULBERRIES;
STEAL ALL THE HONEY FROM THE HUMBLE-BEES, AND MAKE CANDLES OUT OF THEIR WAXEY HIVES.
THEN LIGHT THEM USING FIERY GLOW-WORM EYES. MY LOVE NEEDS LIGHT AT NIGHT, UNTIL SUNRISE. THEN, PLUCK THE WINGS FROM PAINTED BUTTERFLIES SO YOU CAN FAN THE MOONBEAMS FROM HIS EYES.
FLIT
FLIT
BOW TO HIM, MY ELVES, AND CURTSY TO HIM.

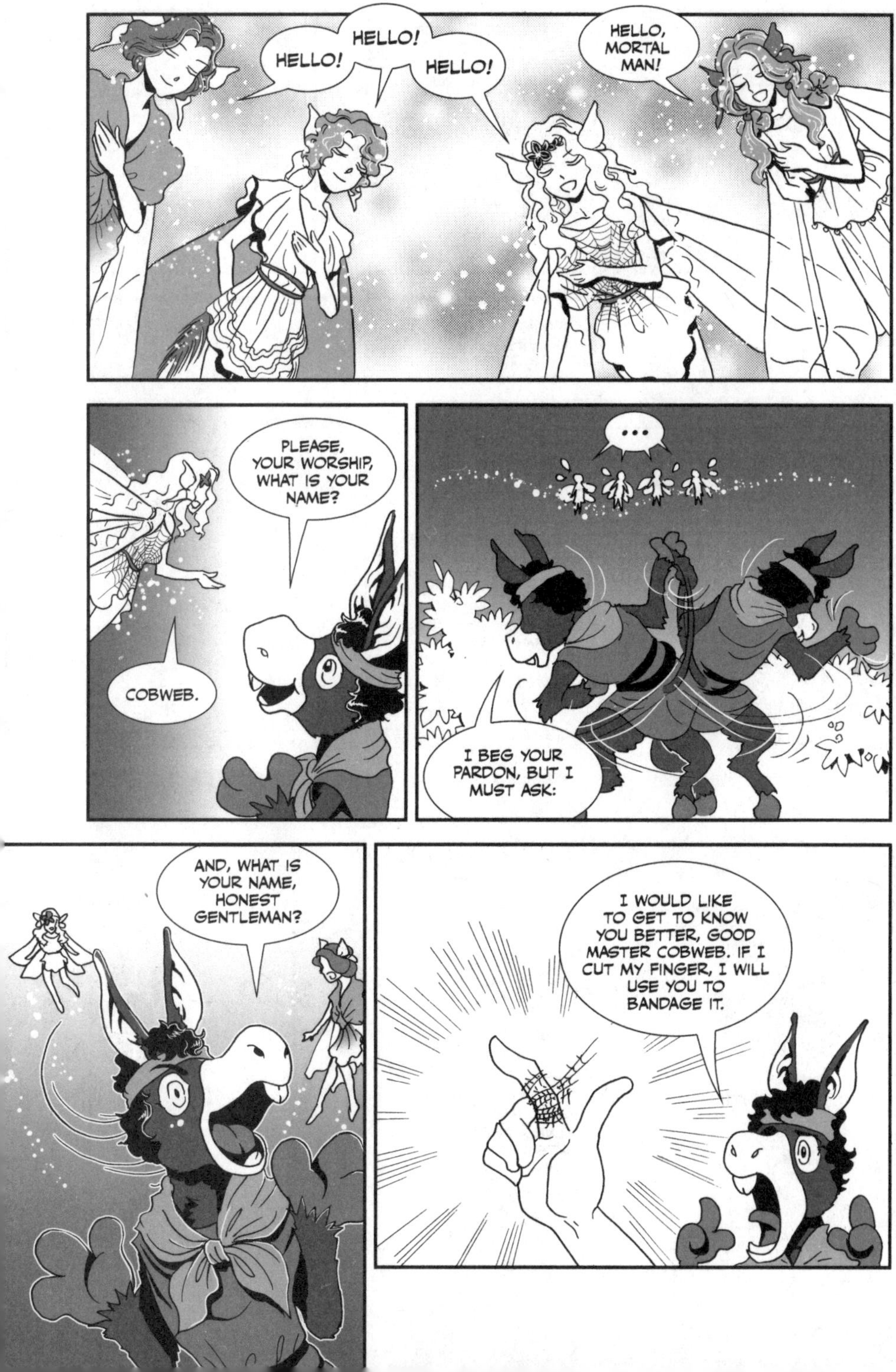
HELLO!
HELLO!
HELLO!
HELLO, MORTAL MAN!
PLEASE, YOUR WORSHIP, WHAT IS YOUR NAME?
COBWEB.
...
I BEG YOUR PARDON, BUT I MUST ASK:
AND, WHAT IS YOUR NAME, HONEST GENTLEMAN?
I WOULD LIKE TO GET TO KNOW YOU BETTER, GOOD MASTER COBWEB. IF I CUT MY FINGER, I WILL USE YOU TO BANDAGE IT.

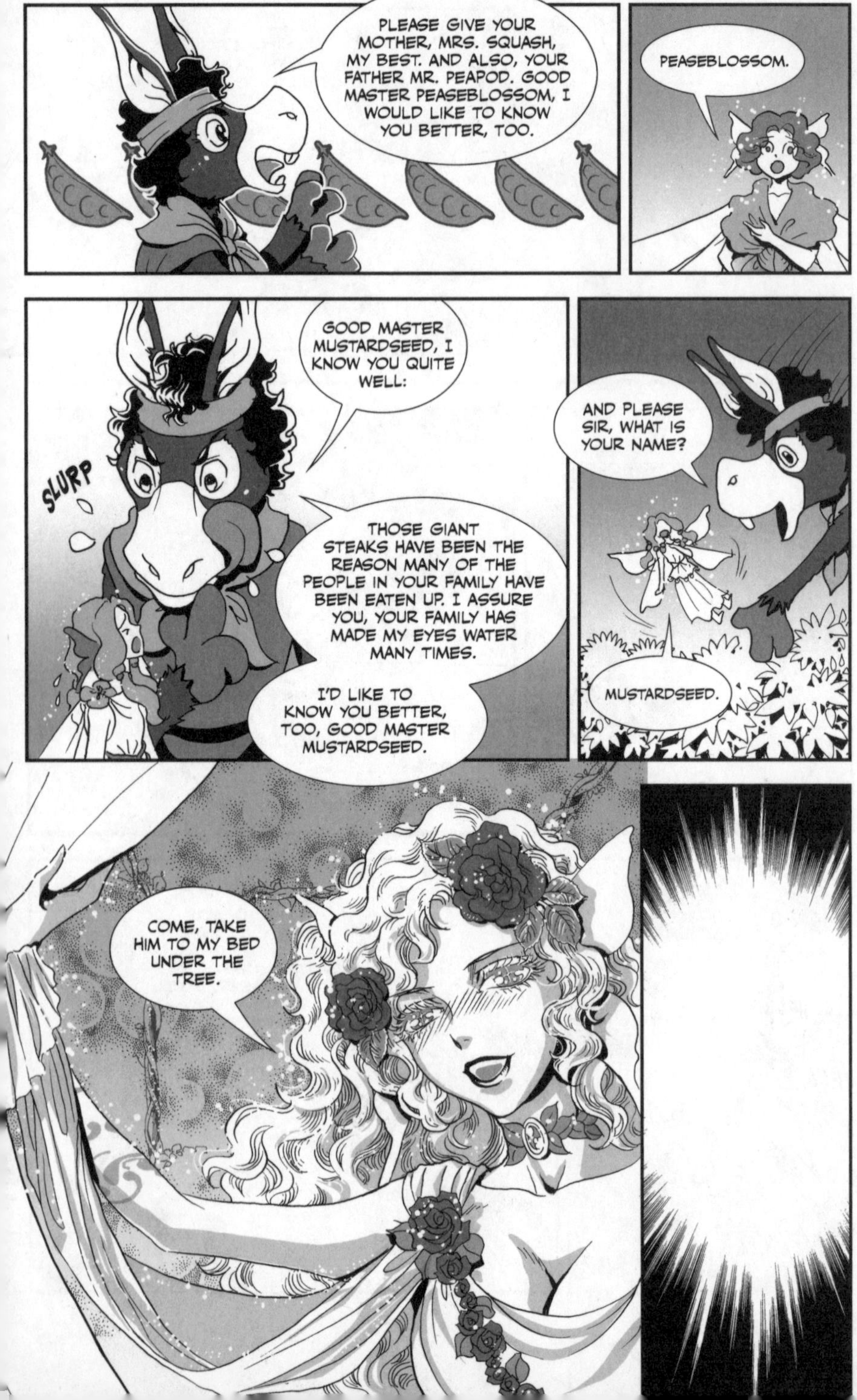
PEASEBLOSSOM.
PLEASE GIVE YOUR MOTHER, MRS. SQUASH, MY BEST. AND ALSO, YOUR FATHER MR. PEAPOD. GOOD MASTER PEASEBLOSSOM, I WOULD LIKE TO KNOW YOU BETTER, TOO.
AND PLEASE SIR, WHAT IS YOUR NAME?
MUSTARDSEED.
GOOD MASTER MUSTARDSEED, I KNOW YOU QUITE WELL:
SLURP
THOSE GIANT STEAKS HAVE BEEN THE REASON MANY OF THE PEOPLE IN YOUR FAMILY HAVE BEEN EATEN UP. I ASSURE YOU, YOUR FAMILY HAS MADE MY EYES WATER MANY TIMES.
I'D LIKE TO KNOW YOU BETTER, TOO, GOOD MASTER MUSTARDSEED.
COME, TAKE HIM TO MY BED UNDER THE TREE.

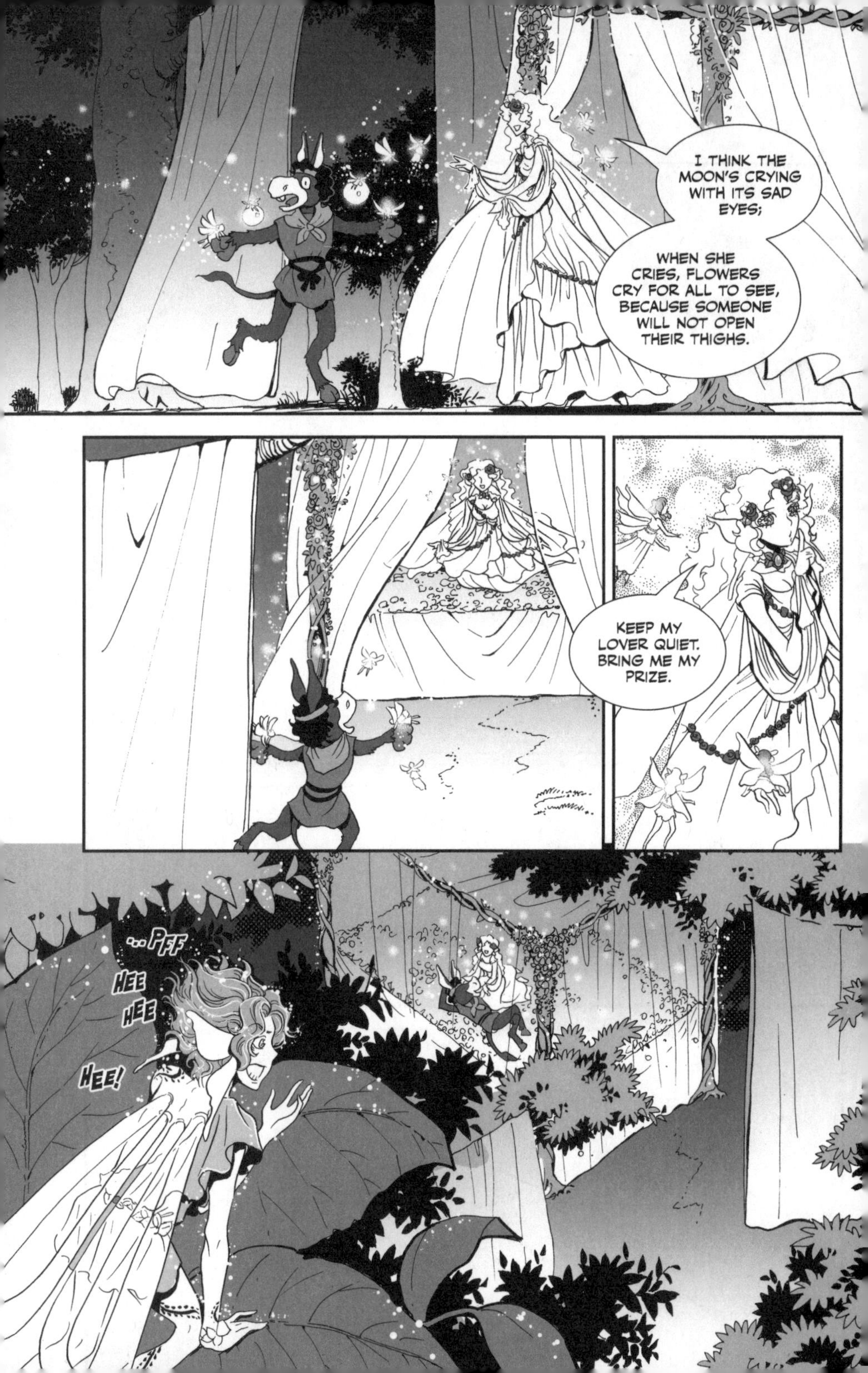
I THINK THE MOON'S CRYING WITH ITS SAD EYES;
WHEN SHE CRIES, FLOWERS CRY FOR ALL TO SEE, BECAUSE SOMEONE WILL NOT OPEN THEIR THIGHS.
KEEP MY LOVER QUIET. BRING ME MY PRIZE.
...PFF
HEE
HEE
HEE!

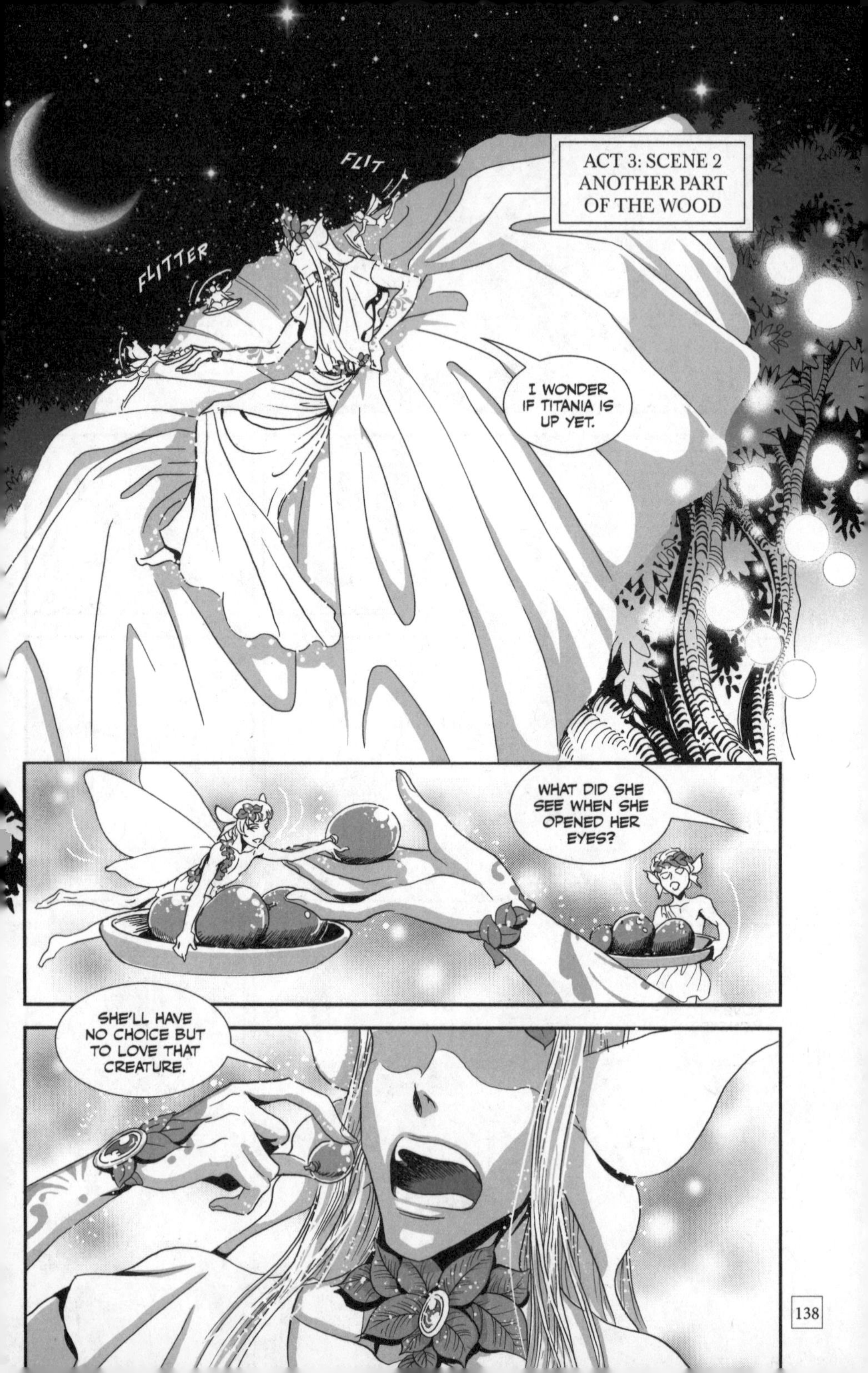
ACT 3: SCENE 2
ANOTHER PART
OF THE WOOD
FLIT
FLITTER
I WONDER IF TITANIA IS UP YET.
WHAT DID SHE SEE WHEN SHE OPENED HER EYES?
SHE'LL HAVE NO CHOICE BUT TO LOVE THAT CREATURE.

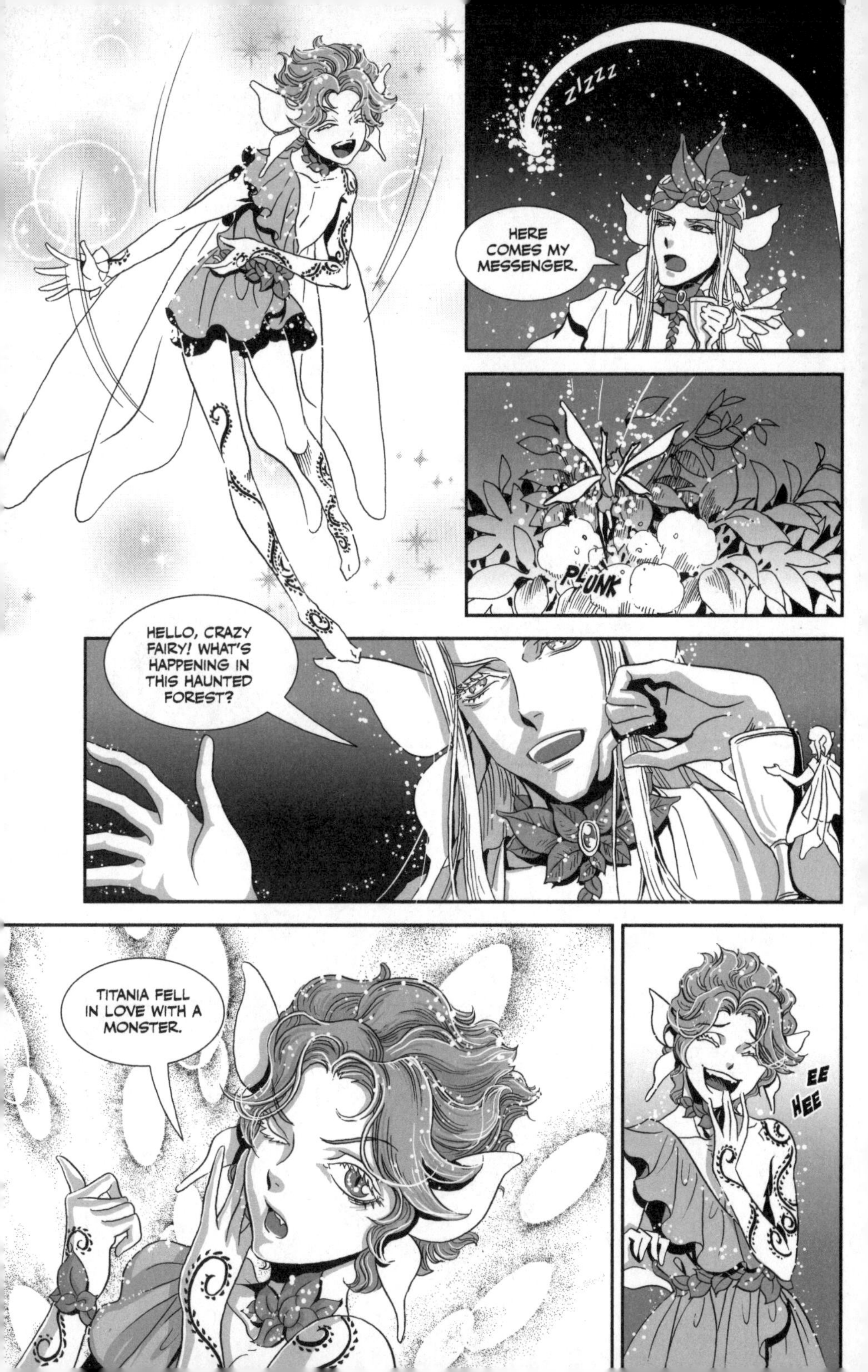
ZIZZZ
HERE COMES MY MESSENGER.
PLUNK
HELLO, CRAZY FAIRY! WHAT'S HAPPENING IN THIS HAUNTED FOREST?
EE HEE
TITANIA FELL IN LOVE WITH A MONSTER.

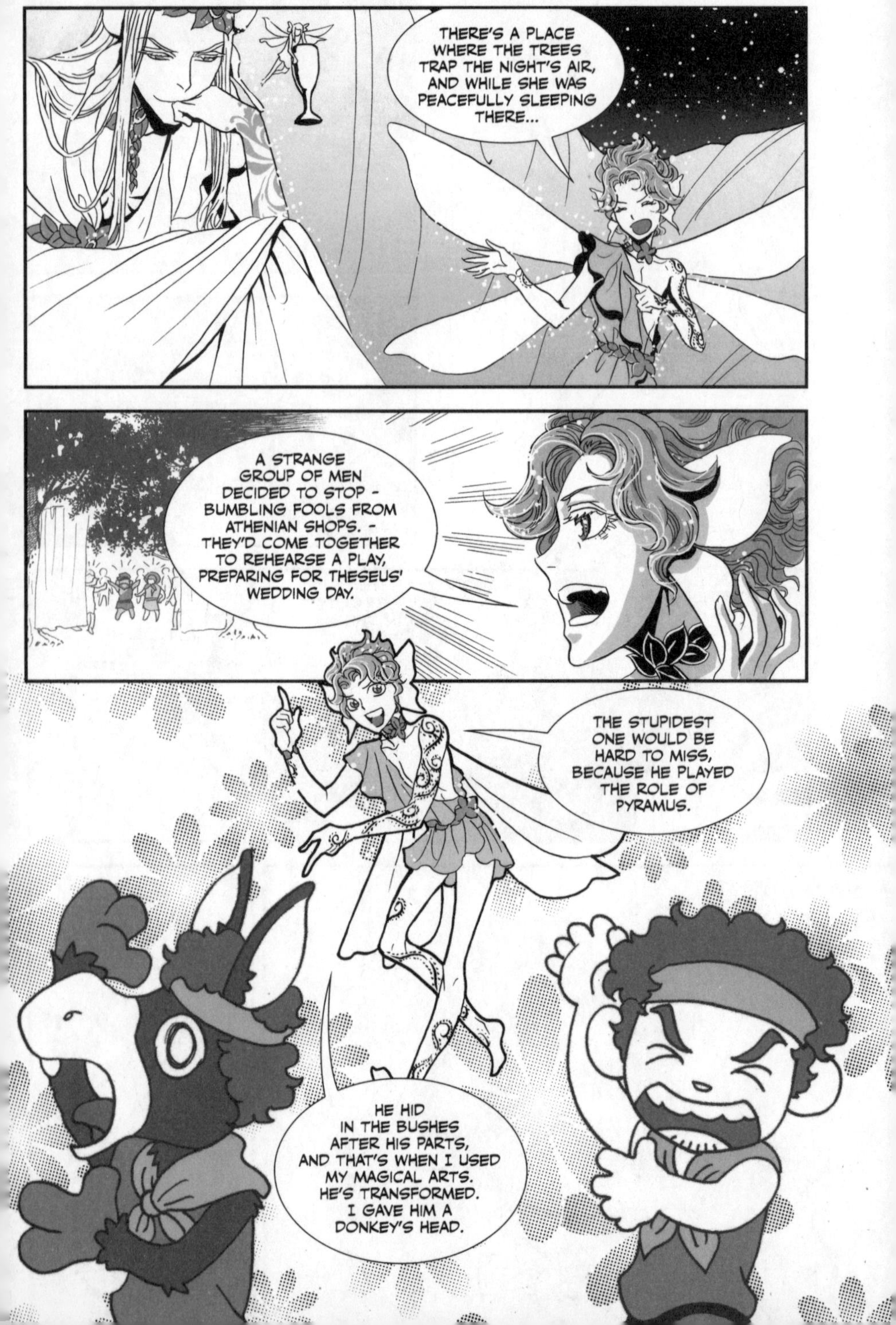
THERE'S A PLACE WHERE THE TREES TRAP THE NIGHT'S AIR, AND WHILE SHE WAS PEACEFULLY SLEEPING THERE...
A STRANGE GROUP OF MEN DECIDED TO STOP - BUMBLING FOOLS FROM ATHENIAN SHOPS. - THEY'D COME TOGETHER TO REHEARSE A PLAY, PREPARING FOR THESEUS' WEDDING DAY.
THE STUPIDEST ONE WOULD BE HARD TO MISS, BECAUSE HE PLAYED THE ROLE OF PYRAMUS.
HE HID IN THE BUSHES AFTER HIS PARTS, AND THAT'S WHEN I USED MY MAGICAL ARTS. HE'S TRANSFORMED. I GAVE HIM A DONKEY'S HEAD.

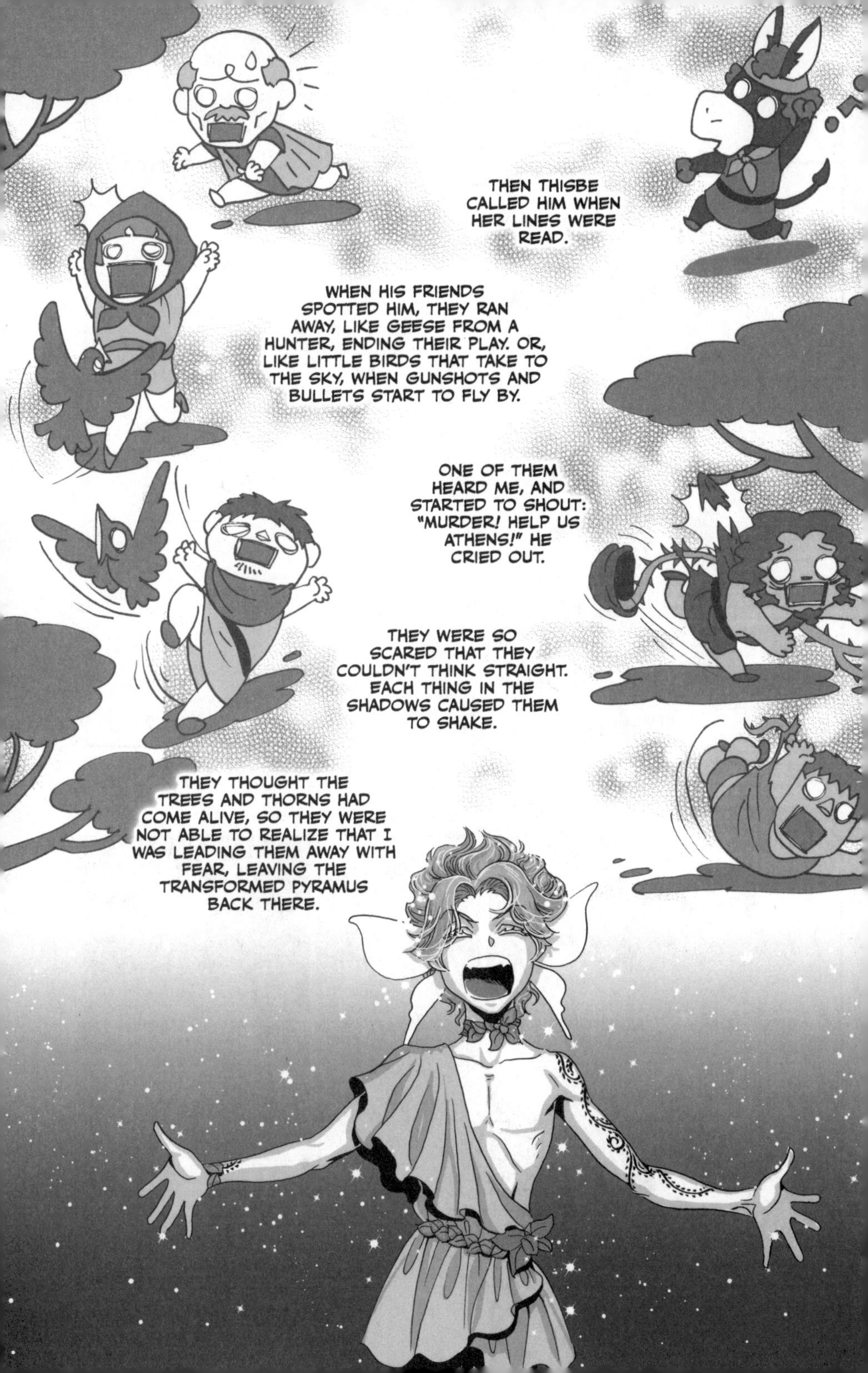
THEN THISBE CALLED HIM WHEN HER LINES WERE READ.
WHEN HIS FRIENDS SPOTTED HIM, THEY RAN AWAY, LIKE GEESE FROM A HUNTER, ENDING THEIR PLAY. OR, LIKE LITTLE BIRDS THAT TAKE TO THE SKY, WHEN GUNSHOTS AND BULLETS START TO FLY BY.
ONE OF THEM HEARD ME, AND STARTED TO SHOUT: "MURDER! HELP US ATHENS!" HE CRIED OUT.
THEY WERE SO SCARED THAT THEY COULDN'T THINK STRAIGHT. EACH THING IN THE SHADOWS CAUSED THEM TO SHAKE.
THEY THOUGHT THE TREES AND THORNS HAD COME ALIVE, SO THEY WERE NOT ABLE TO REALIZE THAT I WAS LEADING THEM AWAY WITH FEAR, LEAVING THE TRANSFORMED PYRAMUS BACK THERE.

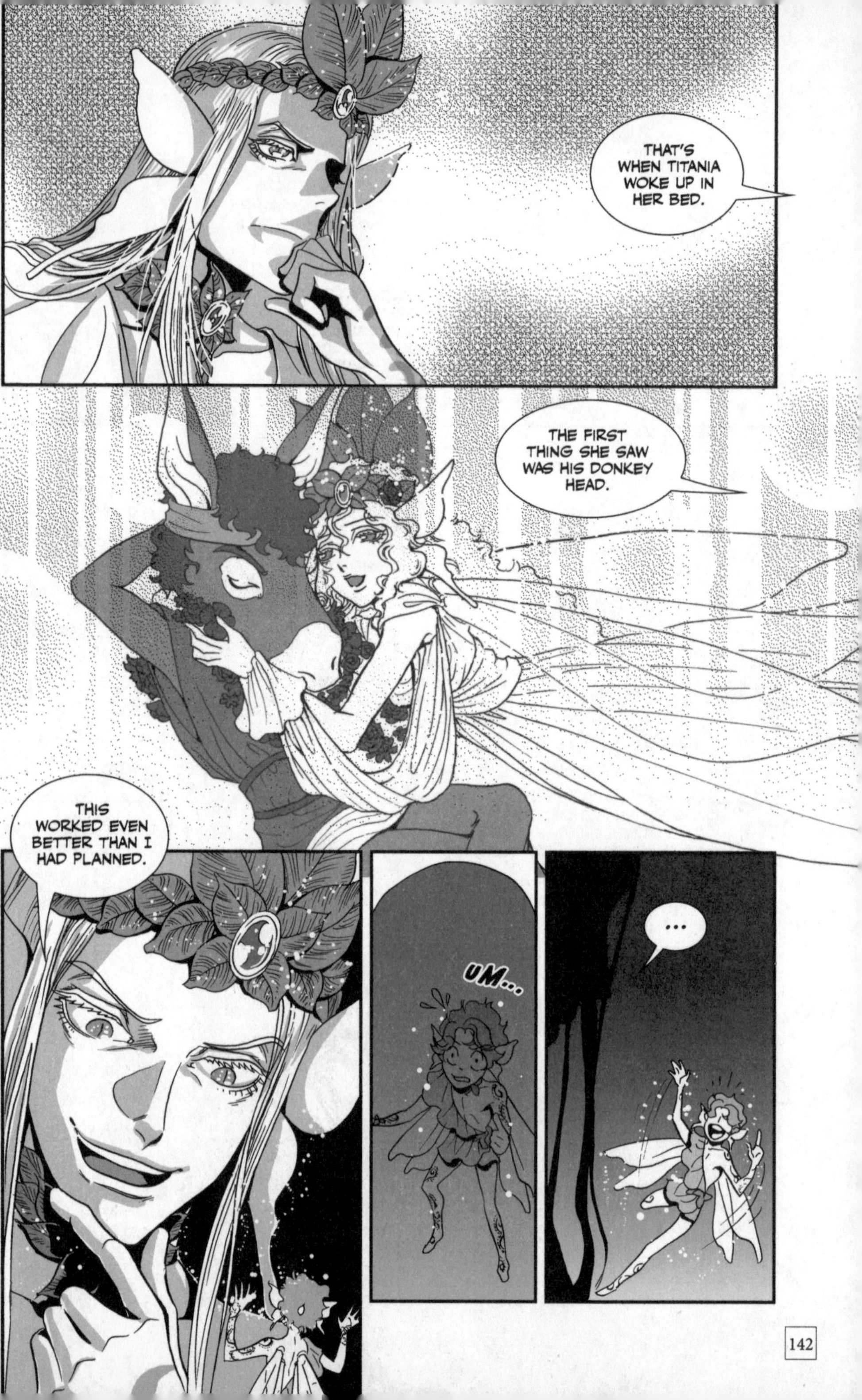
THAT'S WHEN TITANIA WOKE UP IN HER BED.
THE FIRST THING SHE SAW WAS HIS DONKEY HEAD.
...
UM...
THIS WORKED EVEN BETTER THAN I HAD PLANNED.

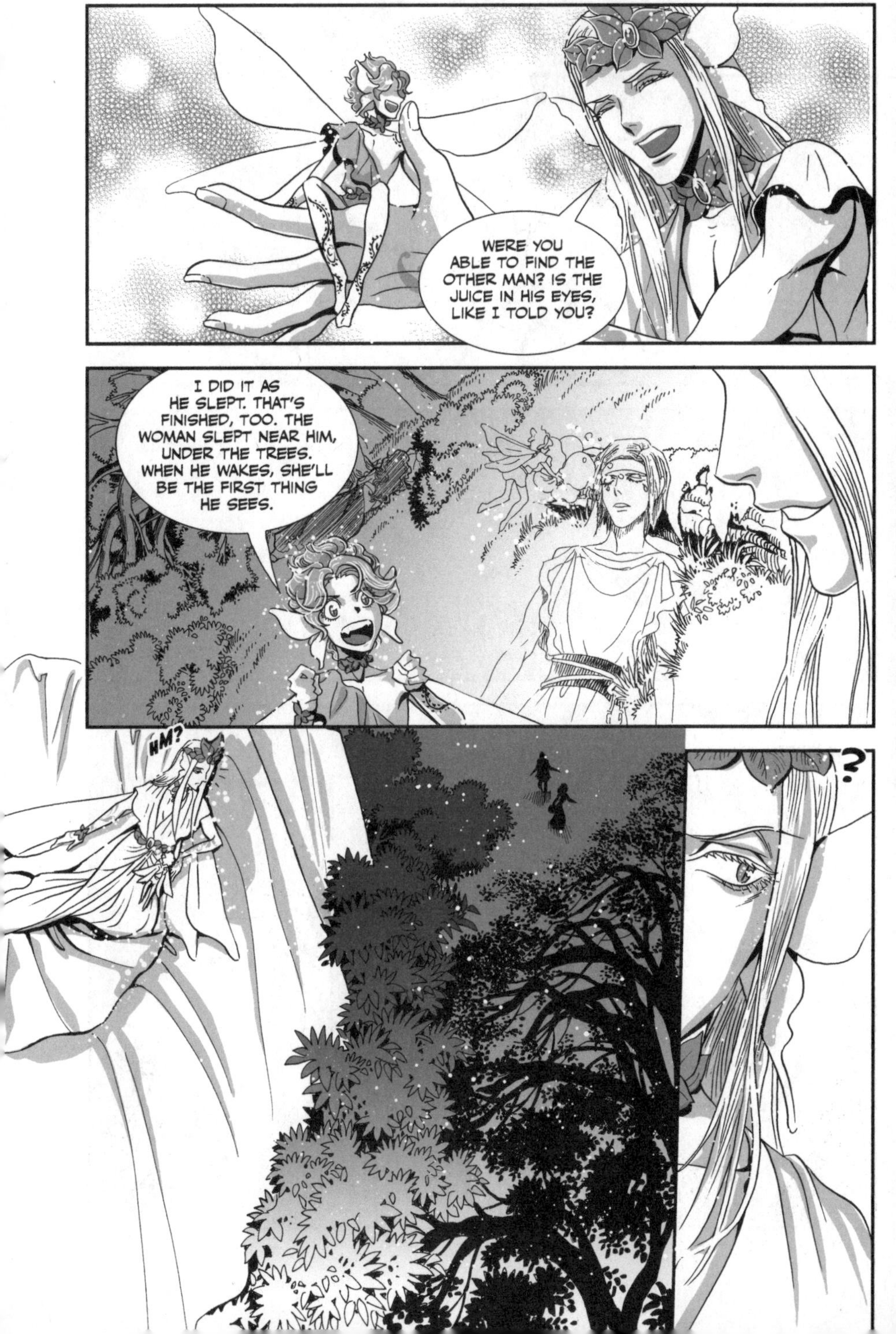
WERE YOU ABLE TO FIND THE OTHER MAN? IS THE JUICE IN HIS EYES, LIKE I TOLD YOU?
I DID IT AS HE SLEPT. THAT'S FINISHED, TOO. THE WOMAN SLEPT NEAR HIM, UNDER THE TREES. WHEN HE WAKES, SHE'LL BE THE FIRST THING HE SEES.
?
HM?

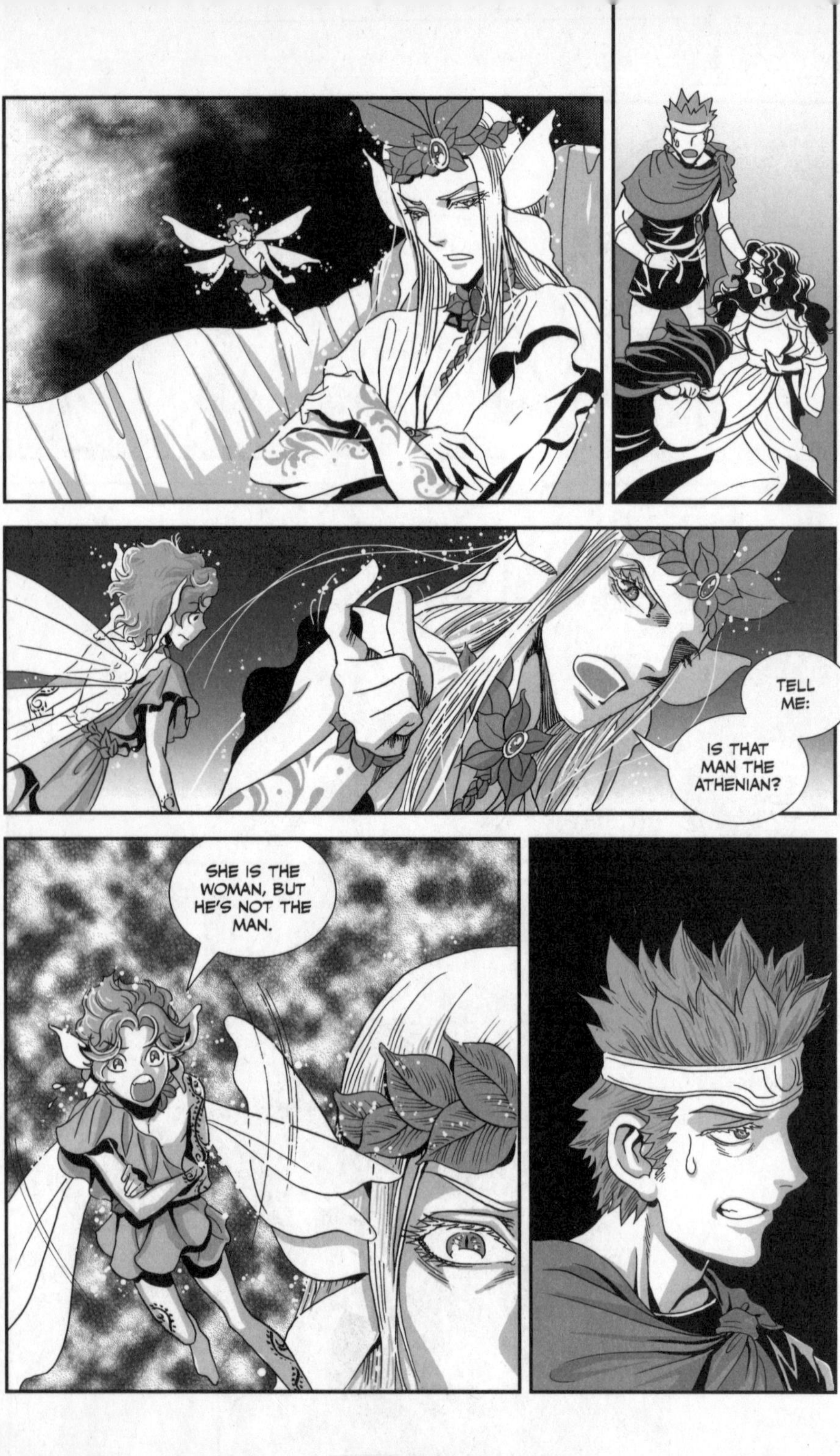
TELL ME:
IS THAT MAN THE ATHENIAN?
SHE IS THE WOMAN, BUT HE'S NOT THE MAN.

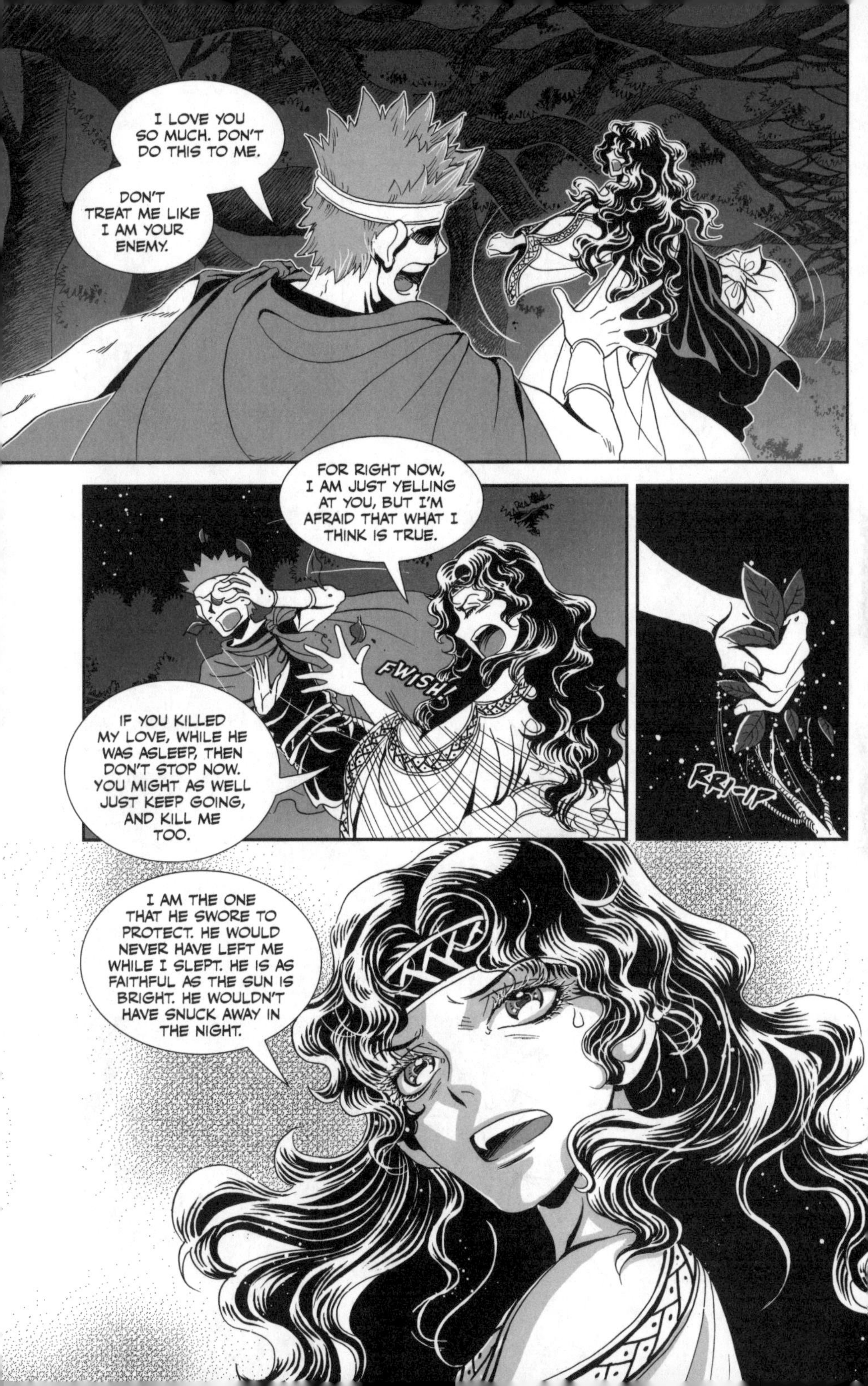
I LOVE YOU SO MUCH. DON'T DO THIS TO ME.
DON'T TREAT ME LIKE I AM YOUR ENEMY.
RRI-IP
FOR RIGHT NOW, I AM JUST YELLING AT YOU, BUT I'M AFRAID THAT WHAT I THINK IS TRUE.
FWISH!
IF YOU KILLED MY LOVE, WHILE HE WAS ASLEEP, THEN DON'T STOP NOW. YOU MIGHT AS WELL JUST KEEP GOING, AND KILL ME TOO.
I AM THE ONE THAT HE SWORE TO PROTECT. HE WOULD NEVER HAVE LEFT ME WHILE I SLEPT. HE IS AS FAITHFUL AS THE SUN IS BRIGHT. HE WOULDN'T HAVE SNUCK AWAY IN THE NIGHT.

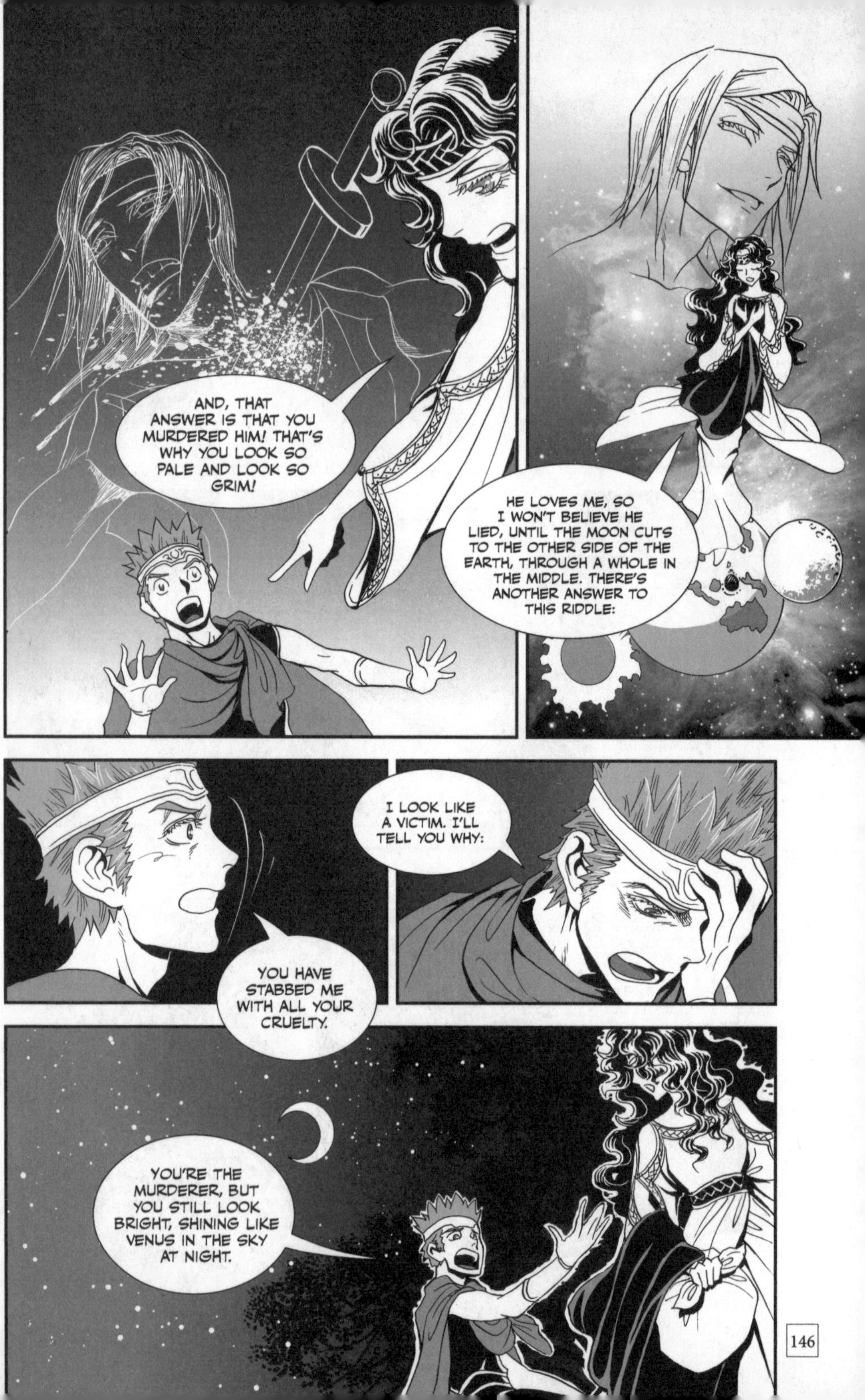
HE LOVES ME, SO I WON'T BELIEVE HE LIED, UNTIL THE MOON CUTS TO THE OTHER SIDE OF THE EARTH, THROUGH A WHOLE IN THE MIDDLE. THERE'S ANOTHER ANSWER TO THIS RIDDLE:
AND, THAT ANSWER IS THAT YOU MURDERED HIM! THAT'S WHY YOU LOOK SO PALE AND LOOK SO GRIM!
I LOOK LIKE A VICTIM. I'LL TELL YOU WHY:
YOU HAVE STABBED ME WITH ALL YOUR CRUELTY.
YOU'RE THE MURDERER, BUT YOU STILL LOOK BRIGHT, SHINING LIKE VENUS IN THE SKY AT NIGHT.

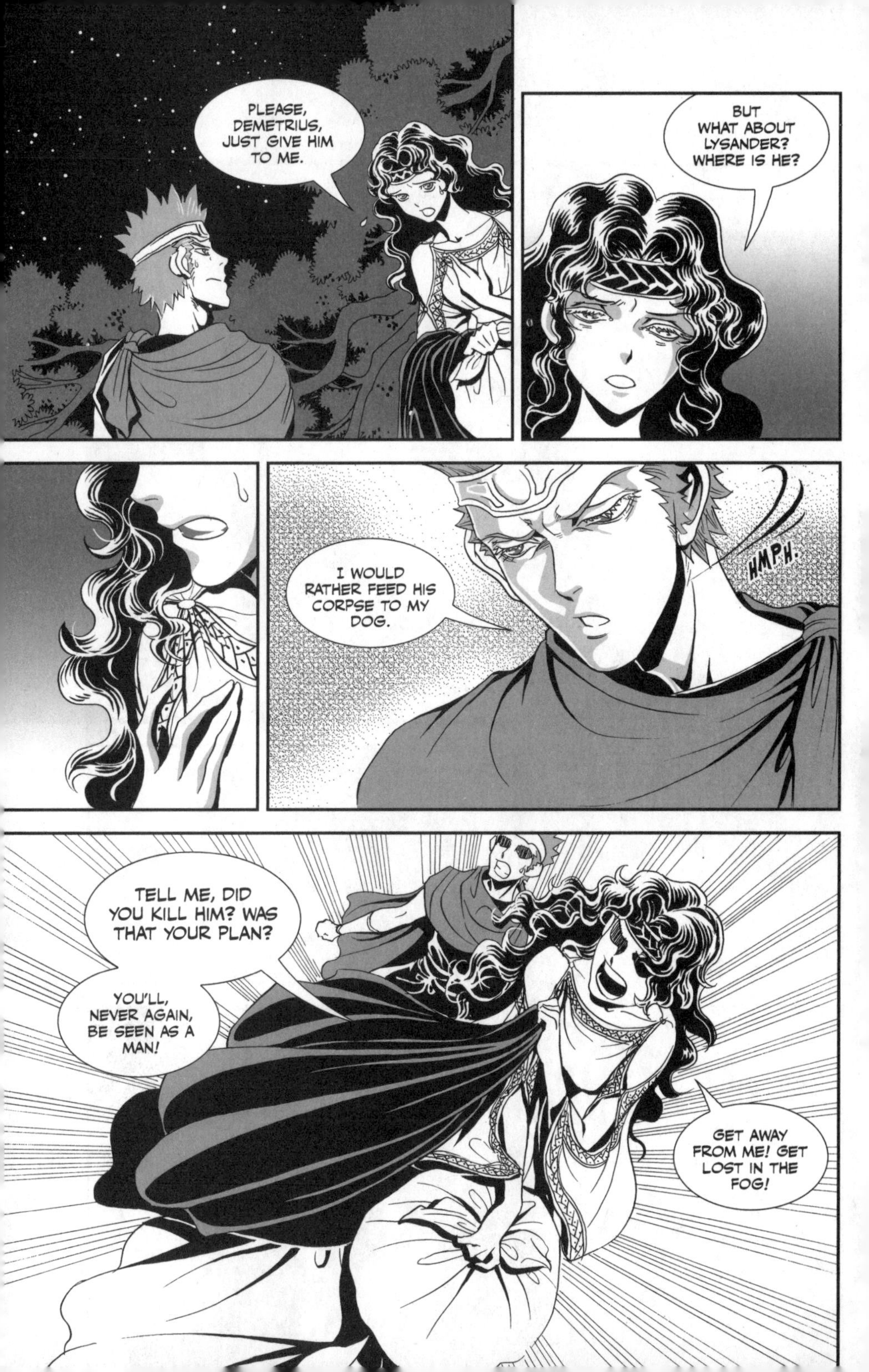
BUT WHAT ABOUT LYSANDER? WHERE IS HE?
PLEASE, DEMETRIUS, JUST GIVE HIM TO ME.
HMPH.
I WOULD RATHER FEED HIS CORPSE TO MY DOG.
TELL ME, DID YOU KILL HIM? WAS THAT YOUR PLAN?
YOU'LL, NEVER AGAIN, BE SEEN AS A MAN!
GET AWAY FROM ME! GET LOST IN THE FOG!

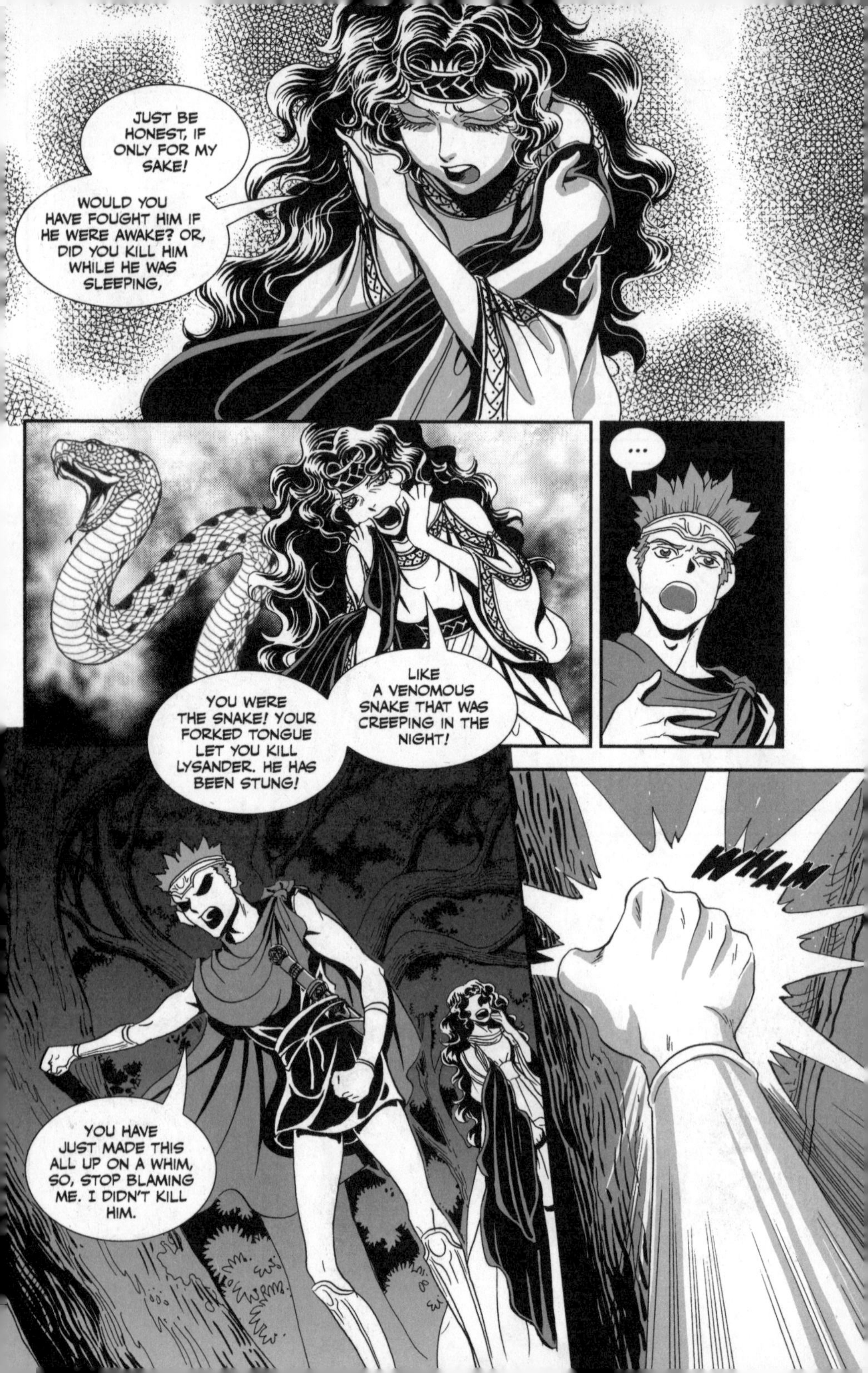
JUST BE HONEST, IF ONLY FOR MY SAKE!
WOULD YOU HAVE FOUGHT HIM IF HE WERE AWAKE? OR, DID YOU KILL HIM WHILE HE WAS SLEEPING,
LIKE A VENOMOUS SNAKE THAT WAS CREEPING IN THE NIGHT!
YOU WERE THE SNAKE! YOUR FORKED TONGUE LET YOU KILL LYSANDER. HE HAS BEEN STUNG!
...
YOU HAVE JUST MADE THIS ALL UP ON A WHIM, SO, STOP BLAMING ME. I DIDN'T KILL HIM.
WHAM

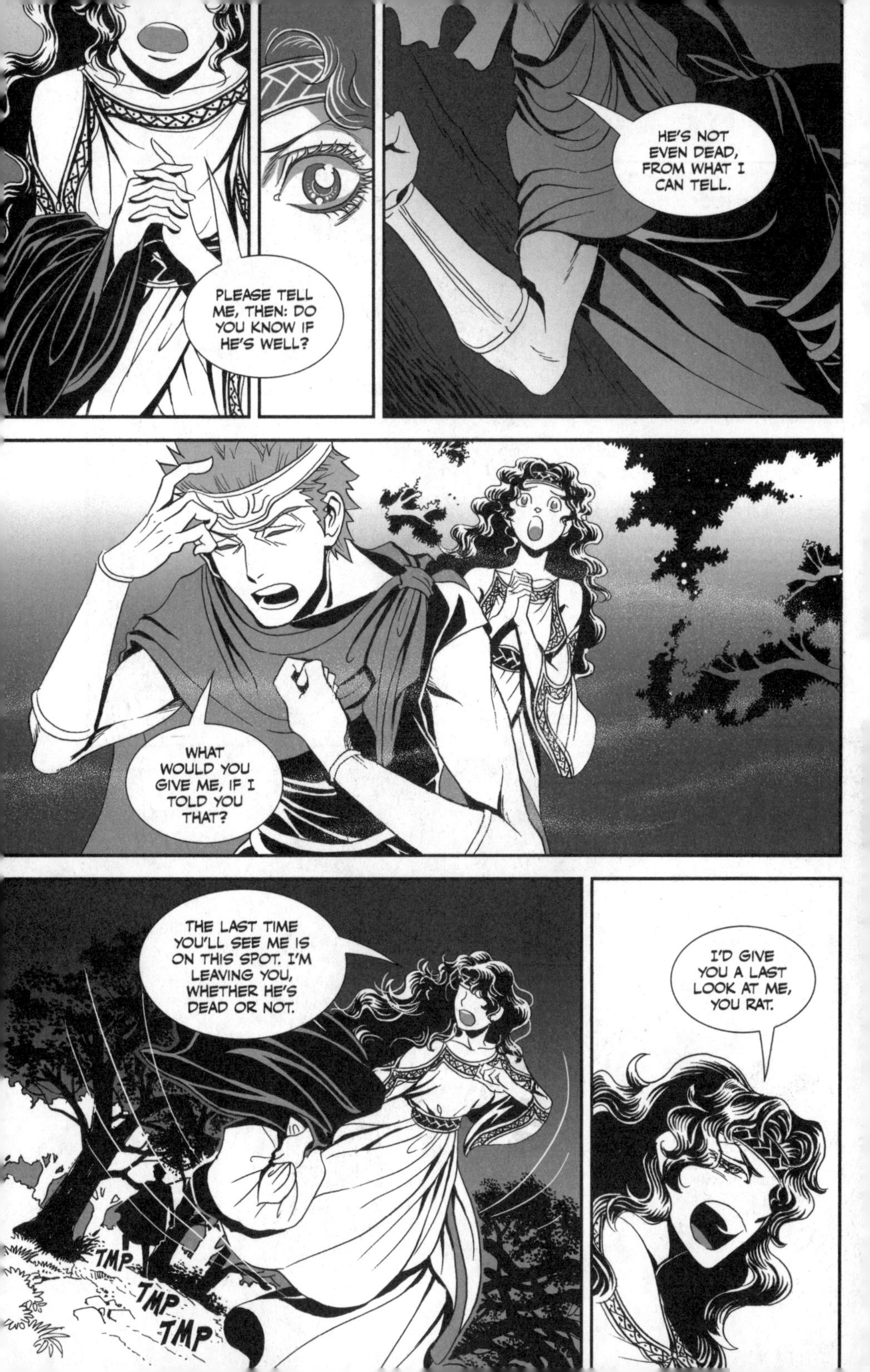
HE'S NOT EVEN DEAD, FROM WHAT I CAN TELL.
PLEASE TELL ME, THEN: DO YOU KNOW IF HE'S WELL?
WHAT WOULD YOU GIVE ME, IF I TOLD YOU THAT?
I'D GIVE YOU A LAST LOOK AT ME, YOU RAT.
THE LAST TIME YOU'LL SEE ME IS ON THIS SPOT. I'M LEAVING YOU, WHETHER HE'S DEAD OR NOT.
TMP
TMP
TMP

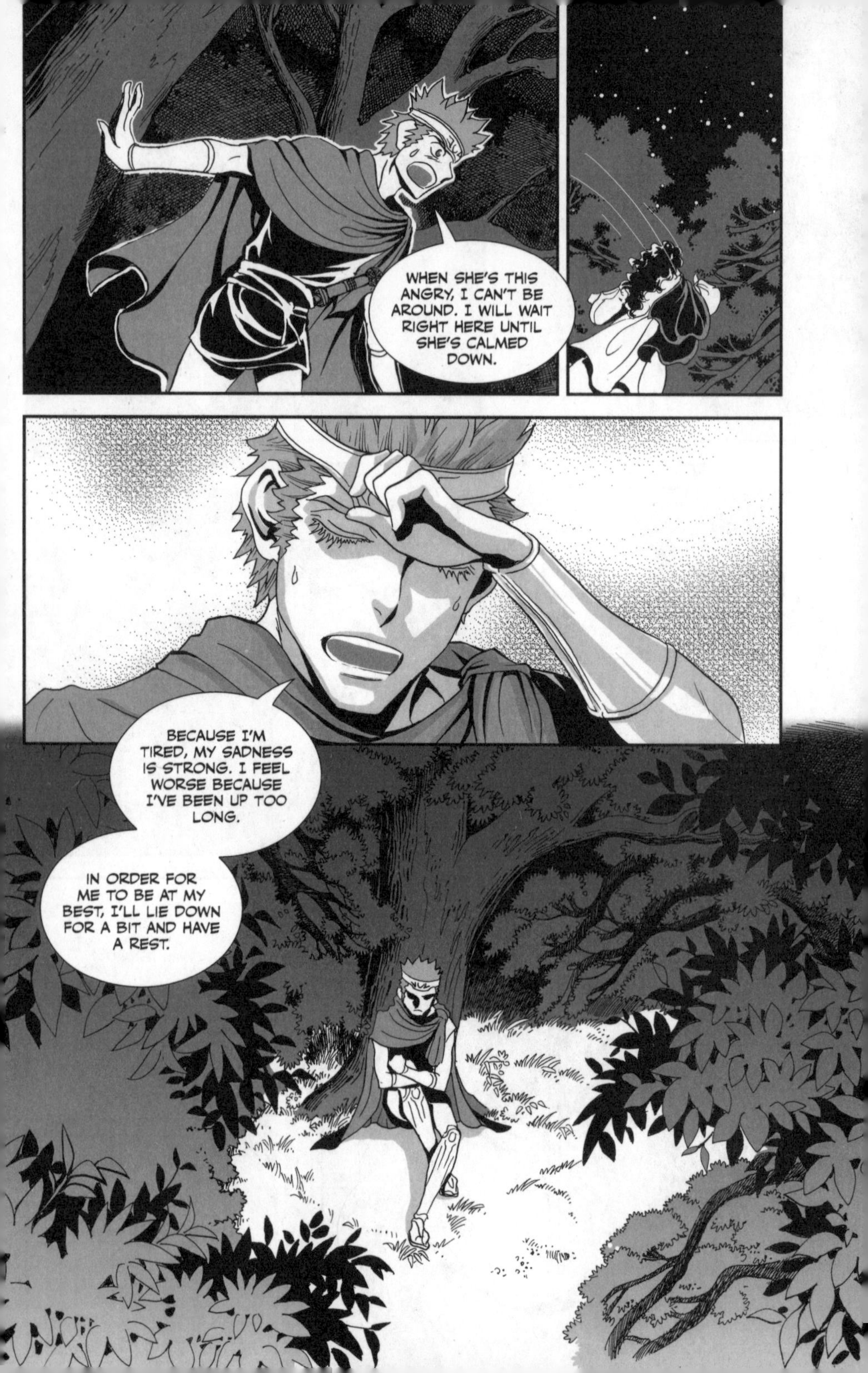
WHEN SHE'S THIS ANGRY, I CAN'T BE AROUND. I WILL WAIT RIGHT HERE UNTIL SHE'S CALMED DOWN.
BECAUSE I'M TIRED, MY SADNESS IS STRONG. I FEEL WORSE BECAUSE I'VE BEEN UP TOO LONG.
IN ORDER FOR ME TO BE AT MY BEST, I'LL LIE DOWN FOR A BIT AND HAVE A REST.

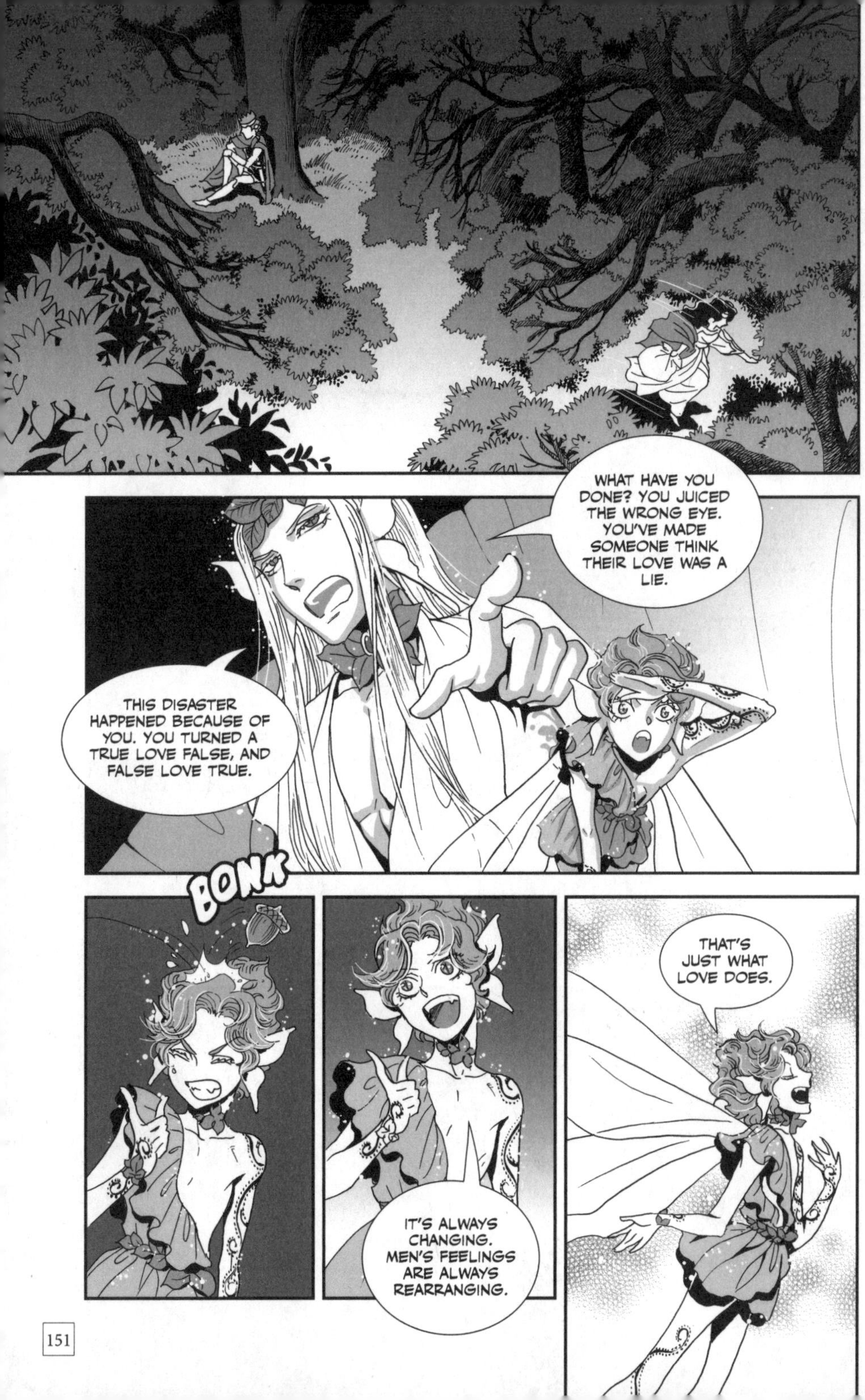
WHAT HAVE YOU DONE? YOU JUICED THE WRONG EYE. YOU'VE MADE SOMEONE THINK THEIR LOVE WAS A LIE.
THIS DISASTER HAPPENED BECAUSE OF YOU. YOU TURNED A TRUE LOVE FALSE, AND FALSE LOVE TRUE.
THAT'S JUST WHAT LOVE DOES.
IT'S ALWAYS CHANGING. MEN'S FEELINGS ARE ALWAYS REARRANGING.
BONK

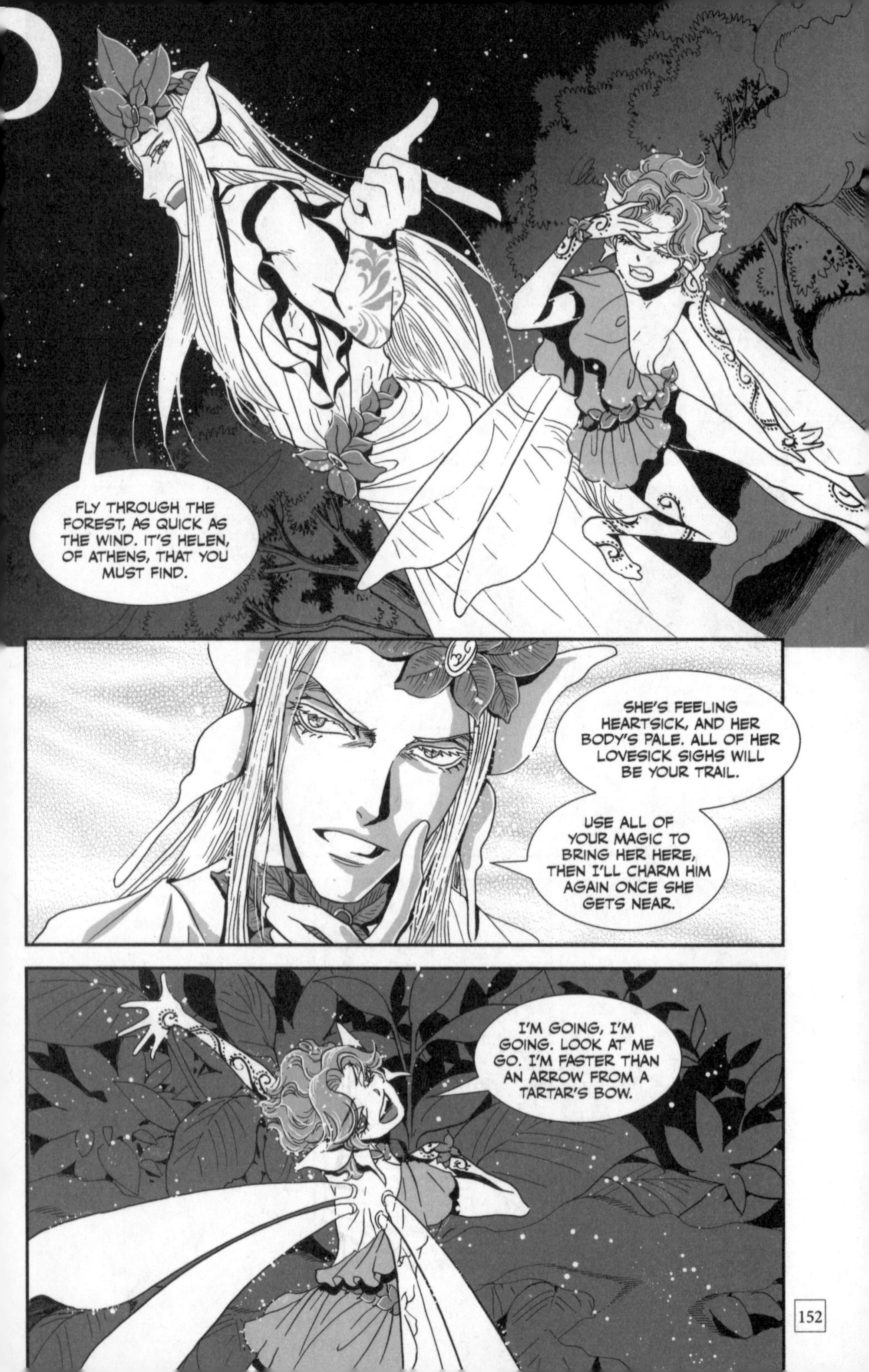
FLY THROUGH THE FOREST, AS QUICK AS THE WIND. IT'S HELEN, OF ATHENS, THAT YOU MUST FIND.
SHE'S FEELING HEARTSICK, AND HER BODY'S PALE. ALL OF HER LOVESICK SIGHS WILL BE YOUR TRAIL.
USE ALL OF YOUR MAGIC TO BRING HER HERE, THEN I'LL CHARM HIM AGAIN ONCE SHE GETS NEAR.
I'M GOING, I'M GOING. LOOK AT ME GO. I'M FASTER THAN AN ARROW FROM A TARTAR'S BOW.

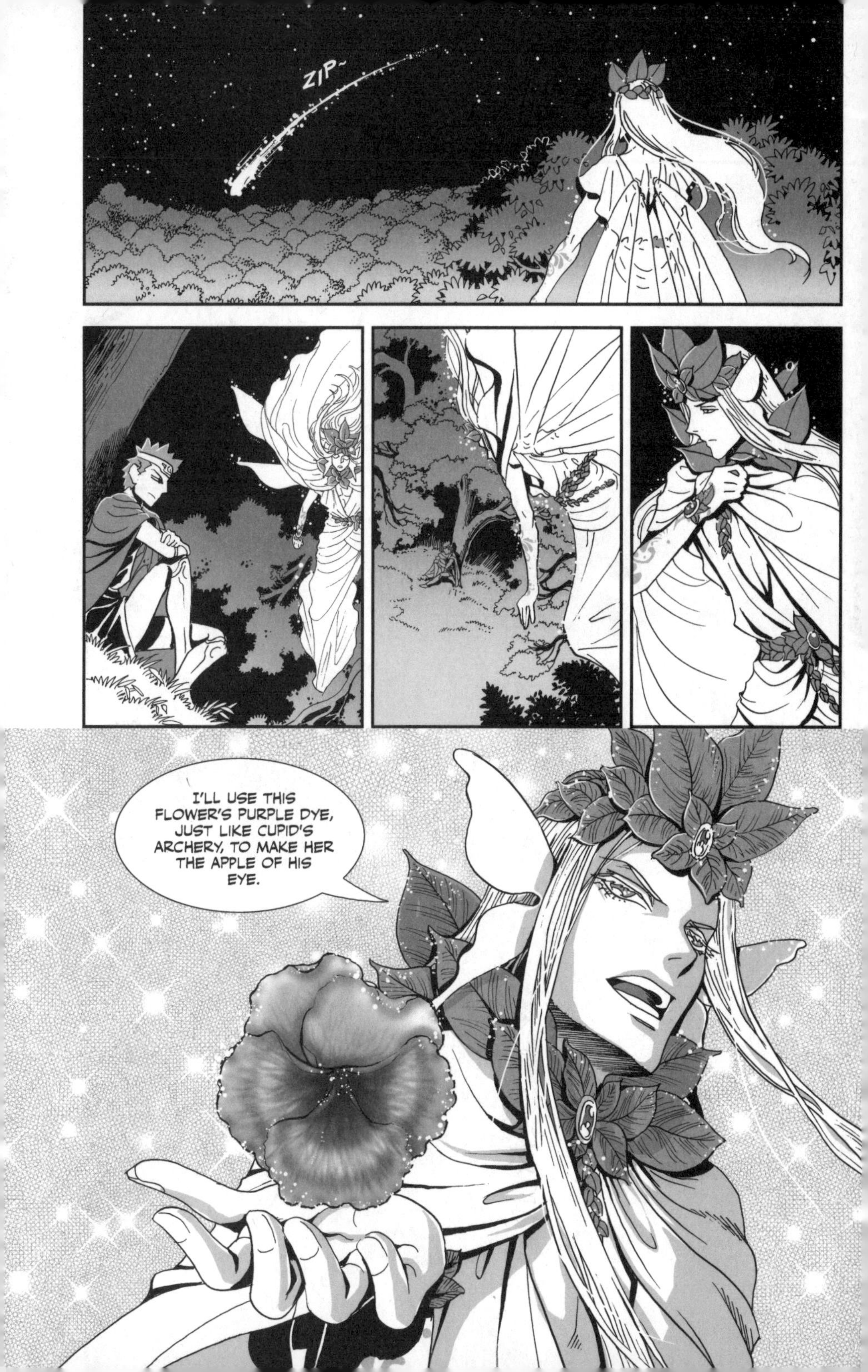
ZIP~
I'LL USE THIS FLOWER'S PURPLE DYE, JUST LIKE CUPID'S ARCHERY, TO MAKE HER THE APPLE OF HIS EYE.

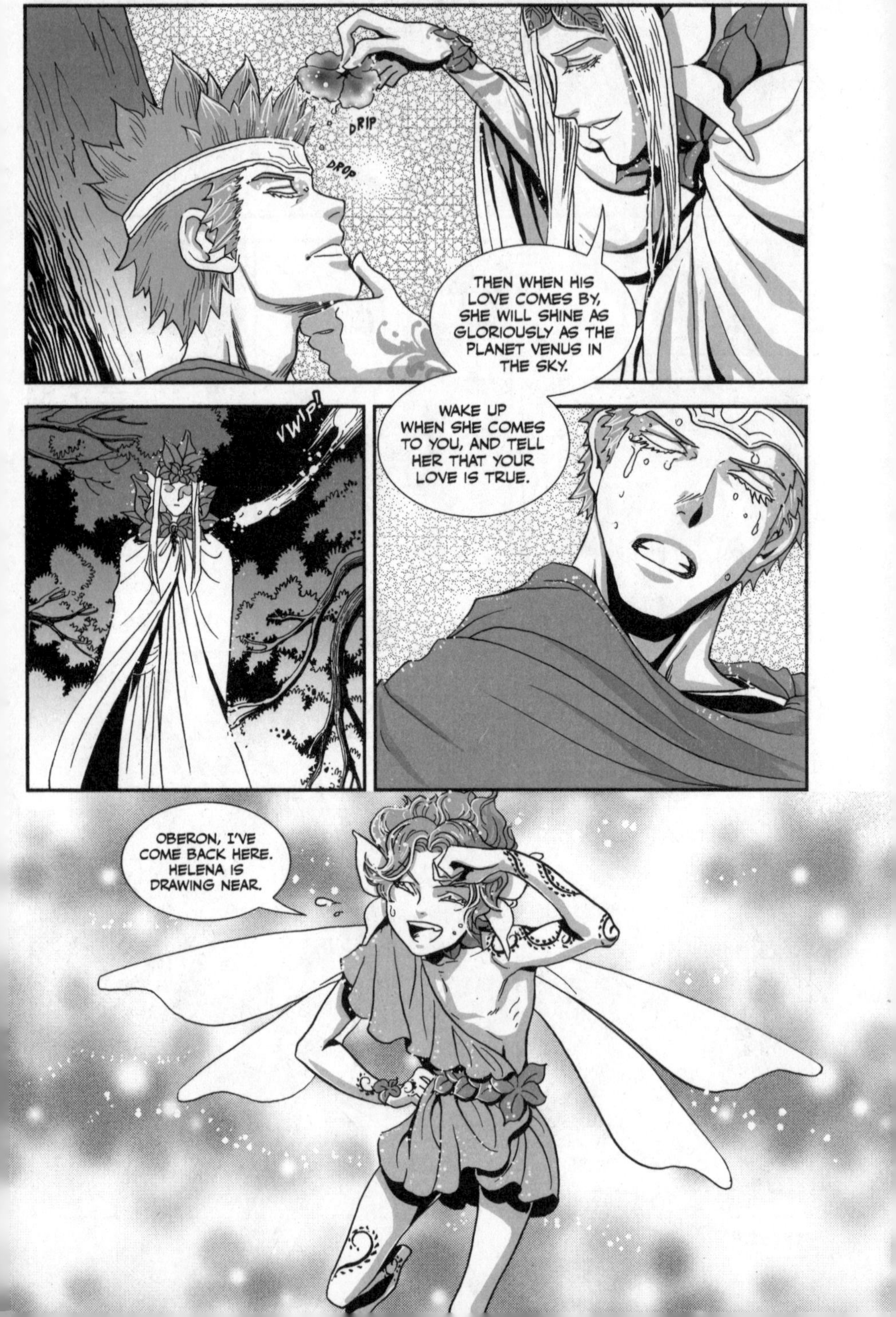
DRIP
DROP
THEN WHEN HIS LOVE COMES BY, SHE WILL SHINE AS GLORIOUSLY AS THE PLANET VENUS IN THE SKY.
WAKE UP WHEN SHE COMES TO YOU, AND TELL HER THAT YOUR LOVE IS TRUE.
VWIP!
OBERON, I'VE COME BACK HERE. HELENA IS DRAWING NEAR.

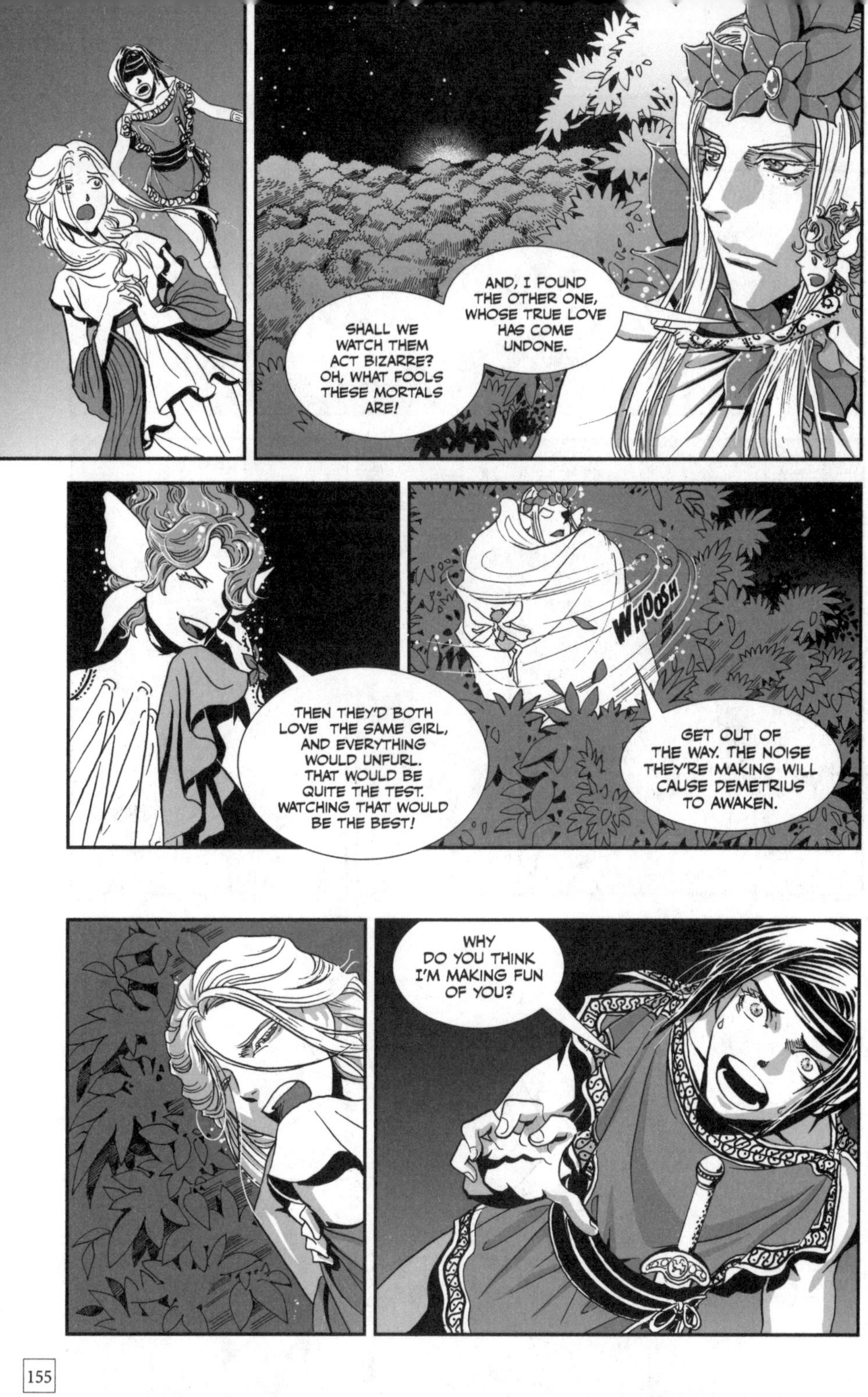
AND, I FOUND THE OTHER ONE, WHOSE TRUE LOVE HAS COME UNDONE.
SHALL WE WATCH THEM ACT BIZARRE? OH, WHAT FOOLS THESE MORTALS ARE!
WHOOSH
GET OUT OF THE WAY. THE NOISE THEY'RE MAKING WILL CAUSE DEMETRIUS TO AWAKEN.
THEN THEY'D BOTH LOVE THE SAME GIRL, AND EVERYTHING WOULD UNFURL. THAT WOULD BE QUITE THE TEST. WATCHING THAT WOULD BE THE BEST!
WHY DO YOU THINK I'M MAKING FUN OF YOU?

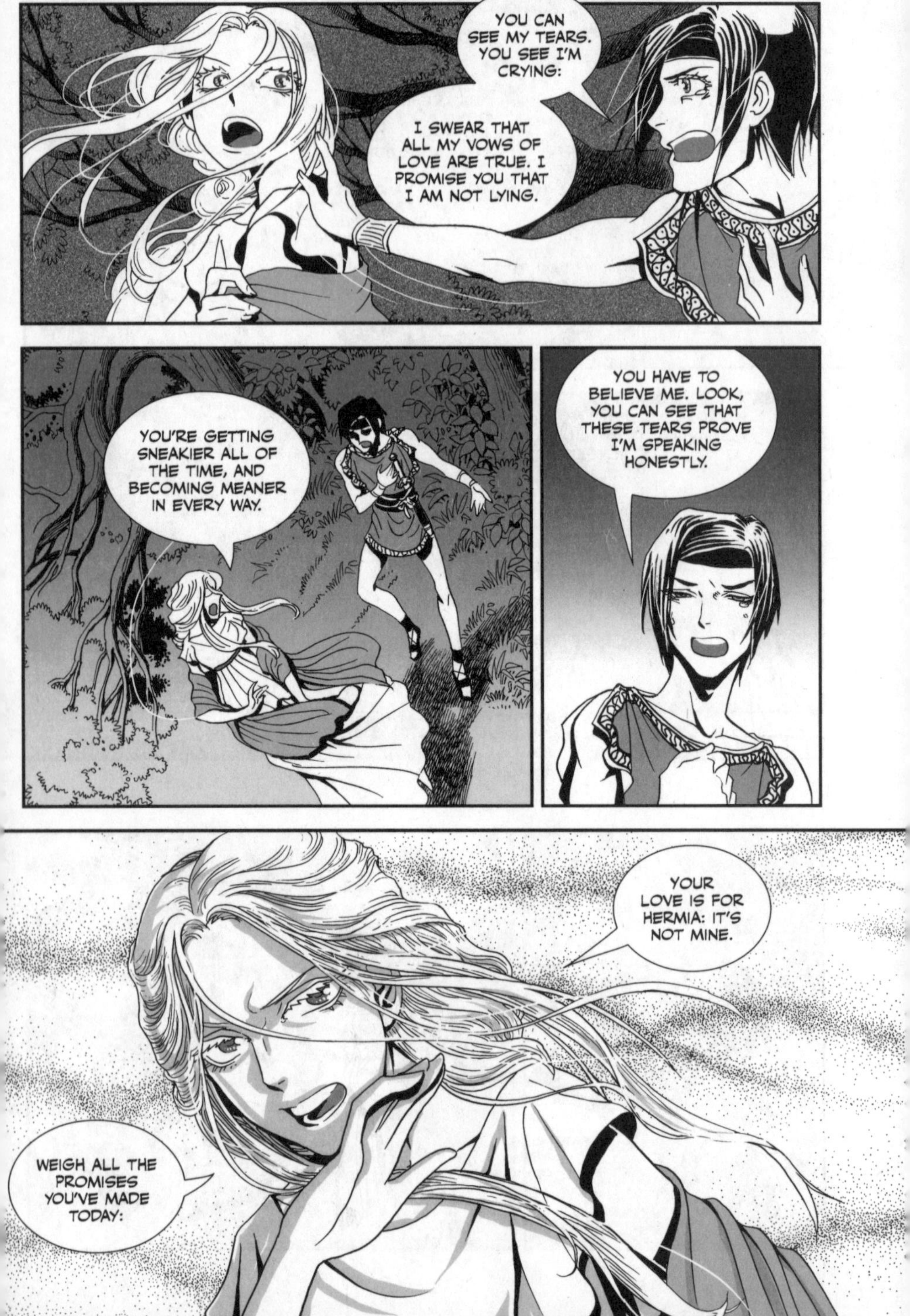
YOU CAN SEE MY TEARS. YOU SEE I'M CRYING:
I SWEAR THAT ALL MY VOWS OF LOVE ARE TRUE. I PROMISE YOU THAT I AM NOT LYING.
YOU HAVE TO BELIEVE ME. LOOK, YOU CAN SEE THAT THESE TEARS PROVE I'M SPEAKING HONESTLY.
YOU'RE GETTING SNEAKIER ALL OF THE TIME, AND BECOMING MEANER IN EVERY WAY.
YOUR LOVE IS FOR HERMIA: IT'S NOT MINE.
WEIGH ALL THE PROMISES YOU'VE MADE TODAY:

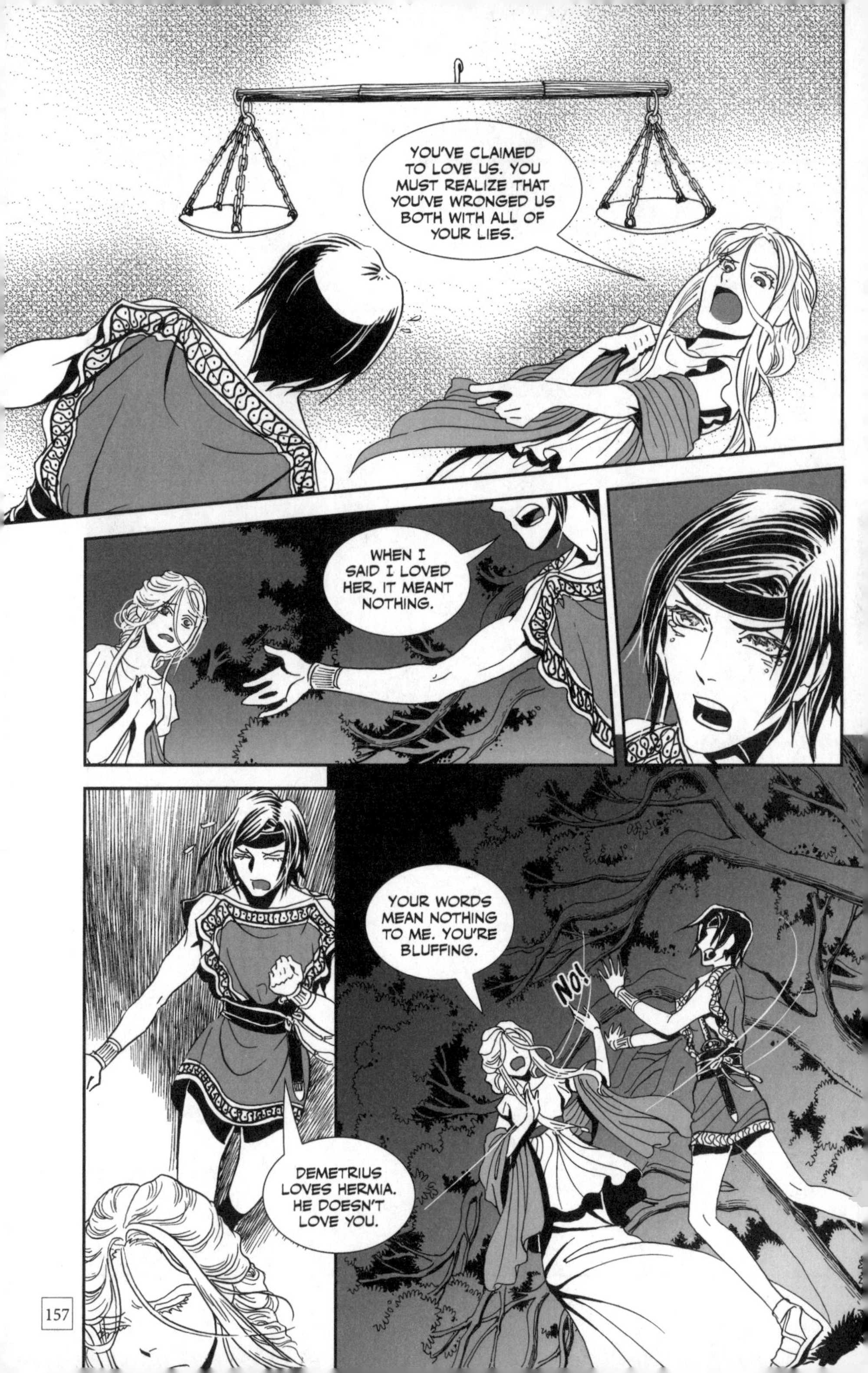
YOU'VE CLAIMED TO LOVE US. YOU MUST REALIZE THAT YOU'VE WRONGED US BOTH WITH ALL OF YOUR LIES.
WHEN I SAID I LOVED HER, IT MEANT NOTHING.
YOUR WORDS MEAN NOTHING TO ME. YOU'RE BLUFFING.
NO!
DEMETRIUS LOVES HERMIA. HE DOESN'T LOVE YOU.

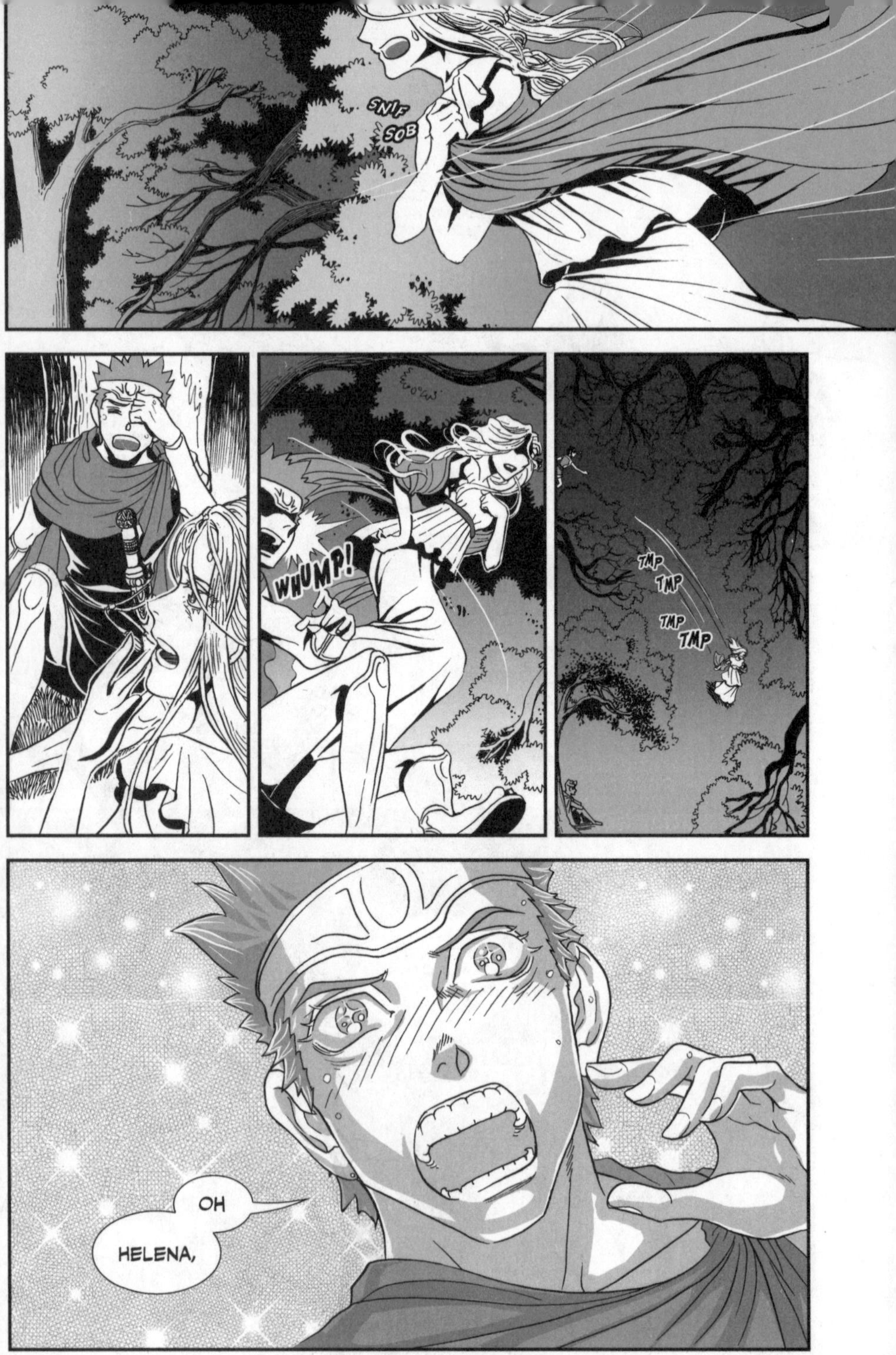
SNIF
SOB
TMP
TMP
TMP
TMP
WHUMP!
OH
HELENA,

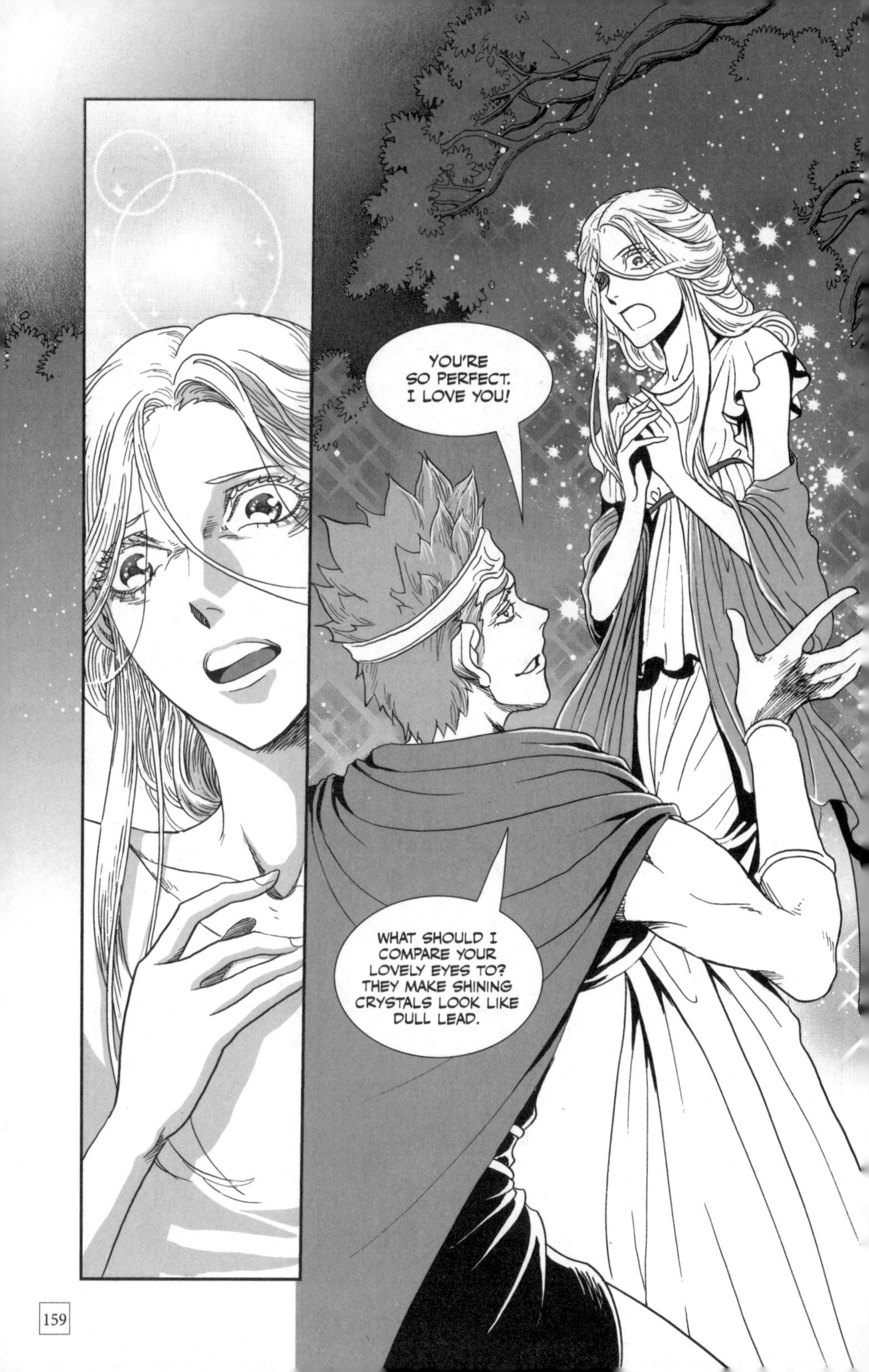
YOU'RE SO PERFECT. I LOVE YOU!
WHAT SHOULD I COMPARE YOUR LOVELY EYES TO? THEY MAKE SHINING CRYSTALS LOOK LIKE DULL LEAD.

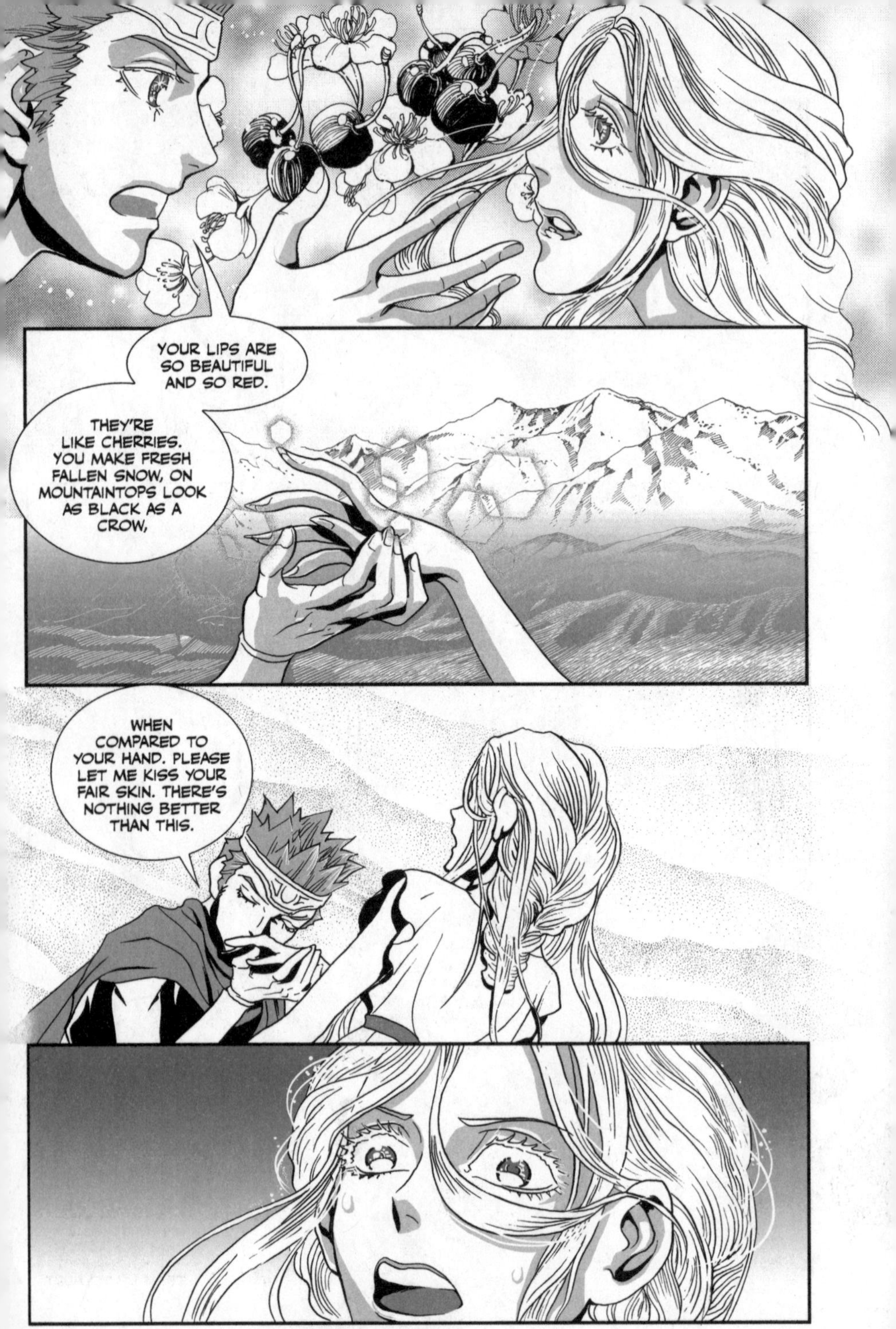
YOUR LIPS ARE SO BEAUTIFUL AND SO RED.
THEY'RE LIKE CHERRIES. YOU MAKE FRESH FALLEN SNOW, ON MOUNTAINTOPS LOOK AS BLACK AS A CROW,
WHEN COMPARED TO YOUR HAND. PLEASE LET ME KISS YOUR FAIR SKIN. THERE'S NOTHING BETTER THAN THIS.

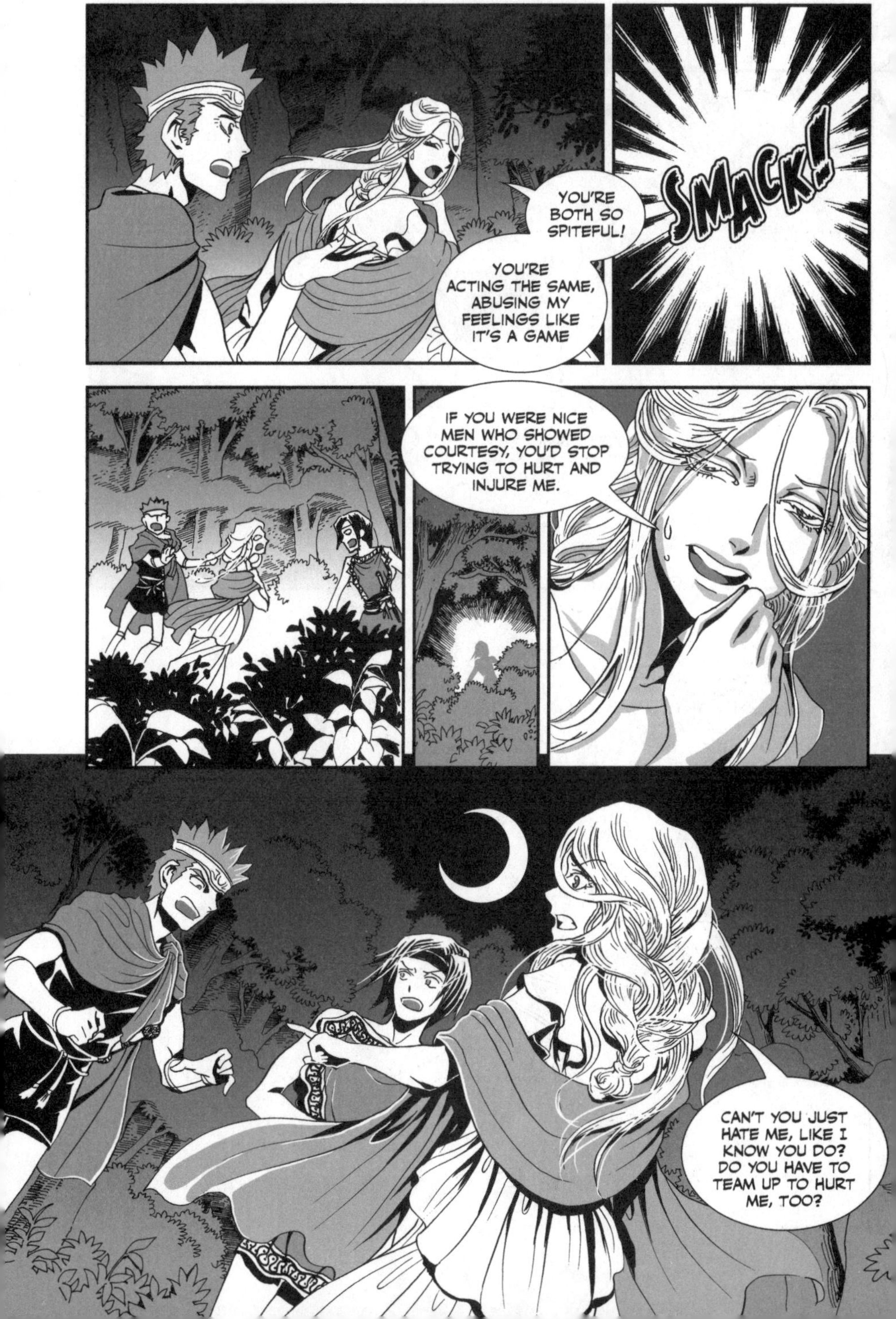
SMACK!
YOU'RE BOTH SO SPITEFUL!
YOU'RE ACTING THE SAME, ABUSING MY FEELINGS LIKE IT'S A GAME
IF YOU WERE NICE MEN WHO SHOWED COURTESY, YOU'D STOP TRYING TO HURT AND INJURE ME.
CAN'T YOU JUST HATE ME, LIKE I KNOW YOU DO? DO YOU HAVE TO TEAM UP TO HURT ME, TOO?

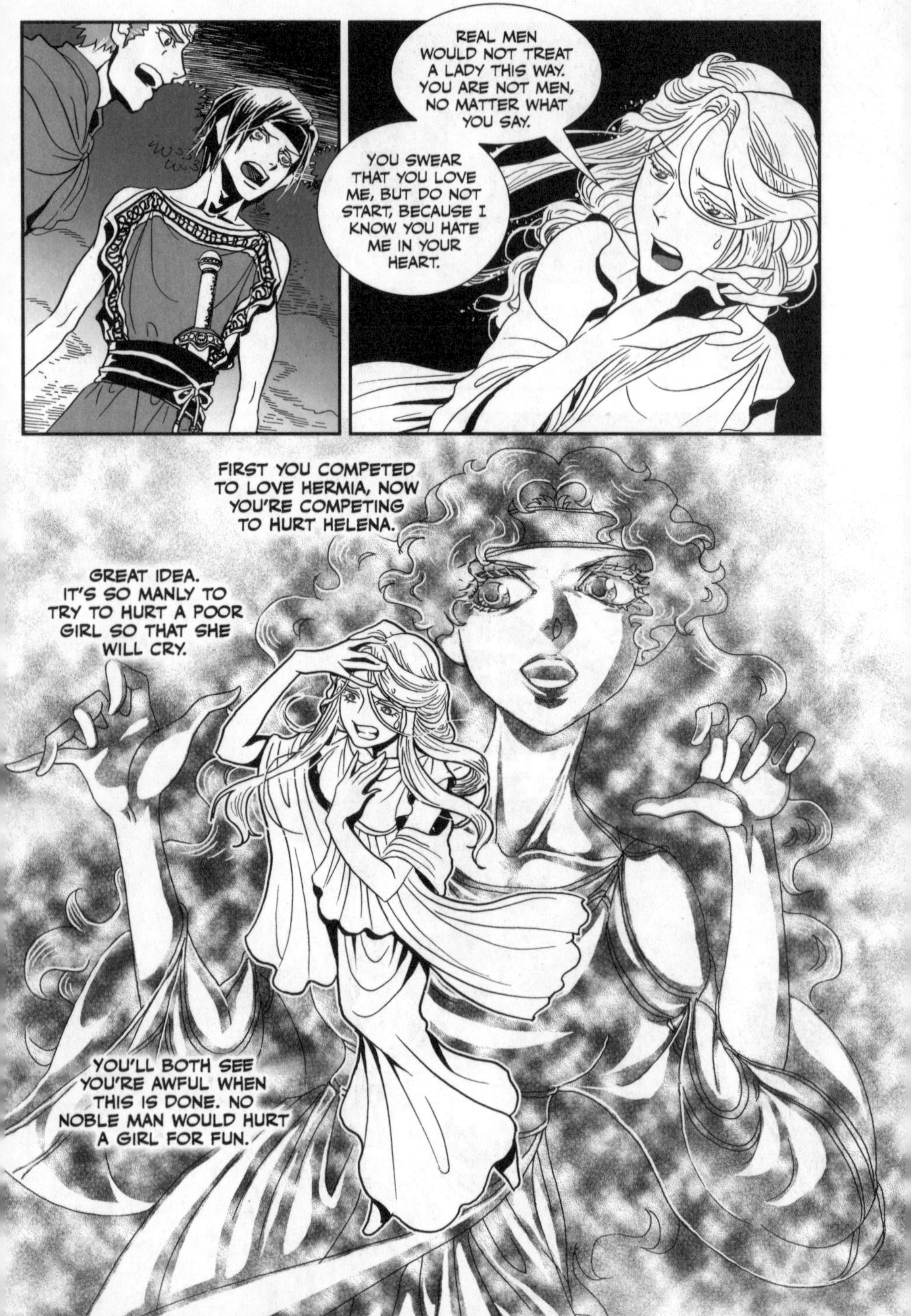
REAL MEN WOULD NOT TREAT A LADY THIS WAY. YOU ARE NOT MEN, NO MATTER WHAT YOU SAY.
YOU SWEAR THAT YOU LOVE ME, BUT DO NOT START, BECAUSE I KNOW YOU HATE ME IN YOUR HEART.
FIRST YOU COMPETED TO LOVE HERMIA, NOW YOU'RE COMPETING TO HURT HELENA.
GREAT IDEA. IT'S SO MANLY TO TRY TO HURT A POOR GIRL SO THAT SHE WILL CRY.
YOU'LL BOTH SEE YOU'RE AWFUL WHEN THIS IS DONE. NO NOBLE MAN WOULD HURT A GIRL FOR FUN.

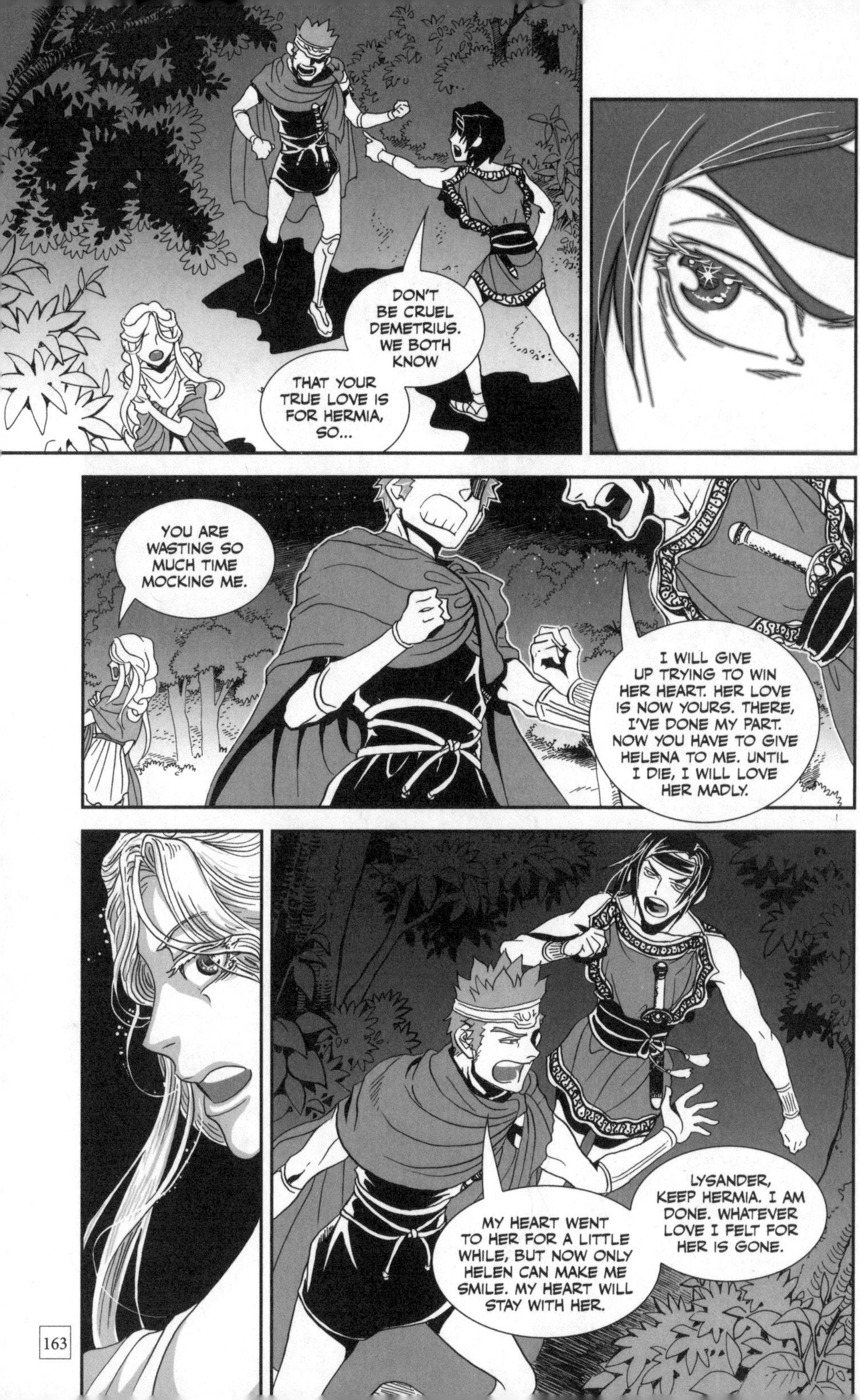
DON'T BE CRUEL DEMETRIUS. WE BOTH KNOW
THAT YOUR TRUE LOVE IS FOR HERMIA, SO...
I WILL GIVE UP TRYING TO WIN HER HEART. HER LOVE IS NOW YOURS. THERE, I'VE DONE MY PART. NOW YOU HAVE TO GIVE HELENA TO ME. UNTIL I DIE, I WILL LOVE HER MADLY.
YOU ARE WASTING SO MUCH TIME MOCKING ME.
LYSANDER, KEEP HERMIA. I AM DONE. WHATEVER LOVE I FELT FOR HER IS GONE.
MY HEART WENT TO HER FOR A LITTLE WHILE, BUT NOW ONLY HELEN CAN MAKE ME SMILE. MY HEART WILL STAY WITH HER.

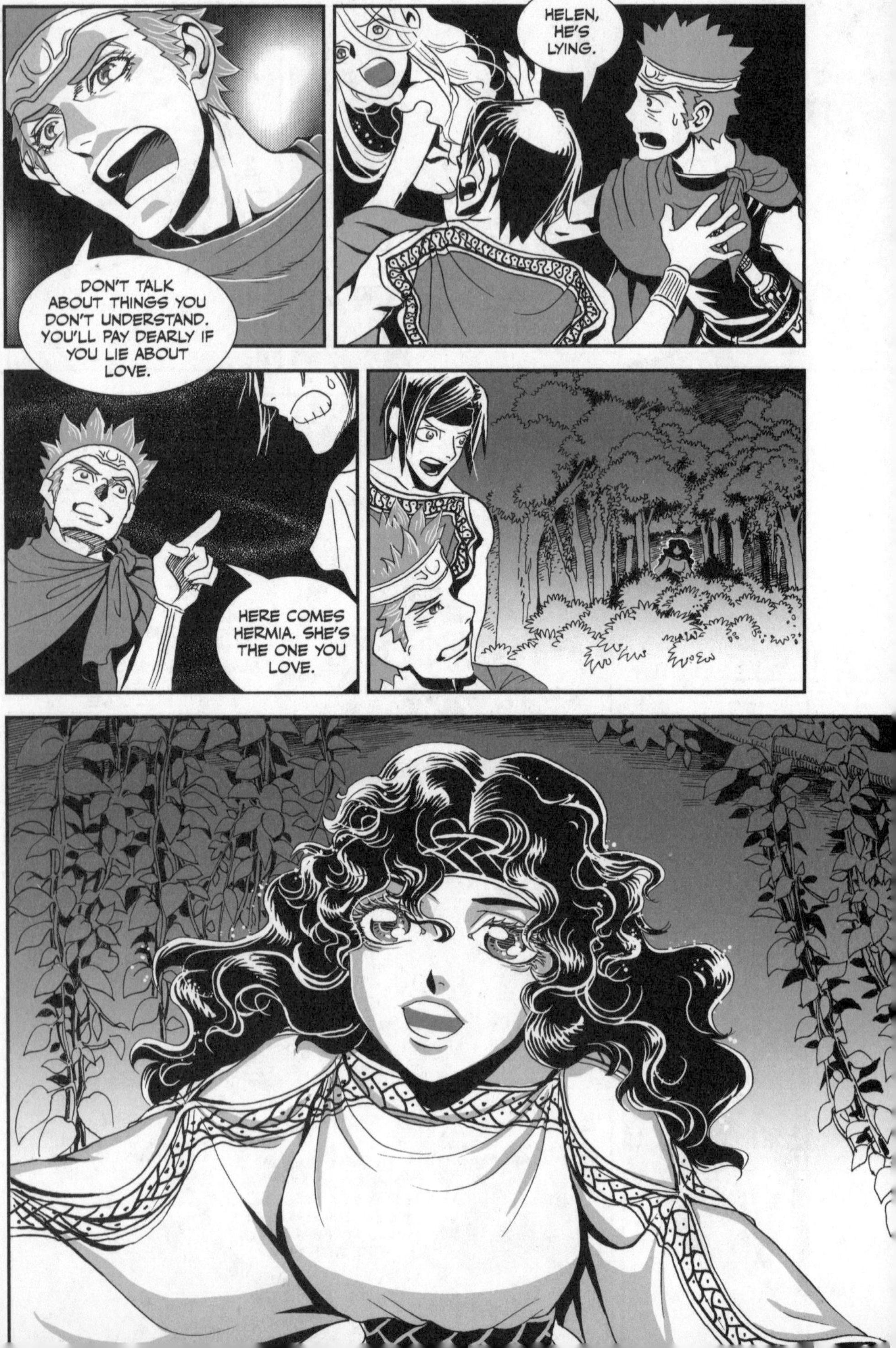
HELEN, HE'S LYING.
DON'T TALK ABOUT THINGS YOU DON'T UNDERSTAND. YOU'LL PAY DEARLY IF YOU LIE ABOUT LOVE.
HERE COMES HERMIA. SHE'S THE ONE YOU LOVE.

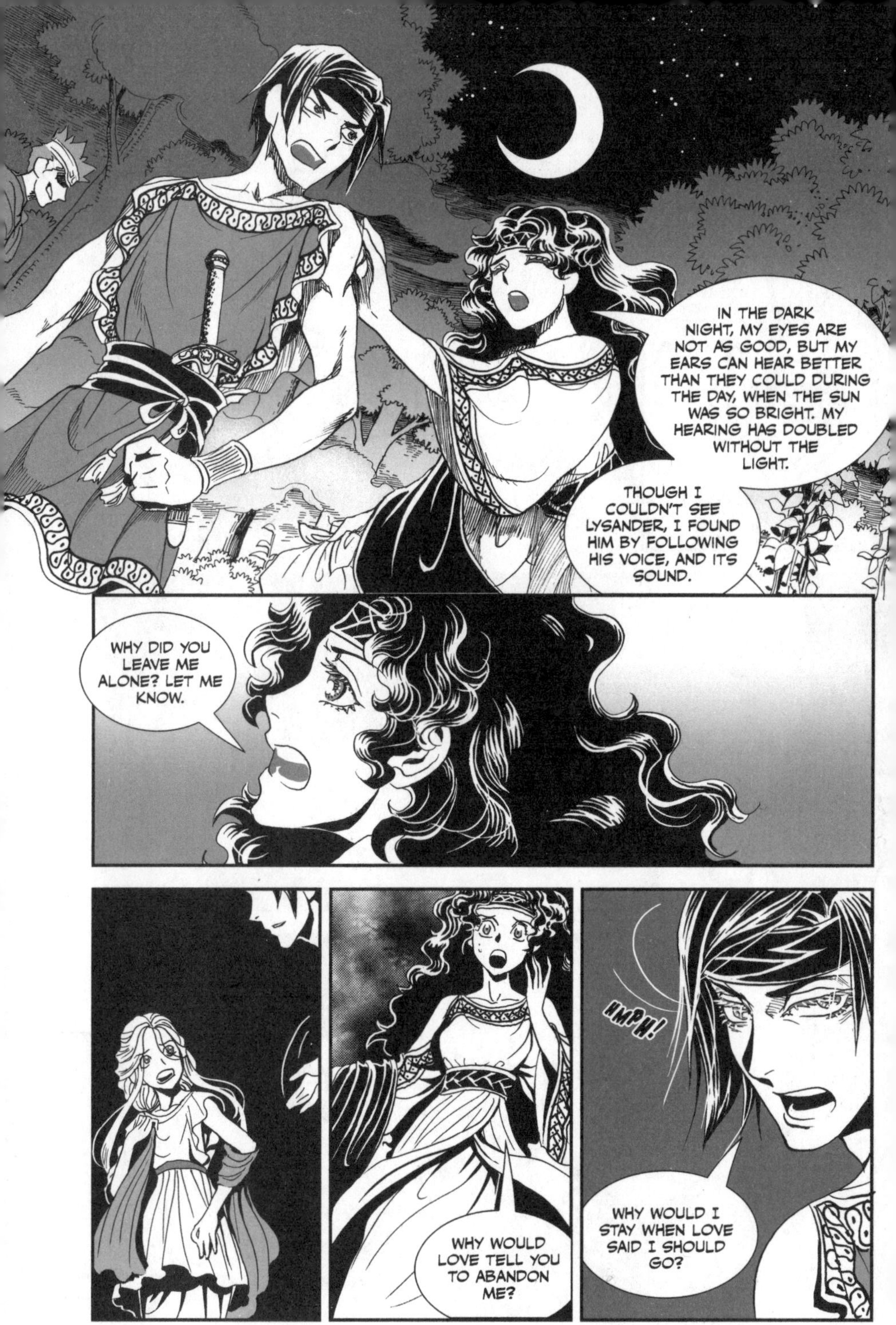
IN THE DARK NIGHT, MY EYES ARE NOT AS GOOD, BUT MY EARS CAN HEAR BETTER THAN THEY COULD DURING THE DAY, WHEN THE SUN WAS SO BRIGHT. MY HEARING HAS DOUBLED WITHOUT THE LIGHT.
THOUGH I COULDN'T SEE LYSANDER, I FOUND HIM BY FOLLOWING HIS VOICE, AND ITS SOUND.
WHY DID YOU LEAVE ME ALONE? LET ME KNOW.
HMPH!
WHY WOULD I STAY WHEN LOVE SAID I SHOULD GO?
WHY WOULD LOVE TELL YOU TO ABANDON ME?

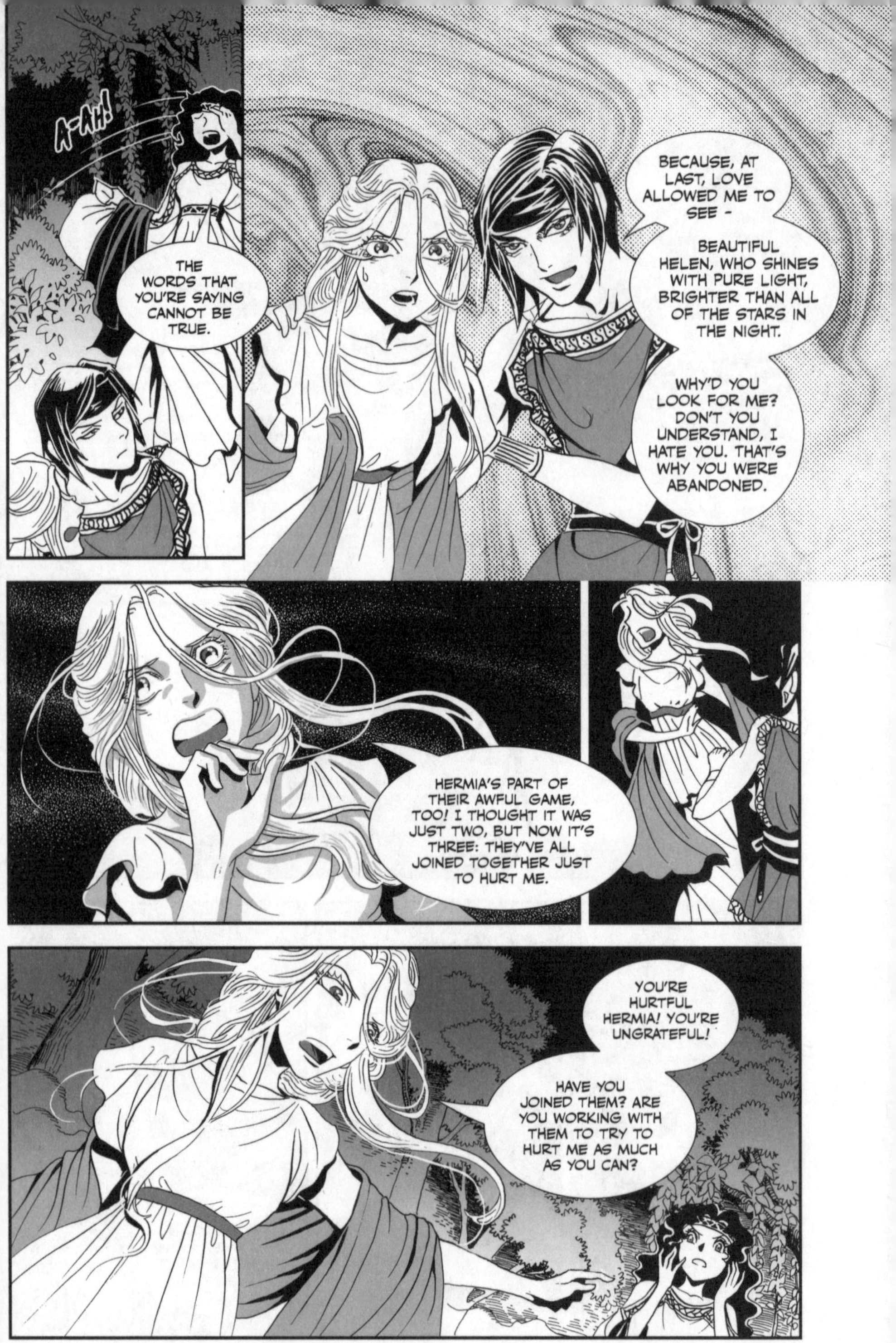
BECAUSE, AT LAST, LOVE ALLOWED ME TO SEE -
BEAUTIFUL HELEN, WHO SHINES WITH PURE LIGHT, BRIGHTER THAN ALL OF THE STARS IN THE NIGHT.
WHY'D YOU LOOK FOR ME? DON'T YOU UNDERSTAND, I HATE YOU. THAT'S WHY YOU WERE ABANDONED.
A-AH!
THE WORDS THAT YOU'RE SAYING CANNOT BE TRUE.
HERMIA'S PART OF THEIR AWFUL GAME, TOO! I THOUGHT IT WAS JUST TWO, BUT NOW IT'S THREE: THEY'VE ALL JOINED TOGETHER JUST TO HURT ME.
YOU'RE HURTFUL HERMIA! YOU'RE UNGRATEFUL!
HAVE YOU JOINED THEM? ARE YOU WORKING WITH THEM TO TRY TO HURT ME AS MUCH AS YOU CAN?

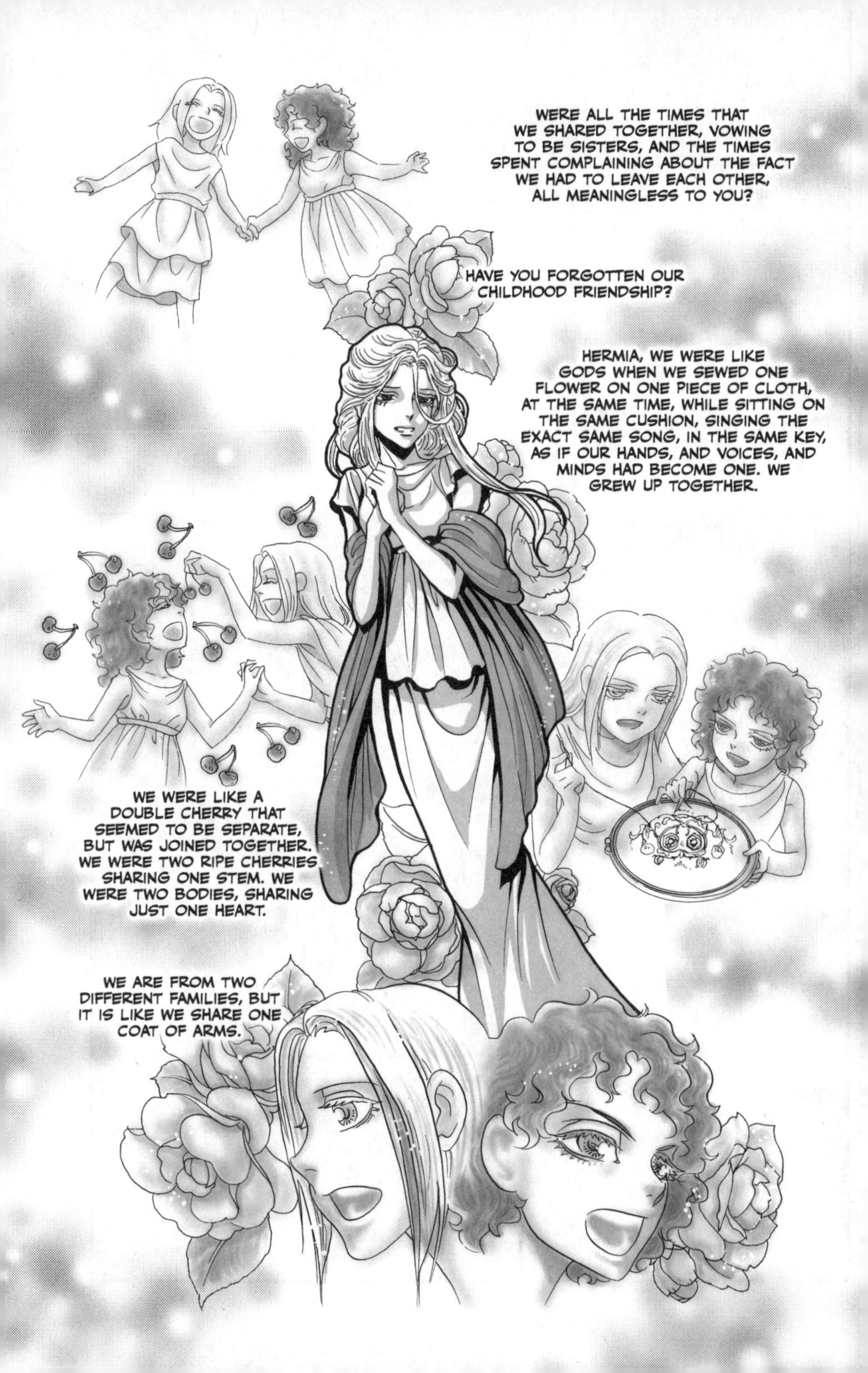
WERE ALL THE TIMES THAT WE SHARED TOGETHER, VOWING TO BE SISTERS, AND THE TIMES SPENT COMPLAINING ABOUT THE FACT WE HAD TO LEAVE EACH OTHER, ALL MEANINGLESS TO YOU?
HAVE YOU FORGOTTEN OUR CHILDHOOD FRIENDSHIP?
HERMIA, WE WERE LIKE GODS WHEN WE SEWED ONE FLOWER ON ONE PIECE OF CLOTH, AT THE SAME TIME, WHILE SITTING ON THE SAME CUSHION, SINGING THE EXACT SAME SONG, IN THE SAME KEY, AS IF OUR HANDS, AND VOICES, AND MINDS HAD BECOME ONE. WE GREW UP TOGETHER.
WE WERE LIKE A DOUBLE CHERRY THAT SEEMED TO BE SEPARATE, BUT WAS JOINED TOGETHER. WE WERE TWO RIPE CHERRIES SHARING ONE STEM. WE WERE TWO BODIES, SHARING JUST ONE HEART.
WE ARE FROM TWO DIFFERENT FAMILIES, BUT IT IS LIKE WE SHARE ONE COAT OF ARMS.

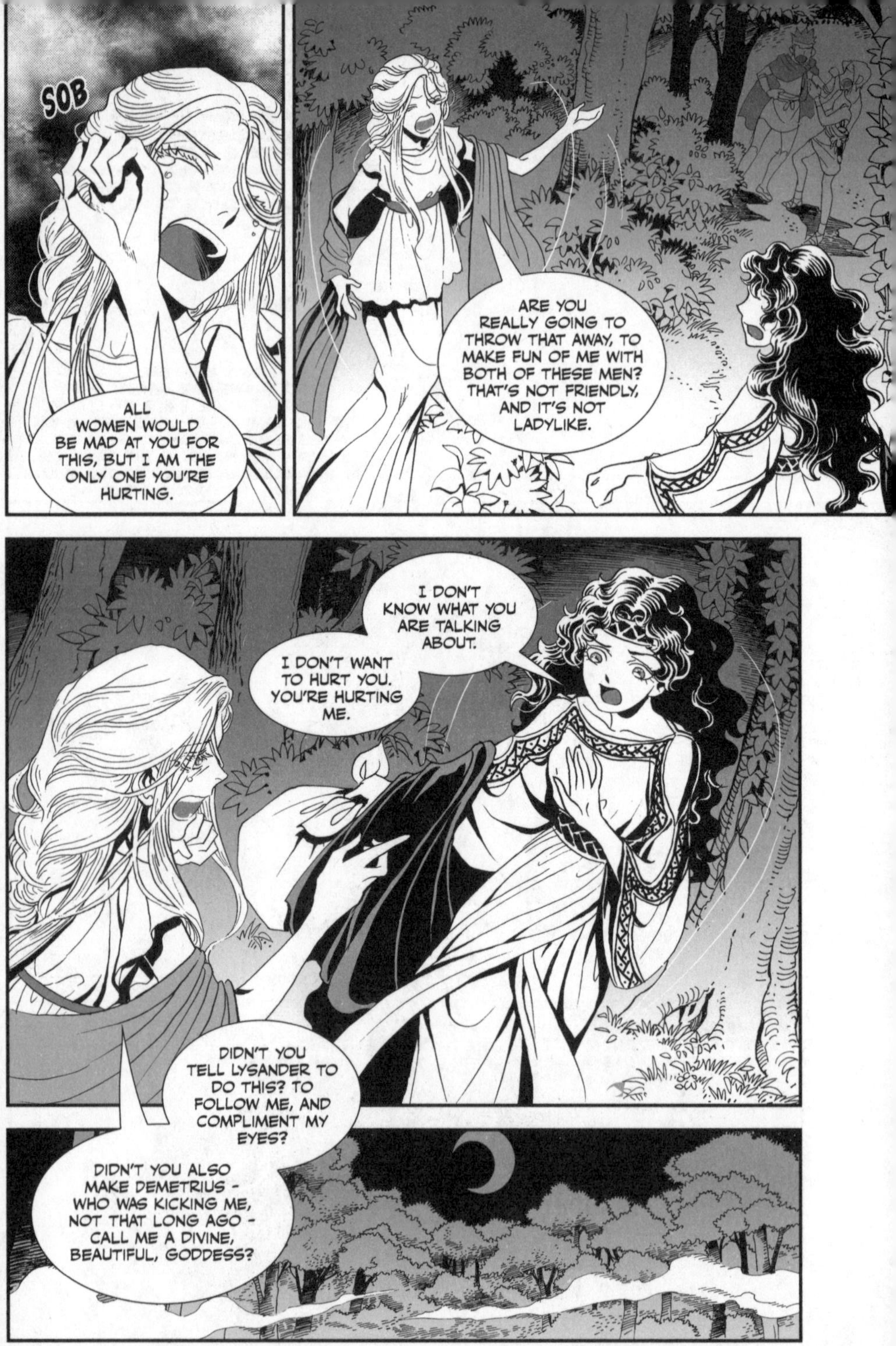
ARE YOU REALLY GOING TO THROW THAT AWAY, TO MAKE FUN OF ME WITH BOTH OF THESE MEN? THAT'S NOT FRIENDLY, AND IT'S NOT LADYLIKE.
SOB
ALL WOMEN WOULD BE MAD AT YOU FOR THIS, BUT I AM THE ONLY ONE YOU'RE HURTING.
I DON'T KNOW WHAT YOU ARE TALKING ABOUT.
I DON'T WANT TO HURT YOU. YOU'RE HURTING ME.
DIDN'T YOU TELL LYSANDER TO DO THIS? TO FOLLOW ME, AND COMPLIMENT MY EYES?
DIDN'T YOU ALSO MAKE DEMETRIUS - WHO WAS KICKING ME, NOT THAT LONG AGO - CALL ME A DIVINE, BEAUTIFUL, GODDESS?

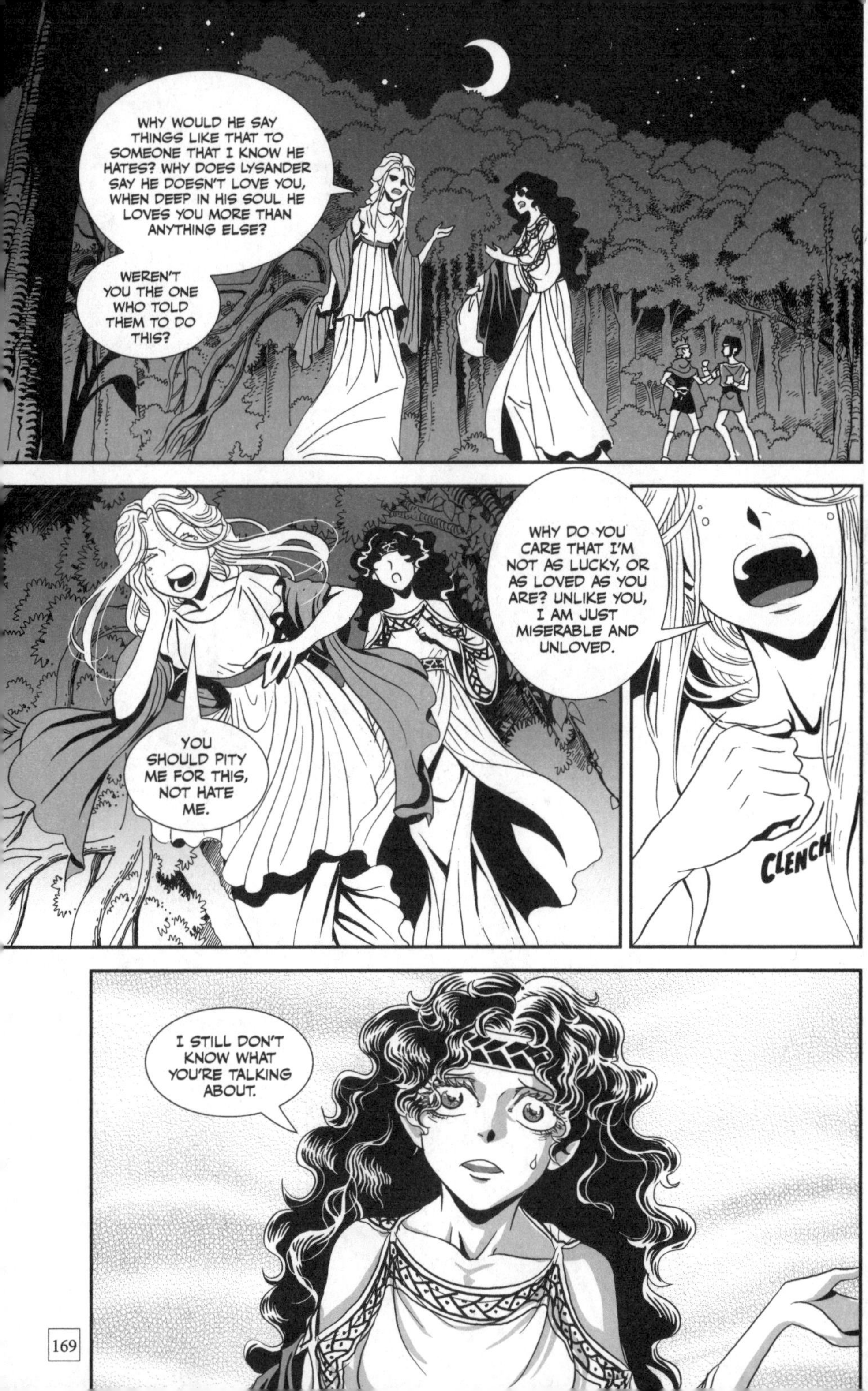
WHY WOULD HE SAY THINGS LIKE THAT TO SOMEONE THAT I KNOW HE HATES? WHY DOES LYSANDER SAY HE DOESN'T LOVE YOU, WHEN DEEP IN HIS SOUL HE LOVES YOU MORE THAN ANYTHING ELSE?
WEREN'T YOU THE ONE WHO TOLD THEM TO DO THIS?
CLENCH
WHY DO YOU CARE THAT I'M NOT AS LUCKY, OR AS LOVED AS YOU ARE? UNLIKE YOU, I AM JUST MISERABLE AND UNLOVED.
YOU SHOULD PITY ME FOR THIS, NOT HATE ME.
I STILL DON'T KNOW WHAT YOU'RE TALKING ABOUT.

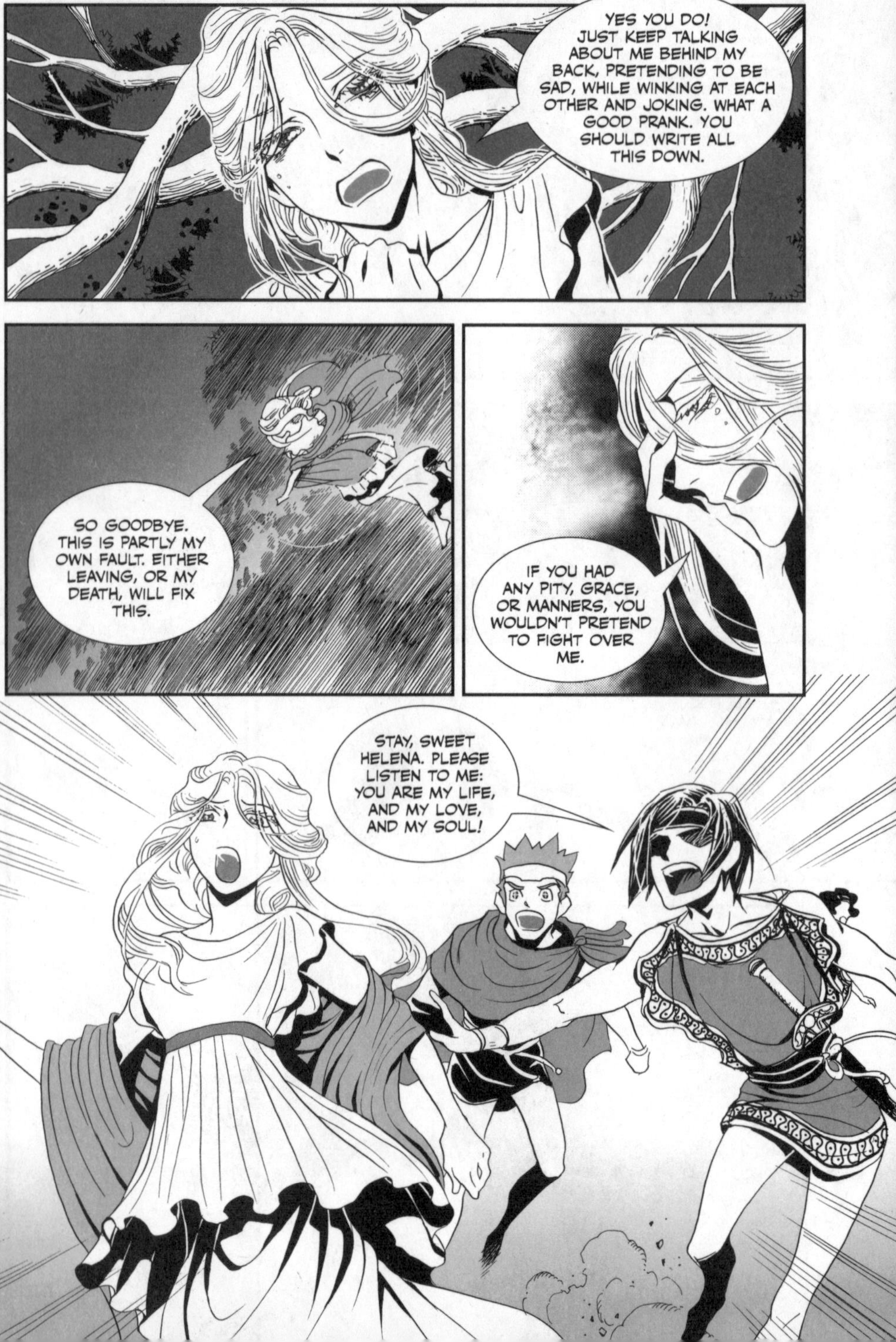
YES YOU DO! JUST KEEP TALKING ABOUT ME BEHIND MY BACK, PRETENDING TO BE SAD, WHILE WINKING AT EACH OTHER AND JOKING. WHAT A GOOD PRANK. YOU SHOULD WRITE ALL THIS DOWN.
IF YOU HAD ANY PITY, GRACE, OR MANNERS, YOU WOULDN'T PRETEND TO FIGHT OVER ME.
SO GOODBYE. THIS IS PARTLY MY OWN FAULT. EITHER LEAVING, OR MY DEATH, WILL FIX THIS.
STAY, SWEET HELENA. PLEASE LISTEN TO ME: YOU ARE MY LIFE, AND MY LOVE, AND MY SOUL!

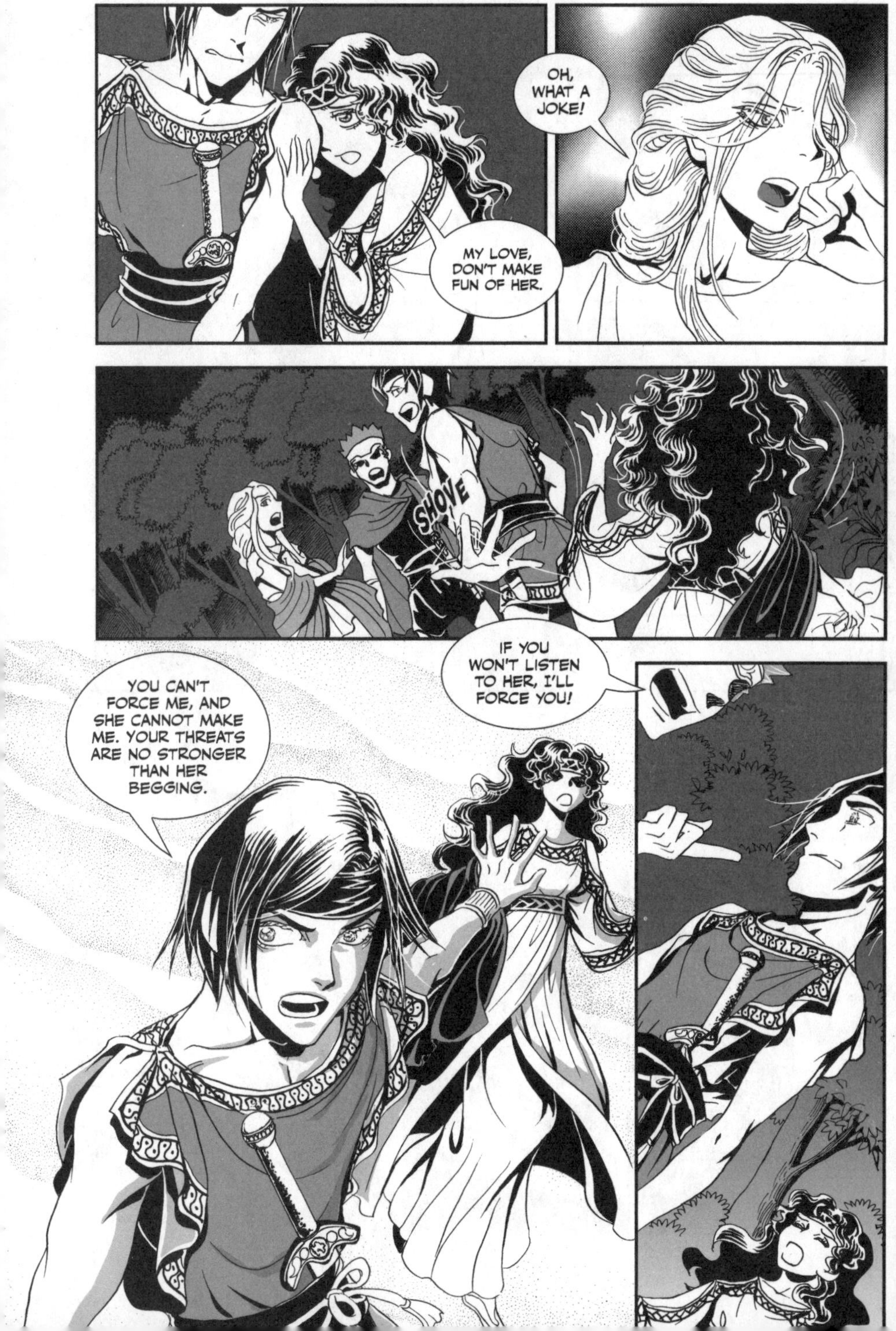
OH, WHAT A JOKE!
MY LOVE, DON'T MAKE FUN OF HER.
SHOVE
IF YOU WON'T LISTEN TO HER, I'LL FORCE YOU!
YOU CAN'T FORCE ME, AND SHE CANNOT MAKE ME. YOUR THREATS ARE NO STRONGER THAN HER BEGGING.

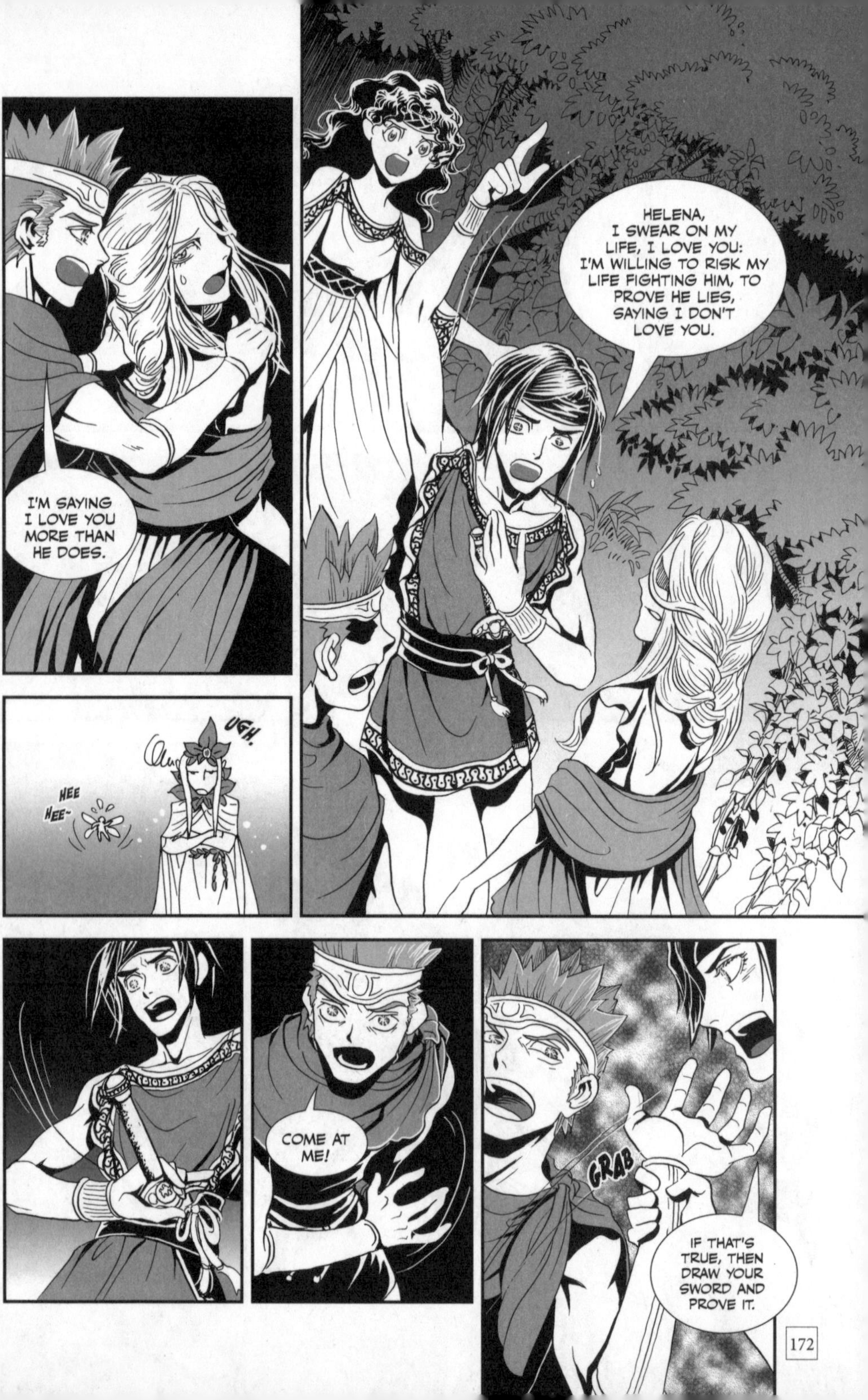
HELENA, I SWEAR ON MY LIFE, I LOVE YOU: I'M WILLING TO RISK MY LIFE FIGHTING HIM, TO PROVE HE LIES, SAYING I DON'T LOVE YOU.
I'M SAYING I LOVE YOU MORE THAN HE DOES.
UGH.
HEE HEE~
GRAB
IF THAT'S TRUE, THEN DRAW YOUR SWORD AND PROVE IT.
COME AT ME!

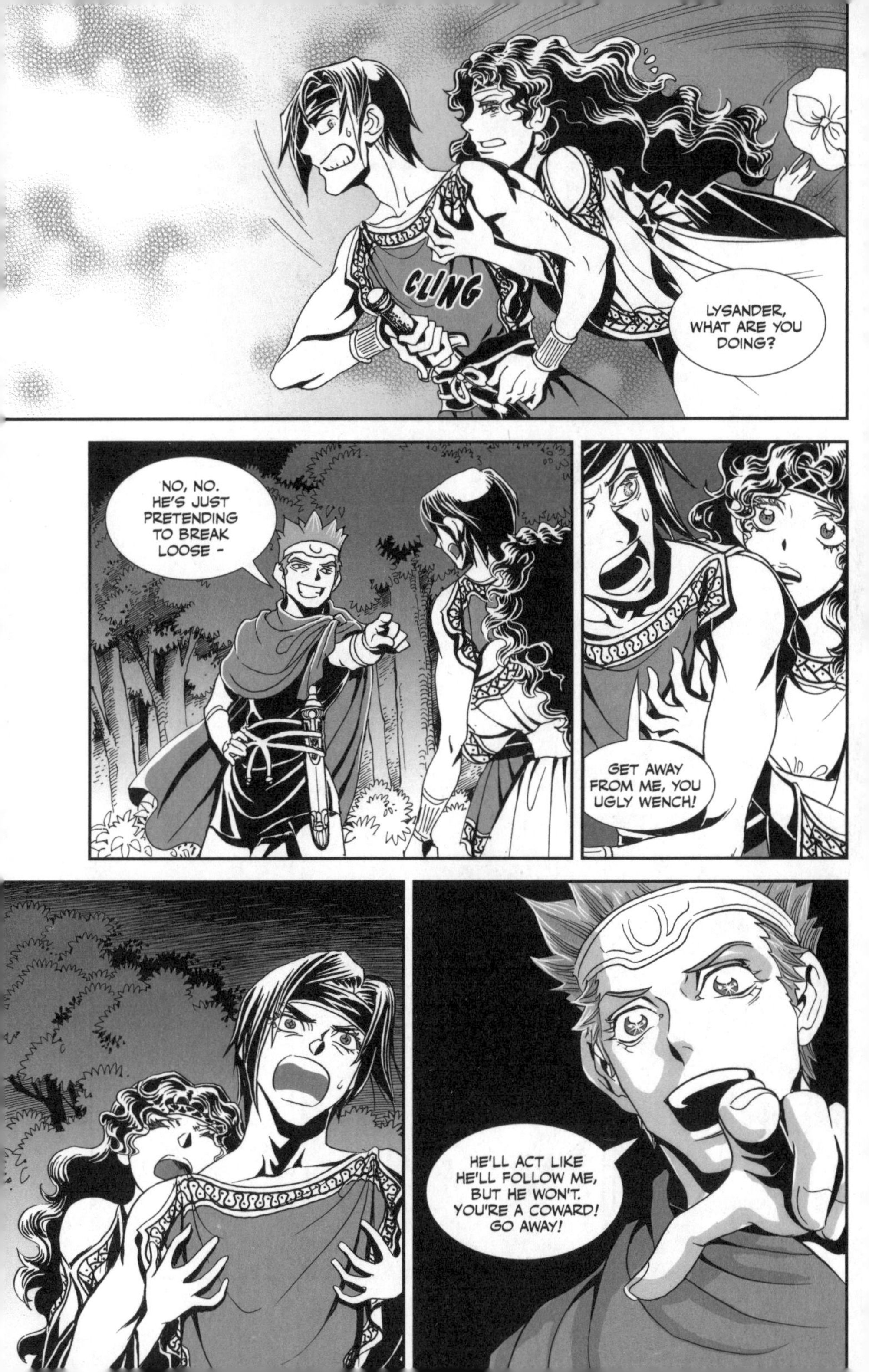
LYSANDER, WHAT ARE YOU DOING?
CLING
GET AWAY FROM ME, YOU UGLY WENCH!
NO, NO. HE'S JUST PRETENDING TO BREAK LOOSE -
HE'LL ACT LIKE HE'LL FOLLOW ME, BUT HE WON'T. YOU'RE A COWARD! GO AWAY!

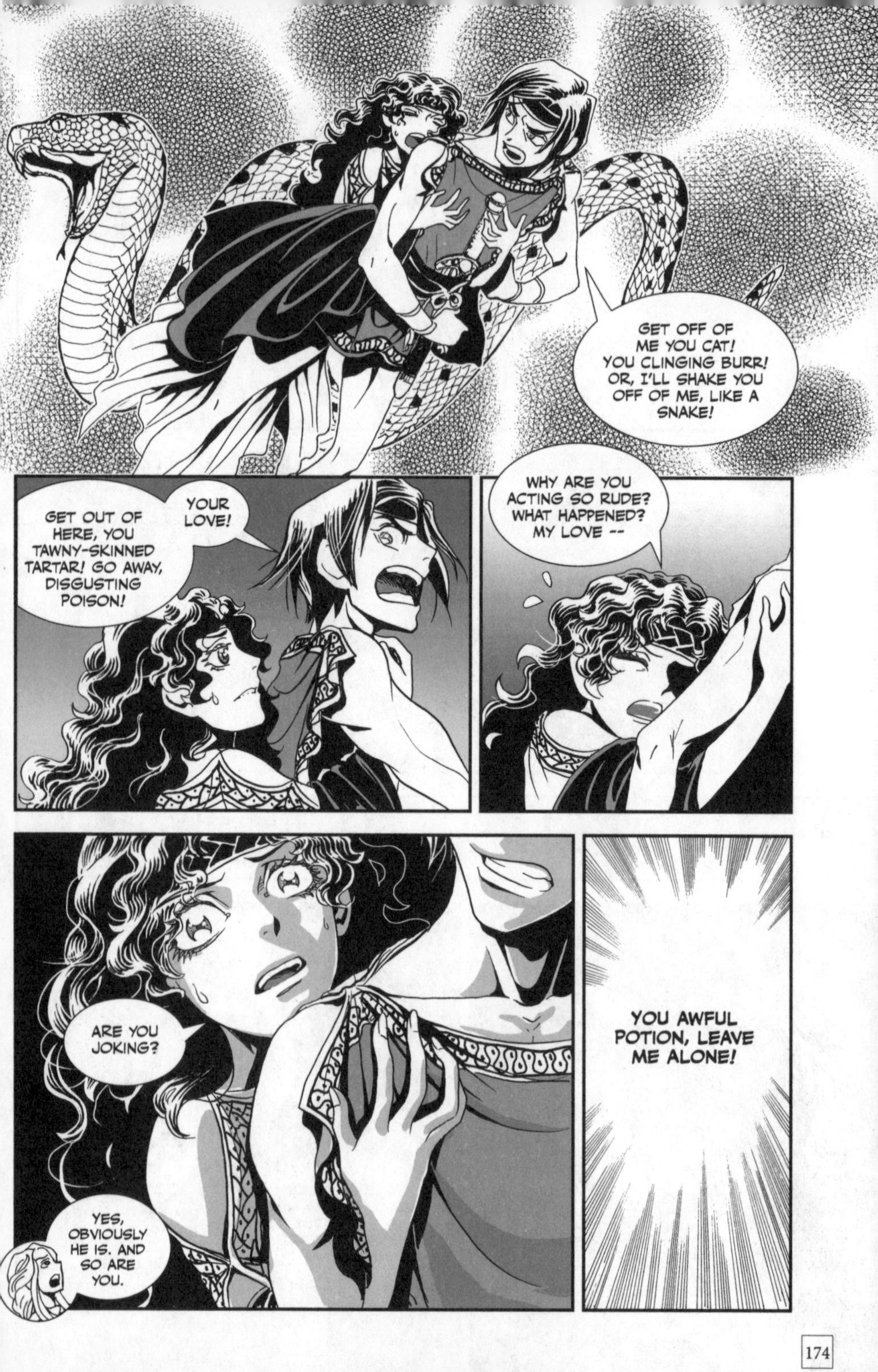
GET OFF OF ME YOU CAT! YOU CLINGING BURR! OR, I'LL SHAKE YOU OFF OF ME, LIKE A SNAKE!
WHY ARE YOU ACTING SO RUDE? WHAT HAPPENED? MY LOVE --
YOUR LOVE!
GET OUT OF HERE, YOU TAWNY-SKINNED TARTAR! GO AWAY, DISGUSTING POISON!
YOU AWFUL POTION, LEAVE ME ALONE!
ARE YOU JOKING?
YES, OBVIOUSLY HE IS. AND SO ARE YOU.

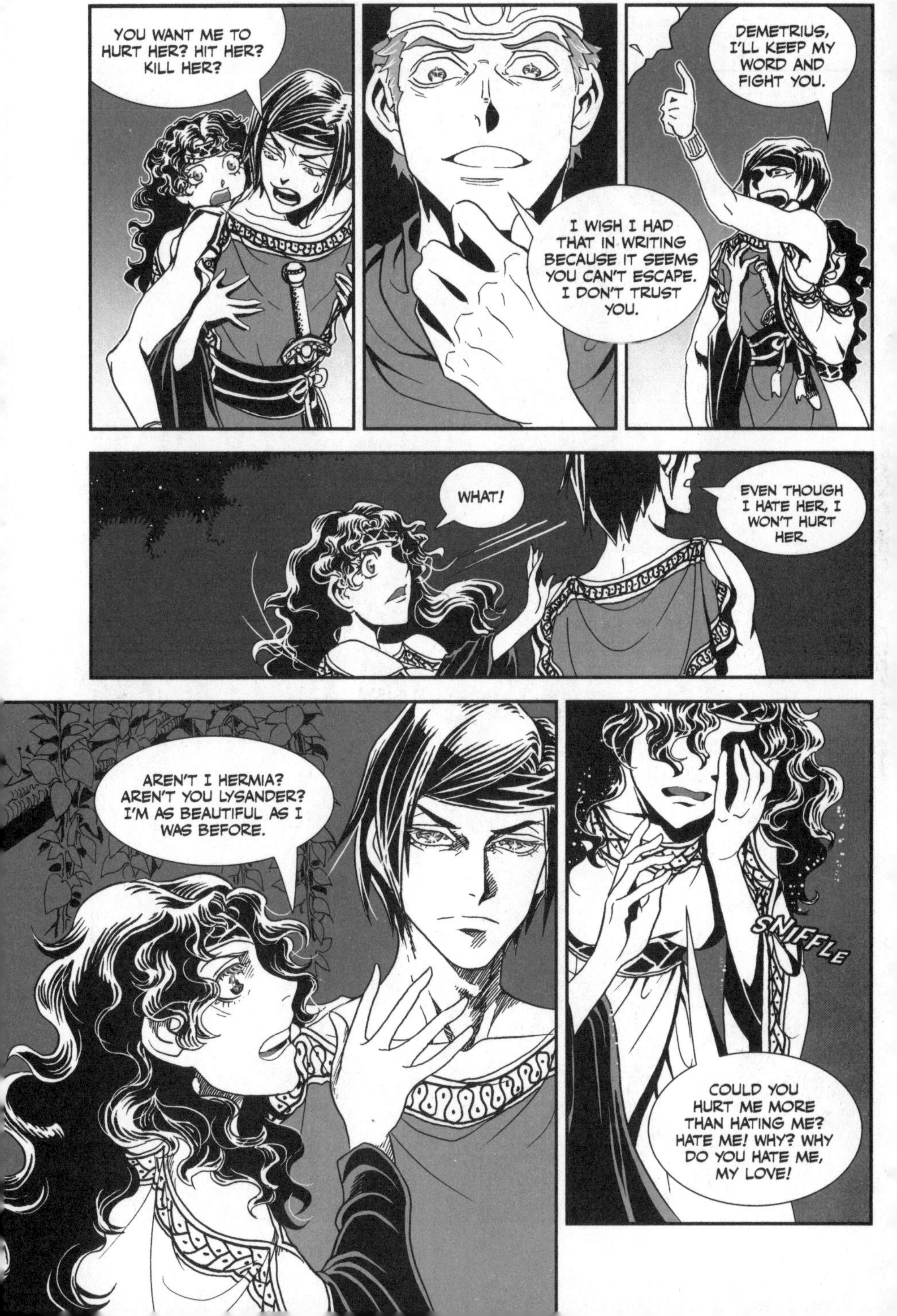
DEMETRIUS, I'LL KEEP MY WORD AND FIGHT YOU.
I WISH I HAD THAT IN WRITING BECAUSE IT SEEMS YOU CAN'T ESCAPE. I DON'T TRUST YOU.
YOU WANT ME TO HURT HER? HIT HER? KILL HER?
EVEN THOUGH I HATE HER, I WON'T HURT HER.
WHAT!
SNIFFLE
COULD YOU HURT ME MORE THAN HATING ME? HATE ME! WHY? WHY DO YOU HATE ME, MY LOVE!
AREN'T I HERMIA? AREN'T YOU LYSANDER? I'M AS BEAUTIFUL AS I WAS BEFORE.

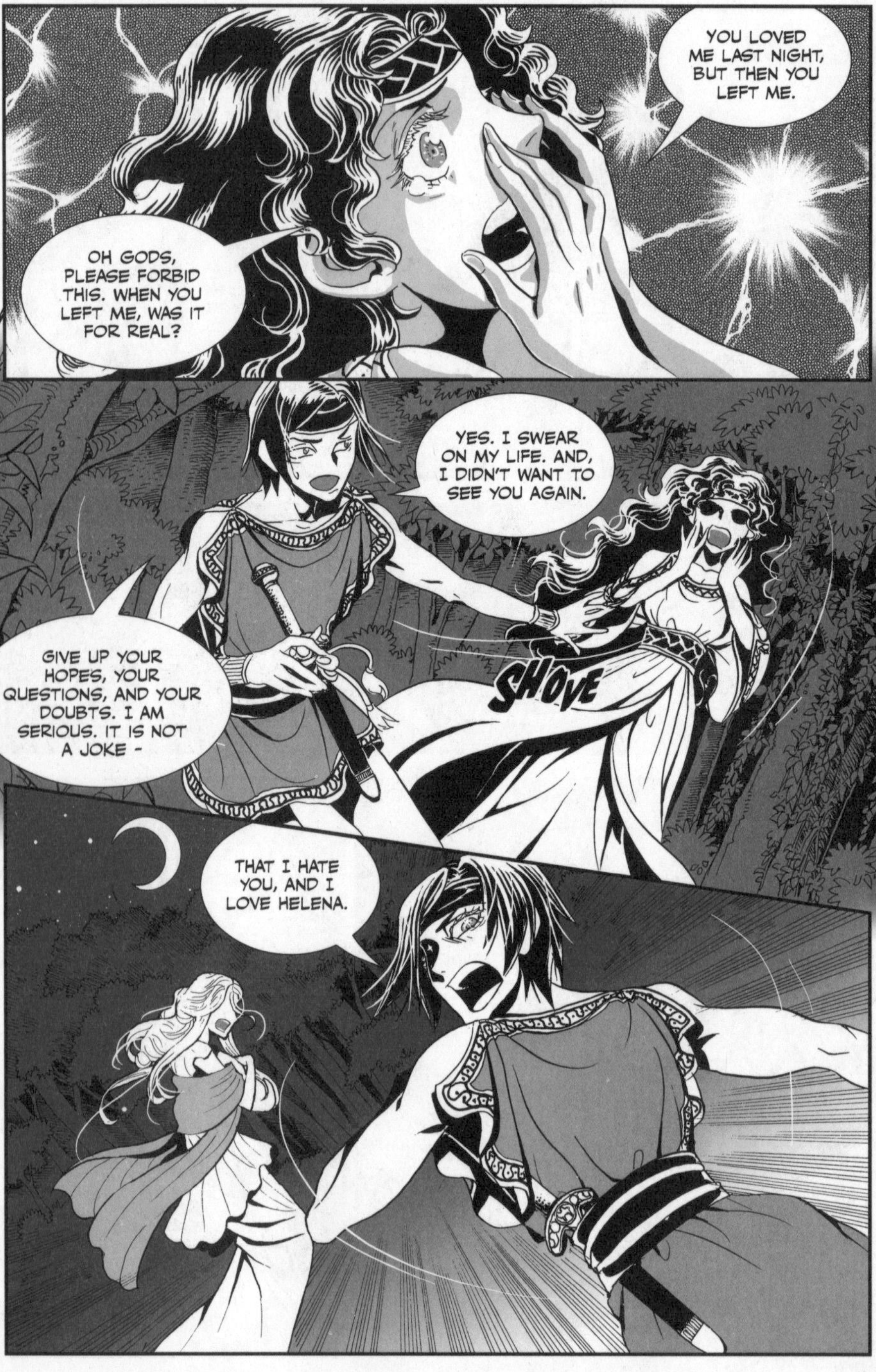

YOU LOVED ME LAST NIGHT, BUT THEN YOU LEFT ME.
OH GODS, PLEASE FORBID THIS. WHEN YOU LEFT ME, WAS IT FOR REAL?
YES. I SWEAR ON MY LIFE. AND, I DIDN'T WANT TO SEE YOU AGAIN.
GIVE UP YOUR HOPES, YOUR QUESTIONS, AND YOUR DOUBTS. I AM SERIOUS. IT IS NOT A JOKE -
SHOVE
THAT I HATE YOU, AND I LOVE HELENA.

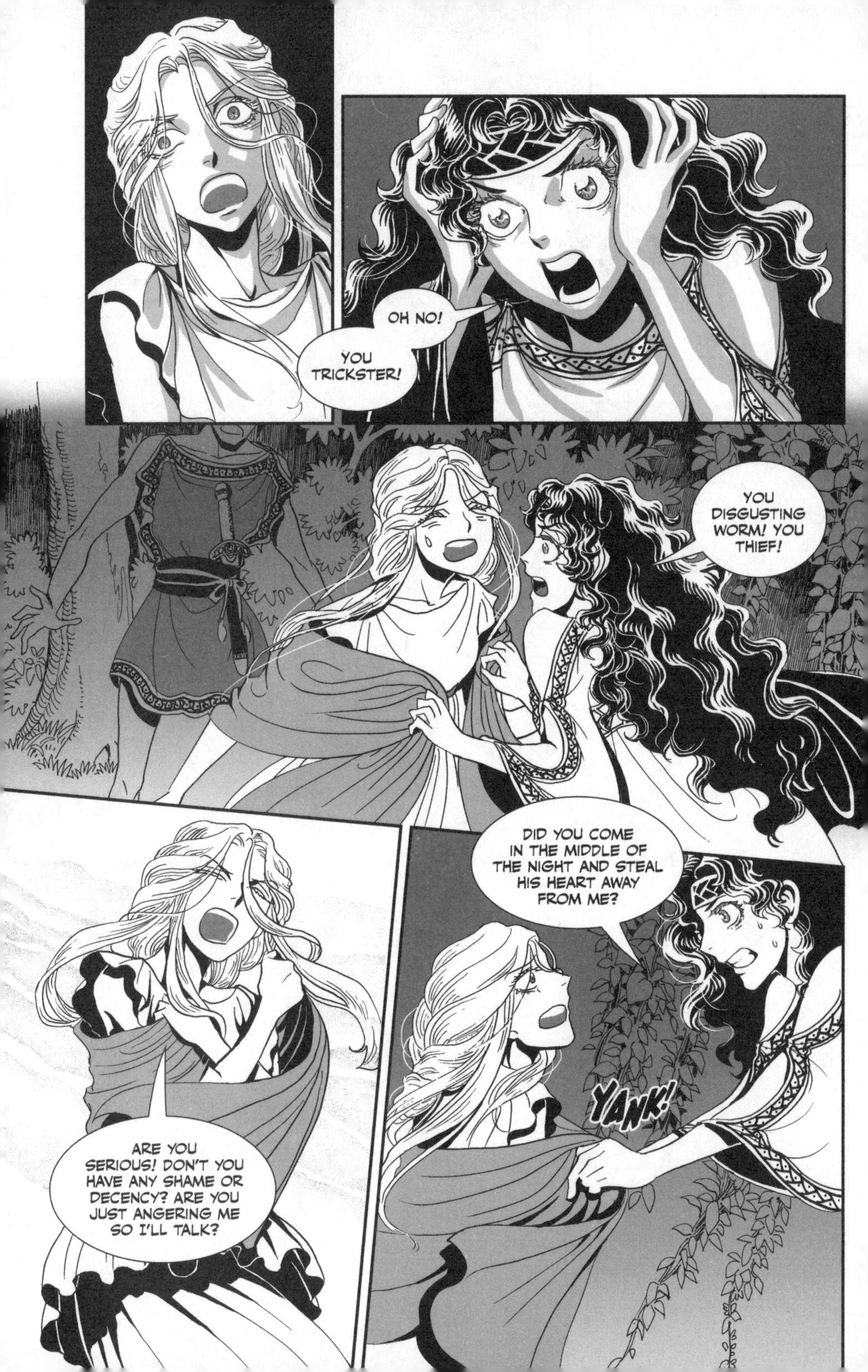
OH NO!
YOU TRICKSTER!
YOU DISGUSTING WORM! YOU THIEF!
DID YOU COME IN THE MIDDLE OF THE NIGHT AND STEAL HIS HEART AWAY FROM ME?
YANK!
ARE YOU SERIOUS! DON'T YOU HAVE ANY SHAME OR DECENCY? ARE YOU JUST ANGERING ME SO I'LL TALK?

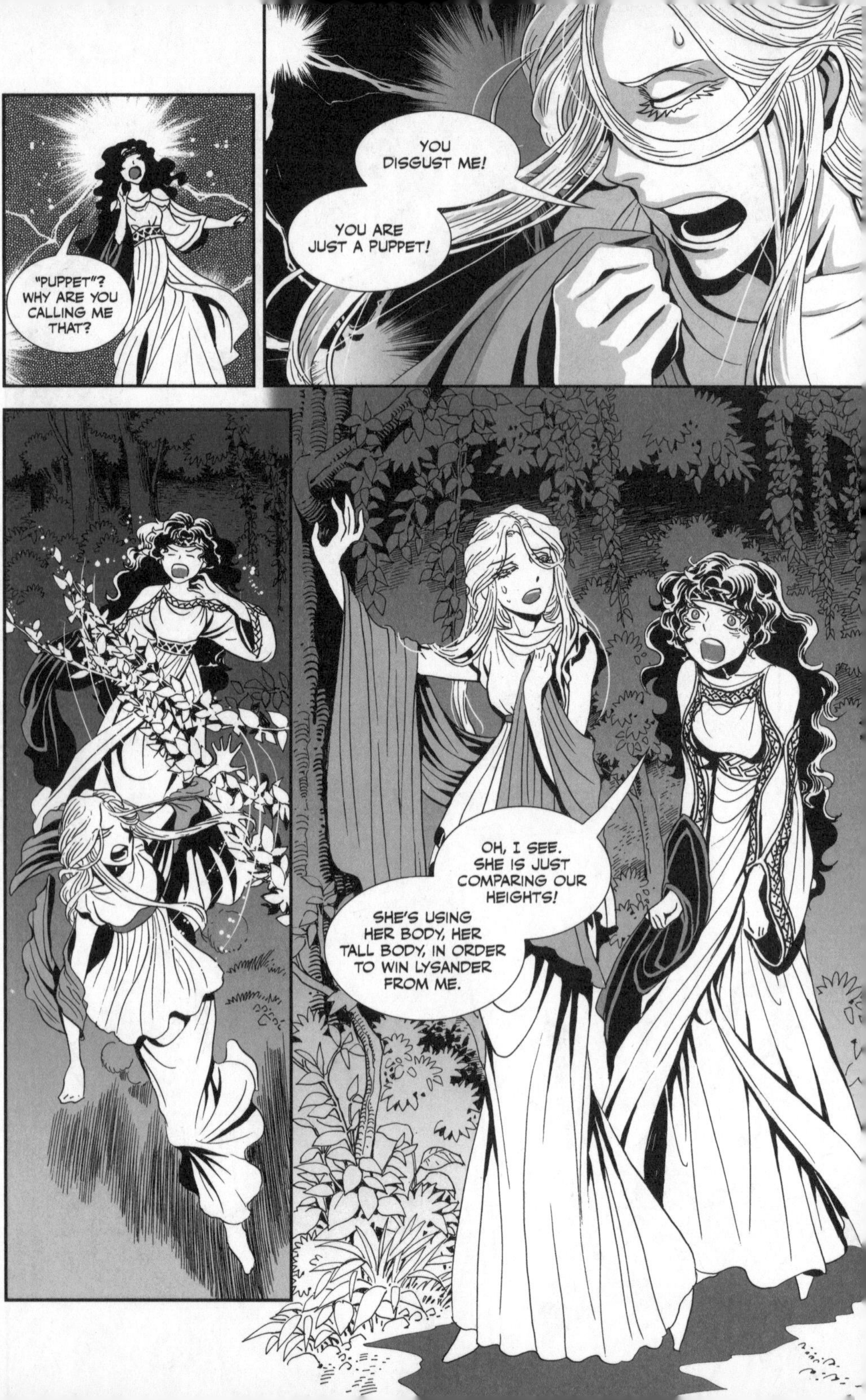
YOU DISGUST ME!
YOU ARE JUST A PUPPET!
"PUPPET"? WHY ARE YOU CALLING ME THAT?
OH, I SEE. SHE IS JUST COMPARING OUR HEIGHTS!
SHE'S USING HER BODY, HER TALL BODY, IN ORDER TO WIN LYSANDER FROM ME.

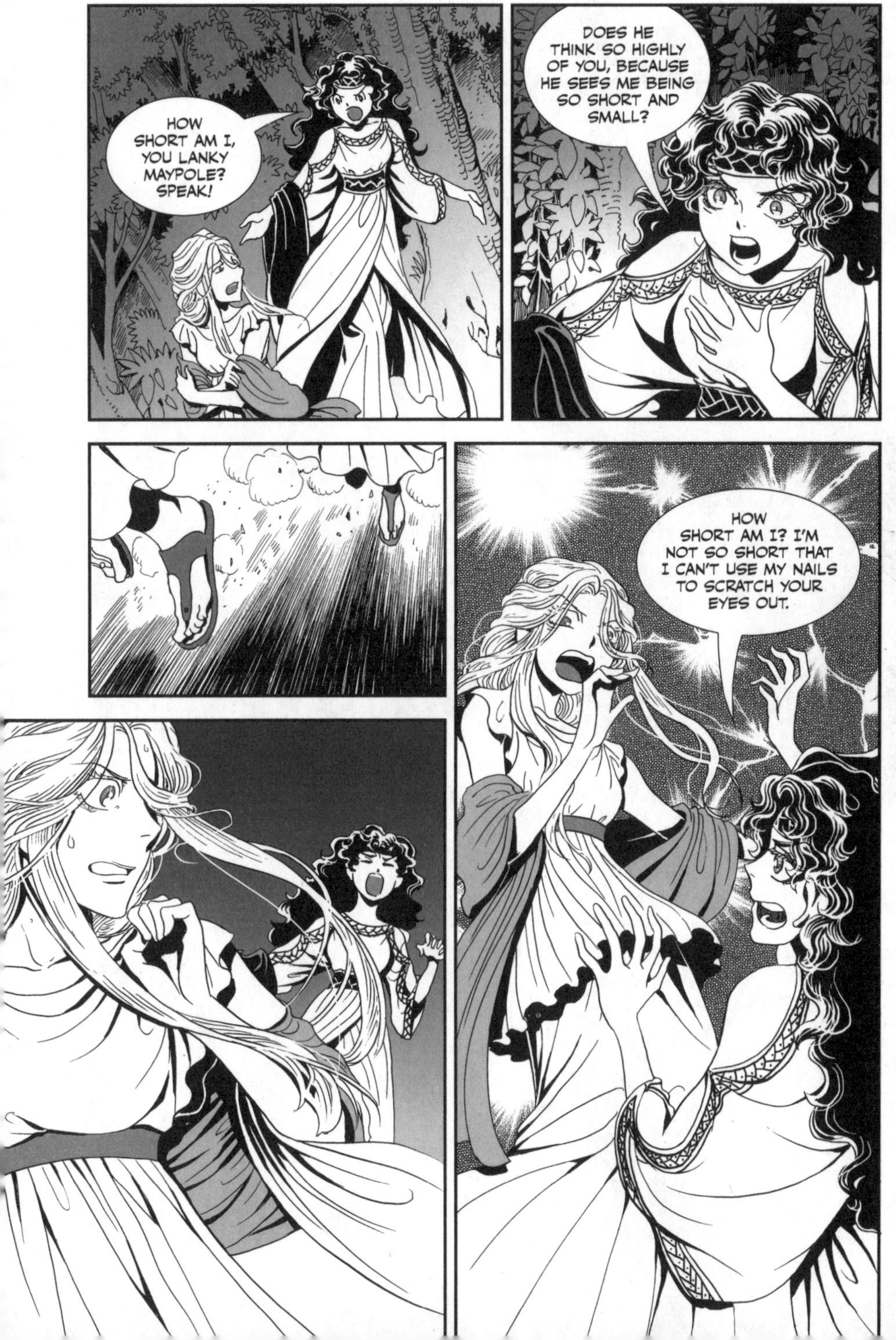
DOES HE THINK SO HIGHLY OF YOU, BECAUSE HE SEES ME BEING SO SHORT AND SMALL?
HOW SHORT AM I, YOU LANKY MAYPOLE? SPEAK!
HOW SHORT AM I? I'M NOT SO SHORT THAT I CAN'T USE MY NAILS TO SCRATCH YOUR EYES OUT.

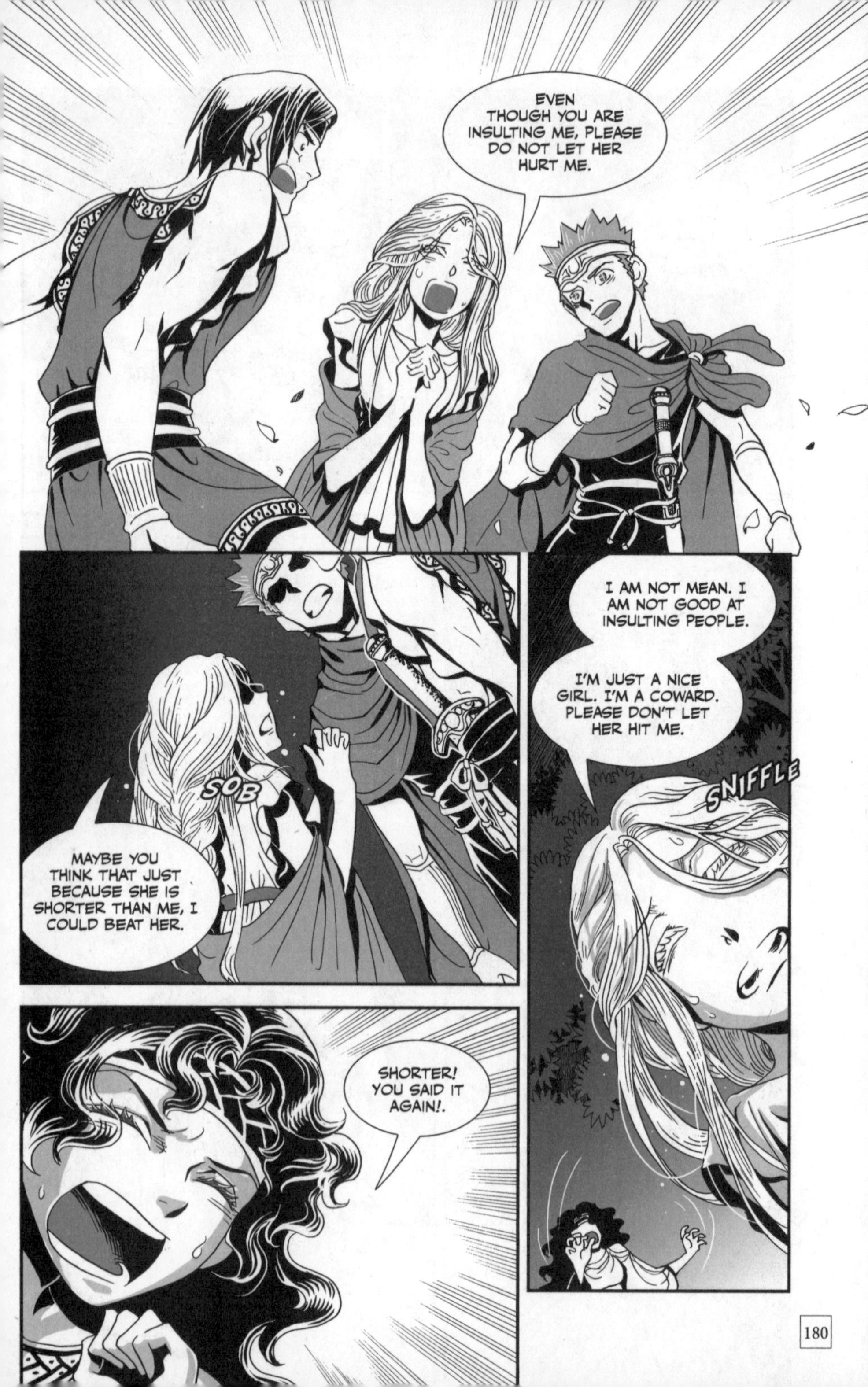
EVEN THOUGH YOU ARE INSULTING ME, PLEASE DO NOT LET HER HURT ME.
I AM NOT MEAN. I AM NOT GOOD AT INSULTING PEOPLE.
I'M JUST A NICE GIRL. I'M A COWARD. PLEASE DON'T LET HER HIT ME.
SNIFFLE
SOB
MAYBE YOU THINK THAT JUST BECAUSE SHE IS SHORTER THAN ME, I COULD BEAT HER.
SHORTER! YOU SAID IT AGAIN!.

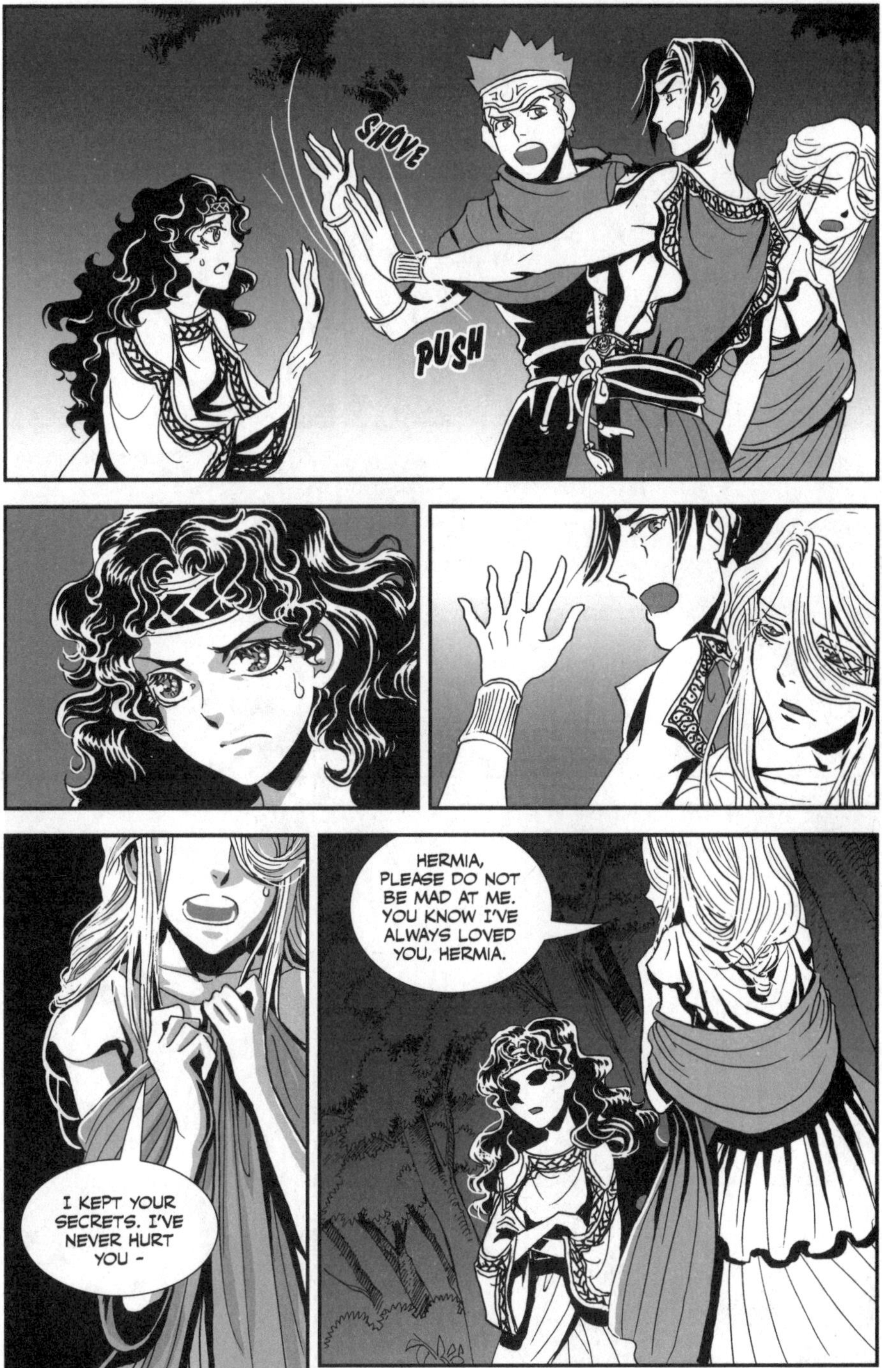
SHOVE
PUSH
HERMIA, PLEASE DO NOT BE MAD AT ME. YOU KNOW I'VE ALWAYS LOVED YOU, HERMIA.
I KEPT YOUR SECRETS. I'VE NEVER HURT YOU -

EXCEPT, BECAUSE I LOVED DEMETRIUS, I TOLD HIM THAT YOU SNUCK INTO THE WOODS. HE FOLLOWED YOU, AND THEN I FOLLOWED HIM.
THEN HE INSULTED ME, AND HE THREATENED TO HIT ME, KICK ME, AND EVEN KILL ME:
PLEASE, IF YOU WILL JUST LET ME GO BACK TO ATHENS, I WILL REGRET WHAT I HAVE DONE, AND WON'T FOLLOW YOU ANY MORE. LET ME GO. YOU CAN SEE THAT I ACTED FOOLISHLY.
THEN LEAVE. WHAT IS IT THAT'S KEEPING YOU HERE?
STOMP
MY FOOLISH HEART, THAT I'M LEAVING BEHIND.

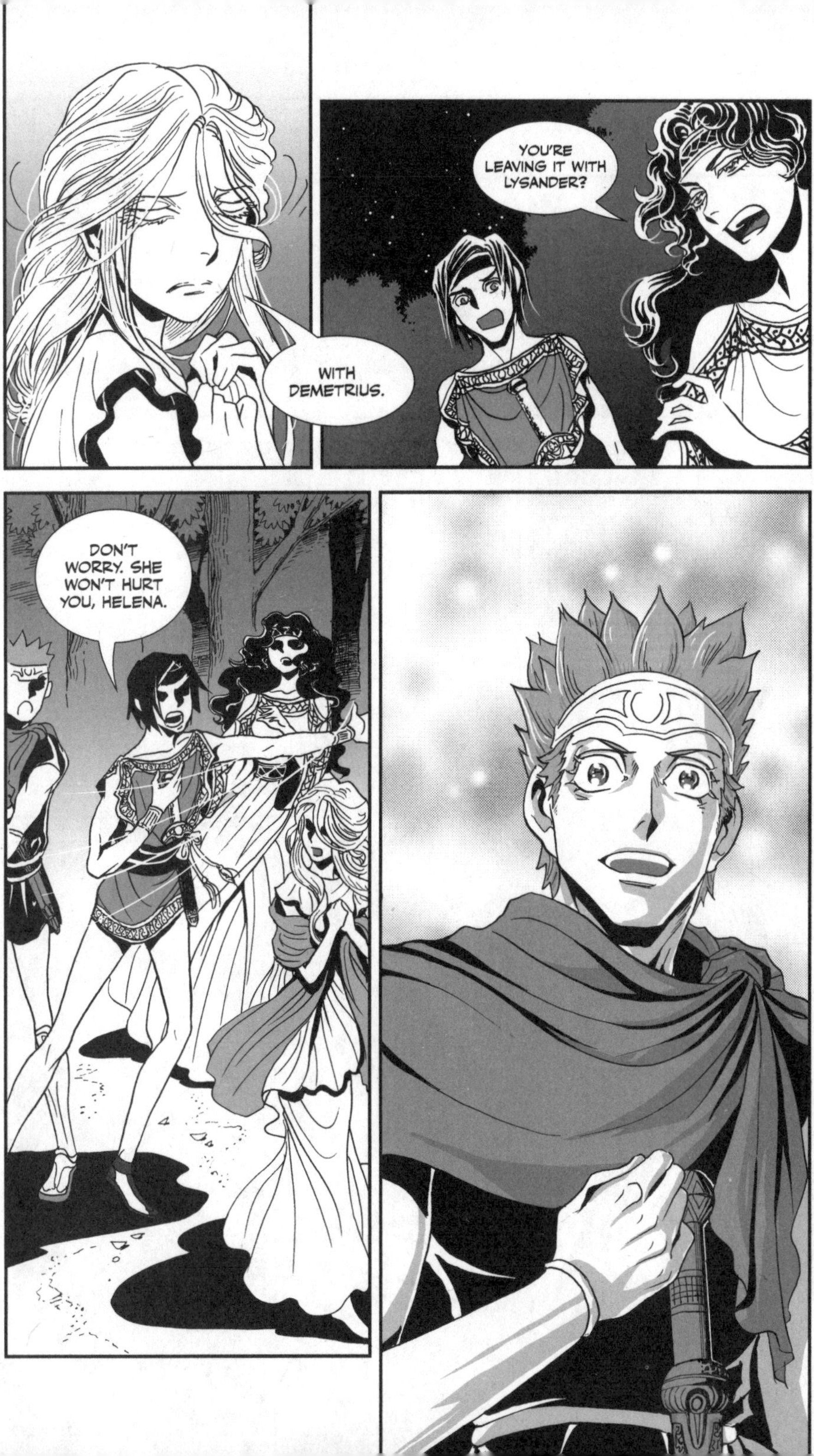
YOU'RE LEAVING IT WITH LYSANDER?
WITH DEMETRIUS.
DON'T WORRY. SHE WON'T HURT YOU, HELENA.

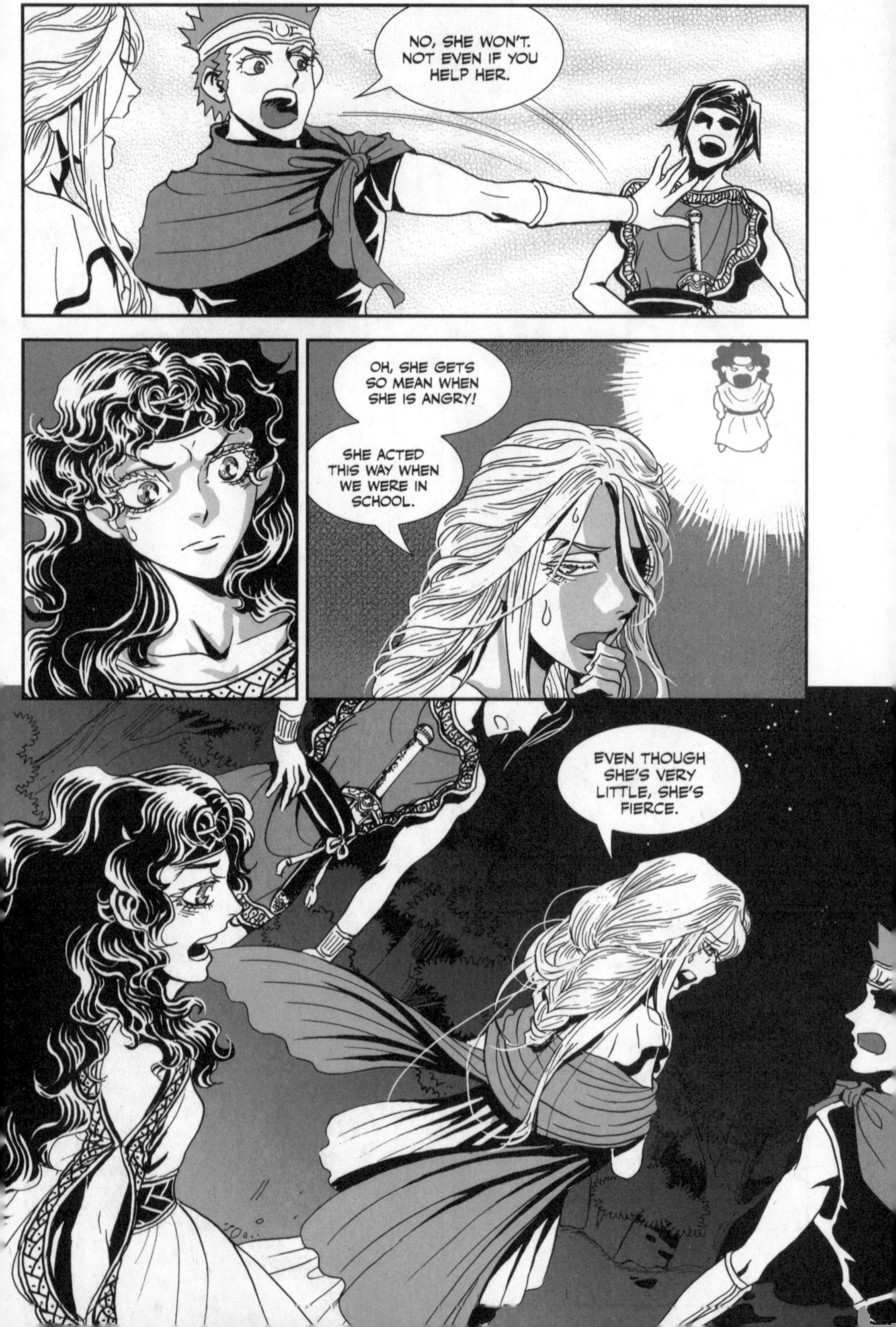
NO, SHE WON'T. NOT EVEN IF YOU HELP HER.
OH, SHE GETS SO MEAN WHEN SHE IS ANGRY!
SHE ACTED THIS WAY WHEN WE WERE IN SCHOOL.
EVEN THOUGH SHE'S VERY LITTLE, SHE'S FIERCE.

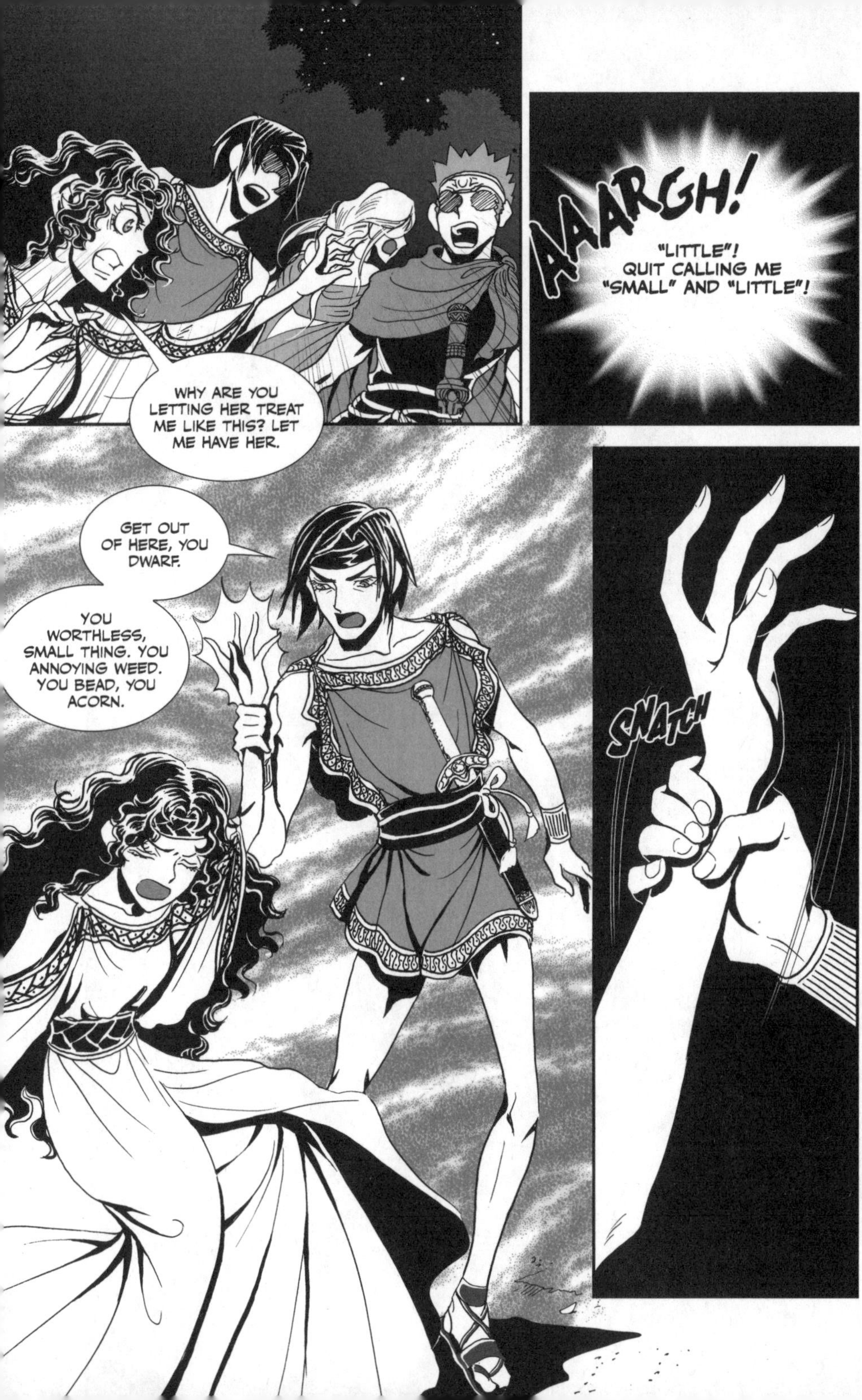
AAARGH!
"LITTLE"! QUIT CALLING ME "SMALL" AND "LITTLE"!
WHY ARE YOU LETTING HER TREAT ME LIKE THIS? LET ME HAVE HER.
SNATCH
GET OUT OF HERE, YOU DWARF.
YOU WORTHLESS, SMALL THING. YOU ANNOYING WEED. YOU BEAD, YOU ACORN.

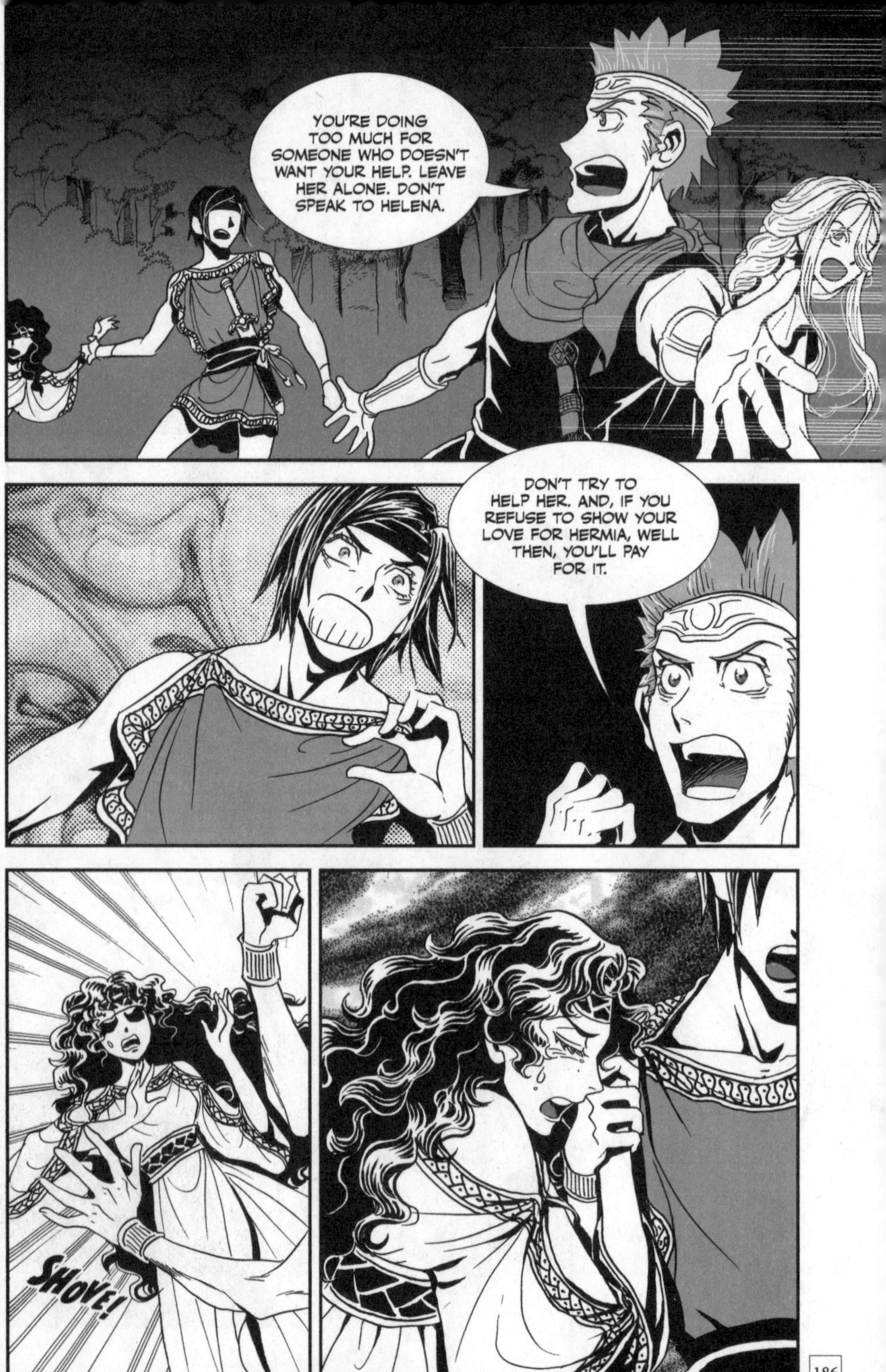
YOU'RE DOING TOO MUCH FOR SOMEONE WHO DOESN'T WANT YOUR HELP. LEAVE HER ALONE. DON'T SPEAK TO HELENA.
DON'T TRY TO HELP HER. AND, IF YOU REFUSE TO SHOW YOUR LOVE FOR HERMIA, WELL THEN, YOU'LL PAY FOR IT.
SHOVE!

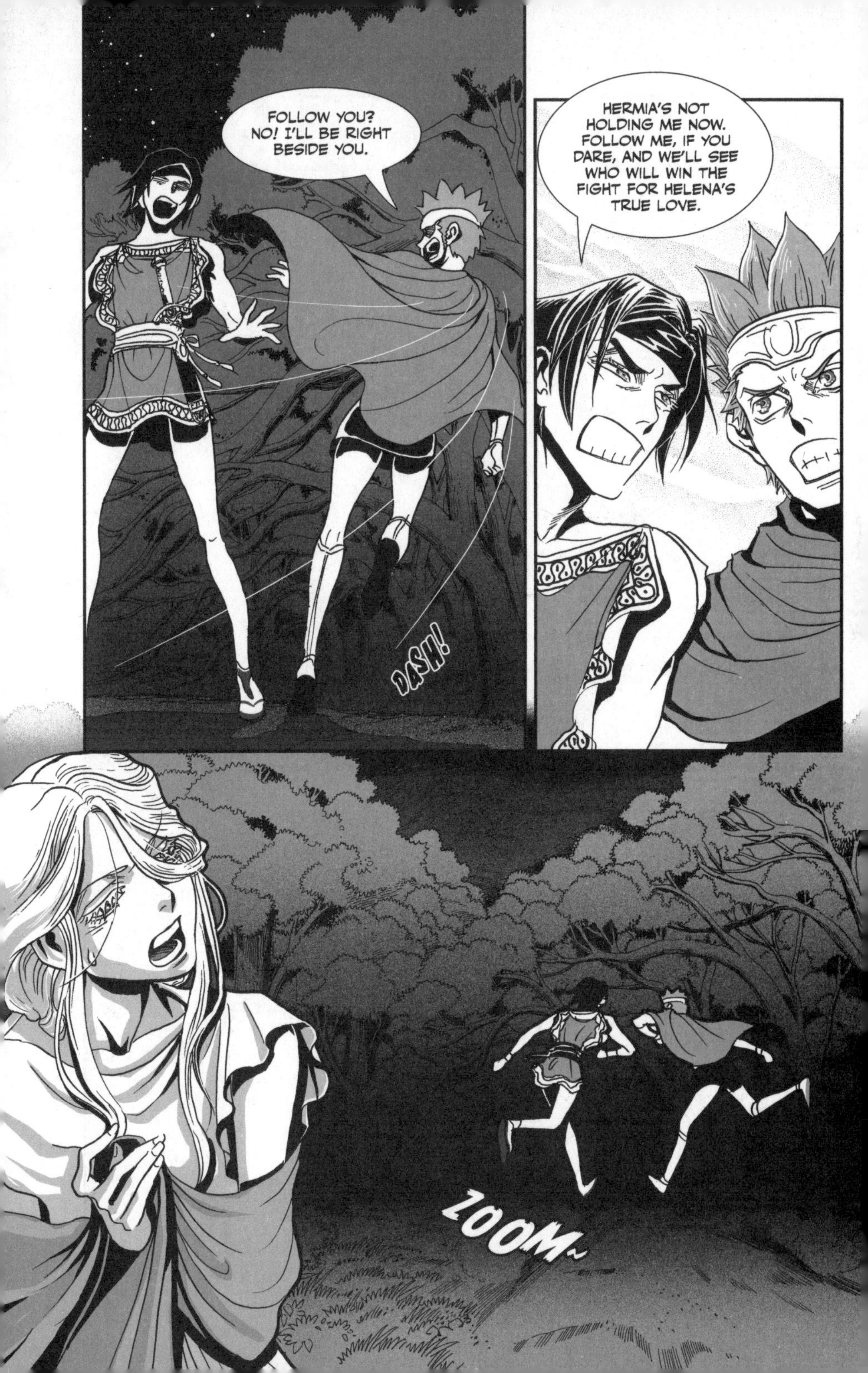
HERMIA'S NOT HOLDING ME NOW. FOLLOW ME, IF YOU DARE, AND WE'LL SEE WHO WILL WIN THE FIGHT FOR HELENA'S TRUE LOVE.
FOLLOW YOU? NO! I'LL BE RIGHT BESIDE YOU.
DASH!
ZOOM~

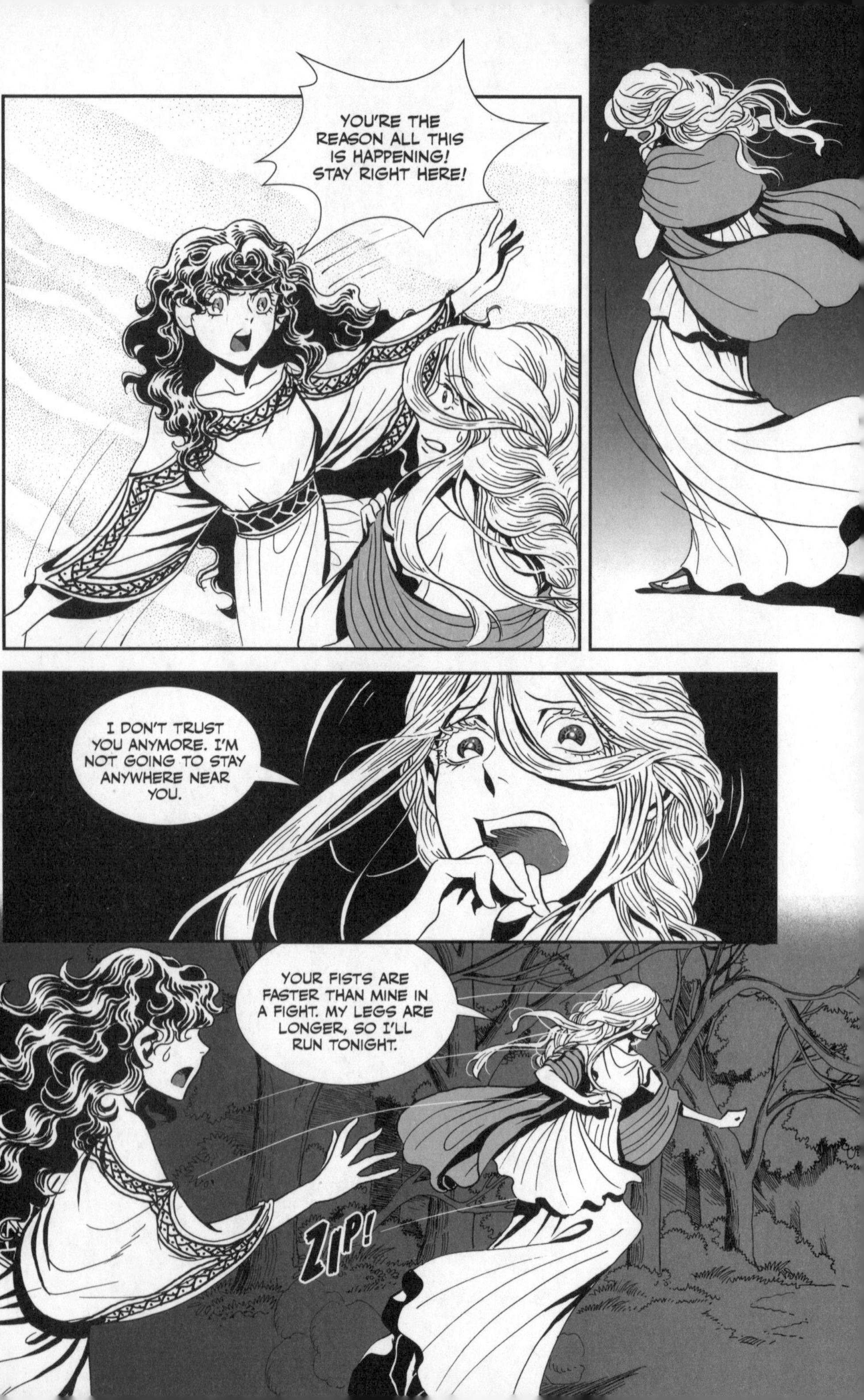
YOU'RE THE REASON ALL THIS IS HAPPENING! STAY RIGHT HERE!
I DON'T TRUST YOU ANYMORE. I'M NOT GOING TO STAY ANYWHERE NEAR YOU.
YOUR FISTS ARE FASTER THAN MINE IN A FIGHT. MY LEGS ARE LONGER, SO I'LL RUN TONIGHT.
ZIP!

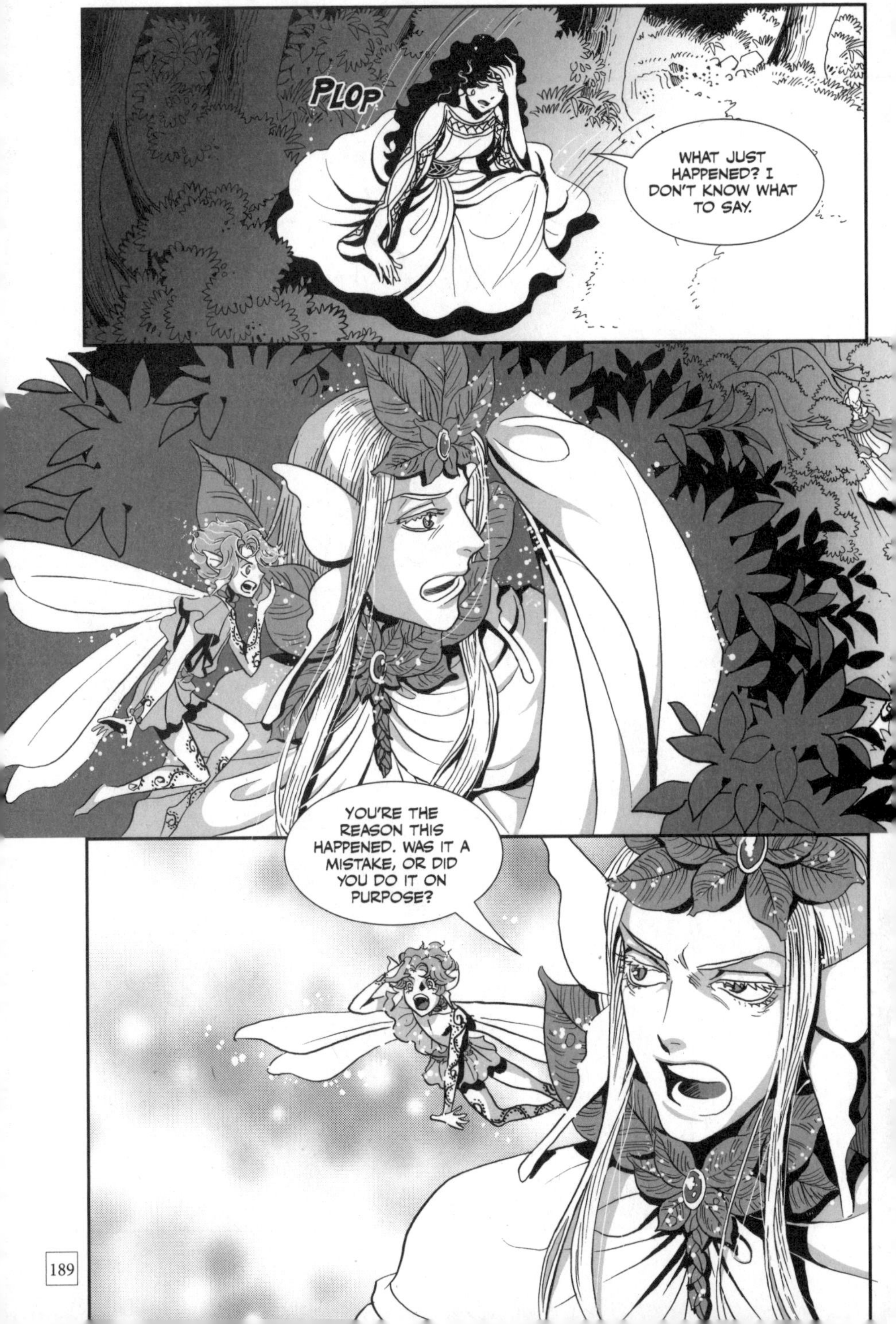
WHAT JUST HAPPENED? I DON'T KNOW WHAT TO SAY.
PLOP
YOU'RE THE REASON THIS HAPPENED. WAS IT A MISTAKE, OR DID YOU DO IT ON PURPOSE?

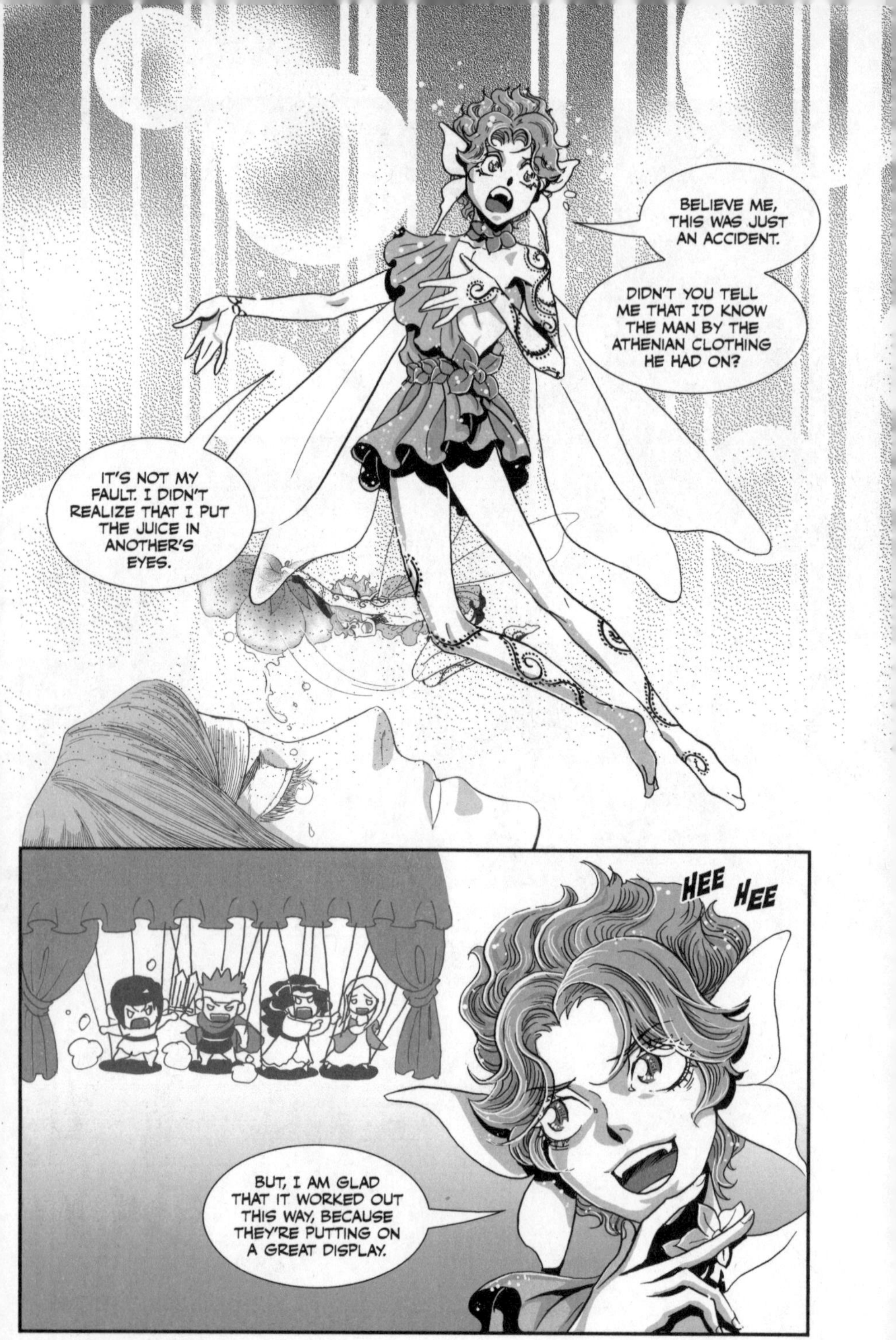
BELIEVE ME, THIS WAS JUST AN ACCIDENT.
DIDN'T YOU TELL ME THAT I'D KNOW THE MAN BY THE ATHENIAN CLOTHING HE HAD ON?
IT'S NOT MY FAULT. I DIDN'T REALIZE THAT I PUT THE JUICE IN ANOTHER'S EYES.
HEE HEE
BUT, I AM GLAD THAT IT WORKED OUT THIS WAY, BECAUSE THEY'RE PUTTING ON A GREAT DISPLAY.

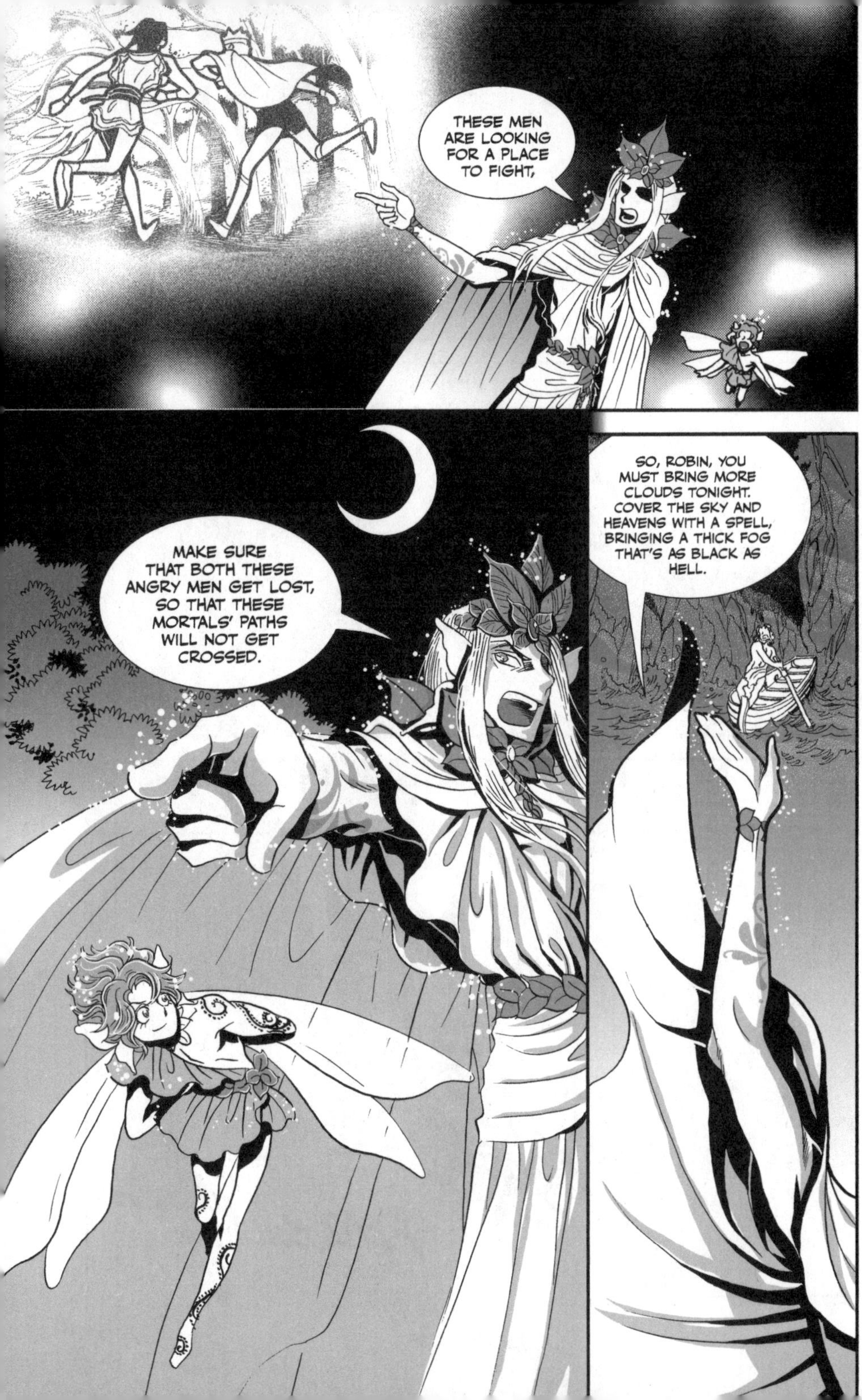
THESE MEN ARE LOOKING FOR A PLACE TO FIGHT,
SO, ROBIN, YOU MUST BRING MORE CLOUDS TONIGHT. COVER THE SKY AND HEAVENS WITH A SPELL, BRINGING A THICK FOG THAT'S AS BLACK AS HELL.
MAKE SURE THAT BOTH THESE ANGRY MEN GET LOST, SO THAT THESE MORTALS' PATHS WILL NOT GET CROSSED.

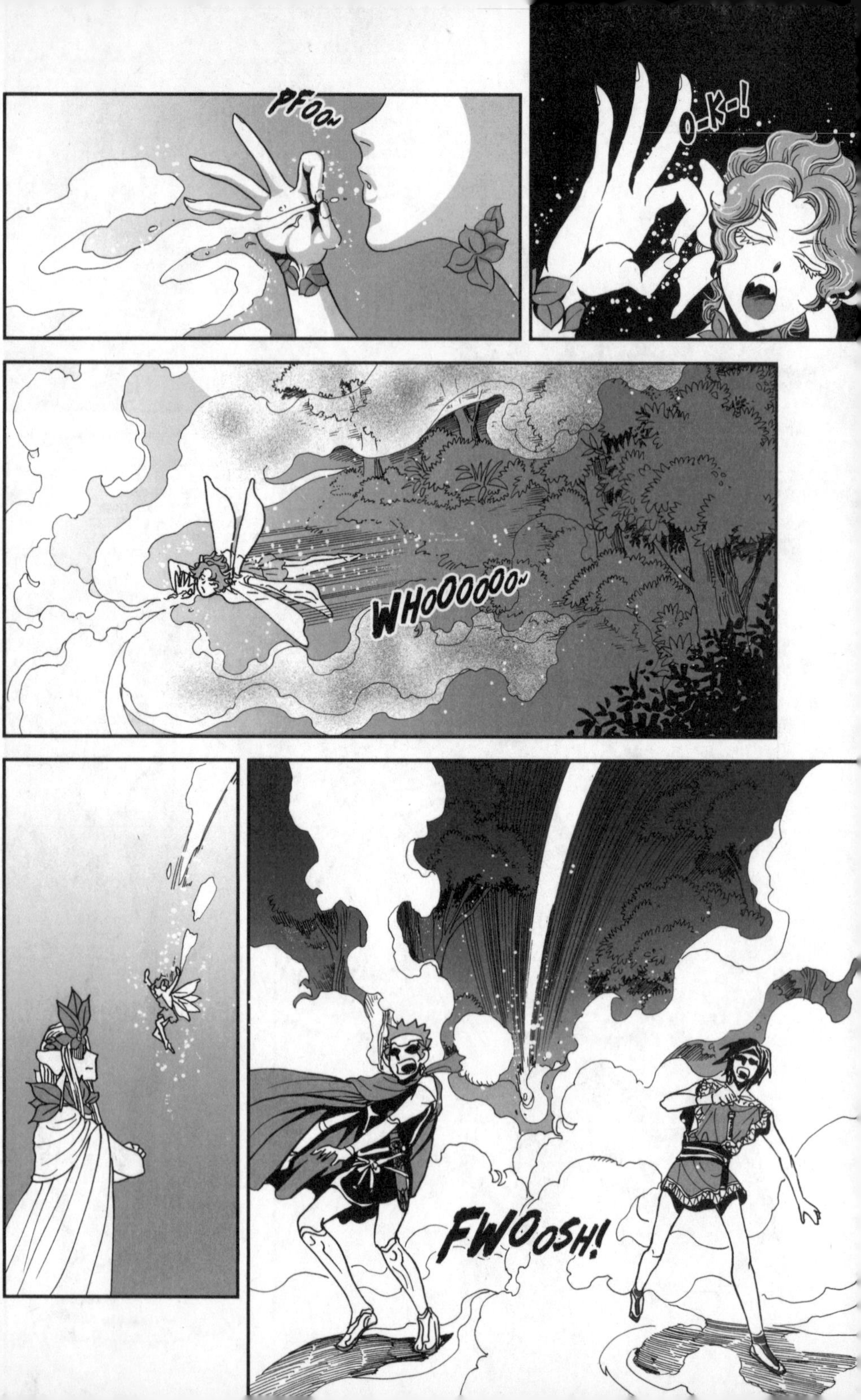
O-K-!
PFOO~
WHOOOOOO~
FWOOSH!

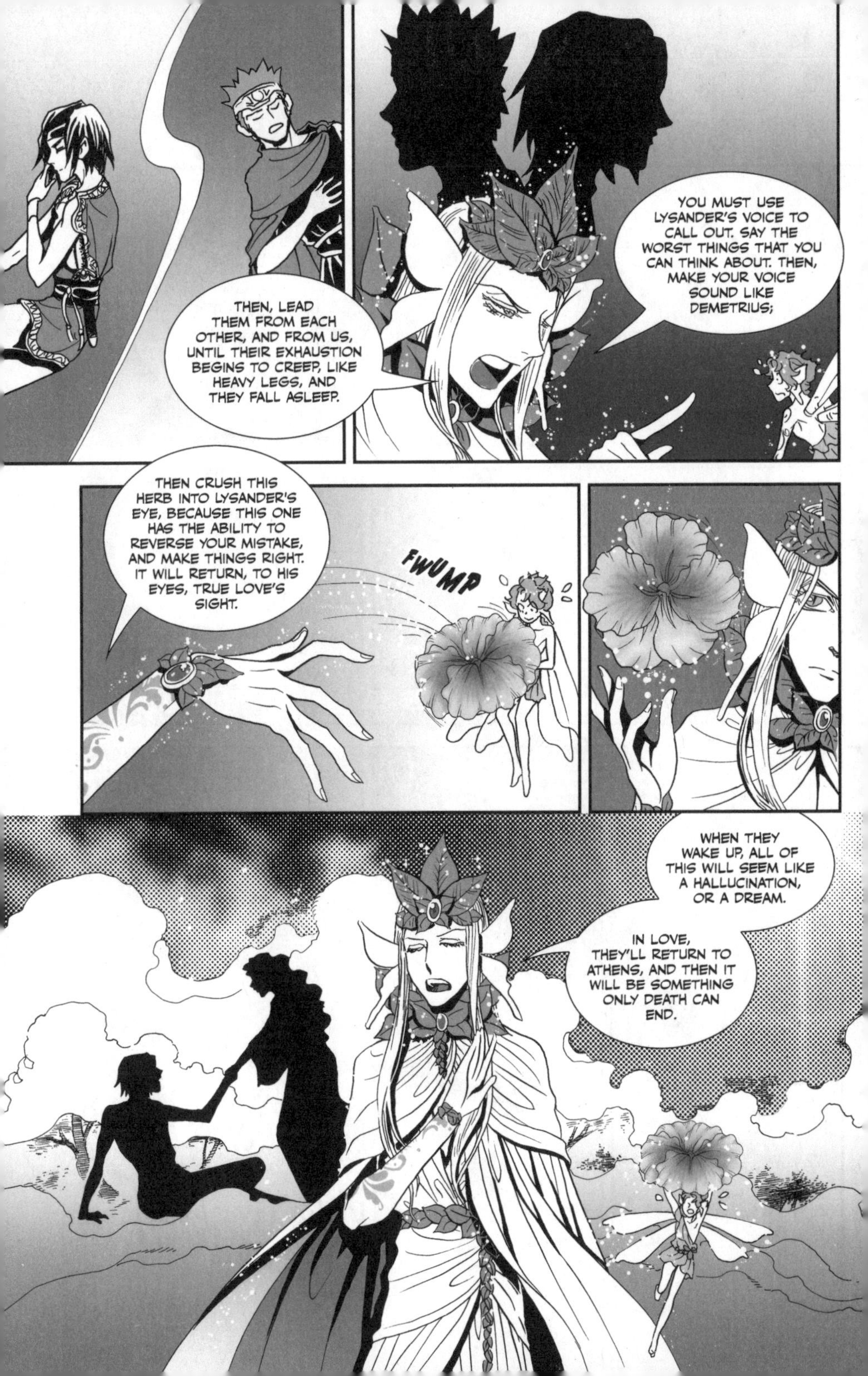
YOU MUST USE LYSANDER'S VOICE TO CALL OUT. SAY THE WORST THINGS THAT YOU CAN THINK ABOUT. THEN, MAKE YOUR VOICE SOUND LIKE DEMETRIUS;
THEN, LEAD THEM FROM EACH OTHER, AND FROM US, UNTIL THEIR EXHAUSTION BEGINS TO CREEP, LIKE HEAVY LEGS, AND THEY FALL ASLEEP.
THEN CRUSH THIS HERB INTO LYSANDER'S EYE, BECAUSE THIS ONE HAS THE ABILITY TO REVERSE YOUR MISTAKE, AND MAKE THINGS RIGHT. IT WILL RETURN, TO HIS EYES, TRUE LOVE'S SIGHT.
FWUMP
WHEN THEY WAKE UP, ALL OF THIS WILL SEEM LIKE A HALLUCINATION, OR A DREAM.
IN LOVE, THEY'LL RETURN TO ATHENS, AND THEN IT WILL BE SOMETHING ONLY DEATH CAN END.

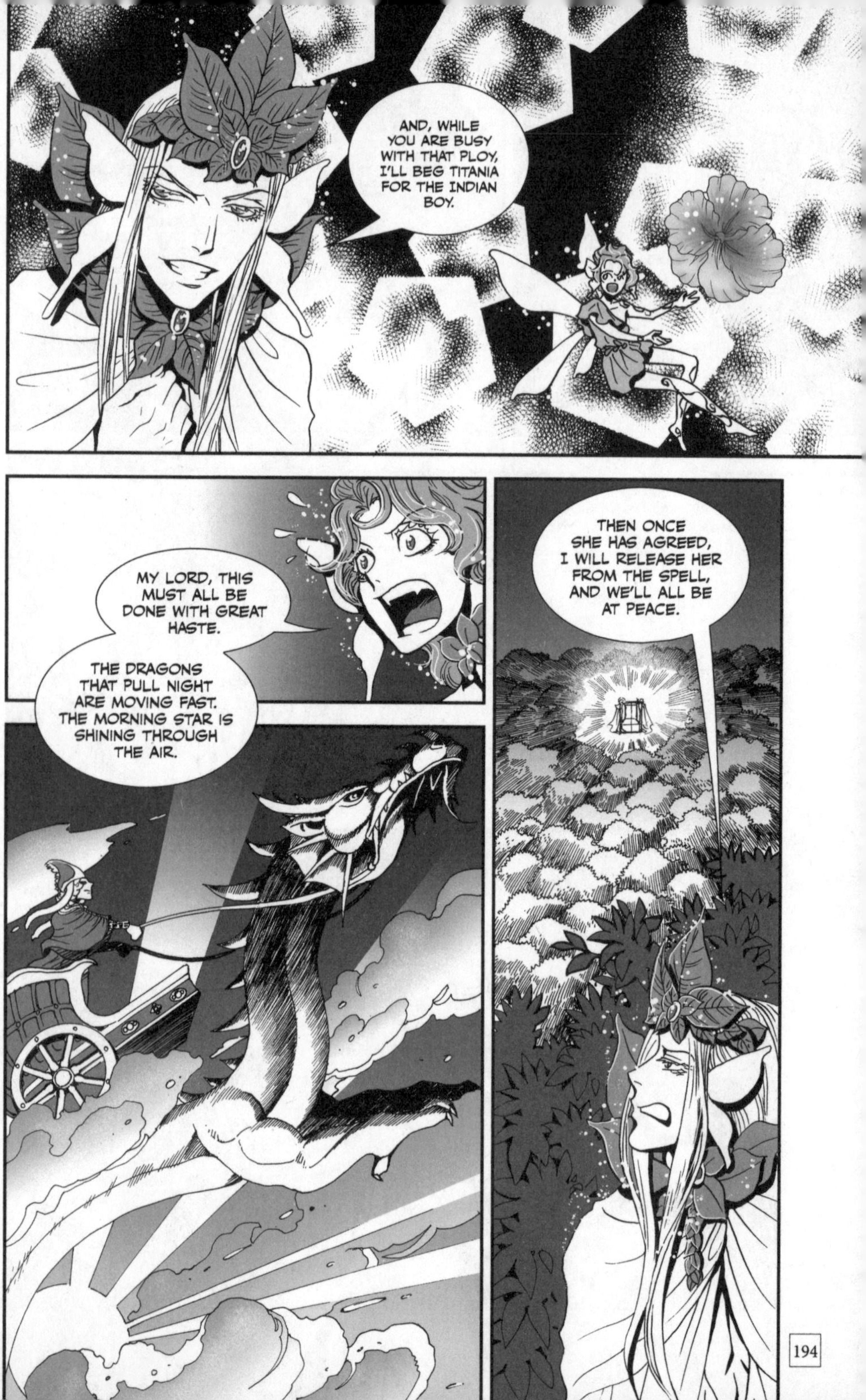
AND, WHILE YOU ARE BUSY WITH THAT PLOY, I'LL BEG TITANIA FOR THE INDIAN BOY.
THEN ONCE SHE HAS AGREED, I WILL RELEASE HER FROM THE SPELL, AND WE'LL ALL BE AT PEACE.
MY LORD, THIS MUST ALL BE DONE WITH GREAT HASTE.
THE DRAGONS THAT PULL NIGHT ARE MOVING FAST. THE MORNING STAR IS SHINING THROUGH THE AIR.

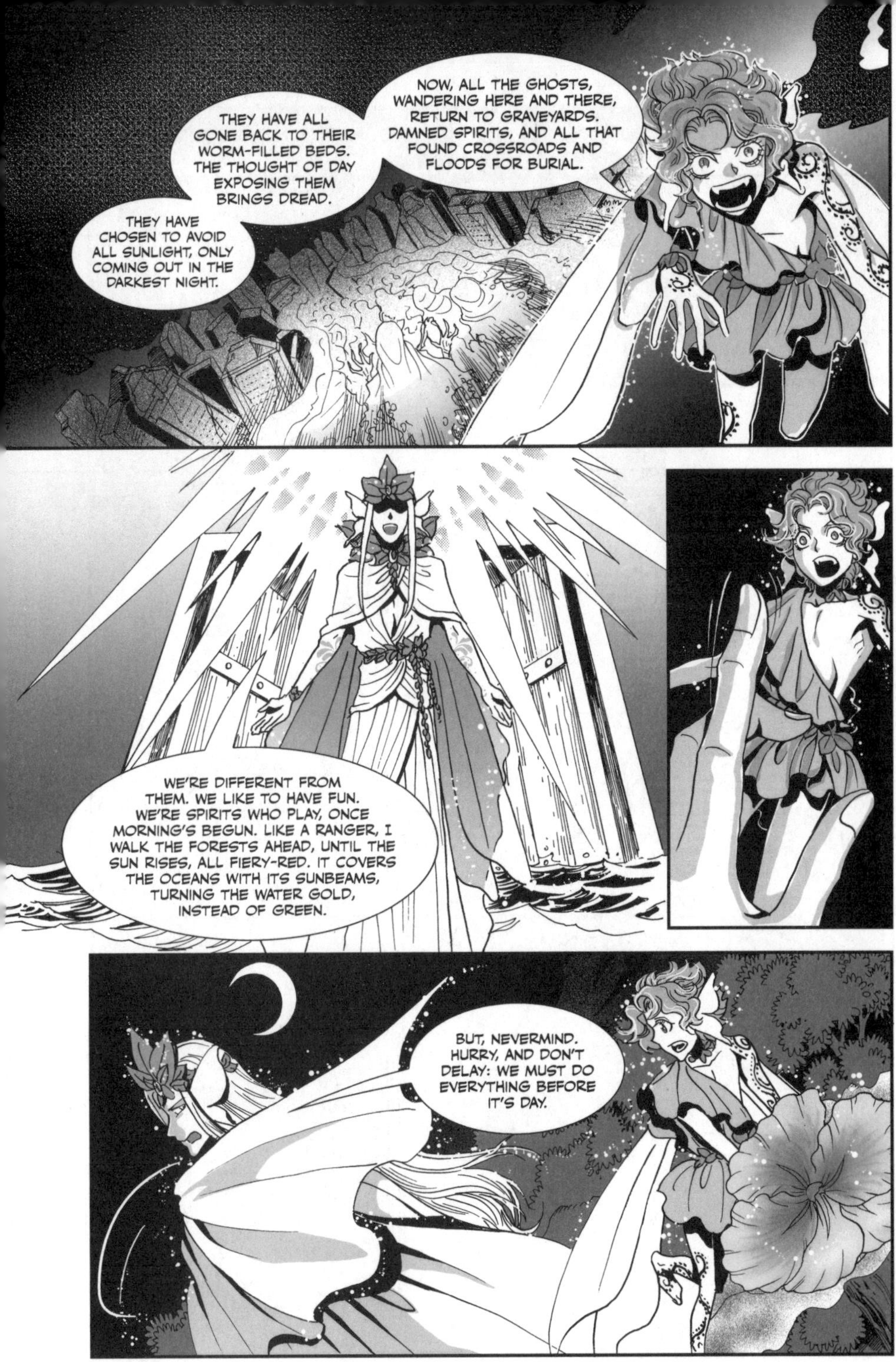
NOW, ALL THE GHOSTS, WANDERING HERE AND THERE, RETURN TO GRAVEYARDS. DAMNED SPIRITS, AND ALL THAT FOUND CROSSROADS AND FLOODS FOR BURIAL.
THEY HAVE ALL GONE BACK TO THEIR WORM-FILLED BEDS. THE THOUGHT OF DAY EXPOSING THEM BRINGS DREAD.
THEY HAVE CHOSEN TO AVOID ALL SUNLIGHT, ONLY COMING OUT IN THE DARKEST NIGHT.
WE'RE DIFFERENT FROM THEM. WE LIKE TO HAVE FUN. WE'RE SPIRITS WHO PLAY, ONCE MORNING'S BEGUN. LIKE A RANGER, I WALK THE FORESTS AHEAD, UNTIL THE SUN RISES, ALL FIERY-RED. IT COVERS THE OCEANS WITH ITS SUNBEAMS, TURNING THE WATER GOLD, INSTEAD OF GREEN.
BUT, NEVERMIND. HURRY, AND DON'T DELAY: WE MUST DO EVERYTHING BEFORE IT'S DAY.

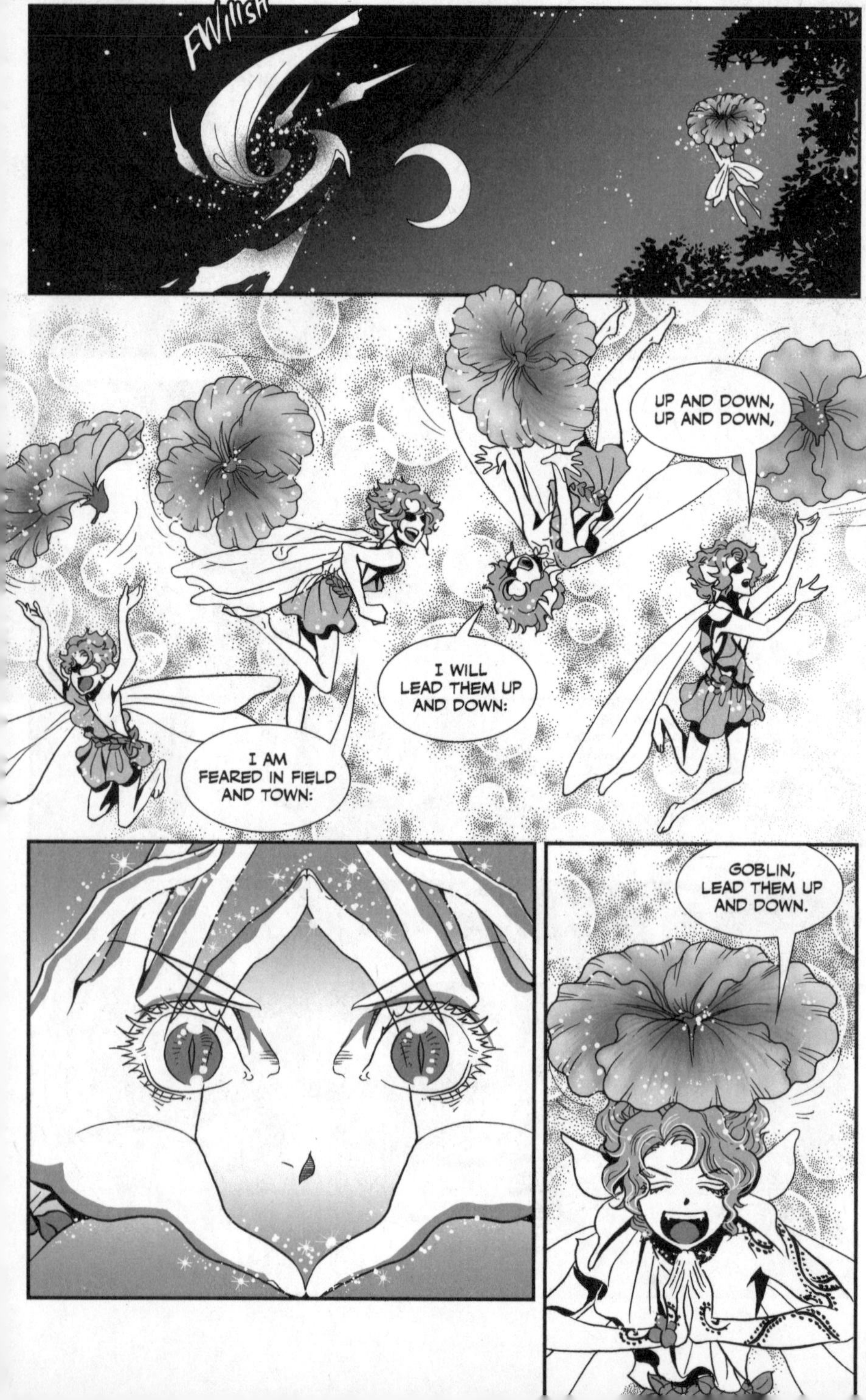
FWIIISH
UP AND DOWN, UP AND DOWN,
I WILL LEAD THEM UP AND DOWN:
I AM FEARED IN FIELD AND TOWN:
GOBLIN, LEAD THEM UP AND DOWN.

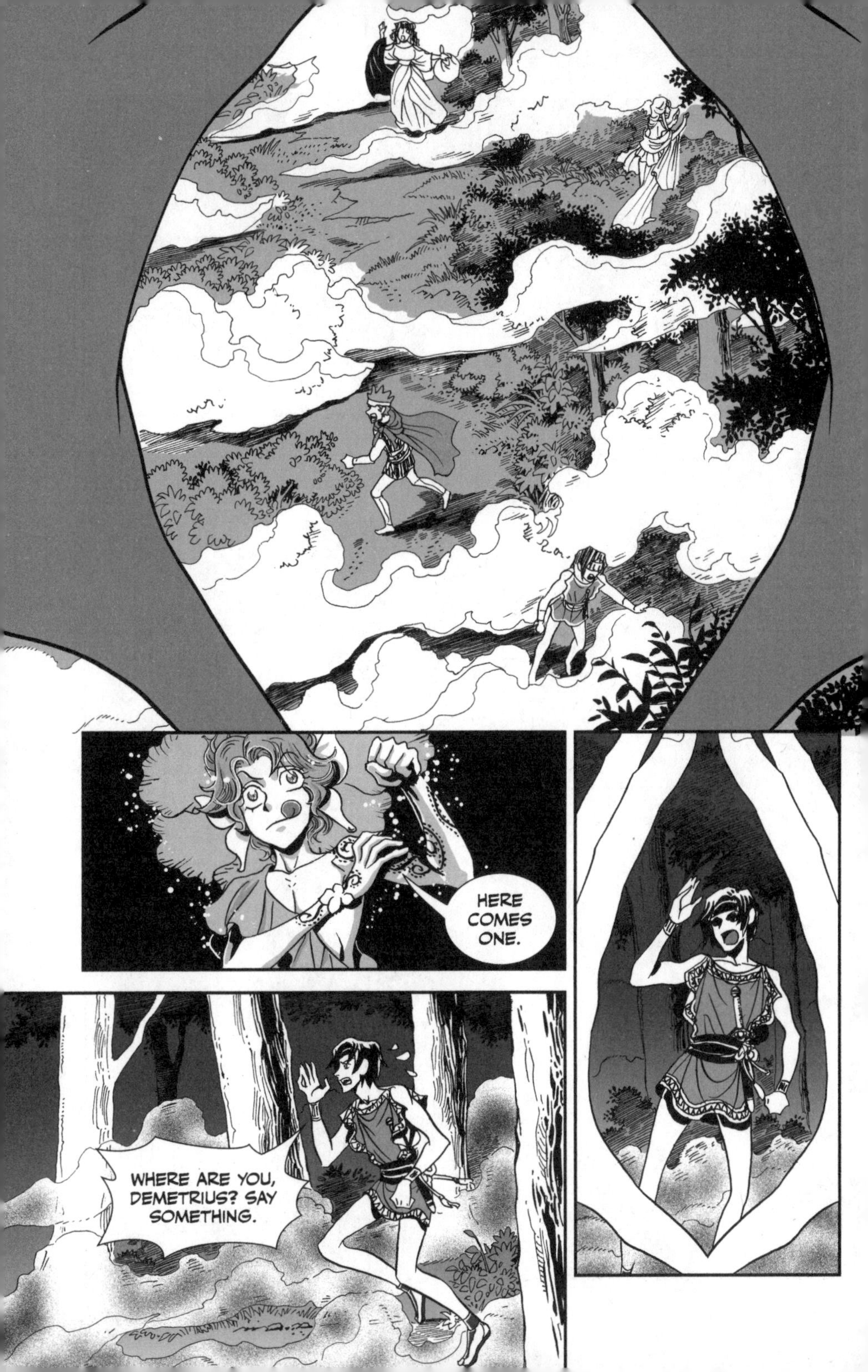
HERE COMES ONE.
WHERE ARE YOU, DEMETRIUS? SAY SOMETHING.

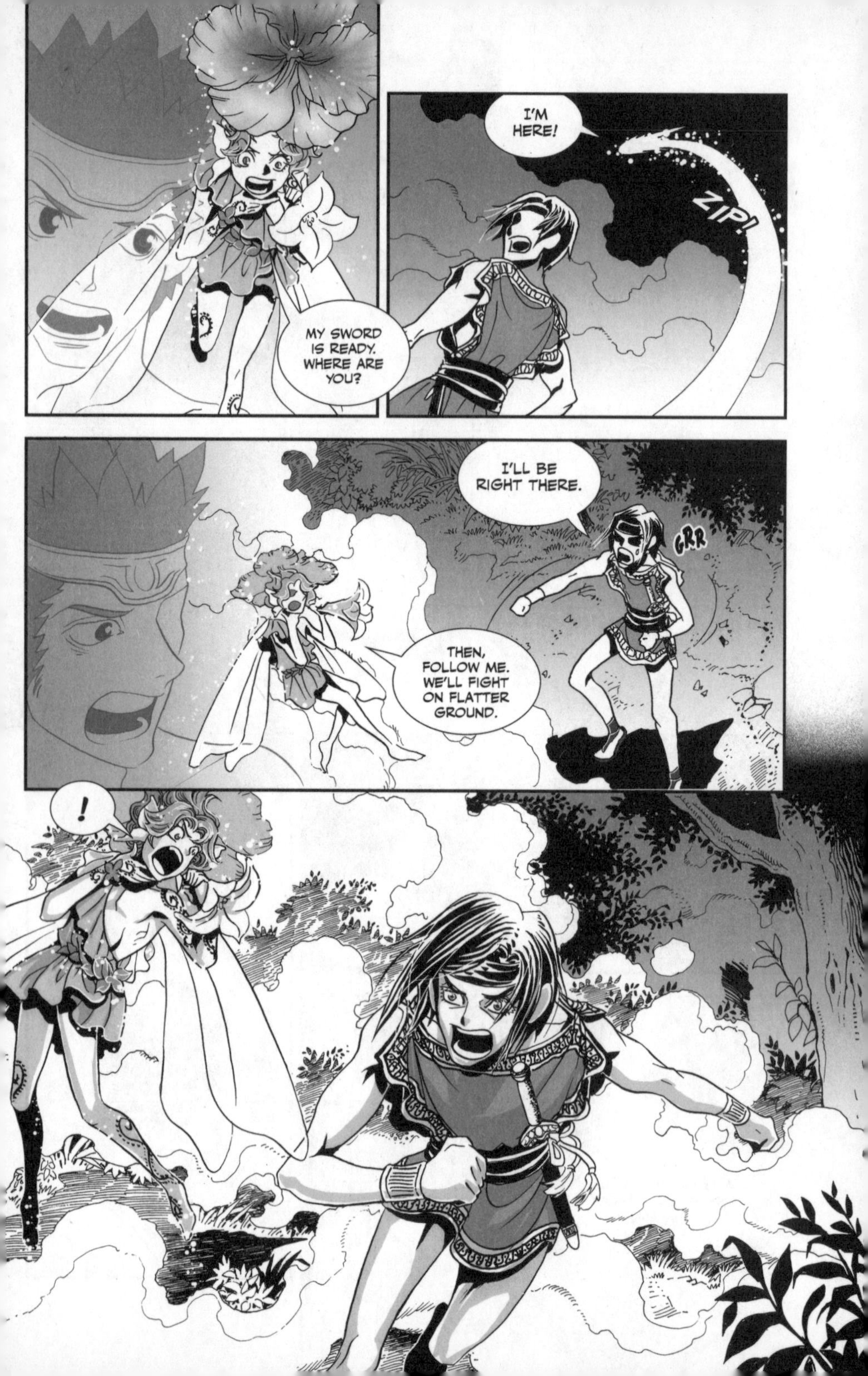
I'M HERE!
ZIP!
MY SWORD IS READY. WHERE ARE YOU?
GRR
I'LL BE RIGHT THERE.
THEN, FOLLOW ME. WE'LL FIGHT ON FLATTER GROUND.
!

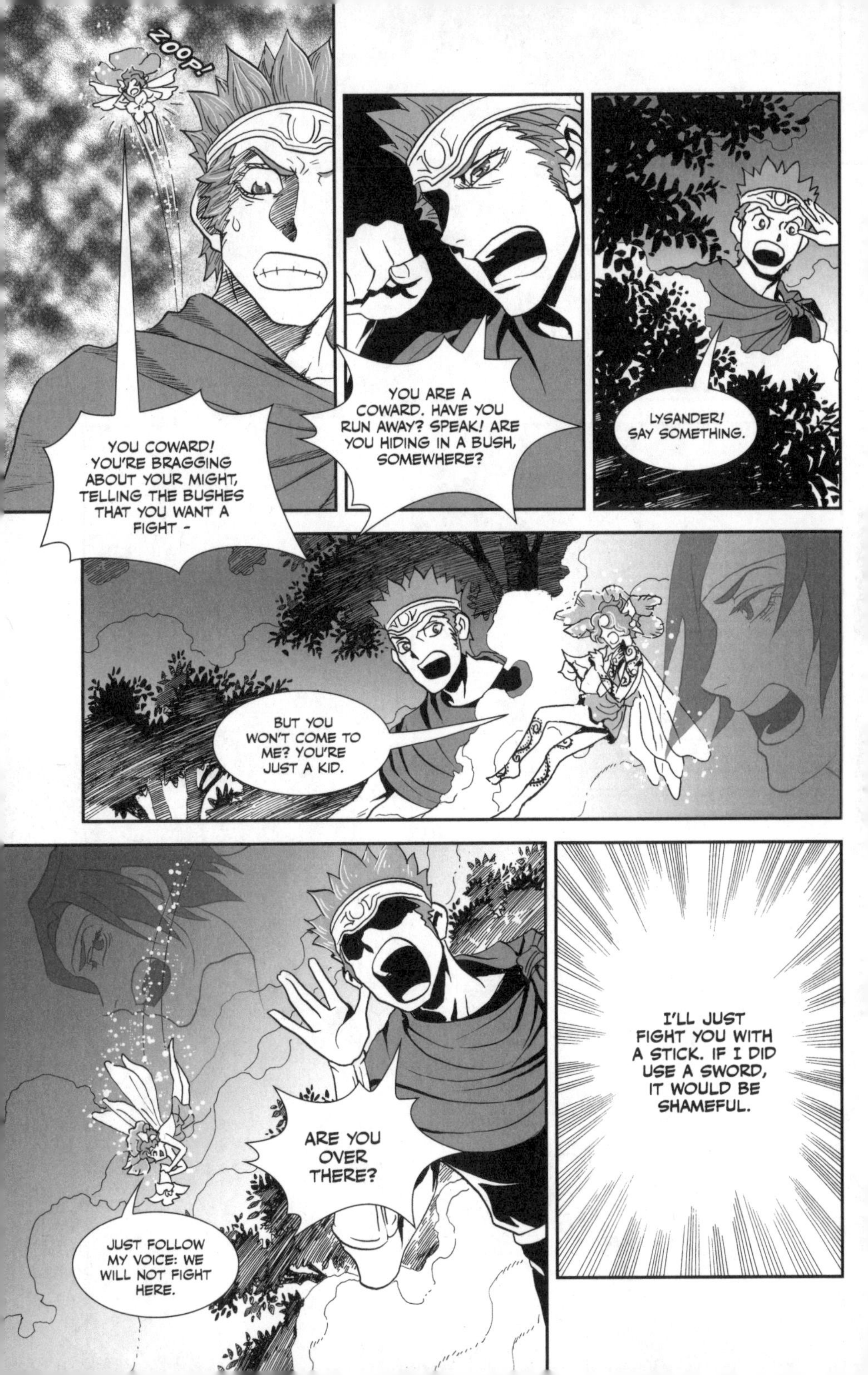
LYSANDER! SAY SOMETHING.
YOU ARE A COWARD. HAVE YOU RUN AWAY? SPEAK! ARE YOU HIDING IN A BUSH, SOMEWHERE?
ZOOP!
YOU COWARD! YOU'RE BRAGGING ABOUT YOUR MIGHT, TELLING THE BUSHES THAT YOU WANT A FIGHT -
BUT YOU WON'T COME TO ME? YOU'RE JUST A KID.
I'LL JUST FIGHT YOU WITH A STICK. IF I DID USE A SWORD, IT WOULD BE SHAMEFUL.
ARE YOU OVER THERE?
JUST FOLLOW MY VOICE: WE WILL NOT FIGHT HERE.

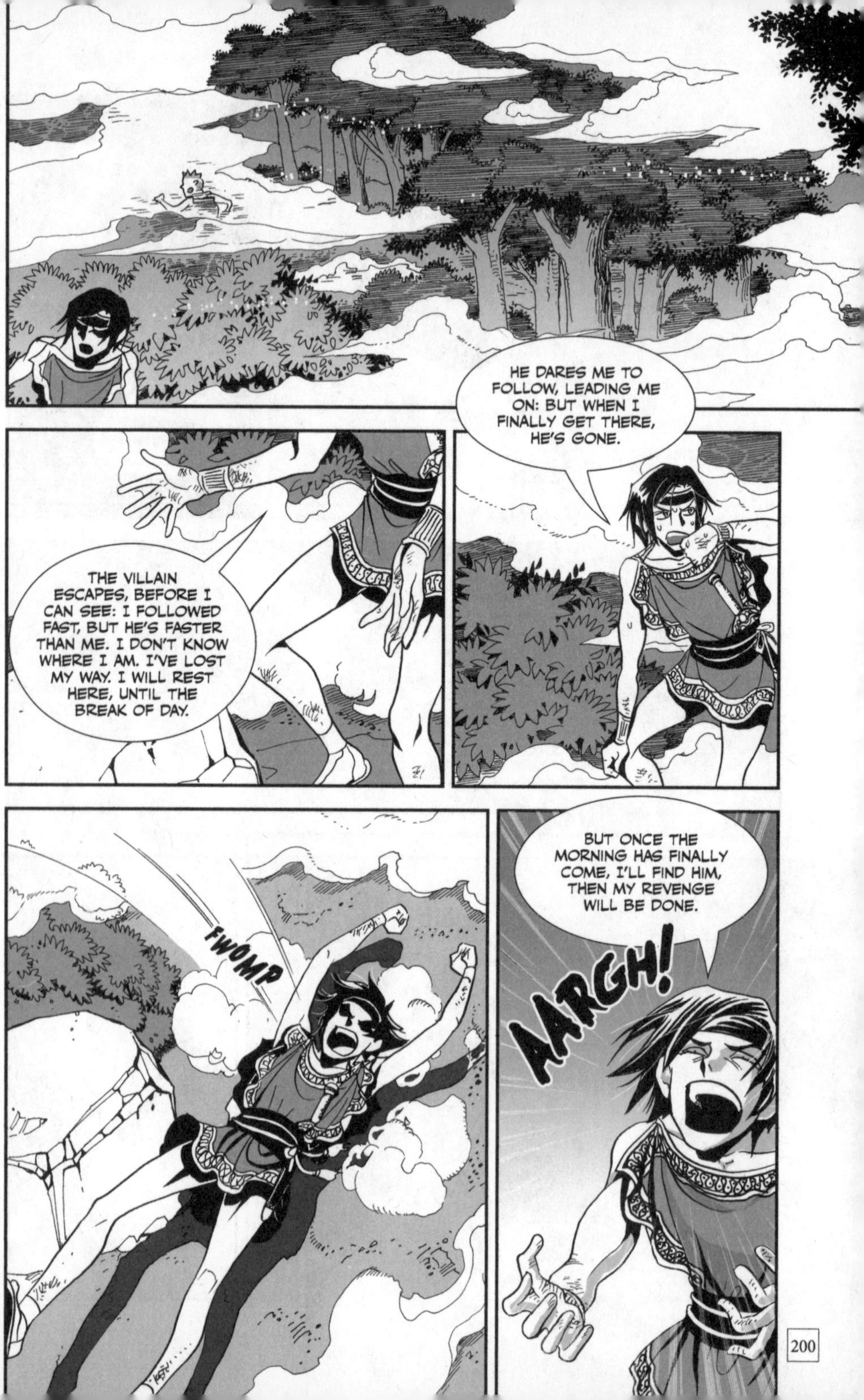
HE DARES ME TO FOLLOW, LEADING ME ON: BUT WHEN I FINALLY GET THERE, HE'S GONE.
THE VILLAIN ESCAPES, BEFORE I CAN SEE: I FOLLOWED FAST, BUT HE'S FASTER THAN ME. I DON'T KNOW WHERE I AM. I'VE LOST MY WAY. I WILL REST HERE, UNTIL THE BREAK OF DAY.
BUT ONCE THE MORNING HAS FINALLY COME, I'LL FIND HIM, THEN MY REVENGE WILL BE DONE.
AARGH!
FWOMP

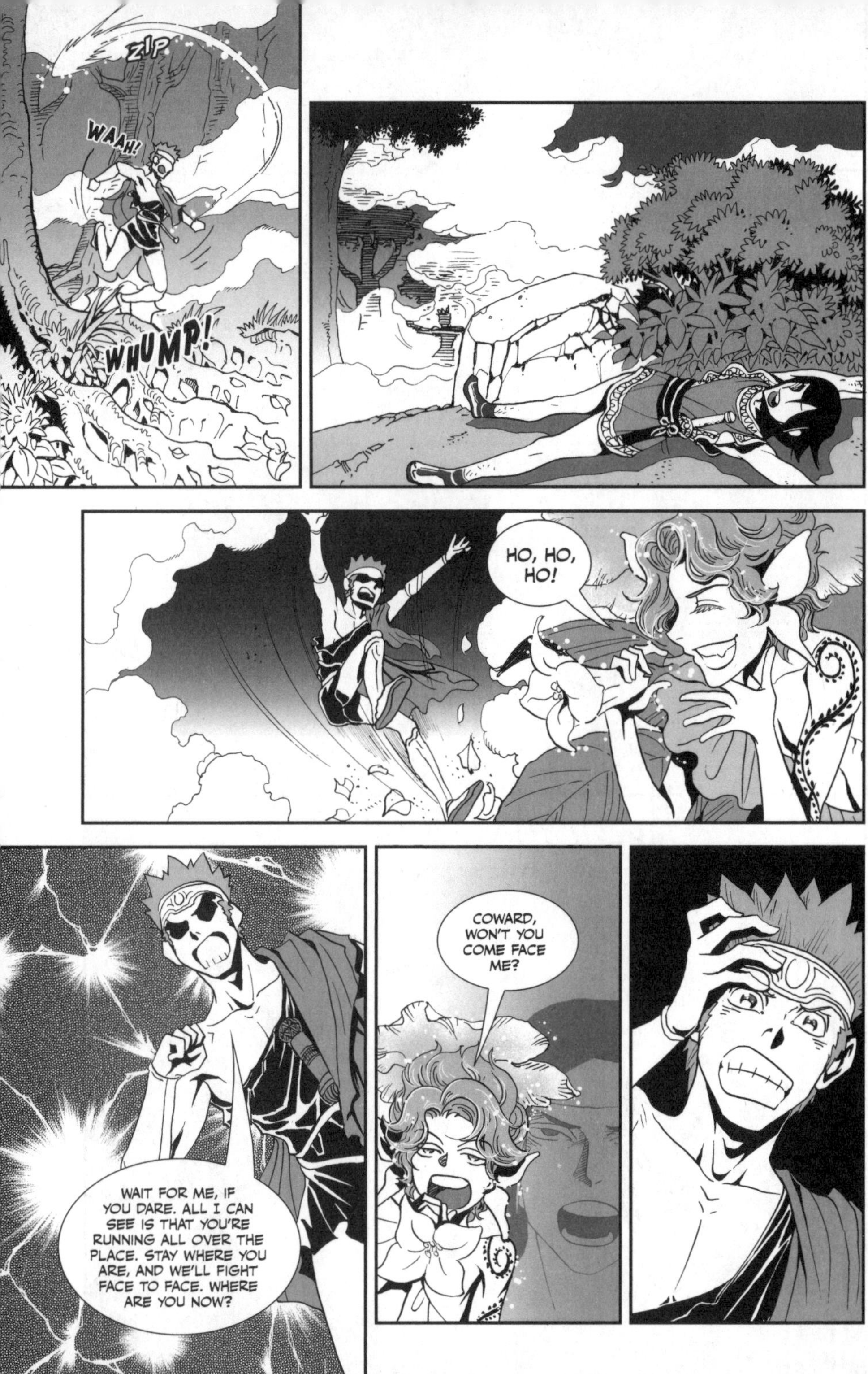
ZIP
WAAH!
WHUMP!
HO, HO, HO!
COWARD, WON'T YOU COME FACE ME?
WAIT FOR ME, IF YOU DARE. ALL I CAN SEE IS THAT YOU'RE RUNNING ALL OVER THE PLACE. STAY WHERE YOU ARE, AND WE'LL FIGHT FACE TO FACE. WHERE ARE YOU NOW?

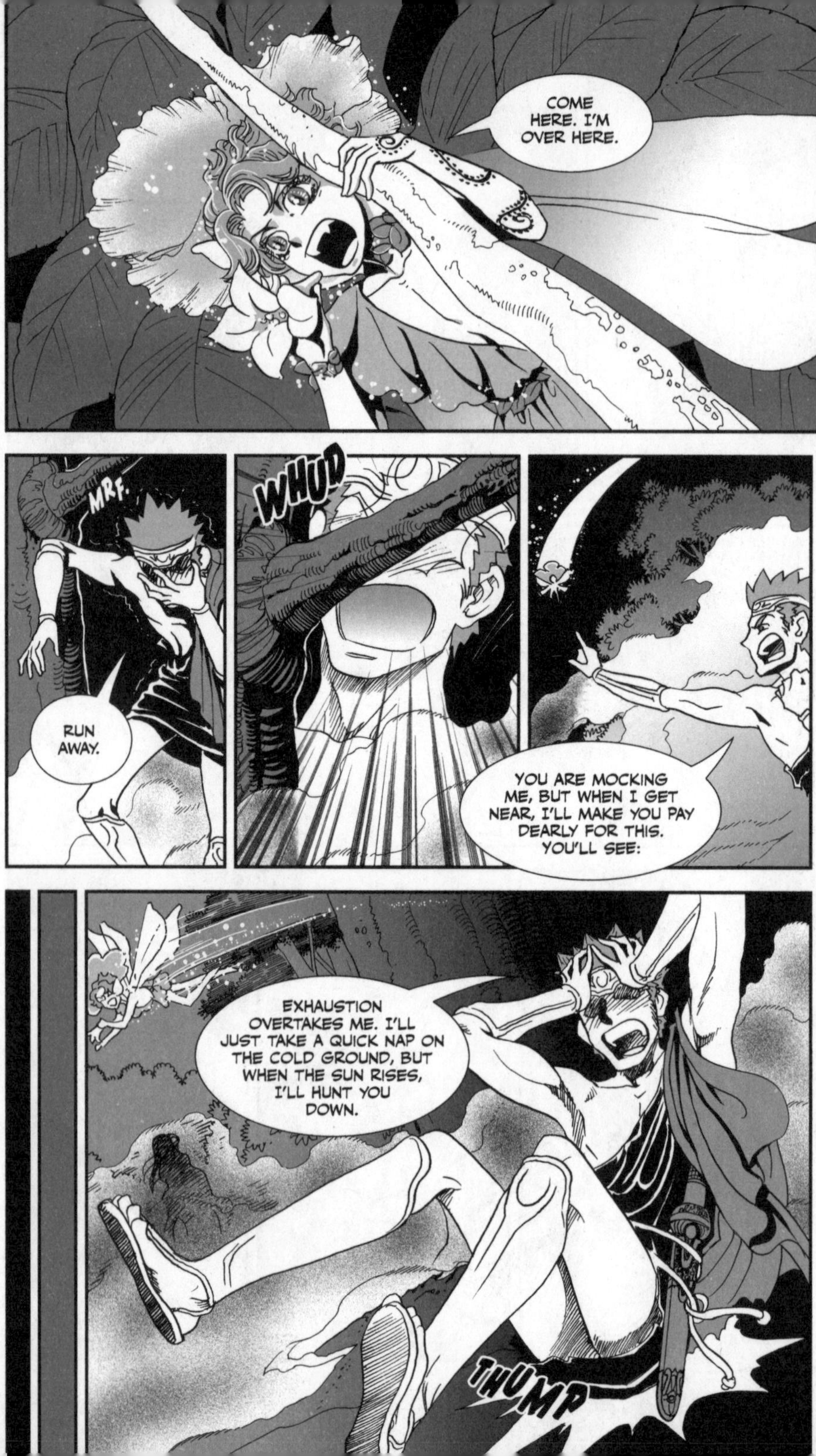
COME HERE. I'M OVER HERE.
YOU ARE MOCKING ME, BUT WHEN I GET NEAR, I'LL MAKE YOU PAY DEARLY FOR THIS. YOU'LL SEE:
WHUD
MRF.
RUN AWAY.
EXHAUSTION OVERTAKES ME. I'LL JUST TAKE A QUICK NAP ON THE COLD GROUND, BUT WHEN THE SUN RISES, I'LL HUNT YOU DOWN.
THUMP

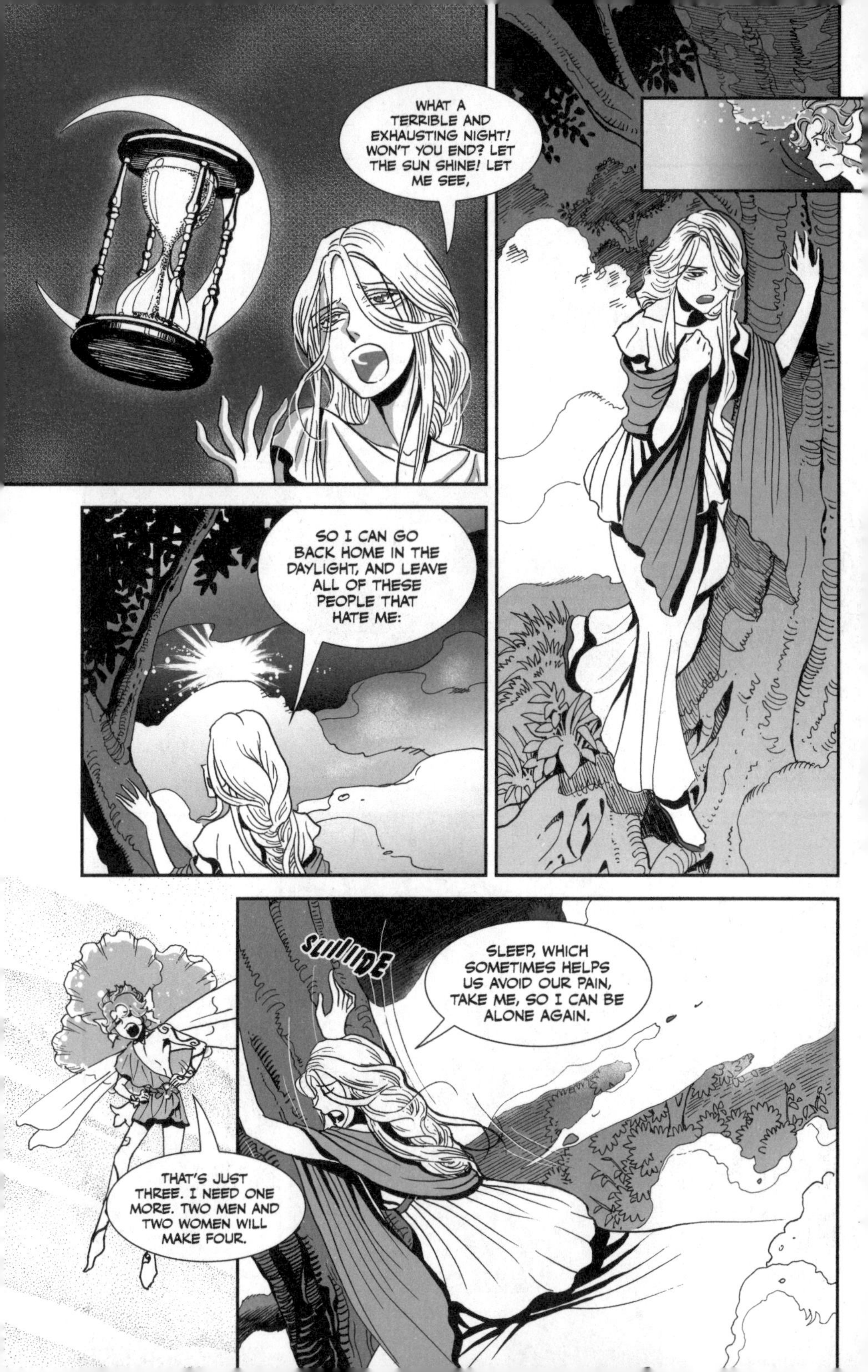
WHAT A TERRIBLE AND EXHAUSTING NIGHT! WON'T YOU END? LET THE SUN SHINE! LET ME SEE,
SO I CAN GO BACK HOME IN THE DAYLIGHT, AND LEAVE ALL OF THESE PEOPLE THAT HATE ME:
SLEEP, WHICH SOMETIMES HELPS US AVOID OUR PAIN, TAKE ME, SO I CAN BE ALONE AGAIN.
SLIIIIDE
THAT'S JUST THREE. I NEED ONE MORE. TWO MEN AND TWO WOMEN WILL MAKE FOUR.

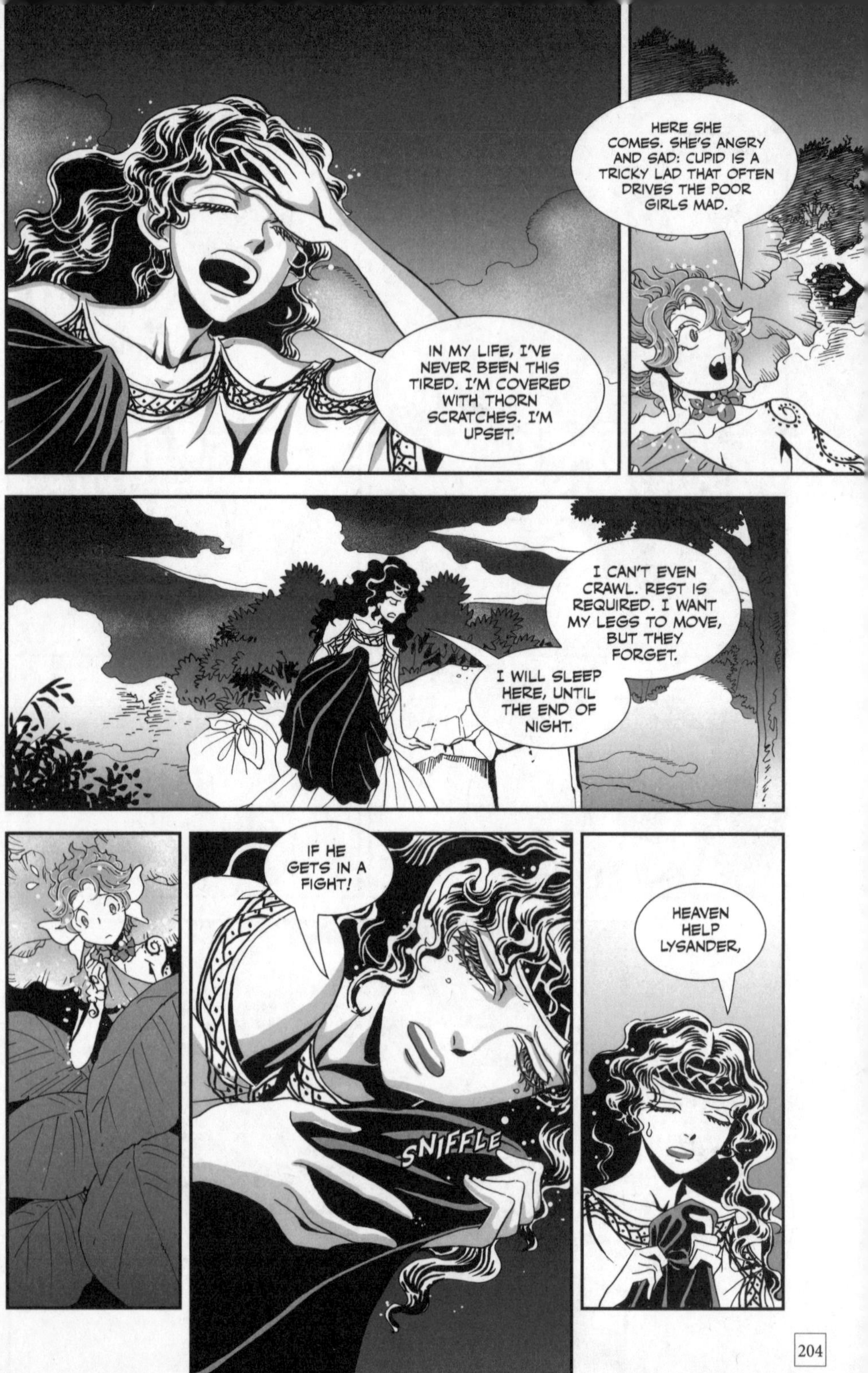
HERE SHE COMES. SHE'S ANGRY AND SAD: CUPID IS A TRICKY LAD THAT OFTEN DRIVES THE POOR GIRLS MAD.
IN MY LIFE, I'VE NEVER BEEN THIS TIRED. I'M COVERED WITH THORN SCRATCHES. I'M UPSET.
I CAN'T EVEN CRAWL. REST IS REQUIRED. I WANT MY LEGS TO MOVE, BUT THEY FORGET.
I WILL SLEEP HERE, UNTIL THE END OF NIGHT.
HEAVEN HELP LYSANDER,
IF HE GETS IN A FIGHT!
SNIFFLE

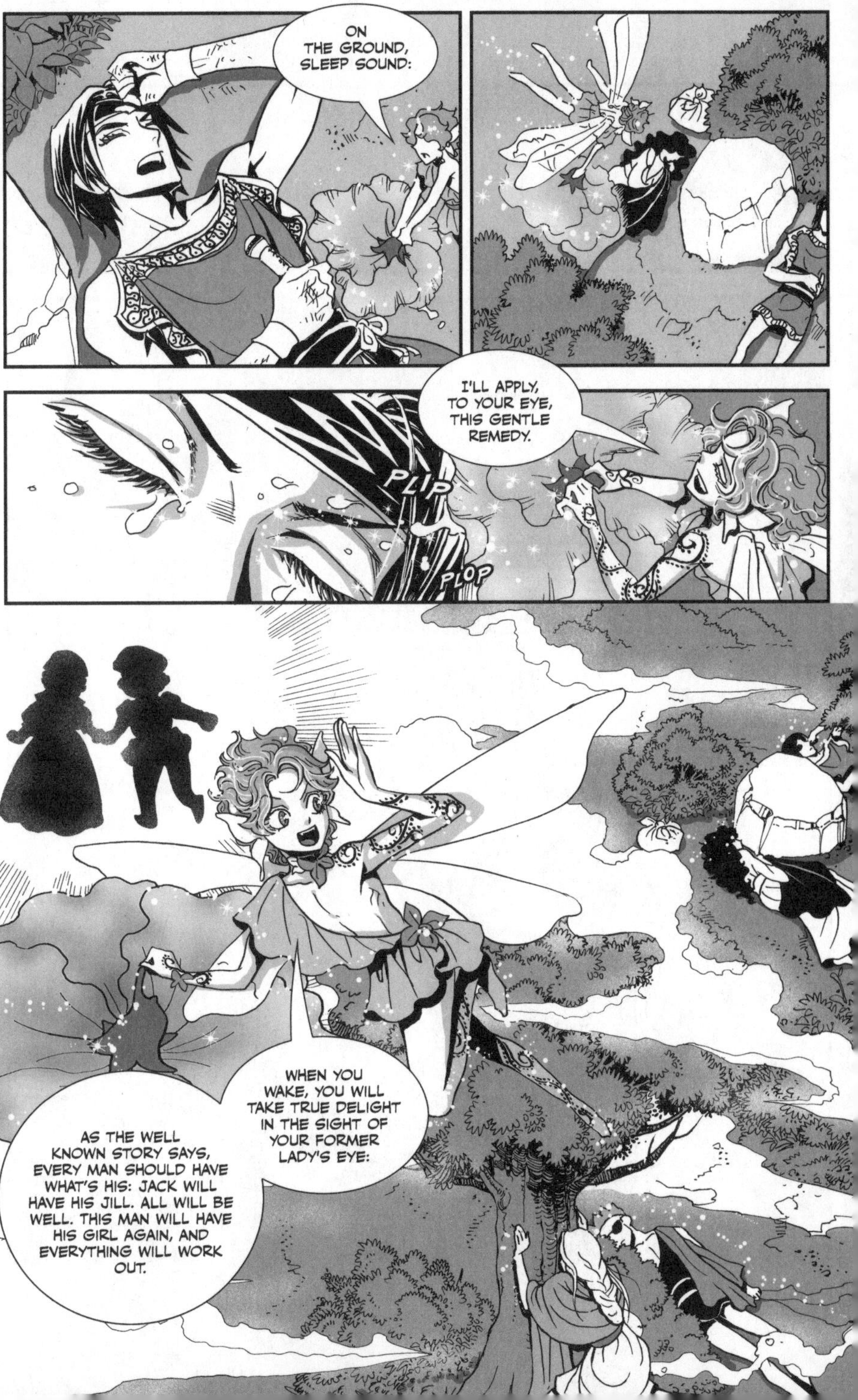
ON THE GROUND, SLEEP SOUND:
I'LL APPLY, TO YOUR EYE, THIS GENTLE REMEDY.
PLIP
PLOP
WHEN YOU WAKE, YOU WILL TAKE TRUE DELIGHT IN THE SIGHT OF YOUR FORMER LADY'S EYE:
AS THE WELL KNOWN STORY SAYS, EVERY MAN SHOULD HAVE WHAT'S HIS: JACK WILL HAVE HIS JILL. ALL WILL BE WELL. THIS MAN WILL HAVE HIS GIRL AGAIN, AND EVERYTHING WILL WORK OUT.

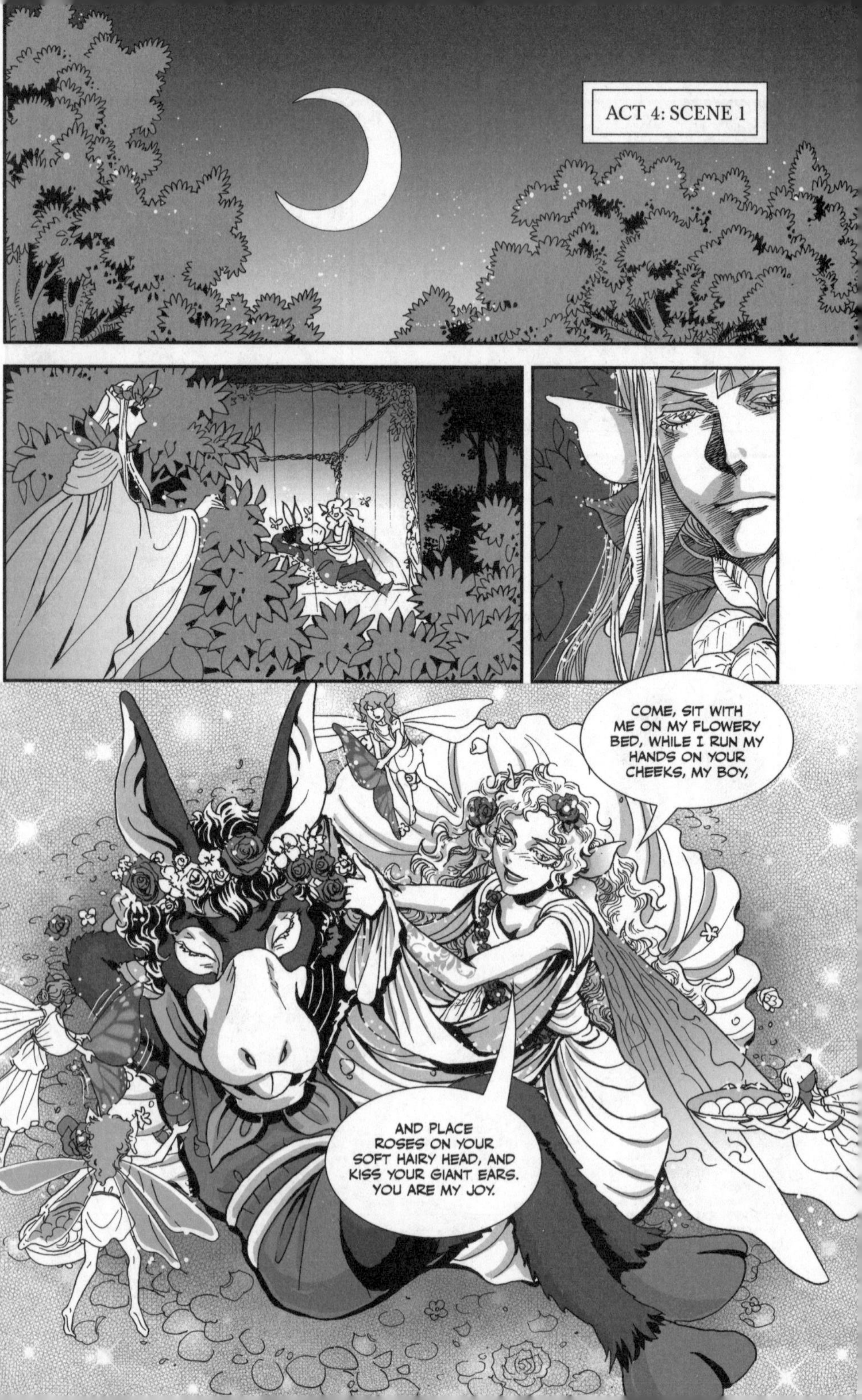
ACT 4: SCENE 1
COME, SIT WITH ME ON MY FLOWERY BED, WHILE I RUN MY HANDS ON YOUR CHEEKS, MY BOY,
AND PLACE ROSES ON YOUR SOFT HAIRY HEAD, AND KISS YOUR GIANT EARS. YOU ARE MY JOY.

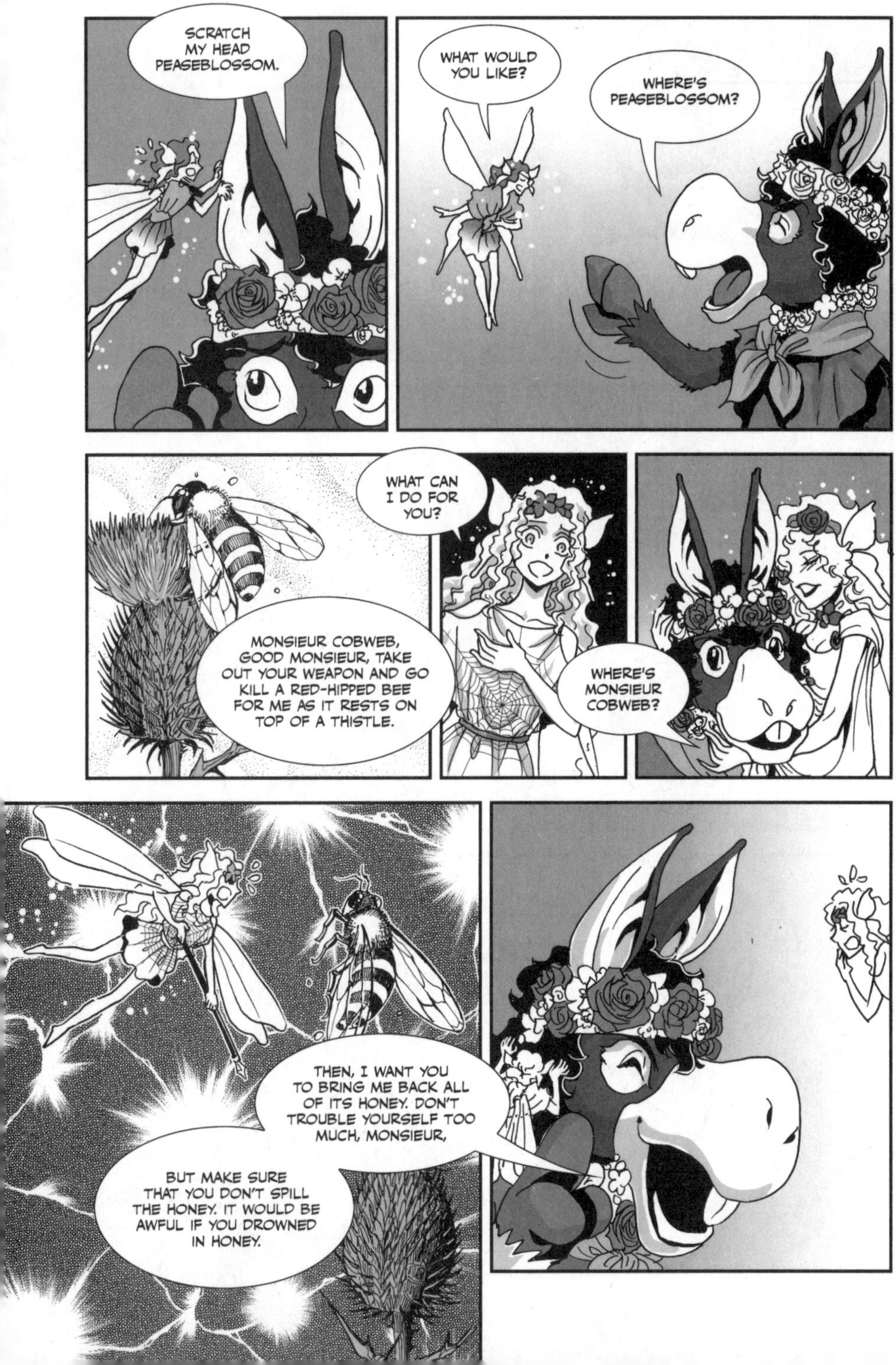
WHERE'S PEASEBLOSSOM?
WHAT WOULD YOU LIKE?
SCRATCH MY HEAD PEASEBLOSSOM.
WHERE'S MONSIEUR COBWEB?
WHAT CAN I DO FOR YOU?
MONSIEUR COBWEB, GOOD MONSIEUR, TAKE OUT YOUR WEAPON AND GO KILL A RED-HIPPED BEE FOR ME AS IT RESTS ON TOP OF A THISTLE.
THEN, I WANT YOU TO BRING ME BACK ALL OF ITS HONEY. DON'T TROUBLE YOURSELF TOO MUCH, MONSIEUR,
BUT MAKE SURE THAT YOU DON'T SPILL THE HONEY. IT WOULD BE AWFUL IF YOU DROWNED IN HONEY.

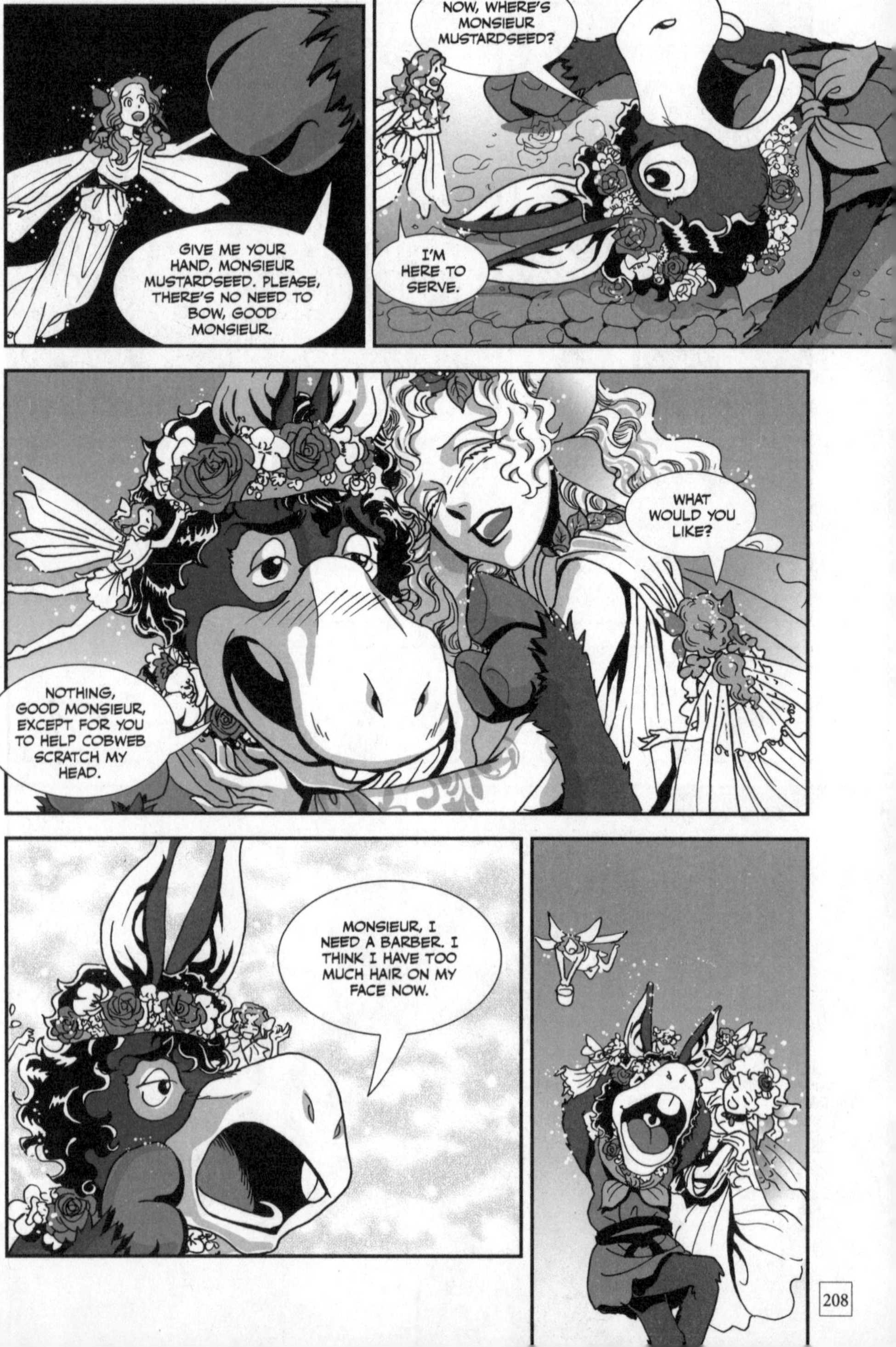
NOW, WHERE'S MONSIEUR MUSTARDSEED?
I'M HERE TO SERVE.
GIVE ME YOUR HAND, MONSIEUR MUSTARDSEED. PLEASE, THERE'S NO NEED TO BOW, GOOD MONSIEUR.
WHAT WOULD YOU LIKE?
NOTHING, GOOD MONSIEUR, EXCEPT FOR YOU TO HELP COBWEB SCRATCH MY HEAD.
MONSIEUR, I NEED A BARBER. I THINK I HAVE TOO MUCH HAIR ON MY FACE NOW.

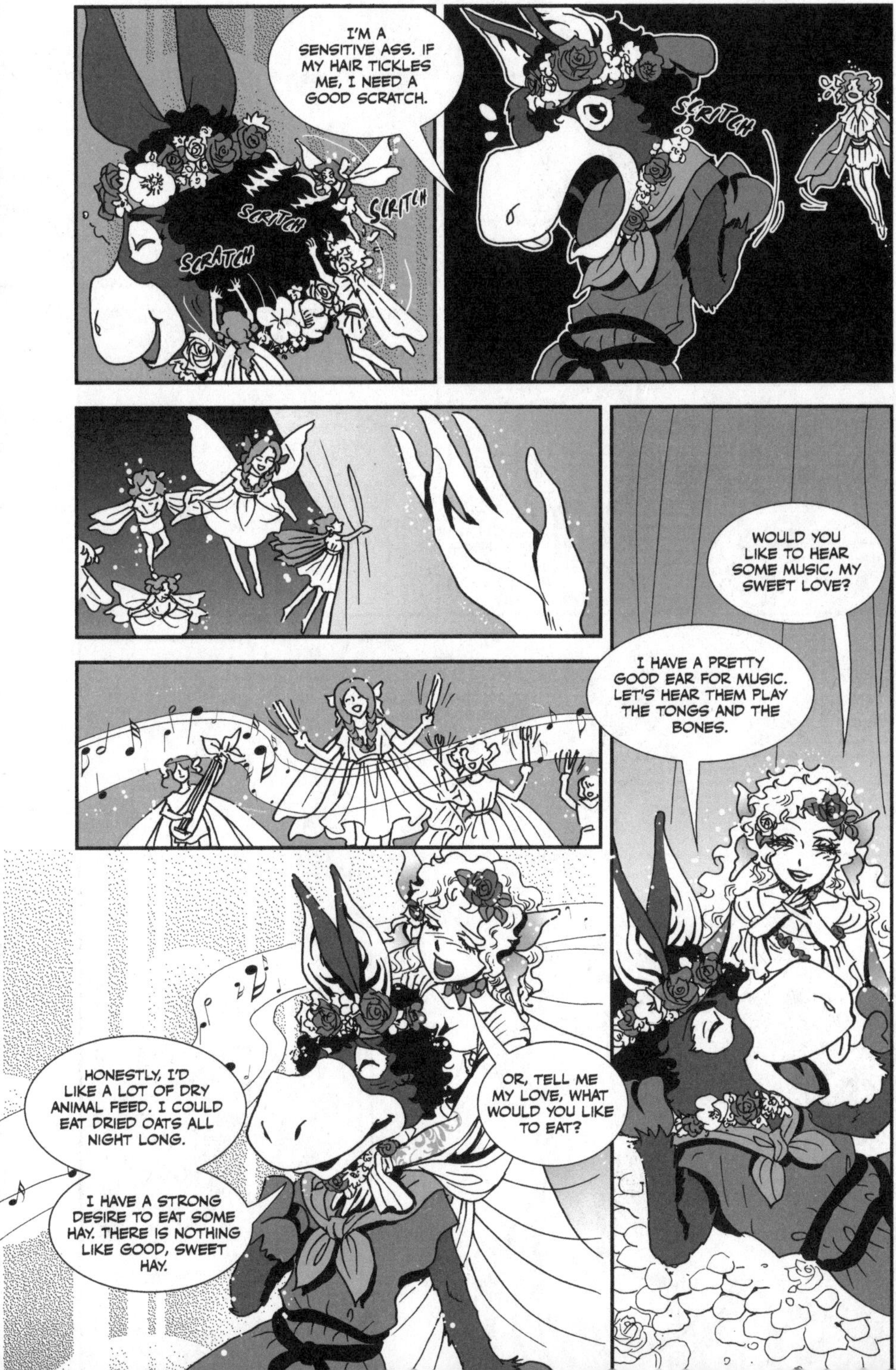
SCRITCH
I'M A SENSITIVE ASS. IF MY HAIR TICKLES ME, I NEED A GOOD SCRATCH.
SCRITCH
SCRITCH
SCRATCH
WOULD YOU LIKE TO HEAR SOME MUSIC, MY SWEET LOVE?
I HAVE A PRETTY GOOD EAR FOR MUSIC. LET'S HEAR THEM PLAY THE TONGS AND THE BONES.
OR, TELL ME MY LOVE, WHAT WOULD YOU LIKE TO EAT?
HONESTLY, I'D LIKE A LOT OF DRY ANIMAL FEED. I COULD EAT DRIED OATS ALL NIGHT LONG.
I HAVE A STRONG DESIRE TO EAT SOME HAY. THERE IS NOTHING LIKE GOOD, SWEET HAY.

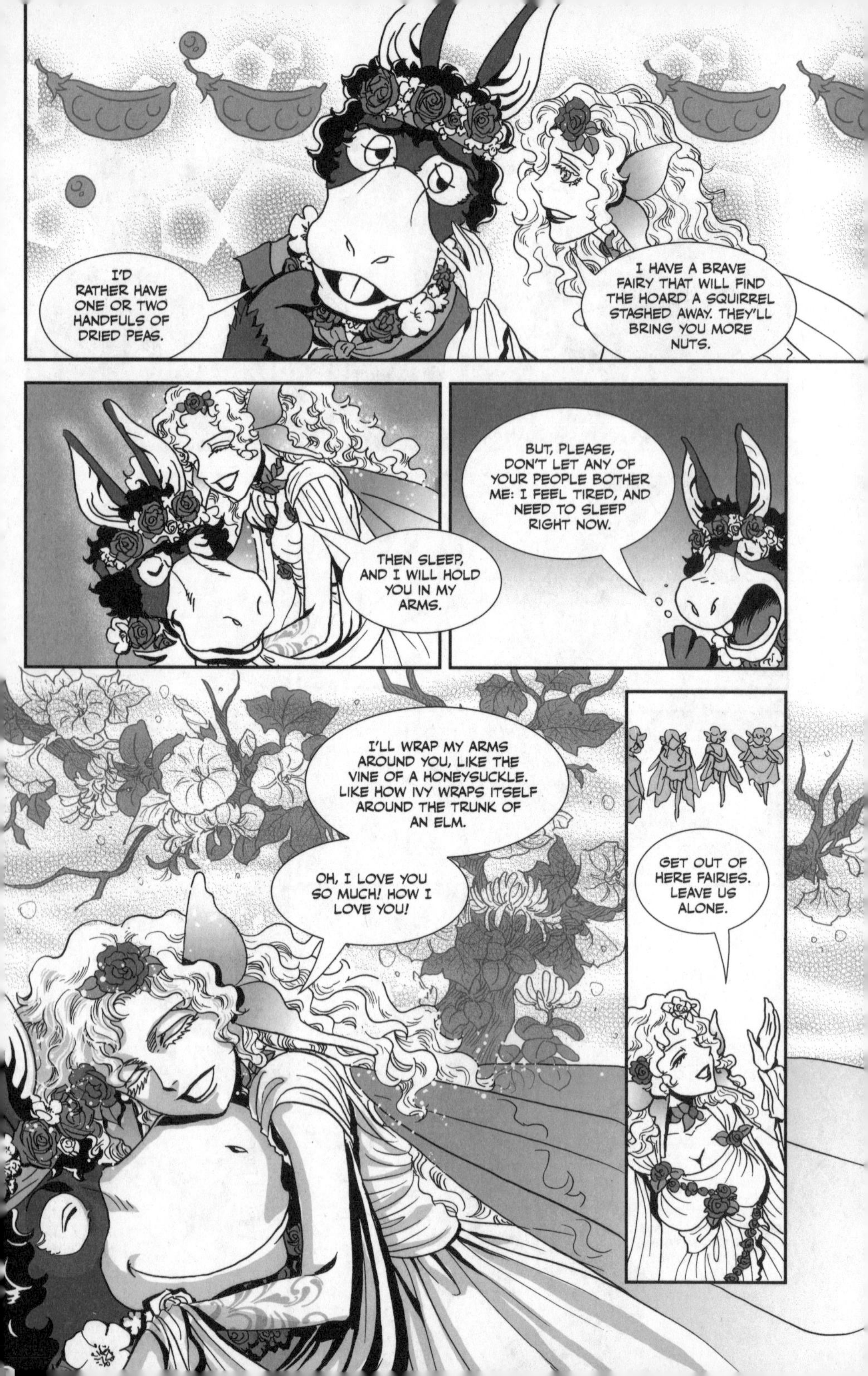
I HAVE A BRAVE FAIRY THAT WILL FIND THE HOARD A SQUIRREL STASHED AWAY. THEY'LL BRING YOU MORE NUTS.
I'D RATHER HAVE ONE OR TWO HANDFULS OF DRIED PEAS.
BUT, PLEASE, DON'T LET ANY OF YOUR PEOPLE BOTHER ME: I FEEL TIRED, AND NEED TO SLEEP RIGHT NOW.
THEN SLEEP, AND I WILL HOLD YOU IN MY ARMS.
GET OUT OF HERE FAIRIES. LEAVE US ALONE.
I'LL WRAP MY ARMS AROUND YOU, LIKE THE VINE OF A HONEYSUCKLE. LIKE HOW IVY WRAPS ITSELF AROUND THE TRUNK OF AN ELM.
OH, I LOVE YOU SO MUCH! HOW I LOVE YOU!

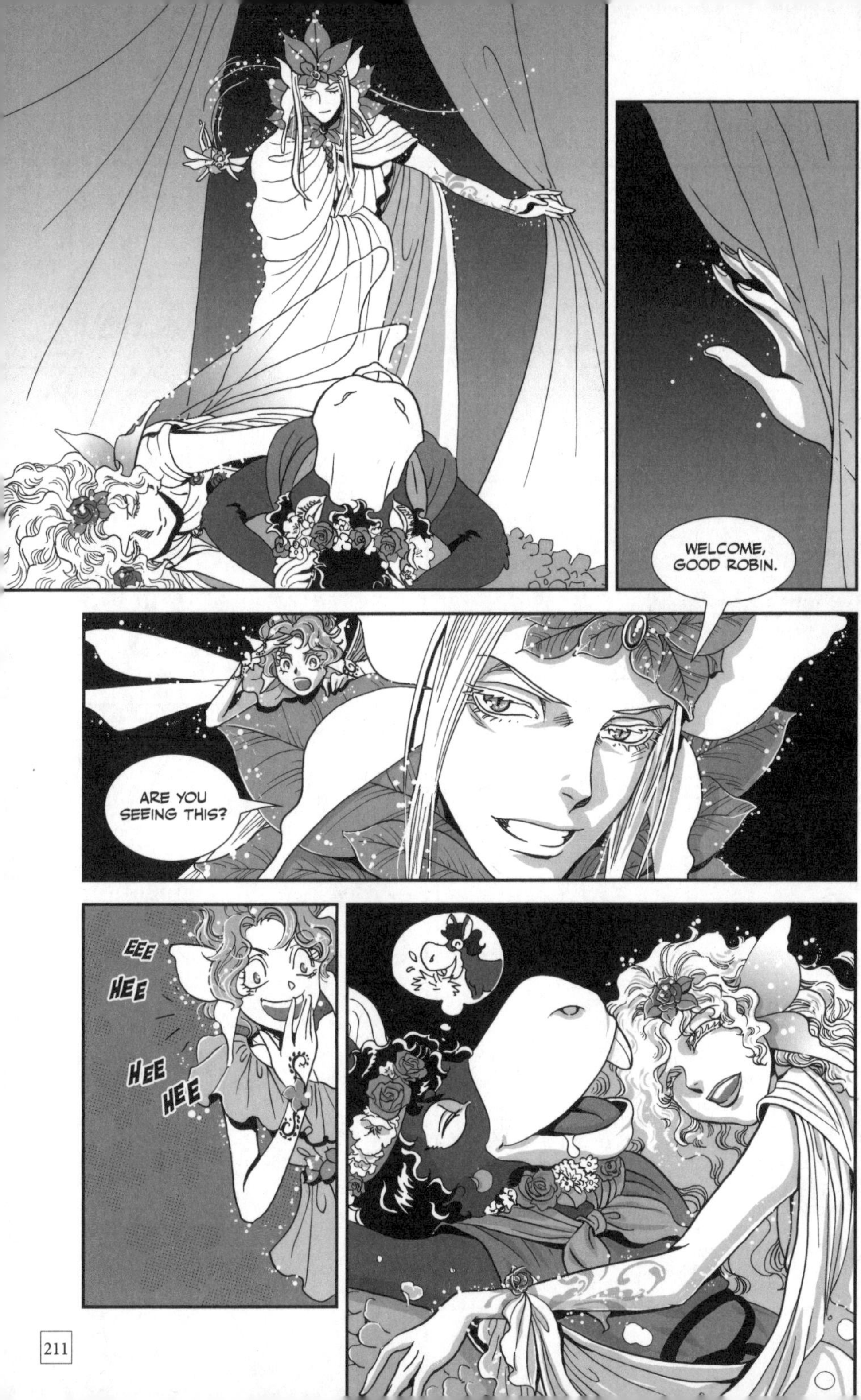

WELCOME, GOOD ROBIN.
ARE YOU SEEING THIS?
EEE HEE HEE HEE

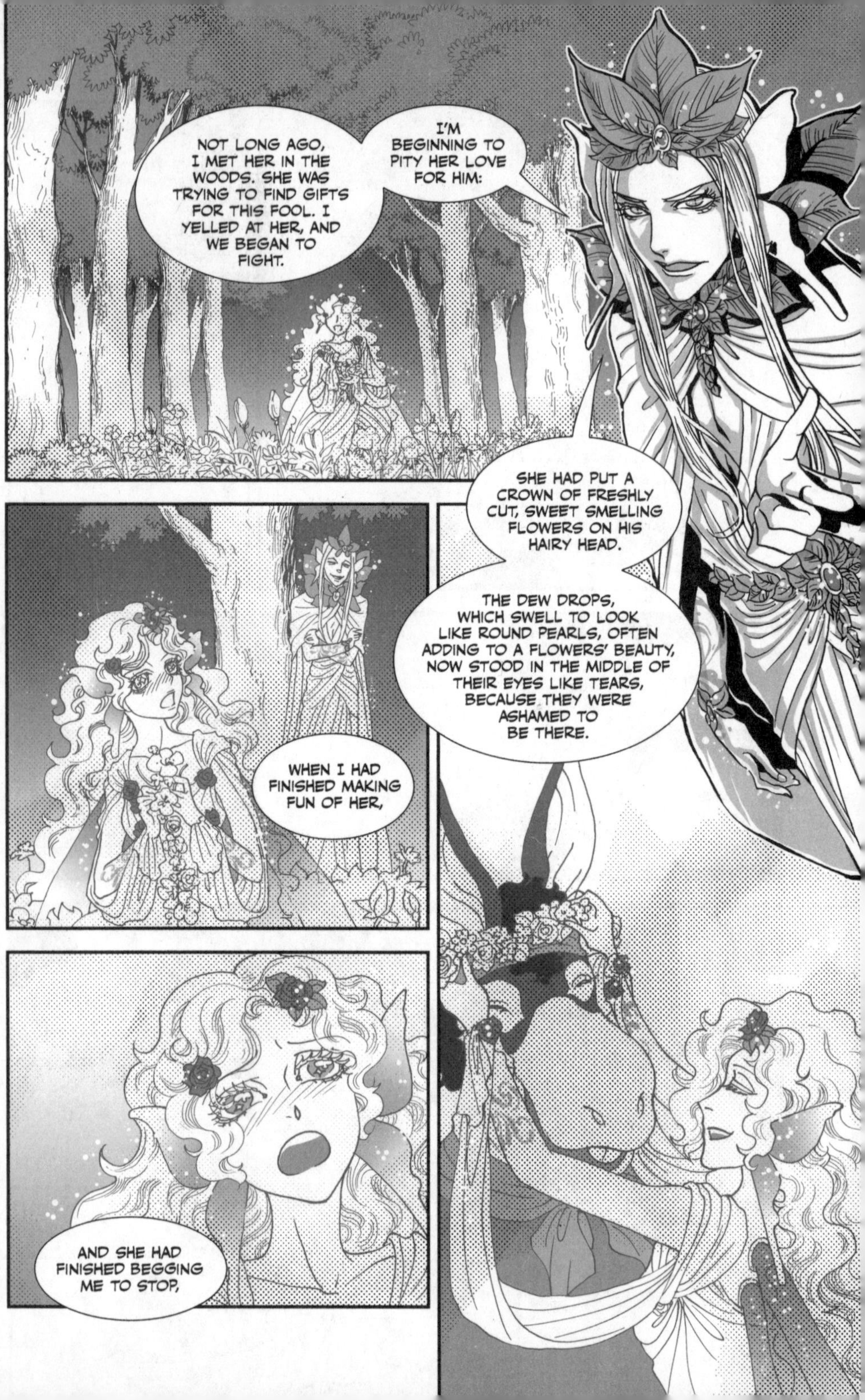
I'M BEGINNING TO PITY HER LOVE FOR HIM:
NOT LONG AGO, I MET HER IN THE WOODS. SHE WAS TRYING TO FIND GIFTS FOR THIS FOOL. I YELLED AT HER, AND WE BEGAN TO FIGHT.
SHE HAD PUT A CROWN OF FRESHLY CUT, SWEET SMELLING FLOWERS ON HIS HAIRY HEAD.
THE DEW DROPS, WHICH SWELL TO LOOK LIKE ROUND PEARLS, OFTEN ADDING TO A FLOWERS' BEAUTY, NOW STOOD IN THE MIDDLE OF THEIR EYES LIKE TEARS, BECAUSE THEY WERE ASHAMED TO BE THERE.
WHEN I HAD FINISHED MAKING FUN OF HER,
AND SHE HAD FINISHED BEGGING ME TO STOP,

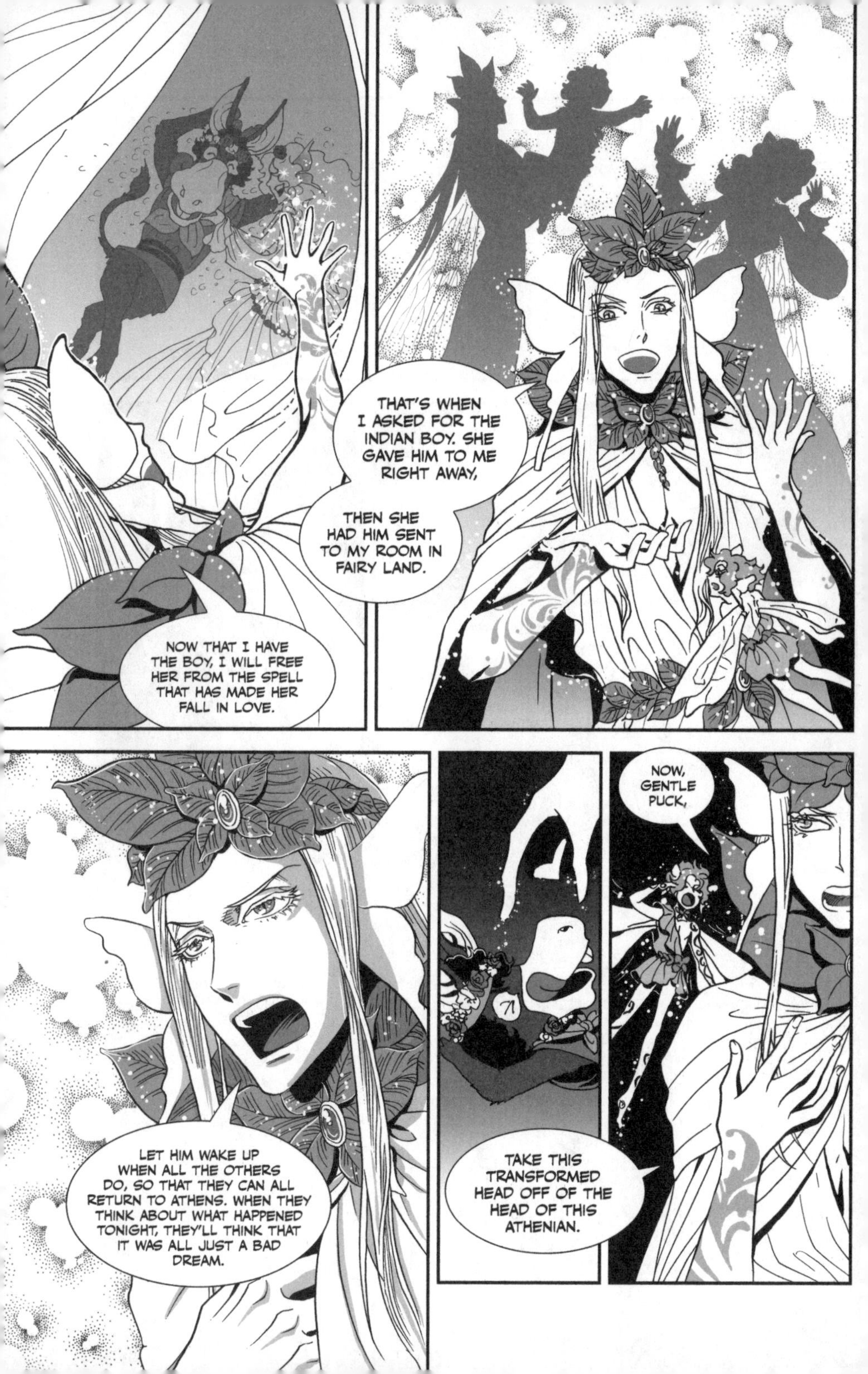
THAT'S WHEN I ASKED FOR THE INDIAN BOY. SHE GAVE HIM TO ME RIGHT AWAY,
THEN SHE HAD HIM SENT TO MY ROOM IN FAIRY LAND.
NOW THAT I HAVE THE BOY, I WILL FREE HER FROM THE SPELL THAT HAS MADE HER FALL IN LOVE.
NOW, GENTLE PUCK,
TAKE THIS TRANSFORMED HEAD OFF OF THE HEAD OF THIS ATHENIAN.
LET HIM WAKE UP WHEN ALL THE OTHERS DO, SO THAT THEY CAN ALL RETURN TO ATHENS. WHEN THEY THINK ABOUT WHAT HAPPENED TONIGHT, THEY'LL THINK THAT IT WAS ALL JUST A BAD DREAM.

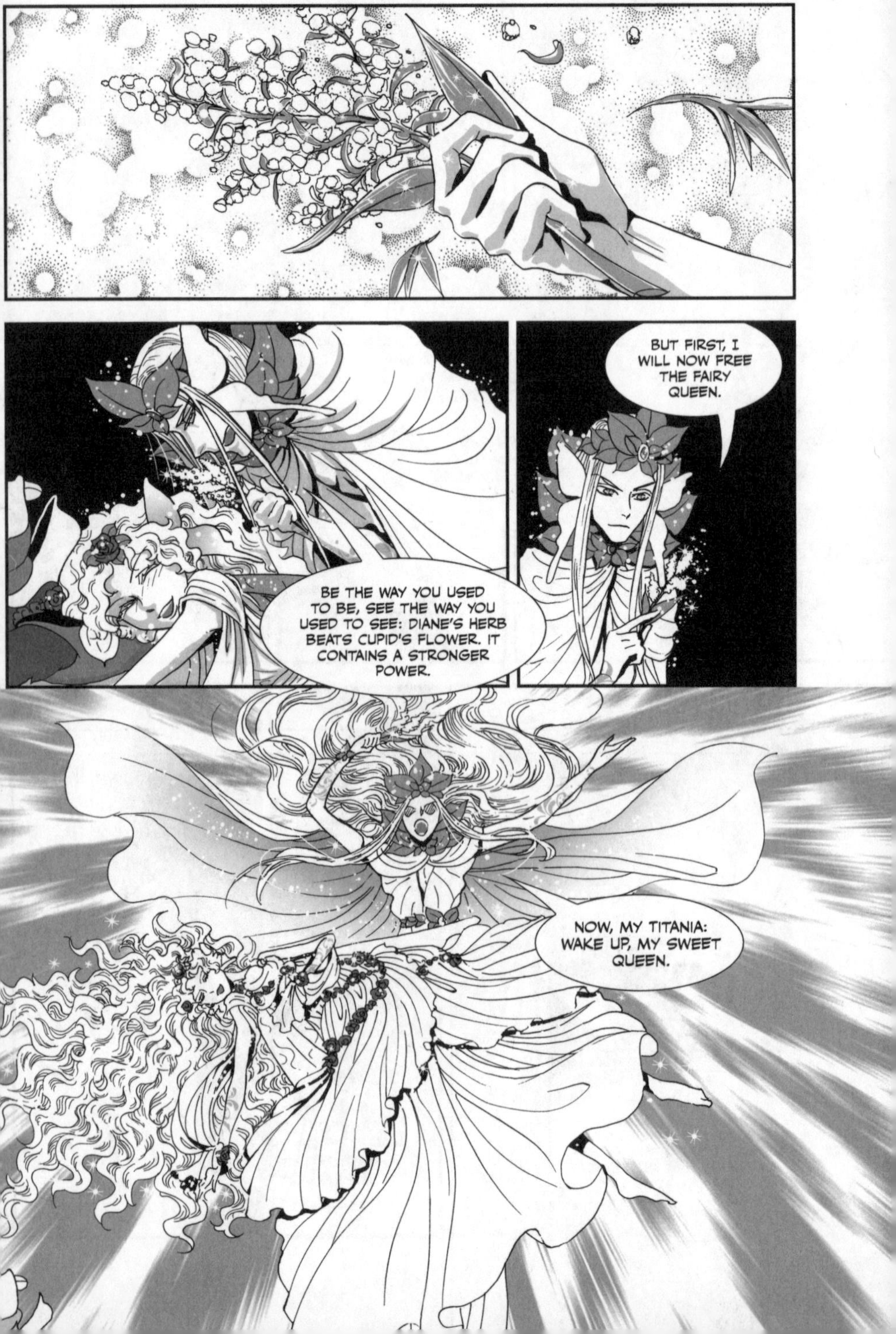
BUT FIRST, I WILL NOW FREE THE FAIRY QUEEN.
BE THE WAY YOU USED TO BE, SEE THE WAY YOU USED TO SEE: DIANE'S HERB BEATS CUPID'S FLOWER. IT CONTAINS A STRONGER POWER.
NOW, MY TITANIA: WAKE UP, MY SWEET QUEEN.

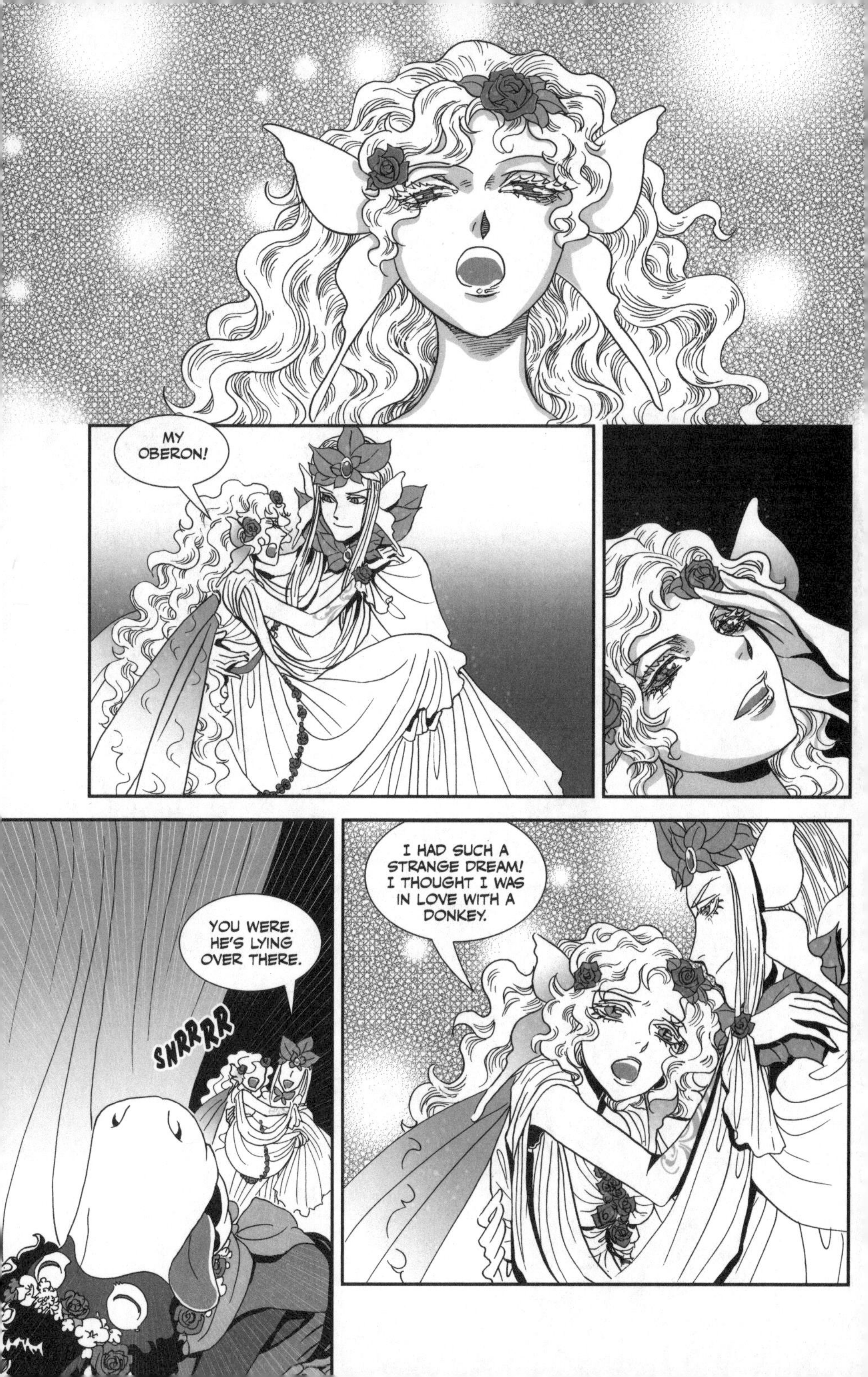
MY OBERON!
I HAD SUCH A STRANGE DREAM! I THOUGHT I WAS IN LOVE WITH A DONKEY.
YOU WERE. HE'S LYING OVER THERE.
SNRRRR

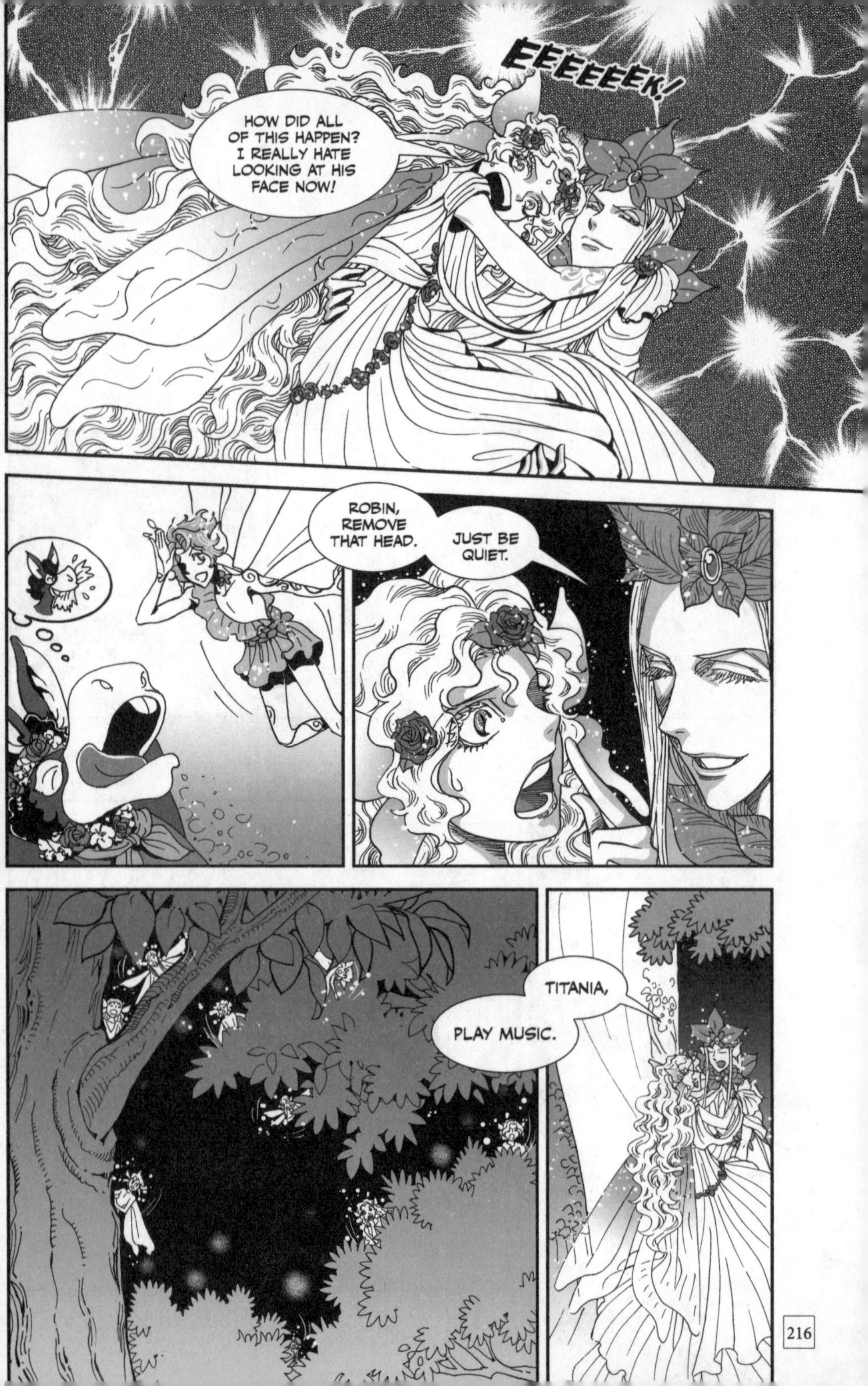
EEEEEEEK!
HOW DID ALL OF THIS HAPPEN? I REALLY HATE LOOKING AT HIS FACE NOW!
JUST BE QUIET.
ROBIN, REMOVE THAT HEAD.
TITANIA,
PLAY MUSIC.

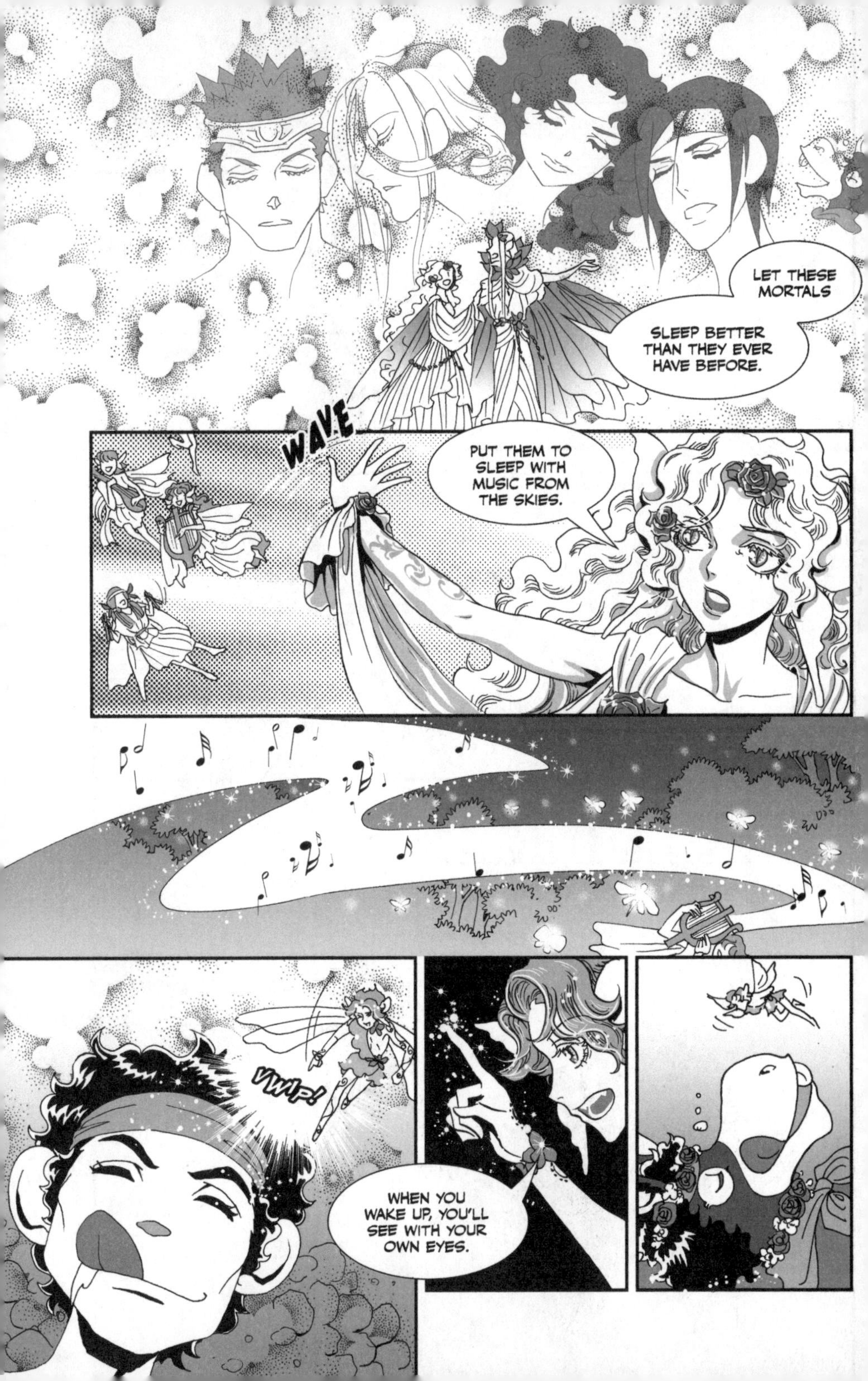
LET THESE MORTALS
SLEEP BETTER THAN THEY EVER HAVE BEFORE.
PUT THEM TO SLEEP WITH MUSIC FROM THE SKIES.
WAVE
WHEN YOU WAKE UP, YOU'LL SEE WITH YOUR OWN EYES.
VWIP!

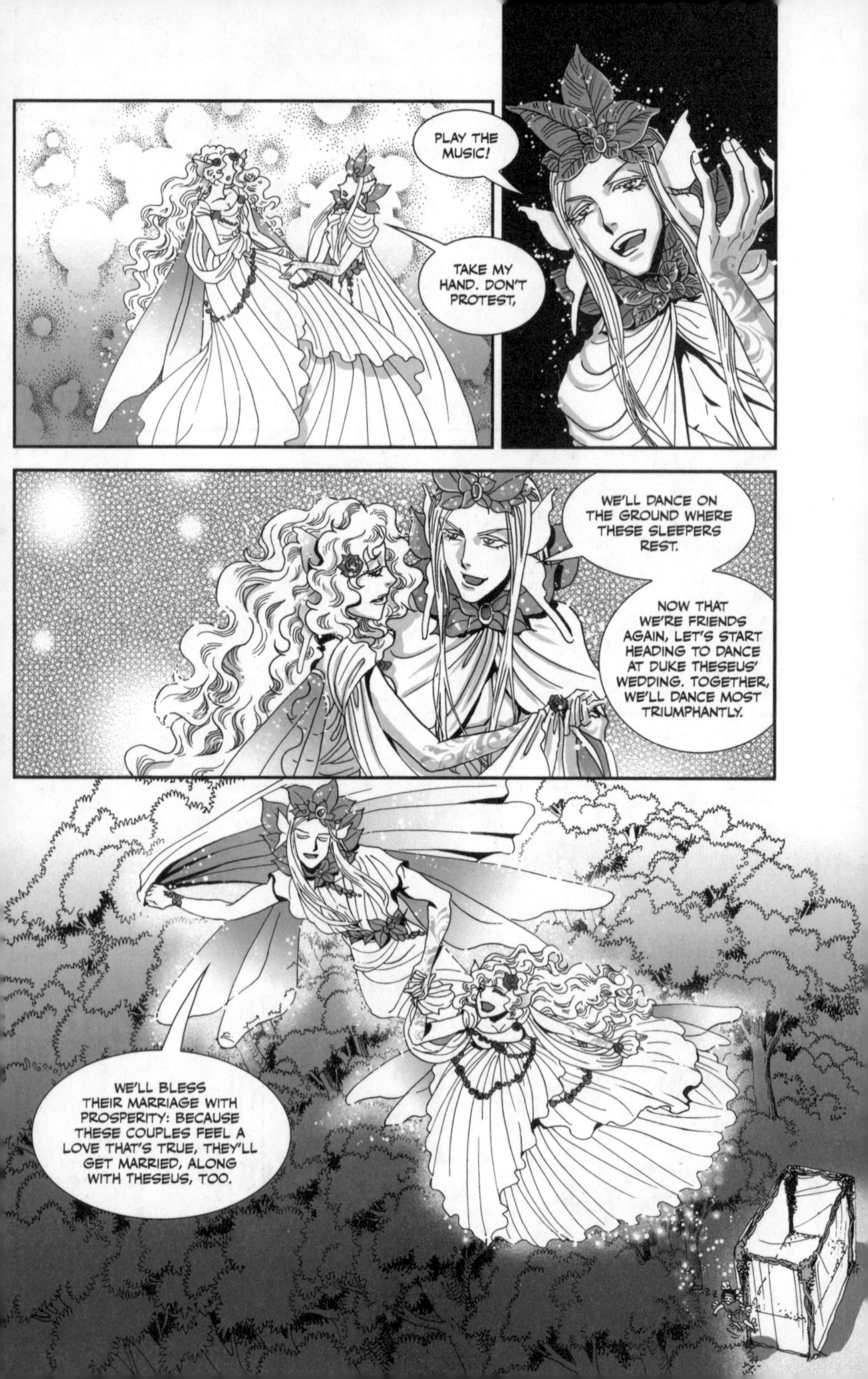
PLAY THE MUSIC!
TAKE MY HAND. DON'T PROTEST,
WE'LL DANCE ON THE GROUND WHERE THESE SLEEPERS REST.
NOW THAT WE'RE FRIENDS AGAIN, LET'S START HEADING TO DANCE AT DUKE THESEUS' WEDDING. TOGETHER, WE'LL DANCE MOST TRIUMPHANTLY.
WE'LL BLESS THEIR MARRIAGE WITH PROSPERITY: BECAUSE THESE COUPLES FEEL A LOVE THAT'S TRUE, THEY'LL GET MARRIED, ALONG WITH THESEUS, TOO.

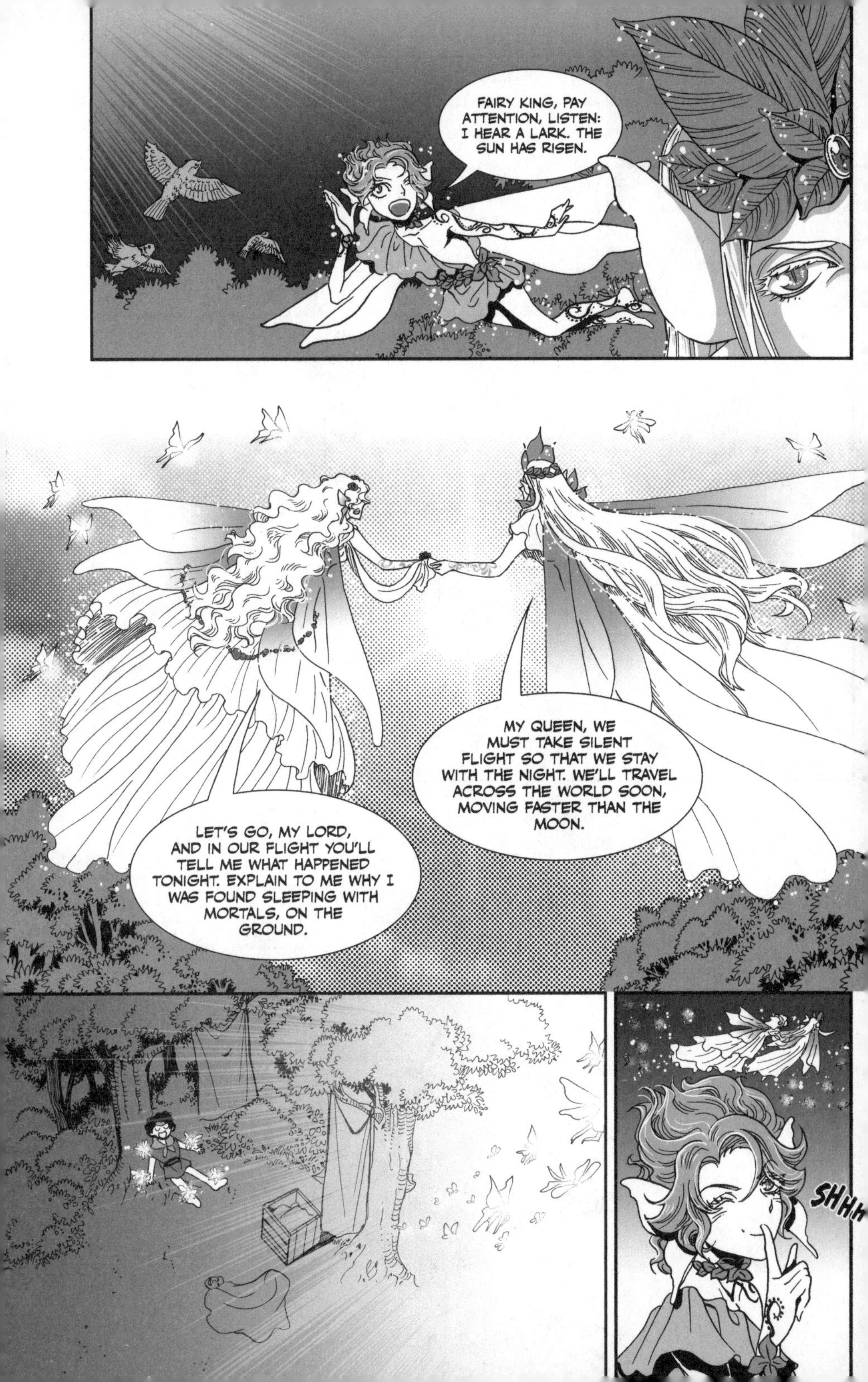
FAIRY KING, PAY ATTENTION, LISTEN: I HEAR A LARK. THE SUN HAS RISEN.
MY QUEEN, WE MUST TAKE SILENT FLIGHT SO THAT WE STAY WITH THE NIGHT. WE'LL TRAVEL ACROSS THE WORLD SOON, MOVING FASTER THAN THE MOON.
LET'S GO, MY LORD, AND IN OUR FLIGHT YOU'LL TELL ME WHAT HAPPENED TONIGHT. EXPLAIN TO ME WHY I WAS FOUND SLEEPING WITH MORTALS, ON THE GROUND.
SHHH

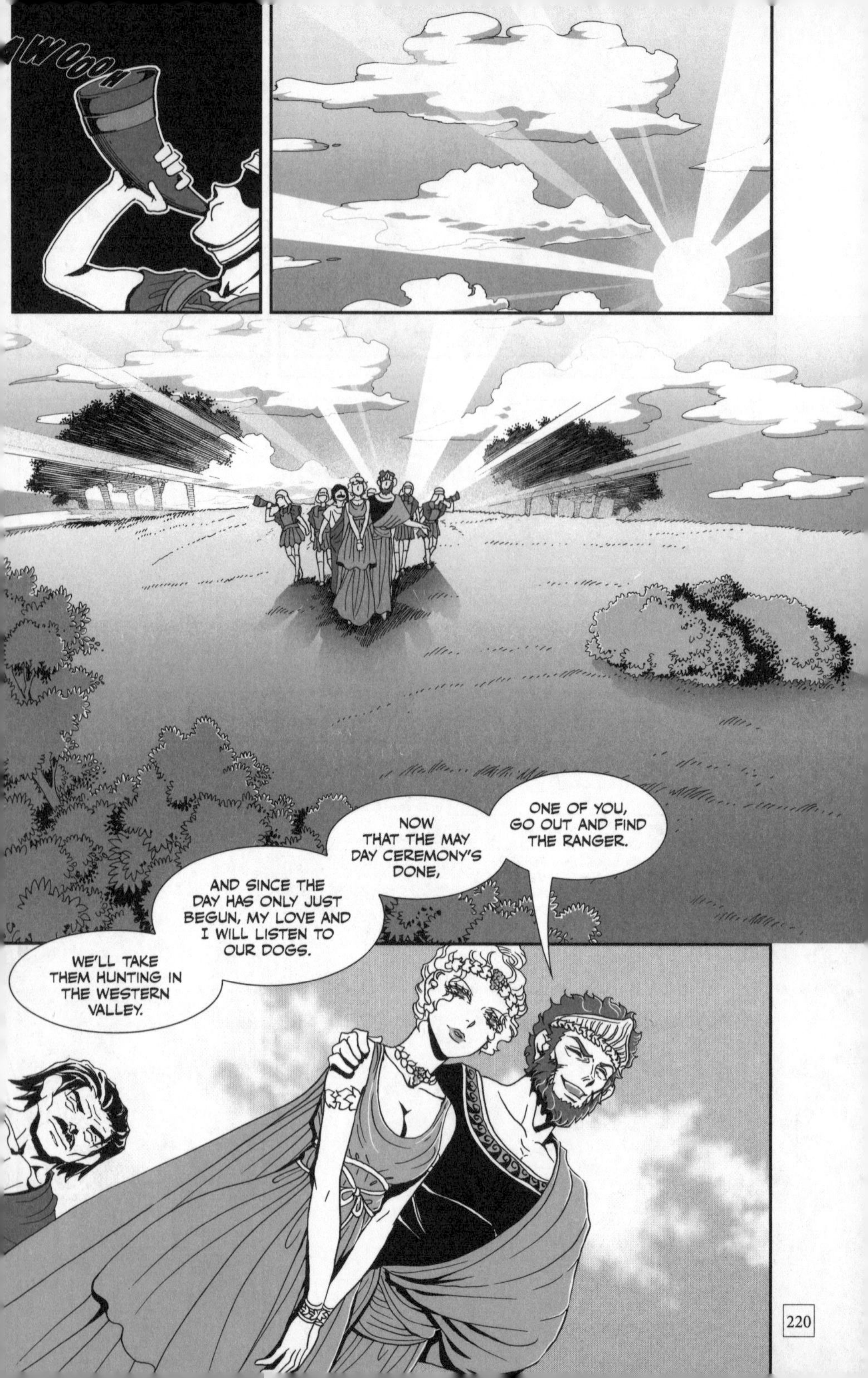
HOOOW
ONE OF YOU, GO OUT AND FIND THE RANGER.
NOW THAT THE MAY DAY CEREMONY'S DONE,
AND SINCE THE DAY HAS ONLY JUST BEGUN, MY LOVE AND I WILL LISTEN TO OUR DOGS.
WE'LL TAKE THEM HUNTING IN THE WESTERN VALLEY.

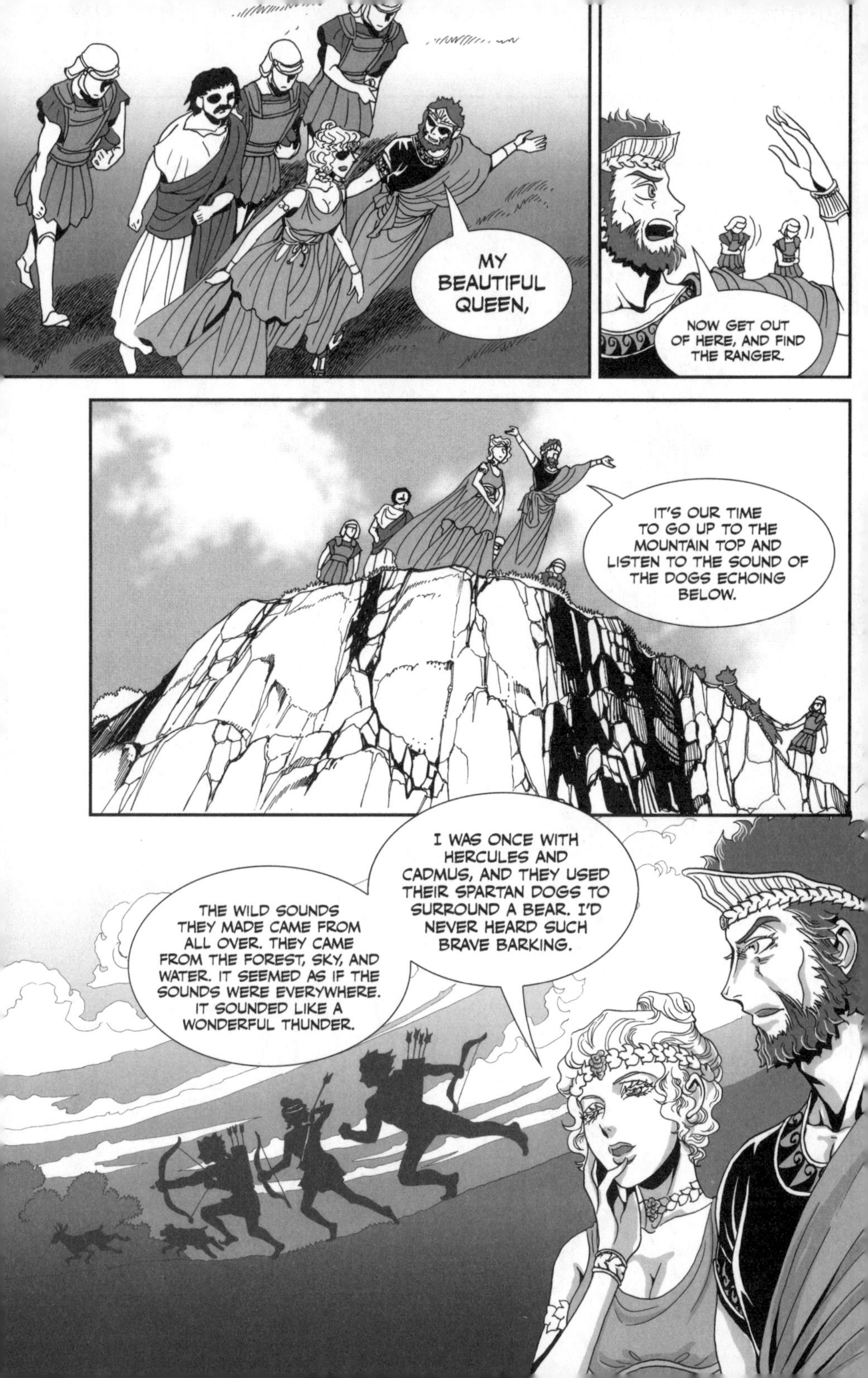
NOW GET OUT OF HERE, AND FIND THE RANGER.
MY BEAUTIFUL QUEEN,
IT'S OUR TIME TO GO UP TO THE MOUNTAIN TOP AND LISTEN TO THE SOUND OF THE DOGS ECHOING BELOW.
I WAS ONCE WITH HERCULES AND CADMUS, AND THEY USED THEIR SPARTAN DOGS TO SURROUND A BEAR. I'D NEVER HEARD SUCH BRAVE BARKING.
THE WILD SOUNDS THEY MADE CAME FROM ALL OVER. THEY CAME FROM THE FOREST, SKY, AND WATER. IT SEEMED AS IF THE SOUNDS WERE EVERYWHERE. IT SOUNDED LIKE A WONDERFUL THUNDER.

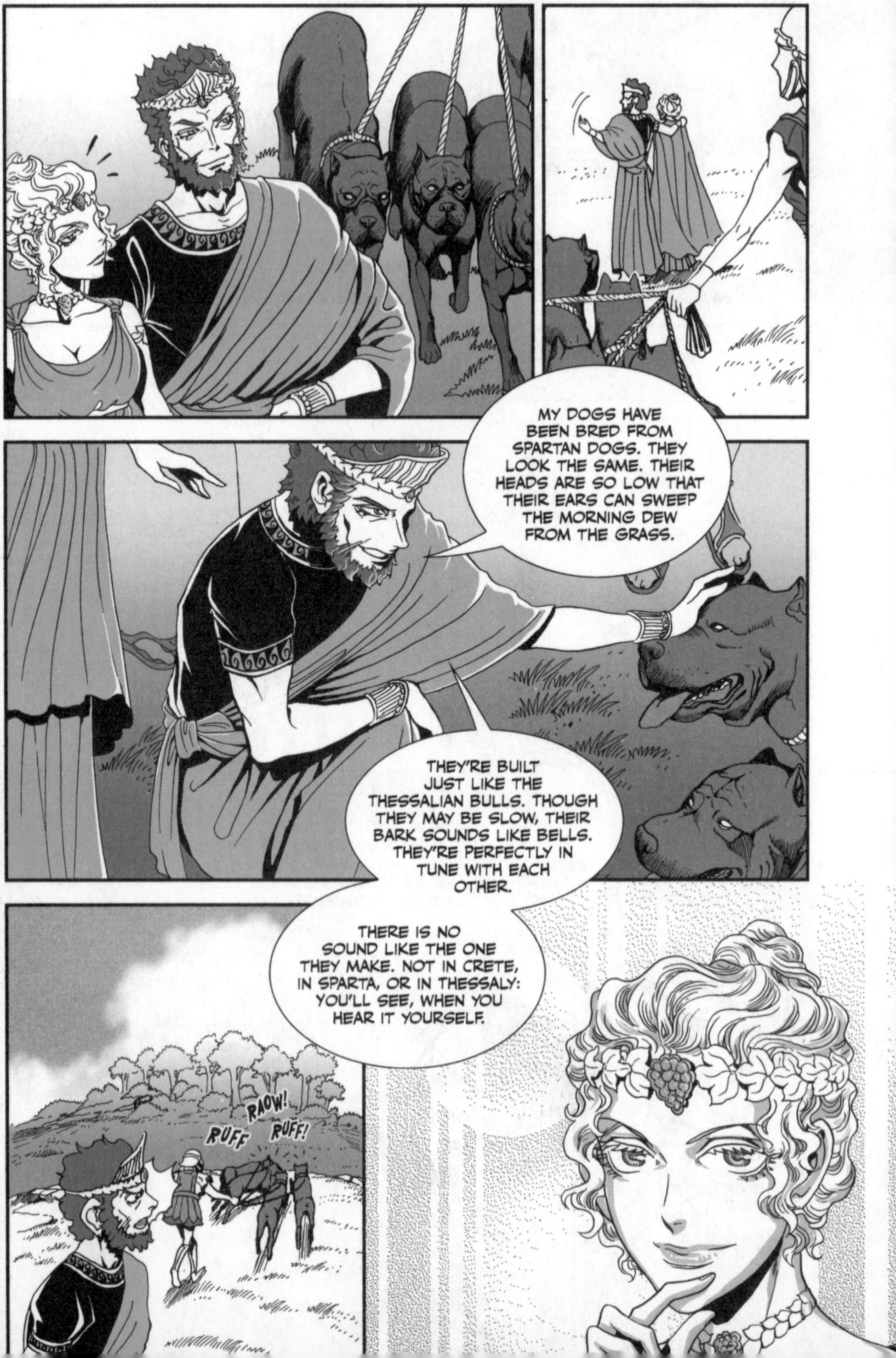
MY DOGS HAVE BEEN BRED FROM SPARTAN DOGS. THEY LOOK THE SAME. THEIR HEADS ARE SO LOW THAT THEIR EARS CAN SWEEP THE MORNING DEW FROM THE GRASS.
THEY'RE BUILT JUST LIKE THE THESSALIAN BULLS. THOUGH THEY MAY BE SLOW, THEIR BARK SOUNDS LIKE BELLS. THEY'RE PERFECTLY IN TUNE WITH EACH OTHER.
THERE IS NO SOUND LIKE THE ONE THEY MAKE. NOT IN CRETE, IN SPARTA, OR IN THESSALY: YOU'LL SEE, WHEN YOU HEAR IT YOURSELF.
RAOW!
RUFF
RUFF!

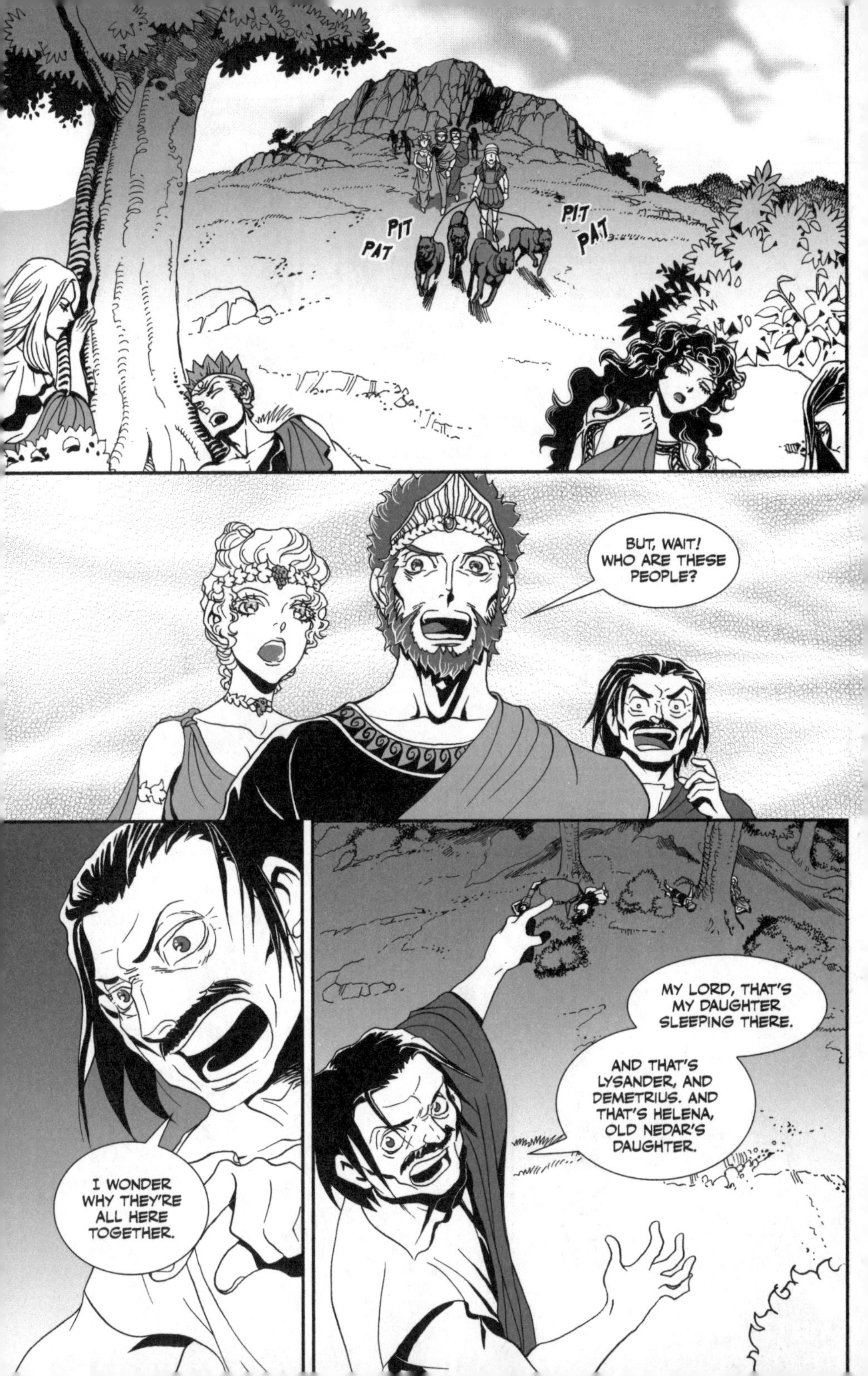
PIT PAT
PIT PAT
BUT, WAIT! WHO ARE THESE PEOPLE?
MY LORD, THAT'S MY DAUGHTER SLEEPING THERE.
AND THAT'S LYSANDER, AND DEMETRIUS. AND THAT'S HELENA, OLD NEDAR'S DAUGHTER.
I WONDER WHY THEY'RE ALL HERE TOGETHER.

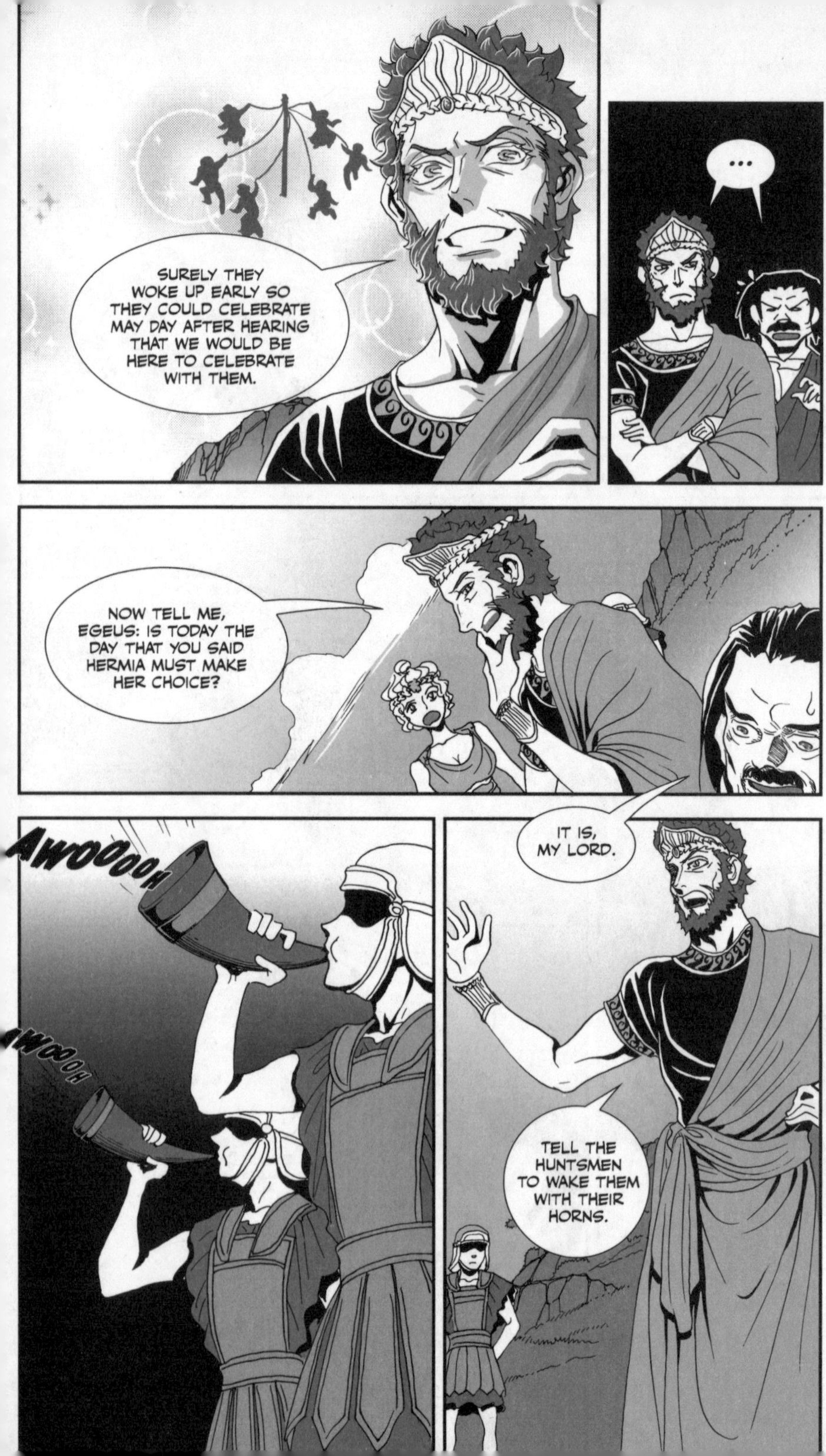
...
SURELY THEY WOKE UP EARLY SO THEY COULD CELEBRATE MAY DAY AFTER HEARING THAT WE WOULD BE HERE TO CELEBRATE WITH THEM.
NOW TELL ME, EGEUS: IS TODAY THE DAY THAT YOU SAID HERMIA MUST MAKE HER CHOICE?
IT IS, MY LORD.
TELL THE HUNTSMEN TO WAKE THEM WITH THEIR HORNS.
AWOOOOH
AWOOOH

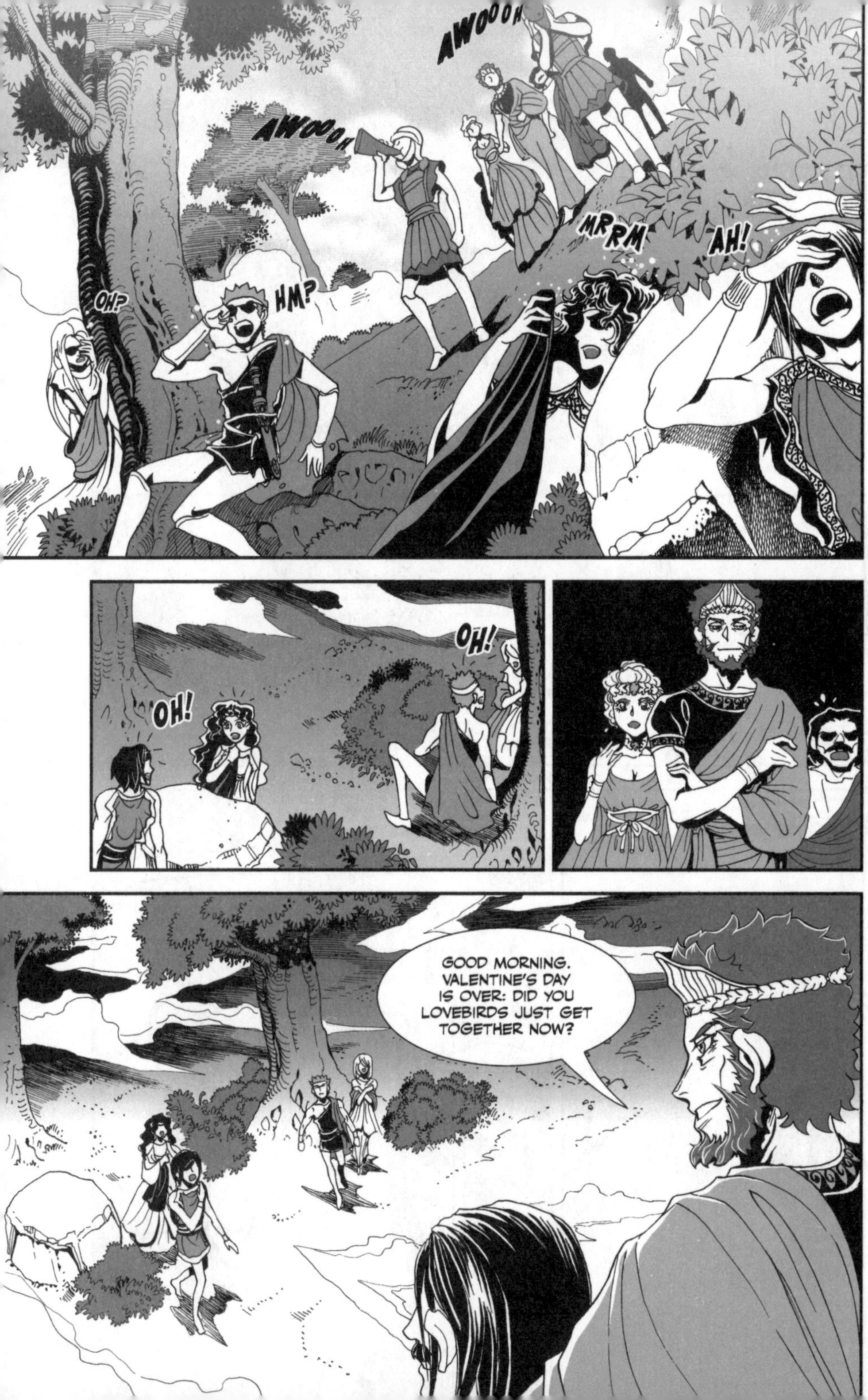
AWOOOH
AH!
AWOOOH
MRRM
HM?
OH?
OH!
OH!
GOOD MORNING. VALENTINE'S DAY IS OVER: DID YOU LOVEBIRDS JUST GET TOGETHER NOW?

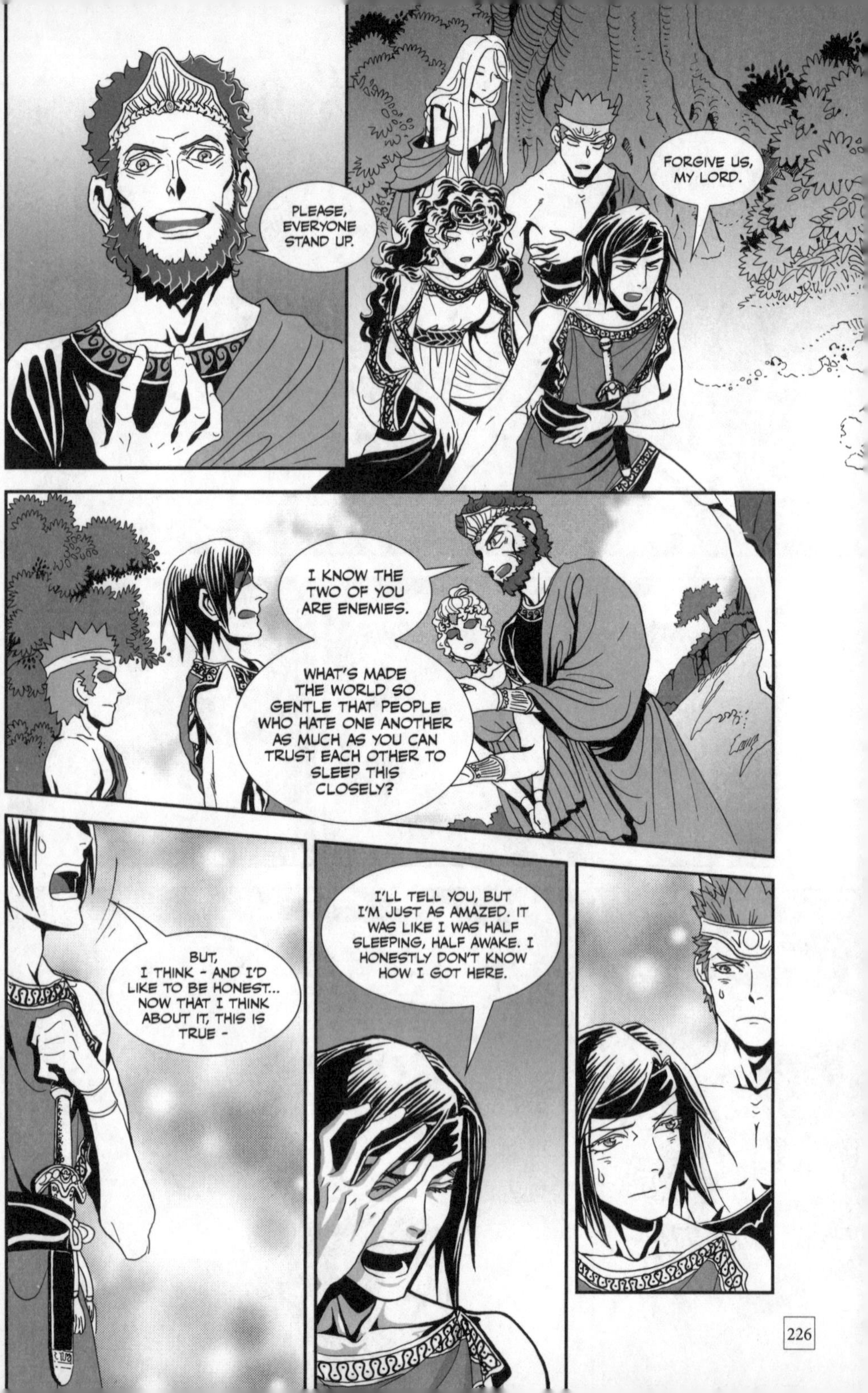
FORGIVE US, MY LORD.
PLEASE, EVERYONE STAND UP.
I KNOW THE TWO OF YOU ARE ENEMIES.
WHAT'S MADE THE WORLD SO GENTLE THAT PEOPLE WHO HATE ONE ANOTHER AS MUCH AS YOU CAN TRUST EACH OTHER TO SLEEP THIS CLOSELY?
I'LL TELL YOU, BUT I'M JUST AS AMAZED. IT WAS LIKE I WAS HALF SLEEPING, HALF AWAKE. I HONESTLY DON'T KNOW HOW I GOT HERE.
BUT, I THINK - AND I'D LIKE TO BE HONEST... NOW THAT I THINK ABOUT IT, THIS IS TRUE -

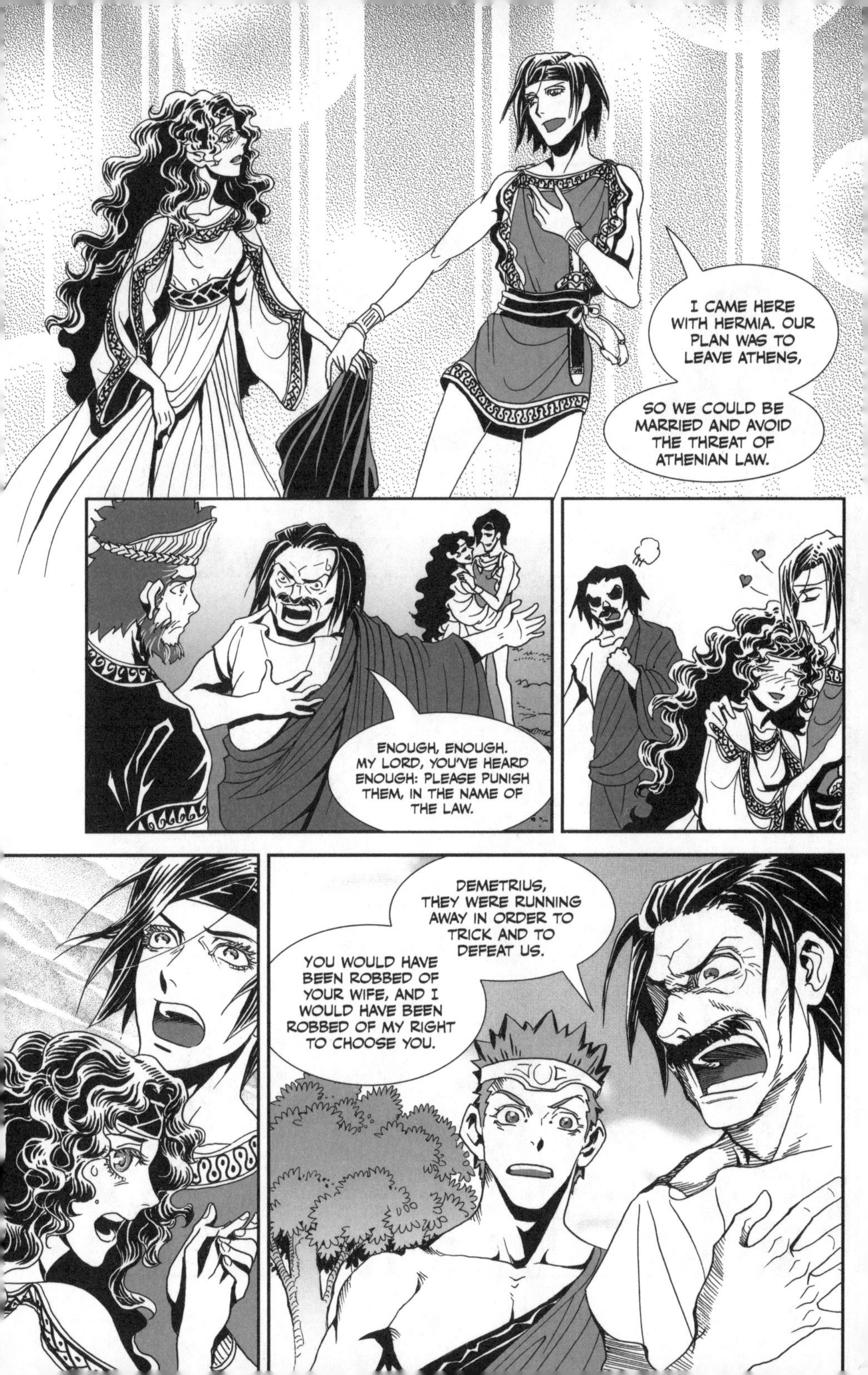
I CAME HERE WITH HERMIA. OUR PLAN WAS TO LEAVE ATHENS,
SO WE COULD BE MARRIED AND AVOID THE THREAT OF ATHENIAN LAW.
ENOUGH, ENOUGH. MY LORD, YOU'VE HEARD ENOUGH: PLEASE PUNISH THEM, IN THE NAME OF THE LAW.
DEMETRIUS, THEY WERE RUNNING AWAY IN ORDER TO TRICK AND TO DEFEAT US.
YOU WOULD HAVE BEEN ROBBED OF YOUR WIFE, AND I WOULD HAVE BEEN ROBBED OF MY RIGHT TO CHOOSE YOU.

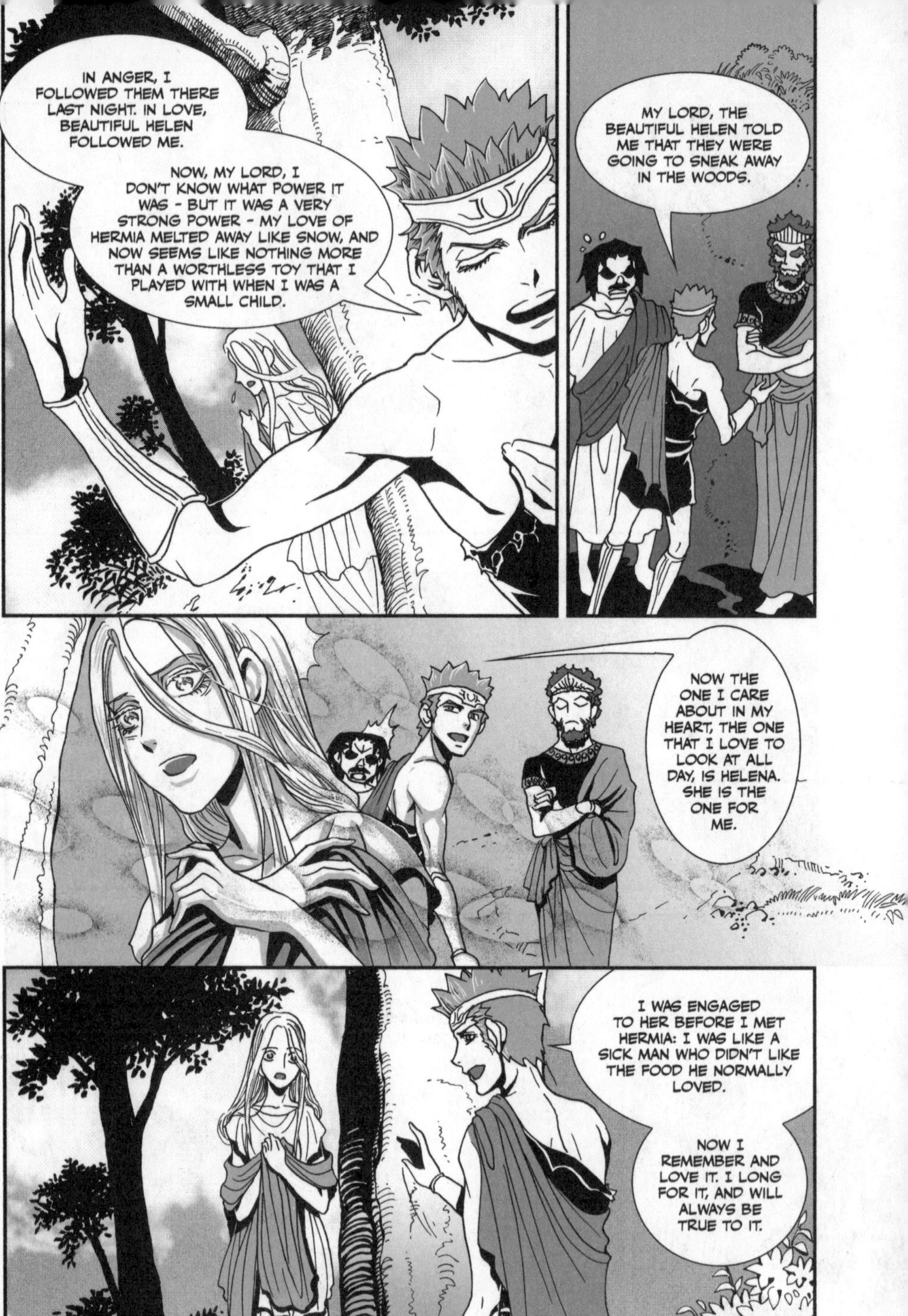
MY LORD, THE BEAUTIFUL HELEN TOLD ME THAT THEY WERE GOING TO SNEAK AWAY IN THE WOODS.
IN ANGER, I FOLLOWED THEM THERE LAST NIGHT. IN LOVE, BEAUTIFUL HELEN FOLLOWED ME.
NOW, MY LORD, I DON'T KNOW WHAT POWER IT WAS - BUT IT WAS A VERY STRONG POWER - MY LOVE OF HERMIA MELTED AWAY LIKE SNOW, AND NOW SEEMS LIKE NOTHING MORE THAN A WORTHLESS TOY THAT I PLAYED WITH WHEN I WAS A SMALL CHILD.
NOW THE ONE I CARE ABOUT IN MY HEART, THE ONE THAT I LOVE TO LOOK AT ALL DAY, IS HELENA. SHE IS THE ONE FOR ME.
I WAS ENGAGED TO HER BEFORE I MET HERMIA: I WAS LIKE A SICK MAN WHO DIDN'T LIKE THE FOOD HE NORMALLY LOVED.
NOW I REMEMBER AND LOVE IT. I LONG FOR IT, AND WILL ALWAYS BE TRUE TO IT.

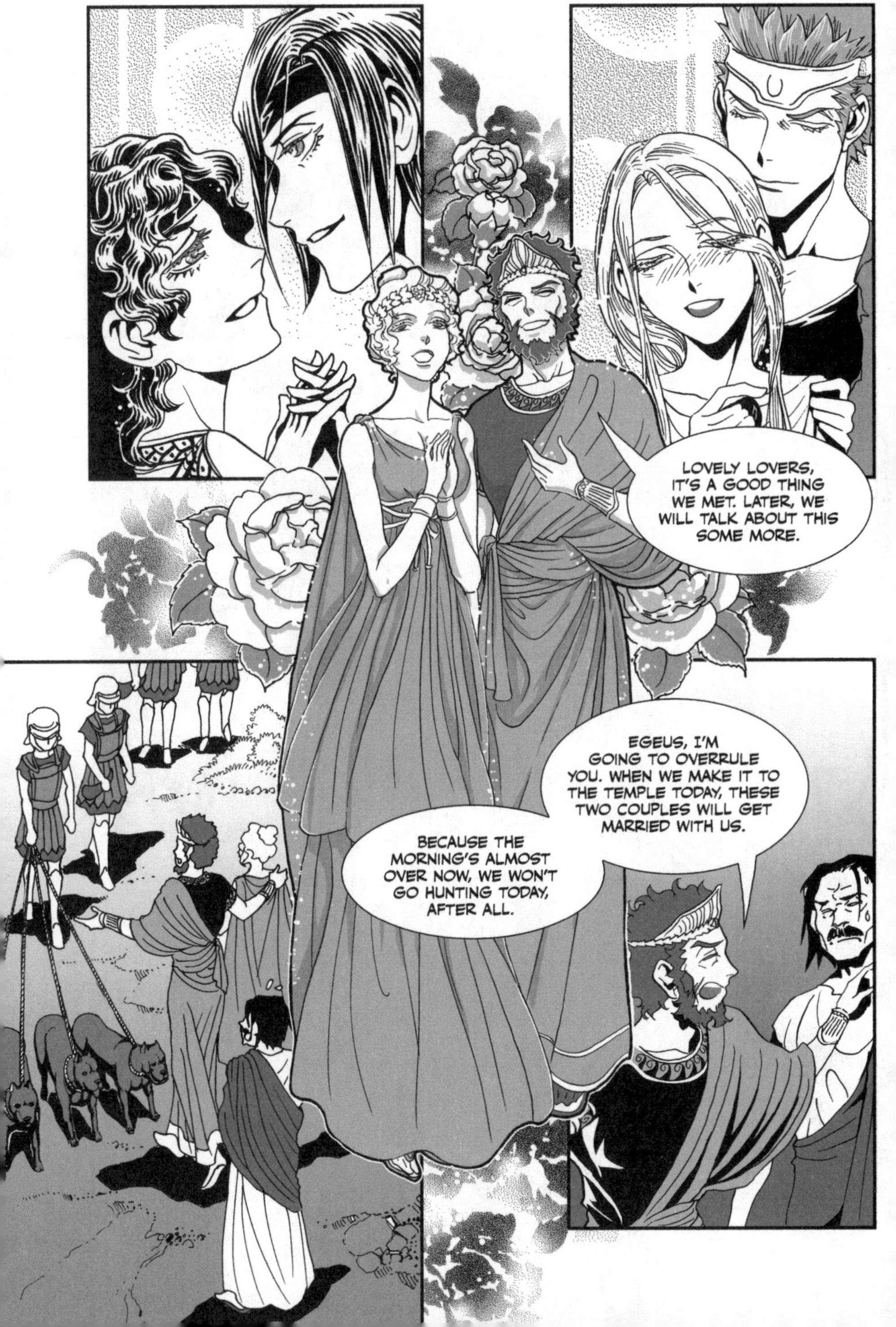
LOVELY LOVERS, IT'S A GOOD THING WE MET. LATER, WE WILL TALK ABOUT THIS SOME MORE.
EGEUS, I'M GOING TO OVERRULE YOU. WHEN WE MAKE IT TO THE TEMPLE TODAY, THESE TWO COUPLES WILL GET MARRIED WITH US.
BECAUSE THE MORNING'S ALMOST OVER NOW, WE WON'T GO HUNTING TODAY, AFTER ALL.

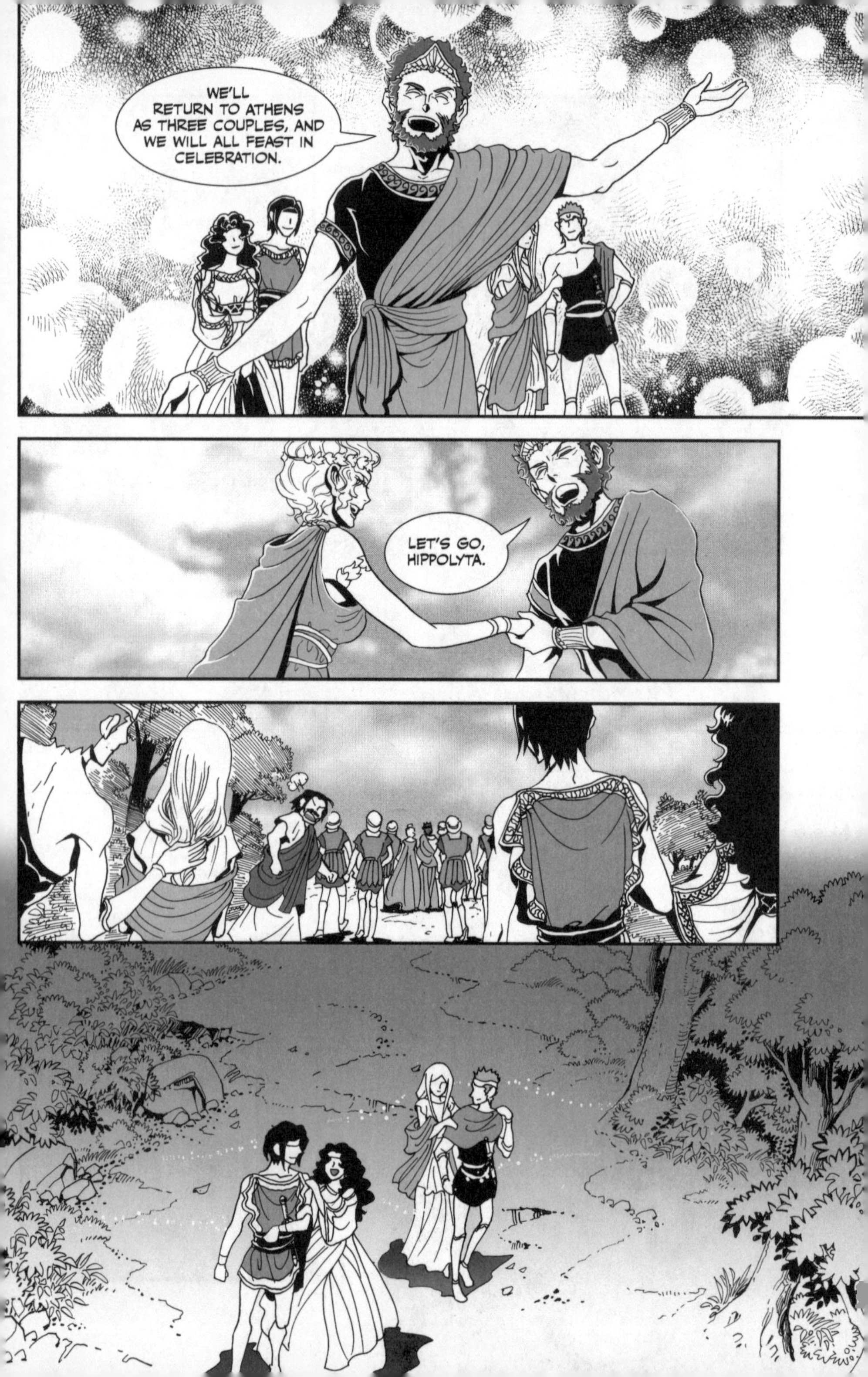
WE'LL RETURN TO ATHENS AS THREE COUPLES, AND WE WILL ALL FEAST IN CELEBRATION.
LET'S GO, HIPPOLYTA.

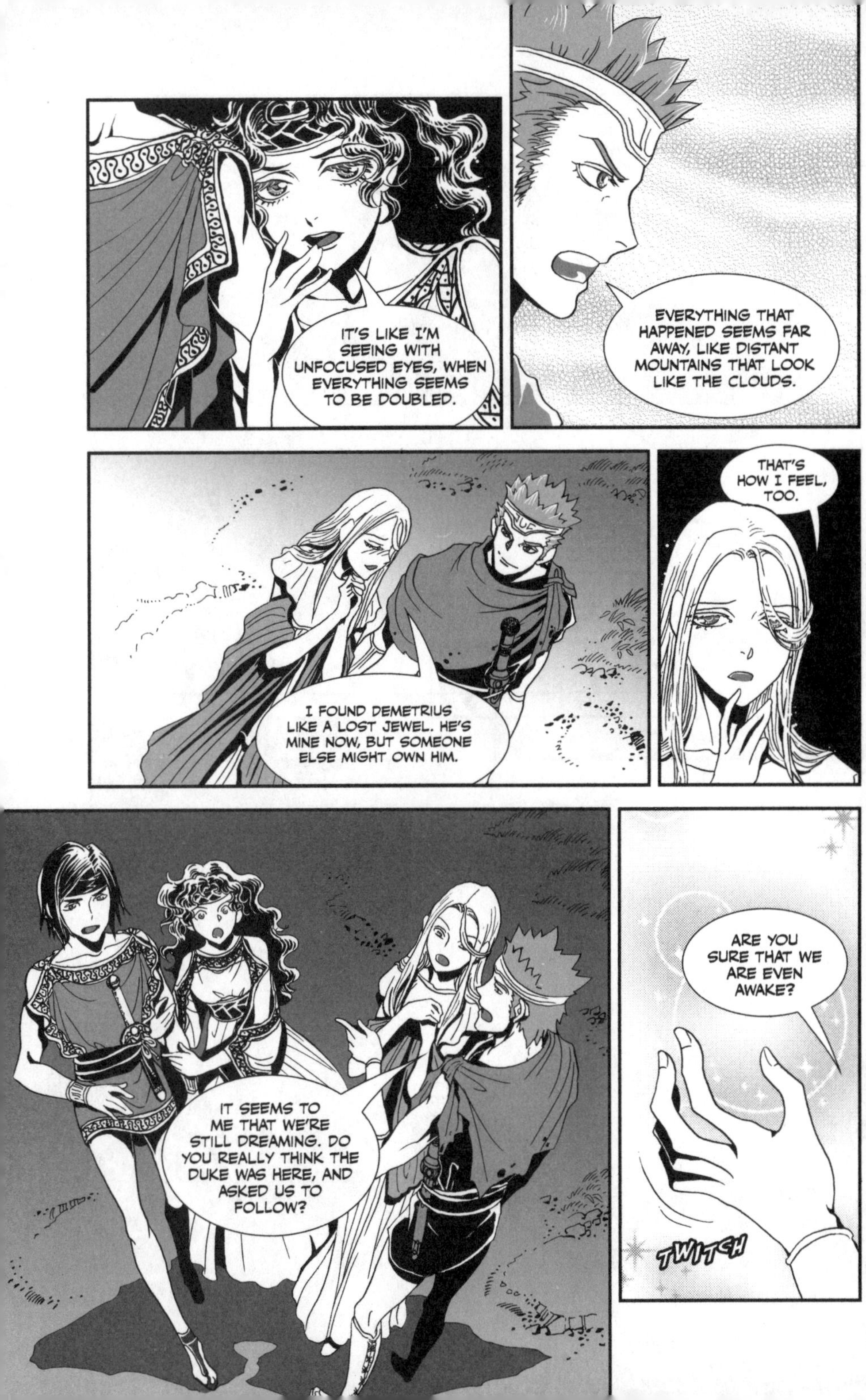
EVERYTHING THAT HAPPENED SEEMS FAR AWAY, LIKE DISTANT MOUNTAINS THAT LOOK LIKE THE CLOUDS.
IT'S LIKE I'M SEEING WITH UNFOCUSED EYES, WHEN EVERYTHING SEEMS TO BE DOUBLED.
THAT'S HOW I FEEL, TOO.
I FOUND DEMETRIUS LIKE A LOST JEWEL. HE'S MINE NOW, BUT SOMEONE ELSE MIGHT OWN HIM.
ARE YOU SURE THAT WE ARE EVEN AWAKE?
TWITCH
IT SEEMS TO ME THAT WE'RE STILL DREAMING. DO YOU REALLY THINK THE DUKE WAS HERE, AND ASKED US TO FOLLOW?

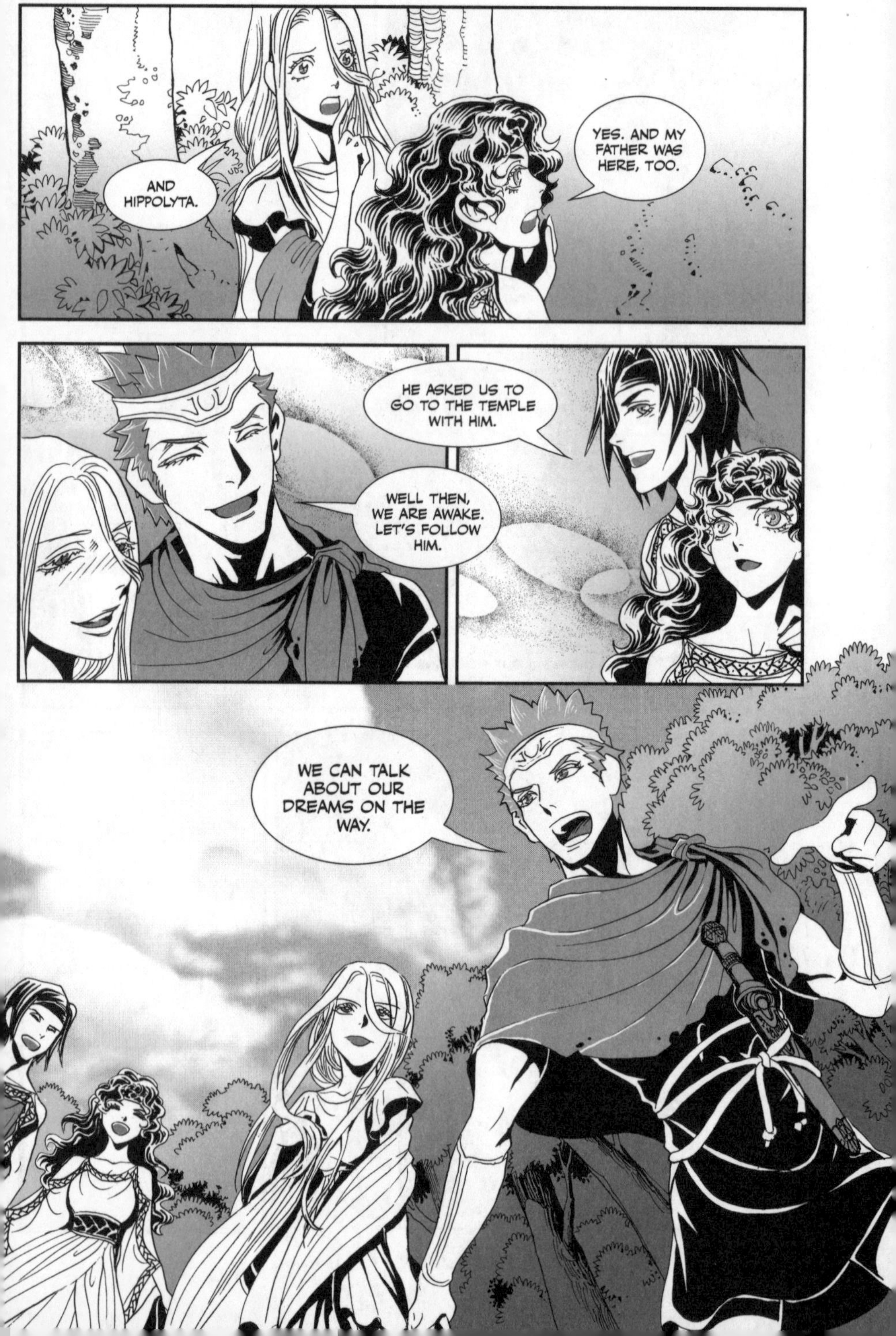
YES. AND MY FATHER WAS HERE, TOO.
AND HIPPOLYTA.
HE ASKED US TO GO TO THE TEMPLE WITH HIM.
WELL THEN, WE ARE AWAKE. LET'S FOLLOW HIM.
WE CAN TALK ABOUT OUR DREAMS ON THE WAY.

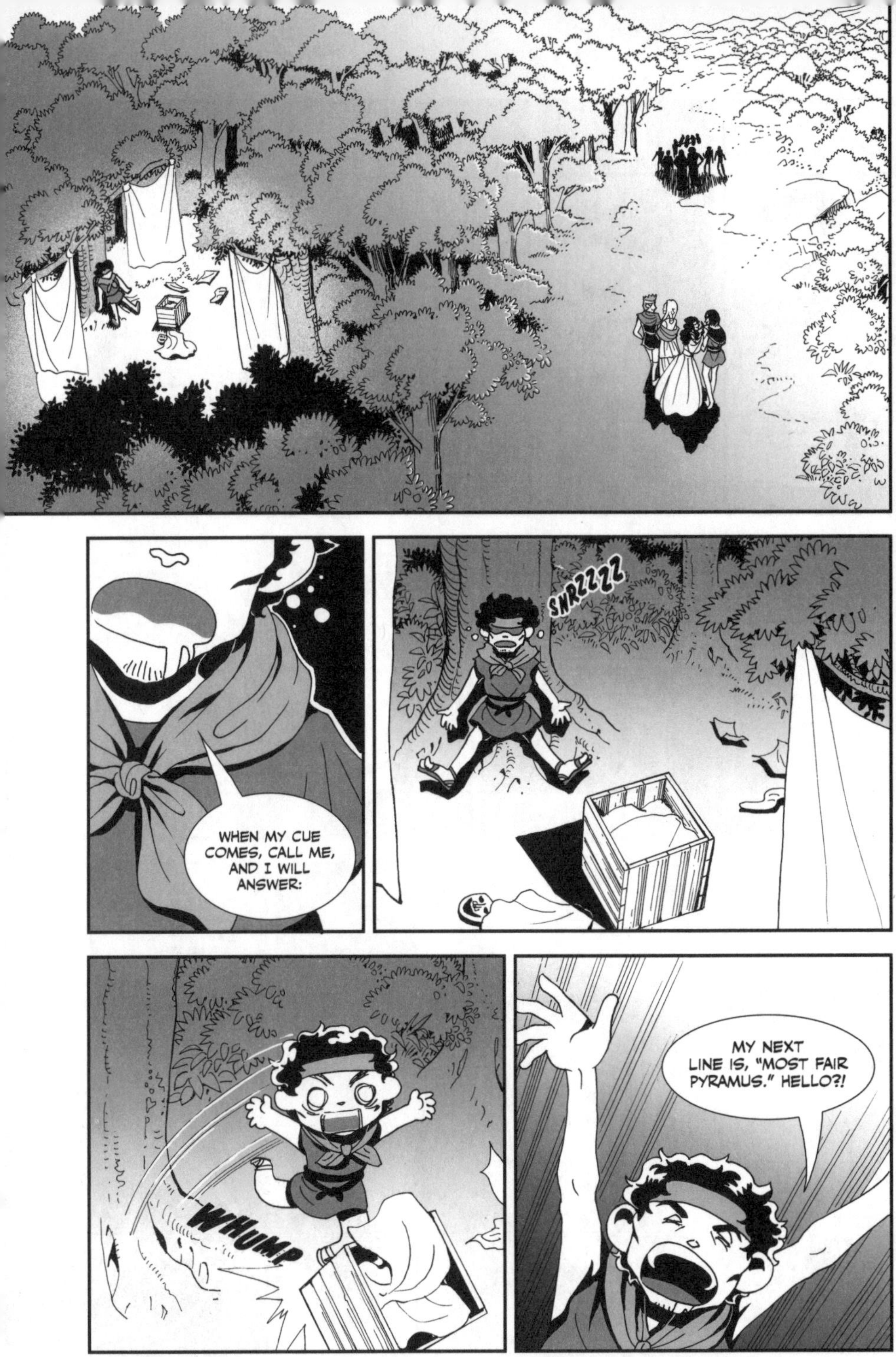
SNRZZZZ
WHEN MY CUE COMES, CALL ME, AND I WILL ANSWER:
MY NEXT LINE IS, "MOST FAIR PYRAMUS." HELLO?!
WHUMP

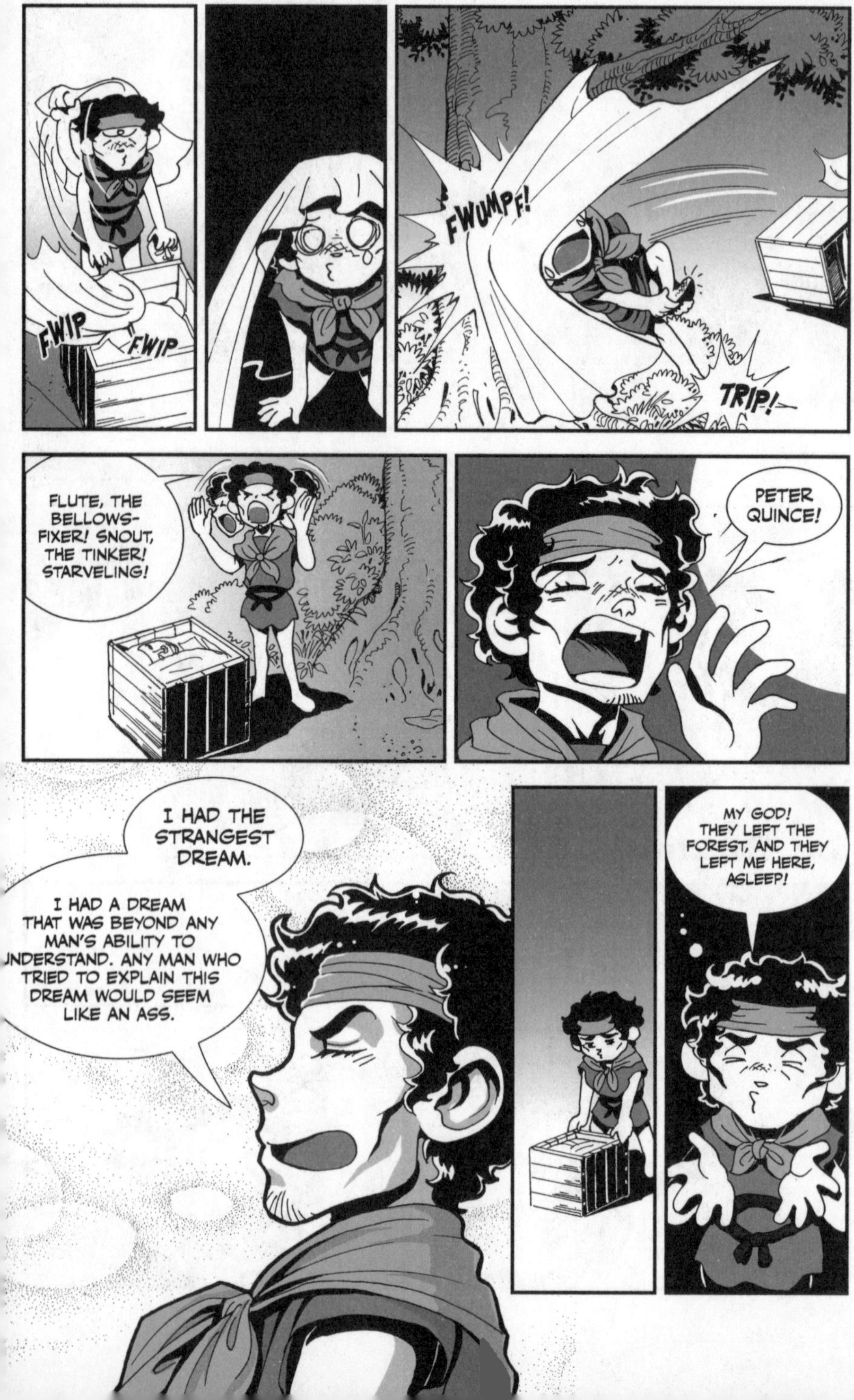
FWUMPF!
TRIP!
FWIP
FWIP
PETER QUINCE!
FLUTE, THE BELLOWS-FIXER! SNOUT, THE TINKER! STARVELING!
MY GOD! THEY LEFT THE FOREST, AND THEY LEFT ME HERE, ASLEEP!
I HAD THE STRANGEST DREAM.
I HAD A DREAM THAT WAS BEYOND ANY MAN'S ABILITY TO UNDERSTAND. ANY MAN WHO TRIED TO EXPLAIN THIS DREAM WOULD SEEM LIKE AN ASS.

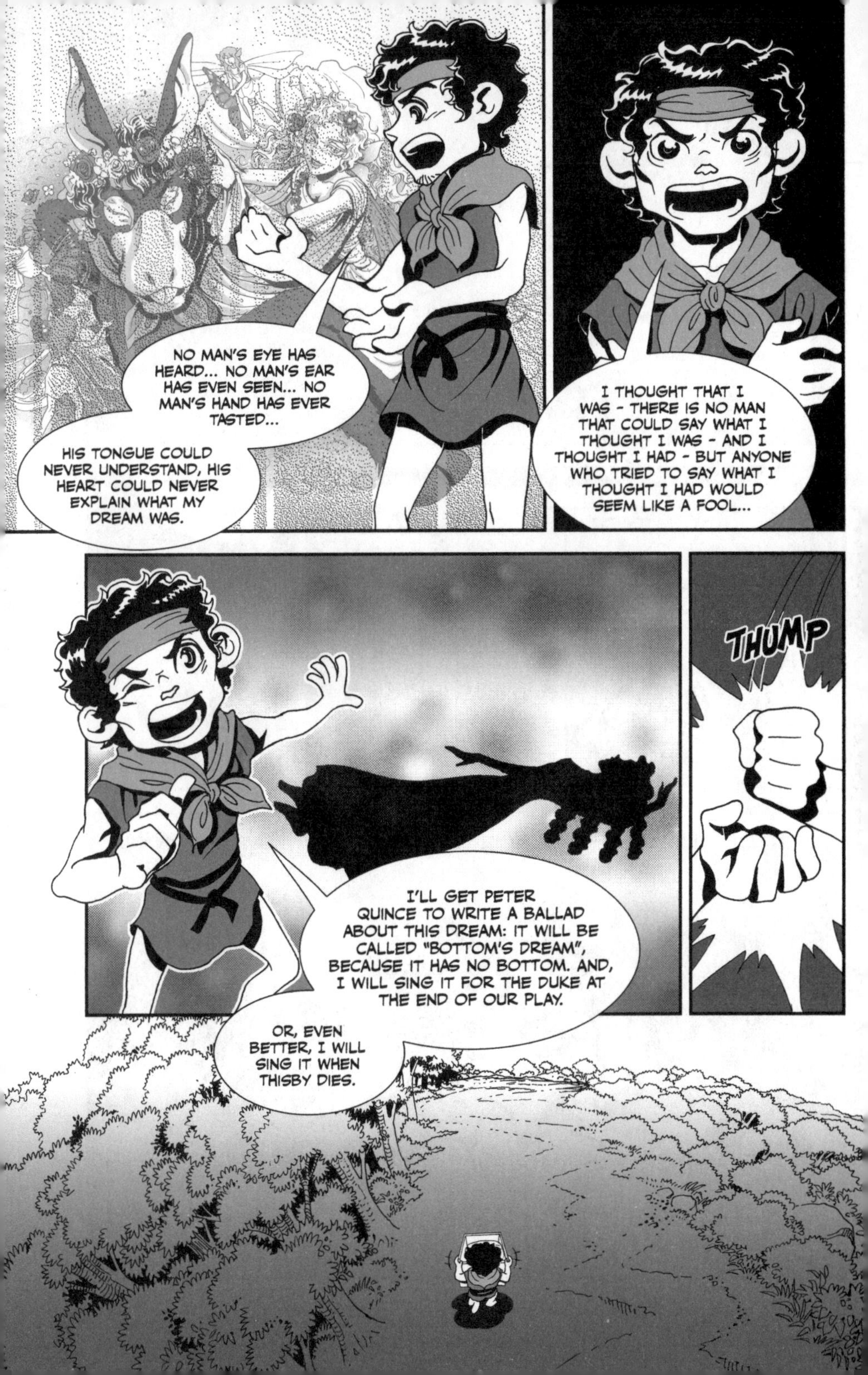
I THOUGHT THAT I WAS - THERE IS NO MAN THAT COULD SAY WHAT I THOUGHT I WAS - AND I THOUGHT I HAD - BUT ANYONE WHO TRIED TO SAY WHAT I THOUGHT I HAD WOULD SEEM LIKE A FOOL...
NO MAN'S EYE HAS HEARD... NO MAN'S EAR HAS EVEN SEEN... NO MAN'S HAND HAS EVER TASTED...
HIS TONGUE COULD NEVER UNDERSTAND, HIS HEART COULD NEVER EXPLAIN WHAT MY DREAM WAS.
THUMP
I'LL GET PETER QUINCE TO WRITE A BALLAD ABOUT THIS DREAM: IT WILL BE CALLED "BOTTOM'S DREAM", BECAUSE IT HAS NO BOTTOM. AND, I WILL SING IT FOR THE DUKE AT THE END OF OUR PLAY.
OR, EVEN BETTER, I WILL SING IT WHEN THISBY DIES.

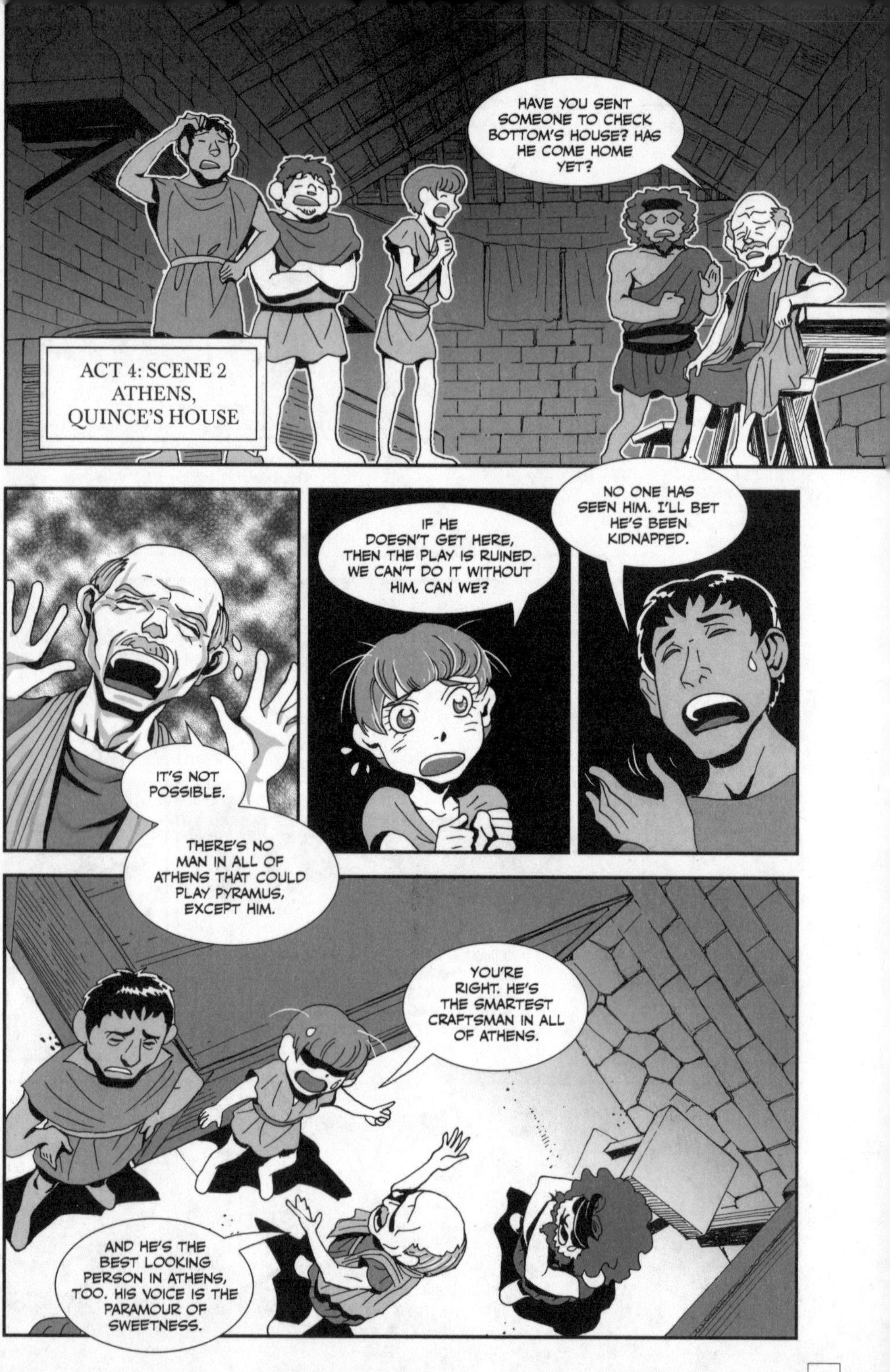
HAVE YOU SENT SOMEONE TO CHECK BOTTOM'S HOUSE? HAS HE COME HOME YET?
ACT 4: SCENE 2
ATHENS,
QUINCE'S HOUSE
NO ONE HAS SEEN HIM. I'LL BET HE'S BEEN KIDNAPPED.
IF HE DOESN'T GET HERE, THEN THE PLAY IS RUINED. WE CAN'T DO IT WITHOUT HIM, CAN WE?
IT'S NOT POSSIBLE.
THERE'S NO MAN IN ALL OF ATHENS THAT COULD PLAY PYRAMUS, EXCEPT HIM.
YOU'RE RIGHT. HE'S THE SMARTEST CRAFTSMAN IN ALL OF ATHENS.
AND HE'S THE BEST LOOKING PERSON IN ATHENS, TOO. HIS VOICE IS THE PARAMOUR OF SWEETNESS.

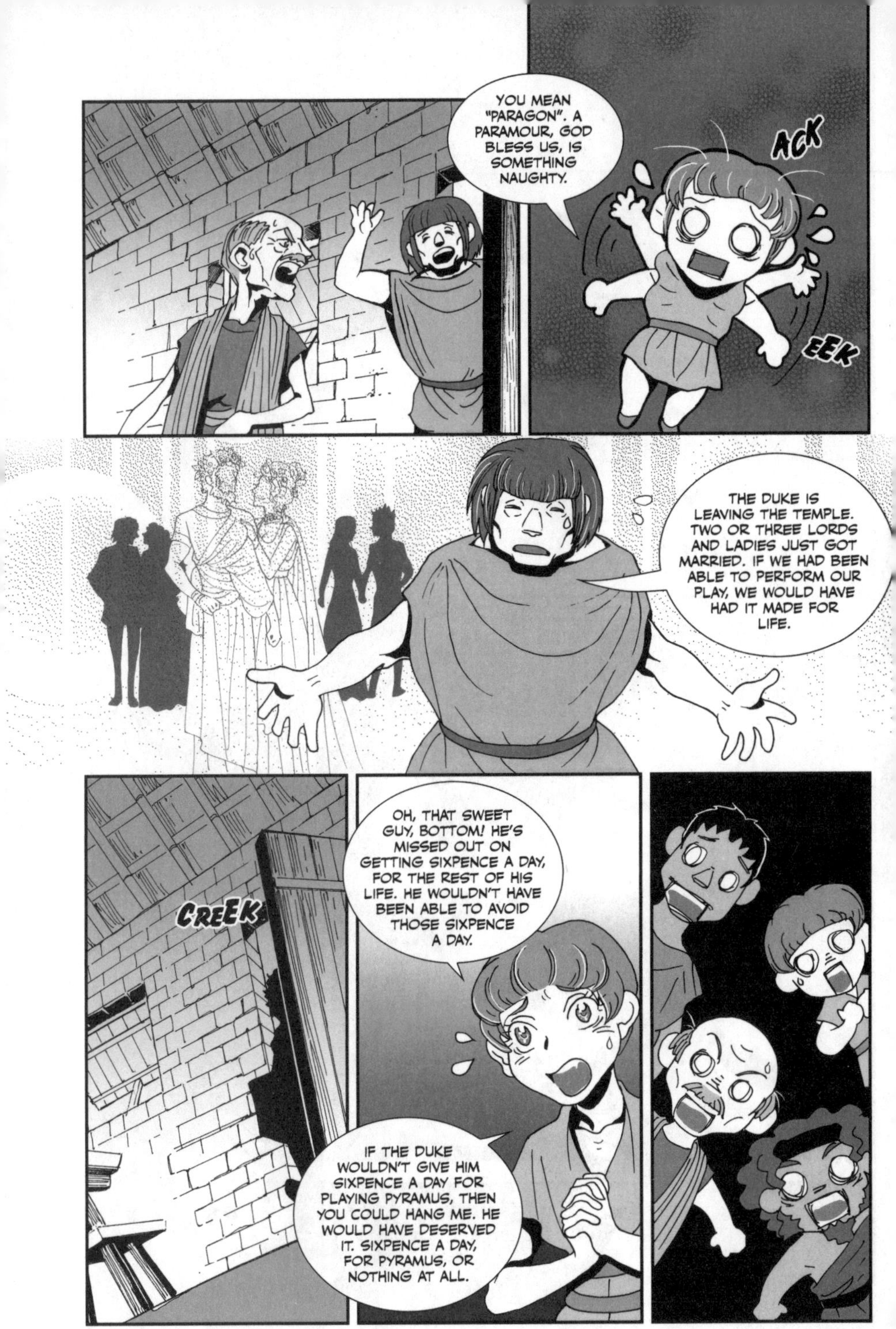

YOU MEAN "PARAGON". A PARAMOUR, GOD BLESS US, IS SOMETHING NAUGHTY.
ACK
EEK
THE DUKE IS LEAVING THE TEMPLE. TWO OR THREE LORDS AND LADIES JUST GOT MARRIED. IF WE HAD BEEN ABLE TO PERFORM OUR PLAY, WE WOULD HAVE HAD IT MADE FOR LIFE.
OH, THAT SWEET GUY, BOTTOM! HE'S MISSED OUT ON GETTING SIXPENCE A DAY, FOR THE REST OF HIS LIFE. HE WOULDN'T HAVE BEEN ABLE TO AVOID THOSE SIXPENCE A DAY.
IF THE DUKE WOULDN'T GIVE HIM SIXPENCE A DAY FOR PLAYING PYRAMUS, THEN YOU COULD HANG ME. HE WOULD HAVE DESERVED IT. SIXPENCE A DAY, FOR PYRAMUS, OR NOTHING AT ALL.
CREEK

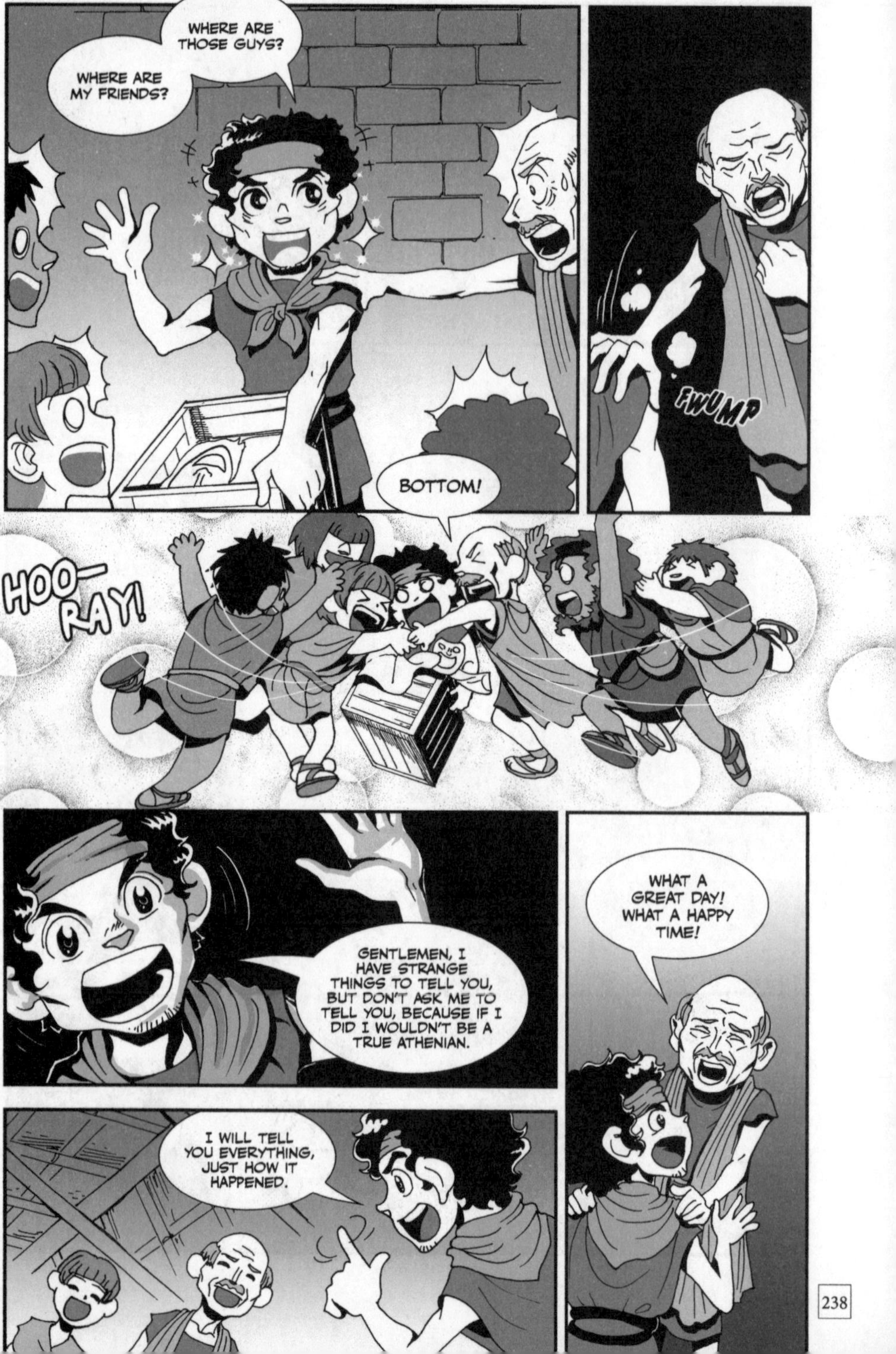
FWUMP
WHERE ARE THOSE GUYS?
WHERE ARE MY FRIENDS?
BOTTOM!
HOO-RAY!
WHAT A GREAT DAY! WHAT A HAPPY TIME!
GENTLEMEN, I HAVE STRANGE THINGS TO TELL YOU, BUT DON'T ASK ME TO TELL YOU, BECAUSE IF I DID I WOULDN'T BE A TRUE ATHENIAN.
I WILL TELL YOU EVERYTHING, JUST HOW IT HAPPENED.

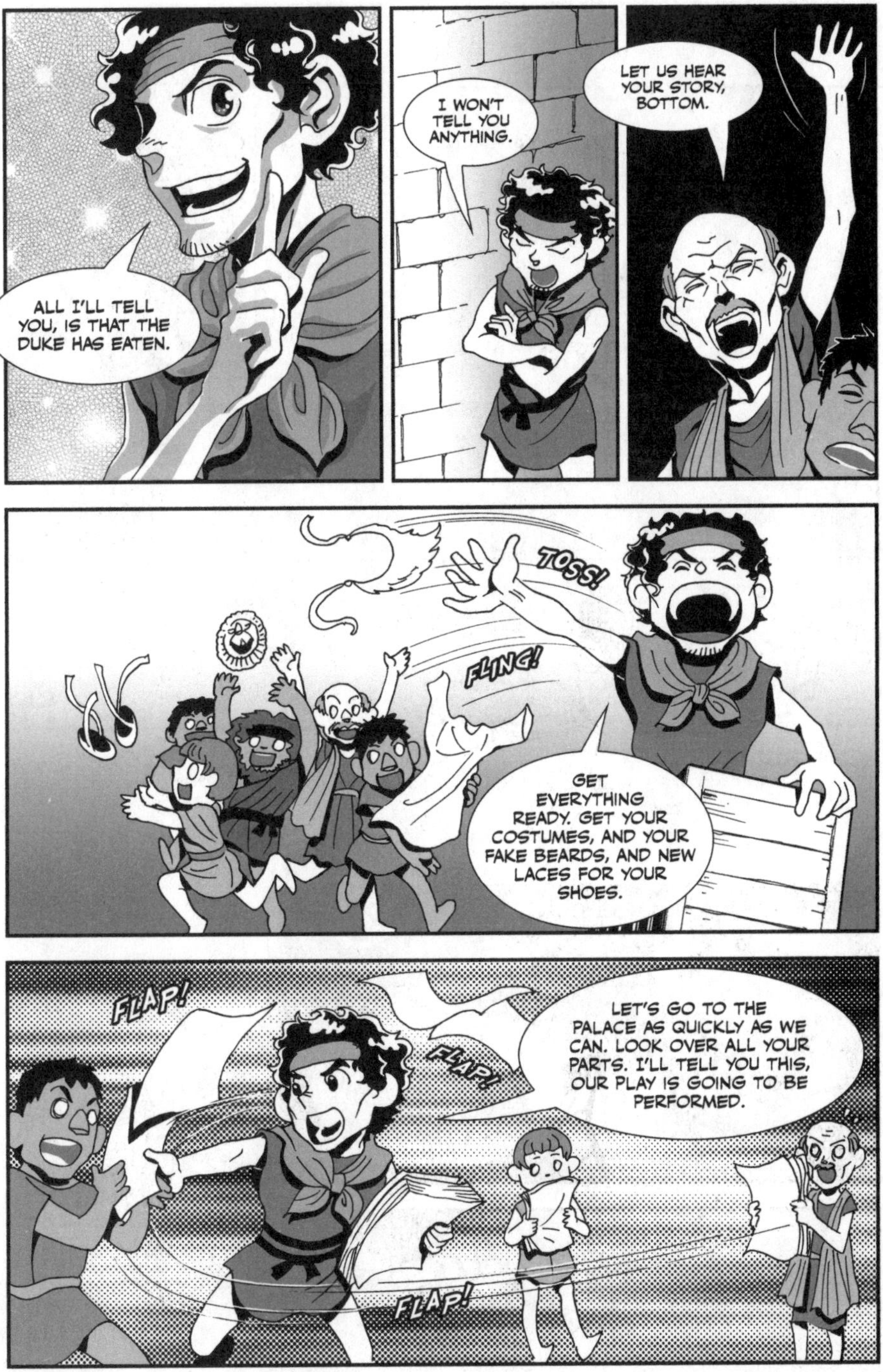
LET US HEAR YOUR STORY, BOTTOM.
I WON'T TELL YOU ANYTHING.
ALL I'LL TELL YOU, IS THAT THE DUKE HAS EATEN.
TOSS!
FLING!
GET EVERYTHING READY. GET YOUR COSTUMES, AND YOUR FAKE BEARDS, AND NEW LACES FOR YOUR SHOES.
LET'S GO TO THE PALACE AS QUICKLY AS WE CAN. LOOK OVER ALL YOUR PARTS. I'LL TELL YOU THIS, OUR PLAY IS GOING TO BE PERFORMED.
FLAP!
FLAP!
FLAP!

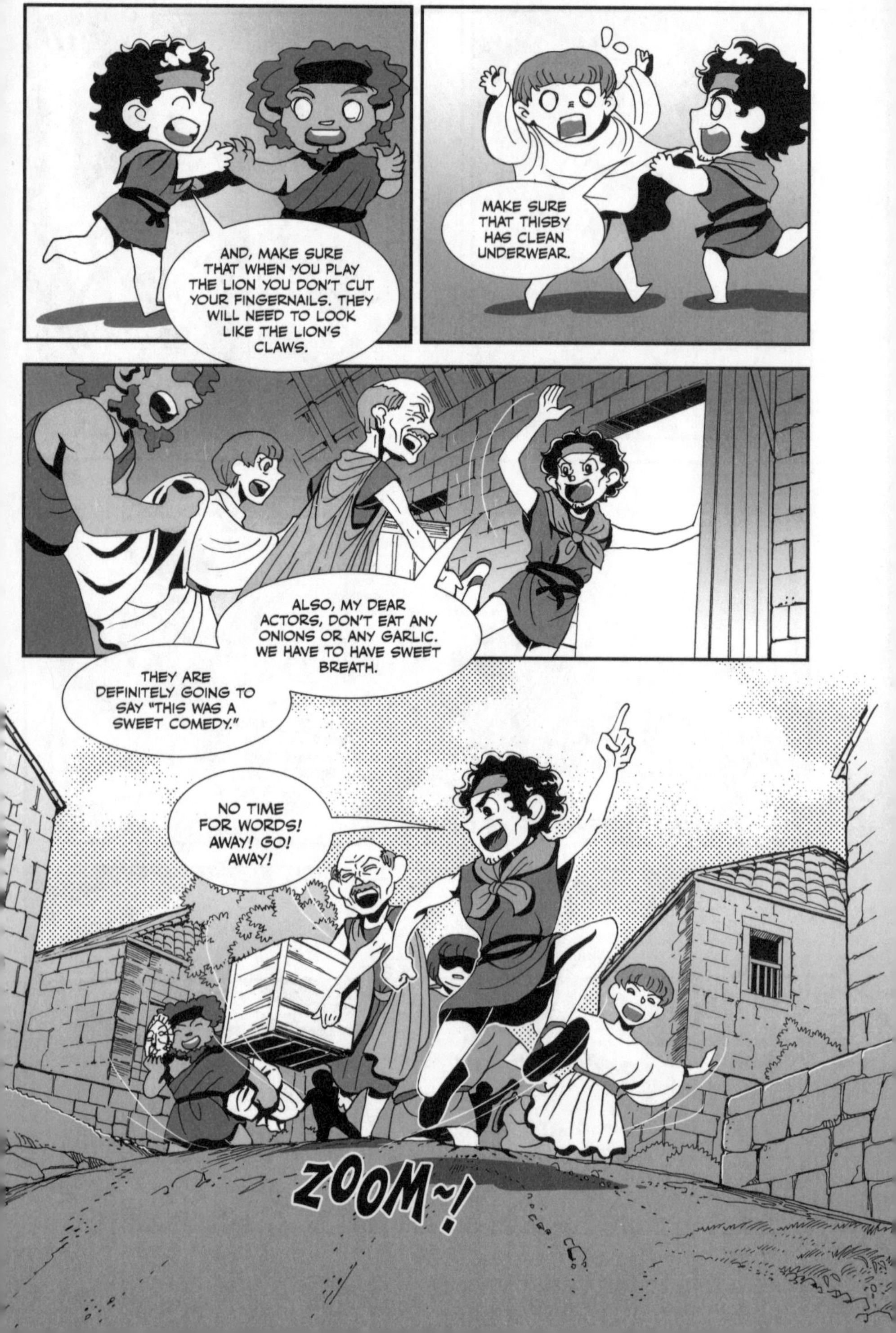
MAKE SURE THAT THISBY HAS CLEAN UNDERWEAR.
AND, MAKE SURE THAT WHEN YOU PLAY THE LION YOU DON'T CUT YOUR FINGERNAILS. THEY WILL NEED TO LOOK LIKE THE LION'S CLAWS.
ALSO, MY DEAR ACTORS, DON'T EAT ANY ONIONS OR ANY GARLIC. WE HAVE TO HAVE SWEET BREATH.
THEY ARE DEFINITELY GOING TO SAY "THIS WAS A SWEET COMEDY."
NO TIME FOR WORDS! AWAY! GO! AWAY!
ZOOM~!

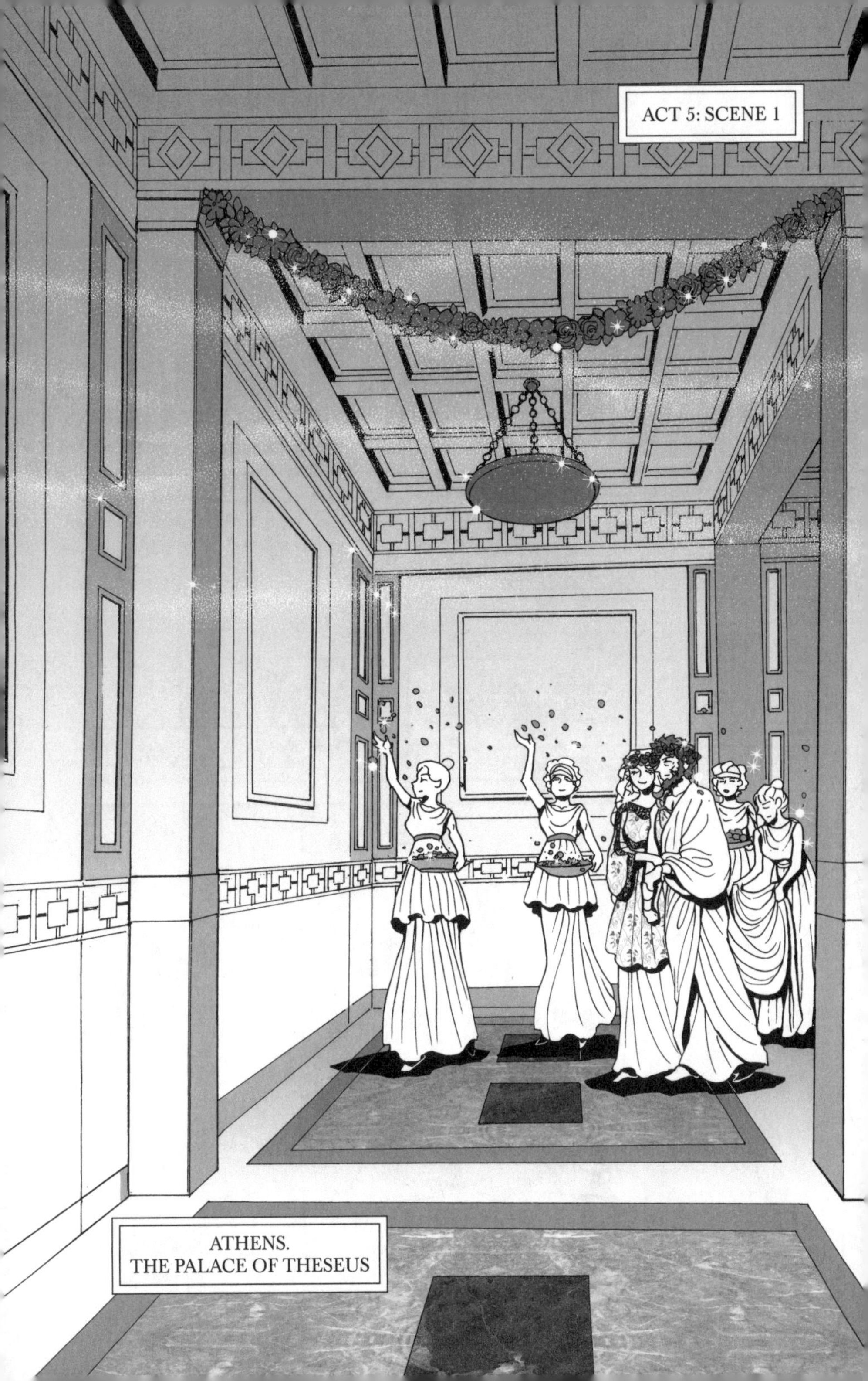
ACT 5: SCENE 1
ATHENS.
THE PALACE OF THESEUS

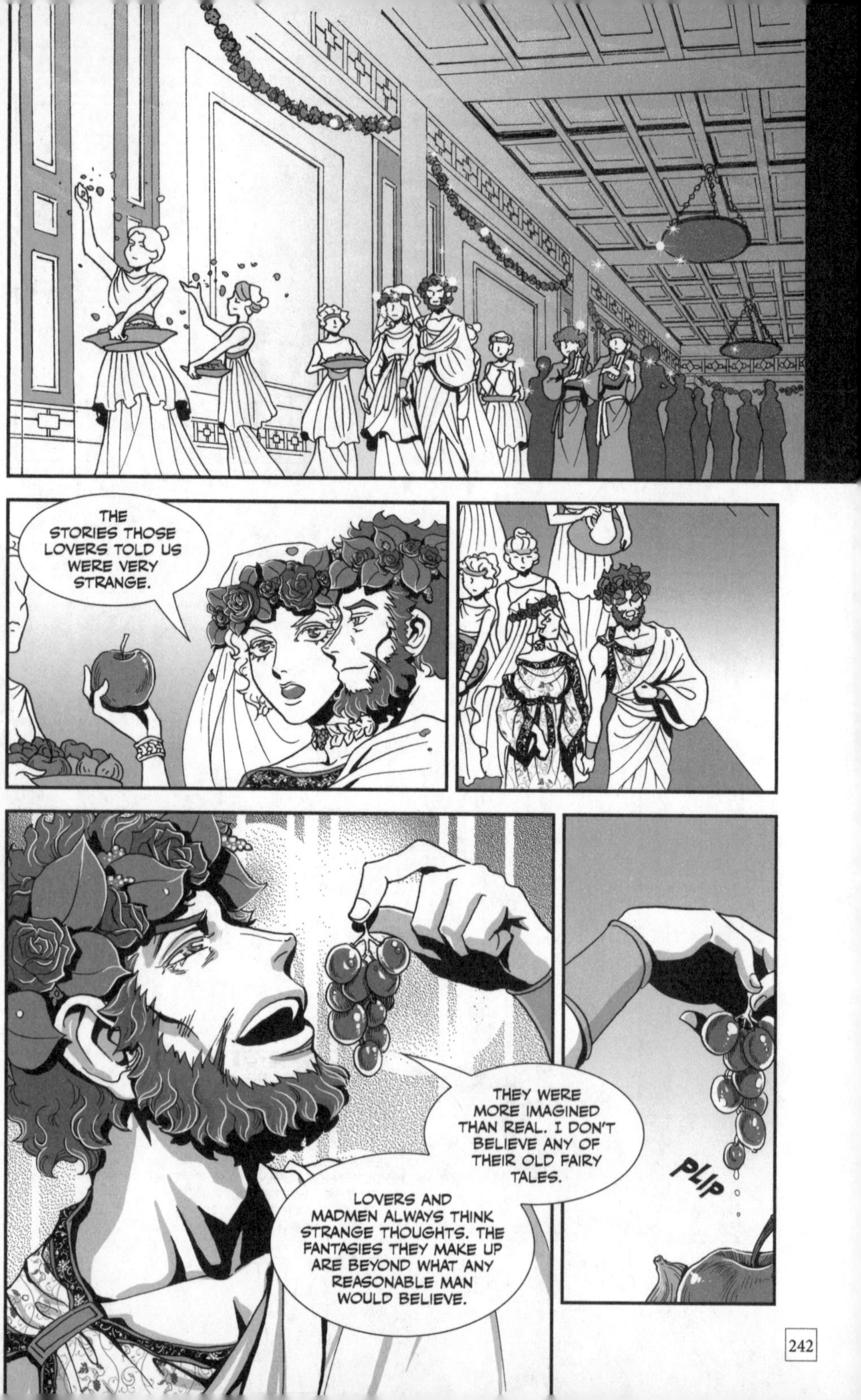
THE STORIES THOSE LOVERS TOLD US WERE VERY STRANGE.
PLIP
THEY WERE MORE IMAGINED THAN REAL. I DON'T BELIEVE ANY OF THEIR OLD FAIRY TALES.
LOVERS AND MADMEN ALWAYS THINK STRANGE THOUGHTS. THE FANTASIES THEY MAKE UP ARE BEYOND WHAT ANY REASONABLE MAN WOULD BELIEVE.

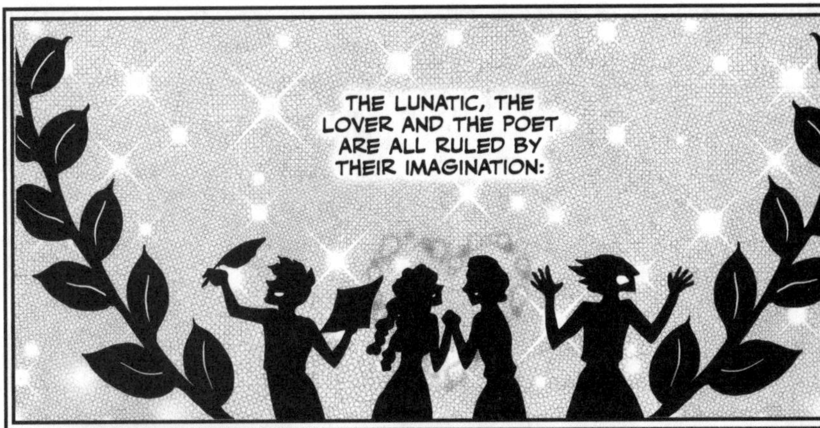
THE LUNATIC, THE LOVER AND THE POET ARE ALL RULED BY THEIR IMAGINATION:

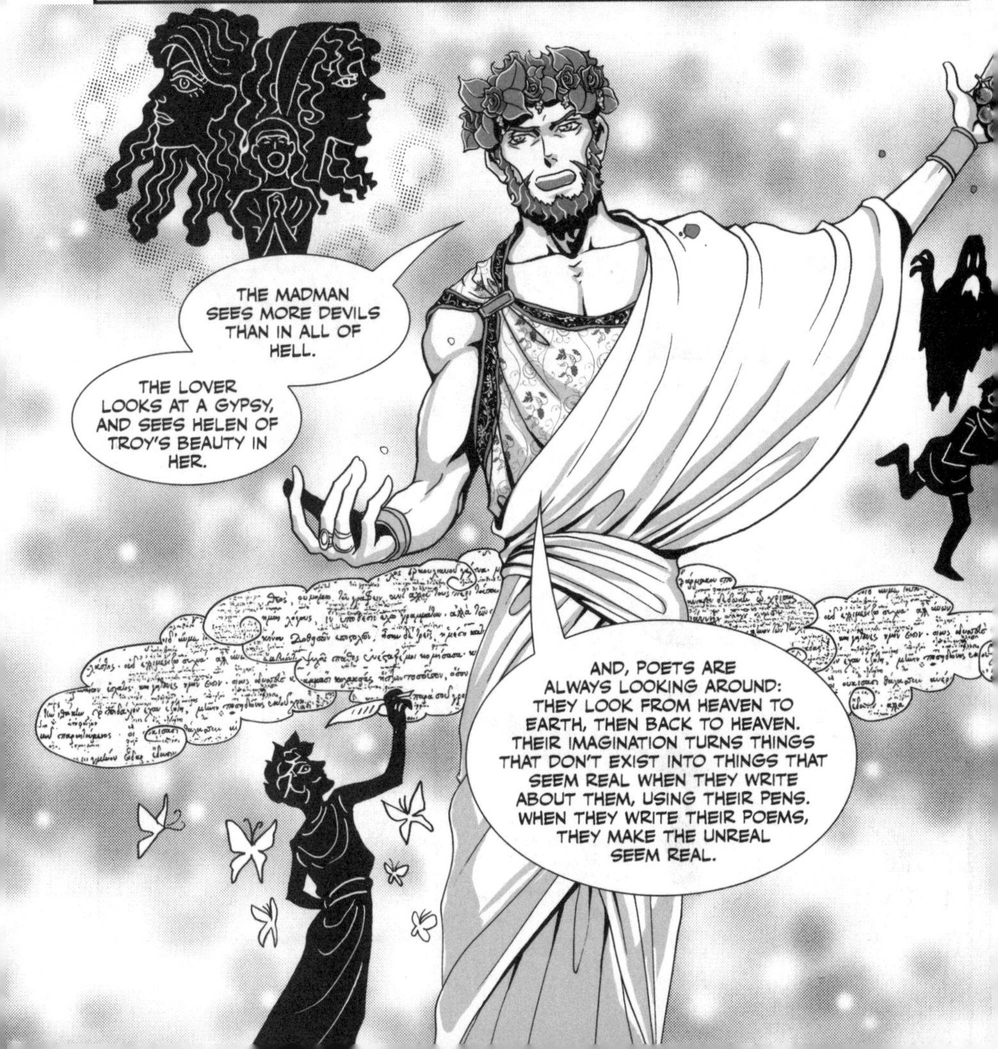
THE MADMAN SEES MORE DEVILS THAN IN ALL OF HELL.
THE LOVER LOOKS AT A GYPSY, AND SEES HELEN OF TROY'S BEAUTY IN HER.
AND, POETS ARE ALWAYS LOOKING AROUND: THEY LOOK FROM HEAVEN TO EARTH, THEN BACK TO HEAVEN. THEIR IMAGINATION TURNS THINGS THAT DON'T EXIST INTO THINGS THAT SEEM REAL WHEN THEY WRITE ABOUT THEM, USING THEIR PENS. WHEN THEY WRITE THEIR POEMS, THEY MAKE THE UNREAL SEEM REAL.

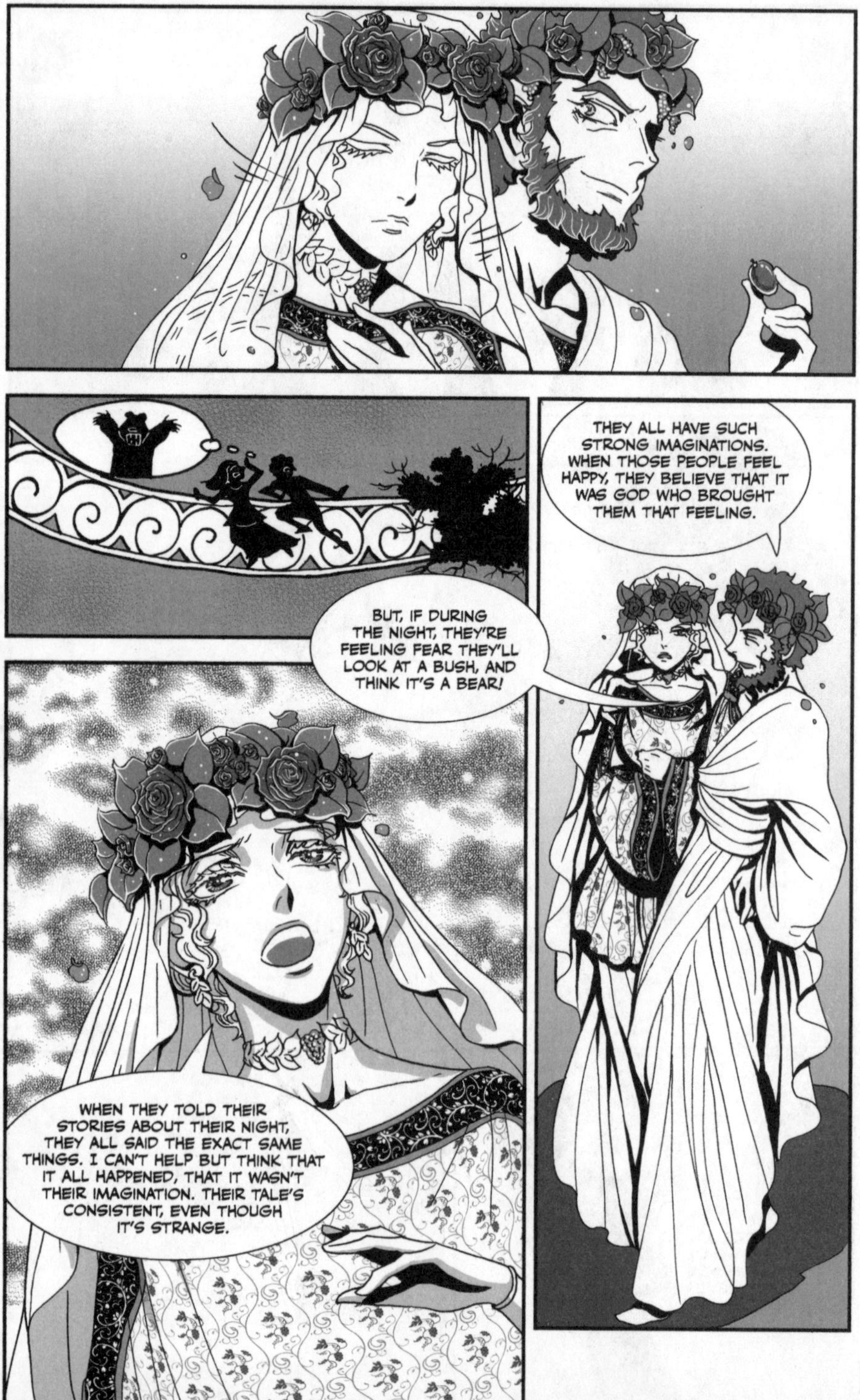
THEY ALL HAVE SUCH STRONG IMAGINATIONS. WHEN THOSE PEOPLE FEEL HAPPY, THEY BELIEVE THAT IT WAS GOD WHO BROUGHT THEM THAT FEELING.
BUT, IF DURING THE NIGHT, THEY'RE FEELING FEAR THEY'LL LOOK AT A BUSH, AND THINK IT'S A BEAR!
WHEN THEY TOLD THEIR STORIES ABOUT THEIR NIGHT, THEY ALL SAID THE EXACT SAME THINGS. I CAN'T HELP BUT THINK THAT IT ALL HAPPENED, THAT IT WASN'T THEIR IMAGINATION. THEIR TALE'S CONSISTENT, EVEN THOUGH IT'S STRANGE.

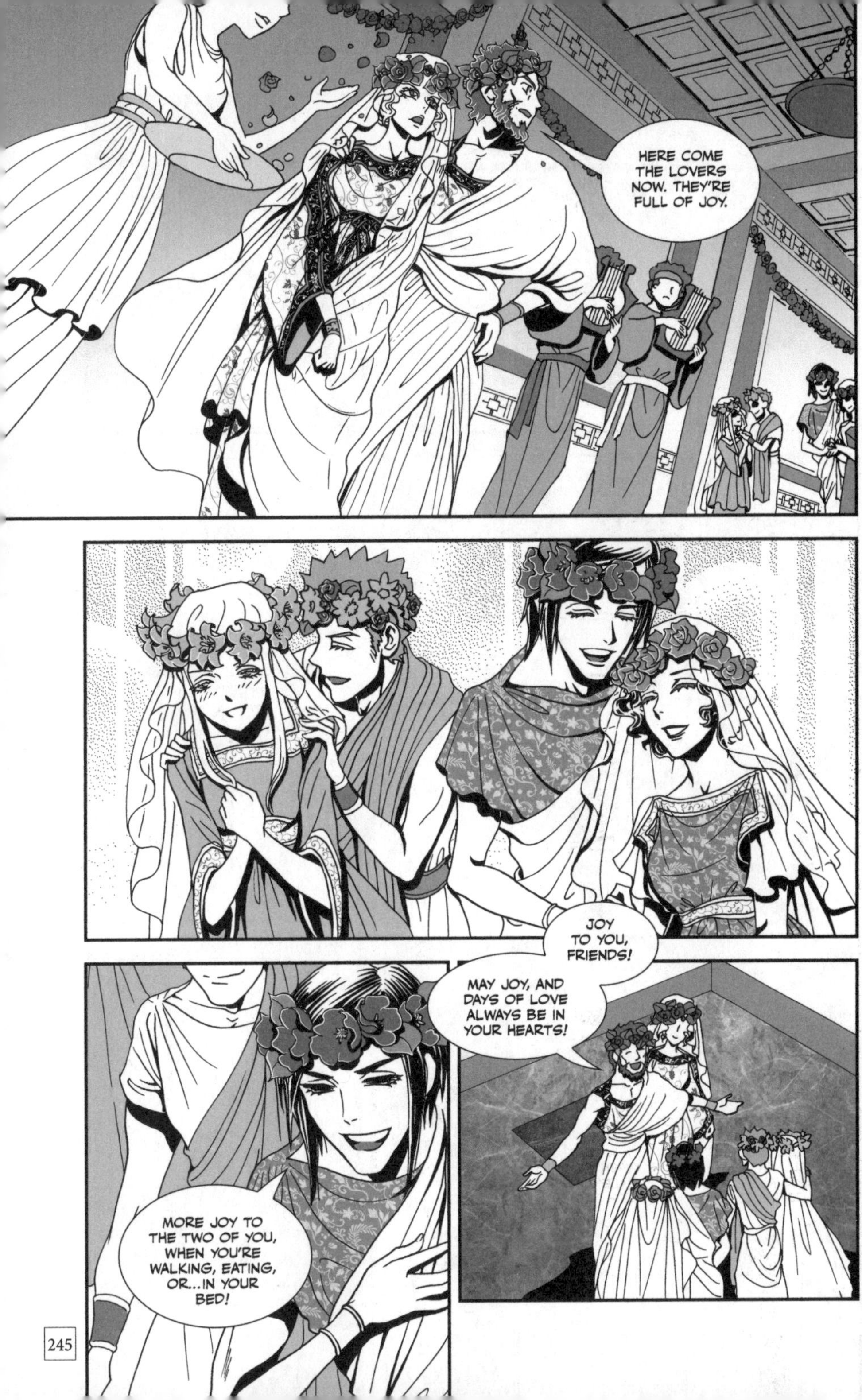
HERE COME THE LOVERS NOW. THEY'RE FULL OF JOY.
JOY TO YOU, FRIENDS!
MAY JOY, AND DAYS OF LOVE ALWAYS BE IN YOUR HEARTS!
MORE JOY TO THE TWO OF YOU, WHEN YOU'RE WALKING, EATING, OR...IN YOUR BED!

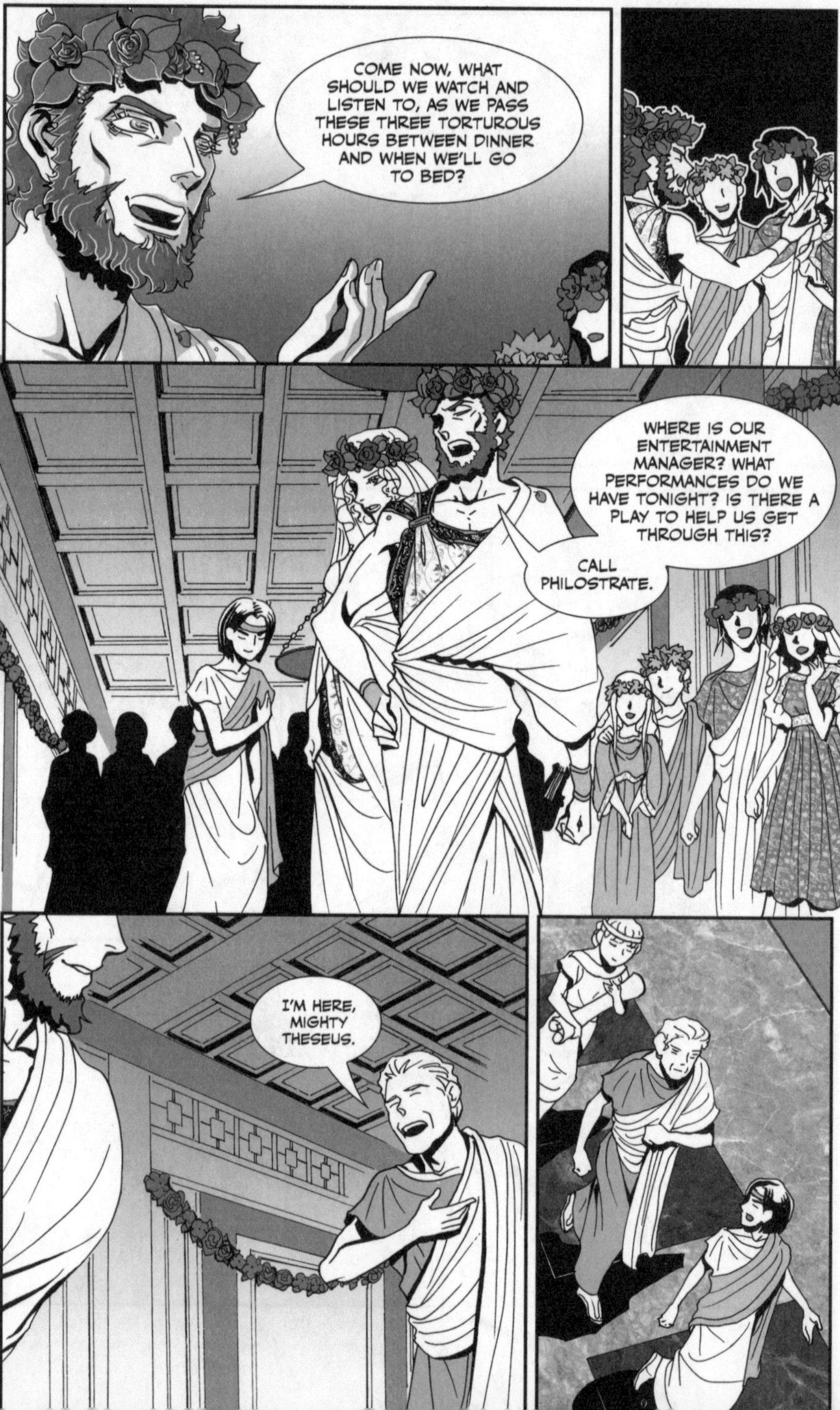
COME NOW, WHAT SHOULD WE WATCH AND LISTEN TO, AS WE PASS THESE THREE TORTUROUS HOURS BETWEEN DINNER AND WHEN WE'LL GO TO BED?
WHERE IS OUR ENTERTAINMENT MANAGER? WHAT PERFORMANCES DO WE HAVE TONIGHT? IS THERE A PLAY TO HELP US GET THROUGH THIS?
CALL PHILOSTRATE.
I'M HERE, MIGHTY THESEUS.

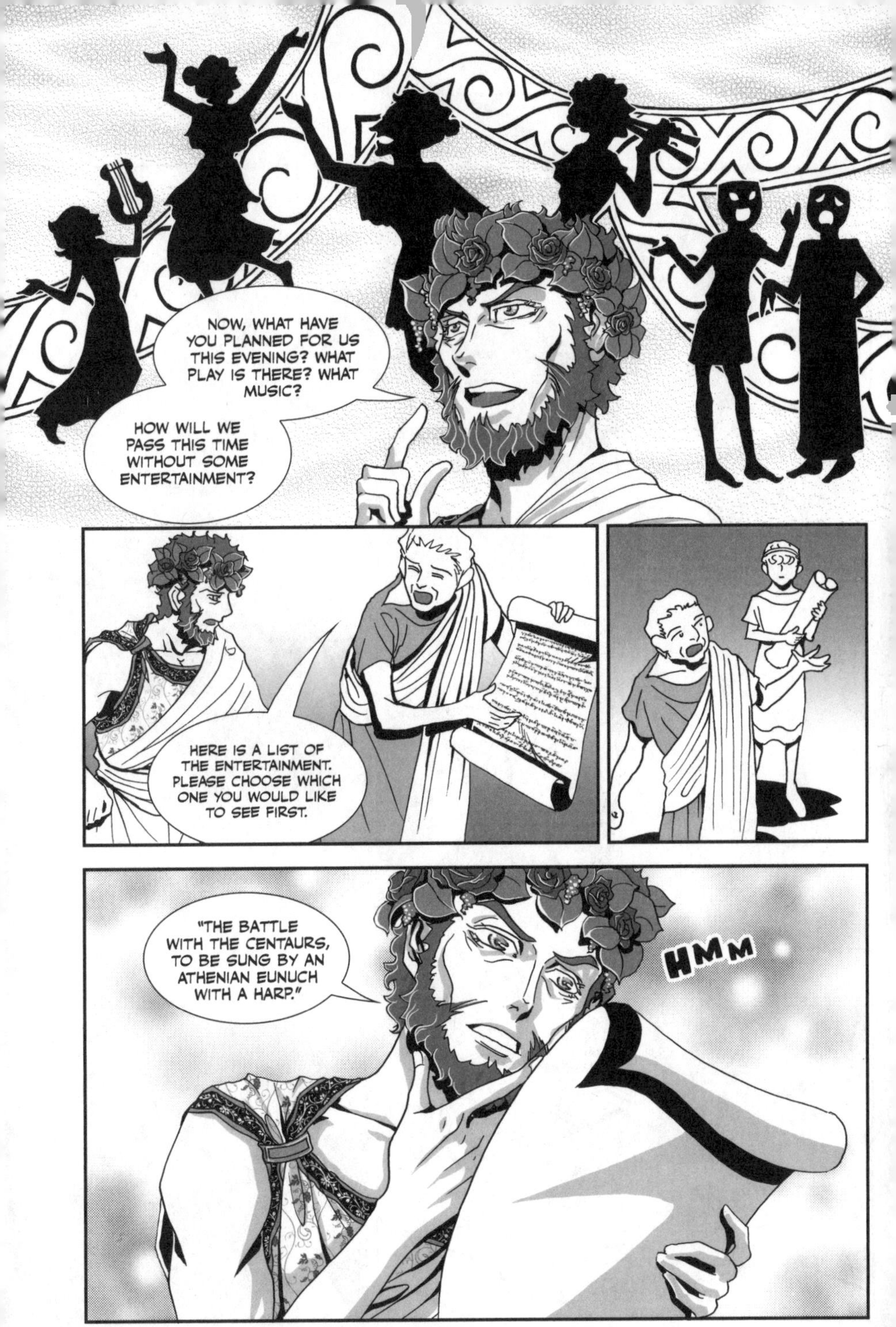
NOW, WHAT HAVE YOU PLANNED FOR US THIS EVENING? WHAT PLAY IS THERE? WHAT MUSIC?
HOW WILL WE PASS THIS TIME WITHOUT SOME ENTERTAINMENT?
HERE IS A LIST OF THE ENTERTAINMENT. PLEASE CHOOSE WHICH ONE YOU WOULD LIKE TO SEE FIRST.
"THE BATTLE WITH THE CENTAURS, TO BE SUNG BY AN ATHENIAN EUNUCH WITH A HARP."
HMM

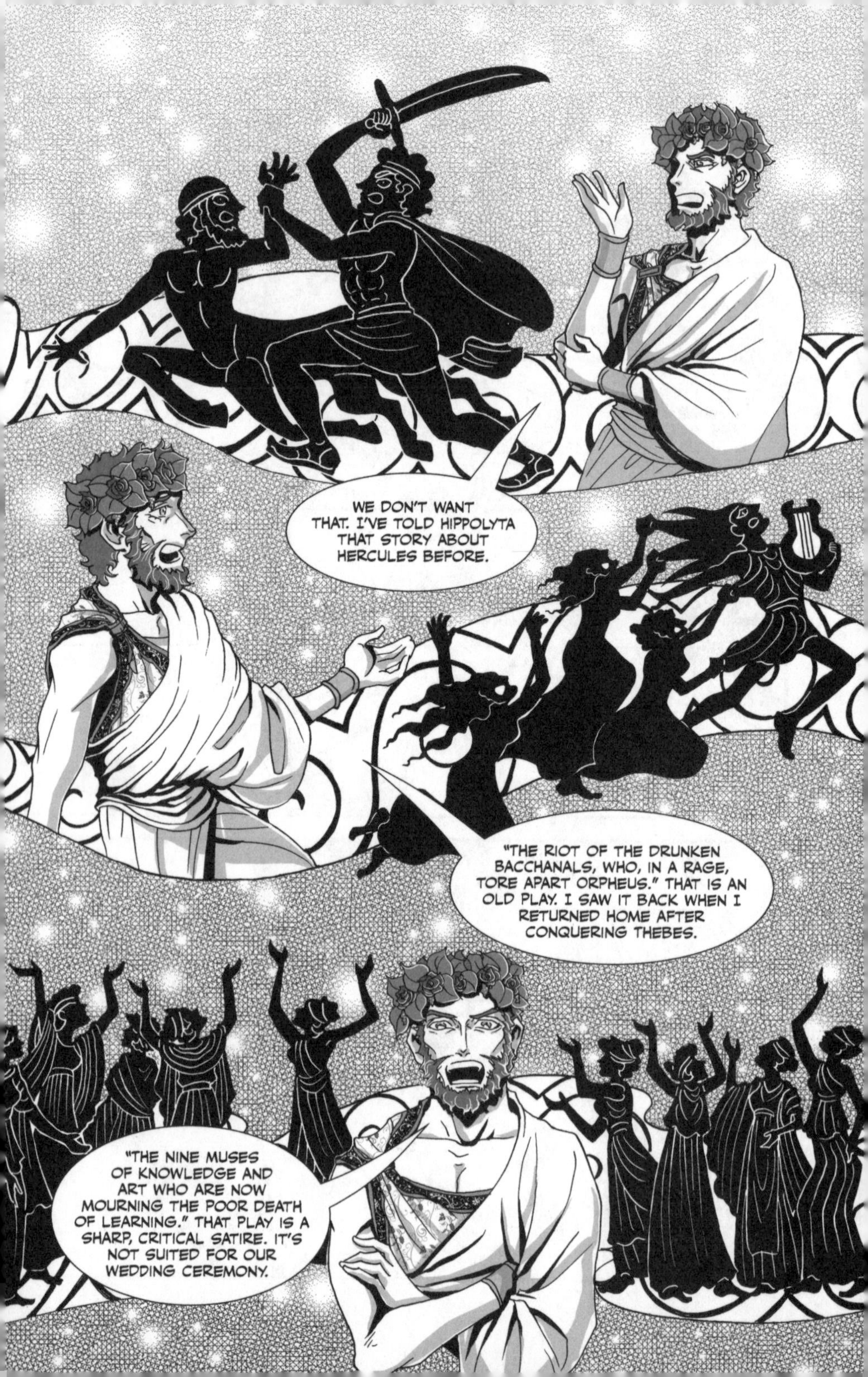
WE DON'T WANT THAT. I'VE TOLD HIPPOLYTA THAT STORY ABOUT HERCULES BEFORE.
"THE RIOT OF THE DRUNKEN BACCHANALS, WHO, IN A RAGE, TORE APART ORPHEUS." THAT IS AN OLD PLAY. I SAW IT BACK WHEN I RETURNED HOME AFTER CONQUERING THEBES.
"THE NINE MUSES OF KNOWLEDGE AND ART WHO ARE NOW MOURNING THE POOR DEATH OF LEARNING." THAT PLAY IS A SHARP, CRITICAL SATIRE. IT'S NOT SUITED FOR OUR WEDDING CEREMONY.

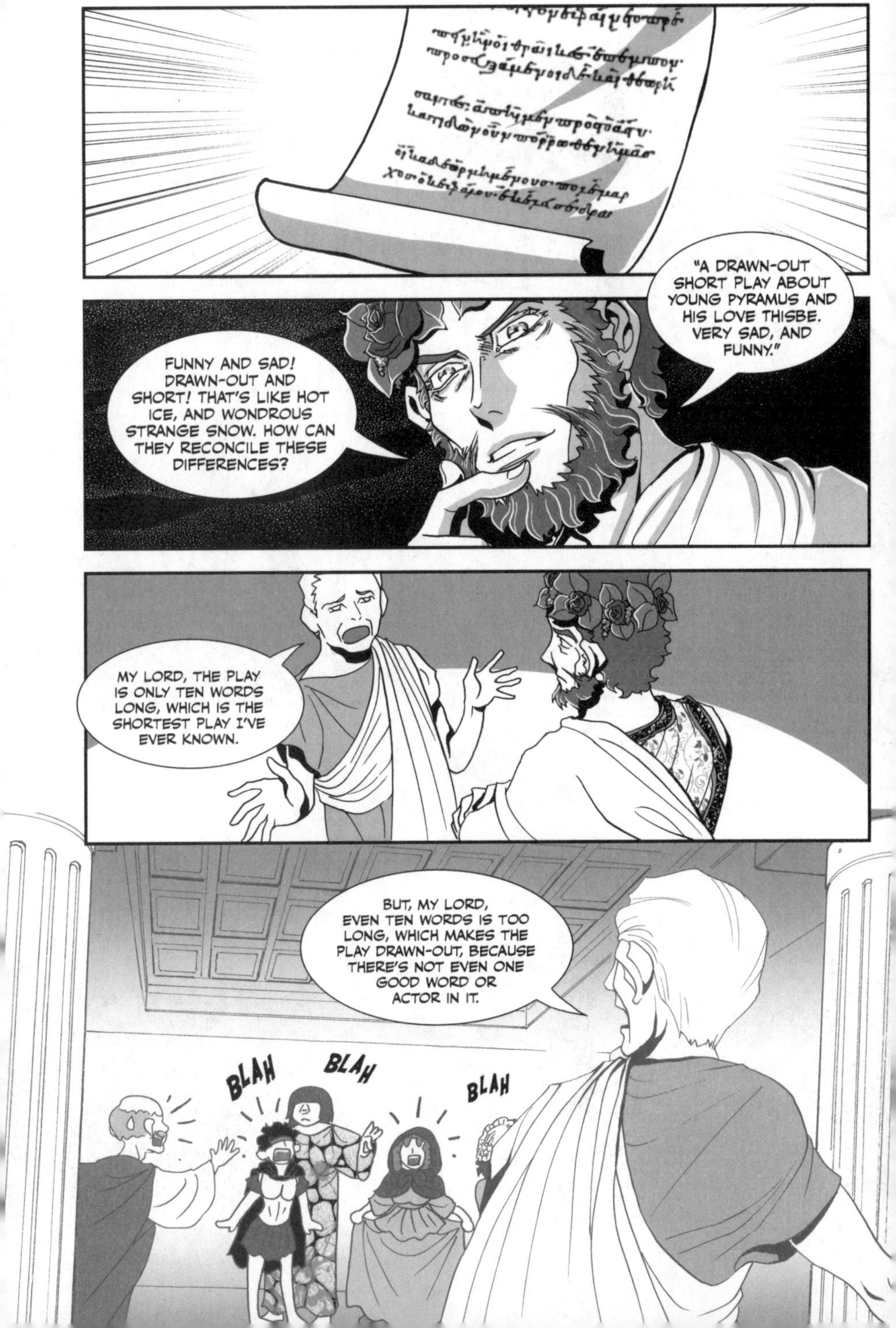
"A DRAWN-OUT SHORT PLAY ABOUT YOUNG PYRAMUS AND HIS LOVE THISBE. VERY SAD, AND FUNNY."
FUNNY AND SAD! DRAWN-OUT AND SHORT! THAT'S LIKE HOT ICE, AND WONDROUS STRANGE SNOW. HOW CAN THEY RECONCILE THESE DIFFERENCES?
MY LORD, THE PLAY IS ONLY TEN WORDS LONG, WHICH IS THE SHORTEST PLAY I'VE EVER KNOWN.
BUT, MY LORD, EVEN TEN WORDS IS TOO LONG, WHICH MAKES THE PLAY DRAWN-OUT, BECAUSE THERE'S NOT EVEN ONE GOOD WORD OR ACTOR IN IT.
BLAH
BLAH
BLAH

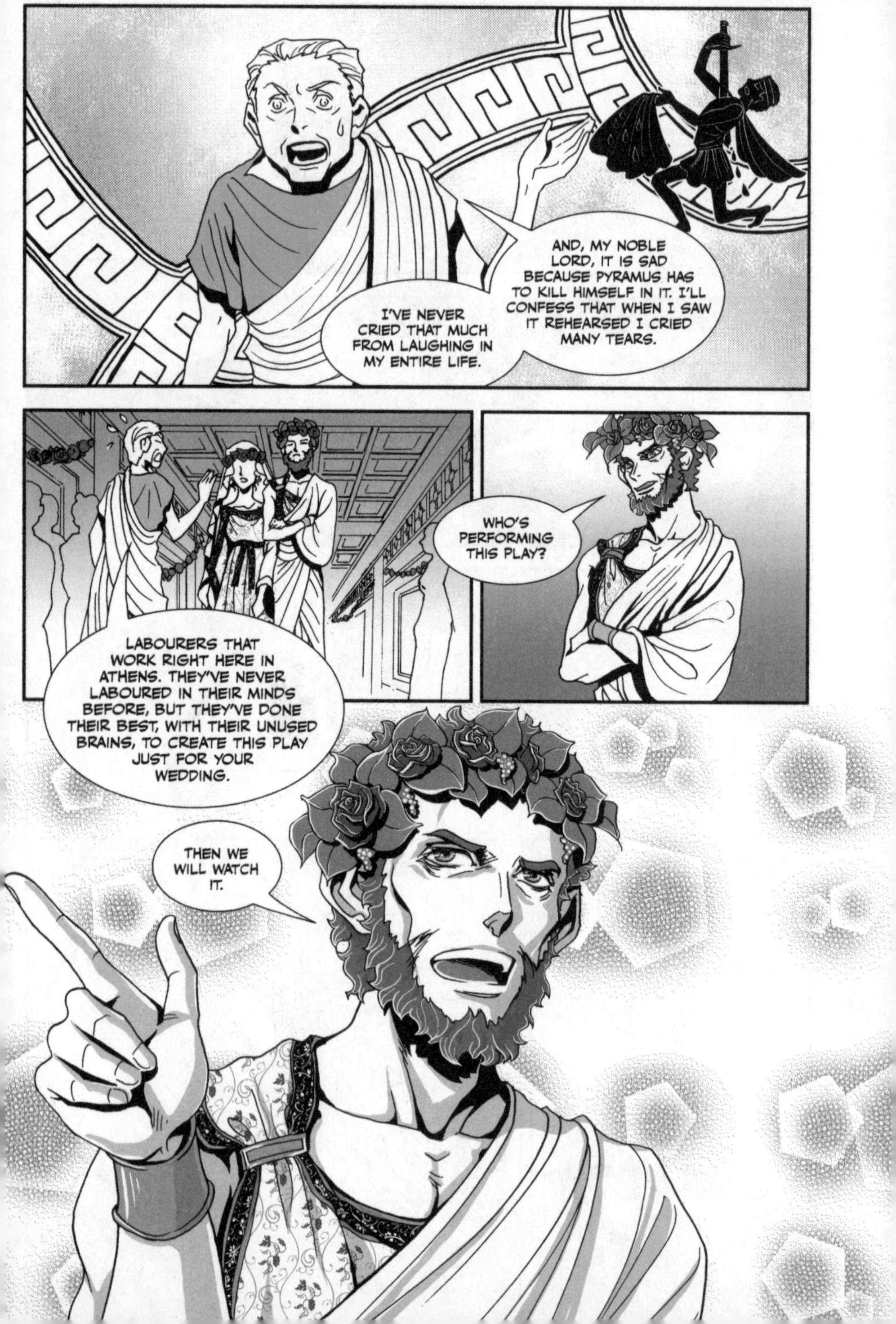
AND, MY NOBLE LORD, IT IS SAD BECAUSE PYRAMUS HAS TO KILL HIMSELF IN IT. I'LL CONFESS THAT WHEN I SAW IT REHEARSED I CRIED MANY TEARS.
I'VE NEVER CRIED THAT MUCH FROM LAUGHING IN MY ENTIRE LIFE.
WHO'S PERFORMING THIS PLAY?
LABOURERS THAT WORK RIGHT HERE IN ATHENS. THEY'VE NEVER LABOURED IN THEIR MINDS BEFORE, BUT THEY'VE DONE THEIR BEST, WITH THEIR UNUSED BRAINS, TO CREATE THIS PLAY JUST FOR YOUR WEDDING.
THEN WE WILL WATCH IT.

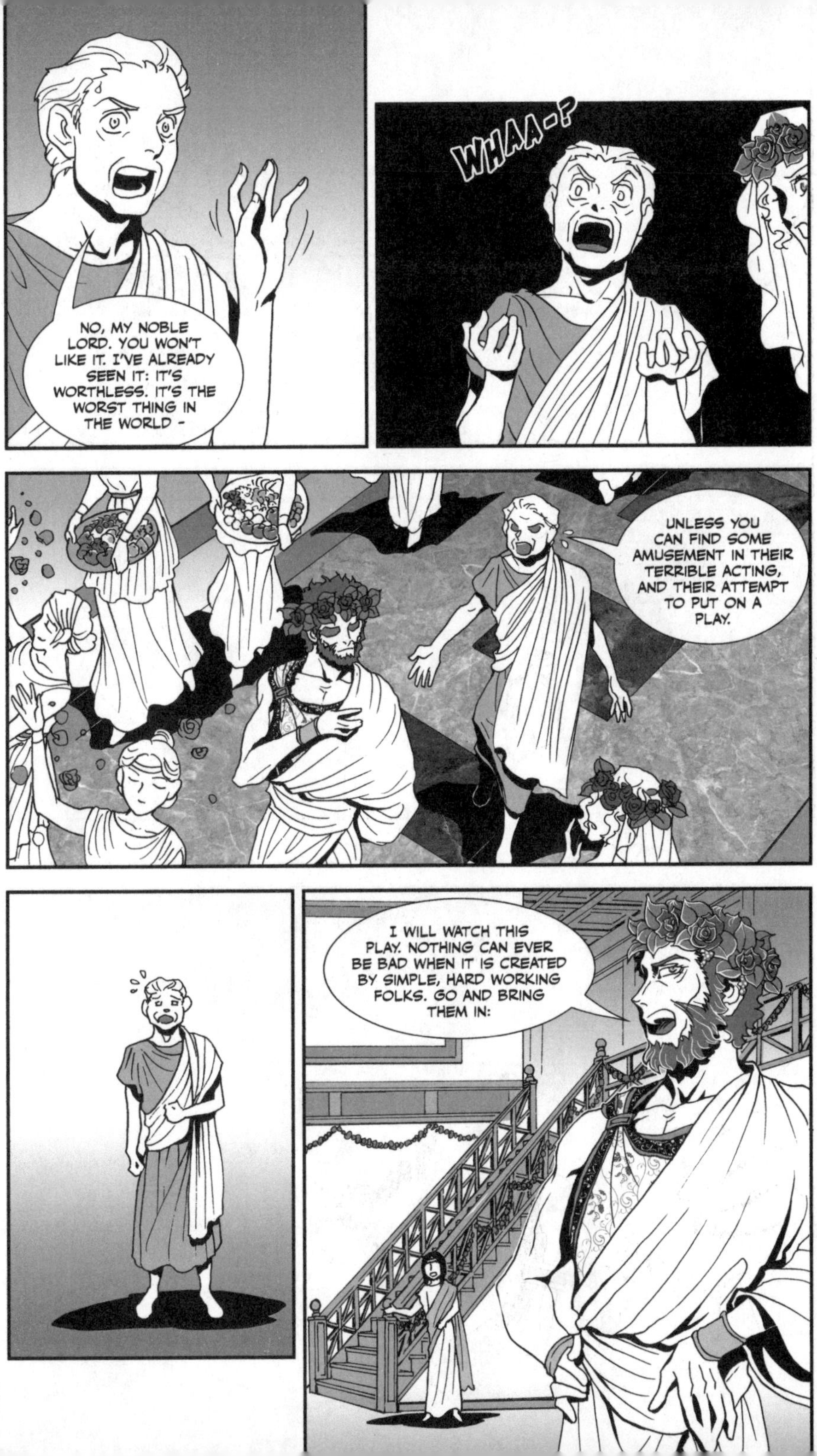
WHAA-?
NO, MY NOBLE LORD. YOU WON'T LIKE IT. I'VE ALREADY SEEN IT: IT'S WORTHLESS. IT'S THE WORST THING IN THE WORLD -
UNLESS YOU CAN FIND SOME AMUSEMENT IN THEIR TERRIBLE ACTING, AND THEIR ATTEMPT TO PUT ON A PLAY.
I WILL WATCH THIS PLAY. NOTHING CAN EVER BE BAD WHEN IT IS CREATED BY SIMPLE, HARD WORKING FOLKS. GO AND BRING THEM IN:

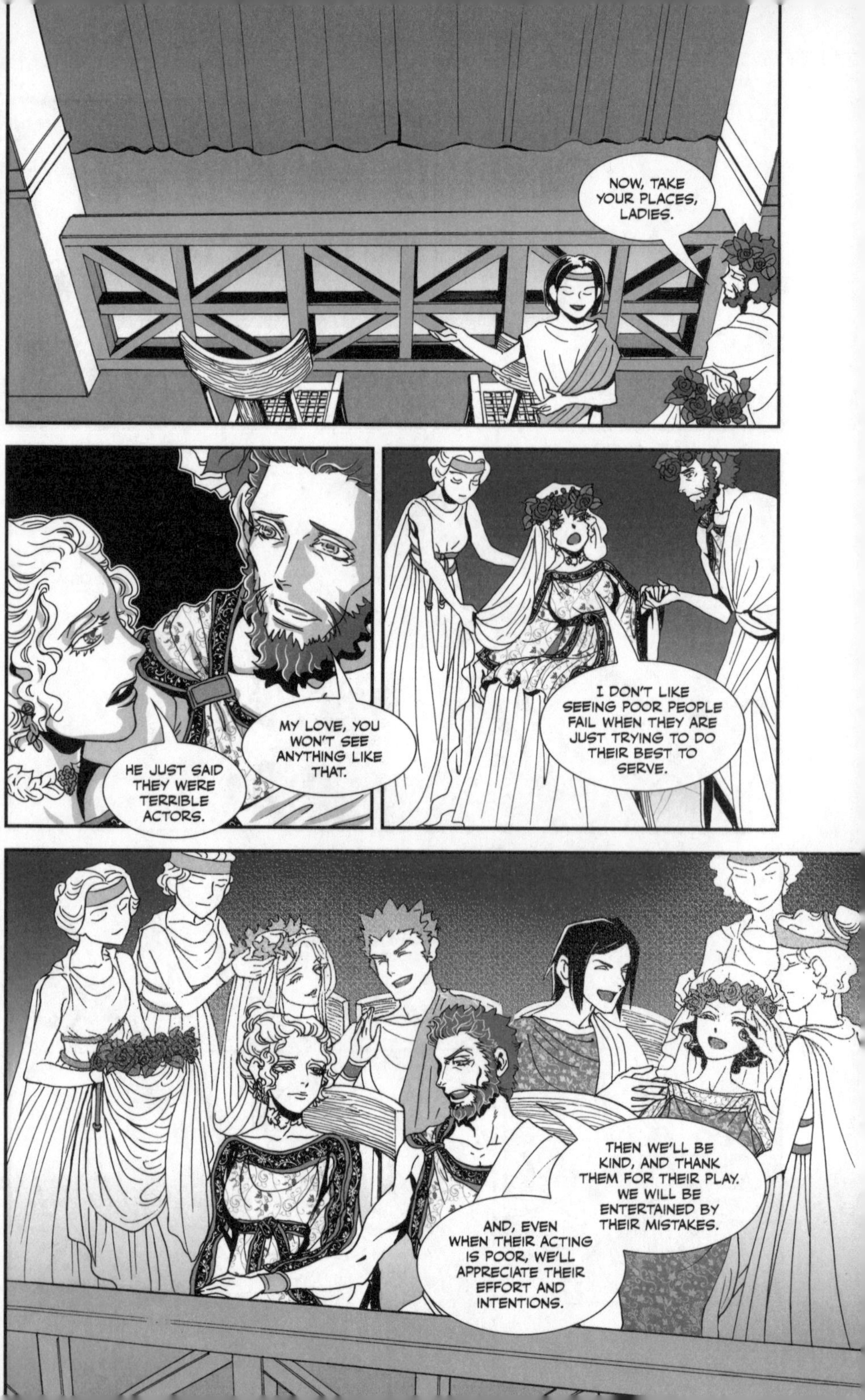
NOW, TAKE YOUR PLACES, LADIES.
I DON'T LIKE SEEING POOR PEOPLE FAIL WHEN THEY ARE JUST TRYING TO DO THEIR BEST TO SERVE.
MY LOVE, YOU WON'T SEE ANYTHING LIKE THAT.
HE JUST SAID THEY WERE TERRIBLE ACTORS.
THEN WE'LL BE KIND, AND THANK THEM FOR THEIR PLAY. WE WILL BE ENTERTAINED BY THEIR MISTAKES.
AND, EVEN WHEN THEIR ACTING IS POOR, WE'LL APPRECIATE THEIR EFFORT AND INTENTIONS.

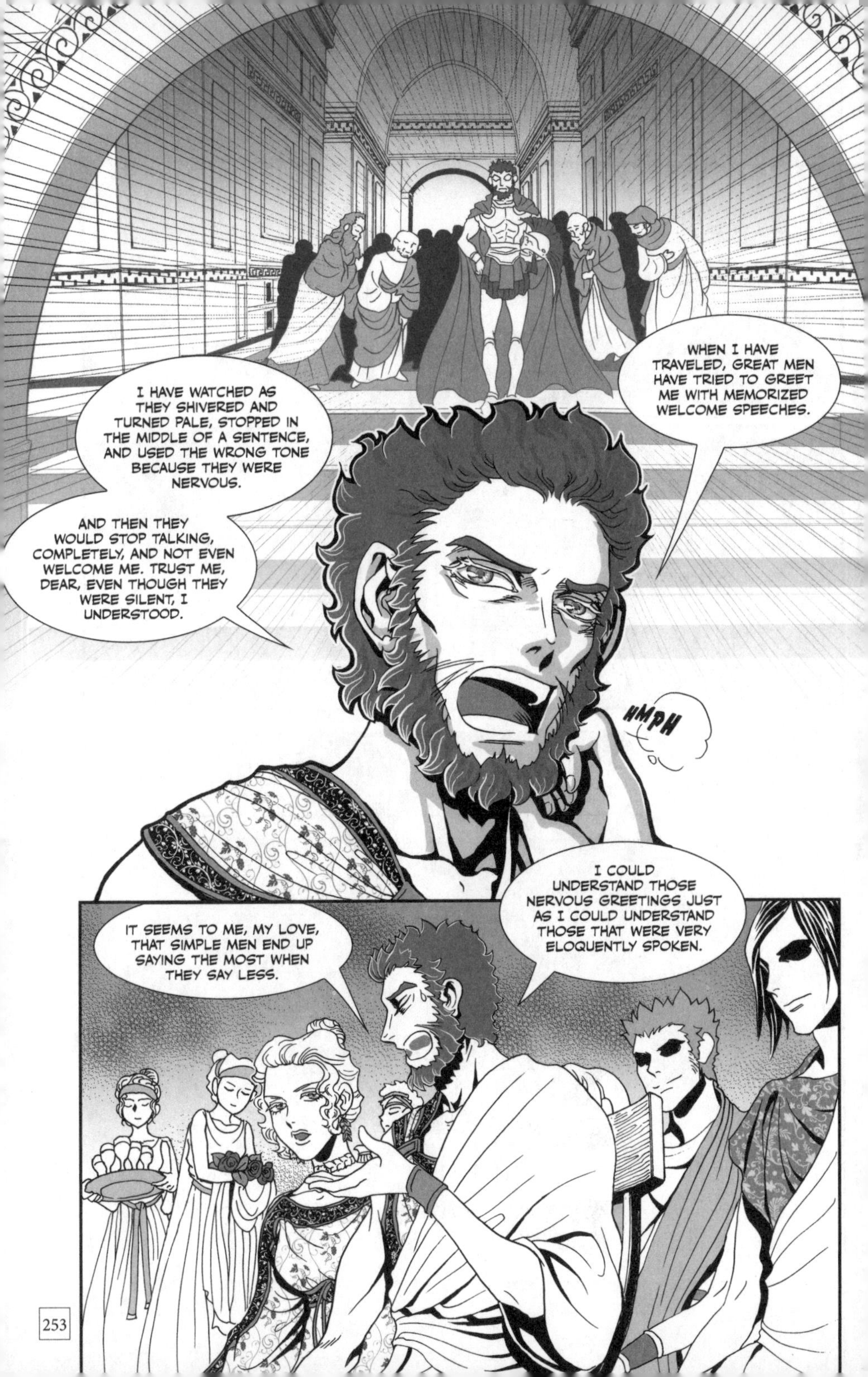
WHEN I HAVE TRAVELED, GREAT MEN HAVE TRIED TO GREET ME WITH MEMORIZED WELCOME SPEECHES.
I HAVE WATCHED AS THEY SHIVERED AND TURNED PALE, STOPPED IN THE MIDDLE OF A SENTENCE, AND USED THE WRONG TONE BECAUSE THEY WERE NERVOUS.
AND THEN THEY WOULD STOP TALKING, COMPLETELY, AND NOT EVEN WELCOME ME. TRUST ME, DEAR, EVEN THOUGH THEY WERE SILENT, I UNDERSTOOD.
HMPH
I COULD UNDERSTAND THOSE NERVOUS GREETINGS JUST AS I COULD UNDERSTAND THOSE THAT WERE VERY ELOQUENTLY SPOKEN.
IT SEEMS TO ME, MY LOVE, THAT SIMPLE MEN END UP SAYING THE MOST WHEN THEY SAY LESS.

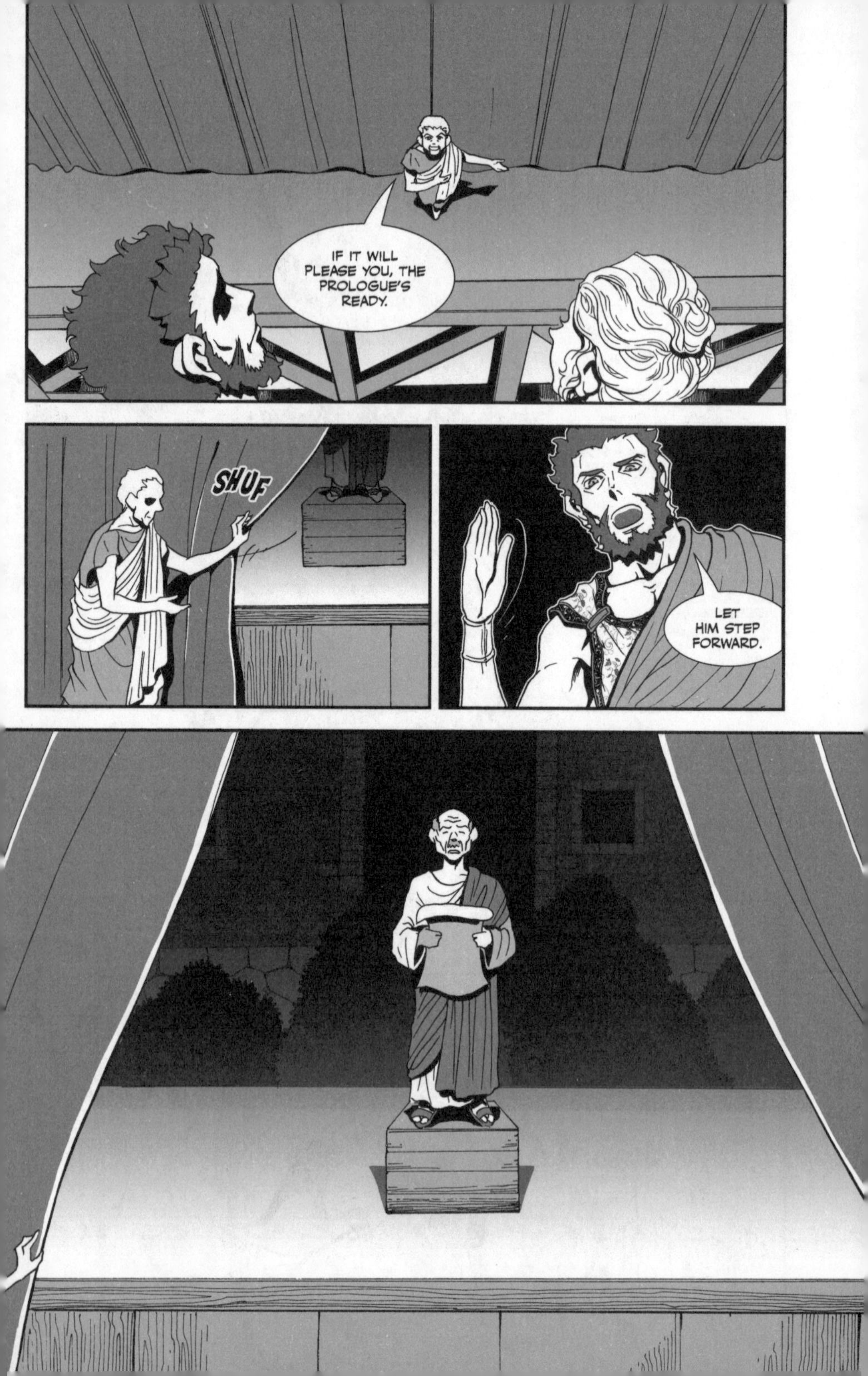
IF IT WILL PLEASE YOU, THE PROLOGUE'S READY.
LET HIM STEP FORWARD.
SHUF

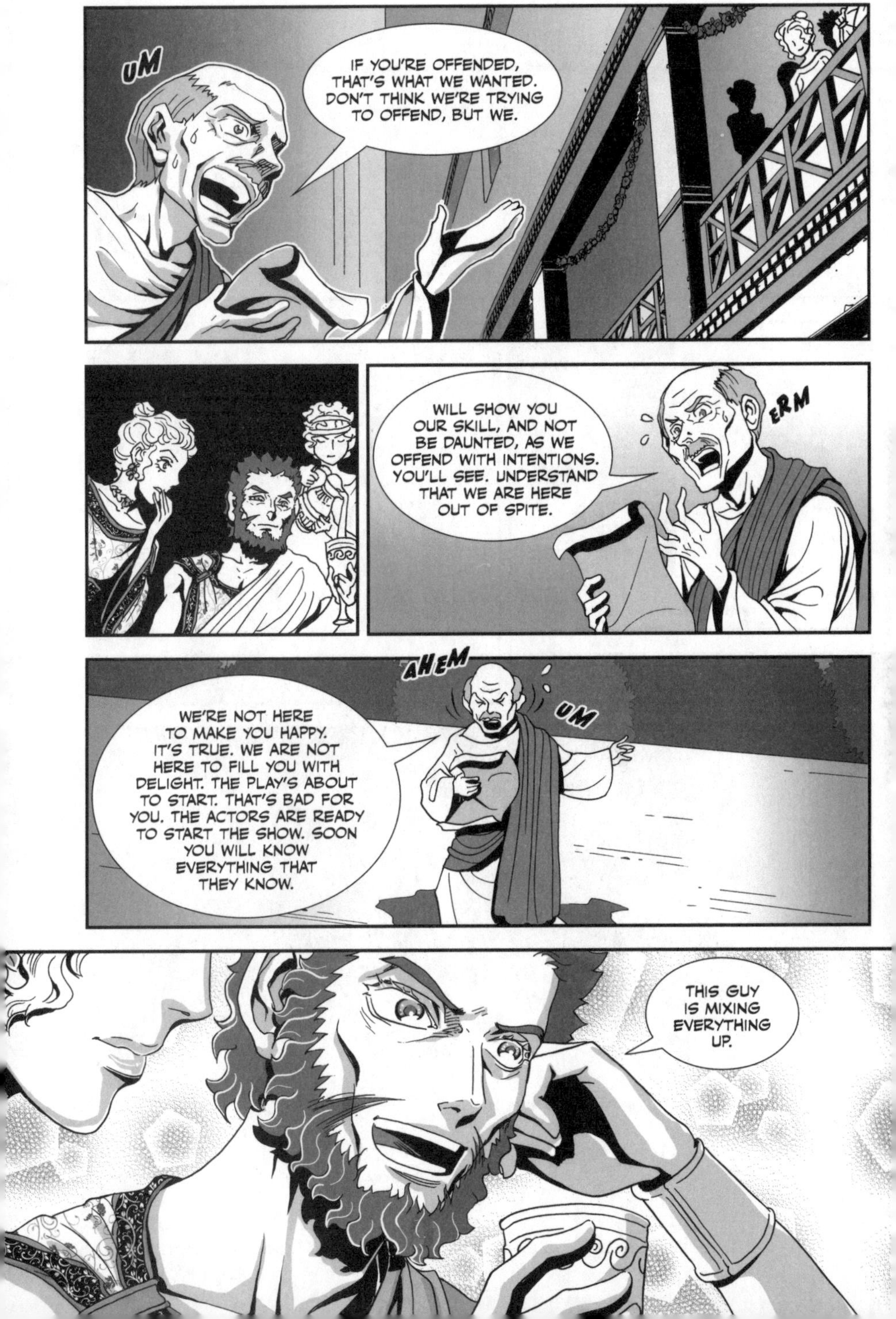
IF YOU'RE OFFENDED, THAT'S WHAT WE WANTED. DON'T THINK WE'RE TRYING TO OFFEND, BUT WE.
UM
ERM
WILL SHOW YOU OUR SKILL, AND NOT BE DAUNTED, AS WE OFFEND WITH INTENTIONS. YOU'LL SEE. UNDERSTAND THAT WE ARE HERE OUT OF SPITE.
AHEM
UM
WE'RE NOT HERE TO MAKE YOU HAPPY. IT'S TRUE. WE ARE NOT HERE TO FILL YOU WITH DELIGHT. THE PLAY'S ABOUT TO START. THAT'S BAD FOR YOU. THE ACTORS ARE READY TO START THE SHOW. SOON YOU WILL KNOW EVERYTHING THAT THEY KNOW.
THIS GUY IS MIXING EVERYTHING UP.

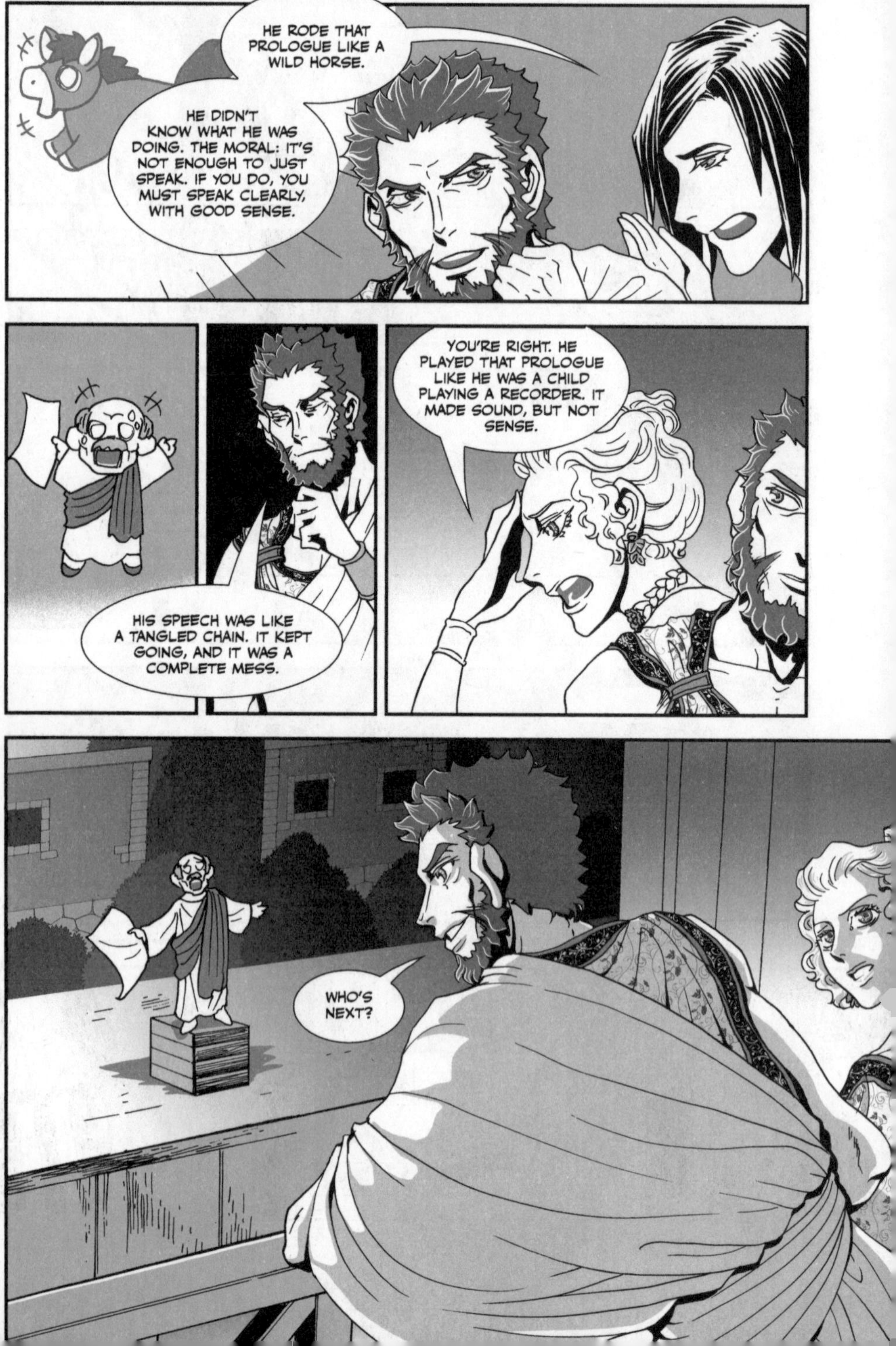
HE RODE THAT PROLOGUE LIKE A WILD HORSE.
HE DIDN'T KNOW WHAT HE WAS DOING. THE MORAL: IT'S NOT ENOUGH TO JUST SPEAK. IF YOU DO, YOU MUST SPEAK CLEARLY, WITH GOOD SENSE.
YOU'RE RIGHT. HE PLAYED THAT PROLOGUE LIKE HE WAS A CHILD PLAYING A RECORDER. IT MADE SOUND, BUT NOT SENSE.
HIS SPEECH WAS LIKE A TANGLED CHAIN. IT KEPT GOING, AND IT WAS A COMPLETE MESS.
WHO'S NEXT?

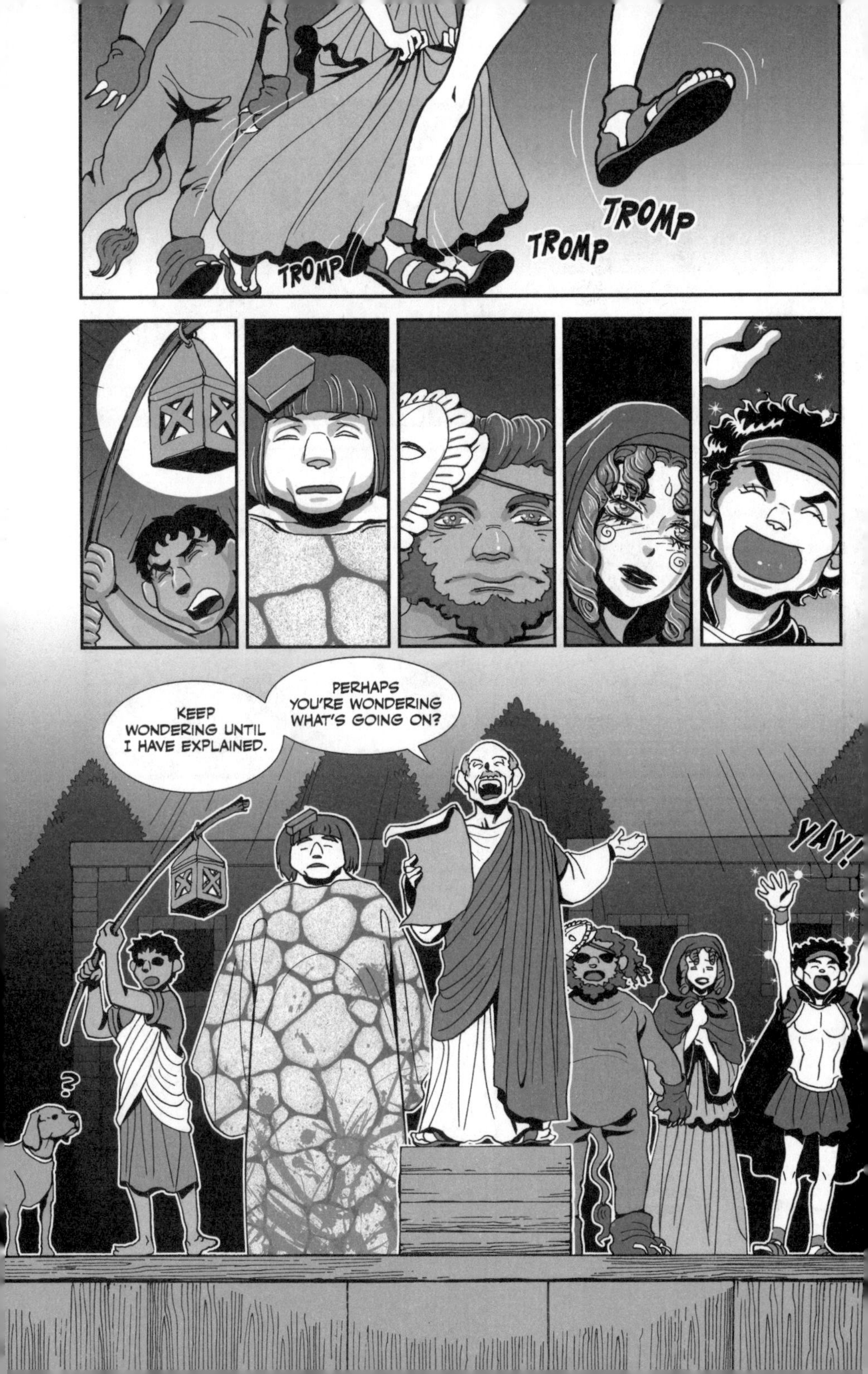
TROMP
TROMP
TROMP
PERHAPS YOU'RE WONDERING WHAT'S GOING ON?
KEEP WONDERING UNTIL I HAVE EXPLAINED.
YAY!

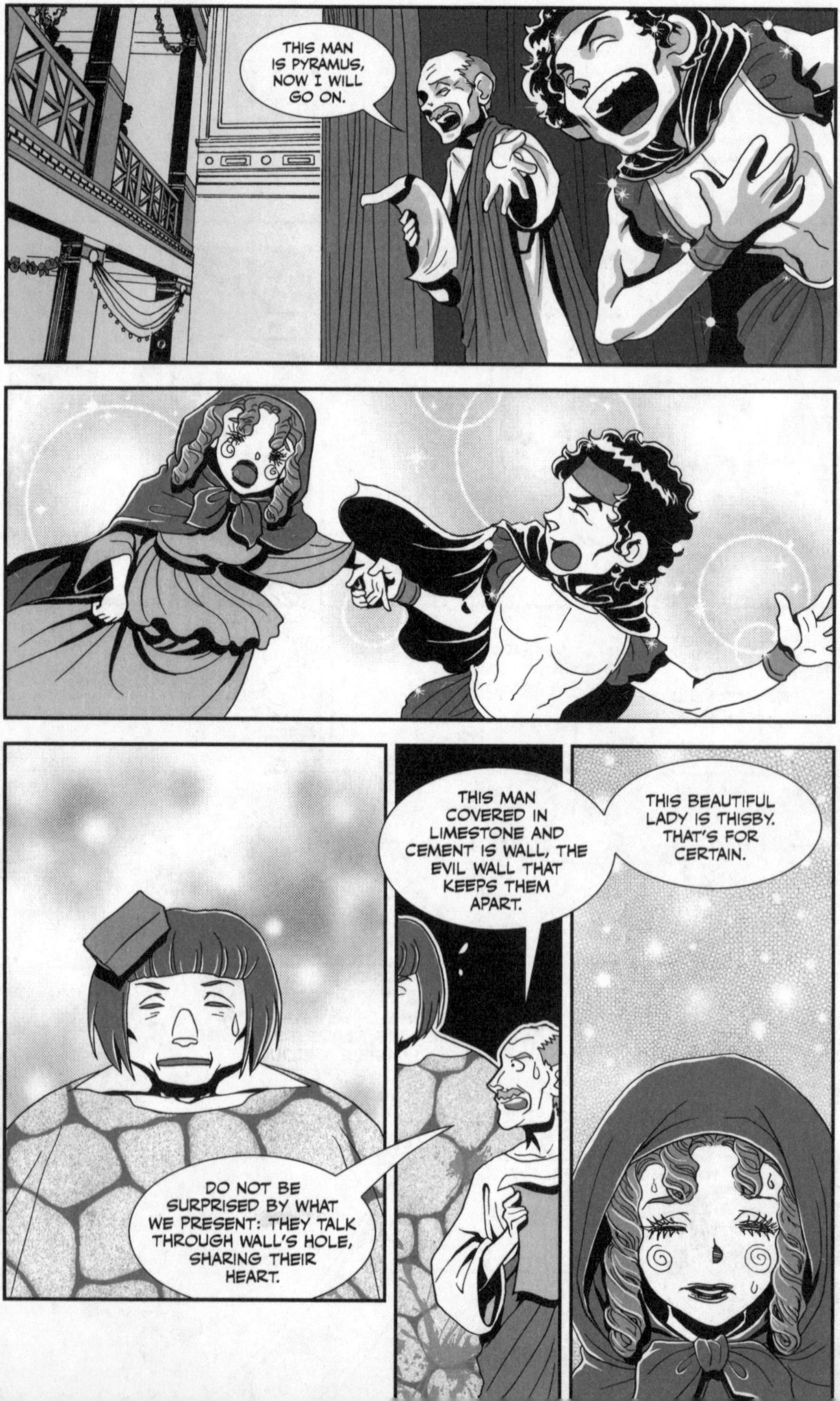
THIS MAN IS PYRAMUS, NOW I WILL GO ON.
THIS BEAUTIFUL LADY IS THISBY. THAT'S FOR CERTAIN.
THIS MAN COVERED IN LIMESTONE AND CEMENT IS WALL, THE EVIL WALL THAT KEEPS THEM APART.
DO NOT BE SURPRISED BY WHAT WE PRESENT: THEY TALK THROUGH WALL'S HOLE, SHARING THEIR HEART.

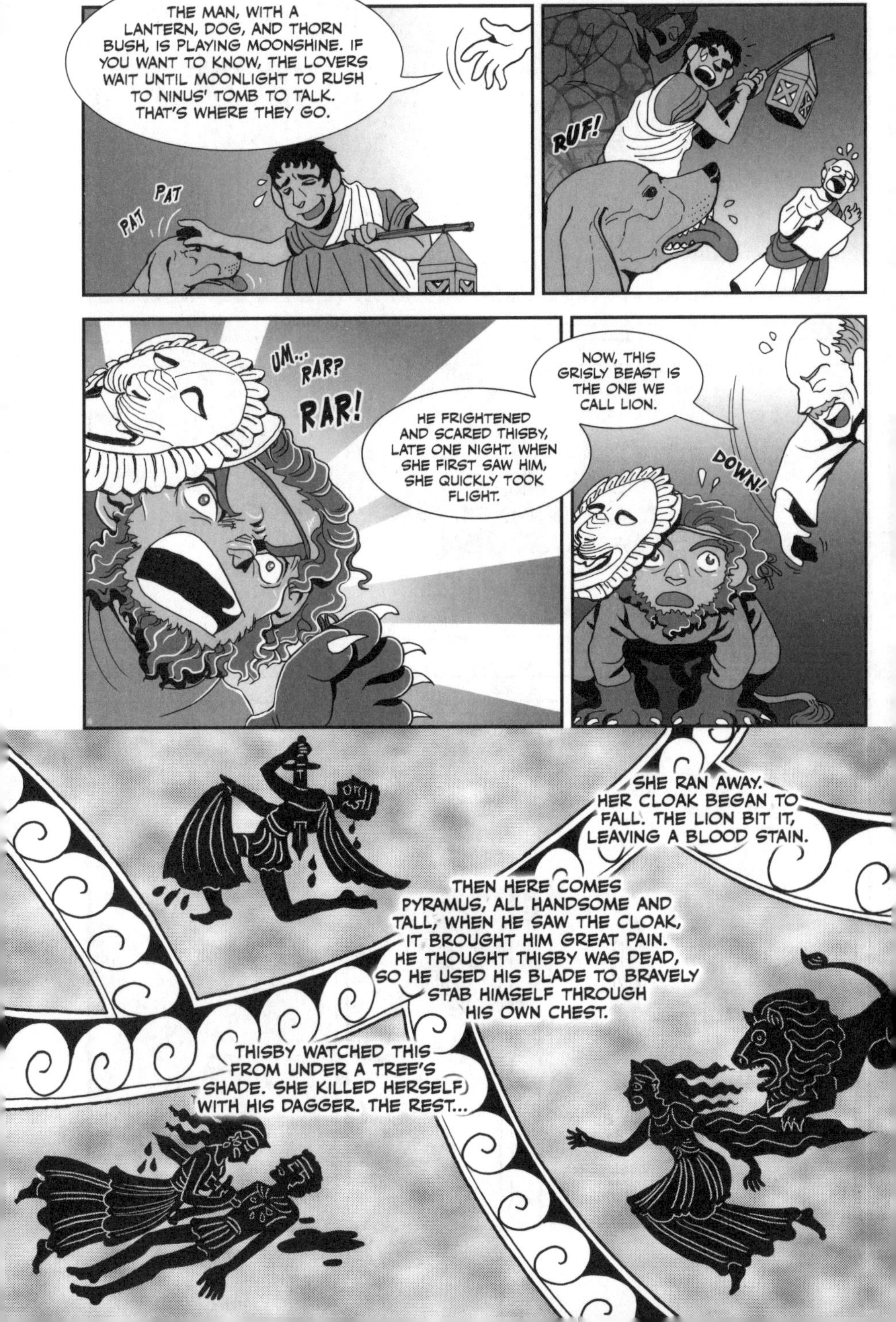
RUF!
THE MAN, WITH A LANTERN, DOG, AND THORN BUSH, IS PLAYING MOONSHINE. IF YOU WANT TO KNOW, THE LOVERS WAIT UNTIL MOONLIGHT TO RUSH TO NINUS' TOMB TO TALK. THAT'S WHERE THEY GO.
PAT PAT
NOW, THIS GRISLY BEAST IS THE ONE WE CALL LION.
DOWN!
HE FRIGHTENED AND SCARED THISBY, LATE ONE NIGHT. WHEN SHE FIRST SAW HIM, SHE QUICKLY TOOK FLIGHT.
UM... RAR?
RAR!
SHE RAN AWAY. HER CLOAK BEGAN TO FALL. THE LION BIT IT, LEAVING A BLOOD STAIN.
THEN HERE COMES PYRAMUS, ALL HANDSOME AND TALL, WHEN HE SAW THE CLOAK, IT BROUGHT HIM GREAT PAIN. HE THOUGHT THISBY WAS DEAD, SO HE USED HIS BLADE TO BRAVELY STAB HIMSELF THROUGH HIS OWN CHEST.
THISBY WATCHED THIS FROM UNDER A TREE'S SHADE. SHE KILLED HERSELF WITH HIS DAGGER. THE REST...

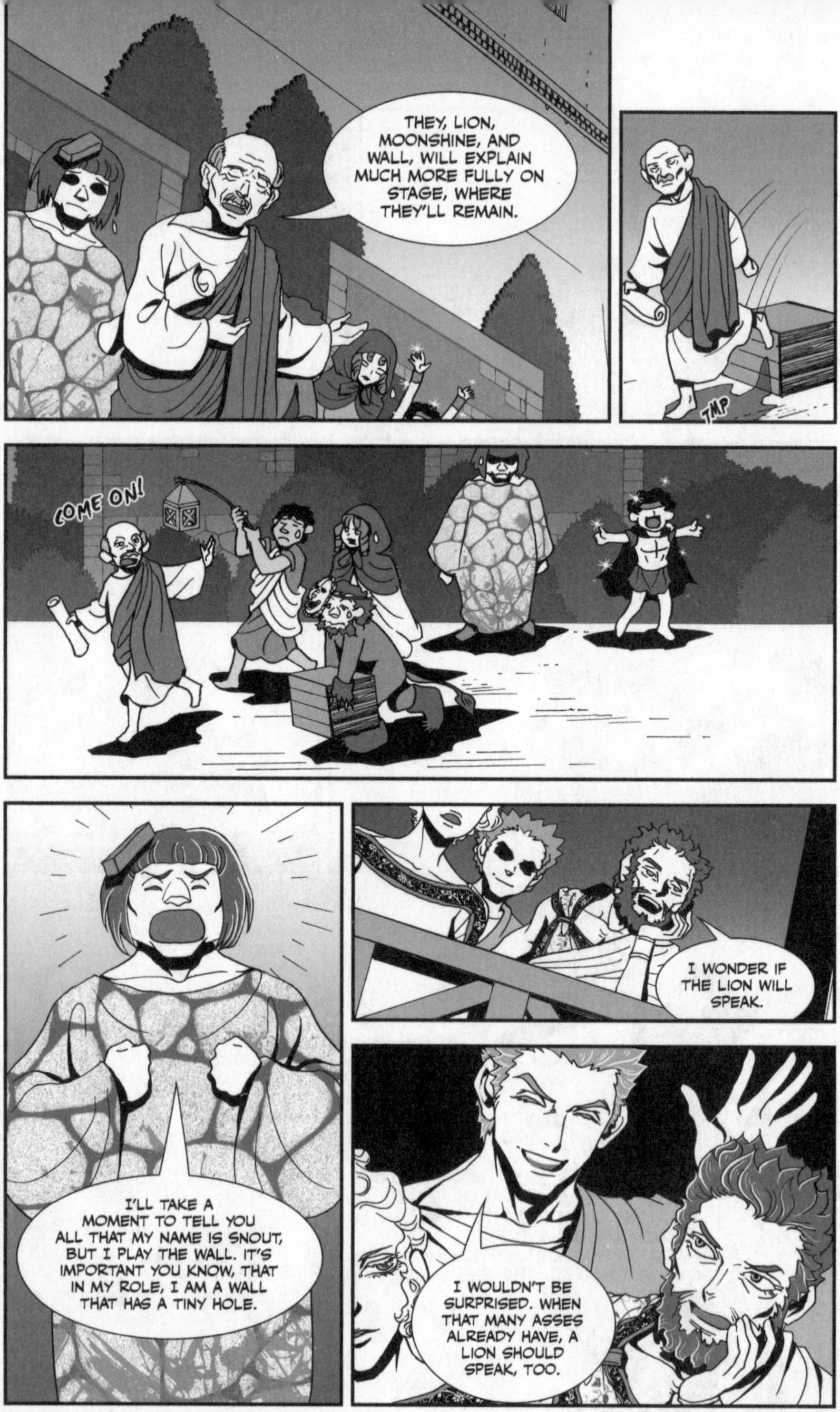
TMP
THEY, LION, MOONSHINE, AND WALL, WILL EXPLAIN MUCH MORE FULLY ON STAGE, WHERE THEY'LL REMAIN.
COME ON!
I WONDER IF THE LION WILL SPEAK.
I WOULDN'T BE SURPRISED. WHEN THAT MANY ASSES ALREADY HAVE, A LION SHOULD SPEAK, TOO.
I'LL TAKE A MOMENT TO TELL YOU ALL THAT MY NAME IS SNOUT, BUT I PLAY THE WALL. IT'S IMPORTANT YOU KNOW, THAT IN MY ROLE, I AM A WALL THAT HAS A TINY HOLE.

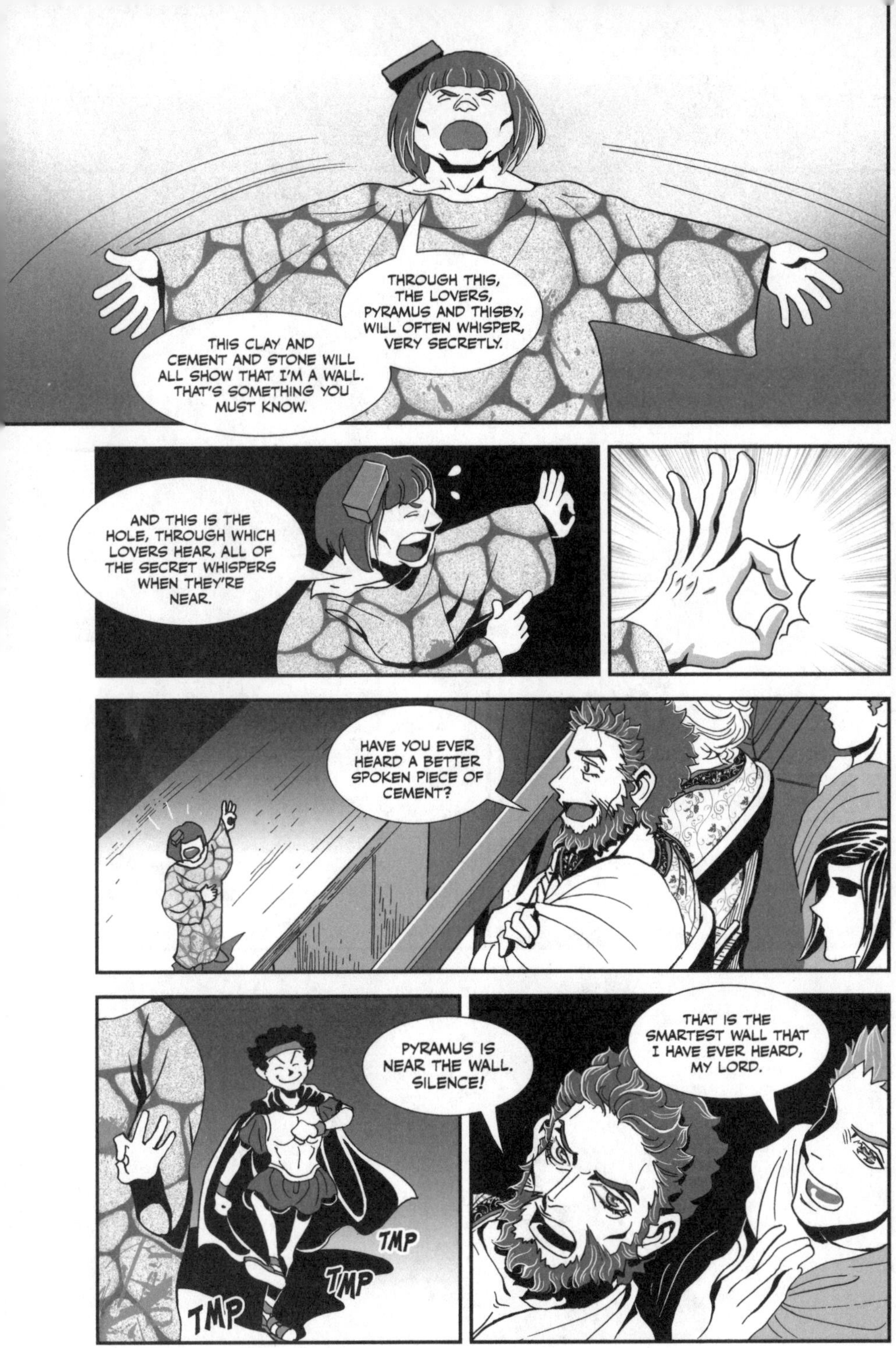
THROUGH THIS, THE LOVERS, PYRAMUS AND THISBY, WILL OFTEN WHISPER, VERY SECRETLY.
THIS CLAY AND CEMENT AND STONE WILL ALL SHOW THAT I'M A WALL. THAT'S SOMETHING YOU MUST KNOW.
AND THIS IS THE HOLE, THROUGH WHICH LOVERS HEAR, ALL OF THE SECRET WHISPERS WHEN THEY'RE NEAR.
HAVE YOU EVER HEARD A BETTER SPOKEN PIECE OF CEMENT?
THAT IS THE SMARTEST WALL THAT I HAVE EVER HEARD, MY LORD.
PYRAMUS IS NEAR THE WALL. SILENCE!
TMP
TMP
TMP

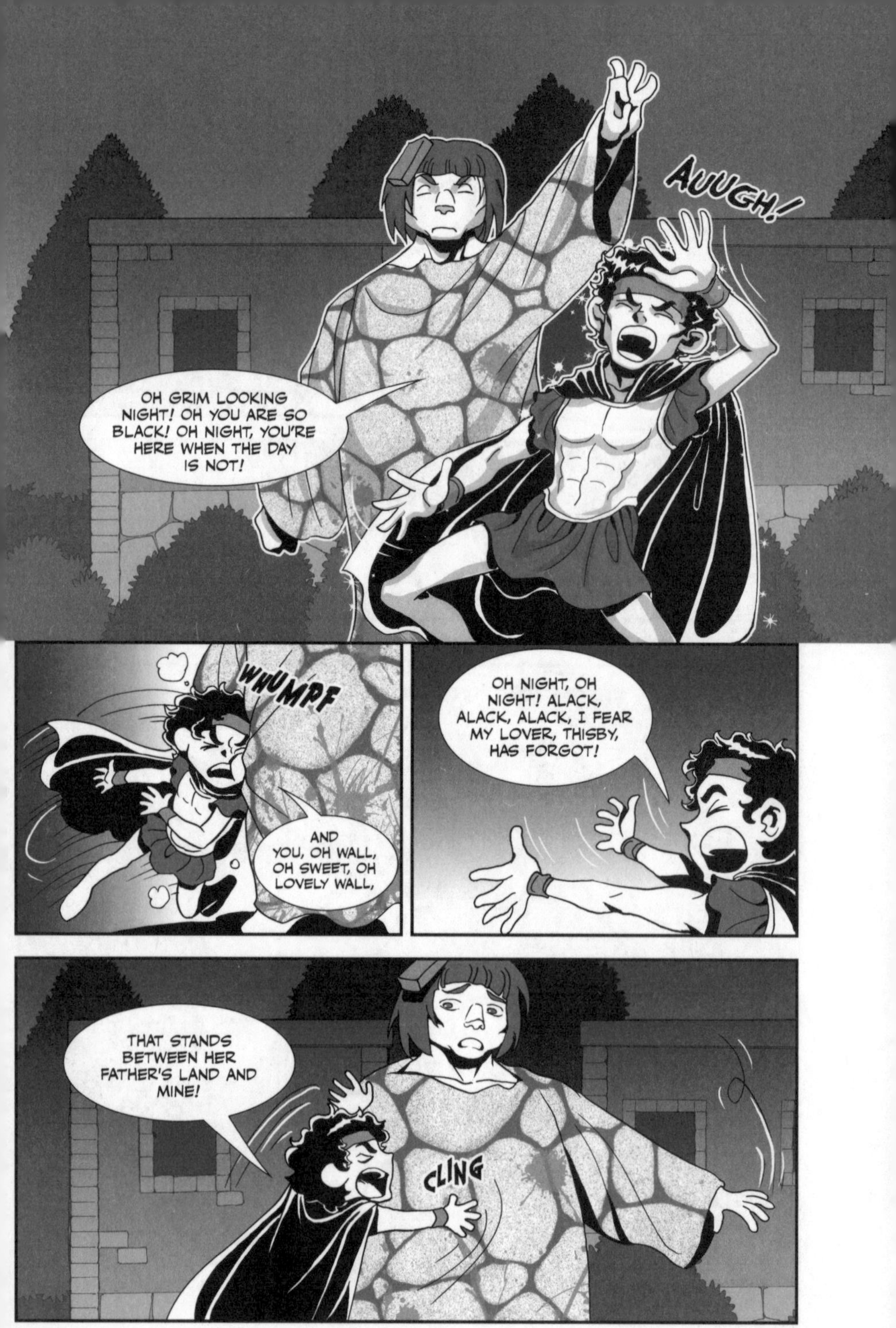
AUUGH!
OH GRIM LOOKING NIGHT! OH YOU ARE SO BLACK! OH NIGHT, YOU'RE HERE WHEN THE DAY IS NOT!
OH NIGHT, OH NIGHT! ALACK, ALACK, ALACK, I FEAR MY LOVER, THISBY, HAS FORGOT!
WHUMPF
AND YOU, OH WALL, OH SWEET, OH LOVELY WALL,
THAT STANDS BETWEEN HER FATHER'S LAND AND MINE!
CLING

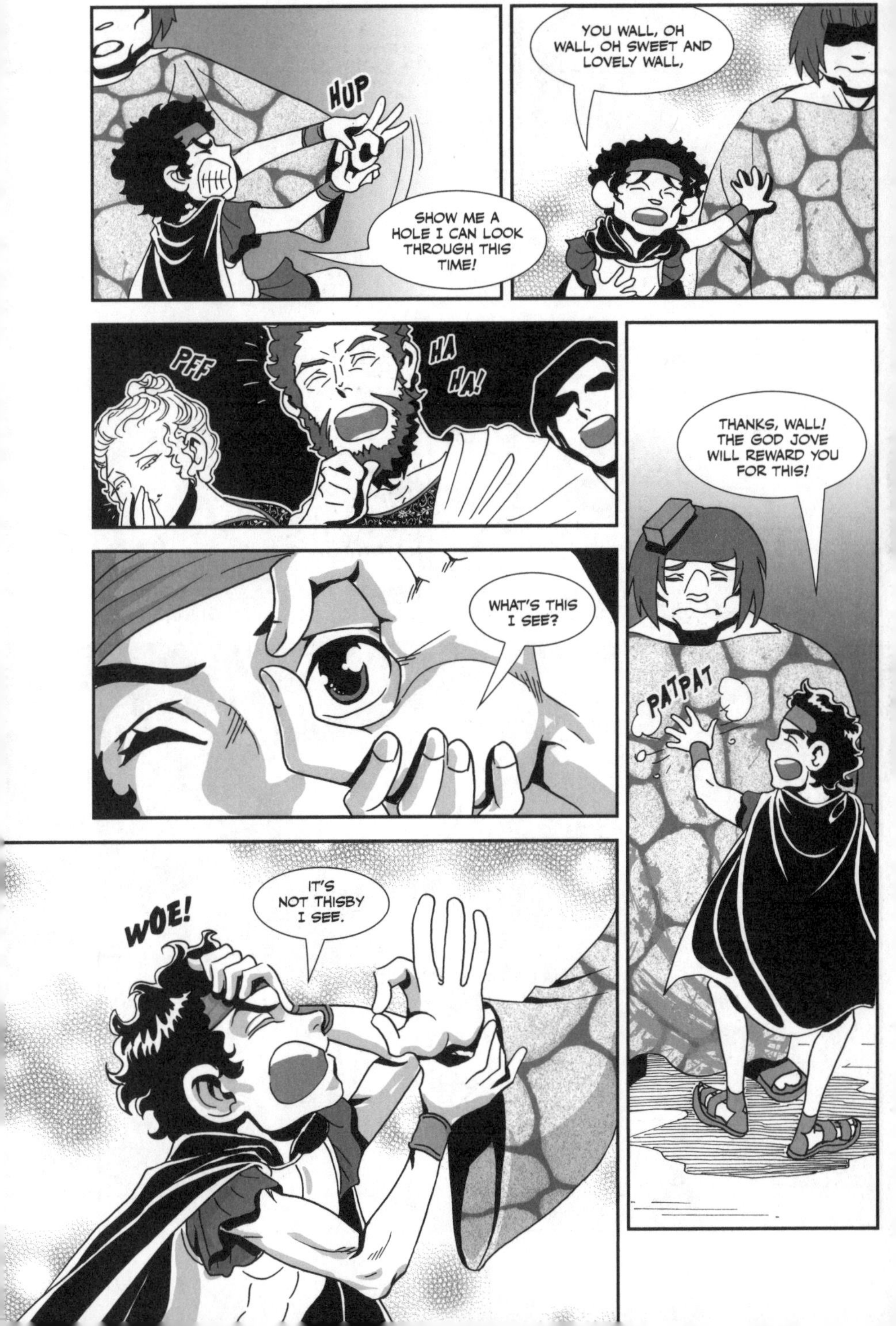
YOU WALL, OH WALL, OH SWEET AND LOVELY WALL,
HUP
SHOW ME A HOLE I CAN LOOK THROUGH THIS TIME!
THANKS, WALL! THE GOD JOVE WILL REWARD YOU FOR THIS!
PATPAT
HA HA!
PFF
WHAT'S THIS I SEE?
WOE!
IT'S NOT THISBY I SEE.

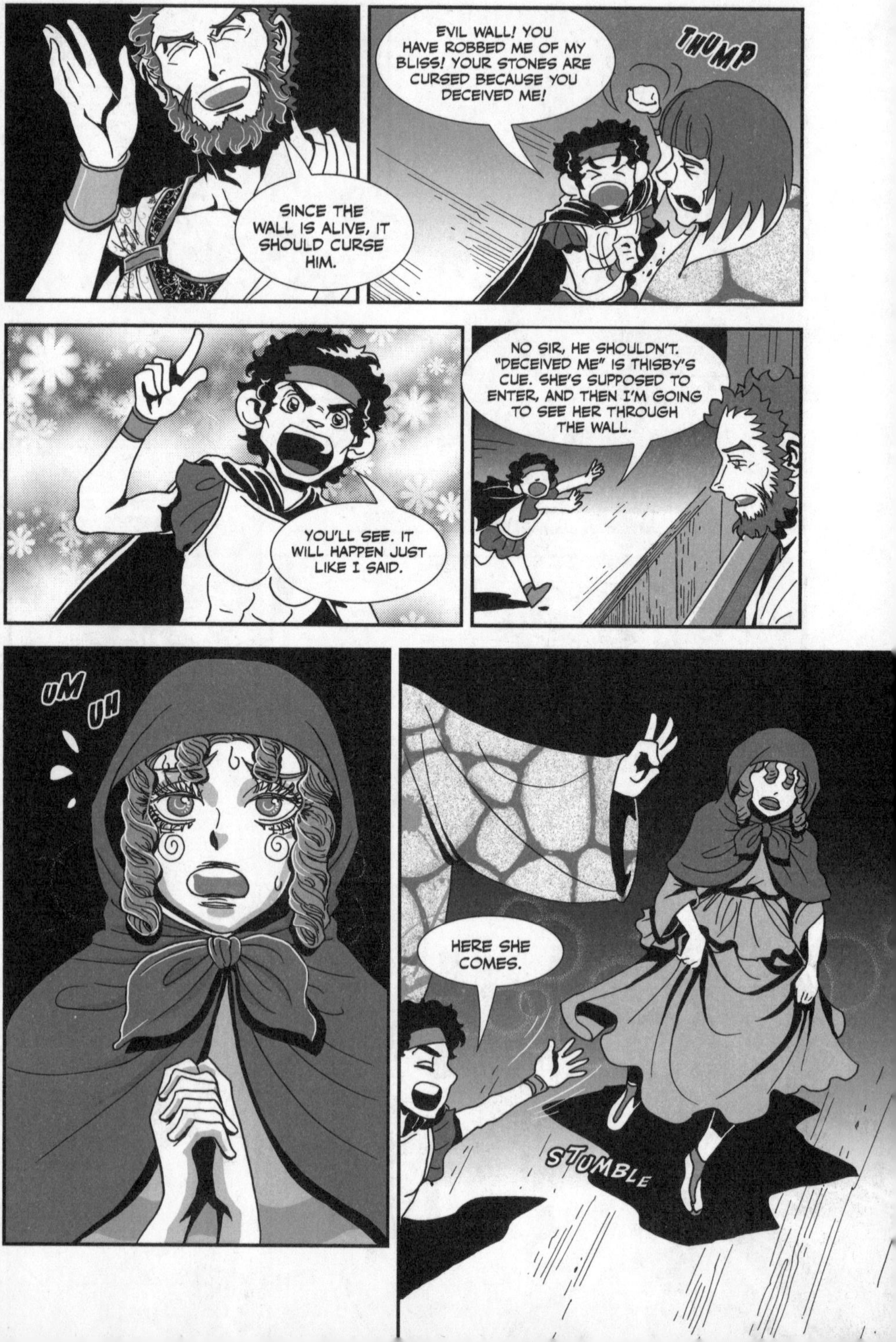
THUMP
EVIL WALL! YOU HAVE ROBBED ME OF MY BLISS! YOUR STONES ARE CURSED BECAUSE YOU DECEIVED ME!
SINCE THE WALL IS ALIVE, IT SHOULD CURSE HIM.
NO SIR, HE SHOULDN'T. "DECEIVED ME" IS THISBY'S CUE. SHE'S SUPPOSED TO ENTER, AND THEN I'M GOING TO SEE HER THROUGH THE WALL.
YOU'LL SEE. IT WILL HAPPEN JUST LIKE I SAID.
HERE SHE COMES.
STUMBLE
UM
UH

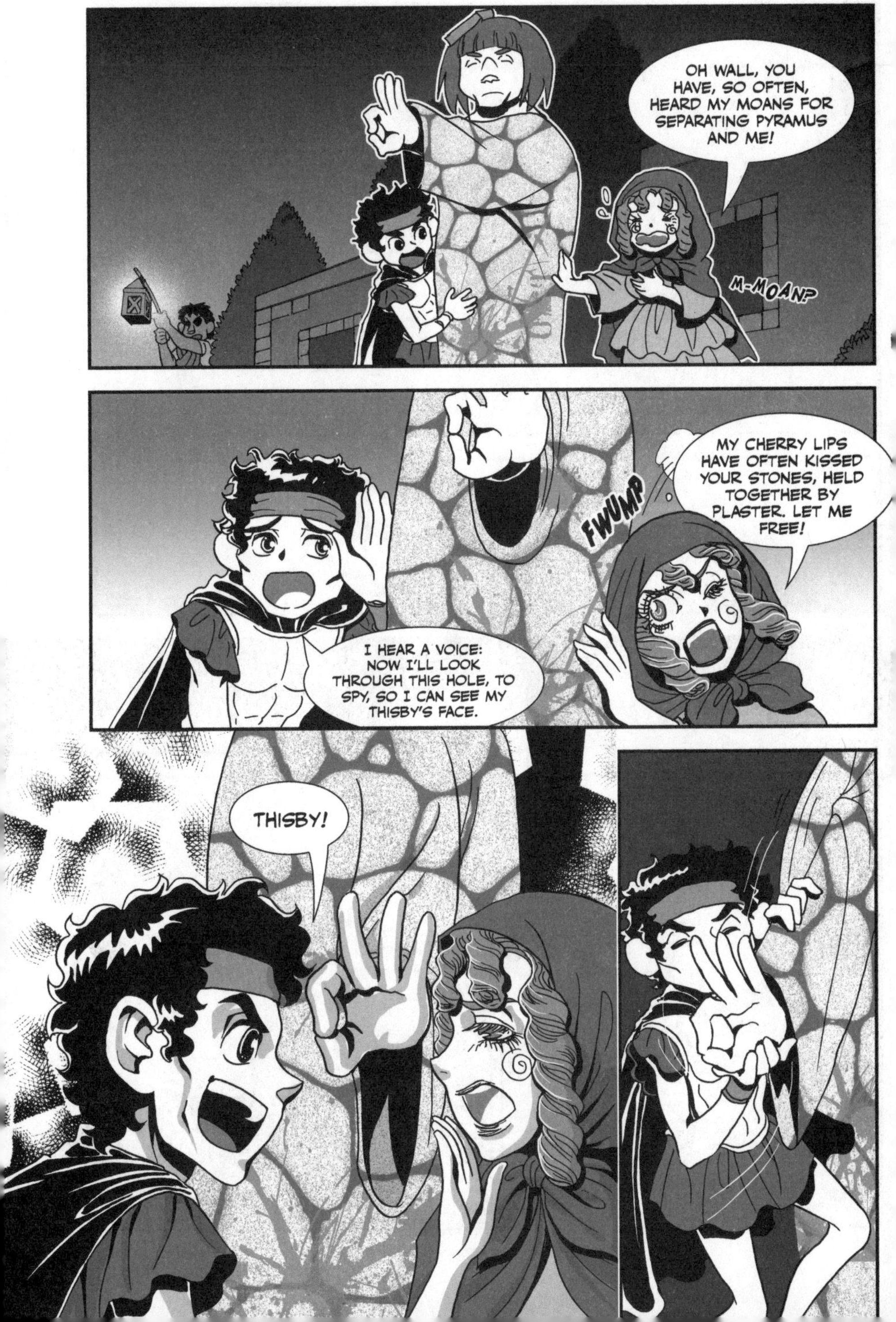
OH WALL, YOU HAVE, SO OFTEN, HEARD MY MOANS FOR SEPARATING PYRAMUS AND ME!
M-MOAN?
MY CHERRY LIPS HAVE OFTEN KISSED YOUR STONES, HELD TOGETHER BY PLASTER. LET ME FREE!
FWUMP
I HEAR A VOICE: NOW I'LL LOOK THROUGH THIS HOLE, TO SPY, SO I CAN SEE MY THISBY'S FACE.
THISBY!

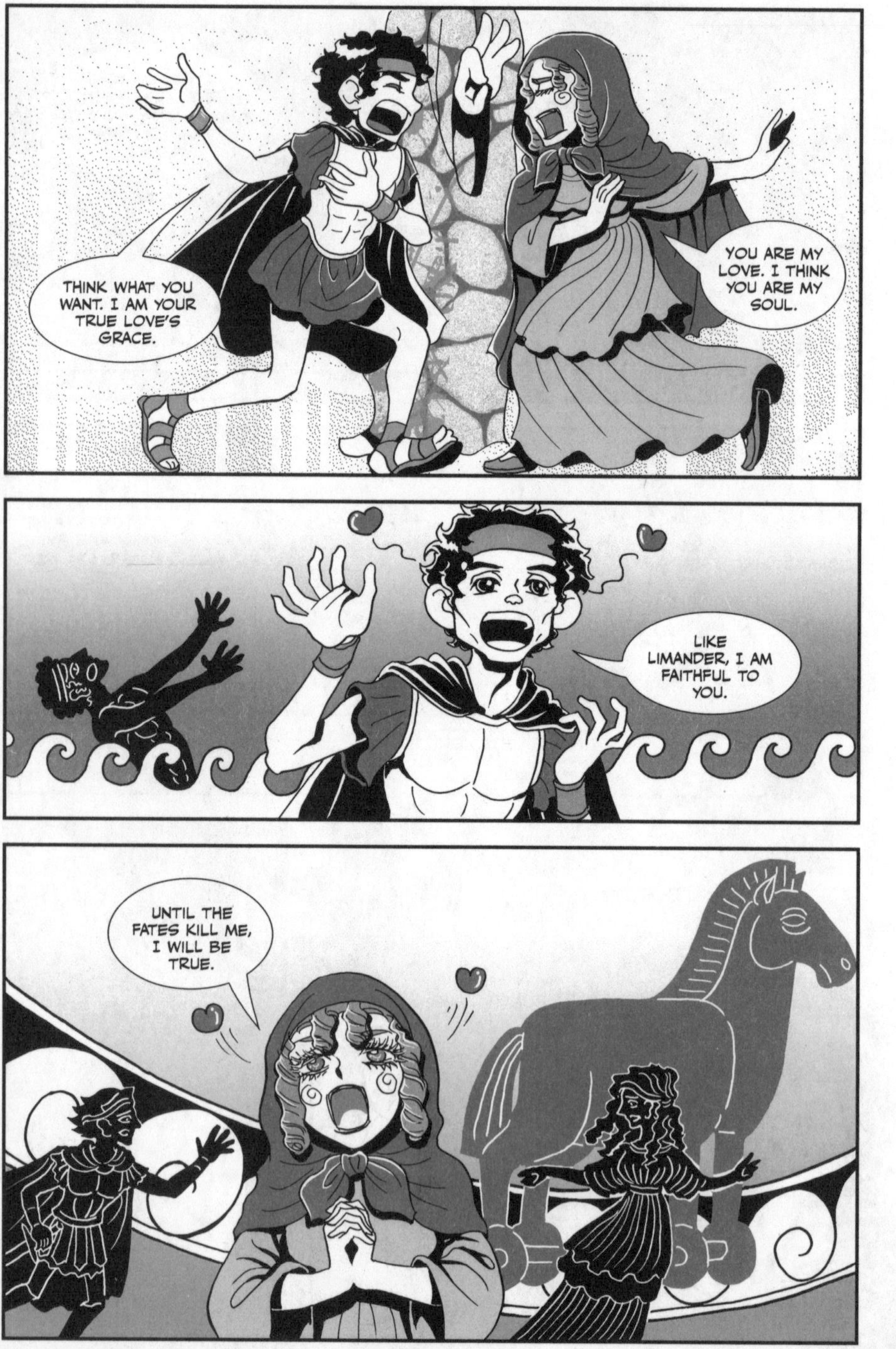
YOU ARE MY LOVE. I THINK YOU ARE MY SOUL.
THINK WHAT YOU WANT. I AM YOUR TRUE LOVE'S GRACE.
LIKE LIMANDER, I AM FAITHFUL TO YOU.
UNTIL THE FATES KILL ME, I WILL BE TRUE.

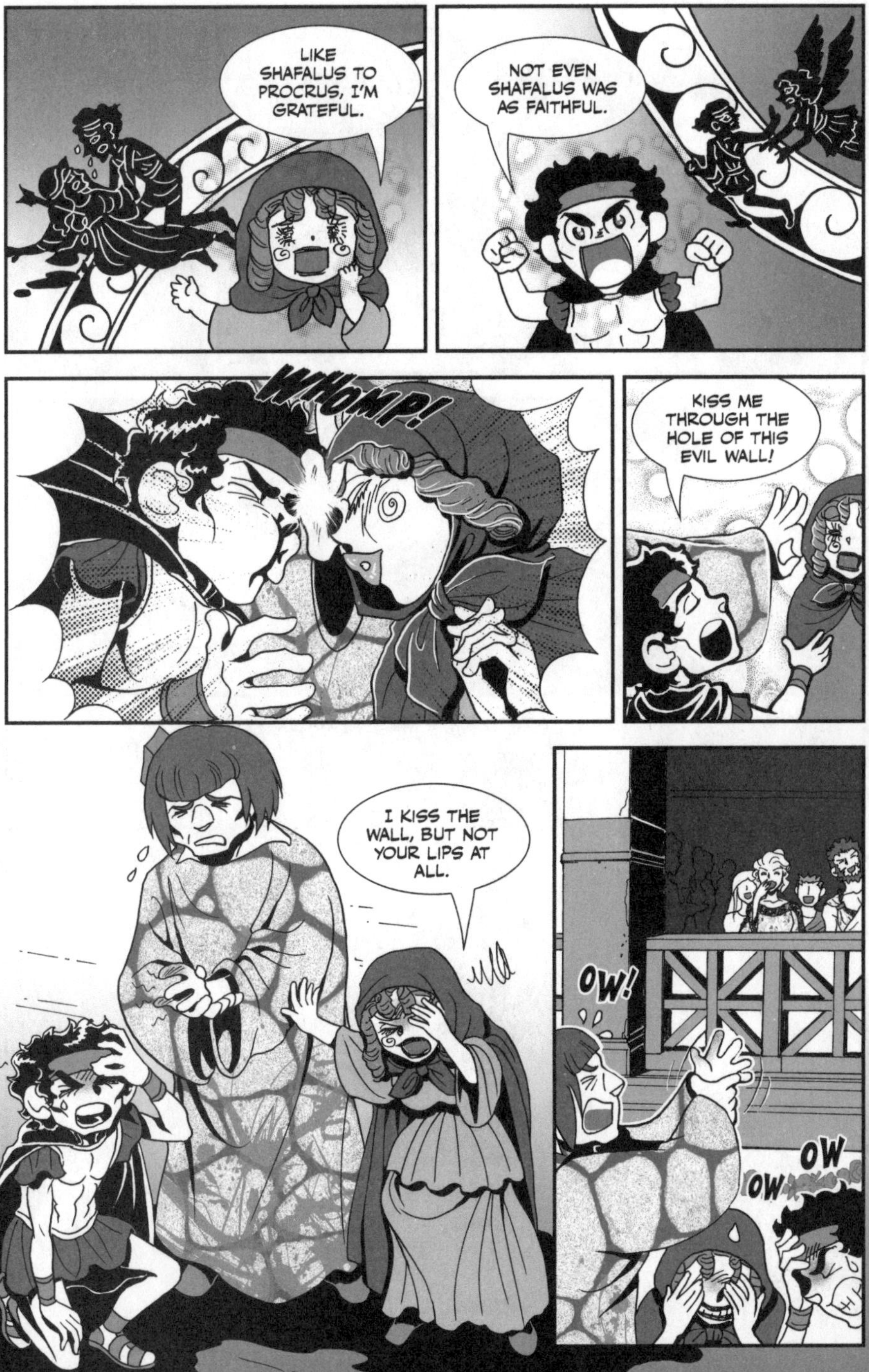
NOT EVEN SHAFALUS WAS AS FAITHFUL.
LIKE SHAFALUS TO PROCRUS, I'M GRATEFUL.
KISS ME THROUGH THE HOLE OF THIS EVIL WALL!
WHOMP!
OW!
OW
OW
I KISS THE WALL, BUT NOT YOUR LIPS AT ALL.

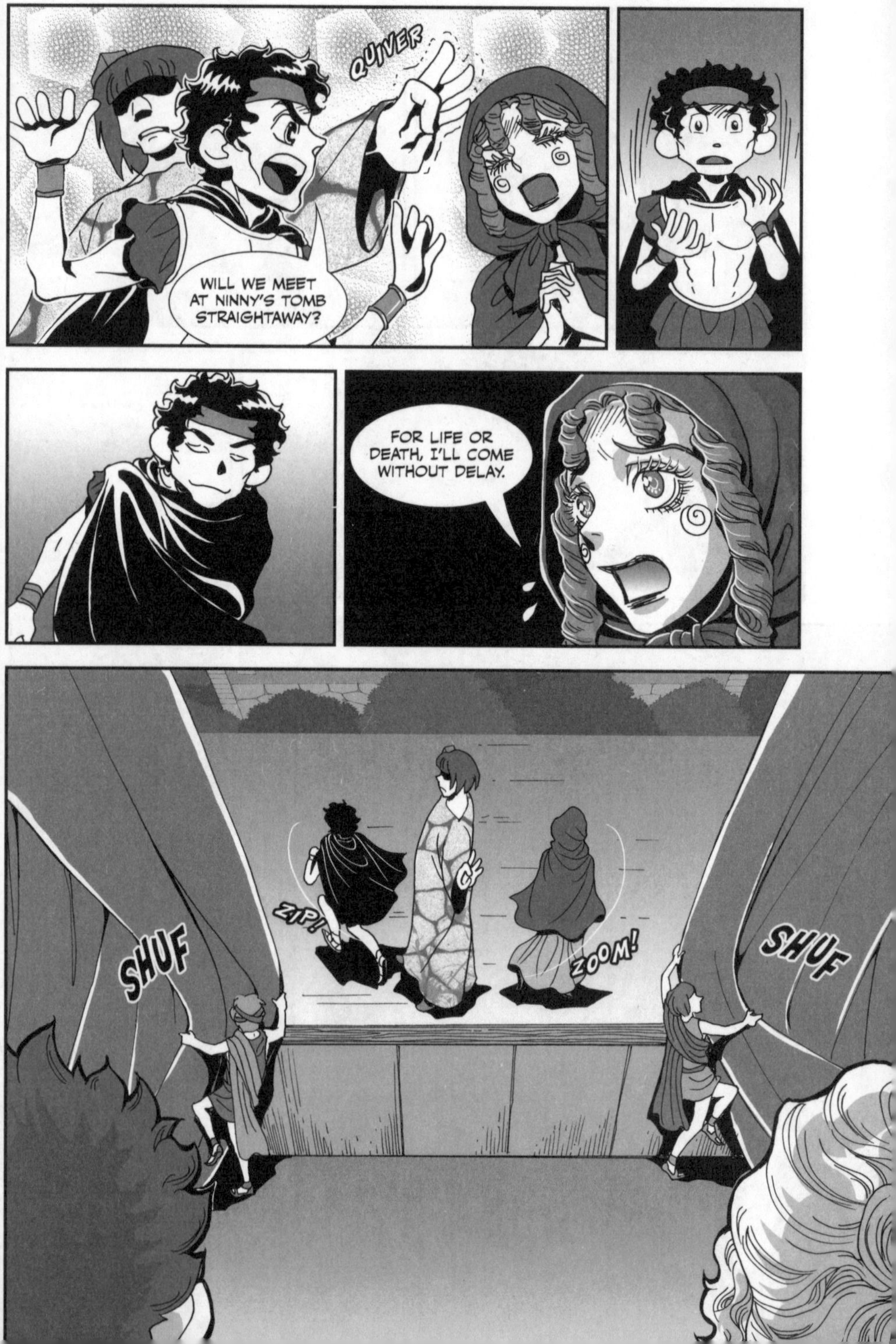
QUIVER
WILL WE MEET AT NINNY'S TOMB STRAIGHTAWAY?
FOR LIFE OR DEATH, I'LL COME WITHOUT DELAY.
ZOOM!
ZIP!
SHUF
SHUF

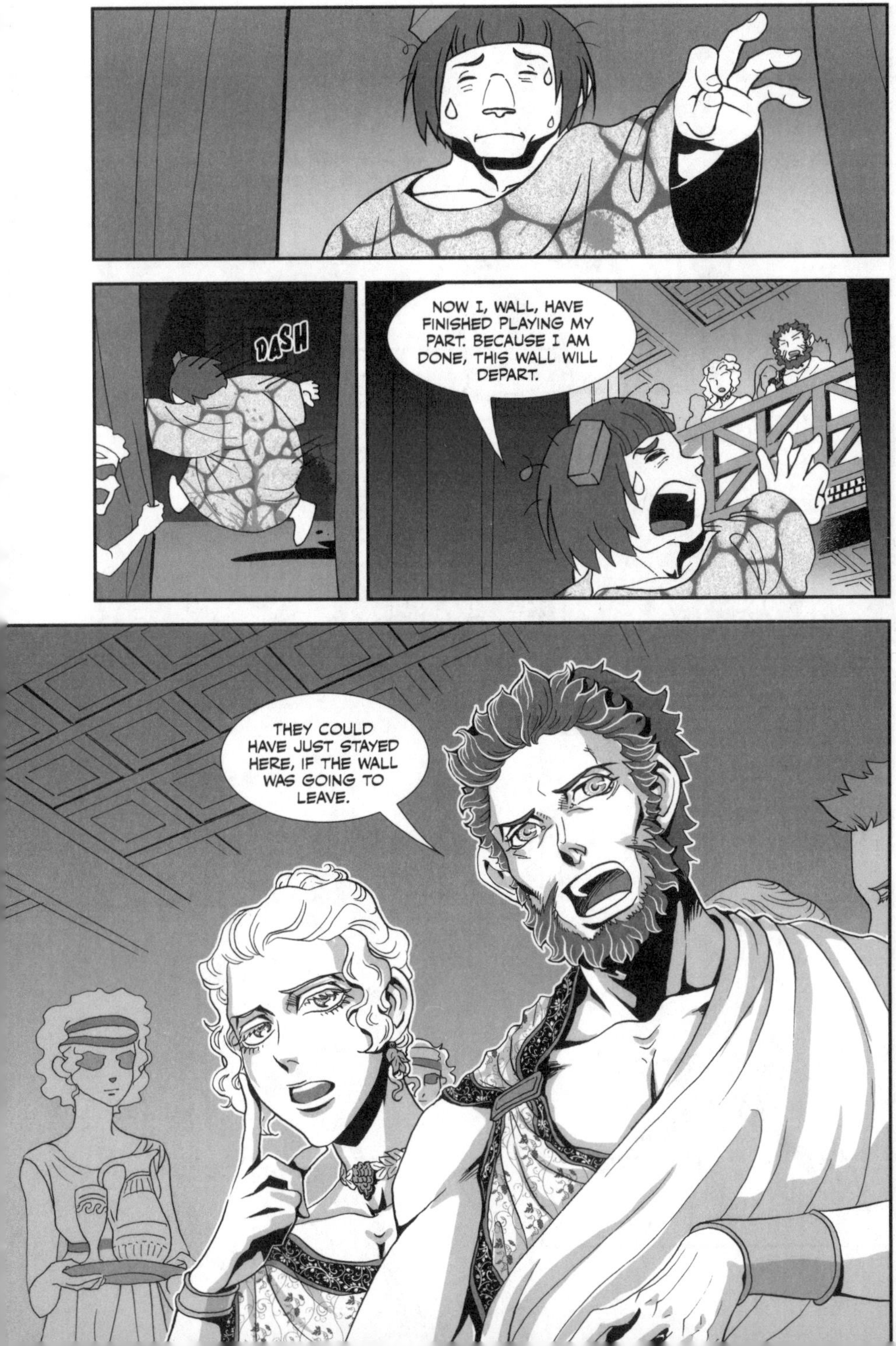
NOW I, WALL, HAVE FINISHED PLAYING MY PART. BECAUSE I AM DONE, THIS WALL WILL DEPART.
DASH
THEY COULD HAVE JUST STAYED HERE, IF THE WALL WAS GOING TO LEAVE.

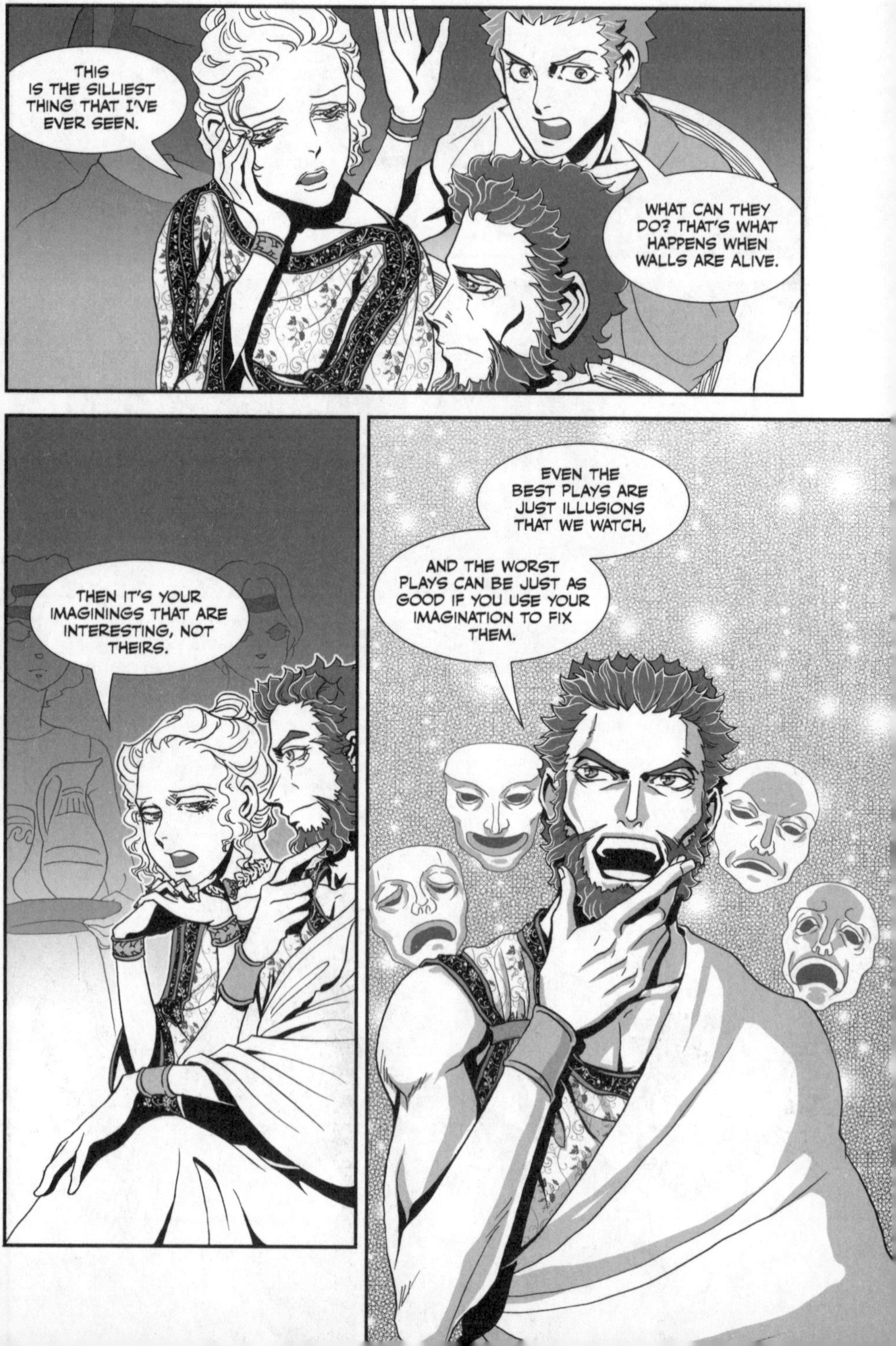
THIS IS THE SILLIEST THING THAT I'VE EVER SEEN.
WHAT CAN THEY DO? THAT'S WHAT HAPPENS WHEN WALLS ARE ALIVE.
EVEN THE BEST PLAYS ARE JUST ILLUSIONS THAT WE WATCH,
AND THE WORST PLAYS CAN BE JUST AS GOOD IF YOU USE YOUR IMAGINATION TO FIX THEM.
THEN IT'S YOUR IMAGININGS THAT ARE INTERESTING, NOT THEIRS.

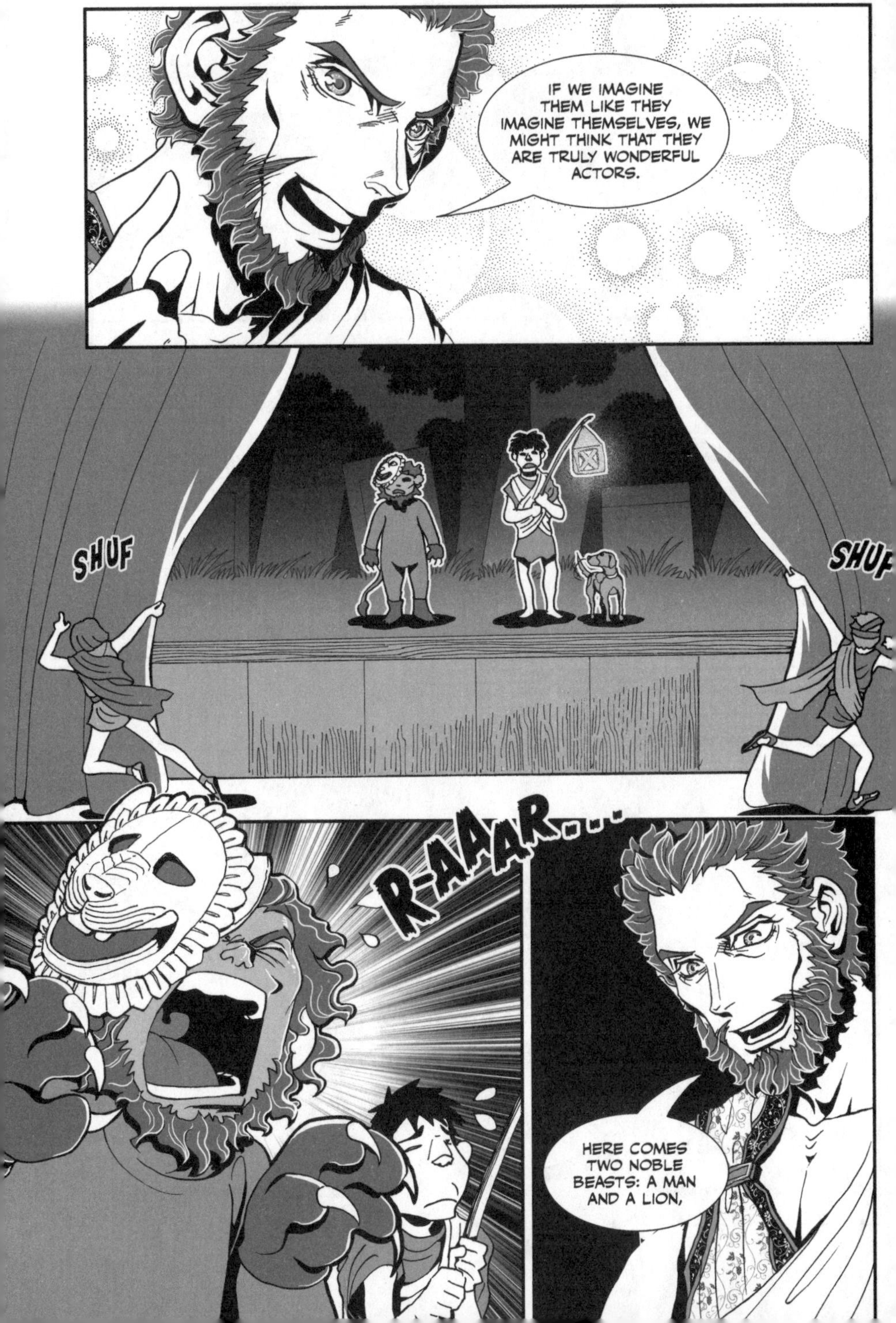
IF WE IMAGINE THEM LIKE THEY IMAGINE THEMSELVES, WE MIGHT THINK THAT THEY ARE TRULY WONDERFUL ACTORS.
SHUF
SHUF
HERE COMES TWO NOBLE BEASTS: A MAN AND A LION,
R-AAAR...

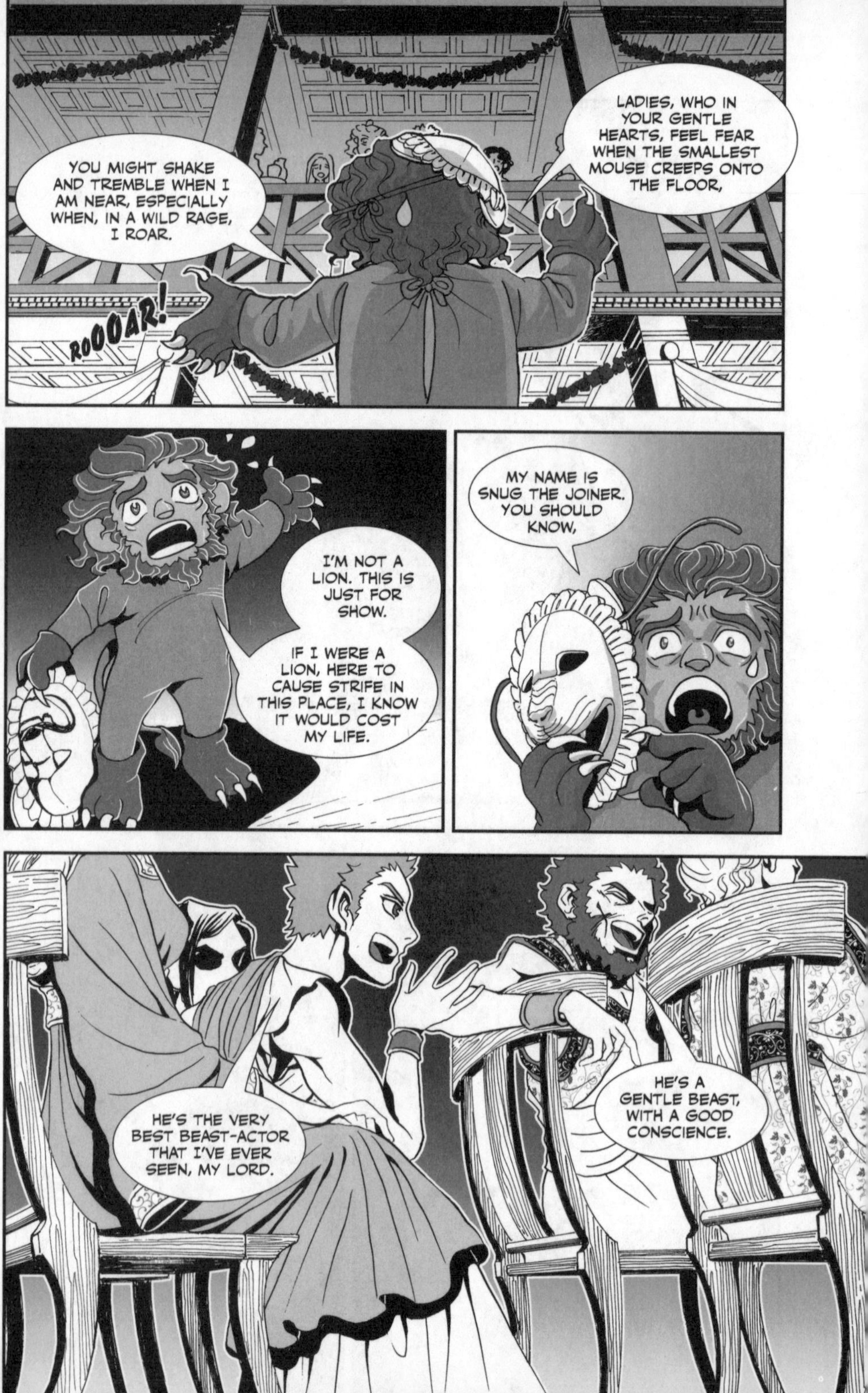
LADIES, WHO IN YOUR GENTLE HEARTS, FEEL FEAR WHEN THE SMALLEST MOUSE CREEPS ONTO THE FLOOR,
YOU MIGHT SHAKE AND TREMBLE WHEN I AM NEAR, ESPECIALLY WHEN, IN A WILD RAGE, I ROAR.
RoOOAR!
MY NAME IS SNUG THE JOINER. YOU SHOULD KNOW,
I'M NOT A LION. THIS IS JUST FOR SHOW.
IF I WERE A LION, HERE TO CAUSE STRIFE IN THIS PLACE, I KNOW IT WOULD COST MY LIFE.
HE'S A GENTLE BEAST, WITH A GOOD CONSCIENCE.
HE'S THE VERY BEST BEAST-ACTOR THAT I'VE EVER SEEN, MY LORD.

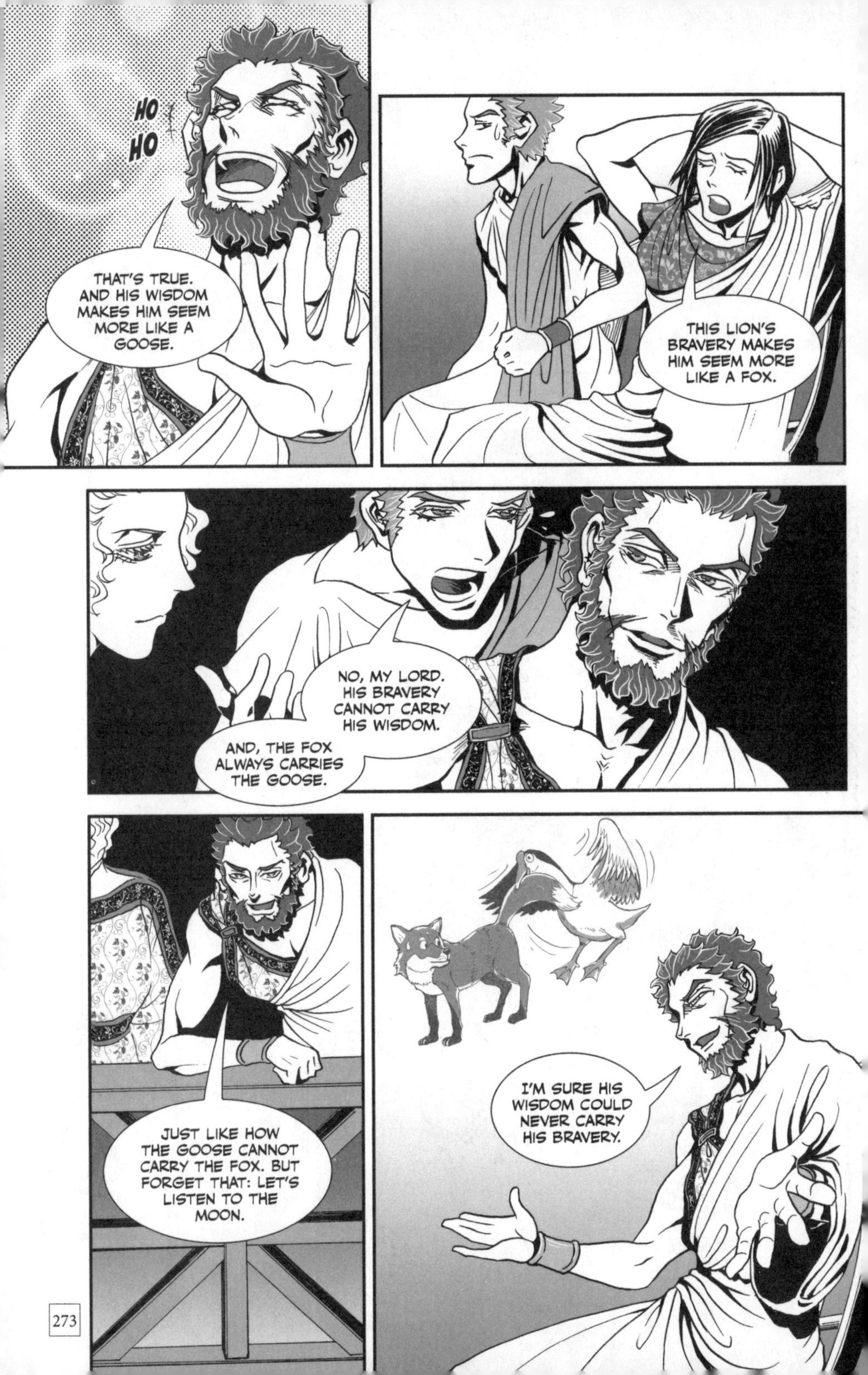

THIS LION'S BRAVERY MAKES HIM SEEM MORE LIKE A FOX.
HO HO
THAT'S TRUE. AND HIS WISDOM MAKES HIM SEEM MORE LIKE A GOOSE.
NO, MY LORD. HIS BRAVERY CANNOT CARRY HIS WISDOM.
AND, THE FOX ALWAYS CARRIES THE GOOSE.
I'M SURE HIS WISDOM COULD NEVER CARRY HIS BRAVERY.
JUST LIKE HOW THE GOOSE CANNOT CARRY THE FOX. BUT FORGET THAT: LET'S LISTEN TO THE MOON.

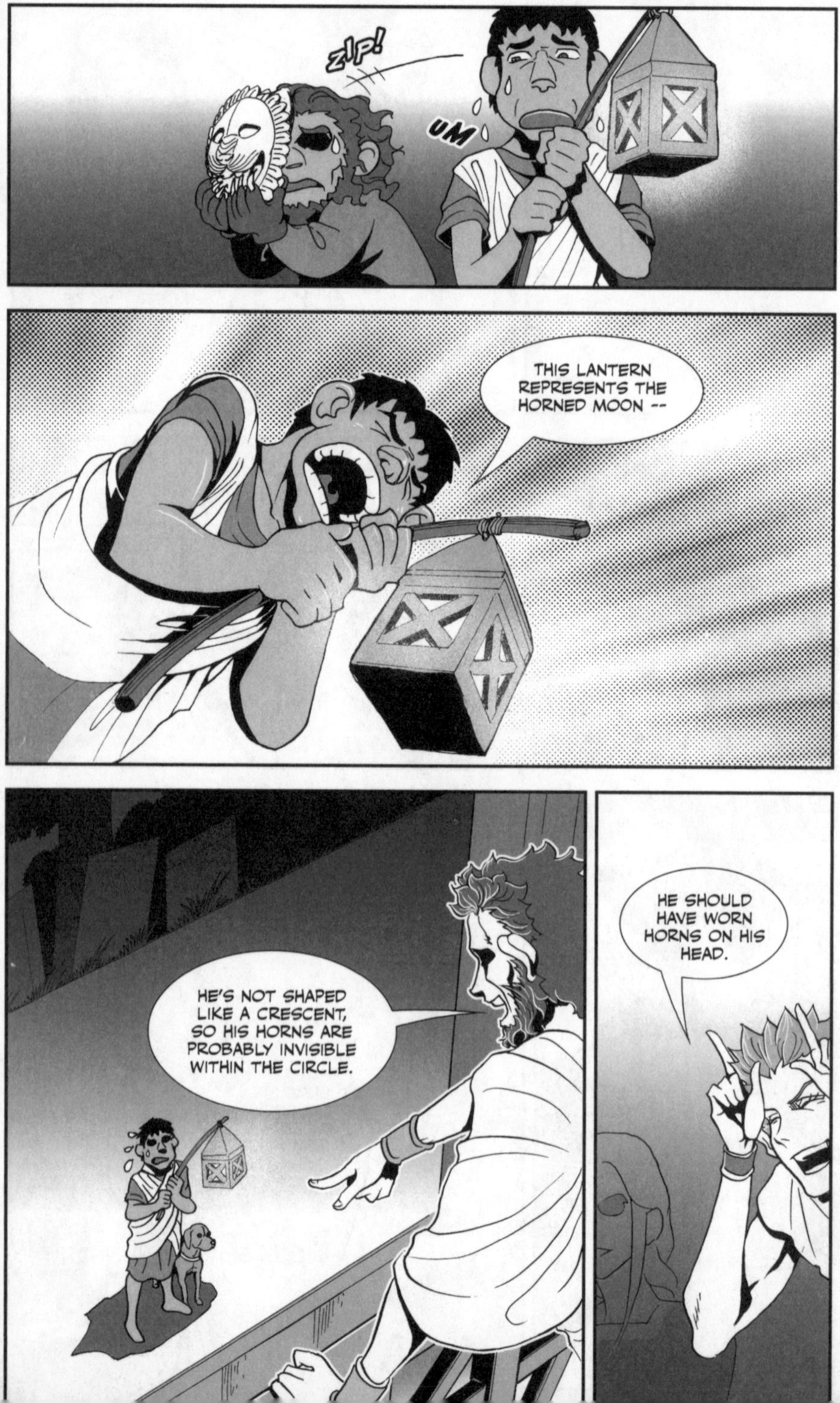
ZIP!
UM
THIS LANTERN REPRESENTS THE HORNED MOON --
HE SHOULD HAVE WORN HORNS ON HIS HEAD.
HE'S NOT SHAPED LIKE A CRESCENT, SO HIS HORNS ARE PROBABLY INVISIBLE WITHIN THE CIRCLE.

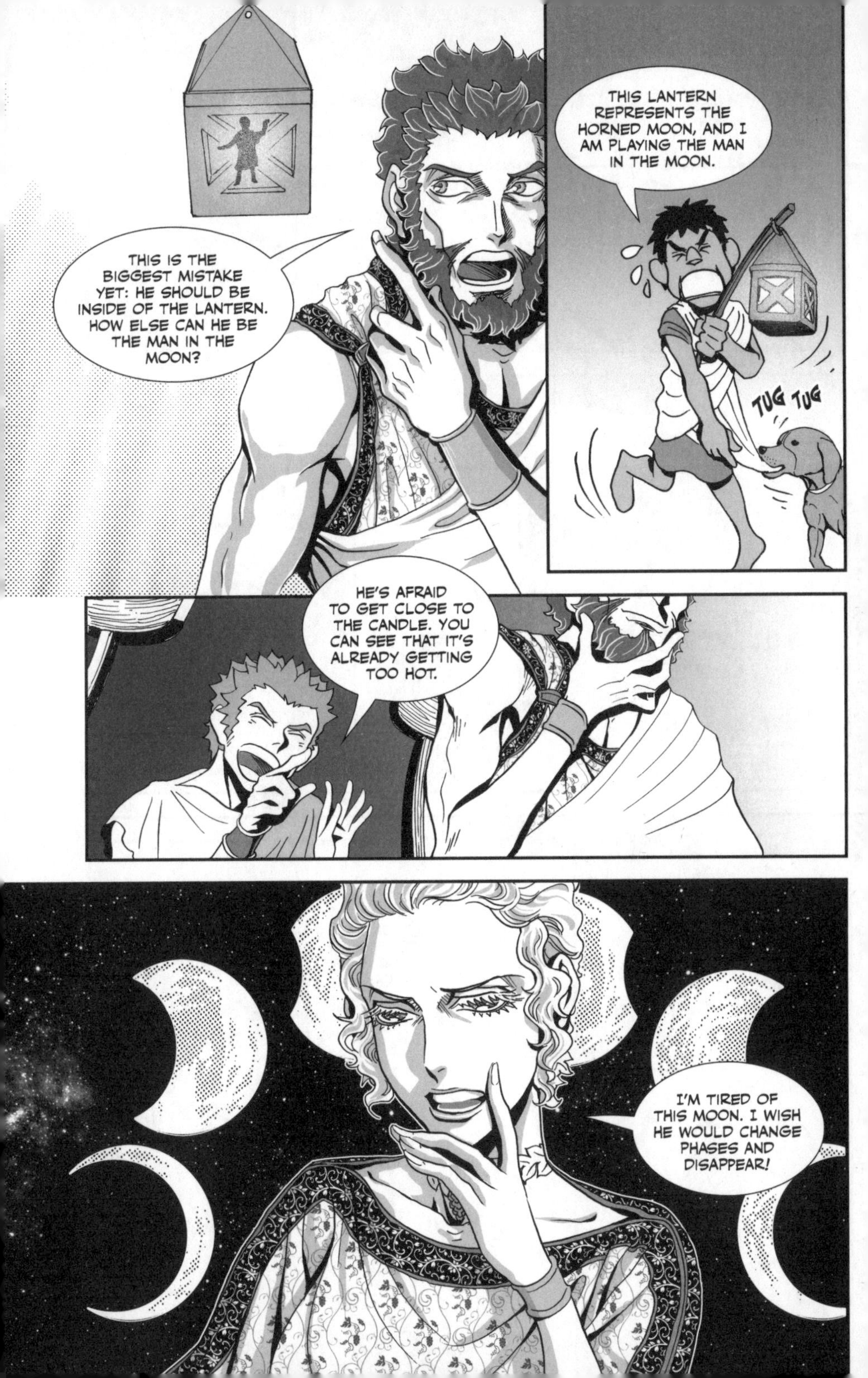
THIS LANTERN REPRESENTS THE HORNED MOON, AND I AM PLAYING THE MAN IN THE MOON.
TUG TUG
THIS IS THE BIGGEST MISTAKE YET: HE SHOULD BE INSIDE OF THE LANTERN. HOW ELSE CAN HE BE THE MAN IN THE MOON?
HE'S AFRAID TO GET CLOSE TO THE CANDLE. YOU CAN SEE THAT IT'S ALREADY GETTING TOO HOT.
I'M TIRED OF THIS MOON. I WISH HE WOULD CHANGE PHASES AND DISAPPEAR!

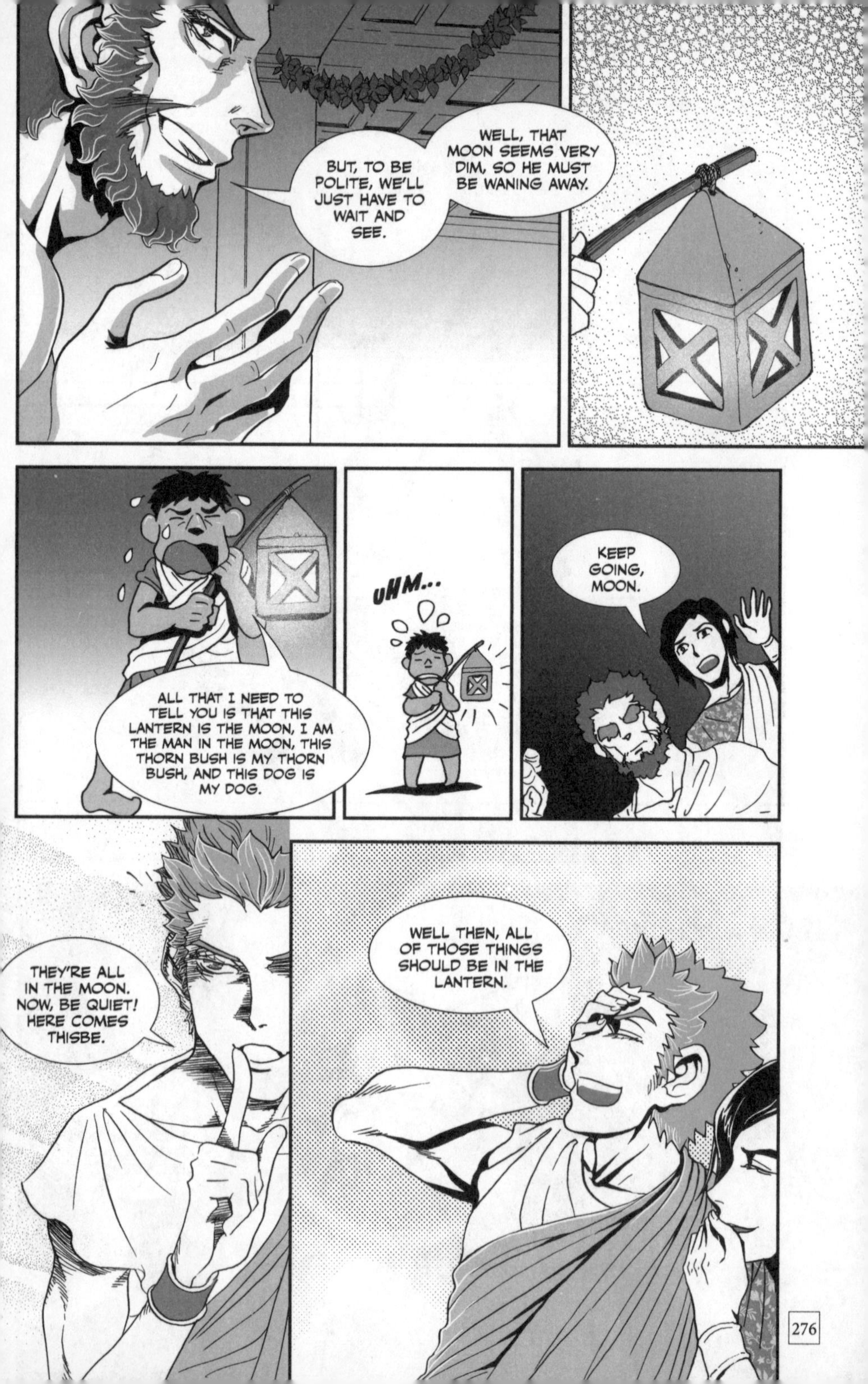
WELL, THAT MOON SEEMS VERY DIM, SO HE MUST BE WANING AWAY.
BUT, TO BE POLITE, WE'LL JUST HAVE TO WAIT AND SEE.
KEEP GOING, MOON.
UHM...
ALL THAT I NEED TO TELL YOU IS THAT THIS LANTERN IS THE MOON, I AM THE MAN IN THE MOON, THIS THORN BUSH IS MY THORN BUSH, AND THIS DOG IS MY DOG.
WELL THEN, ALL OF THOSE THINGS SHOULD BE IN THE LANTERN.
THEY'RE ALL IN THE MOON. NOW, BE QUIET! HERE COMES THISBE.

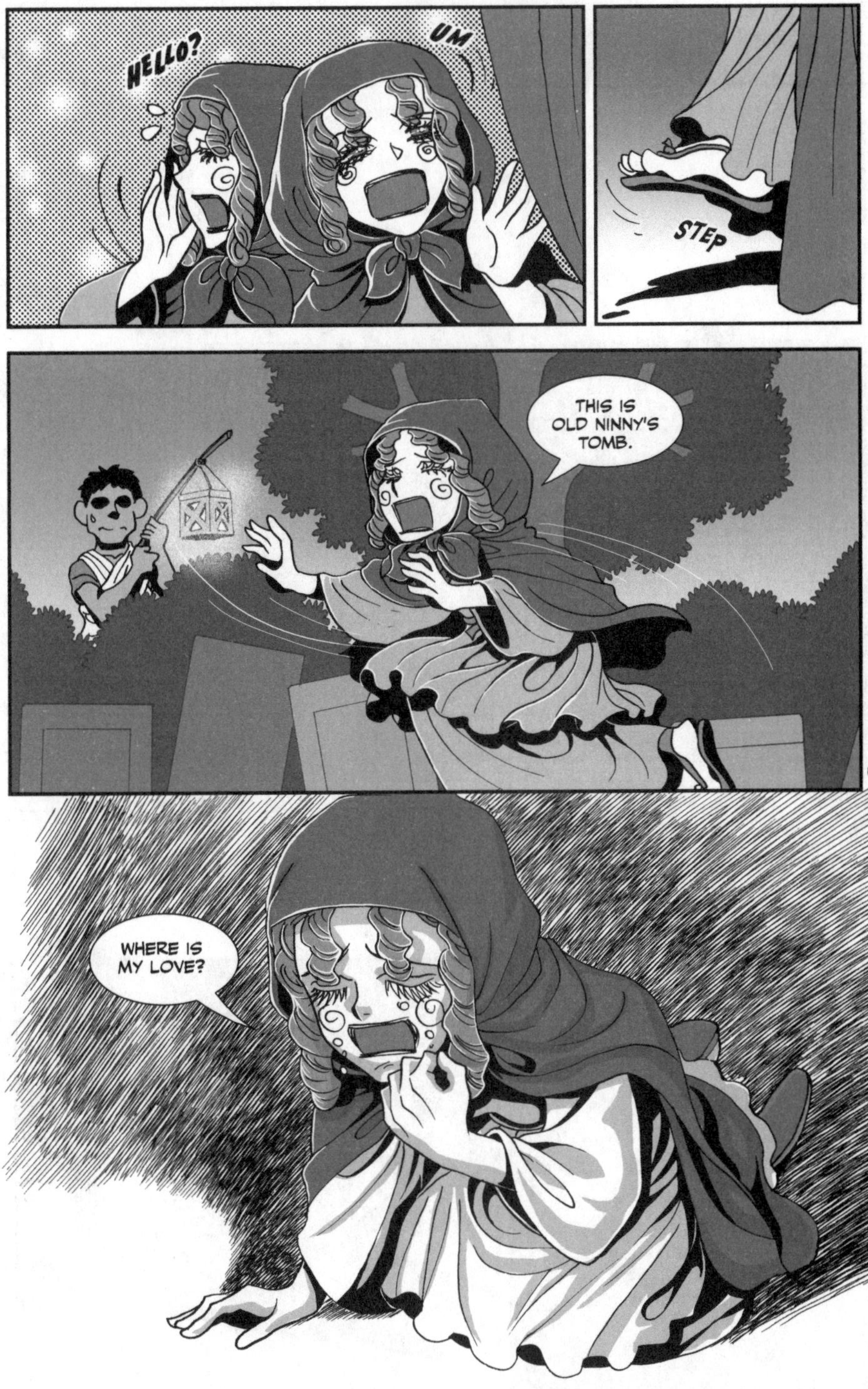
STEP
UM
HELLO?
THIS IS OLD NINNY'S TOMB.
WHERE IS MY LOVE?

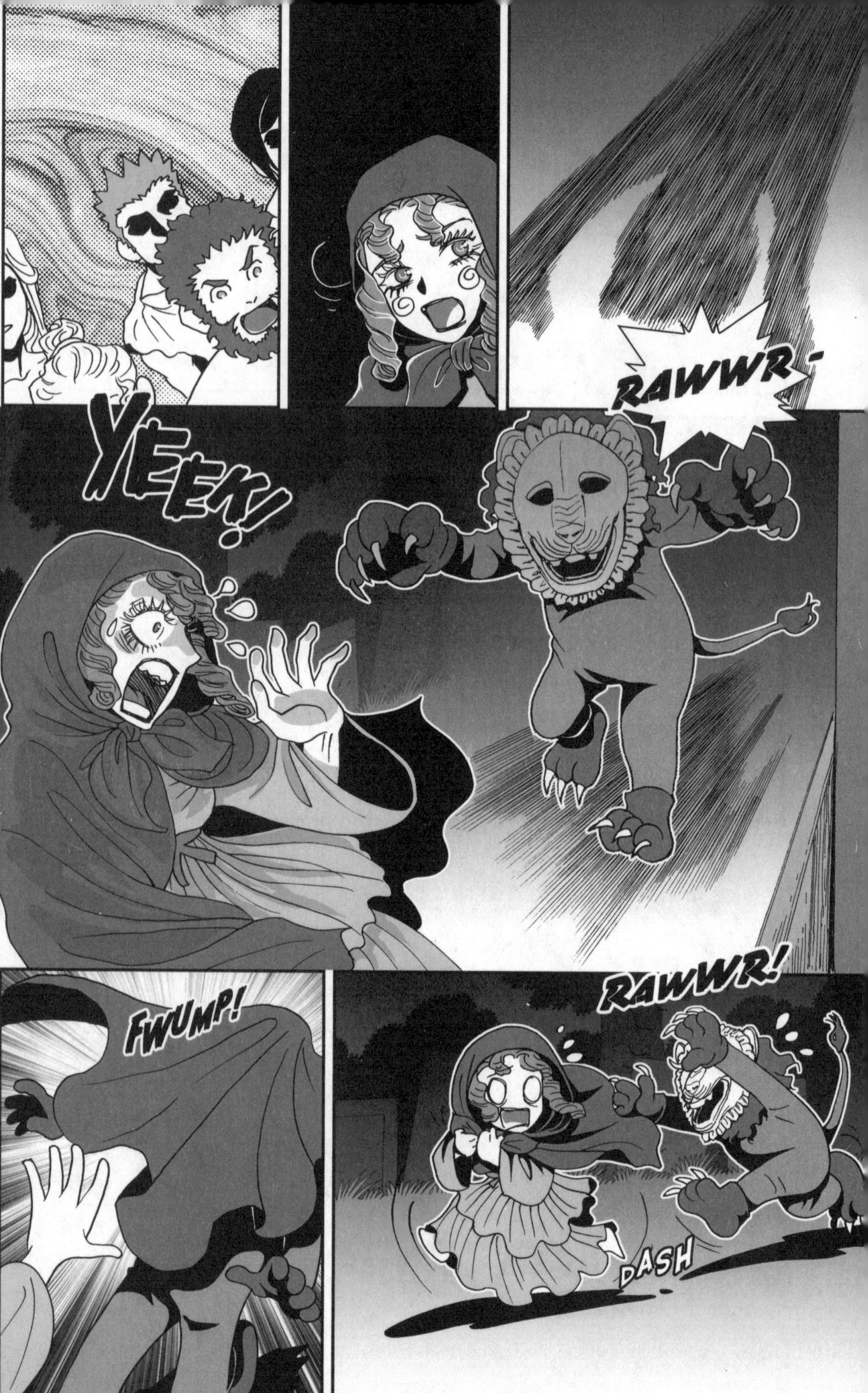
RAWWR -
YEEK!
RAWWR!
DASH
FWUMP!

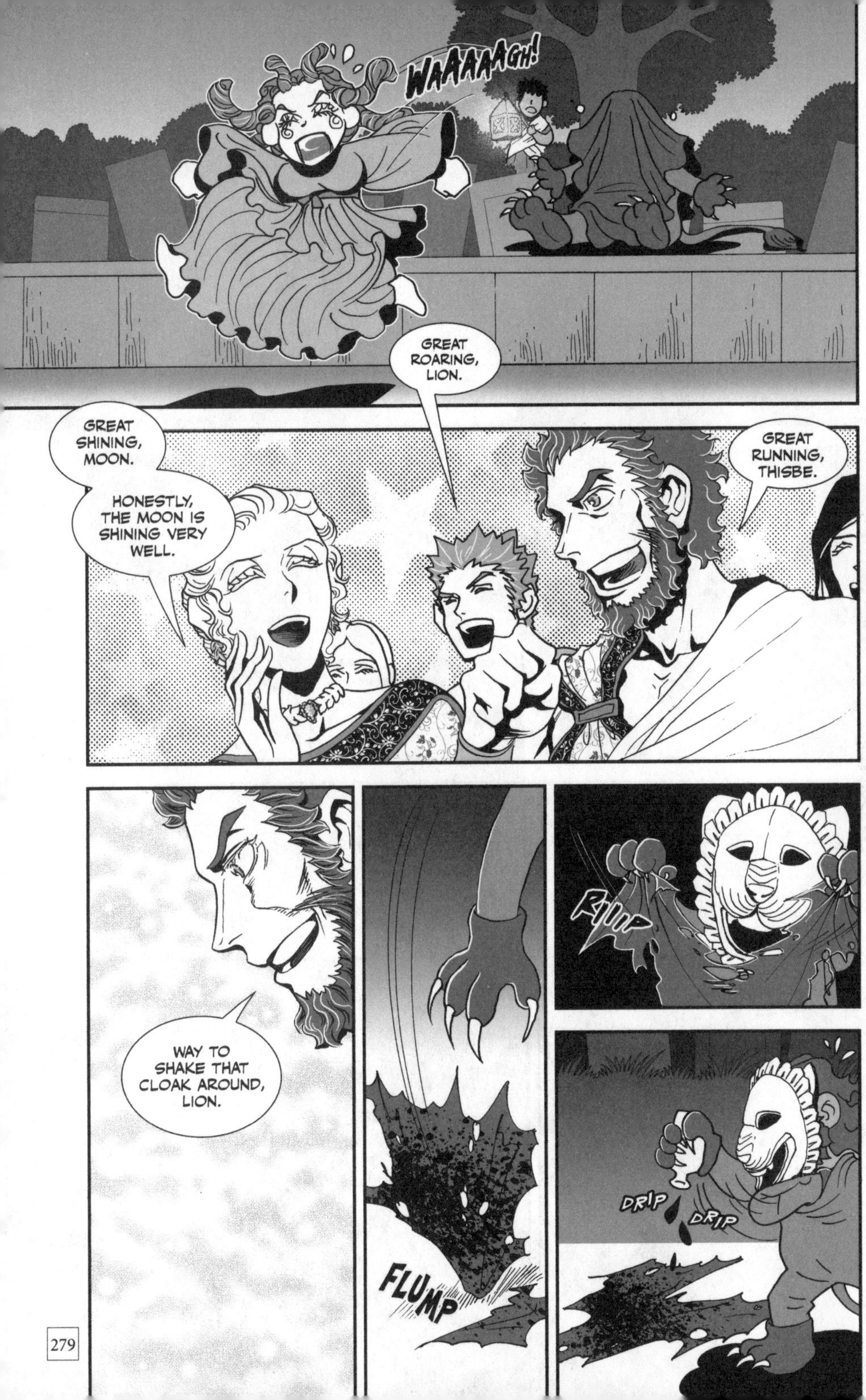
WAAAAAGH!
GREAT RUNNING, THISBE.
GREAT ROARING, LION.
GREAT SHINING, MOON.
HONESTLY, THE MOON IS SHINING VERY WELL.
RIIIP
DRIP
DRIP
FLUMP
WAY TO SHAKE THAT CLOAK AROUND, LION.

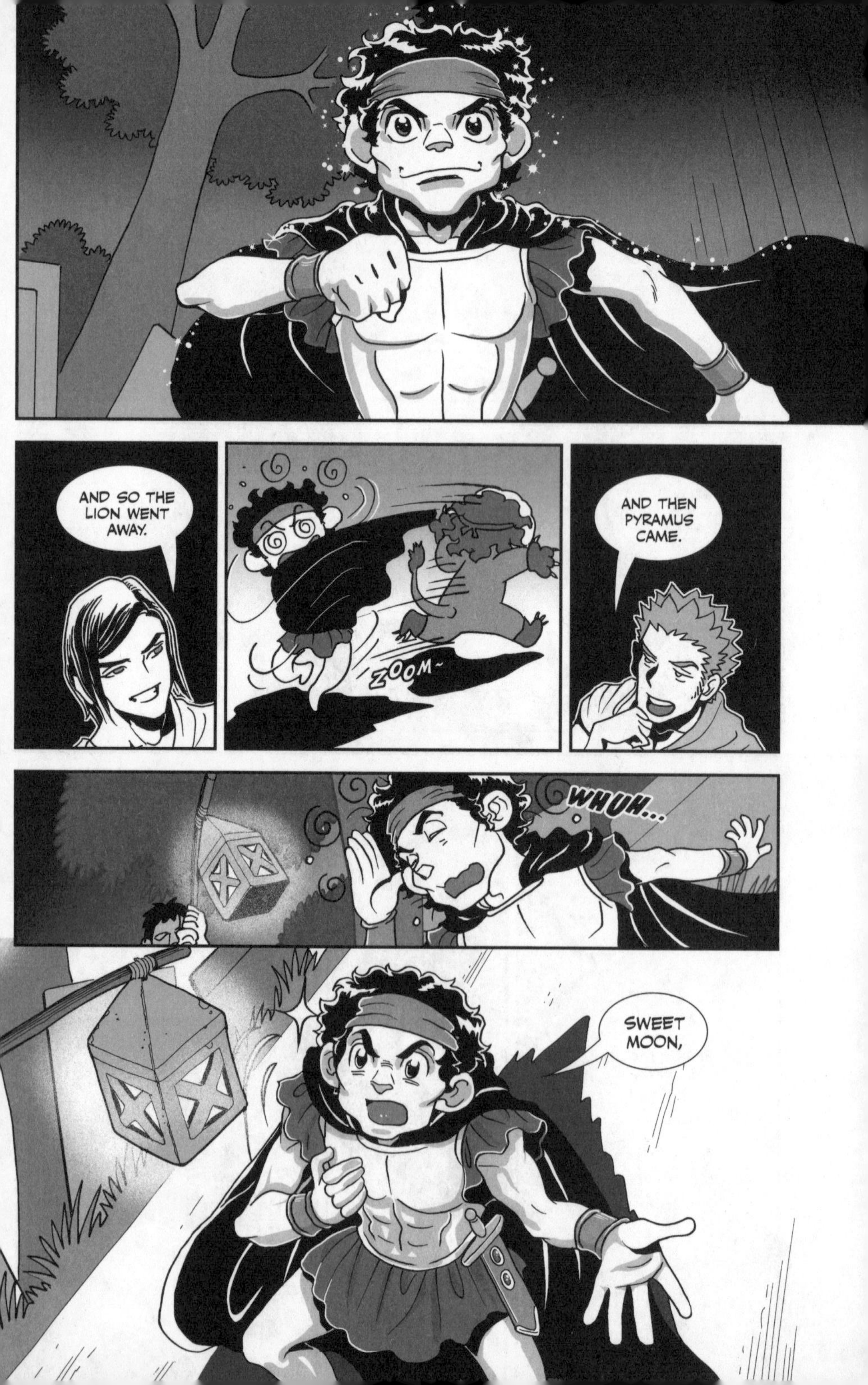
AND THEN PYRAMUS CAME.
ZOOM~
AND SO THE LION WENT AWAY.
WHUH...
SWEET MOON,

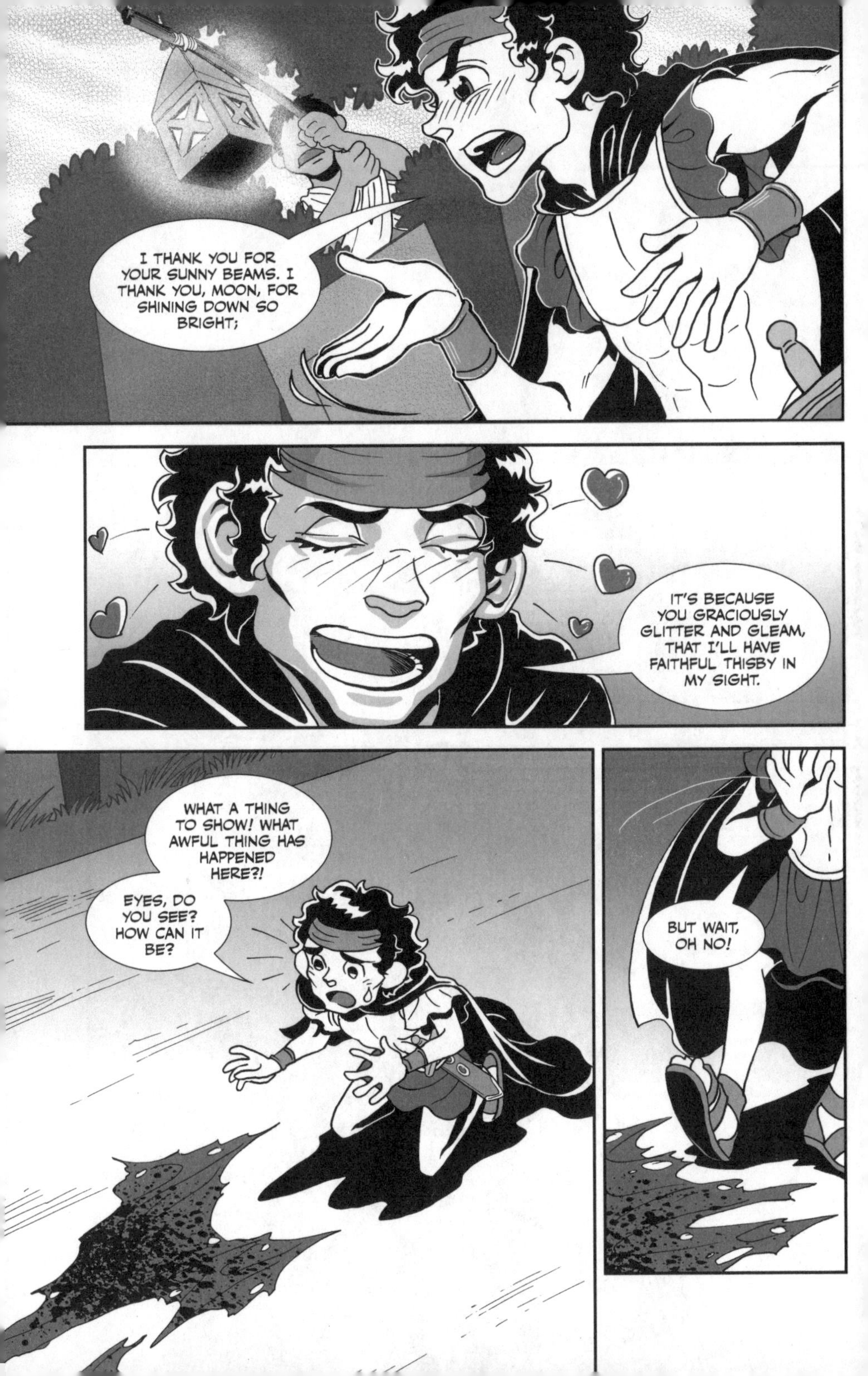
I THANK YOU FOR YOUR SUNNY BEAMS. I THANK YOU, MOON, FOR SHINING DOWN SO BRIGHT;
IT'S BECAUSE YOU GRACIOUSLY GLITTER AND GLEAM, THAT I'LL HAVE FAITHFUL THISBY IN MY SIGHT.
BUT WAIT, OH NO!
WHAT A THING TO SHOW! WHAT AWFUL THING HAS HAPPENED HERE?!
EYES, DO YOU SEE? HOW CAN IT BE?

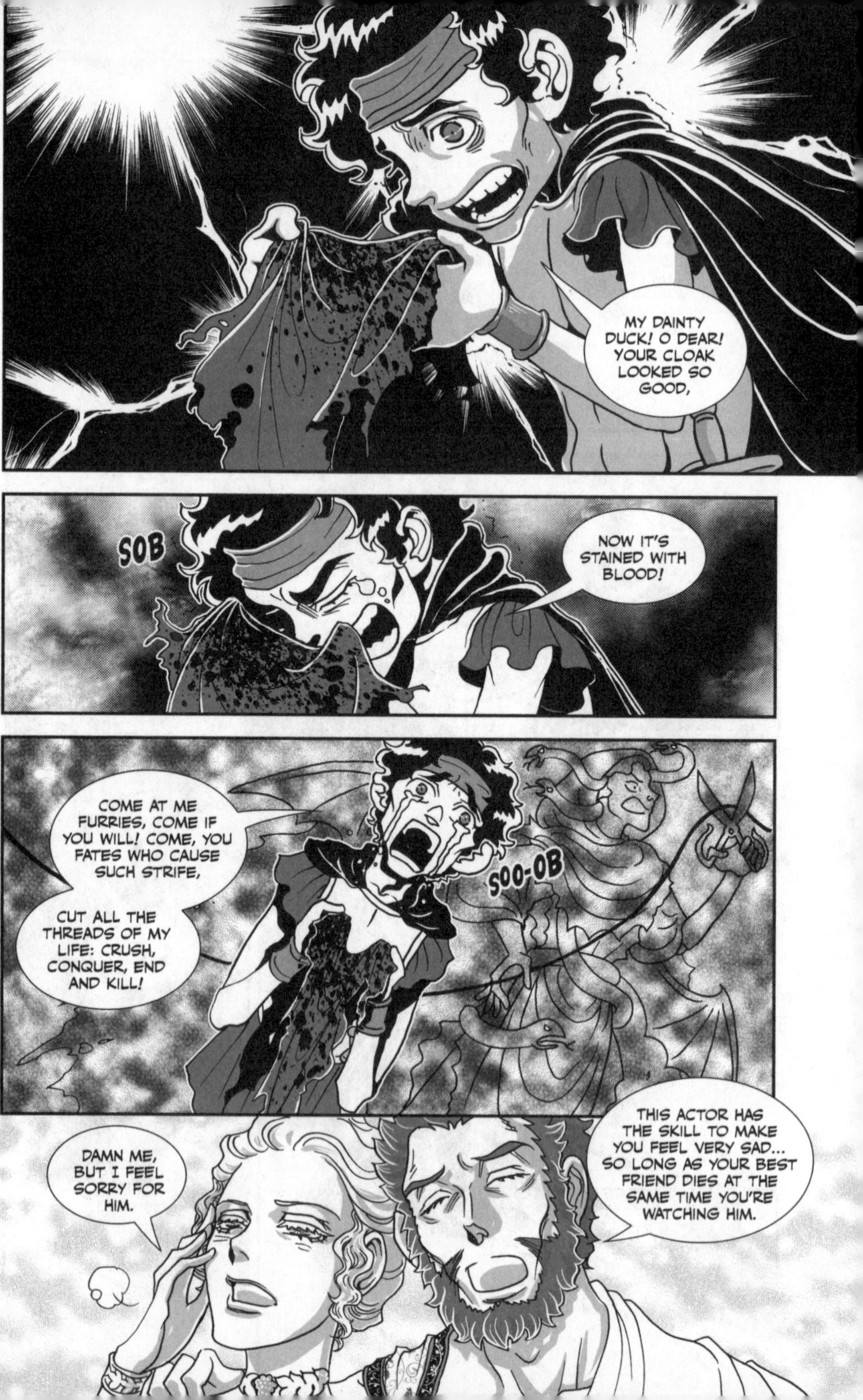
MY DAINTY DUCK! O DEAR! YOUR CLOAK LOOKED SO GOOD,
NOW IT'S STAINED WITH BLOOD!
SOB
COME AT ME FURRIES, COME IF YOU WILL! COME, YOU FATES WHO CAUSE SUCH STRIFE,
SOO-OB
CUT ALL THE THREADS OF MY LIFE: CRUSH, CONQUER, END AND KILL!
THIS ACTOR HAS THE SKILL TO MAKE YOU FEEL VERY SAD... SO LONG AS YOUR BEST FRIEND DIES AT THE SAME TIME YOU'RE WATCHING HIM.
DAMN ME, BUT I FEEL SORRY FOR HIM.

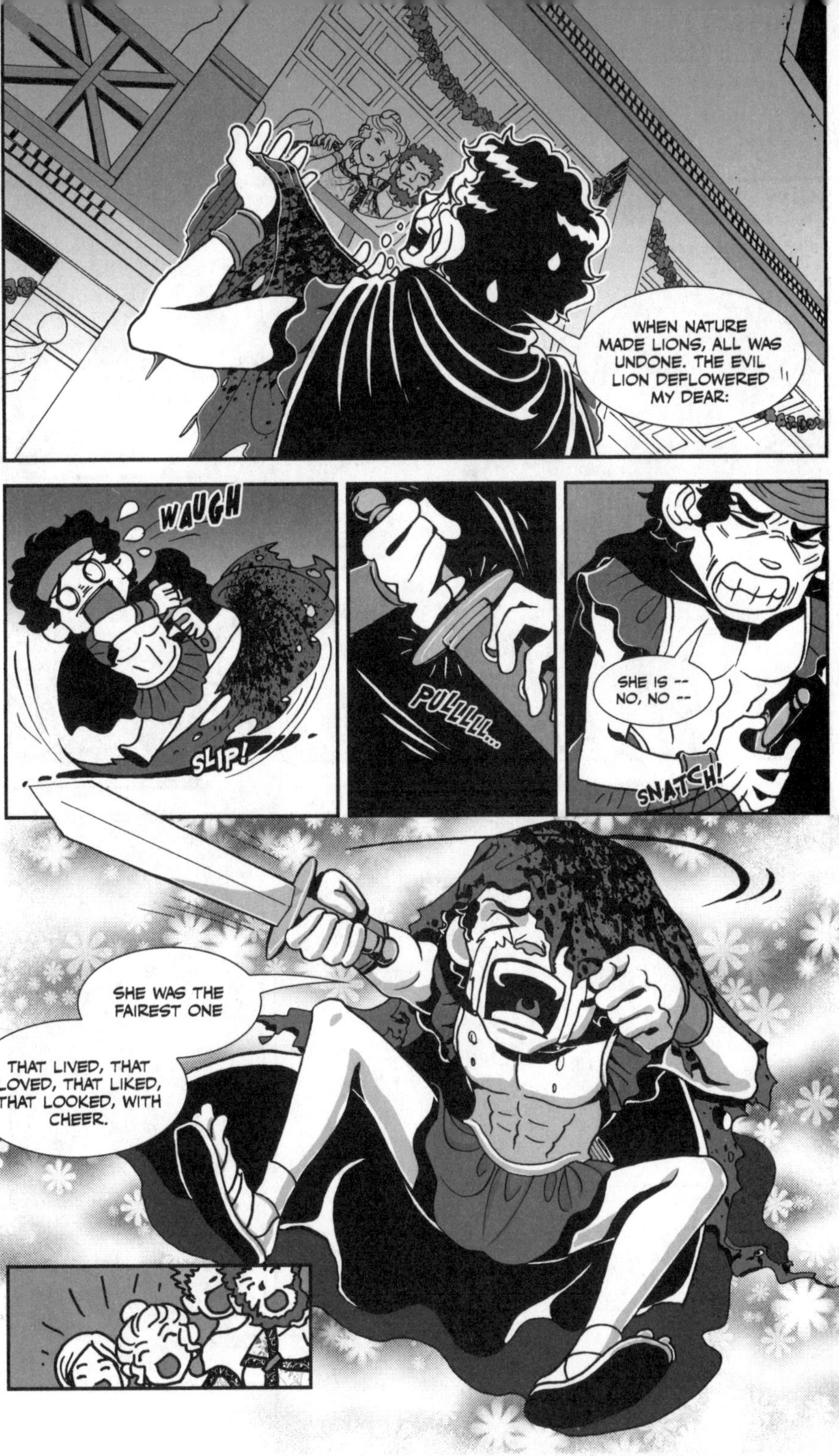
WHEN NATURE MADE LIONS, ALL WAS UNDONE. THE EVIL LION DEFLOWERED MY DEAR:
SHE IS -- NO, NO --
SNATCH!
PULLLLL...
WAUGH
SLIP!
SHE WAS THE FAIREST ONE
THAT LIVED, THAT LOVED, THAT LIKED, THAT LOOKED, WITH CHEER.

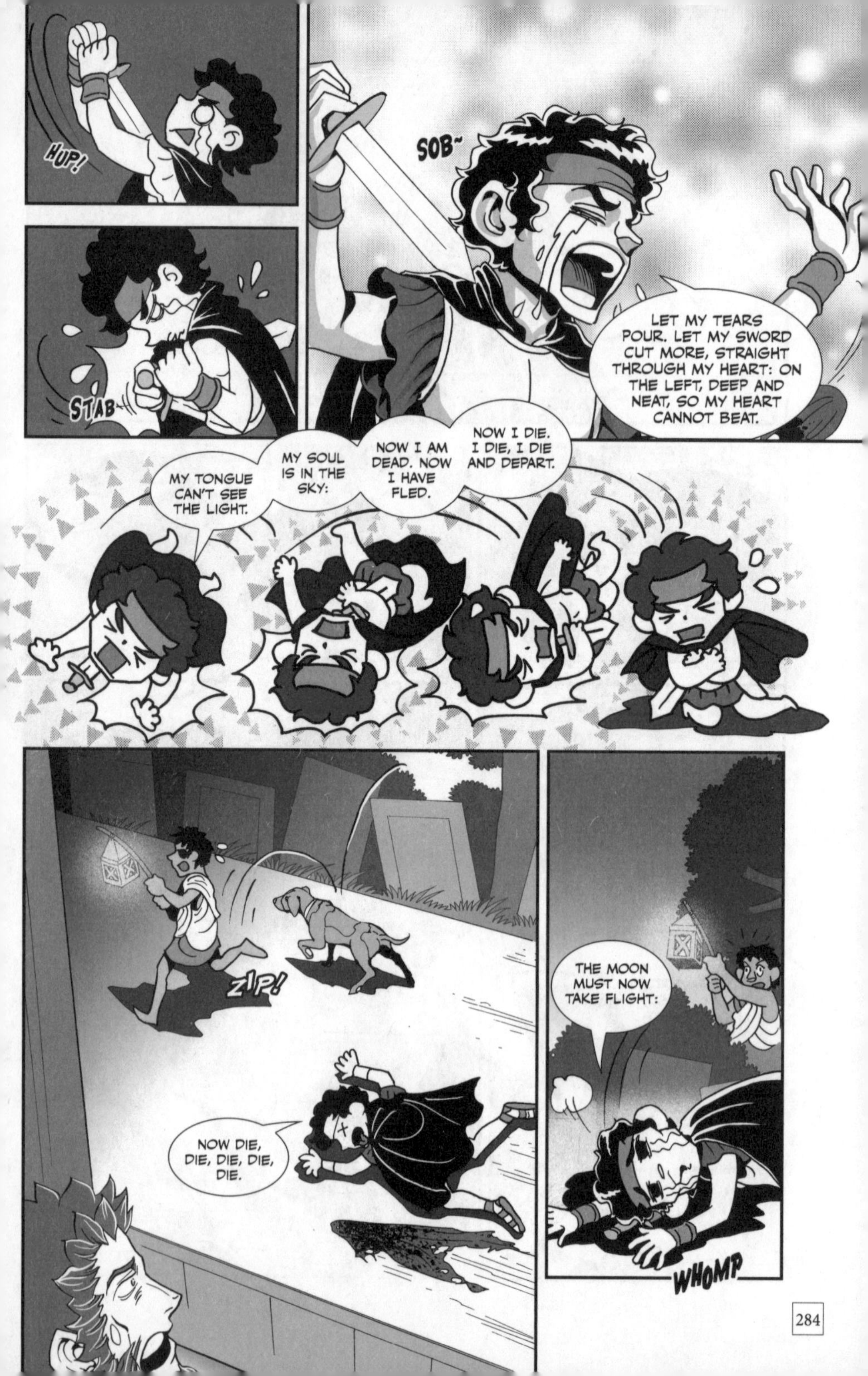
SOB~
LET MY TEARS POUR. LET MY SWORD CUT MORE, STRAIGHT THROUGH MY HEART: ON THE LEFT, DEEP AND NEAT, SO MY HEART CANNOT BEAT.
HUP!
STAB
NOW I DIE. I DIE, I DIE AND DEPART.
NOW I AM DEAD. NOW I HAVE FLED.
MY SOUL IS IN THE SKY:
MY TONGUE CAN'T SEE THE LIGHT.
THE MOON MUST NOW TAKE FLIGHT:
WHOMP
ZIP!
NOW DIE, DIE, DIE, DIE, DIE.

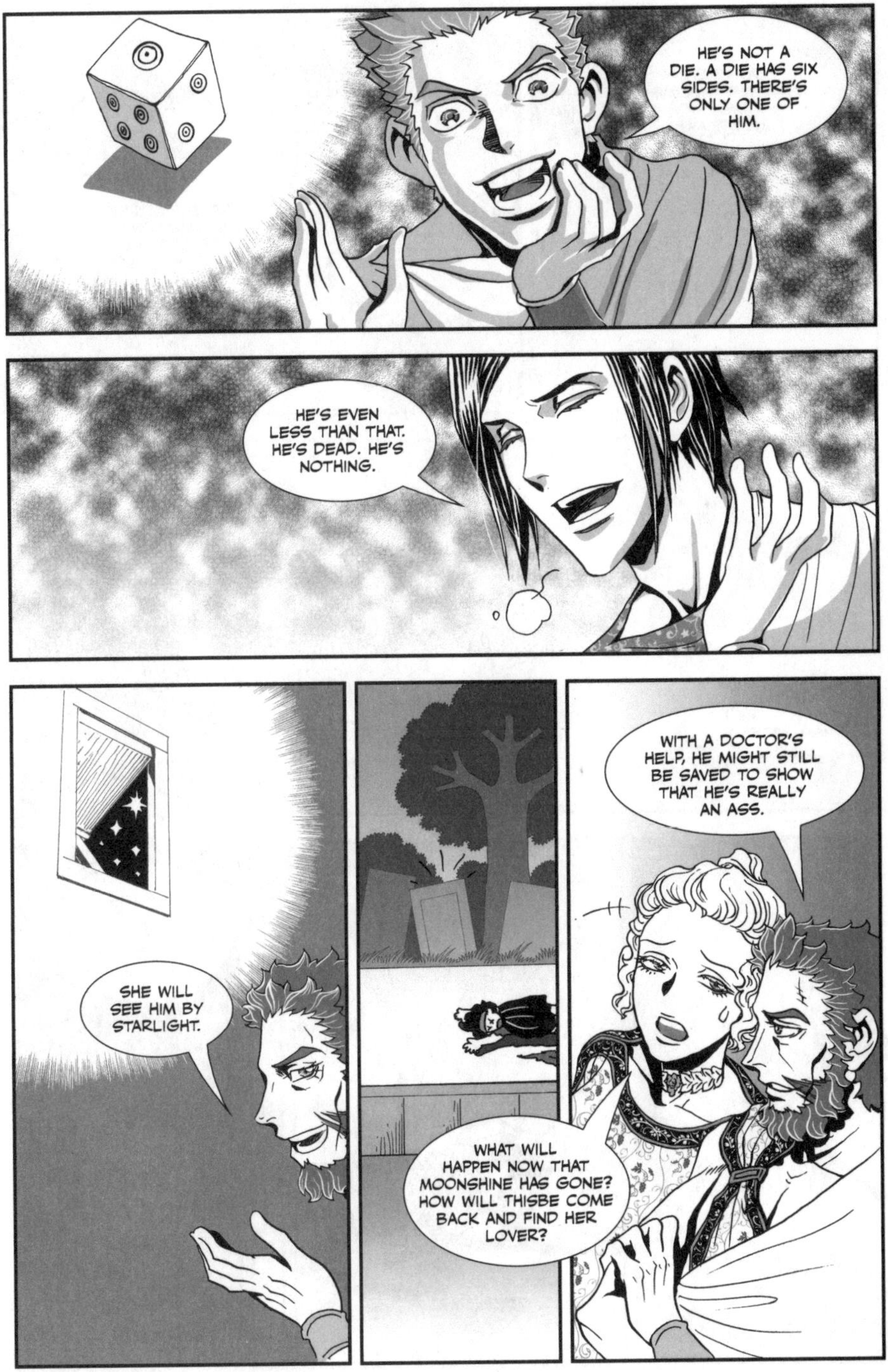
HE'S NOT A DIE. A DIE HAS SIX SIDES. THERE'S ONLY ONE OF HIM.
HE'S EVEN LESS THAN THAT. HE'S DEAD. HE'S NOTHING.
WITH A DOCTOR'S HELP, HE MIGHT STILL BE SAVED TO SHOW THAT HE'S REALLY AN ASS.
WHAT WILL HAPPEN NOW THAT MOONSHINE HAS GONE? HOW WILL THISBE COME BACK AND FIND HER LOVER?
SHE WILL SEE HIM BY STARLIGHT.

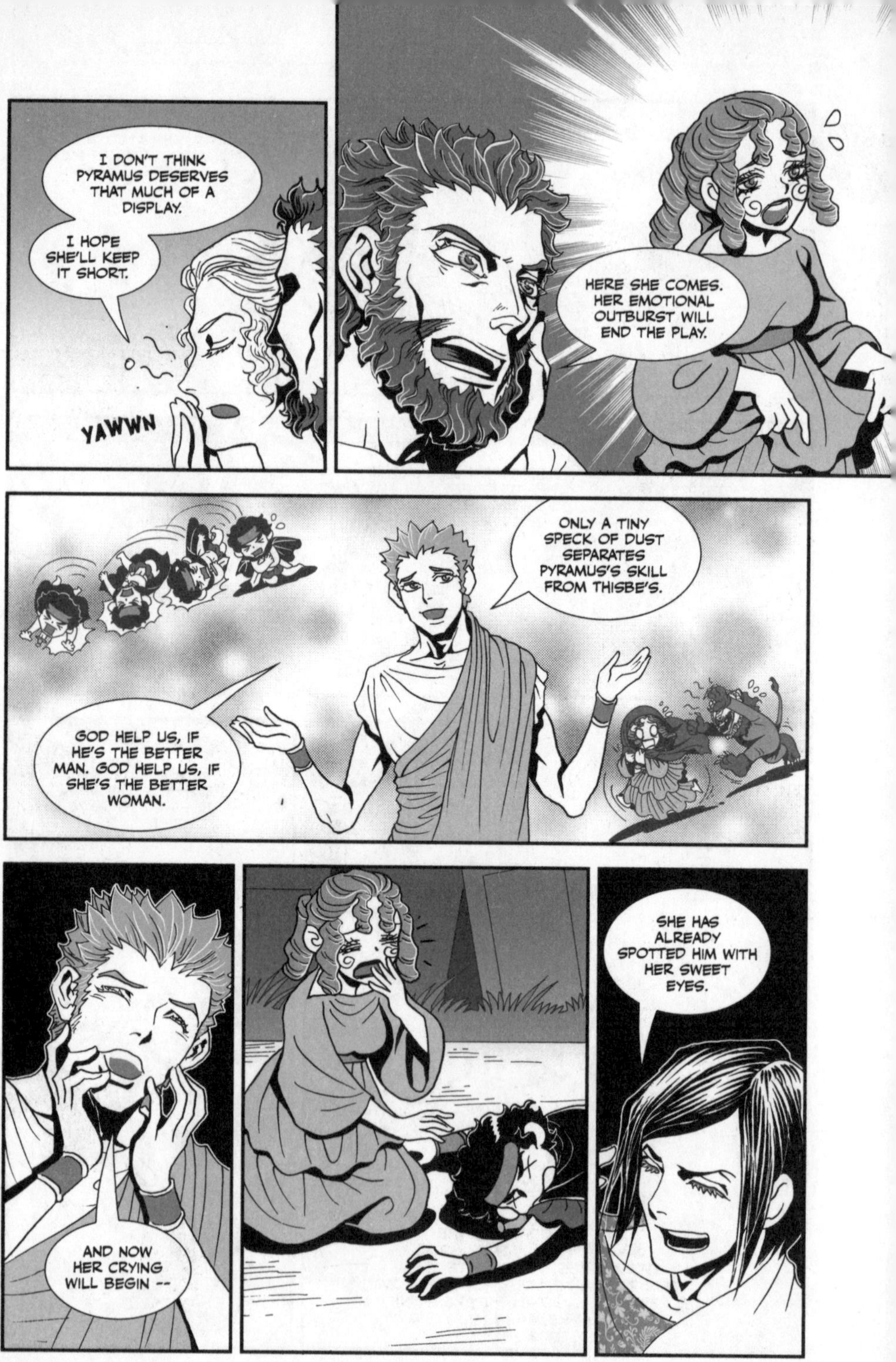
HERE SHE COMES. HER EMOTIONAL OUTBURST WILL END THE PLAY.
I DON'T THINK PYRAMUS DESERVES THAT MUCH OF A DISPLAY.
I HOPE SHE'LL KEEP IT SHORT.
YAWWN
ONLY A TINY SPECK OF DUST SEPARATES PYRAMUS'S SKILL FROM THISBE'S.
GOD HELP US, IF HE'S THE BETTER MAN. GOD HELP US, IF SHE'S THE BETTER WOMAN.
SHE HAS ALREADY SPOTTED HIM WITH HER SWEET EYES.
AND NOW HER CRYING WILL BEGIN --

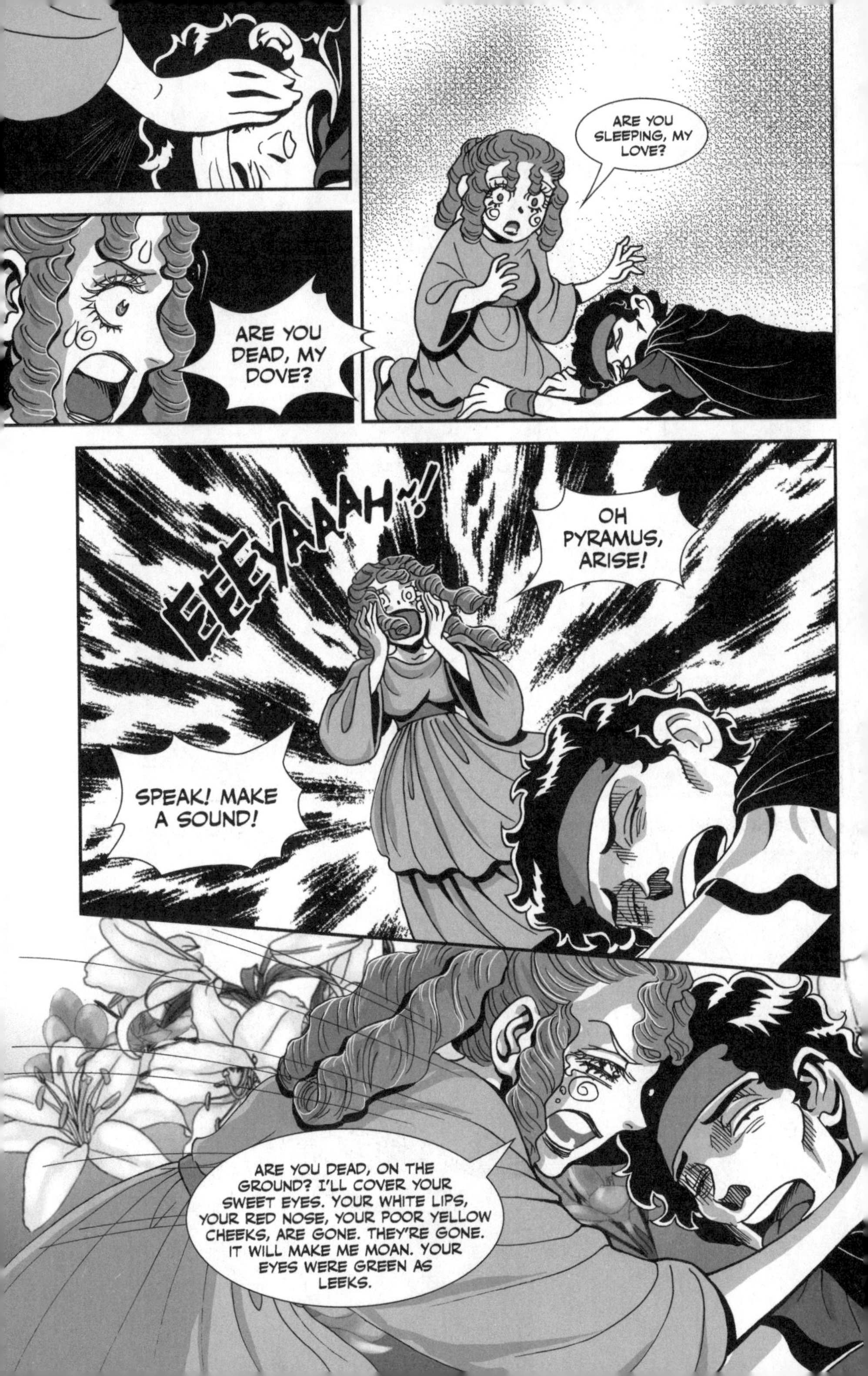
ARE YOU SLEEPING, MY LOVE?
ARE YOU DEAD, MY DOVE?
OH PYRAMUS, ARISE!
EEEYAAAH~!
SPEAK! MAKE A SOUND!
ARE YOU DEAD, ON THE GROUND? I'LL COVER YOUR SWEET EYES. YOUR WHITE LIPS, YOUR RED NOSE, YOUR POOR YELLOW CHEEKS, ARE GONE. THEY'RE GONE. IT WILL MAKE ME MOAN. YOUR EYES WERE GREEN AS LEEKS.

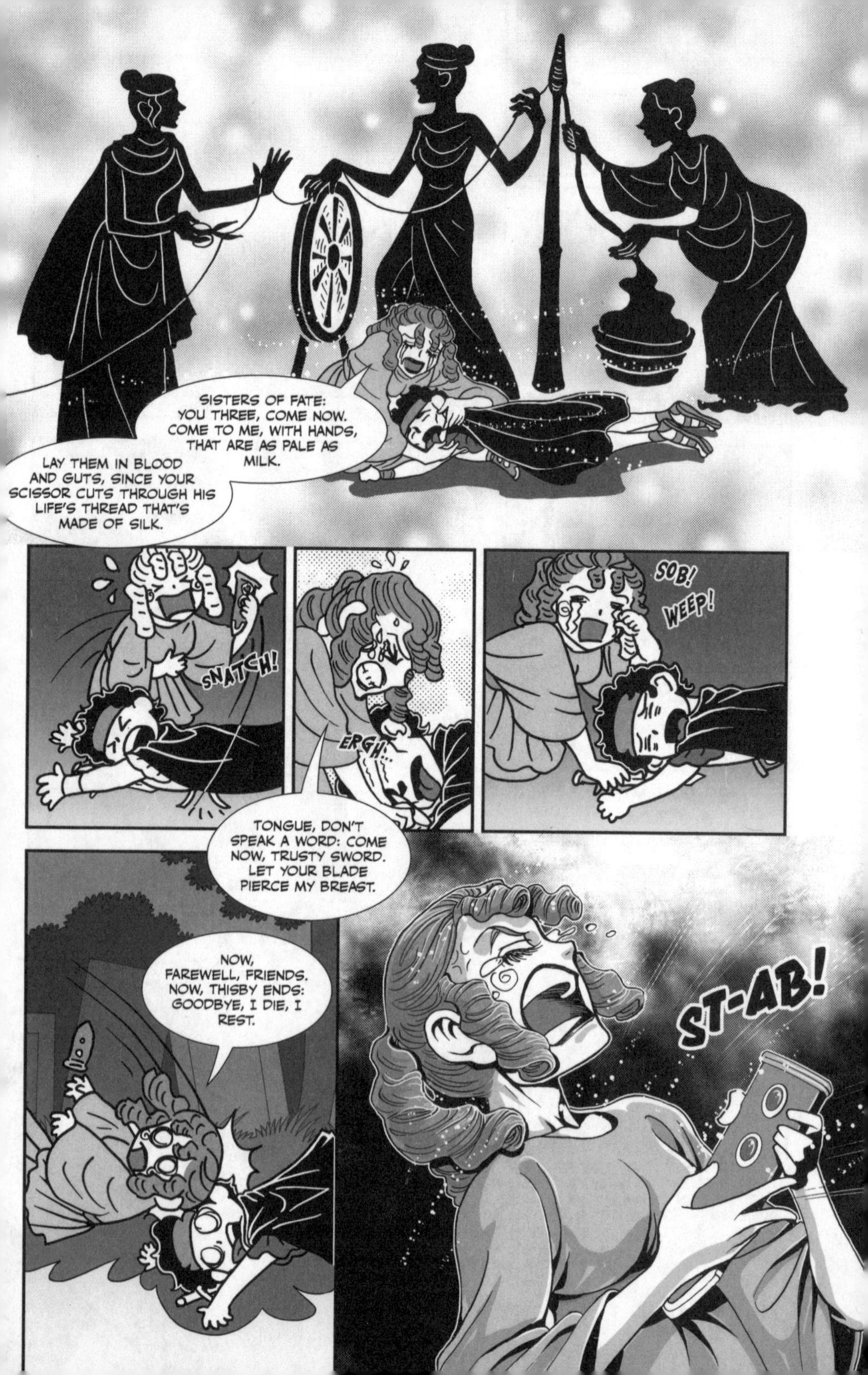
SISTERS OF FATE: YOU THREE, COME NOW. COME TO ME, WITH HANDS, THAT ARE AS PALE AS MILK.
LAY THEM IN BLOOD AND GUTS, SINCE YOUR SCISSOR CUTS THROUGH HIS LIFE'S THREAD THAT'S MADE OF SILK.
SOB!
WEEP!
ERGH...
TONGUE, DON'T SPEAK A WORD: COME NOW, TRUSTY SWORD. LET YOUR BLADE PIERCE MY BREAST.
SNATCH!
ST-AB!
NOW, FAREWELL, FRIENDS. NOW, THISBY ENDS: GOODBYE, I DIE, I REST.

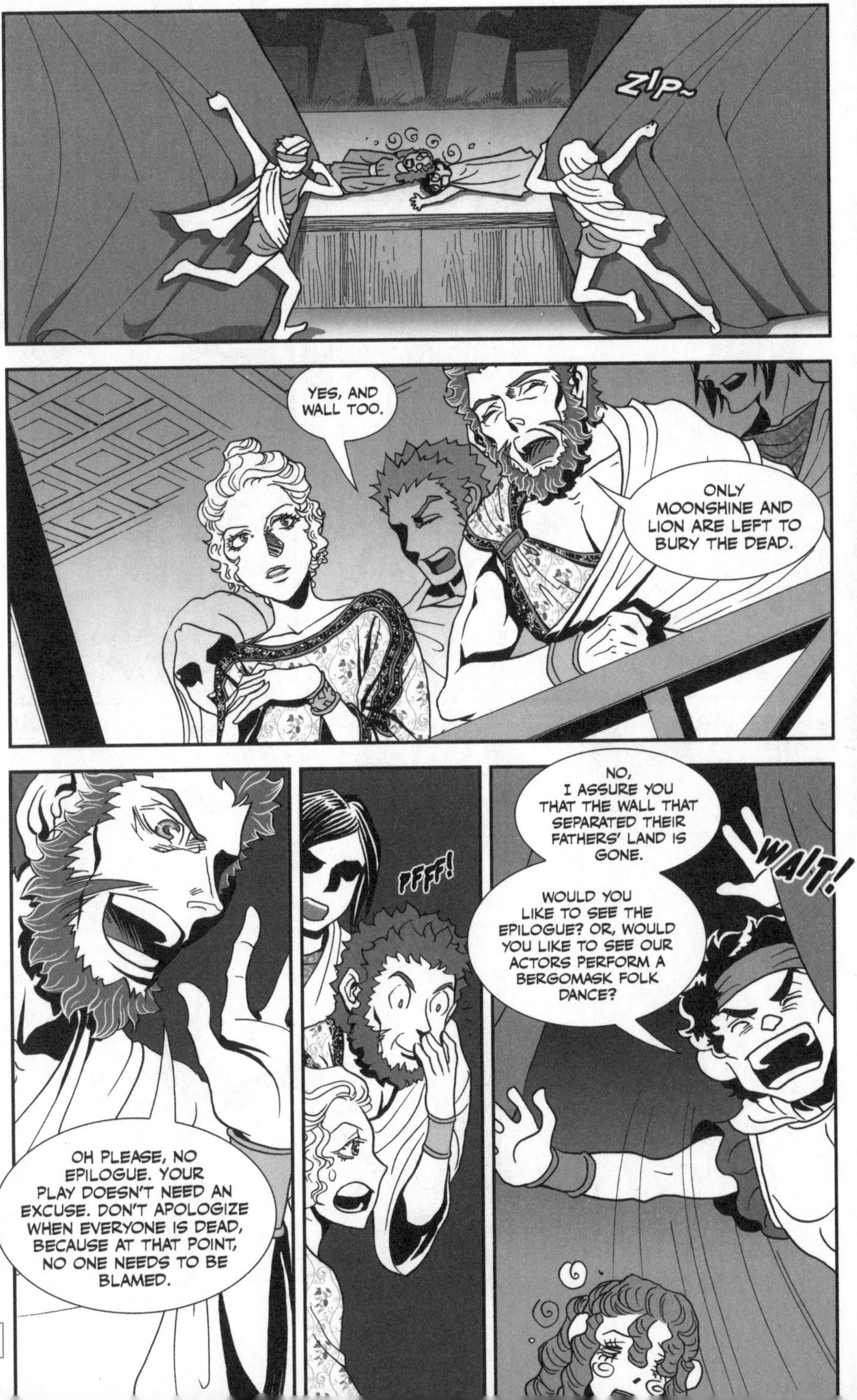
ZIP~
ONLY MOONSHINE AND LION ARE LEFT TO BURY THE DEAD.
YES, AND WALL TOO.
NO, I ASSURE YOU THAT THE WALL THAT SEPARATED THEIR FATHERS' LAND IS GONE.
WAIT!
WOULD YOU LIKE TO SEE THE EPILOGUE? OR, WOULD YOU LIKE TO SEE OUR ACTORS PERFORM A BERGOMASK FOLK DANCE?
PFFF!
OH PLEASE, NO EPILOGUE. YOUR PLAY DOESN'T NEED AN EXCUSE. DON'T APOLOGIZE WHEN EVERYONE IS DEAD, BECAUSE AT THAT POINT, NO ONE NEEDS TO BE BLAMED.

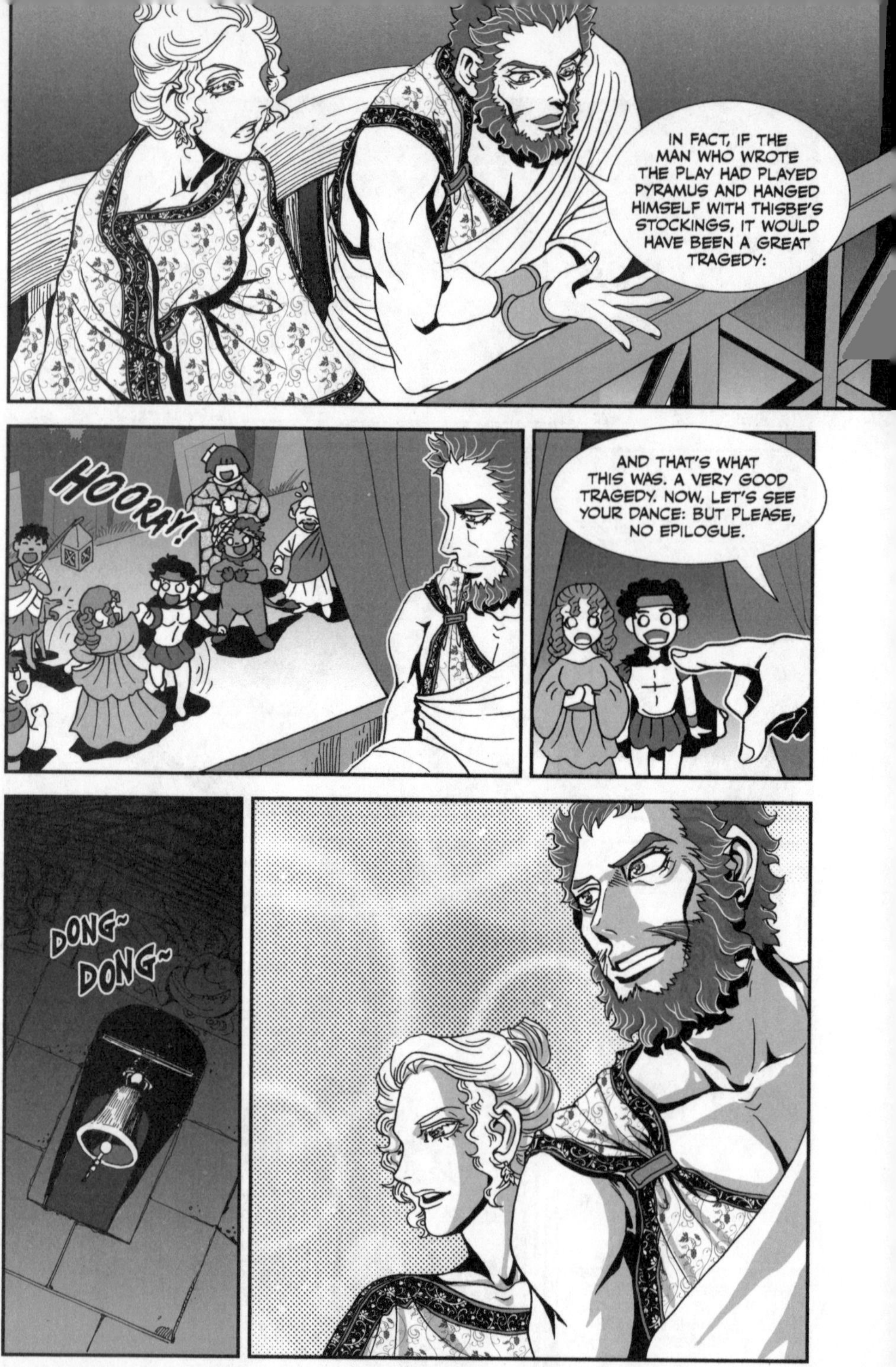
IN FACT, IF THE MAN WHO WROTE THE PLAY HAD PLAYED PYRAMUS AND HANGED HIMSELF WITH THISBE'S STOCKINGS, IT WOULD HAVE BEEN A GREAT TRAGEDY:
AND THAT'S WHAT THIS WAS. A VERY GOOD TRAGEDY. NOW, LET'S SEE YOUR DANCE: BUT PLEASE, NO EPILOGUE.
HOORAY!
DONG~
DONG~

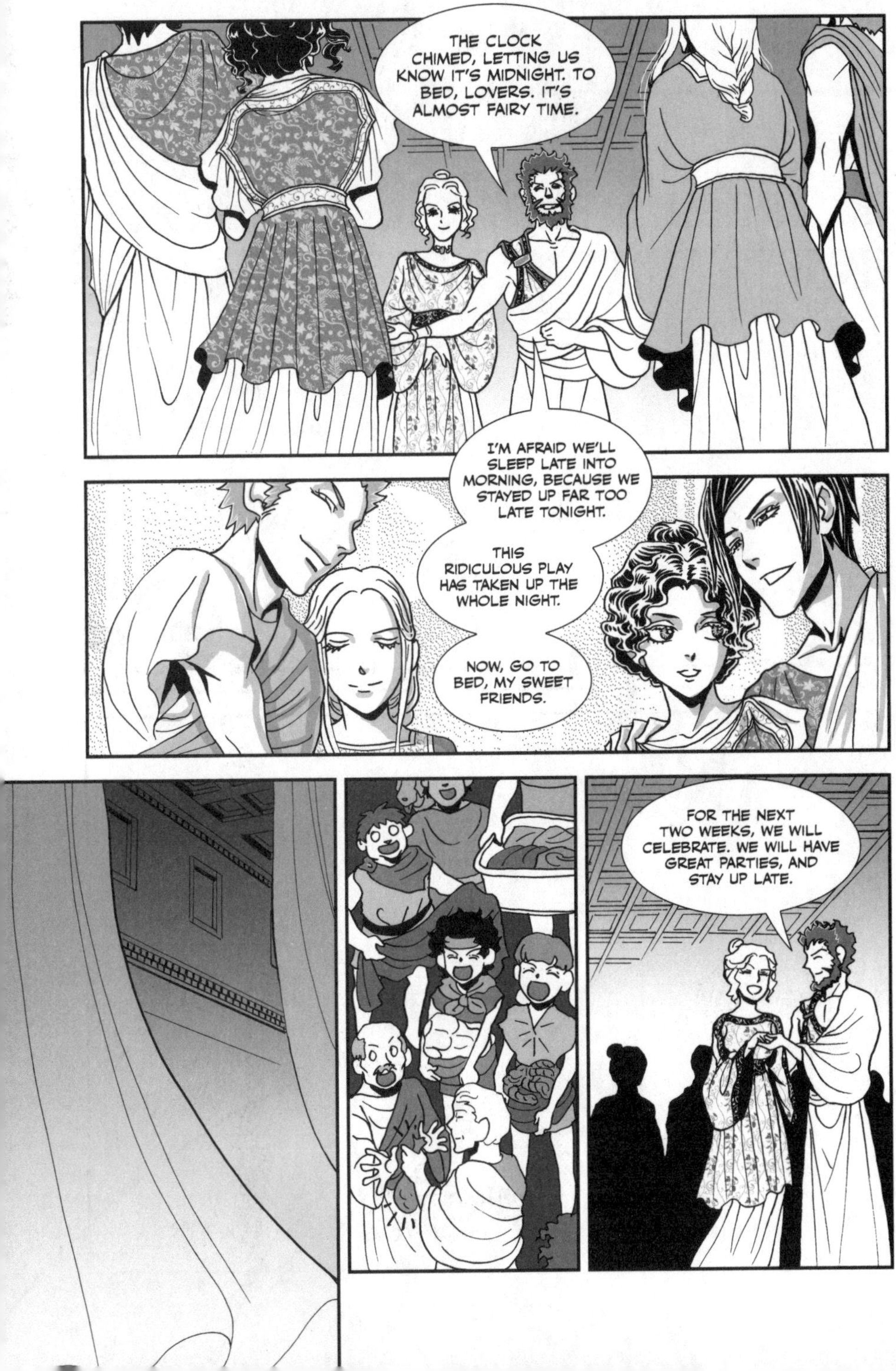
THE CLOCK CHIMED, LETTING US KNOW IT'S MIDNIGHT. TO BED, LOVERS. IT'S ALMOST FAIRY TIME.
I'M AFRAID WE'LL SLEEP LATE INTO MORNING, BECAUSE WE STAYED UP FAR TOO LATE TONIGHT.
THIS RIDICULOUS PLAY HAS TAKEN UP THE WHOLE NIGHT.
NOW, GO TO BED, MY SWEET FRIENDS.
FOR THE NEXT TWO WEEKS, WE WILL CELEBRATE. WE WILL HAVE GREAT PARTIES, AND STAY UP LATE.

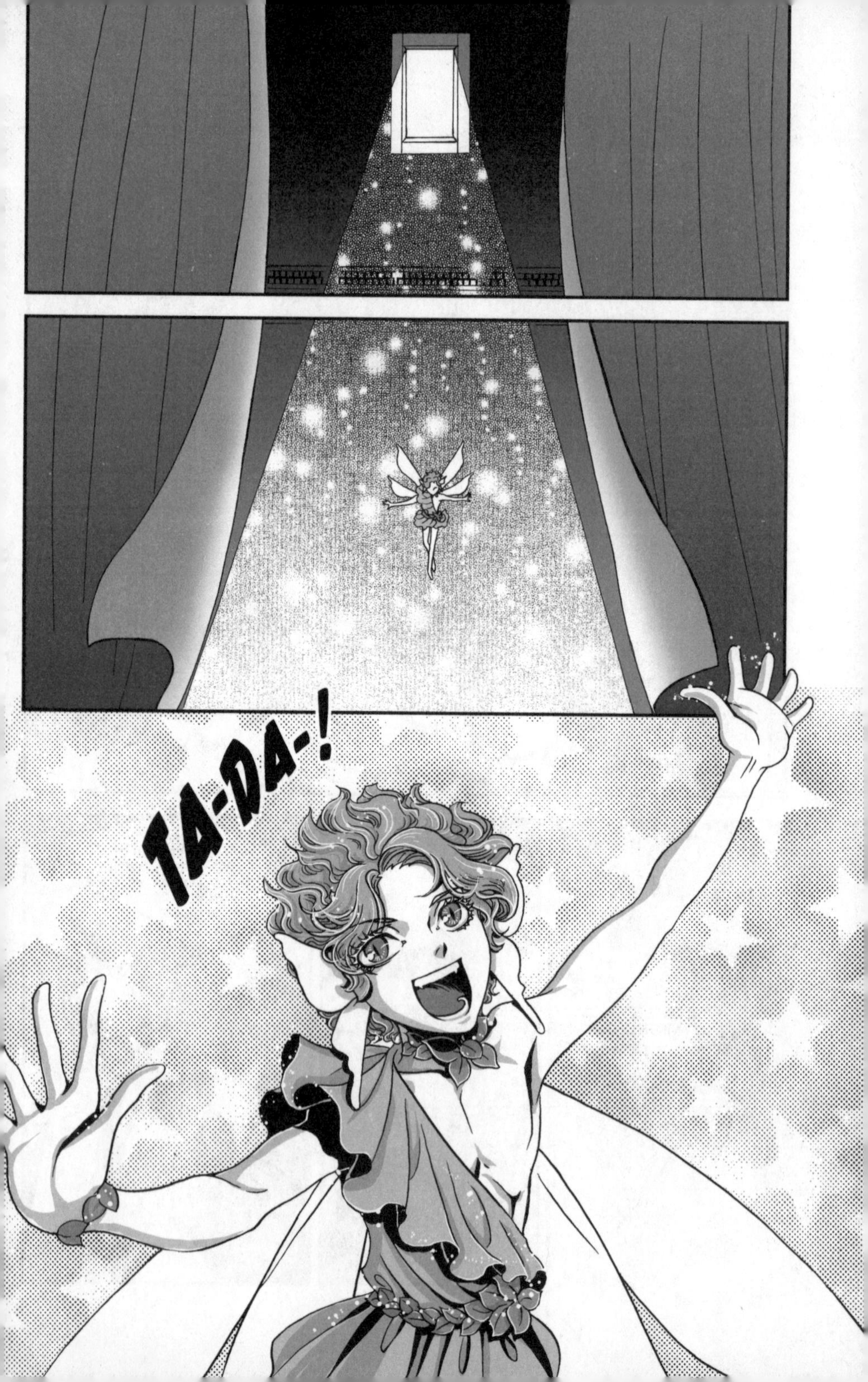
TA-DA-!

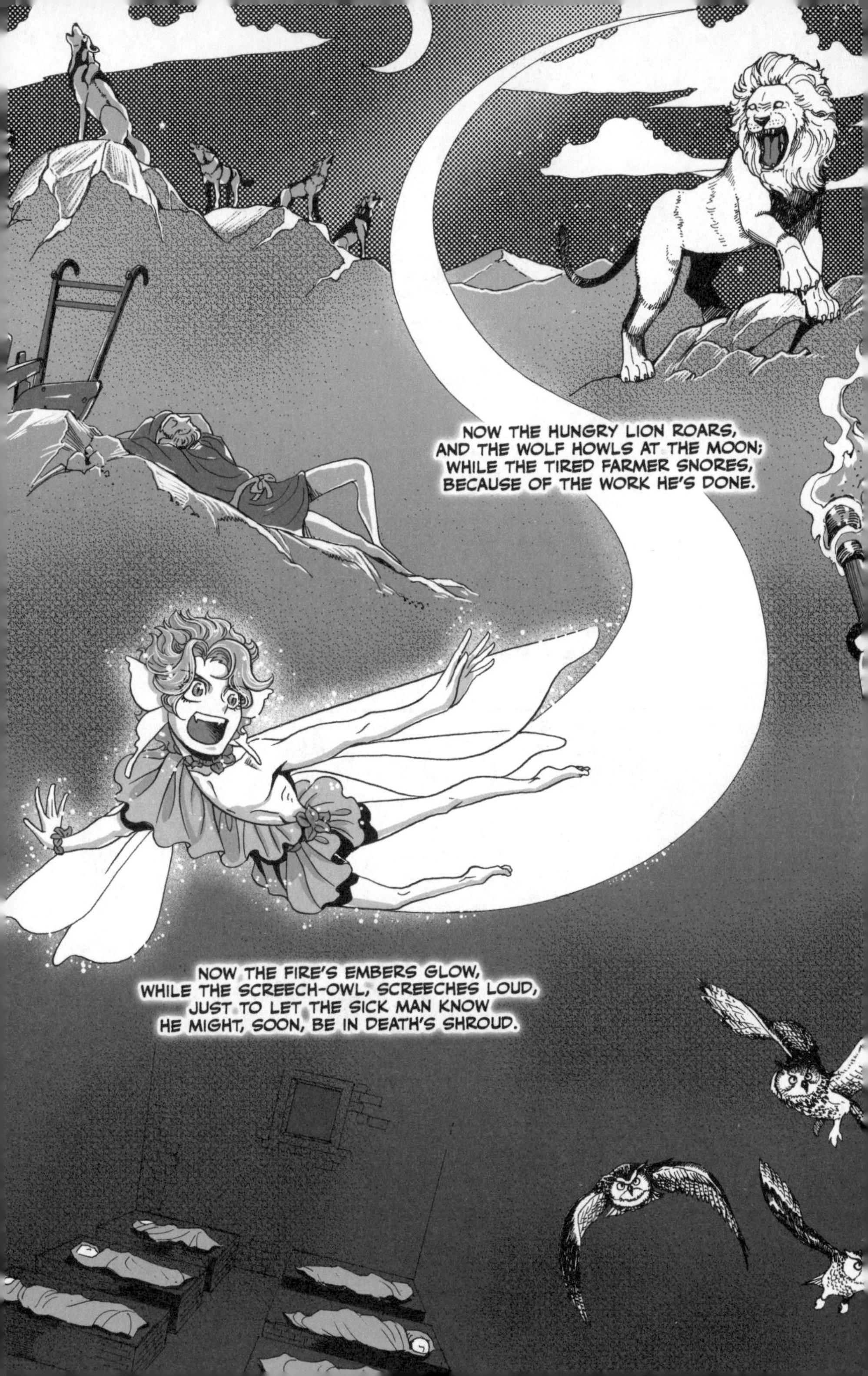
NOW THE HUNGRY LION ROARS,
AND THE WOLF HOWLS AT THE MOON;
WHILE THE TIRED FARMER SNORES,
BECAUSE OF THE WORK HE'S DONE.
NOW THE FIRE'S EMBERS GLOW,
WHILE THE SCREECH-OWL, SCREECHES LOUD,
JUST TO LET THE SICK MAN KNOW
HE MIGHT, SOON, BE IN DEATH'S SHROUD.

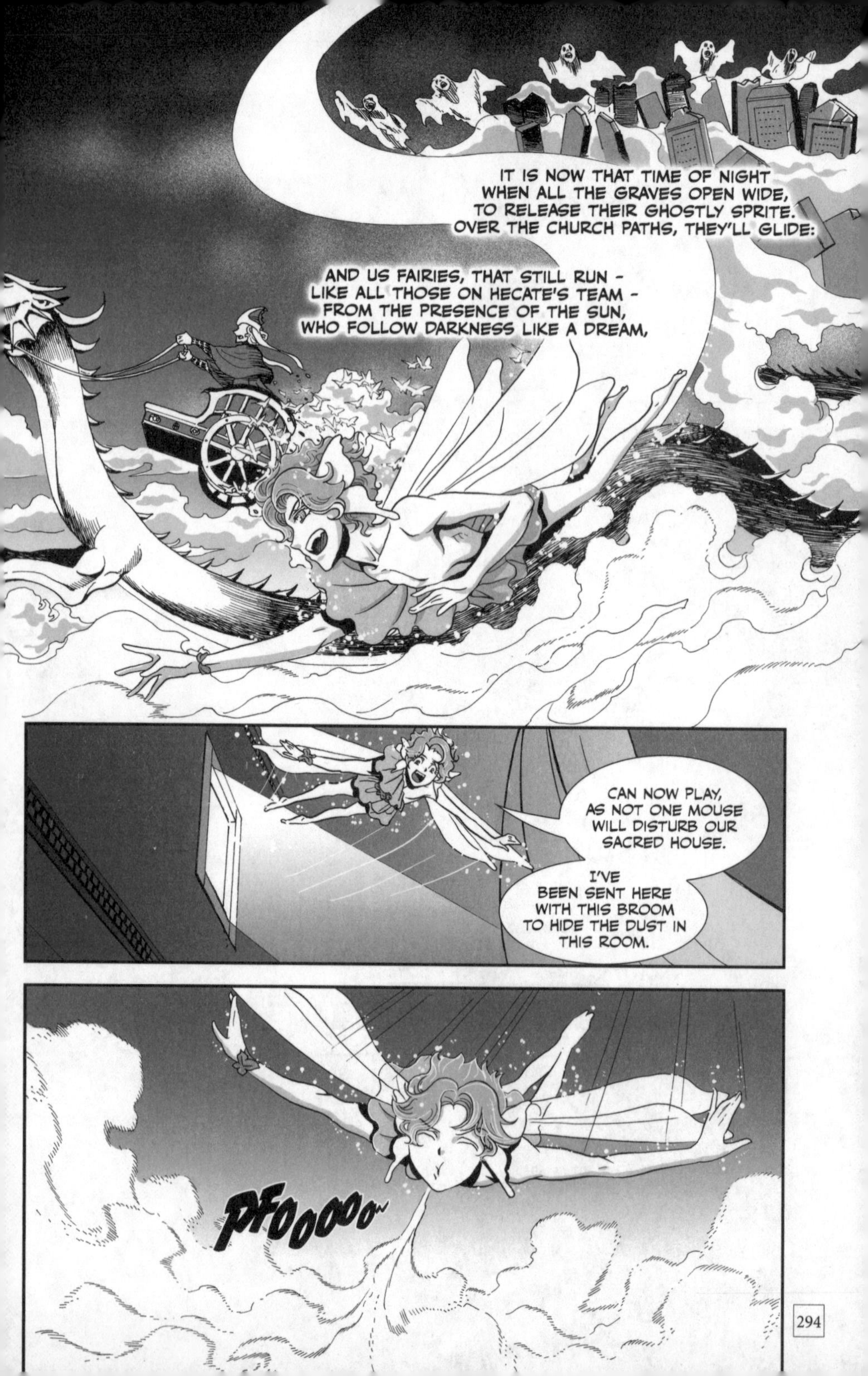
IT IS NOW THAT TIME OF NIGHT
WHEN ALL THE GRAVES OPEN WIDE,
TO RELEASE THEIR GHOSTLY SPRITE.
OVER THE CHURCH PATHS, THEY'LL GLIDE:
AND US FAIRIES, THAT STILL RUN -
LIKE ALL THOSE ON HECATE'S TEAM -
FROM THE PRESENCE OF THE SUN,
WHO FOLLOW DARKNESS LIKE A DREAM,
CAN NOW PLAY,
AS NOT ONE MOUSE
WILL DISTURB OUR
SACRED HOUSE.
I'VE
BEEN SENT HERE
WITH THIS BROOM
TO HIDE THE DUST IN
THIS ROOM.
PFOOOOO

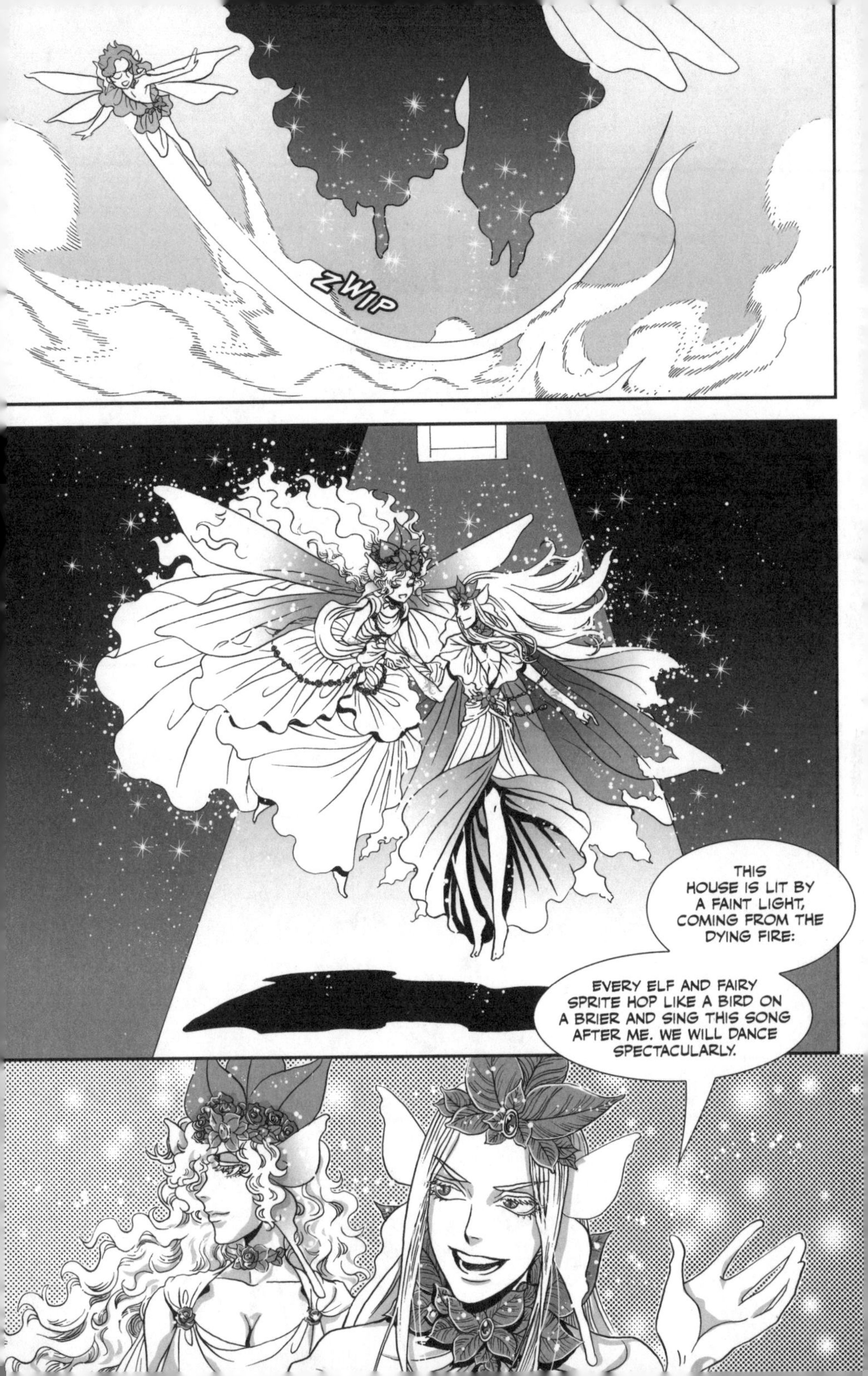
ZWIP
THIS HOUSE IS LIT BY A FAINT LIGHT, COMING FROM THE DYING FIRE:
EVERY ELF AND FAIRY SPRITE HOP LIKE A BIRD ON A BRIER AND SING THIS SONG AFTER ME. WE WILL DANCE SPECTACULARLY.

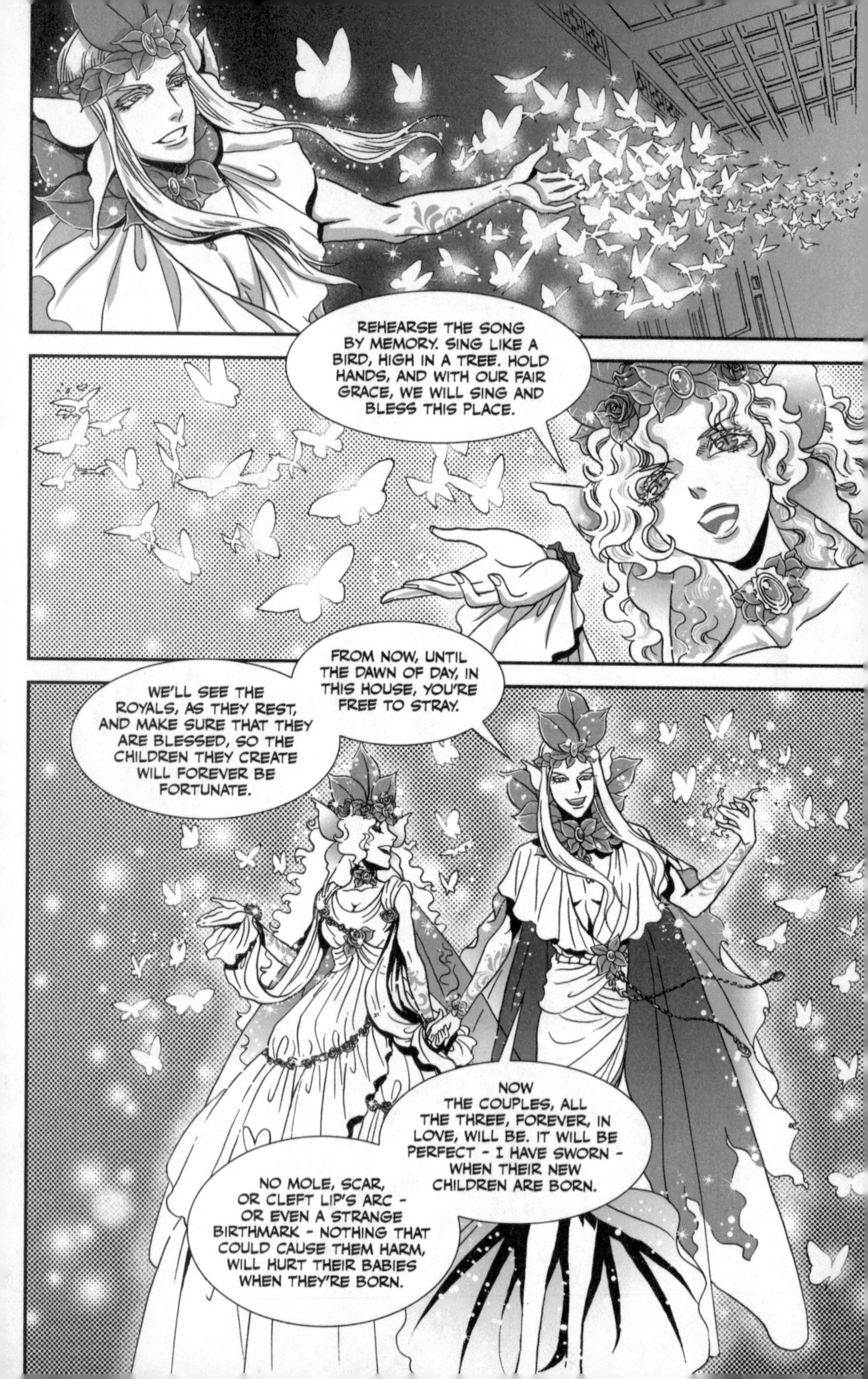
REHEARSE THE SONG BY MEMORY. SING LIKE A BIRD, HIGH IN A TREE. HOLD HANDS, AND WITH OUR FAIR GRACE, WE WILL SING AND BLESS THIS PLACE.
FROM NOW, UNTIL THE DAWN OF DAY, IN THIS HOUSE, YOU'RE FREE TO STRAY.
WE'LL SEE THE ROYALS, AS THEY REST, AND MAKE SURE THAT THEY ARE BLESSED, SO THE CHILDREN THEY CREATE WILL FOREVER BE FORTUNATE.
NOW THE COUPLES, ALL THE THREE, FOREVER, IN LOVE, WILL BE. IT WILL BE PERFECT - I HAVE SWORN - WHEN THEIR NEW CHILDREN ARE BORN.
NO MOLE, SCAR, OR CLEFT LIP'S ARC - OR EVEN A STRANGE BIRTHMARK - NOTHING THAT COULD CAUSE THEM HARM, WILL HURT THEIR BABIES WHEN THEY'RE BORN.

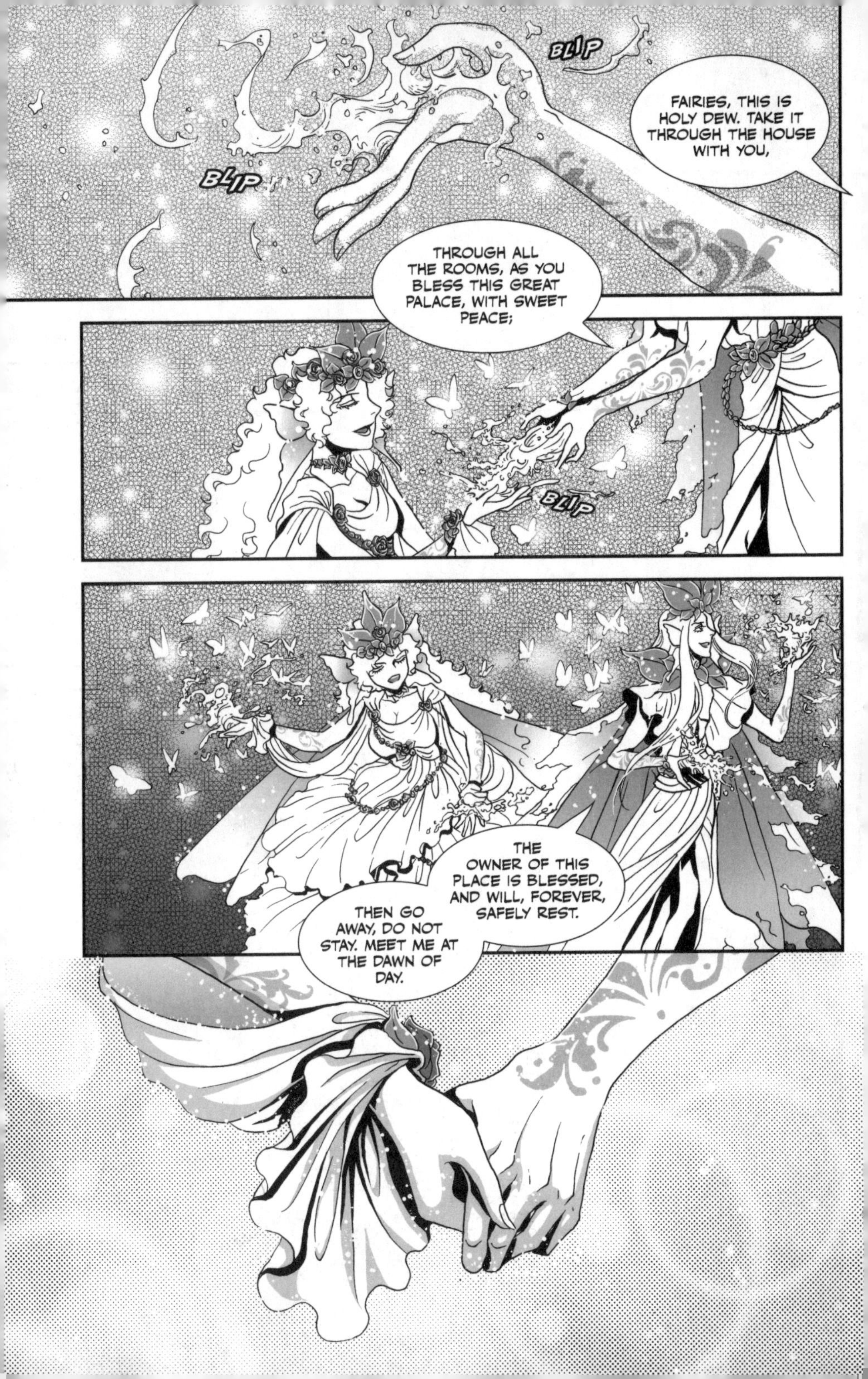
BLIP
FAIRIES, THIS IS HOLY DEW. TAKE IT THROUGH THE HOUSE WITH YOU,
BLIP
THROUGH ALL THE ROOMS, AS YOU BLESS THIS GREAT PALACE, WITH SWEET PEACE;
BLIP
THE OWNER OF THIS PLACE IS BLESSED, AND WILL, FOREVER, SAFELY REST.
THEN GO AWAY, DO NOT STAY. MEET ME AT THE DAWN OF DAY.

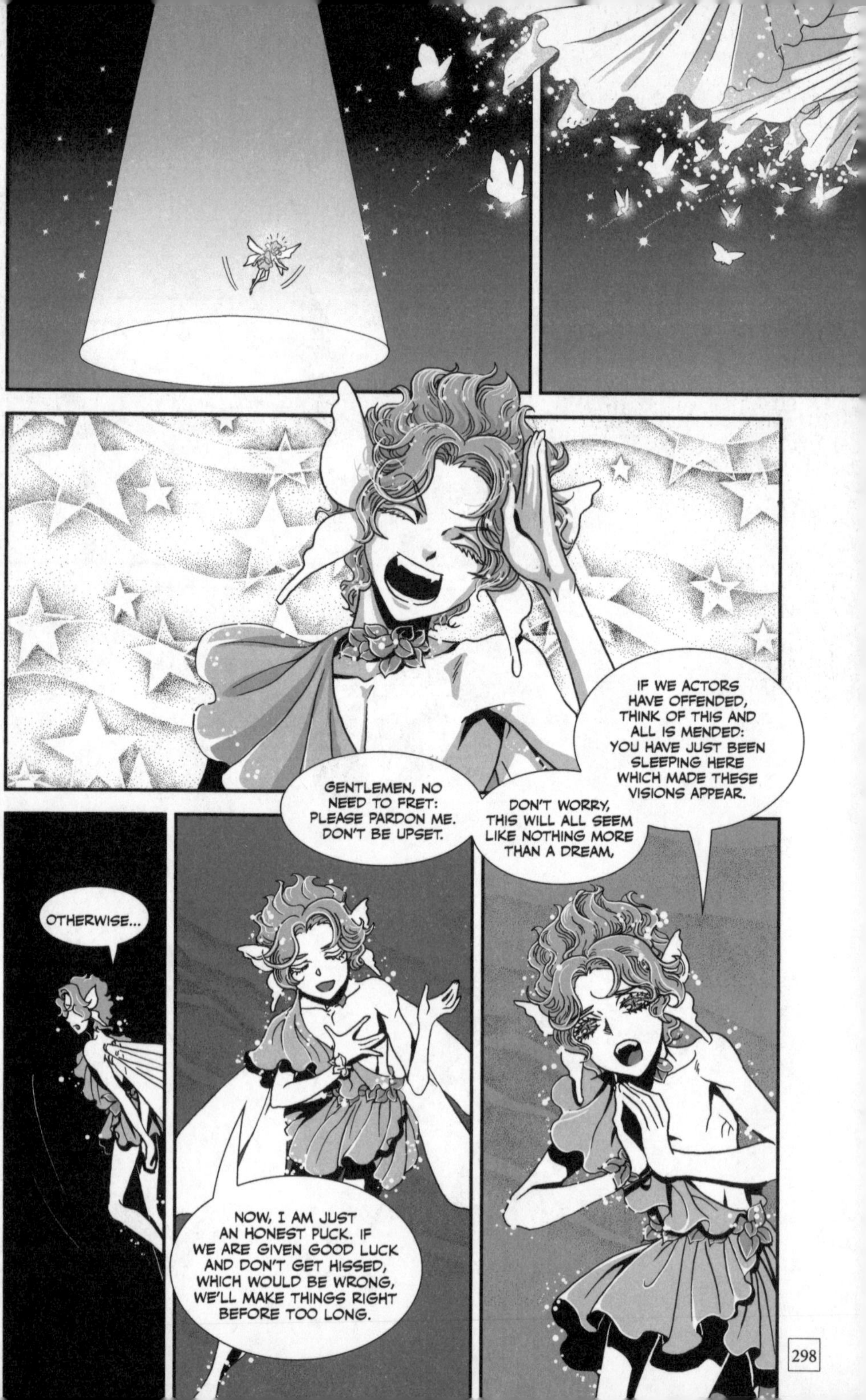
IF WE ACTORS HAVE OFFENDED, THINK OF THIS AND ALL IS MENDED: YOU HAVE JUST BEEN SLEEPING HERE WHICH MADE THESE VISIONS APPEAR.
DON'T WORRY, THIS WILL ALL SEEM LIKE NOTHING MORE THAN A DREAM,
GENTLEMEN, NO NEED TO FRET: PLEASE PARDON ME. DON'T BE UPSET.
NOW, I AM JUST AN HONEST PUCK. IF WE ARE GIVEN GOOD LUCK AND DON'T GET HISSED, WHICH WOULD BE WRONG, WE'LL MAKE THINGS RIGHT BEFORE TOO LONG.
OTHERWISE...

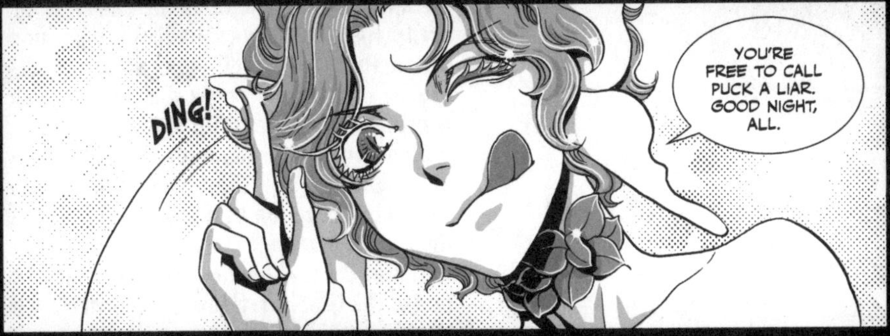
YOU'RE FREE TO CALL PUCK A LIAR. GOOD NIGHT, ALL.
DING!

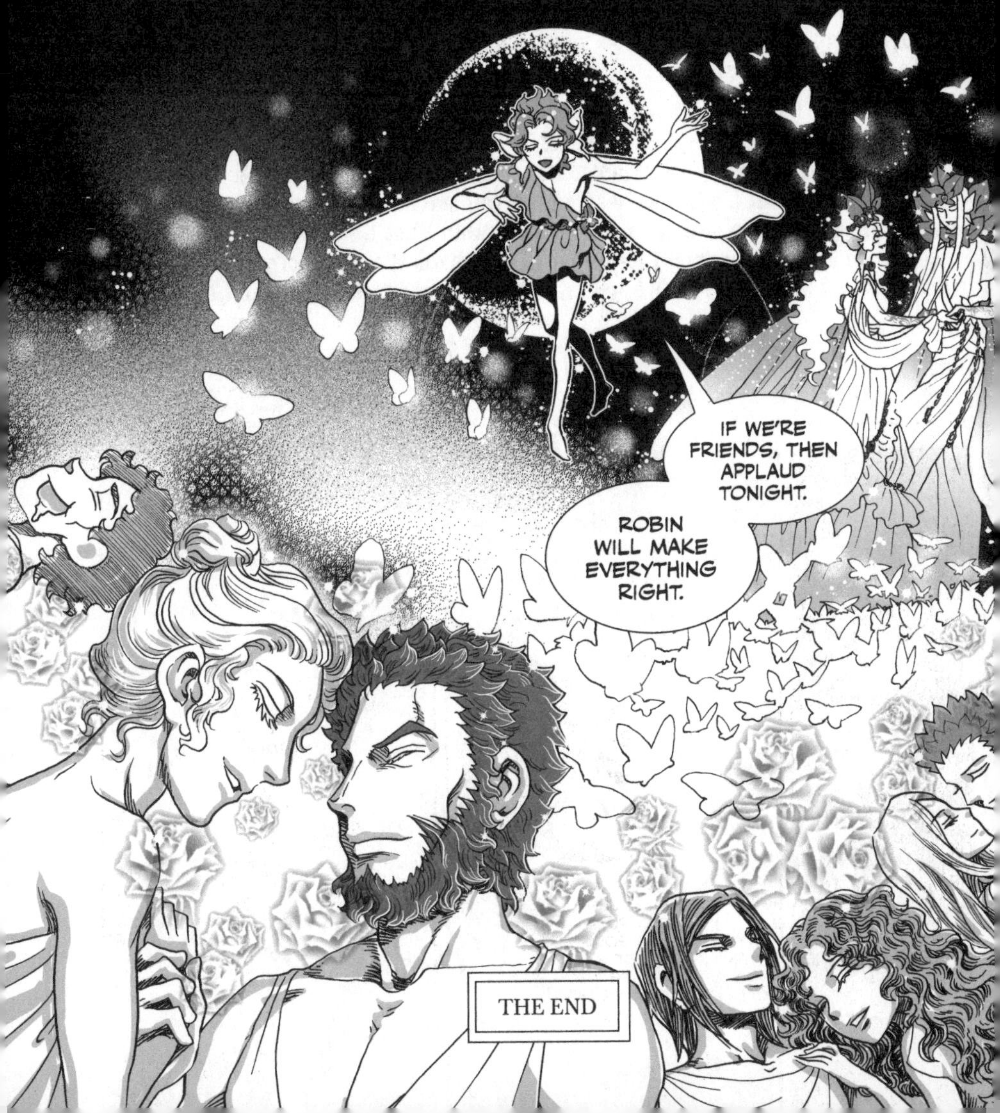
IF WE'RE FRIENDS, THEN APPLAUD TONIGHT.
ROBIN WILL MAKE EVERYTHING RIGHT.
THE END

EARLY BOTTOM DESIGNS

Speaking of Bottom, he is the classic 'fool' archetype. You have to admire his passion for acting (although his actual skills are in question - where did he get such confidence?!) At least he did a spectacular job during the banquet performance, entertaining all the guests with his emotional reaction to his beloved Thisby's death. (Also, it might be interesting to note that the donkey-headed Bottom might be one of the first 'furry' love stories in classic literature!)

Other characters - like the morally-ambiguous Oberon, the brave Hermia, and the self-sacrificing Helena - all remain very memorable to me. I hope you enjoy how I handled them in the manga!

Once again, I wish to thank all my comrades who helped in the production of this book. The team improves with every title. I especially want to thank Julien Choi and Mr. Kuma for their generous help in critical moments! And, last but not least, I wish to say 'thank you' to my dear Jessica, who has been supporting me behind the scenes for all these years. Without her love and encouragement, I would not have been able to have my career as an artist. Of course, I also want to say 'thank you' to all of you readers, who are supporting our books! Let's hope we cross paths again soon - in another book!

Po Tse

EARLY CONCEPT ART

FROM THE ARTIST:

Hello, everyone!

I am so happy that I was able to work on another **Manga Classics** title. I switched from Jane Austen to another master of British literature: the great William Shakespeare himself! It is such an honor to be involved with turning the famous comedy *A Midsummer Night's Dream* into manga. It feels like only yesterday that I started working on Manga Classics titles, but this is my fourth one already! I hope everyone likes what I've done so far.

Although *A Midsummer Night's Dream* is considered to be a light-hearted comedy, it's actually fairly complex - three different social classes (royalty, peasantry, and fairies) all crossing paths in a single, magical night and sharing the same big, messy 'dream'. After the story ends, all of them seem to have found a new perspective on love and relationships!

While I don't have the time - or the space - to talk about everyone in the book, I want to share my opinions on some of my favorites:

Everyone knows that Puck is the most popular character in *A Midsummer Night's Dream*. This little fairy is very powerful and mischievous - and his recklessness causes so much trouble! He's always laughing about the chaos he creates, even laughing at Titania herself after he makes her fall in love with a donkey-headed man. Although his actions are definitely not praise-worthy, it's those same actions that link all the characters together. I made sure to always depict him as energetic and happy-go-lucky - no matter how much of a mess he creates, he's always confident that he can fix everything with his magical powers. Come to think of it, Puck is probably the most powerful of the fairies!

Because of my own personal preferences, I put a lot of effort into drawing Titania, the fairy queen. I've always loved her character. When designing her, I made sure she looked both majestic and romantic; her attire is a little 'out of this world', and her floral accessories combine with the flowing sheerness of her costume to give her a connection to nature and the woods. Titania is probably the most honorable of all the characters, unconditionally loving everyone she holds dear, from her adopted child to the ill-fated Bottom! Even though that sequence is meant to be funny, I still find it tragic.

EARLY DESIGNS OF TITANIA, OBERON, AND PUCK

MATCHING THE ACTIONS TO THE DIALOGUE:

In Shakespeare's plays, there are very few stage instructions provided beyond entrances and exits - only the dialogue was considered important enough to write down. It falls to the director and the actors to decide how the characters should act. When it came to adapting the play for the manga version, therefore, it was my job to provide these instructions to the artist, based on the dialogue and the emotions of the characters.

For example: in Act 2, Scene 1, Demetrius is furious with Helena for tagging along and importuning him. He threatens her by saying, "But I shall do thee mischief in the wood." I used the classic Japanese 'kabedon' action for Demetrius - making him slap his hand against the tree next to her head - to reinforce the idea that he is threatening Helena. Isn't that a more expressive way to show the threat?

ECHOING THE CHARACTERS' EMOTIONS IN THE SCENE:

In addition to showing the characters' actions, I also asked the artist to match the artwork to the characters' emotions. Like in Act 2, Scene 2, Helena is heartbroken after Demetrius abandons her. She envies Hermia's beauty, believing herself to be ugly. Since she was already in the wood, I suggested that we should add a stream to allow her to see her own reflection in the water. When Helena says, "For she hath blessed and attractive eyes," I let her look at the imaginary Hermia in the water with jealousy; when she says, "No, no, I am as ugly as a bear," I had her splash the water in her hatred, demonstrating that she was upset and didn't want to see her own reflection in the water anymore.

Continues on Page 3...

CRYSTAL S. CHAN: ADAPTING A MIDSUMMER NIGHT'S DREAM

EDITOR'S NOTE: These adaptation notes are from the [ORIGINAL TEXT EDITION], therefore the dialogue qouted here are from the original text.

A Midsummer Night's Dream **is one of Shakespeare's most acclaimed comedies, a well-known play. As the readers can well imagine, I needed to make adjustments to the original script to make it better suited to the manga format. At the same time, however, I could put the strengths of the manga format to good use, in order to create an accurate version of the original play. Let me take this opportunity to show you how I create these adaptations.**

EXPRESSING THE FIGURATIVE LANGUAGE THROUGH ART:

Shakespeare often used figurative language (such as metaphors) in his dialogue, to better express the thoughts and feelings of the characters. In the play, these figures of speech could only be expressed by the actors and actresses speaking the words aloud. In the manga version, however, we could use the artwork to our advantage - we could show the reader these things in every panel, making it easier to understand the dialogue.

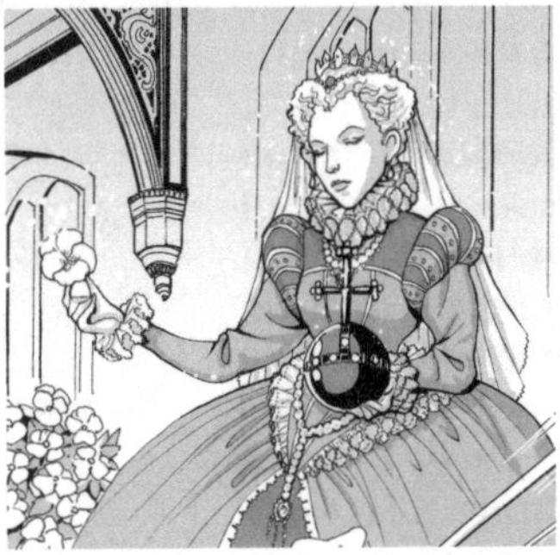

In Act 2, Scene 1, Oberon refers to "a fair vestal throned by the west". Many critics believe that this line refers to Queen Elizabeth I, Shakespeare's patron. I suggested that the artist draw the queen in the corresponding panel.

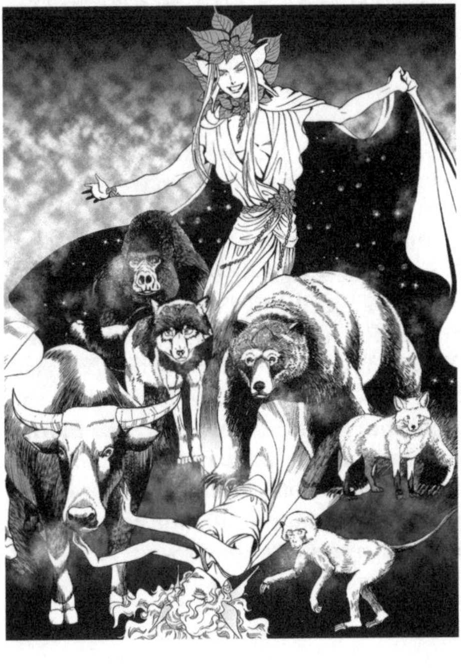

In Act 2, Scene 2, Oberon says, "Be it ounce or cat or bear / Pard or boar with bristled hair". I suggested that the artist should include all of these animals on that page, and make them look wicked and vile, to show that Oberon's plan to make Titania fall in love with animals is also wicked!

Later on, Helena's line "Wings and no eyes figure unheedy haste: and therefore is Love said to be a child" also refers to Cupid, so I suggested that we should combine the two things together. We ended up with the statue of Cupid drawn as a naughty little boy, trying to tease Helena with his bow and arrow. We borrowed ideas from each other, trying our best to tell the story in a playful way that also made good use of the background we designed together.

MANGA'S UNIQUE STORYTELLING ABILITIES:

One of the most well-known classic plot twists in *A Midsummer Night's Dream* is the plight of poor Bottom, who gets turned into a donkey by Puck's magic. The original play called for Bottom's actor to wear a donkey mask - but in the manga version we were free to be as creative as we liked, so we decided to turn

Bottom into a donkey from head to toe, even giving him a long, wagging tail. When he says, "Methinks I have a great desire to a bottle of hay," we gave him the hay!

A FEMINIST NOTE:

When I was working on this adaptation, I couldn't help but feel sympathy for Hermia. Not only did she have no right to decide who to marry, she had to obey her father's order to marry someone she did not love - or else be prosecuted! Wouldn't her fate have been a tragedy, if she hadn't taken that magical journey into the forest? When I talked about this with the artist, I asked him to show Hermia's father behaving unreasonably, in order to help the readers understand that Hermia is a victim of patriarchal society. I hope that some day things like this will only happen in stories; everyone should have the right to marry the ones they love.

In conclusion, we adapted the manuscript of Shakespeare's play for manga without adding or deleting a single line, which took a lot of effort. It was worth it in the end. I hope that the reader will not only gain a better understanding of the original play through this adaptation, but also become more interested in the other Shakespeare books from *Manga Classics*.

Crystal (Silvermoon) Chan

...continued from Page 2

SPECIAL INSTRUCTIONS BASED ON THE STORY:

Although stage directions would have been provided to the actors in the original play, these weren't sufficient for the artist. Therefore, when I worked on the adaptation, I needed to fill in the gaps. Take Act 2, Scene 2 as an example. When Hermia and Lysander are about to go to sleep, Hermia says, "So far be distant," implying that they did not sleep next to each other. Therefore, I reminded the artist to pay attention to the distance between them. But, then, how far apart should they be? That distance would be important to the story later. In Act 3, Scene 2, Lysander, whose eyes had been enchanted by Puck's magic spell, fell in love with Helena the moment he woke up. If Hermia had been sleeping very close by, she absolutely should

have overheard Lysander telling Helena that he loved her - and Helena rejecting him! However, since they were sleeping in the forest and were in danger of being attacked by wild animals, Lysander certainly wouldn't have let Hermia sleep too far away. Therefore, when I gave the script to the artist, I explained my reasoning and let him make the judgment on the distance.

WORKING WITH THE ARTIST:

I mentioned earlier that I wanted to visualize the figurative language in the panels. It really inspired both of us, and sparked our creativity to do so. In Act 1, Scene 1, when Hermia says, "By Cupid's strongest bow, by his best arrow with the golden head," I recommended that the artist draw Cupid in the background. Not only did he agree with me, he also suggested that we should add a statue of Cupid to the decorations when we were designing the palace of Theseus. I thought this was a pretty good idea.

THE MECHANICALS

These guys are good old salt of the Earth Athenians. They labour in shops, they fix tools, they build things, they work hard. They're the labourers who keep the city going. But, even they can create something as wonderful as a play to perform for the Duke.

They don't need to cloud their speech with fancy syllable counts, or enchanted rhyming couplets. They just say what they mean, even if what they mean gets mixed up from time to time.

At the end of the day, these guys mean well. And that's important. They go out there, they do their best, and they're overjoyed by the entire experience. They know they're wonderful, even if others may doubt them. Honestly, who doesn't love Bottom?

MAKING IT SPECIAL:

As I translated this play, I paid close attention to syllable count, rhyme scheme, and the lack thereof. When Shakespeare rhymed, he did it with intent. When he stopped rhyming, that was intentional too. The challenge with this play is that it often combines three unique elements for translation: Modern language, iambic pentameter, and rhyme scheme. When all three come together, there are a number of limitations on how ideas and concepts can be expressed. Still, line by line, and rhyme by rhyme, I ensured that a modern audience could appreciate not only the text, but also the form that Shakespeare intended.

When I finally made it to the tale of Pyramus and Thisby (A little like Romeo and Juliet, isn't it?) everything changed. Those sonnets were written by The Mechanicals, so they could be a bit rougher around the edges, a bit sillier, and a little bit more fun. Just like they are, themselves.

Hopefully, this translation allows you to experience this play in the way it was always intended.

Happy reading.

MICHAEL BARLTROP   HYBT?

Michael Barltrop has been teaching since 2006, integrating Manga, Video Games, and TTRPGs into his classroom. He has been the head of English, Literacy, and Universal Design. Feel free to reach out to him through his website WhatBinder.com or find him on Twitter @MrBarltrop! He thanks his children, Miles and Gwen, and his wife (and editor) Katherine for their constant support.

MICHAEL BARLTROP:
ADAPTING A MIDSUMMER NIGHT'S DREAM INTO MODERN ENGLISH

A Midsummer Night's Dream is not one, but two plays. There is the play that tells the tale of the lovers, the faeries, and the mechanicals (the labourers). And then, of course, there is the play that the mechanicals perform for the lovers: The Most Lamentable Comedy and Most Cruel Death of Pyramus and Thisbe.

Each play, and each group of characters within the play, speak with very different voices. For *A Midsummer Night's Dream* to be properly translated each of these voices must be carefully preserved.

THE THREE VOICES:

As you begin reading you'll notice the way the lovers speak comes off very lofty, and regal. You'll find that there is something magical about how the faeries talk to each other. And the mechanicals? Well they seem just like you and me, don't they?

While the depiction of these characters bring unique qualities to each group, there's more to it than that. How did Shakespeare achieve this differentiation just through the lines read from a page?

That will require a closer look at all three voices.

THE LOVERS

Those who have read *Romeo and Juliet* will be quick to point out that The Lovers speak in iambic pentameter more often than not. Simply speaking, iambic pentameter is a collection of lines that are each ten syllables long (for a more in-depth explanation, read my Translator Notes in *Manga Classics: Romeo and Juliet*).

When these lines are read, it's difficult not to feel the air of nobility baked into each grouping of lines. But, once Shakespeare set up this rule he was granted the power that comes from breaking it. When The Lovers stop speaking in iambic pentameter, what does that mean? Why would they do that? That's for the reader to decide.

THE FAERIES

The faeries speak with a defined rhythm. They also enhance their voice through an additional quality: Rhyme.

In *A Midsummer Night's Dream*, rhyme is used to indicate a sense of magical wonder that falls over the night. When the fairies speak, the audience is lulled into a sense of comfort as each line moves smoothly from one, into the next. They seek to enchant the audience.

When the The Lovers speak in rhyme they prove that the night's enchantment is far reaching, showing that, they too, have fallen under its spell.

WHOOPS

This is the back of the book!

Manga Classics® books follow the Japanese comic (aka Manga!) reading order. Traditional manga is read in a "reversed" format starting on the right and heading towards the left. The story begins where English readers expect to find the last page because the spine of the book is on the opposite side. Flip to the other end of the book and start reading your Manga Classics!

A Midsummer Night's Dream

WILLIAM SHAKESPEARE

MODERN ENGLISH EDITION

Art by: Po Tse
Story Adaptation by: Crystal S. Chan
Modern English Adaptation by: Michael Barltrop
Lettering: Wing-Yin Leung & W.T. Francis

STAFF:

Project Chief North America: Erik Ko
Editor: M. Chandler
Marketing Director: Megan Maiden
Production Manager: Janice Leung
Copy Editing: Michelle Lee

Project Chief Asia: Andy Hung
Production Manager: Yuen Him Tai
Art Assistants: Man Yiu. Peter Mak
J.C.Chow, Stoon

Special thanks to: Michael Gianfrancesco, Eric Kallenborn, Claudia McGivney, & John Shableski.

INTEREST LEVEL: 7-12 READING LEVEL: Grade 9 AGE: Young Adult (12+)

BISAC: YAF010060 YAF010010 YAF009000 YAF010000
CGN00600 DRA000000, FIC004000
Young Adult Fiction, Comics & Graphic Novels, Manga, Classic Adaptation

DEWEY 741.5

LIBRARY SUBJECT: Drama, Manga, Shakespeare, Classic Literature

Manga Classics: A Midsummer Night's Dream - Modern English Edition. Published by Manga Classics, Inc. 118 Tower Hill Road, C1, PO Box 20008, Richmond Hill, Ontario, L4K 0K0, Canada.

First Printing October 2021 Printed in Canada
ISBN # 978-1-947808-24-9

www.mangaclassics.com